RURAL SETTLEMENT

Sidestone Press

RURAL SETTLEMENT

RELATING BUILDINGS, LANDSCAPE, AND PEOPLE IN THE EUROPEAN IRON AGE

edited by Dave C. Cowley, Manuel Fernández-Götz, Tanja Romankiewicz & Holger Wendling

Volume acknowledgements

Our thanks to Fraser Hunter and Rod McCullagh for their role in co-organising the Edinburgh conference on which the volume is based. This conference was sponsored by Historic Environment Scotland, the National Museum of Scotland, the Scottish Archaeological Research Framework, AOC Archaeology Group, CFA Archaeology Ltd, GUARD Archaeology, The Leverhulme Trust and Northlight Heritage to whom we express our sincere thanks.

We are grateful to Historic Environment Scotland and the Leverhulme Trust for supporting this publication.

LEVERHULME TRUST

HISTORIC ENVIRONMENT SCOTLAND | ÀRAINNEACHD EACHDRAIDHEIL ALBA

THE UNIVERSITY of EDINBURGH School of History, Classics and Archaeology

First Millennia FMSG Studies Group

AG EZ Arbeitsgemeinschaft EisenZeit

Published by Sidestone Press, Leiden
www.sidestone.com

Lay-out & cover design: Sidestone Press

Cover: The cover illustration is a composite of the reconstruction of a semi-sunken structure at Josipovac-Selište in southern Pannonia, overlaid on a settlement density distribution in relation to visual coverage from hillforts in the area of Sarmizegetusa Regia, Dacia. (With thanks to Ivan Drnić (reconstruction: source Filipec, K. (ed.) 2009. Josipovac - Selište (AN 14). In Arheološke slike Slavonije. Zagreb: Odsjek za arheologiju Filozofskog fakulteta Sveučilišta u Zagrebu) and João Fonte (map)).

ISBN 978-90-8890-818-7 (softcover)
ISBN 978-90-8890-819-4 (hardcover)
ISBN 978-90-8890-820-0 (PDF e-book)

Contents

PART 2 SETTLEMENT UNITS AND BUILDINGS

Chapter 1

Exploring rural settlement in Iron Age Europe

An introduction

Dave C. Cowley, Manuel Fernández-Götz,
Tanja Romankiewicz & Holger Wendling

1.1 Introduction

> *'Sometime ... perhaps around 600 BC, a farming community ... decided to build a stout palisade and ditch around a low hilltop ... most probably a virgin site, rising gently above fields, open grassland and scattered pockets of woodland ... The builders themselves were probably local, perhaps recently split off from a parent village, or perhaps newly arrived from some other part of the coastal plain'* (Armit & McKenzie 2013, 494).

These words are taken from the narrative picture painted of Broxmouth, one of the most comprehensively excavated Iron Age hillforts in Scotland (Figure 1). This passage conveys a view of the social dynamics within which settlements might have been founded, and the landscape mosaic within which they may have developed. Implicit in this narrative are the many factors that work in concert to structure settlement systems, including concepts of ownership, social group coherence, and the character of wider social networks. Importantly, this interpretation considers such patterns of occupation and activity across the wider landscape, and within a certain continuity of place. Other factors are at play, too, such as production of goods, craft working, and the creation of places for social gathering and worship. All these factors underpin the basic characteristics of settlement systems – where did people live, why there, and for how long? How did they support their lives and in what kind of environment? How resilient or transient were their strategies? Who and where were their nearest neighbours? How did they maintain status, relationships, and subsistence? How did the sacred inform their everyday lives? The answers to these questions, in turn, have a direct impact on broader discussions about past lives.

While the last two decades have witnessed a strong research focus on Iron Age centralisation and urbanisation processes (see, for example, Fernández-Götz *et al.* 2014; Krausse 2010; Sievers & Schönfelder 2012), rural settlements have more often been studied on a site-by-site basis, in their local and regional context, rather than through comparative perspectives from across Europe. The importance of the large agglomerations that developed during the 1st millennium BC in parts of Europe should

In D.C. Cowley, M. Fernández-Götz, T. Romankiewicz & H. Wendling (eds). Rural Settlement. Relating buildings, landscape, and people in the European Iron Age (Leiden 2019: Sidestone Press) 9-18.

Figure 1: Aerial view of the Iron Age site of Broxmouth in southeast Scotland under excavation. (SC714820, © Historic Environment Scotland).

not overshadow the fundamentally rural character of the Iron Age world, with the majority of the population living in small hamlets and farmsteads (Audouze & Buchsenschutz 1989; Malrain *et al.* 2002). In addition, large settlements that in some cases we might identify from the archaeological evidence as 'urban' are restricted to certain regions, and from both a temporal and geographical perspective they were the exception rather than the rule.

Viewed from a world-wide perspective, the 'rural' is the predominant way of life, even in periods that might implicitly be associated with urban lifestyles. For example, it has been calculated that in the early Roman Empire more than 90% of the population of Gaul lived in the countryside (Étienne 1988). According to United Nations official data, 2009 marked the first year in world history during which the number of people living in cities surpassed the rural population (United Nations 2010).

While archaeological perspectives on low-density urbanism in the Americas (Fletcher 2011) and south-east Asia (Evans *et al.* 2013), for example, illustrate the undesirability of simple oppositional distinctions between rural and urban, this book contributes to affirming the necessity of studying rural settlements in the Iron Age. By doing so, we pick up a theme that is attracting interest beyond the period of focus in this volume (*i.e.* the special issue in the *World Archaeology* journal, cf. van Dommelen 2018).

1.2 Rurality as a concept in Iron Age research?

The wider context of this book asks the question of whether 'rurality' is indeed a useful concept (or set of concepts) for Iron Age research. Definitions of 'rural' tend to be framed in opposition to urban settings such as towns and cities, and while there are clearly urban settlements in the Iron Age, their distribution across Europe is very uneven. In Scotland and Scandinavia, for example, any definition of rural that depends on an urban counterpoint cannot really be sustained for the 1st millennium BC. It is perhaps more useful to see the rural and the urban as two broad concepts, within which lesser and greater degrees of aggregation and complexity can be expressed. This position does not depend on superficial linkages such as rural/agricultural or urban/industrial, as fields and pastures have been identified within large-area *oppida* such as Manching (southern Germany; Brestel this volume) and industrial-scale production evidence is attested at smaller settlement sites such as Seafield West (Scotland; Cressey & Anderson 2011).

So too, we think care is needed not to project modern perceptions or prejudices onto the past, such as caricatures that associate urban lives with modernity and progressiveness. In the later prehistoric context, 'rurality' can perhaps best be used as a device to explore small-scale settlement sites (from single farmsteads to groupings of a few households) and the landscapes in which they were embedded.

While rurality may provide a useful frame within which to refer to local Iron Age settlement systems, it is essential to prevent culturally loaded ideas of the 'rural idyll', which owe more to early modern and contemporary sensibilities than the distant past, creeping into use. Heavily romanticised views of the rural landscape and rural life have a long history, which finds expression in the Classical period and the writings of Cicero, Cato, Horace and Vitruvius. These authors praise, often in bucolic scenes, rural and specifically agricultural life, equating rustic simplicity with enviable innocence and integrity (*e.g.* Horace's Ode 2.18; see Baumann 2018). Idealised conceptions of rural life are widespread across Europe in the early modern period, and have also been reinvented in modern anti-urban romantic and uncritical notions of 'life in harmony with nature'. Frequently, such neo-romanticist views are expressed in the revival of esoteric Celticism and neo-paganism (Birkhan 2012). It is also worth noting that ever-increasing proportions of archaeologists, like the rest of the population, have been born, grown up, and now live and work in urban environments, which inevitably makes them less familiar with the patterns and rhythms of the countryside than was the case a century ago. The contemporary agricultural world is also changing, with dramatic developments in the processes of working the land, in the condition of the land itself, and associated ecosystems.

These caveats aside, there is the question of how aware people in the Iron Age may have been of these concepts and differences between urban and rural, centralisation and decentralisation, agricultural and industrial? Certainly in areas with urban centres there is already an awareness of the concept of 'rural living', and large 'aristocratic' establishments were often deliberately built away from the 'urban' centres of the *Fürstensitze* and *oppida* (see Fernández-Götz & Ralston; Fichtl this volume). Moreover, in regions and for time periods without central places that may be characterised as predominantly 'non-urban', large-scale survey (*e.g.* Figure 2) has led to a considerable increase in the variety of known sites, broadening the range of settlement strategies evidenced across the landscape. So too, the increase of diachronic settlement evidence highlights considerable fluctuation in prehistoric settlement dynamics. This broadened spectrum of remains invites more complex interpretations beyond concepts of 'urban', 'central', or 'rural' – and suggests that investigating more abstract concepts such as rurality is useful in understanding Iron Age lives and life-choices. Importantly, as a broadly agricultural rural landscape setting remains the most significant and persistent attribute of most Iron Age sites in northern and central Europe and provided the basis of most subsistence strategies, rural settlement cannot exclusively be defined in contrast to urban, nor implicitly equated with lower status. Indeed, the rural settlements explored in this volume range from everyday farms to highly organised elite country seats, which are set within landscapes that expressed social, economic, political and cultural interactions and organisation.

1.3 Rural settlement in Iron Age Europe: relating buildings, landscape, and people

Investigating these themes and relationships between people, buildings, and landscape under the concept of rurality defined the scope of an international conference, held in Edinburgh, Scotland, between the 19th and the 21st of June 2017, under the title *Rural Settlement – relating buildings, landscape, and people in the European Iron Age.*

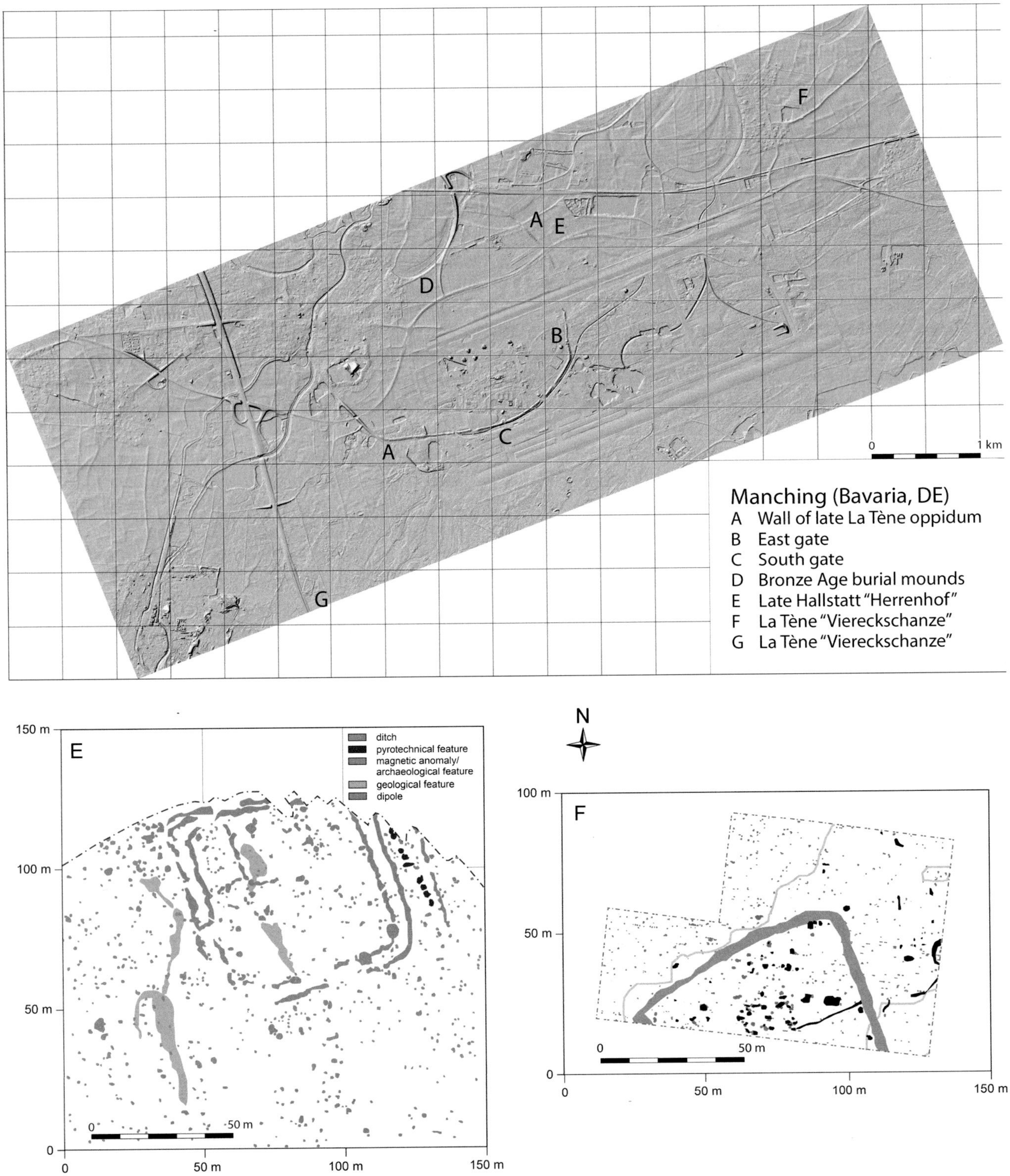

Figure 2: Large-scale geophysical survey and Airborne Laser Scanning data have considerably increased the archaeological record beyond central places like the Manching *oppidum*. These have revealed 'rural' estates contemporary to the Late Iron Age town, and also earlier phases, documenting a dynamic pattern of non-urban settlement. (Data courtesy of Römisch-Germanische Kommission DAI; graphics: H. Wendling).

Figure 3: Artistic reconstruction of White Castle hillfort by David Simon. Such images are compelling but are often based on limited archaeological evidence (Image: permission of East Lothian Council).

Jointly organised by the Arbeitsgemeinschaft Eisenzeit, the First Millennia Studies Group, and the School of History, Classics and Archaeology of the University of Edinburgh, this conference drew together recent research from Austria, Bulgaria, Croatia, the Czech Republic, Denmark, France, Germany, Hungary, Ireland, Italy, Netherlands, Poland, Romania, Serbia, Slovenia, Spain, and the UK, together dealing with the basic element of Iron Age rural settlement: the farm – a unit of land, its buildings, and inhabitants (Cowley *et al.* 2017).

This volume is made up of 28 presentations delivered at the conference dealing with evidence from across the continent – from southern Spain to Scotland and the western Atlantic seaboard to the eastern Alps and the Hungarian plain. This body of material, some of it presented in English for the first time, provides a fascinating insight into the complex, textured landscapes of rural settlement (in its broadest sense) occupied by Iron Age societies (Figure 3).

Many papers include archaeological analyses of farmstead disposition, form, and organisation – basic characteristics that are central to our understanding of the social, economic, and cultural interactions highlighted above. Here we see the range of settlement forms and of landscape setting, factors that can indicate both notable similarities and marked differences in aspects of rural life from area to area, and over time. These chronological and spatial dynamics, from the beginning of the 1st millennium BC to the early centuries of the Common Era, and from households to larger local and regional demographic units, reflect the changing rhythms and textures of inhabitation and land use. Results offer insights into the immediate and intimate relationships that rural settlements had with their surrounding landscape and resources (compare Ingold 1993). Moreover, at a European scale and across the span of the Iron Age, the variations in unit size and density of settlements, and their distribution and roles in wider societal and landscape organisation, for example, offer a basis for exploration of common themes and regional variation in those societies. These themes can be grouped under four key headings to address rurality at different scales, both geographically as well as economically and socially, highlighting both commonalities and diversities in Iron Age societies.

1) Beyond the site: settlement systems and territories

Archaeological thinking has expanded beyond the confines of traditional sites and the increasing availability of landscape-scale datasets, whether from large area excavations or survey data, have contributed to evidence-based exploration of settlement systems and territories. The forms of local and regional settlement patterns as expressions of larger economic, political, and social organisation are amongst the building blocks of Iron Age societies, and the essays collected in this section address how settlement systems and territorial units might be defined. At the heart of this theme is the extent to which identity and cohesion across areas can be identified, against the sense of otherness and differentiation – and where these might represent differences in Iron Age lifeways.

In northern France, large area excavations and aerial survey have produced significant datasets that support the identification of highly structured integrated territorial units. **Cony's** work indicates developed concepts of land-ownership and centralised coordination of economic activity in the period from the 3rd century BC to the early centuries AD. **Runge** takes a wider chronological span of the entire 1st millennium BC in a study of settlement and landscape organisation in Denmark. He explores the extent of regional variation, the inter-relationships of settlement form within different environmental situations, and their dynamics over the period from the Late Bronze Age to the end of the Iron Age. Settlement changes become apparent, from an inherently mobile system of 'wandering villages' towards a pattern of larger, more rigidly structured sites which were more permanently fixed to specific locations. While we see patterns of centralisation in the French data across larger distances, the individual farmstead sites in Denmark seem to adhere to some form of self-sustaining autonomy, despite being situated in relative proximity.

Such questions of where and how people lived are picked up by **Becker** who highlights the range of uses that Iron Age populations in Ireland made of a variety of landscape types. The extensive, as opposed to intensive, use of a landscape, manifested through a network of sites, including those used seasonally for pasture or for exploitation of raw material resources, is a central theme in a pattern of small-scale settlements, that were nonetheless linked within supra-regional networks. Similar relationships between different landscape settings and settlements are explored by **Halkon** in a study of eastern England, with variability evident across both lowland and upland contexts and distinctive forms of enclosure. The identification of social differentiation from the settlement evidence remains difficult, though it is more clearly demonstrated by the burial evidence from the so-called Arras culture. In contrast, analysis of settlement in eastern Iberia by **Grau Mira** presents an integrated range of socially differentiated sites within which dominant centres exercising control over territorial units emerge in the 3rd century BC. Interdependencies between different functional elements of a settlement hierarchy are indicated, including differing morphologies of buildings (*i.e.* round/rectangular), different forms of settlement (farmsteads/villages/*oppida*) and varying permanent and potentially seasonal occupation. The complexity of settlement patterns is also a central theme in the paper by **López-Mondéjar** on the Late Iron Age of southeast Iberia. She highlights the diversity of settlement form and economic activity, but also the wider context of burial monuments and cult centres in the socio-political landscape of the area.

The dynamic pattern of settlement in southern Iberia over the 1st millennium BC is discussed by **Ferrer-Albelda *et al.*** who outline the fluctuating patterns of farms and hamlets within territorial units also dominated by *oppida*. The role of external influences from across the Mediterranean serves to set the local developments in the context of a wider world of emergent common trajectories across very large areas. The varying extent to which external influences and networks may have impacted on lifestyles in settlement networks is explored by **Labeaune** for the Early Iron Age in eastern Burgundy. He identifies very different patterns in the degree to which settlements were integrated into such wider networks, or were essentially 'local' in their outlook. In this context, he also examines the roles of pre-eminent settlements.

2) Settlement units and buildings

Buildings (serving as dwellings, byres, barns, and workshops or a range of other purposes) are core elements of settlement units, whether in farmsteads, villages, or larger aggregated foci of habitation. These buildings and settlement units are amongst the nodes that anchor elements of the wider landscape – they are where people lived, where agricultural produce might be processed and stored, and a forum where economic, social, and political networks were expressed and negotiated. The papers in this section explore the forms of buildings and their context in settlement units, their dating, and how individual sites link to broader patterns. They provide a series of case studies that illustrate the variability in form and function, as well as the landscape context of Iron Age settlement.

The paper by **Cavers & Crone** on southwest Scotland highlights the detailed evidence that wetland sites can provide, including precise dating and unrivalled preservation of organic structural material. On the basis of this type of evidence, the discussion of individual buildings can be framed around human timescales, while the contemporaneity of occupations of buildings and settlements can be established rather than guessed at. This kind of evidence challenges interpretations of dryland sites, where structural evidence for buildings rarely includes more than hints of the organic components that make up most of the superstructure and where dating evidence can be scarce and inherently broad. Nevertheless, **de Vries** analyses house forms in what is now The Netherlands from heavily truncated floor plans and identifies aspects of construction that speak to patterns of occupation and relationships between building forms and settlement structure. By taking a long view across much of the 1st millennium BC to the early centuries AD, she illustrates how specifics of building renovation, extension, or rebuilding, related to processes of nucleation and stabilisation of individual house plots and larger settlement units in specific locations, and their aggregation over time. De Vries also suggests much longer occupation periods of individual structures as evidenced in repairs and rebuilding than has been demonstrated from the Scottish wetland evidence. The benefits of detailed analyses of the remains of buildings are discussed by **Romankiewicz**, who highlights the potential role of turf as a building material in the Iron Age and the implications of this for broader settlement dynamics.

Beyond individual buildings, the forms, functions, and disposition of Iron Age settlements also varies greatly across Europe – with, for example, regional variations in the extents to which enclosures are present, whether buildings are round or rectangular on plan, or incorporate sunken floored elements. These attributes of rural settlement, amongst others, are evident in all the papers in this volume, but the following contributions have a specific focus on local and regional case studies. They highlight the difficulties of defining building functions, considerations of settlement disposition and context, and of reconstructing the life-histories of occupation at particular locations. The paper by **Kovács** reviews the evidence for Iron Age settlement in eastern Hungary, summarising the range of available evidence and the varying concepts of 'house' and 'settlement' implied by the data. The difficulties of defining the purpose(s) of buildings are explored by **Bulas *et al.*** in a case study from Poland. This theme is also evident in the paper by **Tankó & Timár** on Late Iron Age settlement in Hungary, who also discuss the issues of reconstructing building superstructure. **Georgescu** reviews the evidence for rural occupation in the Banat Region of Romania, and **Drnić** for southern Pannonia. Both emphasise the wider connections of these discrete areas. The paper by **Möller & Karl** describes the excavation of an Iron Age enclosure in northwest Wales, illustrating the dynamism of its occupation and the changing expressions of status and place in wider settlement networks. The trajectories of settlement development is also the central theme explored by **Mecking** for La Tène farmsteads in Central and Western continental Europe. She identifies local variations on general themes expressed through individual site histories and common processes of abandonment and continuity across large areas.

Finally, exploring a point made earlier in this introduction about the undesirability of sharp oppositional rural vs urban classifications, **Brestel** describes the incidence of essentially rural settlement forms within urban areas. Through the example of the large *oppidum* of Manching, in Bavaria, he points to the contrasts between high density and dispersed or peripheral occupation, essentially agricultural in character, within the site.

3) Status and settlement hierarchy

The presence of marked settlement hierarchies is referenced in many papers throughout the volume. These include large, elaborate rural settlements that stand out from a background pattern of seemingly unassuming farmsteads, within which the routines of everyday life were lived by the majority of the population. They stand out through factors such as size, complexity, and artefactual richness and can be argued to represent the rural seats of elites. These rural establishments, by analogy to Roman or medieval systems identifiable as 'country estates', were often parts of the mechanisms through which elites exercised and displayed control over land, resources, and populations.

The paper by **Fernández-Götz & Ralston** challenges assumptions that the principal residences of 6th and 5th century BC elites in Central Europe were necessarily within the so-called 'princely seats' (*Fürstensitze*). They note the presence of high status farmsteads and distributions of sumptuous burials lying at a distance from central settlements, and suggest these may indicate that high-status individuals may have spent much of their time on these country estates. Their results chime with **Fichtl** who identifies high status establishments for the later period of the 2nd and 1st century BC, which he equates to aristocratic residences, following his review of the evidence from rescue excavations and research projects in France over the last twenty years. The individuals, and to an extent their family lines, occupying these settlements are identified with aristocrats known from classical written sources. In the rather different context of northern Serbia, **Wendling** describes a monumental Late Iron Age fortification, which is interpreted as a centre of a martial elite resembling some of these large-scale aristocratic residences in Late Iron Age Gaul. Finally, the paper by **Chordá *et al.*** provides a case study on the emergence of *oppida* in Celtiberia. This highlights the role these Iron Age settlements played as centres of elite power, and how that translated into the Roman period.

4) New tools and perspectives

The enormous growth in information from preventive or rescue archaeology over the last 50 years has been highlighted above and is difficult to overstate, with increasingly large area excavations undertaken against a backdrop of big infrastructure projects and urban expansion (*e.g.* see Bradley *et al.* 2012; Demoule 2012; Florjanowicz 2016; Novaković *et al.* 2016). Such interventions have not only produced mass archaeological data, but have also shifted the emphasis of archaeological investigation from single sites to larger landscapes, and from a focus on well-known highly-visible established sites to a broader range of settlement patterns and land use evidence. In France, for example, development-led fieldwork has fundamentally changed understandings of the settlement landscapes in pre-Roman Gaul with the discovery of large numbers of Late Iron Age rural settlements. This information bonanza is explored in some papers in earlier sections of this volume (in particular **Cony**, **Runge**, **Becker**, and **Labeaune**) which illustrate its broad reach and profound impact on knowledge across many parts of Europe. Fresh insights into landscape-scaled patterns are also evident from the increasing use of non-destructive survey techniques. These include aerial survey (*e.g.* **Halkon** and **Tankó & Timár**), geophysics (*e.g.* **Wendling**) and the increasing use of Airborne Laser Scanning (ALS, aka Lidar), that bring the wider landscape firmly into the frame.

This wider landscape-scale perspective, and the analytical opportunities that detailed digital topographic ALS data provide, are explored by **Oltean & Fonte** for Romania. They illustrate the potential of such datasets to examine aspects of settlement disposition and structure. **Laharnar *et al.*** describe in some detail a relatively small block of landscape, illustrating the rich information that good ALS data can provide. Such data, and derivatives such as interpreted mapping, demand the use of Geographical Information Systems (GIS). Indeed, the integration of diverse sources of spatial information increasingly makes GIS a mandatory 'tool-of-the-trade'. The paper by **Bernard** provides a case study that illustrates the importance of easy access to multiple datasets to improve their research value and ensure existing knowledge can inform heritage management across regional and national boundaries. The collation of various sources of information is further explored by **López-Mondéjar** in an example from the southern Iberian Peninsula.

It remains important, however, that tools such as GIS, which cannot be regarded as new anymore, do not become an end in themselves. The availability of digital data and the willingness of archaeologists to engage with them in innovative and imaginative ways to think about observable patterns in the archaeological remains will vary, but remains a challenge in the face of ever-increasing volumes of information. This is not to suggest that the use of GIS automatically produces great insights, as poorly formulated questions asked of badly understood data and uncritically applied analytical routines will produce outcomes that do not advance our understandings of the past.

The need for clear archaeological questions based on thorough understanding of datasets is also a theme of the concluding paper in this volume by **Ruano & Berrocal-Rangel**. They explore the value that an ethnoarchaeological study of post-medieval buildings and land use can bring to the interpretation of Iron Age remains. The positive synergies offered by ethno-archaeological approaches provide archaeologists with an insight on people observably 'doing' things – on the activities and dynamics that the fragments of the archaeological record often struggle to evidence (*i.e.* Binford 1981, 27; Lucas 2010, 32). In this context it remains important not to seek simplistic direct and uncritical transfer of patterns from recently observed examples onto a deeper past, but to broaden our own perspectives through plausible analogies (see also **Runge** who draws on medieval and post medieval analogy). This needs to stretch beyond the assumptions (and preconceptions) that derive from our contemporary 20th and 21st century context.

1.4 Some concluding thoughts

The material presented in this volume illustrates the variety of forms and trajectories for settlement and landscape organisation in Iron Age Europe, with case studies providing windows on their diverse landscape textures. Over the period during which this volume was being compiled the cohesion of the 'European Project' is being challenged, as common values and purpose are set against national differences and interests. This is happening against a background of rapid economic and social change, particularly notable in changing demographics and the resilience of local rural communities. In this time of tendencies to differentiate and segregate, the integrative value of archaeological approaches that transcend modern political boundaries becomes even more significant. Such integration is not always easy, with language and different research traditions being among the major barriers (Kristiansen 2001; Ruiz Zapatero 2011).

Awareness of the intrinsic historical burden is important because our narratives of the past are shaped by our own settings, experiences, and lifeways. Thus, very often our preconceptions (or prejudices) will colour our interpretations as we piece together fragmented archaeological evidence. The permanency and longevity

Figure 4: Iron Age roundhouses in the Iberian Peninsula and the British Isles. Left – The footings of a roundhouse in the Iron Age hillfort of Castrolandín (Pontevedra, Spain). Right – Roundhouses in St David's Head Camp (Pembrokeshire, Wales). (Left image: D. Cowley; Right image: S. Halliday).

of occupation at particular locations is a good case in point, as only rarely does the archaeological evidence provide robust evidence for absolute durations of occupations of buildings and settlements on a generational scale (see **Cavers & Crone** this volume). Even more limited is the capacity of the evidence to establish with any certainty the contemporaneity of occupation within and between sites. Thus, the character of occupation and assumed densities of past settlement patterns, for example, may rely as much on our personal beliefs as on hard evidence, although the increasing use of radiocarbon dates and Bayesian modelling is starting to produce more refined chronologies (*e.g.* Hamilton & Haselgrove 2019). These issues are central to understandings of the textures of local, regional, and supra-regional patterning in Iron Age Europe – how densely and evenly were settlements distributed, how did their characteristics vary, and how did these factors change across space and over time? What, one wonders, would have a person travelling in the 2nd century BC from the Mediterranean coast in what is now Spain, through Gaul, and across the sea to the British Isles, have noticed about the differences in the landscapes they traversed? Topography, climate, and vegetation would have varied greatly along their route, with changes also in land use as the emphasis on arable and stock fluctuated between areas. What would they have noticed changing? – the regional variation in the distribution of *oppida*? or the changing predominance of roughly rectangular settlement enclosures? And would they have been struck by the similarities of roundhouse forms between Iberia and Wales, or noticed subtle differences in style (Figure 4)?

As selected attributes of Iron Age settlement and societies, these examples highlight a fascinating mix of commonality and diversity across Europe, for which this volume presents a series of case studies. These provide windows on the landscapes and settlement systems of the Iron Age, but they also ask questions about what happened in between: where do the boundaries between 'different' places lie?; how can these differences be defined?; and to what degree do different places still exhibit commonality? These factors can express local and regional diversity, but also, when examined at a pan-European scale, shared responses and trajectories. In this mix lies the opportunity to explore the geographies of rural settlement and people in the European Iron Age, an objective to which we hope this volume contributes.

1.5 Acknowledgements

Our thanks to Rod McCullagh for his comments on this introductory chapter. Tanja Romankiewicz would like to thank the Leverhulme Trust for supporting her research as an Early Career Fellowship (Grant No. ECF-2014-424) and Manuel Fernández-Götz for the support offered by the Philip Leverhulme Prize.

1.6 Bibliography

Armit, I. & McKenzie, J. 2013. *An Inherited Place – Broxmouth Hillfort and the South-East Scottish Iron Age*. Edinburgh: Society of Antiquaries of Scotland.

Audouze, F. & Buchsenschutz, O. 1989. *Villes, villages et campagnes de l'Europe celtique*. Paris: Hachette.

Baumann, C. 2018. *Idyllische Ländlichkeit. Eine Kulturgeographie der Landlust*. Bielefeld: Transcript Verlag.

Binford, L. 1981. *Bones. Ancient men and modern myths*. New York: Academic Press.

Birkhan, H. 2012. "Wer hört in unserer hektischen, technokratischen, kapitalistischen Zeit noch die Stimme der Bäume, wer kennt die Weisheit unserer Ahnen?" Beobachtungen zum mysterischen Keltenbild besonders in Österreich. In R. Karl, J. Leskovar

& S. Moser (eds). *Die erfundenen Kelten – Mythologie eines Begriffes und seine Verwendung in Archäologie, Tourismus und Esoterik*. Studien zur Kulturgeschichte von Oberösterreich 31. 53-65. Linz: Oberösterreichisches Landesmuseum.

Bradley, R. Haselgrove, C. Vander Linden, M. & Webley, L. (eds). 2012. *Development-led Archaeology in North-West Europe*. Oxford: Oxbow Books.

Cowley, D., Fernández-Götz, M., Hunter, F., McCullagh, R., Romankiewicz, T. & Wendling, H. 2017. Rural Settlement: Relating Buildings, Landscape, and People in the European Iron Age, Joint International Workshop of the AG Eisenzeit, the First Millennia Studies Group & the University of Edinburgh. Edinburgh, 19-21 June 2017. *The European Archaeologist* 54 Autumn-Fall 2017, 31-33.

Cressey, M. & Anderson, S. 2011. *A Later Prehistoric Settlement and Metalworking Site at Seafield West, near Inverness, Highland*. Scottish Archaeological Internet Reports 47. Edinburgh: Society of Antiquaries of Scotland.

Demoule, J-P. 2012. Rescue Archaeology: A European View. *Annual Review of Anthropology* 41, 611-26.

Étienne, R. 1988. Gaule romaine. In J. Dupâquier (ed.). *Histoire de la population française I. Des origines à la Renaissance*. 65-117. Paris: PUF.

Evans, D., Fletcher, R., Pottier, C., Chevance, J., Soutif, D., Suy Tan, B., Im, S., Ea, D., Tin, T., Kim, S., Cromarty, C., De Greef, S., Hanus, K., Bâty, P., Kuszinger, R., Shimoda, I. & Boornazian, G. 2013. Uncovering archaeological landscapes at Angkor using lidar. *PNAS* July 30, 2013, vol. 110, no. 31, 12595-600.

Fernández-Götz, M., Wendling, H. & Winger, K. (eds) 2014. *Paths to Complexity. Centralisation and Urbanisation in Iron Age Europe*. Oxford: Oxbow Books.

Fletcher, R. 2011. Low-Density, Agrarian-Based Urbanism. In M. Smith (ed.). *The Comparative Archaeology of Complex Societies*. 285-320. Cambridge: Cambridge University Press.

Florjanowicz, P. (ed.) 2016. *When Valletta meets Faro: The reality of European archaeology in the 21st century*. EAC Occasional Paper 11. Budapest: Archaeolingua.

Hamilton, D. & Haselgrove, C. 2019. Exploring settlement dynamics through radiocarbon dating. In T. Romankiewicz, M. Fernández-Götz, G. Lock & O. Buchsenschutz (eds). *Enclosing Space, Opening New Ground: Iron Age Studies from Scotland to Mainland Europe*. 111-9. Oxford: Oxbow Books.

Krausse, D. (ed.) 2010. *„Fürstensitze" und Zentralorte der frühen Kelten*. Forschungen und Berichte zur Vor- und Frühgeschichte in Baden-Württemberg 120. Stuttgart: Theiss.

Kristiansen, K. 2001. Borders of ignorance: research communities and language. In Z. Kobylinski (ed.). *Quo vadis archaeologia? Whither European Archaeology in the 21st century?*. 38-44. Warsaw: Polish Academy of Science.

Ingold, T. 1993. The temporality of the landscape. *World Archaeology* 25(2), 152-74.

Lucas, G. 2010. Triangulating absence: exploring fault lines between archaeology and anthropology. In D. Garrow & T. Yarrow (eds). *Archaeology and Anthropology*. 28-39. Oxford: Oxbow Books.

Malrain, F., Matterne, V. & Méniel, P. 2002. *Les paysans gaulois*. Paris: Errance.

Novaković, P., Horňák, M., Guermandi, M. P., Stäuble, H., Depaepe, P. & Demoule, J.-P. (eds) 2016. *Recent developments in preventive archaeology in Europe*. Ljubljana: Ljubljana University Press.

Ruiz Zapatero, G. 2011. Settlement and landscape in Iron Age Europe: archaeological mainstreams and minorities. In T. Moore & X.-L. Armada (eds). *Atlantic Europe in the First Millennium BC. Crossing the Divide*. 81-108. Oxford: Oxford University Press.

Sievers, S. & Schönfelder. M. (eds) 2012. *Die Frage der Protourbanisation in der Eisenzeit. La question de la proto-urbanisation à l'âge du Fer. Akten des 34. internationalen Kolloquiums der AFEAF vom 13.-16. Mai 2010 in Aschaffenburg*. Kolloquien zur Vor- und Frühgeschichte 16. Bonn: Habelt.

United Nations 2010. *Urban and rural areas 2009*. http://www.un.org/en/development/desa/population/publications/urbanization/urban-rural.shtml, accessed 30 January 2019.

Van Dommelen, P. (ed.) 2018. *Rural Archaeologies*. World Archaeology 50(5) (special issue).

PART 1

BEYOND THE SITE: SETTLEMENT SYSTEMS AND TERRITORIES

Chapter 2

Regional settlement entities or *terroirs* in Late Iron Age northern France

Alexandra Cony

2.1 Introduction

Since the 1990s data on the settlement of the Late Iron Age in France have become abundant. Many settlements have been discovered due to the development of preventive archaeology through which large area excavations have been carried out, over several dozen if not hundreds of hectares. At the end of the 1990s these settlements have been reintegrated into wider environmental and archaeological contexts. For example, more than 150 hectares were explored at Actiparc, near Arras, (Pas-de-Calais: Jacques & Prilaux 2003), where five late La Tène period farms were excavated on a well-defined plateau. The first farm reached by following the path leading to the top of the plateau has been interpreted as the residence of a landowner. At Objec'Ifs Sud, in the Plain of Caen (Calvados), 60 hectares were excavated revealing several enclosures perfectly fitting into an orthogonal field system (Le Goff 2009, 93-107). Finally, for the ZAC des Béliers in Brebières (Pas-de-Calais), which will be discussed in more detail below, 60 hectares have been explored, revealing more than twenty enclosures within a network of field ditches (Lacalmontie 2016, 133-46).

These large area excavations of settlements give the impression that the enclosures belonged to a single socio-economic group. They are named 'terroirs' by the archaeologists that excavated the sites (Jacques & Prilaux 2003; Le Goff 2009, 93-107; Lacalmontie 2016, 133-46). I took up the term, which is originally a word used by geographers. It corresponds to a territory characterised by identical agronomic attributes (Lebeau 1996, 10), but it is also used in medieval archaeology to designate the territory exploited by a village (Favier 1993, 966-7). What I call a *terroir* for the Gallic period in France is therefore a set of domestic, funerary and agricultural areas evolving on a more or less extensive territory and fitting into the wider landscape (Cony 2017a, 71-2). I decided to retain the French word since there is no equivalent term in English and it can only be insufficiently translated as 'regional rural entities'.

The study reported on in this paper was carried out in the context of a PhD thesis presented in April 2017. This focused on the analysis of five *terroirs* defined by excavators (Actiparc [Pas-de-Calais], Brebières [Pas-de-Calais], Boves and Glisy [Somme], La Plaine de Caen [Calvados], Méaulte [Somme]) and eight archaeologically dynamic zones presenting a large number of Late Iron Age enclosed settlements (Batilly-en-Gâtinais [Loiret], Seine/Yonne confluence [Seine-et-Yonne], Croixrault [Somme], Jaux and Venette [Oise], La

In D.C. Cowley, M. Fernández-Götz, T. Romankiewicz & H. Wendling (eds). Rural Settlement. Relating buildings, landscape, and people in the European Iron Age (Leiden 2019: Sidestone Press) 21-30.

Plaine de France [Val d'Oise], Marne-la-Vallée [Seine-et-Marne], Saint-Quentin [Aisne], ZAC de Haute Picardie [Somme]). For this paper, I will examine the attributes of these *terroirs* using the example of Brebières. Then, I will apply these attributes to an archaeologically dynamic zone in the area of the Seine/Yonne confluence.

2.2 Defining the attributes of *terroirs* – the example of Brebières

Brebières is located in the Pas-de-Calais department, in the north of France, southwest of Douai (Figure 1a). This area corresponds to the western part of the alluvial plain of the Scarpe River, which flows from west to east at the south of the study area. Today, the rivers of this area are largely channelled. The relief is not very marked and the altitude is about 50 m above sea level. The ground is covered with silt, which is very suitable for farming. Three excavations have been studied for this paper: the ZAC des Béliers (Huvelle 2006; Huvelle 2007a; Huvelle 2007b; Lacalmontie 2016), Horizon 2000 (Compagnon 1996; Severin 1997) and L'Ermitage (Bernez 2006; Compagnon & Bernez 2006; Sys & Censier 2009). All in all, nearly 65 hectares were explored. On the Horizon 2000 site, an enclosure and field ditches dating to the late La Tène period were discovered. At the ZAC des Béliers, twenty-two enclosures were found which are integrated into a network of field ditches. Their occupation covers a timespan from the middle La Tène period to the Roman period. For the Ermitage, four phases of enclosures dating to the middle and late La Tène periods were excavated – providing a total of twenty-six enclosures for this study. This set of sites has been interpreted as a *terroir* and it is possible to outline its main attributes.

For the ZAC des Béliers, an assumption had been made – that the enclosures were standardized in their morphology and dimensions (Lacalmontie 2016, 133-46). The enclosures all exhibit a similar quadrangular form with three internal structural variants being distinguished: simple enclosures; partitioned enclosures; and complex enclosures (Figure 1b). The dimensions are also standardized with a size of less than 2000 m^2, except five of them. This difference may reflect the position of the enclosures in a settlement hierarchy. Consequently, the first attribute of a *terroir* is the morphological similarity of the domestic enclosures.

For the ZAC des Béliers, the methodology of excavation – the large extended area excavations and the sampling of the field ditches by mechanical digger trenches – made it possible to intercept a maximum of features and understand their layout, function and chronology. The enclosed settlements are part of a network of orthogonal field ditches arranged on an NW/SE and NE/SW orientation. This orientation is also visible in most of the enclosures. Moreover, by extending the field ditches of the ZAC des Béliers to the Ermitage, the enclosures would fit perfectly into the network (Figure 2a). The second attribute of the *terroirs* is the integration and arrangement of the domestic enclosures into a network of plots of land. This grid is visible through the presence of a network of field ditches or in the corresponding orientation of the enclosures.

The sites were dated by artefacts from between the early 3rd century BC and the second half of the 2nd century AD (Figure 2b). Three phases were identified. The first began during the 3rd century and extended to the middle of the 2nd century BC. In the middle of the 2nd century BC, a redevelopment can be observed and new enclosures were created. At the end of the 1st century BC and during the Roman period, an enclosure continued in use in the network of field ditches. Here, we can observe a continuous occupation without any hiatus from the beginning of the 3rd century BC to the Roman period. Thus, temporal continuity is the third attribute of a *terroir*.

The sites lie on the slopes overlooking the Scarpe alluvial plain. They are all located to the north of the Scarpe and to the south of the river Escrebieux. Further north, another area was analysed. It also has the attributes of a *terroir* and the same spatial configuration, lying between two rivers. The fourth attribute that I was able to distinguish is the insertion of a *terroir* into a well-defined unit of the landscape (a small plateau or a confluence, for example).

In earlier research a hypothesis was formulated – that one larger and richer (*i.e.* dominant) settlement seemed to control the others (Lacalmontie 2016, 133). This phenomenon can be analysed through the distribution of activities and wealth in the enclosures which constitute the *terroir*. Little data on agricultural production is available as bones are poorly preserved and only a few tools indirectly attest to cattle breeding. The complex network of field ditches can be interpreted as animal pens. Likewise, agriculture is attested by grain storage in small buildings. Site 74 includes a dozen of them. Also at site 74, an anvil as well as metallurgical waste illustrating craft activity were discovered. Hierarchical classification of the sites was developed based on morphological criteria and the temporal dimensions of the settlements. Again, site 74 stands out from the others, covering about 1.5 ha and with a complex form combining spaces for domestic and agricultural activities. Artefacts are more numerous than on the other sites and traces of craft activities were discovered. Finally, a significant number of buildings and continuity of occupation over a longer period were observed. This settlement also occupies a central location in the *terroir*. The other, smaller settlements are located at a distance of 400 m around it (Figure 2a). The fifth and last attribute corresponds to a hierarchical distribution of

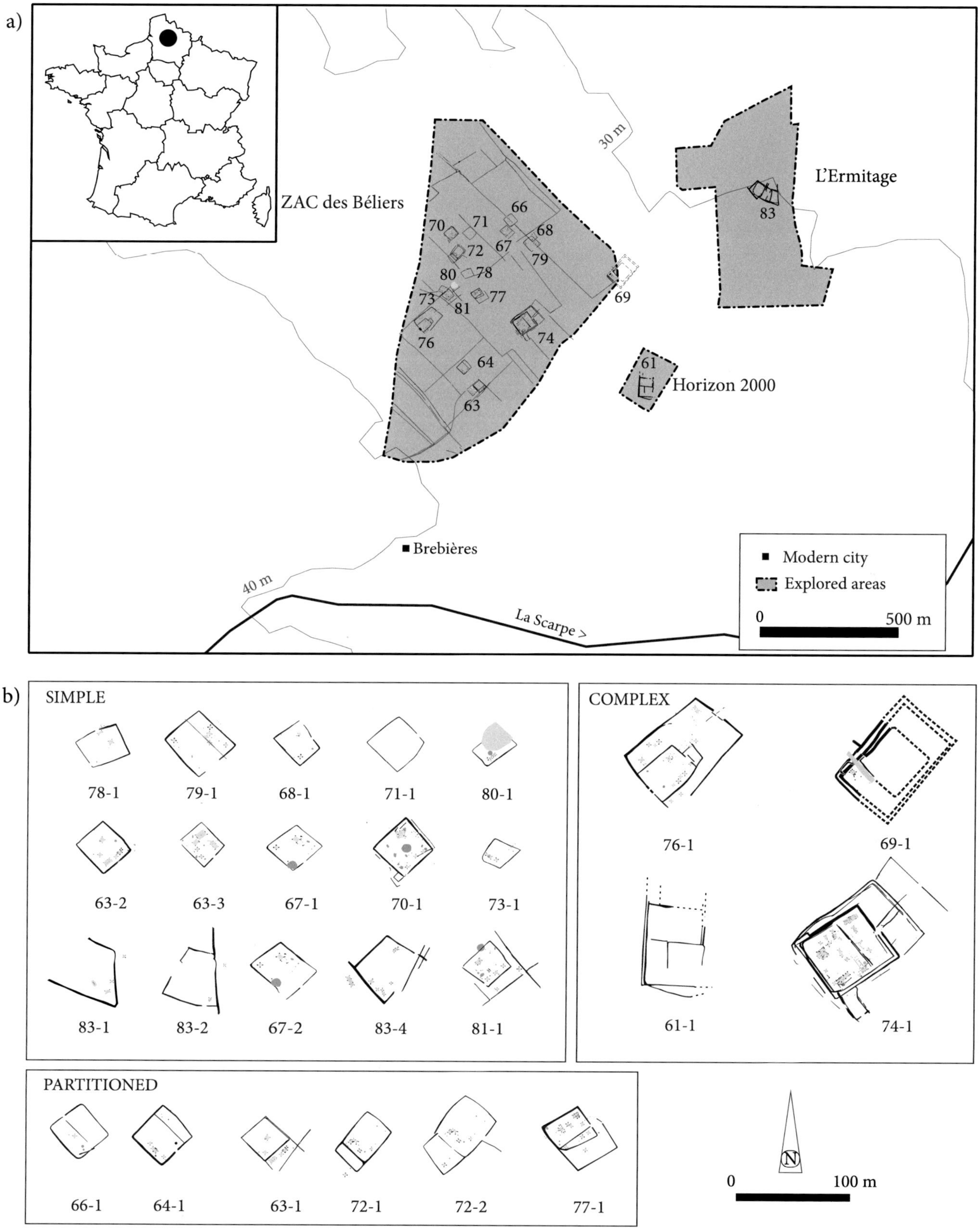

Figure 1: a) Site location plan of the terroir of Brebières (Drawing: A. Cony); b) Enclosures of the terroir of Brebières. (Drawing: A. Cony after the excavation reports and Lacalmontie 2016).

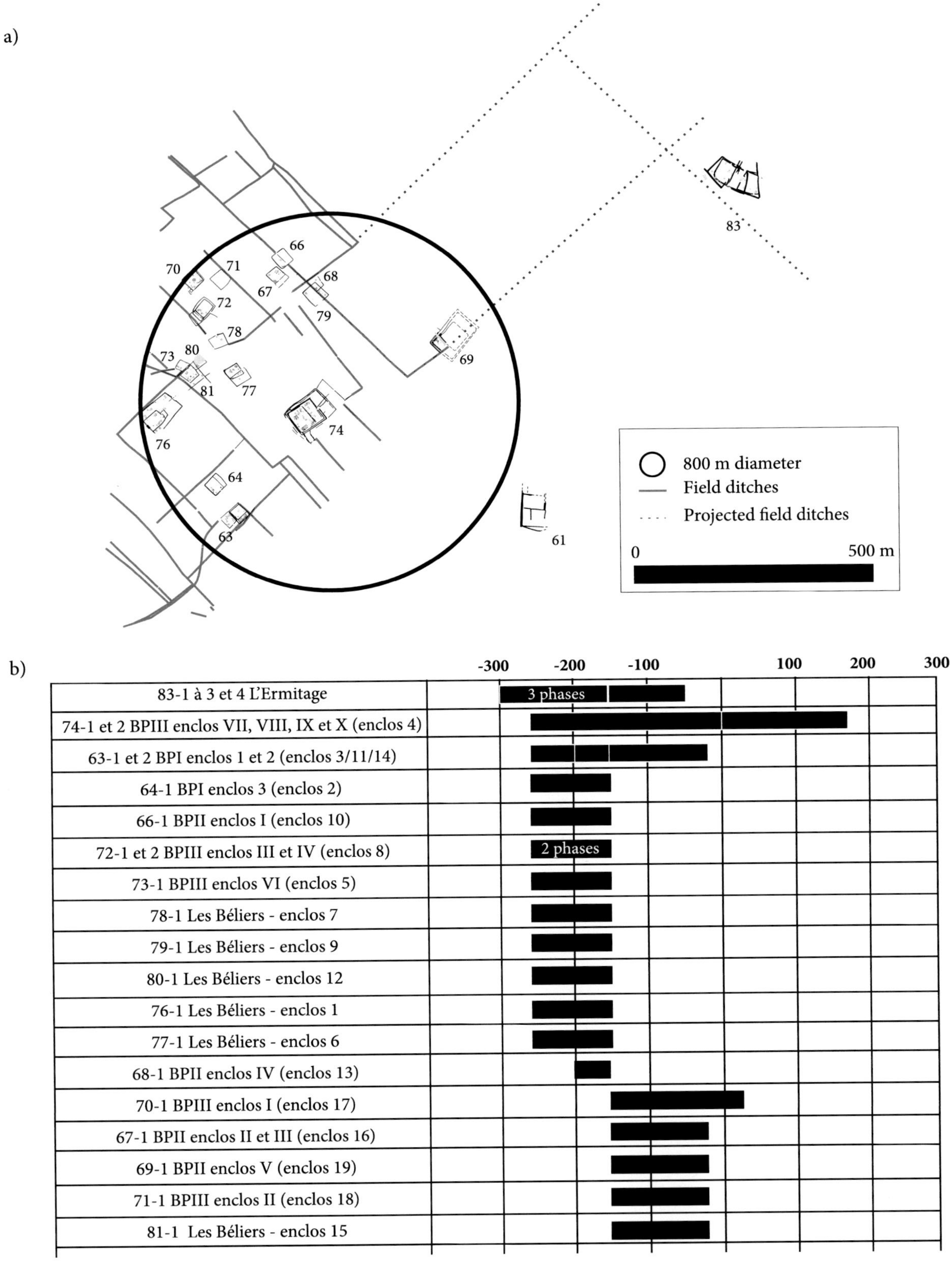

Figure 2: a) Plan of ZAC des Béliers extending to L'Ermitage (83); b) Chronology of the terroir of Brebières. (Drawing: A. Cony).

TERROIR OF BREBIÈRES: ATTRIBUTES
1 - Morphological similarity of the domestic enclosures
- Standardized enclosures - Three organizations (simple, partitioned, complex) based on a quadrangular form - Standardized sizes
2 - Insertion in a network of field ditches
- A visible network of orthogonal field ditches - Similar orientation of the enclosures: NW/SE and NE/SW
3 - Continuous occupation without a hiatus
- Three phases and no hiatus: from the 3rd c. BC to the 2nd c. AD
4 - Insertion into a well-defined unit of the landscape
- The slopes overlooking the Scarpe alluvial plain
5 - Hierarchical distribution of activities and wealth
- Site 74 stands out based on morphological criteria and duration in time plus its central location in the terroir

Table 1: Summary of the attributes of the terroir of Brebières. (A. Cony).

activities and wealth, which could indicate the presence of an elite controlling these entities.

These five attributes were identified from attested *terroirs* like Brebières, and used for identification elsewhere (Table 1). The classification can be applied to archaeologically dynamic zones with several contemporary settlements such as the Seine/Yonne confluence area.

2.3 Testing the attributes of a *terroir* on the Seine/Yonne confluence area

The Seine/Yonne confluence lies southeast of Paris, in the Seine-et-Marne Department (Figure 3a). It corresponds to the alluvial plains of the Seine and the Yonne rivers which are delimited by silty plateaux. Three topographical and geomorphological entities are defined for this zone: the interfluvial plain downstream of the confluence; the interfluvial plain upstream of the confluence; and La Bassée, which corresponds to a corridor about 40 km long and about 5 km wide.

This study area has been extensively explored in the course of quarrying for alluvial aggregates since the 1960s, and around 5000 ha have been explored. The data from these operations has been inventoried, classified and analysed since the early 1990s and Jean-Marc Séguier has studied the area from the Iron Age to the Roman Period for many years (Gouge & Séguier 1994; Horard-Herbin *et al.* 2000; Nouvel *et al.* 2009; Séguier 2012). The corpus of the sites includes 16 enclosed settlements dating to the end of the middle La Tène and the late La Tène period. Burial areas and field ditches are also known in the area, which has been intensely occupied since the Bronze Age.

Some constraints of research have to be mentioned. The first constraint is historiographical. Indeed, before 2003, evaluations of archaeological capability of sites were carried out using large-scale excavations, but after 2003, following a new legislation in France, evaluations are based on trenches covering at least 10 % of the area to be explored. By comparison to open area excavation, this provides a limited insight on certain areas of study. The second constraint is geological and environmental. The area has always undergone major periods of flooding, and erosion is sometimes profound. The sites preserved today are those located on sand and gravel mounds separated by palaeo-channels. Thus, the known occupation evidence in the studied area is unlikely to be complete.

Keeping in mind these limitations, the study area nevertheless includes a large number of enclosed settlements that form two groups – one in the west and the other in the east. These settlements were occupied from the middle to the late La Tène period. This begs the question if the disposition of evidence points to the presence of *terroirs* here. And if so, how many? One? Two? Let us apply the attributes defined before.

As for the morphological similarity of the domestic enclosures, the Seine/Yonne confluence area shows three morphologies: complex enclosures that can be partitioned, co-joined or maybe nested; U-shaped enclosures, enclosed by ditches on only three sides; and simple enclosures (Figure 3b). By mapping this data and in particular the complex enclosures, it is possible to identify the two groups defined above. All the partitioned enclosures are located in the eastern group while the western group combines the co-joined and nested enclosures as well as most of the simple enclosures. The two groups of enclosures are thus defined, each characterised by specific layouts and structures. The first attribute for the identification of *terroirs* is verified.

Concerning the insertion and arrangement of domestic spaces in a network of plots of land, few field ditches have been discovered and these are not organised in a large network as in the ZAC des Béliers. But from the analysis of the orientation of enclosures a possible grid system might be deduced. In fact, in the western group, nine out of ten enclosures share the same orientation (N/S and E/W) thus verifying the attribute. For the eastern group, it is less obvious and the characteristic cannot be easily attested.

Regarding continuity of occupation (Figure 4a), the first settlements date to the beginning of the 3rd century BC and were occupied until the beginning of the 1st century AD. The oldest settlements correspond to the western group. They also present a greater time-depth (except for the site of Le Petit Noyer, which was created later). The settlements of the eastern group were established at the beginning of the 2nd century BC and were abandoned in

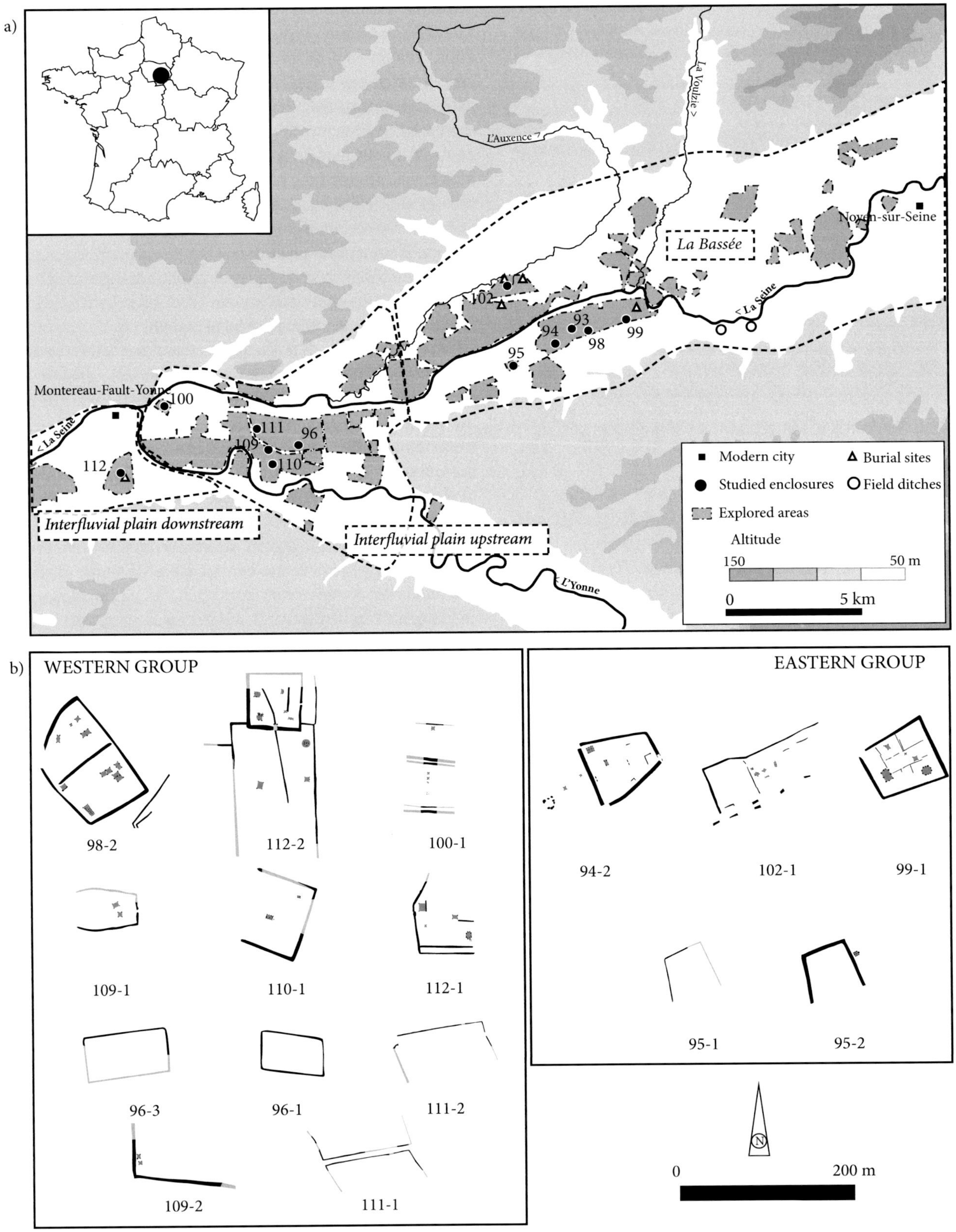

Figure 3: a) Map of the Seine/Yonne confluence area (Drawing: A. Cony); b) Enclosures in the Seine/Yonne confluence area. (Drawing: A. Cony after the excavation reports).

a)

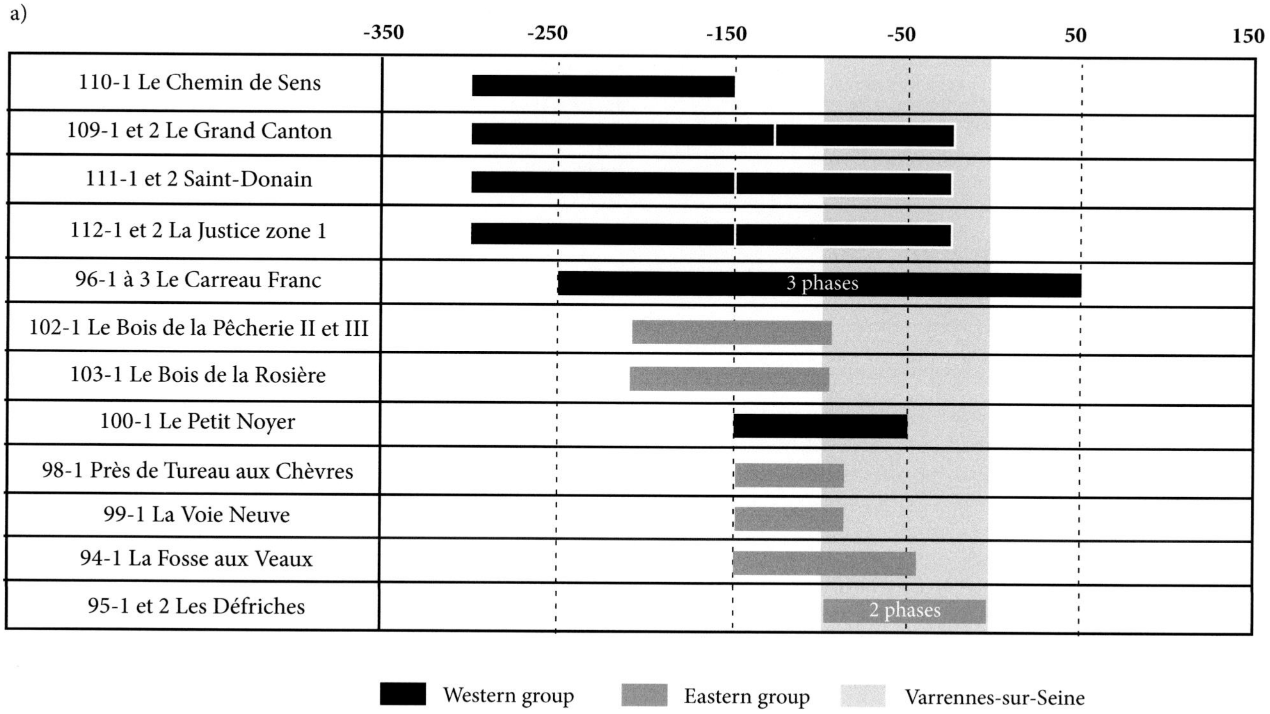

b)

Western group : rich sites

Eastern group : rich sites

B = big XR : extra regional
M = medium R : regional

SG : simple gate w = wine
MD : monumental door c = ceramic

	MORPHOLOGY OF THE ENCLOSURES									PRODUCTION	CONSUMPTION				TRADE		WAR	CULT AND FEAST		
Studied sites	Dimensions of the enclosure	Compartimentation	Size of the ditches (in m)	Monumental gate	Burial site associated	Remarquable localisation	Number of buildings	Multiplication of plans	elaborated plans of the buildings	Association of agriculture and craft	Good quality meat based diet	Precious goods	Wine, oil and salt	Mediterranean exported	Exchanged goods	Provenance	Warrior status	Cult activities	Feast	Number of criteria considered
112-2 La Justice zone 1	B	X	1,18	MD	X		11	X	X	X	X	X	w	X	w+c	XR	X	X	X	5
99-1 La Voie Neuve	M	X	1,60	SG			5	X	X	X	X		w	X	w	XR	X	X	X	13
100-1 Le Petit Noyer	?	X	0,60				5			X	X		w	X	w+c	XR + R	X	X	X	9
98-2 Près de Tureau aux Chèvres	M	X	1				10	X	X		X		w	X	w+c	XR				8
112-1 La Justice zone 1	M		1,50				6	X		X		X	w	X	+c	XR				8
102-1 Le Bois de la Pêcherie II et III	M	X	?		X		5						w				X			5
94-2 La Fosse aux Veaux	M	X	1,20				4	X	X				w							5
109-1 Le Grand Canton Sud			1,35				2						w		c	R				3
109-2 Le Grand Canton Sud			2,30				2						w		c	R				3
95-1 Les Défriches			0,50						X											2
95-2 Les Défriches			1				1						w							2
110-1 Le Chemin de Sens			1,50										w					X		2
111-1 Saint-Donain	M		0,65				2		X											1
111-2 Saint-Donain			1,20																	1
96-1, 2 et 3 Le Carreau Franc			?																	0
103-1 Le Bois de la Rosière	M		?																	0

Figure 4: a) Chronology of the Seine/Yonne confluence area; b) Classification of the sites of the Seine/Yonne confluence area. (Drawing: A. Cony).

WESTERN TERROIR	EASTERN TERROIR
1 - Morphological similarity of the domestic enclosures	
Co-joined or nested enclosures	Partitioned enclosures
2 - Insertion in a network of field ditches	
Two orientations used: N/S and E/W	Not visible
3 - Continuous occupation without a hiatus	
3rd c. – middle 1st c. BC Long time-depth	Beginning 2nd c. – middle 1st c. BC Short time-depth
4 - Insertion into a well-defined unit of the landscape	
Confluence	Western Bassée
5 - Hierarchical distribution of activities and wealth	
La Justice and Le Petit Noyer	La Voie Neuve and Près de Tureau aux Chèvres

Table 2: Table summarising the attributes of the two terroirs of the Seine/Yonne confluence area. (A. Cony).

the later 1st century BC. The settlements of each group are contemporary and present a continuous occupation without any hiatus. The enclosures of each group also cover similar time-spans.

Regarding the proximity of the settlements and their integration into well-defined geographical units, the sites lie in two areas bounded by rivers. The western group is concentrated around the confluence, while the eastern group is located on the two banks of the river, in the western *Bassée*. Thus, the fourth attribute is also verified.

The fifth attribute of *terroirs* is the existence of a hierarchical distribution of economic activities and wealth. The classification of the sites according to their wealth is based on a range of criteria: morphology of the enclosures; dimensions of the enclosures; size of the ditches; number of buildings; social and religious diversity (feasts, cult, warrior status); and the quality of the artefacts. Duration of occupation is also taken into account (Cony 2017b). The classification shows two wealthier settlements, at La Justice and La Voie Neuve (Figure 4b). Two other settlements at Le Petit Noyer and Près de Tureau aux Chèvres also conform to a significant number of criteria. La Justice and Le Petit Noyer belong to the western group and La Voie Neuve and Près de Tureau aux Chèvres to the eastern group. Therefore, each group has two apparently rich settlements that could correspond to the residence of an elite controlling the rest of the sector.

This evidence supports the suggestion that two *terroirs* exist in the Seine/Yonne confluence area (Table 2). It is then possible to develop the interpretation of these sets of settlements and to try to understand the ways in which they functioned.

2.4 Further interpretation of two terroirs

The two groups of sites discussed above have already been highlighted by Marie-Pierre Horard-Herbin (Horard-Herbin *et al.* 2000, 196) through the study of faunal remains, in particular by the proportions of canines, which are more frequent in the western group, and equines, which are more frequent in the eastern group.

Similarly, archaeozoological, palynological and paleoethnobotanocal analyses show a distribution of agro-pastoral production activities. Archaeozoological analyses indicate that the site of La Justice did not produce meat (Séguier 2013, 335-7), while the pollen and plant remains show specialisation in cereal production. Tools and storage buildings are numerous. Data from the other sites in the western group also indicate an economy based on cereal production rather than on animal husbandry.

On the other hand, the settlements of the eastern group indicate meat production, with areas interpreted as animal pens and the bones of very young animals identified. However, it is too early to envisage such a strict separation of agro-pastoral productions between these two *terroirs*. Further analysis of these data is needed to verify these suggestions.

However, we can further develop the interpretation of the links between these two *terroirs* and their archaeological environment. In fact, the unenclosed nucleated settlement of Varennes-sur-Seine is located 600 m north of the site of La Justice. It was occupied at the earliest in LT D1b, and lasted until just before the Augustan period, its maximum development being in LT D2 (Séguier 2013, 345-8; Viand & Séguier accepted). Crafts are strongly represented and the site fits into an important exchange network illustrated through the presence of imported goods. This unenclosed nucleated settlement developed in parallel to the rural settlements of the study area and could be interpreted as a market place.

Chronological analysis of each site suggests that the first *terroir* to be created is the western one followed by the eastern one. Therefore, these two *terroirs* and their economic and wealth activities (agro-pastoral production) have created a commercial hub area materialised by the unenclosed nucleated settlement of Varennes-sur-Seine (Viand & Séguier accepted).

To conclude in the Seine/Yonne confluence area, two *terroirs* were clearly identified but several questions remain. The uneven distribution of wealth and economic activities between settlements has revealed a hierarchy and a degree of centralisation. This indicates the presence of an elite, which is nevertheless difficult to characterise precisely. Are the elites aristocrats or only landowners? Furthermore, how did they divide the territory? It is likely that production activities show the complementarity and interconnection of the two *terroirs*. Chronology also suggests an evolution leading to the establishment of an unenclosed nucleated settlement that can be interpreted as a market place. The links between the three entities – the two terroirs and the agglomeration – will require further work to define more precisely, but, for now, it is tempting to argue that Varennes-sur-Seine was managed or maybe even founded by the elite living in these two *terroirs*.

2.5 Conclusion and perspectives

The two *terroirs* presented here have been studied as part of a comprehensive analysis of the Late Iron Age countryside of the north of France (Cony 2017a). This larger study examined thirteen *terroirs*, demonstrating the shared attributes of these sets of settlements, and also to analyse their chronology, production activities and social organisation. This form of land use is known from the early La Tène period up to the Roman period. It is particularly visible during the middle and late La Tène period.

Several hypotheses can be put forward to define what these *terroirs* were. For the ZAC des Béliers in Brebières, it is suggested that this land was the property of a landowner. For Object'Ifs Sud, near to Caen, it is proposed that an agricultural community brought together several landowners and exploited the land in a coordinated way (Le Goff 2009). We can perhaps also consider a family property that grew through inheritances and demise of lineages as another explanatory model (cf. Wendling 2010). The hinterland of the nucleated settlements must also be considered, as suggested for Actiparc and Arras (Jacques & Prilaux 2003). Eventually, as for the Seine/Yonne confluence area, a *terroir* and its social and economic activities can generate an agglomeration.

More studies of this kind are needed to provide a frame of reference that would allow for further interpretation. Furthermore, this phenomenon raises the issue of land tenure and ownership at the end of the Iron Age. The *terroirs* have to be considered in their natural environment. Multidisciplinary studies (paleoethnobotany, archaeozoology, geology, etc.) are needed to develop hypotheses. Finally, after describing this French model of occupation of the countryside, it would be interesting to see if it can be applied to other regions of Iron Age Europe.

2.6 Bibliography

Bernez, S. 2006. *Lambres-lez-Douai, L'Ermitage, Rapport de diagnostic*. Communauté de l'Agglomération du Douaisis. Direction de l'Archéologie Préventive. Douai: SRA Nord-Pas-de-Calais.

Bertrand, I., Duval, A., Gomez de Soto, J. & Maguer, P. 2009. *Habitats et paysages ruraux en Gaule et regards sur d'autres régions du monde celtique, Actes du 31e colloque international de l'AFEAF, 17-20 mai 2007*. Chauvigny: AFEAF.

Blancquaert, G. & Marion, S. 2000. *Les installations agricoles de l'âge du Fer en France septentrionale*. Paris: Editions rue d'Ulm.

Blancquaert, G. & Malrain, F. 2016. Évolution des sociétés gauloises du second âge du Fer, entre mutations internes et influences externes, Actes du 38*e Colloque international de l'AEFAF, Amiens du 29 mai au 1er juin 2014*. Revue Archéologique de Picardie. n° spécial 30. Amiens: AFEAF.

Buchsenschutz, O. & Méniel, P. (eds) 1994. *Les installations agricoles de l'âge du Fer en Ile-de-France. Actes de Colloque de Paris 1993*. Collection Etudes d'histoire et d'archéologie. Paris: Edition d'Ulm.

Carpentier, V. & Marcigny, C. 2012. *Des hommes aux champs. Pour une archéologie des espaces ruraux du Néolithique au Moyen* Âge. Rennes: Presses universitaires de Rennes.

Compagnon, É. 1996. Brebières, Parc industriel Horizon 2000. *Bilan Scientifique Régional*. Lille: SRA Nord-Pas-de-Calais.

Compagnon, É. & Bernez, S. 2006. *Lambres-lez-Douai, L'Ermitage, Rapport de diagnostic*. Communauté de l'Agglomération du Douaisis. Direction de l'Archéologie Préventive. Douai: SRA Nord-Pas-de-Calais.

Cony, A. 2017a. *Les terroirs en Gaule à la fin de l'âge du Fer*. Thèse de doctorat sous la direction de Stephan Fichtl. Université de Tours. Soutenue en avril 2017.

Cony, A. 2017b. Hiérarchie de l'habitat rural à la fin de l'âge du Fer. L'importance de définir les critères de hiérarchisation en fonction de l'environnement archéologique. *Revue Archimède* n°4. Mis en ligne le 06/06/2017.

Favier, J. 1993. *Dictionnaire de la France medieval*. Paris: Fayard.

Gouge, P. & Séguier, J.-M. 1994. L'habitat rural de l'âge du Fer en Bassée et à la confluence Seine-Yonne (Seine-et-Marne): un état de la recherché. In Buchsenschutz, O. & Méniel, P. (eds). *Les installations agricoles de l'âge du Fer en Ile-de-France. Actes de Colloque de Paris 1993*. 45-70. Collection Etudes d'histoire et d'archéologie. Paris: Edition d'Ulm.

Horard-Herbin, M.-P., Méniel, P. & Séguier, J.-M. 2000. La faune de dix sites ruraux de la fin de l'âge du Fer de La Bassée (Seine-et-Marne). In G. Blancquaert, & S. Marion. *Les installations agricoles de l'âge du Fer en France septentrionale*. 181-208. Paris: Editions rue d'Ulm.

Huvelle, G. 2006. *Brebières, Les Béliers, Phase 1, Rapport de diagnostic*. Communauté de l'Agglomération du

Douaisis. Direction de l'Archéologie Préventive. Inrap. Douai: SRA Nord-Pas-de-Calais.
Huvelle, G. 2007. *Brebières, Les Béliers, Phase 2, Rapport de diagnostic*. Communauté de l'Agglomération du Douaisis. Direction de l'Archéologie Préventive. Douai: Inrap, SRA Nord-Pas-de-Calais.
Huvelle, G. 2007. *Brebières, Les Béliers, Phase 3, Rapport de diagnostic*. Communauté de l'Agglomération du Douaisis. Direction de l'Archéologie Préventive. Douai: Inrap, SRA Nord-Pas-de-Calais.
Jacques, A. & Prilaux, G. 2003. *Dans le sillage de César. Traces de romanisation d'un territoire, les fouilles d'Actiparc à Arras, Catalogue d'exposition du musée des Beaux-Arts à Arras du 27 septembre 2003 au 4 janvier 2004*. Arras.
Lacalmontie, A. 2016. L'occupation du second âge du Fer à Brebières (Pas-de-Calais), un habitat rural standardisé? In G. Blancquaert & F. Malrain 2016. Évolution des sociétés gauloises du second âge du Fer, entre mutations internes et influences externes, Actes du 38*e Colloque international de l'AEFAF, Amiens du 29 mai au 1er juin 2014*. 133-46. Amiens: Revue Archéologique de Picardie. n° spécial 30.
Lebeau, R. 1996. *Les grands types de structures agraires dans le monde*. Collection Initiation aux études de géographie. 6e édition mise à jour (première édition: 1969). Paris.
Le Goff, E. 2009. Habitats, terroir et paysage rural: aménagement et structuration du territoire et de la campagne gauloise: Ifs, ZAC Object'Ifs Sud. In I. Bertrand, A. Duval, J. Gomez de Soto & P. Maguer 2009. *Habitats et paysages ruraux en Gaule et regards sur d'autres régions du monde celtique, Actes du 31e colloque international de l'AFEAF, 17-20 mai 2007*. 93-107. Chauvigny: AFEAF.
Nouvel, P., Barral, P., Defressigne, S., Riquier, V., Séguier, J.-M., Tikonoff, N. & Zehner, M. 2009. Rythmes de création, fonctionnement et abandon des établissements ruraux de la fin de l'âge du Fer dans l'est de la France. In I. Bertrand, A. Duval, J. Gomez de Soto & P. Maguer 2009. *Habitats et paysages ruraux en Gaule et regards sur d'autres régions du monde celtique, Actes du 31e colloque international de l'AFEAF, 17-20 mai 2007*. 109-51. Chauvigny: AFEAF.
Séguier, J.-M. 2012. Fermes, terroirs et territoires du deuxième âge du Fer à l'époque romaine dans le secteur Seine-Yonne (Seine-et-Marne). In V. Carpentie & C. Marcigny. *Des hommes aux champs. Pour une archéologie des espaces ruraux du Néolithique au Moyen Âge*. 391-408. Rennes: Presses universityaires de Rennes.
Séguier, J.-M. 2013. *Varennes-sur-Seine La Justice, Le marais de la Fontaine du Cœur (Île-de-France, Seine-et-Marne), Rapport de fouille*. Paris: Inrap, SRA Île-de-France.
Séguier, J.-M. 2014. *Varennes-sur-Seine, Le Petit Fossard (Île-de-France, Seine-et-Marne), Rapport de fouille*. Paris: Inrap, SRA Île-de-France.
Severin, C. 1997. *Brebières, Parc industriel Horizon 2000, Rapport de sondage – diagnostic*. Lille: SRA Nord-Pas-de-Calais.
Sys, D. & Censier, D. 2009. *Lambres-lez-Douai, L'Ermitage, Rapport de fouille*. Communauté de l'Agglomération du Douaisis. Direction de l'Archéologie Préventive. Douai: SRA Nord-Pas-de-Calais.
Viand, A. & Séguier, J.-M. accepted. Les agglomérations de la fin de l'âge du Fer et du début de l'époque augustéenne en Île-de-France. In Fichtl, St., Barral, Ph., Pierrevelcin, G. & Schönfelder, M. *Les agglomérations celtiques du IIIe-Ier s. av. J.-C. Keltische Großsiedlungen des 3.-1. Jhs. v. Chr. Actes de la table ronde tenue à Bibracte, octobre 2015*. Mainz: RGZM.
Wendling, H. 2010. Landbesitz und Erbfolge. Ein ethnographisches Modell zur Sozialstruktur und Raumgliederung der mitteleuropäischen Latènezeit. In P. Trebsche, N. Müller-Scheeßel & S. Reinhold (eds). *Der gebaute Raum. Bausteine einer Architektursoziologie vormoderner Gesellschaften*. 325-54. Münster, New York, München & Berlin: Waxmann.

Chapter 3

Regional aspects of landscape exploitation and settlement structure in Denmark in the Late Bronze Age and Early Iron Age

Mads Runge

In D.C. Cowley, M. Fernández-Götz, T. Romankiewicz & H. Wendling (eds). Rural Settlement. Relating buildings, landscape, and people in the European Iron Age (Leiden 2019: Sidestone Press) 31-43.

3.1 Introduction

Over recent decades, Denmark has seen a massive increase in archaeological empirical research, not least on Bronze Age and Iron Age settlements. This is driven by a boom in construction projects and the introduction of a new Museum Act, providing new opportunities for a more systematic approach to archaeological investigations. At the same time analysis of big data has become possible, while developments in archaeological science have created a better understanding of living conditions and better chronologies. Coupled with new theory formation these factors have facilitated a more detailed analysis of the development of settlements and the subsistence economy than was previously possible (Gerritsen 2003; Arnoldussen 2008; Kveiborg 2008; Herschend 2009; Runge 2009; Holst 2010).

As a result, it is no longer appropriate to rely exclusively on the classic settlement studies in Central and Southern Jutland undertaken between the 1960s and the 1980s (Hvass 1983; 1985; Jensen 2003; Rindel 2011). Other parts of the country are now also well-covered by settlement studies from the Bronze and Iron Ages and the contours of distinctive regional patterns are emerging.

This paper will first introduce a model for Danish settlement archaeology of the Late Bronze Age (1000-500 BC) and Early Pre-Roman Iron Age (500 BC-AD 1) in a regional perspective. Thereafter some general trends in settlement structure in three regions will be discussed: the classic picture in Central and Southern Jutland; Northern Jutland; and Eastern Denmark. Thereafter, concepts of the organisation of land, social aspects and cultural interaction, will be outlined based on 'new' material from Northern Jutland and Eastern Denmark as the material from Central and Southern Jutland can be found in already published literature (*e.g.* Hvass 1983; 1985; Jensen 2003; Rindel 2011).

3.2 Regional settlement patterns

3.2.1 Model

In my PhD thesis, I analysed the formation of regional settlement patterns in the Late Bronze Age and Early Iron Age (Runge 2012a; 2014). The analyses of regionality take

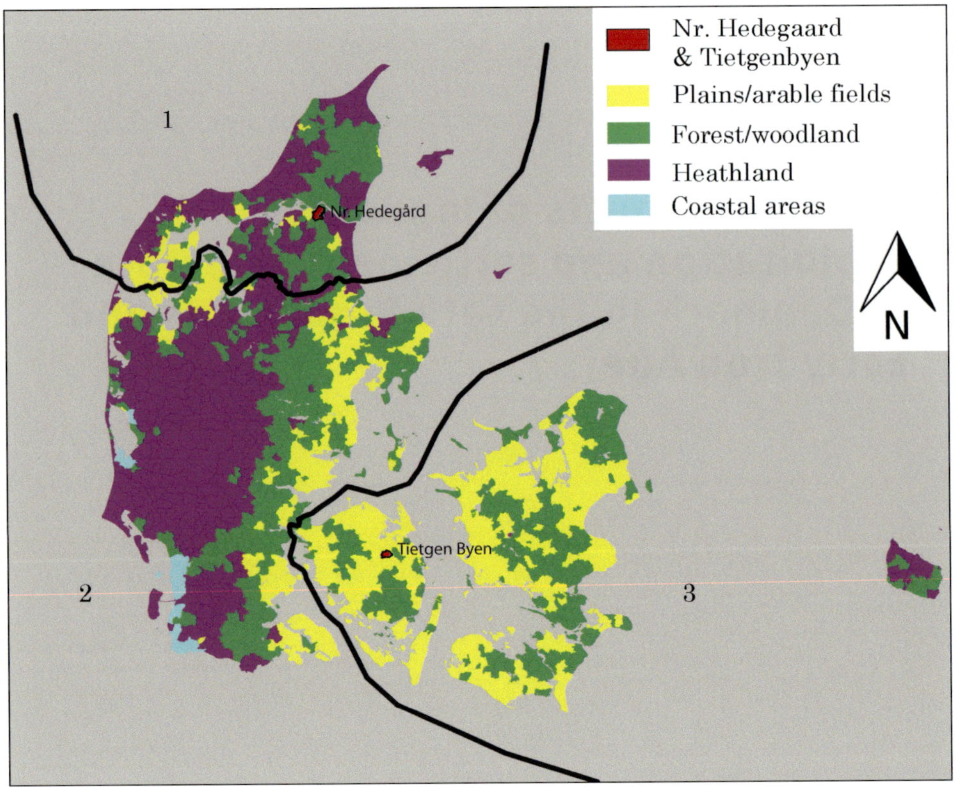

Figure 1: Historical division of the cultural landscape (after Møller & Porsmose 1997) and the three investigation areas, with the case studies of Trandersbakkeøen and Tietgenbyen also shown. (Drawing: Kristine Stub Precht & Mads Runge, Odense City Museums).

their point of departure in the term *bygd* (hamlet) and the formation of *bygder* (hamlets) from the late 1600s until the agricultural reforms around the beginning of the 1800s. The term *bygd* is used here in two interwoven senses: 1) organisational, as the term for an inhabited area with a social fellowship or communality; and 2) an ecological sense, as the term for an overall region – an ecological area – of predominantly uniform topography and vegetation and, as a consequence, a relatively uniform human subsistence base.

The division into *bygder* means that a number of specific natural conditions are linked to certain types of settlements and structural forms, and it is essential that agriculture in the period from the late 1600s onwards has parallels to the Late Bronze Age and Early Iron Age in respect of the basic agro-technological methods, as for instance rotation of fields and a non-mechanical concept (Fabech & Ringtved 2009, 143, 167; Näsman 2009, 104). However, there are variations in patterns of land use and the degree of exploitation between the two periods. This may be a consequence of a stronger connection between the sacral and the profane in the Late Bronze Age and Early Iron Age than in the historical period and thus a minor focus on profit (Fabech & Ringtved 2009, 167; Herschend 2009, 18; Odgaard & Rømer 2009).

At a general scale (Figure 1), the Danish landscape can be divided up into *slette-/agerbygd* (plains/arable fields), *skovbygd* (forest/woodland), *hedebygd* (heathland), *kystbygd* (coastal areas) and *marskbygd* (saltmarsh/marshland). These divisions underpin Møller and Porsmose's assessment of elements in the formation of the historic *bygder* (Møller & Porsmose 1997), aspects of which provide a useful context within which to consider prehistoric settlement patterns.

While coastal areas and saltmarsh/marshlands constitute special landforms that are outside the scope of this article, a rough three-part division of the landscape is evident, with an eastern area of arable fields, forest/woodland comprising till plains and heavy soil, a Central and Southern Jutland heathland area featuring moorland and lighter, sandy soils, and a Northern Jutland area characterised by heathland, forest/woodland – with additional large expanses of post-glacial risen marine plains. Eastern Jutland from Djursland and to the south bears a great resemblance to Eastern Denmark in respect of vegetation and landscape. Even so, the link with the Central and Southern Jutland area has been maintained, since the Eastern Jutland settlement system with fenced-in farms at Vendehøj and elsewhere (Ejstrud & Jensen 2000, 58-61), for example, resembles the Central and Southern Jutland system rather than the one found in Eastern Denmark.

The formation of prehistoric *bygder* in the Late Bronze Age and Early Iron Age came about as a consequence of a combination of: 1) natural conditions, 2) the cultural landscape resources, 3) the internal settlement structure (organisation and dynamics of the settlements) and 4) the regional settlement pattern (interaction, hierarchy and organisation of the landscape) (Runge 2014, 165). The elements in the formation of the prehistoric *bygder* draws heavily on Møller and Porsmose's (1997) assessment of elements in the formation of the historic *bygder*.

The three-part division of the landscape into areas of arable fields with forest/woodland, heathland, and heath and forest/woodland suggests, on the one hand, how the communities were organised on a general level, but should not be taken as a detailed picture since numerous studies have pointed out that this three-part division is too broad (Lund 1994; Nielsen 1998; Ejstrud & Jensen 2000, 61-5, 110-3; Ringtved 1988) and does not adequately capture the complexity of the settlement structure at the time (Møller 2011; Kjær Nielsen 2015). Never-the-less, the three-part division does provide an analytical framework for comparing the three regions (Runge 2014, 164-5).

In the case of Northern Jutland and Eastern Denmark, Trandersbakkeøen and Tietgenbyen are used as cases; both areas which I have investigated in depth in my primary studies (see *e.g.* Runge 2009; 2010; 2011; 2012a; 2012b; 2013; Harvig *et al.* 2014). The description of Central and Southern Jutland is based on literary studies.

3.3 Main points of regional settlement patterns

3.3.1 Central and Southern Jutland

The landscape of Central and Southern Jutland is characterised by heathland and *bakkeøer* (flat-topped hills). The great open wide expanses were well-suited to large field systems and relatively large animal flocks and herds, primarily cattle. The area is characterised by a number of classic Iron Age localities which have contributed to our perception of the settlement of the period. During the Late Bronze Age – Early Pre-Roman Iron Age, the area was dominated by small labile units, moving around in the landscape. From the Late Pre-Roman Iron Age – Early Roman Iron Age onwards, a village society became established and a general tendency is seen towards larger, more rigidly-structured and more permanent settlements. With this came an increased need for regulation. A characteristic feature comprises the so-called 'wandering villages', while well-preserved remains of fences around farms and/or villages enable detailed analyses of the development and structure of the settlements, including the social variation. The term 'wandering' village is a classic term in Danish settlement archaeology. It describes the situation where a village moves around in a resource area from generation to generation, exploiting the good fertile land formerly occupied by the village as a field in the next (Hvass 1988; 1993). Recent studies suggest that these movements do not reflect synchronous relocations of entire villages, but rather gradual relocations resulting from the division of land by heritage (Holst 2010).

3.3.2 Northern Jutland. Trandersbakkeøen and Nr. Hedegaard

The heathland and forest/woodland landscape of Northern Jutland, especially around Aalborg, is highly varied, with its flat-topped hills and marine forelands. The Nr. Hedegaard tell site (series of settlement phases lying on top of each other, thereby forming a visible mound) is located on Trandersbakkeøen, one of the Aalborg area's striking flat-topped hills. In the Iron Age, the flat-topped hills were intensively exploited. These conditions led to the development of specialised economies and, as a consequence, a greater degree of interaction amongst settlements. It is suggested elsewhere that this specialization and intensive exploitation of the landscape needed strong leaders in the largest, most important of the villages, the tells (Runge 2012a; 2018, 66).

3.3.3 Eastern Denmark. Tietgenbyen

Eastern Denmark was characterised by arable fields and forest/woodland, with Tietgenbyen located in the arable fields southeast of Odense. The heavy soils of Eastern Denmark were difficult to cultivate in prehistoric times. Within the past decade, large parts of an approximately 350 hectares commercial area have been investigated at Tietgenbyen, revealing a Bronze Age and Early Pre-Roman Iron Age cultural landscape. The settlement system comprises predominantly small labile units, in a system that can in general be recognised across the rest of Eastern Denmark and Scania. The settlement structure from the Late Bronze Age/Early Pre-Roman Iron Age was retained until the beginning of the Late Roman Iron Age (Runge 2012a; 2014).

3.4 Comparing the three regions

Regional trends stand out clearly from the middle of the Pre-Roman Iron Age, perhaps due to the fact that pressure on resources peaked at that time. Virtually the whole country and a series of different landscape forms seem to have been put to use and there was now a growing need to find local answers to the problems that would have been caused by pressure on resources.

While Central and Southern Jutland developed autonomous, self-regulating mechanisms, Northern Jutland continued its development of strong leadership and a regional subsistence economy, and Eastern Denmark largely maintained the system handed down from the Late Bronze Age/Early Pre-Roman Iron Age with small mobile units and a few strong central localities. Correspondingly, the unifying points in the landscape of Central and Southern Jutland were the large areas of cremation graves while the tell sites served the same purpose in Northern Jutland. In Eastern Denmark, the cooking pit sites, sites consisting of a large number of cooking pits but no houses, played a unifying role (Runge 2012a, 2018: 71-2).

3.5 Case study 1: Trandersbakkeøen, Northern Jutland

3.5.1 Settlement structure

In the Pre-Roman Iron Age, Trandersbakkeøen was divided into seven or eight resource areas located at a distance of less than one kilometre, representing extremely intensive exploitation (Figure 2). The character of the settlement varies from tell sites with fixed locations lasting around seven hundred years to the 'wandering villages' which, for generations, moved around within the resource area in order to benefit from the reciprocal effect of settlement and cultivation. As a hybrid between the tell sites and the 'wandering villages', there are settlements with an accumulation of cultural strata resulting from a certain degree of continuity of occupation, but without the formation of a tell site (Runge 2009, 181-3).

At Trandersbakkeøen there are two tell sites – Nr. Hedegaard to the south and Nr. Tranders to the north – and it has been suggested that their fixed location over several hundred years and their large size may have been special markers in the landscape, constituting some form of significant centre (Lund 2009, 195). The excavation of a few extensive strata supports the assessment of the development of the settlement at village level and not, as

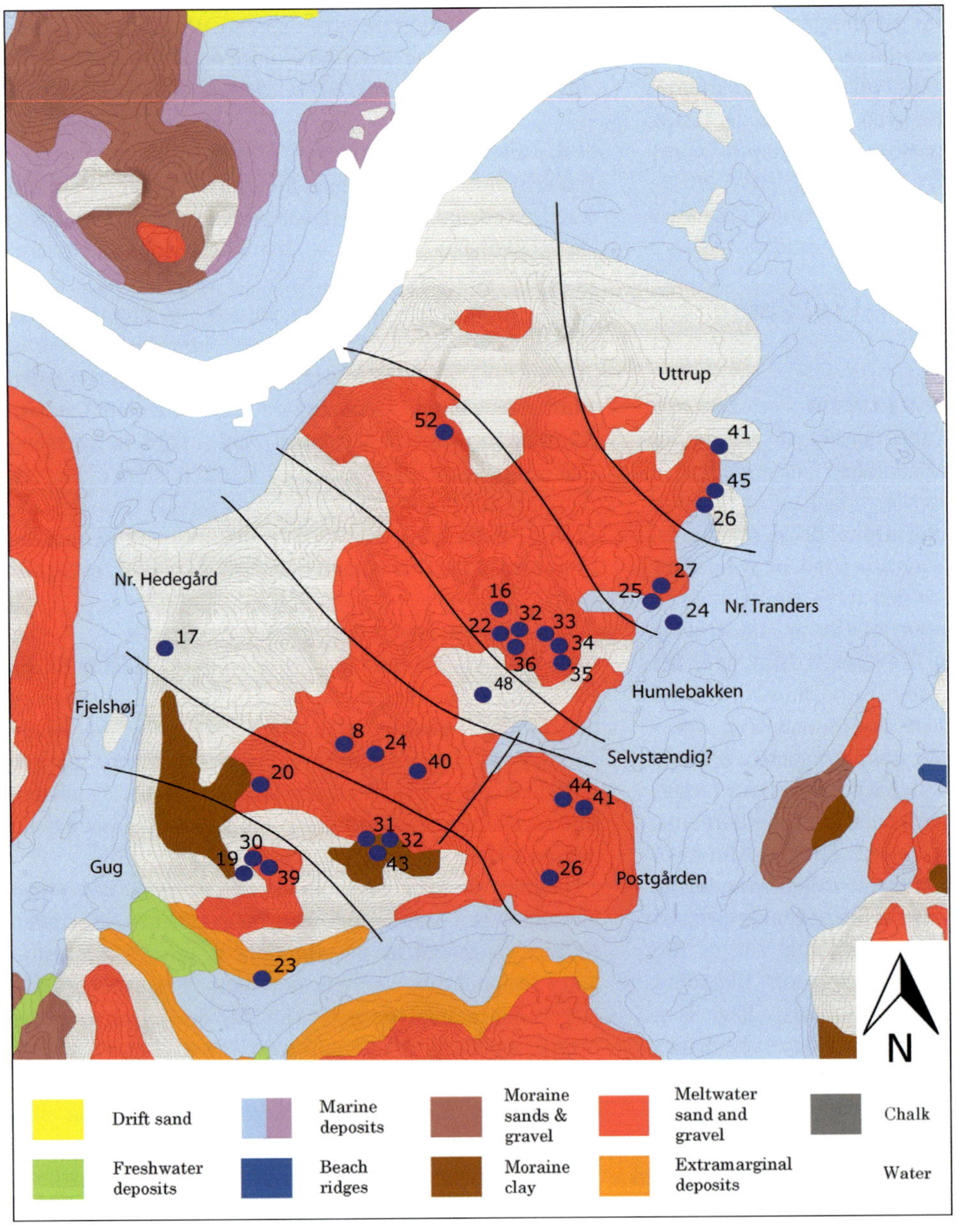

Figure 2: The geology of Trandersbakkeøen and its possible division during the Pre-Roman and Early Roman Iron Ages into eight resource areas. (Map source: Geological Survey of Denmark and Greenland).

had been the norm for tell sites, to be restricted to looking at development within various phases of single farmsteads (Bech 1984, 40; 1985, 133; Runge 2014, 52).

The oldest village phases at Nr. Hedegaard were established at the Bronze Age/Iron Age transition and can be traced through a number of phases into the middle of the Early Roman Iron Age. The oldest phases consist of relatively large and unstructured houses covering most of the south-facing slope where the settlement is located. From the Late Pre-Roman Iron Age, the settlement was structured into a couple of rows of buildings orientated east to west, with the positions of the individual farmsteads fixed through several phases. The presence of social stratification is evident in large houses, generally sited discretely from other buildings, whose size or distinct constructional features set them apart (*e.g.* distinctive entrance areas), but is not reflected in the finds assemblage (Runge 2009, 35-53, 165-72).

3.5.2 Subsistence strategies and exploitation of land

The resource areas on Trandersbakkeøen apparently had a primary resource area on the fertile, well-drained land near the settlement with fields and grazing, as well as a secondary resource area on the lower post-glacial risen marine plains. The secondary resource area may have been an uninhabited and extensively exploited area, perhaps woodland (Runge 2009, 253-6).

Nr. Hedegaard is located some 3.5 km from Limfjorden on the south side of a drumlin to the south/south-east of which there is a valley, probably characterised by wet meadowlands suitable for grazing and haymaking. The higher ground north of the site may have been predominantly heathland, and maps from the 1700s/1800s indicate that the heath was fairly extensive in the vicinity of the site. Indeed, the existence of heathland in the Early Iron Age is implied by twigs of heather retrieved in samples from the settlement, where it was probably used for a wide varity of purposes. Shifting sand has been a strong factor throughout most of the Early Iron Age, as indicated by sectional views of thick dunes between the settlement strata (Figure 3). The distance to marine resources in the Limfjord was not great, so these were exploited, too. Finds of wells on the site indicate access to freshwater (Dalsgaard 2009; Henriksen *et al.* 2009; Runge 2009, 17-20, 253-6).

Figure 3: Longitudinal section through a series of overlapping chalk floors separated by cultural layers and shifting sand at the tell site Nr. Hedegaard. There are ard marks in the subsoil. (Photo: Jens N. Nielsen, Historical Museum of Northern Jutland).

The heathlands provided a stable resource for grazing and winter fodder and was especially suitable for sheep. From the large quantities of preserved animal bones, sheep proved to be the predominant species. Cattle was also common. Pigs, horses, dogs, and game are represented but not in great numbers (Hesel 2009).

Fishing was important to an extent, but in no way a predominant feature. A common method was net fishing, notably for flounder. Besides this, a fair amount of greater weever, a few eels, garpike, salmon/trout, sculpin, and turbot/brill are evident. Besides fish bones, needles for knotting fishing nets were retrieved. Other marine resources exploited include molluscs and possible seaweed (Enghoff 2009; Runge 2009, 256).

3.5.3 Social aspects and cultural interaction

At Trandersbakkeøen and Nr. Hedegaard there are finds that indicate the linkages between the profane and the sacred. These are predominantly minor settlement offerings, which should presumably be attributed to individuals or households. Examples include a small ritual area measuring 3 by 3 m in the southeastern part of the settlement comprising a pit, a fireplace, and two close-set concentrations of burnt material over which had been placed an angled sickle. The finds are dated to the transition period between Bronze and Iron Age. Among other things the pit contained an almost complete clay vessel and other sherds, a fragment of what could be an iron needle, two bone points, several burnt and unburnt bones, and charcoal. The two areas affected by fire contained almost identical archaeo-botanical material with many charred grains and a few seeds. The contents are interpreted as stored, threshed, and cleaned grain (Runge 2009, 125-6).

Mention must also be made of a couple of unusual finds of what might be gaming pieces. One consists of 69 knucklebones, the so-called astragalus bones, and two burnt bones of unspecified type. The bones were buried in a shallow trench and are stratigraphically dated to the transition between the Early and Late Pre-Roman Iron Age (Runge 2009, 123-5). The second find comprises a collection of 67 small light-coloured quartz stones mainly measuring between 0.5 and 2.0 cm in diameter, with some up to 4 cm in size, stratigraphically dated to the Early Pre-Roman Iron Age (Haue 2009, 143). The similarity in the number of pieces in both finds is striking, and both are interpreted as collections of gaming pieces (see Michaelsen 1992, 11-3, 17-23). It is uncertain whether these are complete sets or just a store of potential gaming pieces; in any case, the equal quantities of potential gaming pieces as well as the presence of a few pieces different in size to the others is noteworthy (Runge 2011, 58-60).

Another example of a significant deposit is a Late Pre-Roman Iron Age vessel decorated with a man's face set into a hearth in a house, (Lund 1992). The vessel lay against one of the stones in the base of the fireplace, covered by its red-burned clay capping (Runge 2009, 87). Furthermore, other finds that are interpreted as offerings have been found near entrances and in walls, including fossilised sea urchins, flint axes ('thunderbolts'), a human femur, the cranium of a dog, and a pit containing a ram and a suckling pig (Runge 2009, 87-8).

The skeleton of an infant dating from the very Late Bronze Age/Early Pre-Roman Iron Age had been placed without grave goods in a shallow feature. The deposition of child skeletons, and infant skeletons in particular, in postholes, pits, or similar in settlements is by no means uncommon during the Early Iron Age and it is the subject of much discussion as to whether these are sacrificial offerings or burials (Bantelmann 1955, 34, 173; Haarnagel 1979, 230-8; Runge 2009, 120).

Finally, there is a sacrificial find at Nr. Hedegaard which may have united the entire settlement or even suggest a function for the entire hamlet. An intact skeleton of a young, probably male, individual was buried in an almost rectangular grave orientated east-west and measuring approximately 0.6 by 1.1 m. The grave pit is 0.4 m deep, with vertical sides and a flat base. The deceased was buried face down with his head turned to the east and his hands on his chest with the palms facing in towards the body. The legs were tucked up to the chest and the feet lay about 0.4 m higher than the cranium. The skeleton almost assumes a hocker position, but the position with the face and chest facing downwards suggests that the skeleton had been roughly buried. There were no grave goods, but the grave is dated stratigraphically to the Late Bronze Age/Early Pre-Roman Iron Age (Runge 2009, 120-3).

The burial method, the absence of grave goods, and the orientation of the skeleton combined with the prevalence of cremation accompanied with grave goods at this period, suggest that this is no ordinary burial. Moreover, inhumations from earlier and later tend to be placed with the head in the west and the body on the back or in a variation of hocker (J. Jensen 2003, 56-63, 158-76). Rather, the find shows certain similarities with contemporary bog bodies, some of which are presumed to be punished or possibly sacrificed people. The tradition of sacrificial offerings of humans in wetlands is known from the Late Bronze Age until the beginning of the Early Roman period (Fabech 1991, 284; J. Jensen 2003, 176-87) The skeleton from Nr. Hedeaard does however differ from these as it lies in a settlement area (Runge 2009, 120-3).

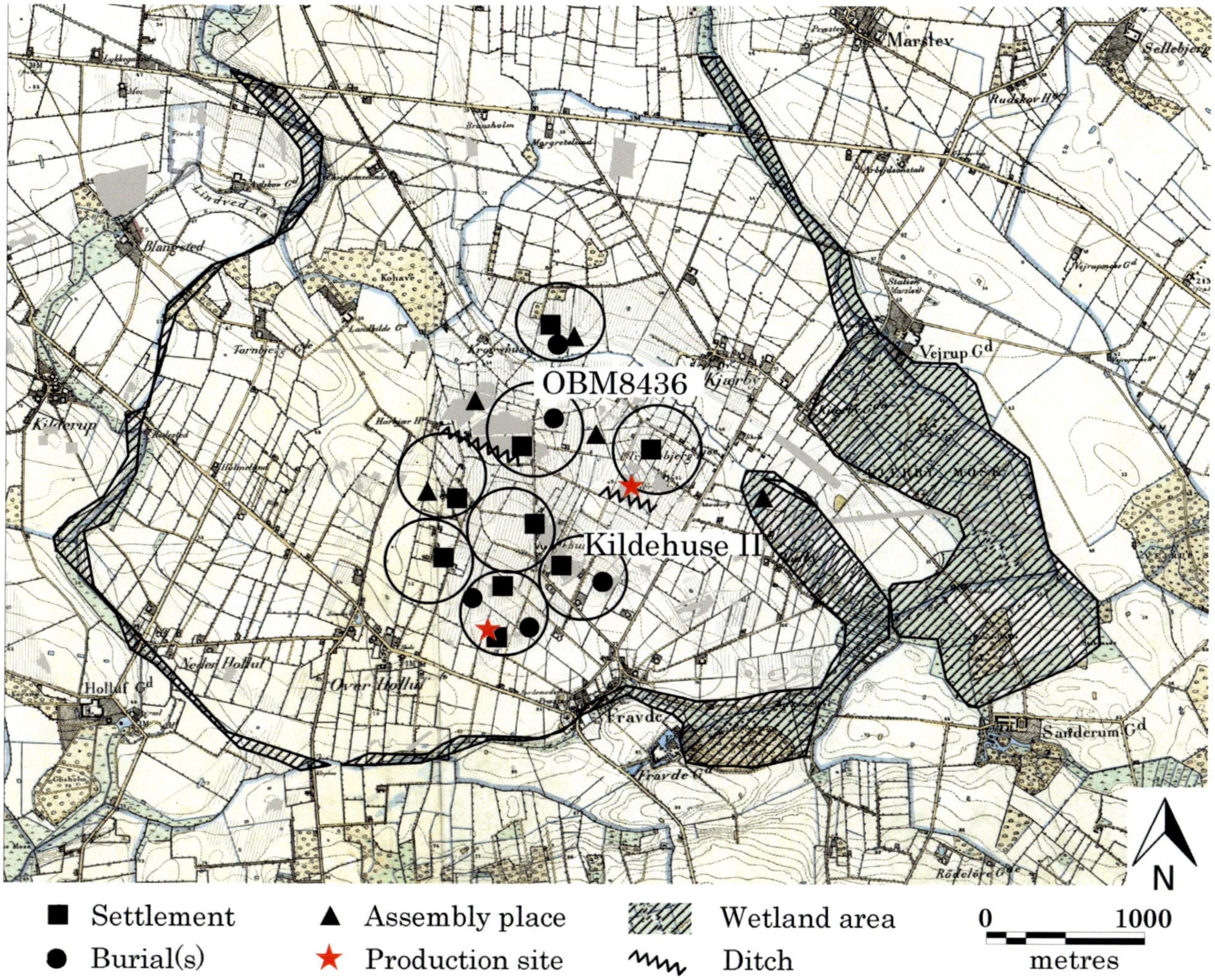

Figure 4: Hypothetical division of the cultural landscape at Tietgenbyen into eight resource areas. (Drawing: Allan Larsen & Mads Runge).

3.6 Case study 2: Tietgenbyen, Eastern Denmark

3.6.1 Settlement structure

Approximately 350 hectares of Tietgenbyen has been archaeologically investigated in the face of gradual ongoing industrial expansion over the last 10-15 years, with some 70-80 % of the total cadastral district explored so far. The area has produced striking finds from the Bronze Age and Early Iron Age showing a regular cultural landscape featuring houses, graves, meeting places, and production areas. The coupling of archaeology, geology and topography provides a unique glimpse of the spatial divisions of the various sites in the landscape.

The Bronze Age and Early Pre-Roman Iron Age material can be divided into roughly eight resource areas, each with house and burial sites (Figure 4). In the Late Pre-Roman and Early Roman Iron Age, the excavated area was apparently entirely deserted while the area was once again heavily exploited in the Late Roman/Early Germanic Iron Age (Runge 2012b, 133). The Bronze Age and Early Pre-Roman Iron Age resource areas are positioned at a distance of 500 and 900 m between each other. House and burial sites lie on flat, heavy moraines, while cooking pits and a production area (Runge & Henriksen 2007) are predominantly placed in wet low-lying areas. The large cooking pit section (and possibly to some extent the burial sites) served as meeting places and were relatively permanent points of orientation within the resource area while the settlement tended to be labile, shifting gradually within the resource area (Runge 2012b, 129-31).

The settlements are generally small and consist of between one and three farmsteads. Only one settlement, OBM 8436, distinguishes itself by comprising a large number of houses (Figure 5). Around 50 longhouses and minor houses date to the (Late) Bronze Age/Pre-Roman Iron Age while about 30 houses can be dated to the Neolithic period/Early Bronze Age PII (c. 3500-1500 BC). Although practically no overlap exists between the houses within each of these three main phases, it is difficult to imagine that this number of houses were in use simultaneously (Runge 2010, 91-102; 2012b, 122-3). On the other hand, the apparent layout of the settlement with traces of two to three east-west orientated rows of houses would seem to indicate some kind of correlation. At any rate, the number of contemporaneous houses does not only seem very high when compared to other localities in Tietgenbyen, but also compared to other localities in the country with large numbers of houses during this period (Becker 1972, 8; 1982; Rasmussen & Adamsen 1993, 141). The locality constitutes a central area in the *bygd* (hamlet), supported by the fact that it, unlike the others, can be traced back to the Neolithic. The area can thus be defined as the 'mother settlement' of the *bygd* (Runge 2014, 169).

3.6.2 Subsistence strategies and exploitation of land

Tietgenbyen covers about one third of a relatively flat, large expanse of moraine clay, broken by a couple of strips of outwash sand deposits, lying about 10km from the fjord (Runge 2010, 15-6). The flat terrain is intersected by a few deep and several shallow depressions.

Pollen analysis indicates an open landscape with scattered trees and bushes in the Early Bronze Age. Pollen from herbs and grasses suggests the existence of periodically uncultivated fields. In conjunction with other scientific analyses, the landscape can be characterised as open agricultural land offering excellent opportunities for cattle and other livestock to graze and as small plots of land with a relatively broad-based composition of cultivated species. Woodlands, including mature oaks were also in existence (Mikkelsen 2010) and the adjacent wetlands may have been used for hunting and, possibly, fishing. Exploitation of the fjord cannot be ruled out (Runge 2012b, 115-7). The general organisation of the landscape with house and burial sites on the heavy moraine plains and cooking pit sections and production areas in wet low-lying ground shows that practically the whole area – as the secondary and primary resource areas at Trandersbakkeøen indicate – was exploited.

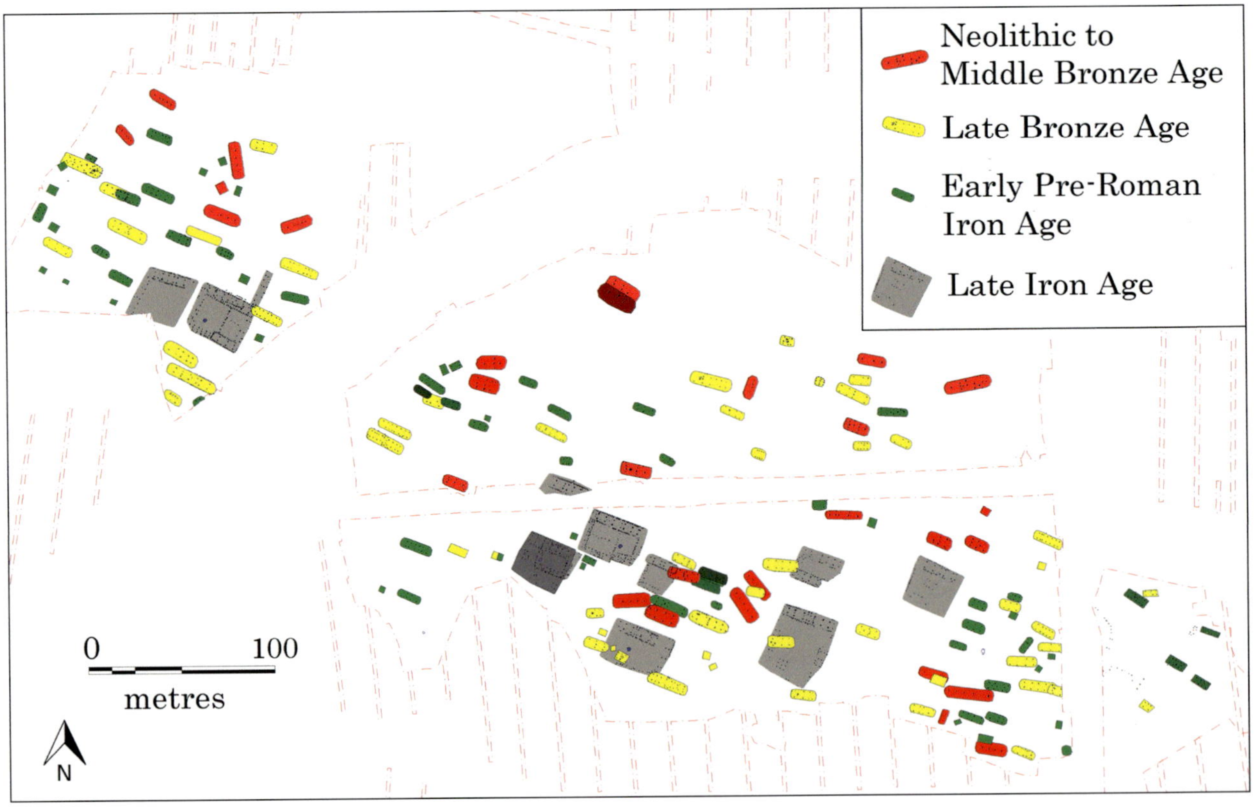

Figure 5: The large settlement, OBM8436, in Tietgenbyen. (Drawing: Kristine Stub Precht).

A special type of production is evident on a low-lying wet area below the margin of a settlement on higher ground. Within a very limited area almost 40 wells were investigated, as well as a number of pits, cooking pits, and cultural layers suggesting extensive use of fire. Macrofossil analyses show that some of the wells were used for production of flax. Three AMS dates place the activities in the Late Bronze Age and Early Pre-Roman Iron Age and this area of activity is thus contemporary with the settlement. The flax production here is so far the oldest in the country (Runge & Henriksen 2007).

3.6.3 Social aspects and cultural interaction

The comprehensive investigations of Tietgenbyen allow us to look behind the physical structures and delve into social and mental aspects. For example, on the burial sites a series of rituals and activities were carried out, which show these sites were not merely used as a place to bury the dead, but were important meeting places, not only for the living, but also between the living and the deceased. A fine example is the Late Bronze Age and Early Iron Age cremation burial site Kildehuse II. The site comprises 42 cremation graves of different types, for the most part placed between two ancient barrows, and presumably represents use by two families over a period of several generations (Runge 2010).

Extending from the north-western corner of the southernmost barrow there are two parallel, south-west to north-east orientated rows of cooking pits. The cooking pits in the western row contain practically no cooking stones and only a very thin layer of charcoal along the bottom. The subsoil at the bottom of the pits is characterised by a strong red colour, possibly indicating that the cooking pits were exposed to high temperatures. The cooking pits in the eastern row are largely filled by cooking stones and a thick charcoal layer. However, there is no red colouring of the subsoil. The difference between the two rows might indicate that the western row contained open fires while food was prepared in the eastern row. The western row could thus have been a marked symbolic boundary to the settlement area west of the burial site (Runge 2010, 83-8).

Another feature providing a clue to the contemporary world of ideas is the relationship of these features to the earlier barrows, which presumably indicated a strong attachment to the forefathers. A similar situation is evident in a burial site to the south where 19 flat graves – about the same number of graves found in each of the groups at Kildehuse II – were placed adjacent to an older barrow. At Kildehuse II, the link to the barrows is emphasised by the fact that the richest graves are placed closest to the barrow while the most poorly equipped graves, for the most part, are placed furthest away from the barrows. Further, there is a tendency to bury children and young people in groups, which might indicate that special areas of the burial site were reserved for children (Runge 2010, 73-9).

Other traces of ritual gatherings on the burial sites are square platforms and pits placed adjacent to the south-western edge of the barrows. Such cult structures are also known from other parts of Denmark and Northern Germany (Hornstrup 1999, 125-31; M. Mikkelsen 2003; Nielsen & Bech 2004, 147-9; Clemmensen 2005; Hornstrup 2005) and perhaps Sweden, too (Svanberg 2005).

Finally, traces have been found in Tietgenbyen of a hollow way beside a possibly contemporary presumably Bronze Age barrow (Figure 6). The roadway can be traced for about 30 m and is open to several interpretations. One possibility might be that it is a concrete testimonial to the linking of Bronze Age barrows and siting of roads (Müller 1897, 299-300; Egeberg 2004). Another possibility could be that it was built for transport of materials for the barrow construction. A processional road in connection with rituals linked to burials in the barrow could be a third scenario (Runge 2010, 93-102).

The cult structures on the burial sites are interpreted as local meeting places. By contrast, in Tietgenbyen, large groups – perhaps the entire *bygd* – presumably gathered at the extensive cooking pit sites. In Tietgenbyen, there are three sites comprising between 100 and 300 cooking pits and one comprising 30-40 cooking pits. Besides cooking pits, the sites comprised a few raw materials pits/waste pits, but no traces of houses (Runge 2010, 91-102). Taken as a whole, the sites are interpreted as meeting places on a par with similar sites elsewhere on Funen and in the country generally (Henriksen 2005; Prangsgaard & Andersen 2008; Kjær Kristensen 2008). It is possible that the large cooking pit sections were the gathering place of the small settlement units and the place where the chieftain from the central settlement, OBM8436, could show his power (Runge 2014, 172-3).

In contrast to the meeting places, there are traces in Tietgenbyen of features dividing up the landscape, such as up to 1.4 km long ditch following, or running parallel to, an east-west bound depression in the terrain. The ditch may have been a contributing factor to separate (some of) the resource areas mentioned earlier and is just over 2 m wide and 0.5-0.8 m deep with a U-shaped profile (Runge 2018, 68). The ditch is undated but based on similar examples at other sites on Funen it most probably dates from the Late Bronze Age or Early Iron Age (Wåhlin 2006; Henriksen 2005, 97-102).

Another contrast is evident in the relationship between the sacred and the profane. At the Kildehuse II burial site a barrier separated the profane and the sacred. In other cases, the sacred and the profane are interwoven to a greater extent, for example at a settlement where pits are enclosed by a flimsy fencing structure. In several cases, the pits contained large

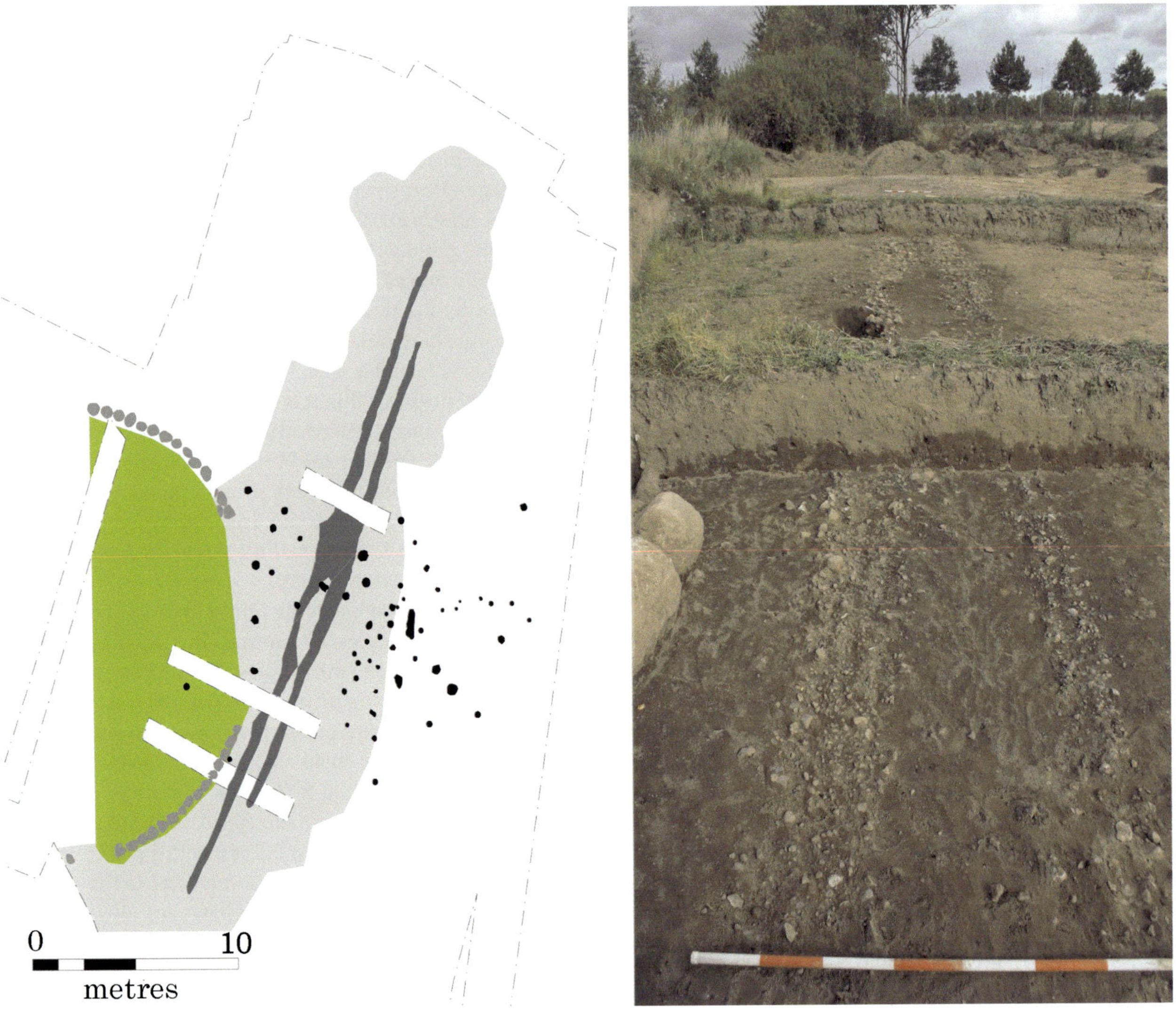

Figure 6: The hollow way (dark grey) near by the burial mound (green) in Tietgenbyen. Drawing: Allan Larsen. (Photo: Charlotte Kolmos).

quantities of burnt animal bones, fire cracked stones, and charcoal, all suggesting extensive use of fire. Further, the pits contained large quantities of pot sherds, three hartshorn axes, three billhooks, and a stone with symbolic signs – undoubtedly representing a special selection of objects. Finally, inside the fenced area two buried large clay vessels were found, one of which was placed upside down. The fenced area and the pits inside it are generally interpreted as a place of sacrifice (Runge 2010, 95; Andreasen *et al.* 2011).

3.7 Conclusion

The systematic approach to archaeology in Denmark practiced in recent decades has, together with new theories and methods, laid the foundation of an empirical method that can go beyond analyses of individual houses and settlements, and reveals considerable complexity.

With the investigation of entire cultural landscapes as at Tietgenbyen, or a series of sites with unusually fine preservation conditions as at Trandersbakkeøen, it is now possible to present alternative versions of the classical model of the Late Bronze Age and Early Iron Age in Denmark as known from Central and Southern Jutland, and to discuss regional variation. It is also possible to go beyond the typology of artefacts, graves, houses and settlements to glimpse the ideas and thoughts of prehistoric people, and to reject linear, simplistic developmental patterns.

3.8 Bibliography

Andersen, H. 1951. Tomme høje. *KUML* 1951, 91-135.

Andreasen, M.H., Kveiborg, J., Rau, R.M., Runge, M. & Skriver, C. 2011. Offerfund fra bronzealderen. *Fynske Minder* 2011, 83.

Arnoldussen, S. 2008. *A living Landscape. Bronze Age settlement sites in the Dutch river area (c. 2000-800 BC).* Leiden: Sidestone.

Bantelmann, A. 1955. *Tofting eine vorgeschichtliche Warft an der Eidermündung.* Neumünster: Wachholtz.

Bech, J.-H. 1984. Heltborg – en ny byhøj fra Thylands ældre jernalder. *Hikuin* 10, 39-56.

Bech, J.-H. 1985. The Iron Age Village Mound at Heltborg, Thy. *Journal of Danish Archaeology* vol. 4, 1985, 129-46.

Becker, C.J. 1972. Hal og hus i yngre bronzealder. *Nationalmuseets Arbejdsmark* 1972, 5-16.

Becker, C.J. 1982. Siedlungen der Bronzezeit und der vorrömischen Eisenzeit in Westjütland. *Offa* 39, 53-71.

Clemmensen, B. 2005. Bronzealderens kultanlæg – en undersøgelse af anlæggene uden for gravhøjene. In J. Goldhahn (ed.). *Mellan sten och järn.* Del 1, 305.

Dalsgaard, K. 2009. Landskabet, bopladslag og marksystem. In M. Runge, 2009. Nørre Hedegård. En nordjysk byhøj fra ældre jernalder. 197-208. Nordjyllands Historiske Museum og Jysk Arkæologisk Selskab.

Egeberg, T. 2004. Høje og hjulspor i tusindvis – færdsel i det vestjyske landskab. *FRAM. Fra Ringkøbing Amts Museer* 2004, 44-51.

Ejstrud, B. & Jensen, C.K. 2000. *Vendehøj – landsby og gravplads. Kronologi, organisation, struktur og udvikling i en østjysk landsby fra 2. årh. f.Kr. til 2. årh.* e.Kr. Kulturhistorisk Museums skrifter 1. Jysk Arkæologisk Selskab.

Enghoff, I.B. 2009. Fiskeri fra Nr. Hedegård. In M. Runge 2009. *Nørre Hedegård. En nordjysk byhøj fra ældre jernalder.* 241-6.Nordjyllands Historiske Museum og Jysk Arkæologisk Selskab.

Ericsson, A. & Runcis, J. 1995. Gravar utan begravningar. Teoretisk diskussion påkallad av en arkeologisk undersökning inom RAÄ 40 vid Skalunda i Sköldinge socken, Södermanland. In *Teoretiska perspektiv på gravundersökningar i Södermanland.* Riksantikvarieämbetet. Arkeologiska undersögningar. Skrifter nr. 8, Studier från UV Stockholm, 31-40.

Fabech, C. & Ringtved, J. 2009. Arealanvendelse og landskabstyper i det 1. årtusinde. In B. V. Odgaard, & J.R. Rømer (eds). *Danske landbrugslandskaber gennem 2000 år.* 143-76. Aarhus: Aarhus Universitetsforlag.

Frisberg, K.H. 2005. Where are the Dead? Empty graves from early iron age Uppland. In T. Artelius & F. Svanberg (eds). *Dealing with the dead. Archaeological Perspectives on Prehistoric Scandinavian Burial Ritual.* Riksantikvarieämbetet. Arkeologiska undersökningar. Skrifter 65, 143-58.

Gerritsen, F.A. 2003. *Local Identities. Landscape and communication in the late prehistoric Meuse-Demer-Scheldt region.* Amsterdam: Amsterdam University Press.

Haarnagel, W. 1979. *Die Grabung Feddersen Wierde. Methode, Hausbau, Siedlungs- und Wirtschaftsformen sowie Sozialstruktur. Bd. I. Textband. Bd. II. Tafelband.* Wiesbaden: Steiner.

Harvig. L., Runge, M. & Borre Lundø, M. 2014. Typology and function of Late Bronze Age and Early Iron Age cremation graves – a microregional study. *Danish Journal of Archaeology* 2014, 1-16.

Haue, N. 2009. Genstande af metal, sten, ben og ler på bopladsen. In Runge, M. 2009. *Nørre Hedegård. En nordjysk byhøj fra ældre jernalder.* Nordjyllands Historiske Museum og Jysk Arkæologisk Selskab, 127-54.

Henriksen, M. B. 2005. En motorvej tilbage til Fyns fortid. *Fynske Minder* 2005, 81-109.

Henriksen, P.S., Harild, J.A. & Jensen, P.M. 2009. De arkæobotaniske analyser af materialet fra Nr. Hedegård. In M. Runge 2009. *Nørre Hedegård. En nordjysk byhøj fra ældre jernalder.* 247-52.Nordjyllands Historiske Museum og Jysk Arkæologisk Selskab.

Herschend, F. 2009. *The Early Iron Age in South Scandinavia. Social Order in Settlement and Landscape.* Västerås: Department of Archaeology and Ancient History, Uppsala university.

Hesel, A. 2009. Husdyr og vildt fra Nr. Hedegård. In M. Runge 2009. *Nørre Hedegård. En nordjysk byhøj fra ældre jernalder.* 209-40. Nordjyllands Historiske Museum og Jysk Arkæologisk Selskab.

Holst, M.K. 2010. Inconstancy and stability – Large and small farmsteads in the village of Nørre Snede (Central Jutland) in the first millennium AD. *Siedlungs- und Küstenforschung im südlichen Nordseegebiet* 33, 155-79.

Hornstrup, K.M. 1999. Brandgrave fra yngre bronzealder. Muligheder og perspektiver. *KUML* 1999, 99-145.

Hornstrup, K.M. 2005. Kultanlæg og stenrækker – højenes funktion i yngre bronzealder. In J. Goldhahn (ed.). *Mellan sten och järn.* Del 1, 279-89. Göteborg: Göteborgs universitet.

Hvass, S. 1983. Vorbasse. The Development of a Settlement through the First Millennium A.D. *Journal of Danish Archaeology* 2, 127-36.

Hvass, S. 1985. *Hodde. Et vestjysk landsbysamfund fra ældre jernalder.* Arkæologiske Studier Vol. VII. København: Akademisk forlag Universitetsforlaget i København.

Hvass, S. 1988: Jernalderens bebyggelse. In P. Mortensen & B.M. Rasmussen (eds). *Fra Stamme til Stat i Danmark 1. Jernalderens stammesamfund.* 53-92. Jysk Arkæologisk Selskabs Skrifter XXII. Aarhus: Jysk Arkæologisk Selskab.

Hvass, S. 1993: Bebyggelsen. In S. Hvass & B. Storgaard (eds). *Da klinger i muld...25 års arkæologi i Danmark.* 187-94. København: Kgl. Nordiske oldskriftselskab.

Jensen, J. 2003. *Danmarks Oldtid. Ældre Jernalder 500 f.Kr.-400 e.Kr.* København.

Kaul, F. 1998. *Ships on Bronzes. A Study in Bronze Age Religion and Iconography.* PNM. Publications from the National Museum. Studies in Archaeology & History Vol. 3:1 og 3:2. København: National Museum.

Kjær Nielsen, S. 2015. Brud eller kontinuitet. Bebyggelsesstrukturer på overgangen mellem ældre og yngre førromersk jernalder i Nordjylland. *Kuml* 2015, 99-130.

Kjær Kristensen, I. 2008. Kogegruber – i klynger eller på rad og række. *KUML* 2008, 9-57.

Kveiborg, J. 2008. Fårehyrder, kvægbønder eller svineavlere. En revurdering af jernalderens dyrehold. *KUML* 2008, 59-100.

Lund, J. 1994. Enkeltgård og – eller landsby? In J. Lund & J. Ringtved (eds). *Sandflugt, dyrkning og bebyggelse i Limfjordsområdet. Limfjordsprojektet.* 91-109. Rapport nr. 7. Århus: Århus University.

McKinley, J.I. 1997. Bronze Age 'Barrows' and Funerary Rites and Rituals of Cremation. *Proceedings of the Prehistoric Society* 63, 129-45.

Mikkelsen, M. 2003. 321 Toruphøje. *Arkæologiske Udgravninger i Danmark* 2003, 93-4.

Michaelsen, K.K. 1992. *Bræt og spil. Spil i jernalderen.* Højbjerg,

Mikkelsen, P.H. 2010. Vedanatomiske undersøgelser. In M. Runge 2010. *Kildehuse II. Gravpladser fra yngre bronzealder og vikingetid i Odense Sydøst.* 55-8. Fynske Studier 23. Odense.

Müller, S. 1897. *Vor Oldtid. Danmarks Forhistoriske Archæologi.* København.

Møller, N. A. 2011. Dynamiske bebyggelsesmønstre? Ældre jernalders bebyggelser i landskabet. In N.A. Møller, S.S. Qvistgaard & S.F. Jensen (eds). *Nyt fra Vestfronten! Jyske bebyggelser fra ældre jernalder.* 155-71. Arkæologiske Skrifter 10. København: Danmarks Universitetsforlag.

Møller, P.G. & Porsmose, E. 1997. *Kulturhistorisk inddeling af landskabet.* København: Miljø- og Energiministeriet. Skov- og Naturstyrelsen.

Nielsen, B.H. 1998. Jernalderfund fra Egådalen. *Kuml* 1997-98, 105-26.

Nielsen, B.H. & Bech, J.-H. 2004. Bronzealderens kulthuse. Anlæg med relation til gravkulten. *KUML* 2004, 129-59.

Näsman, U. 2009. Jernalderens driftformer i arkæologisk belysning. In B.V. Odgaard & J.R. Rømer (eds). *Danske landbrugslandskaber gennem 2000 år*, 99-113.

Prangsgaard, K. & Andersen, A. B. 2008. 3000 år gamle kultpladser ved Søndersø. *Fynske Minder* 2008, 131-41.

Prangsgaard, K., Andersen, S.Th., Breuning-Madsen, H., Holst, M., Malmros, C. & Robinson, D. 1999. Gravhøje ved Lejrskov. Undersøgelse af fem høje. *KUML* 1999, 53-97.

Rasmussen, M. & C. Adamsen 1993. Bebyggelsen. In S. Hvass & B. Storgaard (eds). *Da klinger i muld...25 års arkæologi i Danmark.* 136-41. København.

Rindel, P. O. 2011. Jernalderbebyggelsen ved Grøntoft i forskningshistorisk perspektiv In N. A. Møller, S. S. Qvistgaard & S.F. Jensen (eds). Nyt fra Vestfronten! Jyske bebyggelser fra ældre jernalder. *Arkæologiske Skrifter* 10, 99-110.

Ringtved, J. 1988. Jyske gravfund fra yngre romertid og ældre germanertid. Tendenser i samfundsudviklingen. *KUML* 1986, 95-231.

Runge, M. 2009. *Nørre Hedegård. En nordjysk byhøj fra ældre jernalder.* Nordjyllands Historiske Museum og Jysk Arkæologisk Selskab.

Runge, M. 2010. *Kildehuse II – gravpladser fra yngre bronzealder og vikingetid i Odense Sydøst.* Fynske Studier. Bind 23.

Runge, M. 2011. Nørre Hedegård – et dansk Pompei. Anvendelsen af bopladser med usædvanlige bevaringsforhold til perspektivering af det "ordinære" bopladsmateriale. In N. A. Møller, S. Qvistgaard, S. & Jensen S.F. (eds). *Nyt fra Vestfronten! Jyske bebyggelser fra ældre jernalder.* Arkæologiske Skrifter 10. København 2011, 51-69.

Runge, M. 2012a. *Dannelsen af regionale bebyggelsesmønstre i sen bronzealder og ældre jernalder.* Ph.d.-afhandling.

Runge, M. 2012b. Yngre bronzealders bebyggelse indenfor et 350 hektar stort undersøgelsesområde sydøst for Odense. In S. Boddum, M. Mikkelsen & N. Terkildsen (eds). *Bebyggelsen i yngre bronzealders kulturlandskab. Seminarrapport fra seminariet "Bebyggelsen i yngre bronzealders lokale kulturlandskab" afholdt i Holstebro, 10. marts 2011.* Yngre bronzealders kulturlandskab vol. 2, 2012, 113-39.

Runge, M. 2013. Yngre bronzealders dødekult indenfor et 350 hektar stort undersøgelsesområde sydøst for Odense. In S. Boddum, M. Mikkelsen & N. Terkildsen (eds). *Dødekulten i yngre bronzealders kulturlandskab. Seminarrapport fra seminariet "Bebyggelsen i yngre bronzealders lokale kulturlandskab" afholdt i Viborg, 8. marts 2011.* Yngre bronzealders kulturlandskab vol.3, 2013, 9-23.

Runge, M. 2014. Forskning på museerne. Ph.d.-projektet "Dannelsen af regionale bebyggelsesmønstre i sen bronzealder og ældre jernalder". *Fynske Minder*, 161-79.

Runge, M. 2018. Regionale aspekter af hierarki og samfundsstruktur på overgangen mellem bronze- og jernalder. In S. Boddum, M. Mikkelsen & N. Terkildsen (eds) *Status og samfundsstruktur i yngre bronzealders kulturlandskab. Seminarrapportfra seminariet " Status og samfundsstruktur i yngre bronzealders lokale kulturlandskab" afholdt i Viborg, 8. marts 2011.* 59-76. Yngre bronzealders kulturlandskab vol. 6, 2018.

Runge, M. & Henriksen, P. S. 2007. Danmarks ældste hørindustri. *Fynske Minder* 2007, 145-65.

Svanberg, F. 2005. Kulthus, tempel och artistokratiske husgravar. In J. Goldhahn (ed.). *Mellan sten och järn.* Del 1, 308-31.

Wåhlin, S. 2006. OBM 2726, Herluf Trollesvej – Arkæologisk udgravning af grav og gård fra yngre romertid, en oldtidsgrøft, brønde og gruber fra oldtiden samt et hus fra middelalder. *Arkæologisk rapport* no. 7, Odense Bys Museer. Unpublished.

Chapter 4

Iron Age settlement in mid-west Ireland

Katharina Becker

4.1 Introduction

Difficulties in answering the question of where and how people lived has for a long time been one of the central obstacles to understanding of Iron Age lifeways in Ireland. The earlier part of this period between 800 or 600 BC is very poorly understood and largely characterised by low levels of archaeological evidence. In its later part, from about 400 BC to AD 400, a rather biased dataset has been highlighted as only reflecting particular, select aspects of human activity (*e.g.* Raftery 2006; 1994; 1998).

A period of crucial interest is the Developed Iron Age between ca. 400 BC and about the turn of the millennium (Becker *et al.* 2008; Becker 2012a; Armit *et al.* 2013) that saw the re-emergence of significant levels of human activity. Demographic change has been argued to be reflected in the large set of radiocarbon-dated sites (Armit *et al.* 2013) and the construction of large scale earthworks, the floruit of Royal Sites, the large-scale adoption of iron working technology, and the introduction of La Tène styles, indicate cultural change (Becker 2012 a, b).

While special sites, such as the so-called 'Royal Sites' and large-scale structures like linear earthworks, as well as the La Tène artefact record, indicate human presence and activity, no clear evidence for everyday settlement had been recognised (*e.g.* Raftery 1994). Biases in preservation, and difficulties in recognising settlement or mobile lifeways with low archaeological visibility have been debated as possible explanations for this (*e.g.* Raftery 1994). In combination with a lack of pottery and palynological evidence for an emphasis on pastoral agriculture, this has increasingly consolidated in a narrative of nomadic or semi-nomadic pastoralists (Raftery 1994; Lynn 2003; Armit 2007; Becker 2010; Dolan 2014), with highly visible special enterprises such as the Royal Sites seen as monumental expressions of otherwise invisible communities. In this context the absence of evidence for settlement has served as evidence for mobility – despite the significant methodological challenges that the positive identification of non-sedentary lifeways and the various degrees of mobility presents.

In D.C. Cowley, M. Fernández-Götz, T. Romankiewicz & H. Wendling (eds). Rural Settlement. Relating buildings, landscape, and people in the European Iron Age (Leiden 2019: Sidestone Press) 45-55.

4.2 New light on settlement and settling

However, a richer dataset is beginning to provide evidence that allows this issue to be addressed. It suggests that mobility may have been much more small-scale and complex than previously envisaged. Thus, while pastoralism clearly played an important part in society there is ample evidence for arable agriculture, possibly culminating in the large-scale processing of grains in kilns in the early centuries AD (Monk & Power 2014). As discussed for the Early Medieval period (O'Sullivan *et al.* 2013), taphonomy and sampling strategies may favour the representation of animal bones, particular those of large mammals, over that of cereals. Thus, the picture may have been biased towards pastoral, over arable agricultural practices. Further evidence for largely sedentary lifeways is implied by the fact that pigs play an important role in the animal bone assemblages, including those of the Royal Sites (*e.g.* McCormick 1997). While nomadic societies can be engaged in arable agriculture and pigs are at times integrated in transhumance practices, the evidence suggests a rather complex system of agriculture and land-use that makes the vision of a fully or strongly mobile society unlikely (Becker in press). The record of house sites that can with relative confidence be dated to this period raises many questions, but seems to demonstrate the existence of formal settlement (*e.g.* Becker *et al.* 2017).

The challenge now is to formulate evidence-based hypotheses of land-use, utilising the large number of excavations undertaken during large-scale infrastructure schemes over recent decades (*e.g.* Becker *et al.* 2017). Patterns observed in the distribution of sites are the result of recovery processes and taphonomy, as well as prehistoric reality. Large linear infrastructural schemes expose only narrow slices of land, but their sheer length and course across a variety of regions, landscapes and eco-habitats provides a large-scale cross-section of past activity. These contrast with and add to the distributions of sites and monuments that are otherwise impacted by research driven agendas as well as the above ground visibility of sites (Armit *et al.* 2013; Becker *et al.* 2017) or other survey methods that are subject to taphonomic processes (*e.g.* Cowley 2016). However, the impact of route selection criteria, whereby a route might be designed to avoid known monuments or landscapes that offer particular construction challenges, such as higher elevations or wetlands (see Armit *et al.* 2013), require consideration. Assessment of variable survey and testing strategies within and between infrastructure schemes can also be helpful to explore the influence of such strategies on the numbers and disposition of sites detected (Bermingham *et al.* 2013b, 7-8).

However, there is also a view that assessment of mass aggregated data such as radiocarbon dates provide insights on broad demographic trends (Armit *et al.* 2013; Bevan *et al.* 2017), exploiting the apparently non-discriminatory recovery processes at work in infrastructural schemes and the sheer volume of data. Thus, for radiocarbon dating, after the exclusion of dates that are unlikely to relate to the contexts within they were found, large-scale change in quantities of radiocarbon dates and their contexts observed over time are argued to reflect actual fluctuations in prehistoric activity. However, there may be some exceptions. It is for example notable that within the study region the dating programme of the Gas Pipeline to the West scheme (Grogan *et al.* 2006), appears to target likely Bronze Age sites in particular, as there is a notable lack of dates for potential Iron Age or Early Medieval sites. It is likely that in a vast dataset such differences will not have a significant impact, and in any case, this paper does not consider chronological changes over time but focuses on a particular period – the Developed Iron Age (ca. 400BC to 1BC/AD). A qualitative comparison of the association of certain types of sites with particular forms of landscapes within the extent of these schemes is conducted that should not be affected by sampling biases. Moreover, the absence of sites from particular parts of these schemes can be argued to reflect a prehistoric reality (cf Cowley 2016). However, the ranges of different methodologies applied make systematic comparison between the archaeology of the landscapes uncovered in infrastructure schemes and those only subject to targeted research excavations difficult.

An inherent problem of the dataset is that the limited dating evidence for most sites prohibits fine chronological differentiation or Bayesian modelling of site dating. Thus, dates falling within the study period between 400 BC and the turn of the first millennium BC and AD are treated summarily, focusing on broad patterns in the record and thus playing to the strength of this dataset.

4.3 Patterns of settlement in North-West Munster

4.3.1 The landscapes

The region discussed here covers parts of Counties Clare, Tipperary and Limerick, located within the province of North Munster. The routes of the infrastructural schemes considered run through a diverse landscape, including floodplains, wetlands but also higher elevations. This is augmented by data from survey work in the Shannon estuary as well as the research excavations of some upland sites.

In the preceding Late Bronze Age North Munster was a focus of settlement activity with the hillfort of Moghaun lying at the nexus of a wider network of sites and of deposits of metalwork such as the large gold hoard 'The Great Clare find' found near nearby (Grogan 2005). Recent decades have seen a number of archaeological investigations. Two recent road-schemes traverse this landscape, the M18 Ennis Bypass and N85 Western Relief Road (Bermingham *et al.* 2012), the M18 Gort to Crusheen (Delaney *et al.* 2012) and the M18 Newmarket on Fergus sections located in central Clare within the Fergus estuary (Figure 1). On the eastern side of the Shannon estuary, the Limerick Southern ring road (Bermingham *et al.* 2013a), the Limerick Main Drainage Scheme and the N7 are located in the River Shannon estuary and river valley,

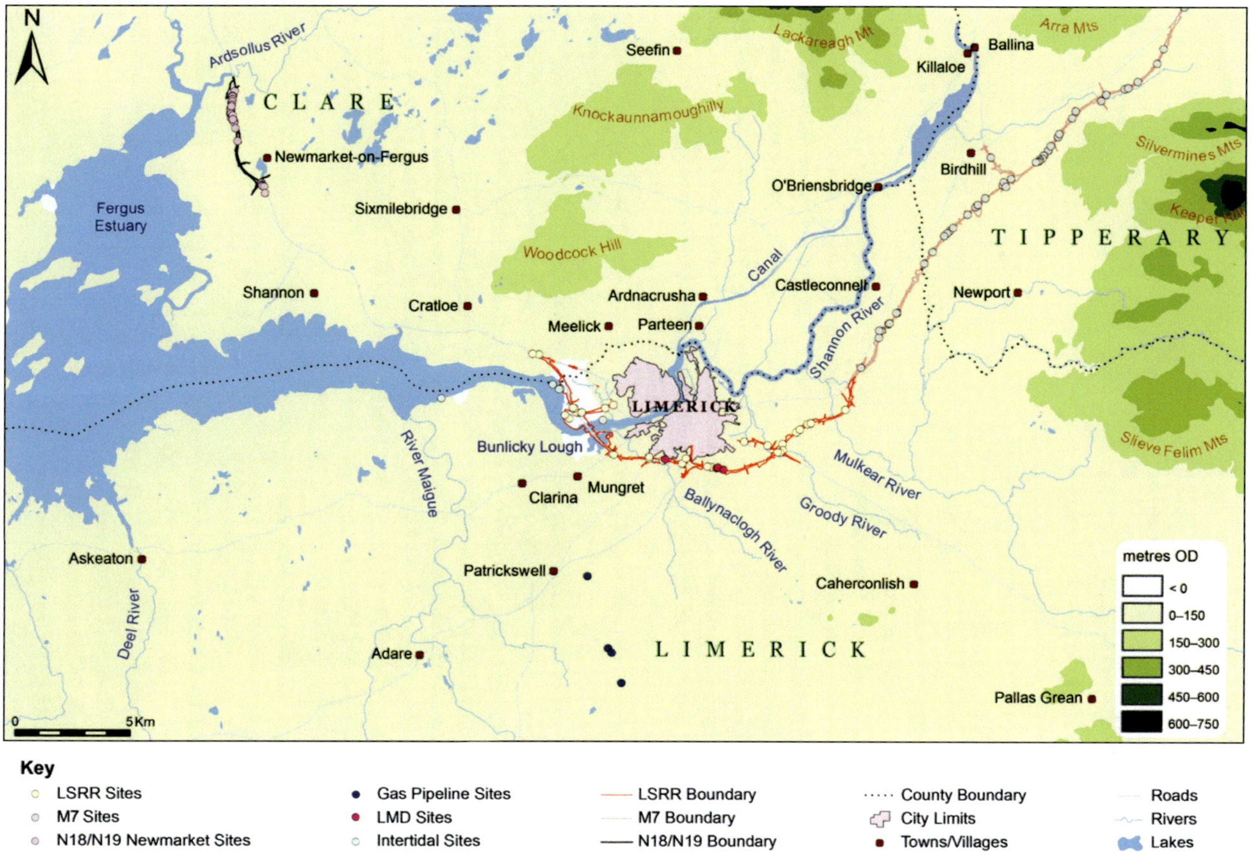

Figure 1: Location of development schemes in the centre of the study region ((TVAS (Ireland) Ltd, courtesy of Transport Infrastructure Ireland)).

from Limerick north-east wards into Tipperary (Figure 1). The 'Gas Pipeline to the West' (Grogan *et al.* 2006) also traversed the area, and the intertidal and estuary sites of the Fergus and Shannon estuaries were surveyed (O'Sullivan 2001; O'Sullivan *et al.* 2010).

The route along the river Fergus valley is generally exceptionally low-lying and wet, with bogs and badly drained soil predominating. In particular the M18 Newmarket on Fergus section is located in a low-lying landscape with a high proportion of water bodies, wetlands including bogs, and today liable to flooding in spring and winter (Bermingham *et al.* 2012, 5-8), with occasional drumlins and glacial ridges. Similarly low-lying are parts of the route around Limerick City where they pass across the Shannon floodplain (Limerick ringroad). In contrast, the N7 Nenagh to Limerick traverses a gently undulating landscape of lowland pasture broken only by a large peat basin that straddles the border between Counties Limerick and Tipperary. The region is overlooked by the Silvermines Mountains to the east and the Arra Mountains to the north and west with the N7 clipping the foothills of both.

A broad contrast can be noted between sites in the low-lying wetter regions and those that are located on the higher elevations on the fringes of the Arras and Silvermines mountains. Whereas burial and iron-working sites dominate in the lower elevations, a greater diversity of sites, including occupation sites can be found in the higher elevations (Figure 2).

4.3.2 The locations of burial and iron working sites

Along the Fergus estuary ring-ditches and pit cemeteries have been identified within the low-lying and wet landscape on small elevations that offer good vistas over the surrounding landscape. The ring-ditches at Ballyboy were located at heights of 39 and 33 m OD below the crest of an east-facing valley ridge (McNamara 2010a, b). The cemetery at Manusmore 100 (Taylor 2006) was located on the top of a south-facing incline at a height of about 8 m OD about 120 m from the nearest river and with views across the Fergus estuary. Nearby, Manusmore 102 was located at about 11-14 m OD (Hull 2006a). A flat cemetery at Killow AR104, consisting of eight possible cremation

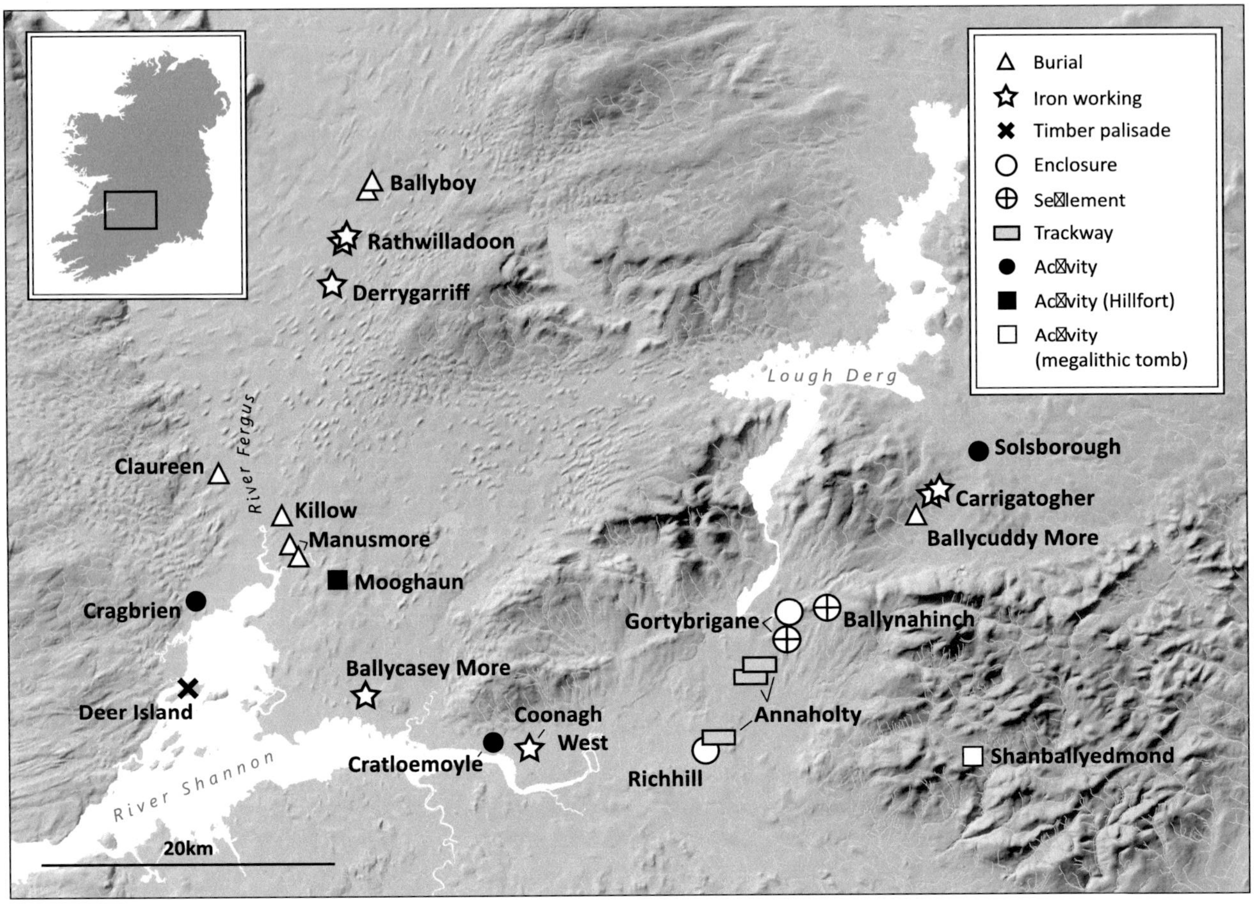

Figure 2: Distribution map of Developed Iron Age sites in the study region.

pits, was located on two drumlin gravel islands at a height of less than 6 m OD, at the interface of deep bog to its north and east and higher and drier land to the south and west (Taylor 2006, 2, 4-6). In the higher elevations along the N7 in the foothills of the Arra Mountains at 80 m OD, only one possible cemetery has been identified at Ballycuddy More (E2483). Nine pits, some with evidence of *in situ* burning and containing cremated bones are suggested to be a cremation cemetery (Taylor 2011, 9), although no human bone was identified.

The sites at Manusmore, Killow and possibly Ballycuddy More would usually be considered flat cemeteries, consisting of pits with pyre debris, some including small amounts of human remains. Such deposits may be considered pyre deposits, rather than actual formal burials involving the deposition of the cremated remains. Instead, after the removal of the human remains, the content of the pyre ashes had to be disposed of in a formal manner, possibly also representing charged and potentially problematic material (Becker 2014). This would explain the amount of less than 700 g of identifiable human cremated bone from 27 pits with bone at Manusmore AR100 (Anthony 2006a) and the presence of only flecks of bone in five pits. Similar patterns were observed at Manusmore AR102 (Anthony 2006b), where only about 150 g of cremated bone, partially identifiable as human, were identified in five pits, ranging in date from the Early to the Developed Iron Age (after Becker *et al.* 2008). At Killow all the identifiable human bone from three pits comprised only 18 g (Anthony 2006c, table 3) and at the ring-ditch at Claureen AR131 (Anthony 2006d), multiple deposits of human bone only comprised 117 g. Fire-reddened ground at Manusmore had been discussed as evidence for the pyre location and also at Killow AR104 evidence for *in situ* burning in three pits was noted (Bermingham *et al.* 2012, 51). The presence of grave goods in association with the more substantial cremation deposits at the ring-ditch sites of Ballyboy creates a supportive contrast to the lack of finds in the flat cemeteries. At Ballyboy 1 (McNamara 2010a) two cremation deposits had been placed in pits cut into the ditch fills. These contained a decorated antler die, glass beads, an amber bead and some undeterminable iron fragments (Figure 3). A third cremation of a female individual was situated within the interior of the ditch and was possibly the focus

Figure 3: Ballyboy 1. Top: ring ditch. Bottom: selection of finds (after McNamara 2010a, plates 6 and 8) , TVAS (Ireland) Ltd, courtesy of Transport Infrastructure Ireland).

of the ring-ditch. At Ballyboy 2 (McNamara 2010b), a ring-ditch enclosed four cremation pits and contained a number of cremations in a sequence of ditch fills, pit cuts and ditch recuts (Figure 4), associated with a number of glass beads and iron fragments.

The actual act of cremation taking place in these locations could add a further dimension to the range of possible cosmological and social reasons for the placement of burial sites in this environment. The availability of fuel sources for the energy-consuming process of cremation in the form of wood, but also peat, may be a factor and, in fact, at Killow evidence for the burning of peat has been noted (Bermingham *et al.* 2012, 51).

Considerations regarding the availability of fuels may have played a role in the siting of iron smelting and apparently also smithing activities in these wet landscapes, in addition to the likely exploitation of bog ore deposits. Similarly positioned on elevations within wetlands, sites like Rathwilladoon 5 (Lyne 2009a) would appear to represent evidence for small-scale iron working in the form of a possible furnace pit with slag, and, if contemporary, charcoal production in an adjacent kiln. Nearby, a curved slot-trench also produced an Iron Age date on charcoal. The slot trench may be reconstructed as a 10 m diameter roundhouse or as a semi-circular windbreak or shelter. These two sites lie at 28 m OD and 31 m OD respectively on the southeast-facing slopes of a hill overlooking a sizeable area of wetland, with Rathwilladoon 2 sitting on a near-level shelf on the hillside (Lyne 2009b, 27). More significant levels of iron production and processing are indicated at Derrygarriff 2 (Nunan 2009), also located on raised ground at 26 m OD within a wetland area. Here 10 kg of ferrous

Figure 4: Ballyboy 2. Top: ring ditch. Bottom: selection of finds (after McNamara 2010b, fig. 4 and plate 8) , (TVAS (Ireland) Ltd, courtesy of Transport Infrastructure Ireland).

slags, indicative of iron smelting (Young 2009, Appendix 2.3) were retrieved from what appeared to be a collapsed shaft furnace. Smithing hearth cakes and hammerscale indicate also smithing took place on site (Young 2009, 10). Also in the south-east of the study area at Coonagh West 4, an iron smelting furnace was located on a gravel ridge on the edge of the Shannon estuary within its tidal mud flats (Ruttle & Taylor 2013, 4, 11).

4.3.3 Settlement and movement

Further north-east in the higher elevations of the foothills of the Arras and the Silvermines mountain ranges, Iron Age activity is of decidedly different character than that observed in the lower-lying areas. At Ballynahinch 2 a cluster of probably at least five circular slot trenches representing house structures is spread out over a site that was in the Early Medieval period enclosed with a ditch (Figure 5). Ballynahinch 2 (Scotland 2011) is situated at 118 m OD in an area of current pasture land, that gently sloped from north to south and offered wide views. Bronze Age burial activity was followed in the site sequence by the creation of a number of foundation trenches, of which structure 1 produced two Iron Age dates falling into the Developed Iron Age. The other trenches remain undated, although structure 3 produced a Late Bronze Age date. It is possible that the remainder

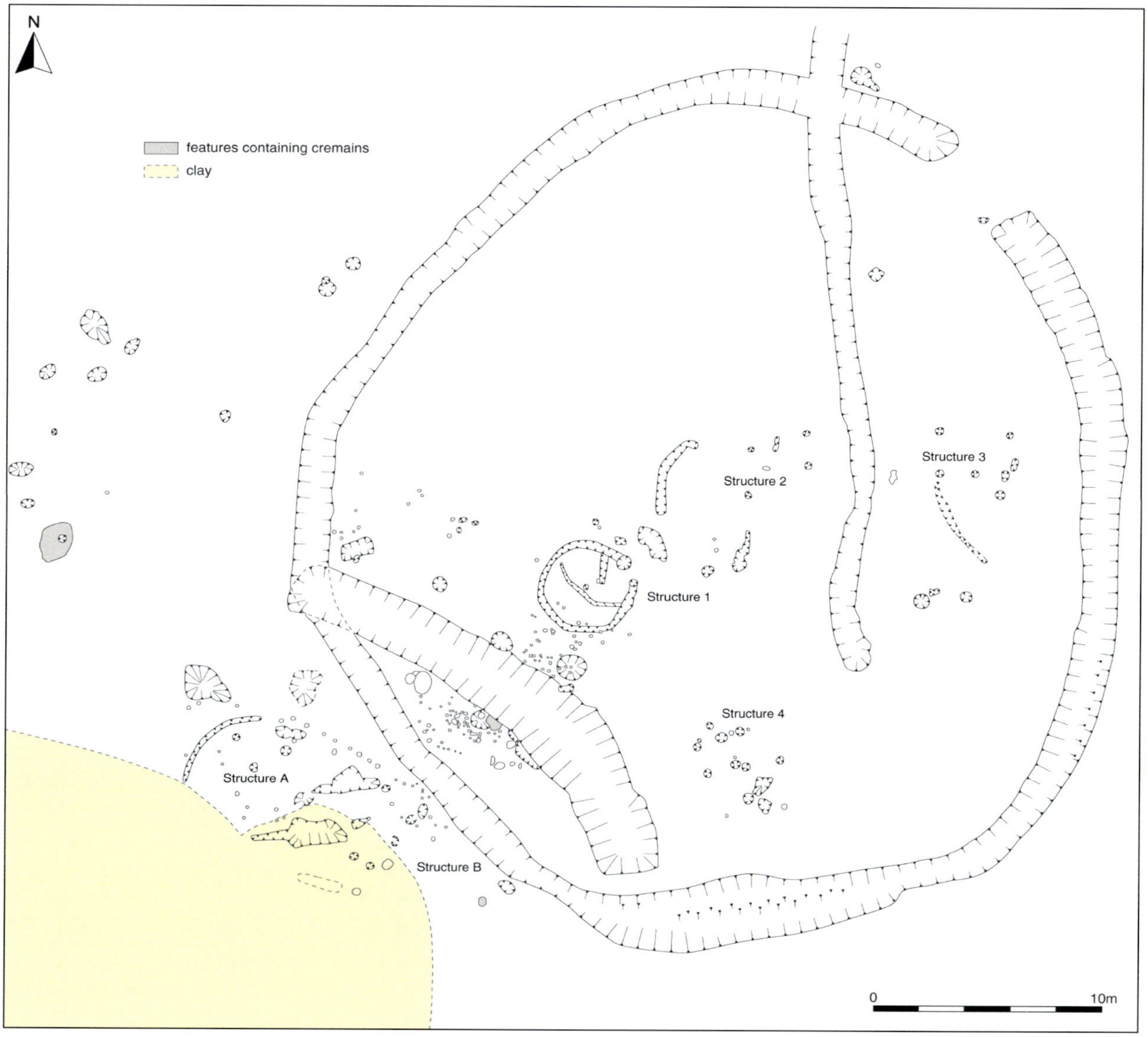

Figure 5: Ballynahinch 2 excavation plan (after Scotland 2011, fig. 6 , Aegis Archaeology Limited, courtesy of Transport Infrastructure Ireland).

of the houses are of Iron Age date. The medieval dates are from postholes that have no clear structural relationship to the slot trenches. The early medieval enclosure trench cuts through the distribution of houses, suggesting the possibility that the entire group of house structures may indeed be of Iron Age date. Further northeast, at Solsborough (Murphy & Clarke 2001), features including some kilns produced Iron Age dates at the very end of the study period on unidentified charcoal and hence may not be of relevance here.

Some tentative evidence for the maintenance or modification of the enclosures in the Iron Age has been discussed in the case of Mooghaun, where a Hallstatt plateau date was derived from a bank built against the middle rampart (UB-4277 on animal bone, Grogan 2005, 241, table 7.2, 244). This appears to represent the latest Late Bronze Age horizon of activity after the abandonment of the Bronze Age occupation area (Grogan 2005, 181). A radiocarbon date was derived on bone from deposits in the inner enclosure in area A between cal. 47 BC and AD 133 (Grogan 2005, 244). These deposits contained evidence for industrial activity consisting of iron and bronze working, and production of rotary querns and iron nails, found to fill hollows on the site in area A (Grogan 2005, 131-7, 244). These artefacts were originally considered to be of Medieval date (Grogan 1996, 56-7; Henderson 2007, 183) and it has to remain unclear if the Iron Age date relates to this assemblage or is residual.

Nearby at Cooleen (McNamara 2012) in a similar location at 76 m above OD on a slope with wide views, a possible roundhouse and a four poster structure produced two Hallstatt plateau dates allowing for a date in the Developed Iron Age or indeed earlier (not on map).

To the west at Gortybrigane 2 an early Medieval ditched enclosure is located on the summit of a hill that slopes steeply towards a basin of waterlogged bog, located within a poorly drained lowland landscape (Clark & Long 2010, 6). The enclosure contained several features, including remains of what appears to be a rectangular Middle Bronze Age house as well as further undated possible structures. The only feature currently datable to the Iron Age is a pit containing human bones, iron working residue and grains. Rather than settlement, specialised activities such as metalworking may have taken place here. An apparent focus of the enclosure on the cluster of features that includes the likely Iron Age pit may hint at an earlier origin of the enclosure.

This site cluster is separated from a further enclosure to the south at Richhill 2 by a large bog basin. The double-ditched enclosure at Richhill 2 is located on a slope and the Iron Age date relates to the re-cutting of a Bronze Age ditch in the 4th to 2nd centuries BC, followed by the later addition of a second ditch in the Early Medieval period (Clark & McLeod 2010). The dating of the sequence is based on hazel charcoal pieces without a clear functional relationship to the ditch and hence possibly residual within it. The stratigraphic and chronological order of the dates makes it possible that this enclosure was indeed re-cut in the Iron Age. The enclosure was only partially excavated, but no structures or other clear evidence for its purpose was recovered within the excavated extent.

One or two trackways are located in the bog basin connecting the two areas of activity, indicating habitual movement between the areas either end of the bog. The two segments of trackway at Annaholty 8 connect two islands of dry gravel land, creating a causeway at the narrowest part of the bog (Taylor & Bermingham 2013, 7). This trackway showed evidence for at least two phases of construction in the 1st century BC (Taylor & Bermingham 2013, 10-8) with the heavily worn timbers of the trackway showing the movement of cattle or vehicles. The presence of animals in this landscape, possibly passing along the trackway, is also indicated in a nearby pollen profile by spores associated with dung parasites (O'Brien 2013, 57-9). At Annaholty/Sallymount remains of a trackway were dated to broadly the same period as Annaholty 8 (McCooey *et al.* 2010).

The enclosure at Richhill (Clark & MacCleod 2010) may have been used for stock-keeping, perhaps for summer pasture within this low-lying and wetter area as part of small-scale transhumance practice. The pollen record from Annaholty bog, while allowing the reconstruction of a relatively densely overgrown, wet landscape, supports this hypothesis with a combination of herbaceous taxa suggesting the local grazing of animals. Small amounts of cereal pollen also indicate small-scale arable farming in the vicinity (O'Brien 2013). Chronologically the building of the trackway appears to correlate with a period of land-clearance represented in the pollen record (Taylor & Bermingham 2013, 8).

A substantial investment is not only reflected in the construction of the trackways, but also in the evidence for the management of the woodland around the site. Evidence of coppicing at Annaholty 8 suggests the utilisation of local wood resources, adding to the evidence provided by the pollen record, the trackway and other sites, for the intense use, management and habitual movement between different parts of the landscape.

4.3.4 Farming communities

Like that from Annaholty, the pollen record from Mooghaun Lough also suggests pastoral as well as arable agriculture being practiced in this area during the Developed Iron Age. While the dating of the record is broad, the chronological model suggests substantial pastoral and arable farming in the period between 650 and 300 BC. Interestingly, an increase in activity in the latter part of this period is followed by a period of apparently steady farming activity that includes a significant cereal-growing component (300 BC-AD 1, Molloy 2005, 274-5). In County Clare on the M18 at Caheraphuca Lough a period of substantial clearance of the existing elm population in zone 6c (Molloy & O'Connell 2012, 119) may possibly be contemporary to the burial and iron working sites in this area (Molloy & O'Connell 2012, 114).

In addition to the pollen record, cereal and animal bone finds from a number of dated contexts on the road scheme provide information on subsistence methods. At Manusmore AR100, two pit deposits contained significant amounts of charred cereal, including wheat grains, wheat chaff and barley. Few animal bones have been recorded on these sites, with a pit at Killow producing horse and possibly sheep bones (Bermingham *et al.* 2012, 51). At Killow pit 27A also contained charred barley and wheat remains, as well as bread wheat, six row barley and what are most likely wild oats. The aforementioned pit at Gortybrigane that produced an Iron Age date on human bone also produced (wild) oat and barley grains. At Coonagh West 4, a possibly deliberate deposit of animal bone comprising mainly cattle jaw bones, was associated with a whetstone. The deposit was dated on charcoal (Ruttle & Taylor 2013) – which makes an Iron Age date of the deposit possible, if not secure.

While there is no clear evidence for the exploitation of wild animal resources in this landscape, hunting and fishing may have played an important role in these wetland environments. A double palisade dating to this part of the Iron Age at Deer Island in the Fergus Estuary has been discussed as possibly having played a role in fishing (O'Sullivan *et al.* 2010), as may an earlier Iron Age post-and-wattle structure in the Fergus Estuary that produced a radiocarbon date of 748-556 BC (O'Sullivan 2001, 170-120; Appendix 1).

While the possible settlement sites uncovered are largely void of finds, the wooden artefacts surviving due to their reuse in the construction of the Annaholty 8 trackway provide important insights into lifeways of the period, such as stave-built kegs, a losset-type vessel, a yoke and possibly a cart (Moore 2013). Traction (presumably by cattle), the transport of goods, possibly the making of bread and butter or other milk products, all add to the evidence for substantive settlement activity in the area. A lathe-turned wooden bowl from a bog at the edge of the Killow burial site either sits chronologically late within or post-dates the calibration range of 777 and 407 cal. BC (95%) obtained directly on the ash wood (UBA 6287; Hull 2012b, 135-6).

4.4 Models of settlement

The archaeology of the Developed Iron Age in the North-West of Munster provides a picture of differential landscape use, likely to relate to landscape type and its resources.

Based on the distribution of sites across these landscapes it is possible to hypothesize a model of landscape-specific land-use and settlement where occupation sites are located in the drier, elevated parts of the landscape surrounded by land with pastoral and arable potential. They are linked into a wider network of sites, which may be used seasonally for pasture or the exploitation of fuel and raw material resources for burial and iron working in lower elevations. The range of Iron Age activity extends across the entire range of landscape forms, with activity in the truly elevated parts of this landscape also evidenced in the, rather ephemeral, re-use of a court tomb at Shanballyedmonduff as well of the Bronze Age Mooghaun hillfort.

Employing a mixed agricultural regime and habitually moving between different parts of the landscape, possibly to access seasonal resources, Iron Age communities have left a significant footprint on the landscapes of North Munster. Extrapolation of the site distributions encountered on the linear schemes to the surrounding areas would imply a densely inhabited landscape. Cemeteries are in some areas of the route closely spaced, with the two ring-ditches at Ballyboy 1 and Ballyboy 2, or the cemeteries at Manusmore and the site at Killow, located at a distance of about 1 km apart respectively. This density may suggest groups living in the vicinity (cf Jones 2012, 55) and the repeated use of the burial sites suggests that they were the burial grounds of small family units. While set apart spatially, they nevertheless aligned themselves within the same landscapes. At the same time the burial sites link the Iron Age of this region most visibly into wider Iron Age cultural trends both in terms of the forms of monuments as well as the artefacts found within them. While at the margins of the La Tène distribution in Ireland, the range of glass beads and toggles, and the bone dice, relate closely to the range of artefacts found in other parts of the country (cf Eogan 2012) and show how the local, small scale settlement was linked into the supra-regional networks of Iron Age of Ireland.

4.5 Acknowledgements

The author would like to thank Kate Taylor TVAS (Ireland) Ltd; Nick Hogan (UCC), James Eogan and Michael Stanley (Transport Infrastructure Ireland).

4.6 Bibliography

Anthony, S. 2006a. Human and animal bone. In G. Hull. *N18 Ennis Bypass and N85 Western Relief Road. Site AR100, Manusmore, Co. Clare.* 16-18. Final Archaeological Excavation Report, TVAS Ireland Ltd.

Anthony, S. 2006b. Human and animal bone In G. Hull. *N18 Ennis Bypass and N85 Western Relief Road. Site AR102, Manusmore, Co. Clare.* 9-11. Final Archaeological Excavation Report, TVAS Ireland Ltd.

Anthony, S. 2006c. Human and animal bone. In K. Taylor. *N18 Ennis Bypass and N85 Western Relief Road, Site AR104, Killow, Co. Clare.* 10-4. Final Archaeological Excavation Report, TVAS Ireland Ltd.

Anthony, S. 2006d. Bone analysis. In G. Hull. *N18 Ennis Bypass and N85 Western Relief Road Site AR131, Claureen, Co. Clare.* 5-6. Final Archaeological Excavation Report. TVAS Ireland Ltd.

Armit, I. 2007. Social landscapes and identities in the Irish Iron Age. In C. Haselgrove & T. Moore (eds). *The Later Iron Age in Britain and beyond.* 130-9. Oxbow: Oxford.

Armit, I., Swindles, G. & Becker, K. 2013. From dates to demography in later prehistoric Ireland? Experimental approaches to the meta-analysis of large 14 C data-sets. *Journal of Archaeological Science*, 40 (1), 433-8.

Becker, K. 2010. Iron Age Ireland. Finding an invisible people. In G. Cooney, K. Becker, J. Coles, M. Ryan, & S. Sievers (eds). *Relics of old decency. Archaeological studies in later prehistory.* 353-62. Bray: Wordwell.

Becker, K. 2012a. Redefining the Irish Iron Age. In M. Potterton & C. Corlett (eds). *Life and death in Iron Age Ireland.* Bray: Wordwell.

Becker, K. 2012b. The introduction of iron working to Ireland. In A. Kern & J. Koch (eds). *Technologieentwicklung und -transfer in der Eisenzeit. Tagungsbericht der AG Eisenzeit, Hallstatt 2009.* Langenweissenbach: Beiträge zur Ur-und Frühgeschichte Mitteleuropas.

Becker, K. 2014. Token explanations – Rathgall and the interpretation of cremation deposits in later prehistoric Ireland. *Archaeology Ireland* 28 (1.107), 13-5.

Becker, K. in press. Irish Iron Age Settlement and Society - Reframing Royal Sites. *Proceedings of the Prehistoric Society* (2019).

Becker, K., Armit, I., & Swindles, G. 2017. The contribution of NRA archaeology to the understanding of the Irish Iron Age. In M. Stanley, R. Swan & A. O'Sullivan. *Stories of Ireland's past*. 85-100. Dublin: Transport Infrastructure Ireland.

Becker, K., Ó Néill, J. & O'Flynn, L. 2008. Iron Age Ireland: Finding an invisible people. *Archaeology Ireland*, 22.2, 3.

Bermingham, N., Coyne, F., Hull, G., Reilly, F. & Taylor, K. 2013a. *River Road. The archaeology of the Limerick Southern Ring Road*. NRA Scheme Monograph 14. Dublin: NRA.

Bermingham, N., Hull, G., O'Keeffe, P. & Taylor, K. 2013b. Searching for a past. In N. Bermingham, F. Coyne, G. Hull, F. Reilly & K. Taylor. *River Road. The archaeology of the Limerick Southern Ring Road*. 1-28. NRA Scheme Monograph 14. Dublin: NRA.

Bermingham, N. & Hull, G. 2012. Introduction. In N. Bermingham, G. Hull & K. Taylor 2012. *Beneath the Banner. Archaeology of the M18 Ennis Bypass and N85 Western Relief Road, Co. Clare*. 1-30. Dublin: NRA.

Bermingham, N., Hull, G. & Taylor, K. 2012. *Beneath the Banner. Archaeology of the M18 Ennis Bypass and N85 Western Relief Road, Co. Clare*. Dublin: NRA.

Bevan, A., Colledge, S., Fuller, D., Fyfe, R., Shennan, S. & Stevens, C. 2017. Holocene fluctuations in human population demonstrate repeated links to food production and climate. *Proceedings of the National Academy of Sciences*, 115 (15) E3597.

Clark, L. & Long, P. 2010. *N7 Nenagh to Limerick High Quality Dual Carriageway Archaeological Resolution Project. Gortybrigane Site 2, E2488 Co. Tipperary*. Final Excavation Report.

Clark, L. & MacLeod, R. 2010. *N7 Nenagh to Limerick High Quality Dual Carriageway Archaeological Resolution Project Richhill Site 2, E2311, Co. Limerick*. Final Excavation Report.

Cowley, D.C. 2016. What do the patterns mean? Archaeological distributions and bias in survey data. In M. Forte & S. Campana (eds). *Digital methods and Remote sensing in Archaeology*. 147-70. New York: Springer.

Delaney, S., Bayley, D., Lyne, E. McNamara, S., Nunan, J. & Molloy, K. 2012. *Borderlands. Archaeological investigations on the route of the M18 Gort to Crusheen road scheme*. Dublin: NRA.

Dolan, B. 2014. Beyond Elites. Reassessing Irish Iron Age Society. *Oxford Journal of Archaeology* 33.4, 361-77.

Eogan, J. 2012. An Iron Age penannular ring-ditch at Ballybronoge South, Co. Limerick. In C. Corlett & M. Potterton (eds). *Life and Death in Iron Age Ireland in the Light of Recent Archaeological Excavations*. 105-19. Dublin: NRA.

Grogan, E., O'Donnell, L., Johnston, P. & Gowen, M. 2006. *The Bronze Age landscapes of the Pipeline to the West: an integrated archaeological and environmental assessment*. Bray: Wordwell.

Grogan, E. 2005. *The North Munster Project*. 255-88. The Discovery Programme. Bray: Wordwell.

Henderson, J. 2011. *The Atlantic Iron Age: Settlement and Identity in the First Millennium BC*. London: Routledge.

Hull, G. 2006a. *N18 Ennis Bypass and N85 Western Relief Road Site AR102, Manusmore, Co. Clare Final Archaeological Excavation Report 04E0189*. TVAS Ireland Ltd.

Hull, G. 2006b. The wooden bowl. In K. Taylor. *N18 Ennis Bypass and N85 Western Relief Road Site AR104, Killow, Co. Clare*. Final Archaeological Excavation Report Licence No: 04E0191. TVAS (Ireland) Ltd.

Lynn, C. 2003. Ireland in the Iron Age - A basket case? *Archaeology Ireland*, 17(2), 20-3.

Lyne, E. 2009a. *N18 Gort to Crusheen Road Scheme. E3657 Rathwilladoon 5, County Galway*. Final excavation report, IAC.

Lyne, E. 2009b. *N18 Gort to Crusheen Road Scheme. Rathwilladoon 2 and 3. E3656*. Final excavation report, IAC.

McCooey, J, Ruttle, E & Taylor, K, 2010. *N7 Nenagh to Limerick High Quality Dual Carriageway, E3462, Monitoring of Wetlands Cos Limerick and Tipperary*, Archaeological monitoring report. TVAS (Ireland) Ltd.

McCormick, F. 1997. The Animal bones from Site B. In D. M. Waterman. *Excavations at Navan Fort 1961-1971*. 117-20. Ed. C. J. Lynn. Belfast: Stationary Office.

McNamara, M. 2012. *N7 Nenagh to Limerick High Quality Dual Carriageway Archaeological Resolution Project. E3370, Cooleen Site 1, Co. Tipperary*. Final Archaeological Excavation Report. TVAS Ireland Ltd

McNamara, S. 2010a. *N18 Gort to Crusheen Road Scheme. Ballyboy 1. E3719*. Final report. IAC.

McNamara, S. 2010b. *N18 Gort to Crusheen Road Scheme. Ballyboy 2*. E3718. Final report. IAC.

Molloy, K. 2005. Holocene vegetation and land-use history at Mooghaun, south-east Clare, with particular refernce to the Bronze Age. In E. Grogan. *The North Munster Project*. 255-88. The Discovery Programme. Bray: Wordwell.

Molloy, K. & O'Connell, M. 2012. Prehistoric farming in western Ireland: pollen analysis at Caheraphuca, Co. Clare. In S. Delaney, D. Bayley, E. Lyne, S. McNamara, J. Nunan & K. Molloy. *Borderlands. Archaeological investigations on the route of the M18 Gort to Crusheen road scheme*. 109-23. Dublin: NRA.

Monk, M. & Power, O. 2014. Casting Light from the Fires of Corn-Drying Kilns in the Later Irish Iron Age. *Archaeology Ireland* 28.3, 39-42.

Moore, C. 2013. Wood Technology. In K. Taylor & N. Bermingham. *N7 Nenagh to Limerick High Quality Dual Carriageway Archaeological Resolution Project E3530, Annaholty Site 8, Co. Tipperary.* 17-38. Final Archaeological Excavation Report for Limerick County Council. TVAS Ireland Ltd.

Murphy, D. & Clarke, L. 2001. *Nenagh By-pass project N-52 Link road. Report on resolution of archaeological sites. 00E0210-227, 00E0385, 00E0552.* Archaeological Consultancy Services Ltd.

Nunan, J. 2009. *N18 Gort to Crusheen Road Scheme. E3711. Derrygarriff 2. Charcoal kiln and metallurgy furnace.* Final Report. IAC.

O'Brien, C. 2013. Pollen Analysis. In K. Taylor & N. Berminham. *N7 Nenagh to Limerick High Quality Dual Carriageway Archaeological Resolution Project E3530, Annaholty Site 8, Co. Tipperary.* 55-9. Final Archaeological Excavation Report for Limerick County Council TVAS Ireland Ltd.

O'Sullivan, A. 2001. *Foragers, Farmers and Fishers in a Coastal Landscape.* Discovery Programme Mongraph 5. Dublin: Royal Irish Academy.

O'Sullivan, A., Dillon, M., Sands, R., McDermott, C., Shaw, R. & Devlin, G. 2010. *The Fergus Estuary and Islands: discovering a maritime historic landscape in Co. Clare.* Dublin: University College Dublin School of Archaeology in association with the Discovery Programme.

O'Sullivan, A., McCormick, F., Kerr, T.R. & Harney, L. 2013. *Early Medieval Ireland, AD 400-1100. The evidence from Archaeological Excavations.* Dublin: Royal Irish Academy Monographs.

Raftery, B. 1994. *Pagan Celtic Ireland. The Enigma of the Irish Iron Age.* London: Thames and Hudson.

Raftery, B. 1998. Kelten und Keltizismus in Irland: Die archäologischen Belege. In A. Müller-Karpe, H. Brandt, H. Jöns, D. Krauße & A. Wigg (eds). *Studien zur Archäologie der Kelten, Römer und Germanen in Mittel- und Westeuropa. Alfred Haffner zum 60. Geburtstagi.* 465-75. Rahden/Westfalen: Verlag Marie Leidorf GmbH.

Raftery, B. 2006. Celtic Ireland: Problems of Language, History and Archaeology. *Acta Archaeologica Academiae Scientiarium Hungaricae* 57, 273-79.

Ruttle, E. & Taylor, K. 2013. *Limerick Southern Ring Road, Phase II. E2091, Coonagh West Site 4, Co. Limerick.* Final Archaeological Excavation Report, TVAS Ireland Ltd.

Scotland, L. 2011. *N7 Nenagh to Limerick High Quality Dual Carriageway. Archaeological Resolution Project E2400: Ballynahinch Site 2. Final Excavation Report.* Aegis Archaeology Limited.

Taylor, K. 2006. *N18 Ennis Bypass and N85 Western Relief Road Site AR104, Killow, Co. Clare.* Final Archaeological Excavation Report Licence No: 04E0191

Taylor, K. 2011. *N7 Nenagh to Limerick High Quality Dual Carriageway Archaeological Resolution Project E2483, Ballycuddy More Site 1, Co. Tipperary.* Final Archaeological Excavation Report. TVAS Ireland Ltd.

Taylor, K. & Bermingham, N. 2013 *N7 Nenagh to Limerick High Quality Dual Carriageway Archaeological Resolution Project E3530, Annaholty Site 8, Co. Tipperary.* Final Archaeological Excavation Report, TVAS Ireland Ltd.

Young, T. 2009. Analysis of archaeometallurgical residues Derrygarriff 2, Co. Clare, E3711. In J. Nunan. *N18 Gort to Crusheen Road Scheme, Derrygarriff 2. Charcoal Kiln and metallurgy furnace.* Final Report, IAC. ixi.

Chapter 5

Recent research on the Arras Culture in its landscape setting

Peter Halkon

5.1 Introduction

Between 1815 and 1817 the Reverend William Stillingfleet, Barnard Clarkson and Dr Thomas Hull, with the aid of an unspecified number of workmen, undertook the excavation of a series of burial mounds at Arras Farm, near the East Yorkshire town of Market Weighton (Stillingfleet 1847; Stead 1979). Their discoveries included several chariot burials and other graves containing prestigious items. The distinctive style of the burials and the objects within them, paralleled on the near continent of Europe, eventually led to the coining of the term "Arras culture". Although such constructs have been questioned and modified (*e.g.* Harding 2015, 4), there are definite differences between the material culture of this region and elsewhere in Iron Age Britain (Cunliffe 2005). The bicentenary of the end of the first Arras excavations, and new discoveries in 2017, provide an opportunity to reflect on the landscape context of these Iron Age people. The primary focus here will be on presenting the settlements and landscape changes, gained through developer funded archaeological excavation and other research projects, particularly those conducted by the author.

5.2 The landscape background

The study area, which covers eastern Yorkshire north of the River Humber, is bounded to the east by the North Sea (Figure 1). It can be divided into a number of discrete topographical zones. The plain of Holderness is low-lying, with a surficial geology comprising glacial till deposits, with gravel ridges interrupting its general flatness (Catt 1990). The Holderness coast is one of the fastest eroding coastlines in Europe and it is certain that much land has been lost to the sea since the Iron Age (De Boer 1996). Holderness contains former glacial lakes or meres, all drained apart from Hornsea Mere. The valley of the River Hull, comprising substantial wetlands, forms a sub-region of Holderness (Van de Noort & Ellis 1995).

The main relief of East Yorkshire is provided by the rolling crescentic Cretaceous chalk hills of the Yorkshire Wolds, extending from the River Humber near Hessle to Flamborough Head. The highest point on the western escarpment rises to 246 m OD (Catt 1990). The chalk plateau is crisscrossed by many valleys formed by glacial activity, now mostly dry, apart from the Z-shaped Great Wold Valley, which contains the Gypsy Race, a stream of great significance in determining the location of major ritual monuments. These include

In D.C. Cowley, M. Fernández-Götz, T. Romankiewicz & H. Wendling (eds). Rural Settlement. Relating buildings, landscape, and people in the European Iron Age (Leiden 2019: Sidestone Press) 57-68.

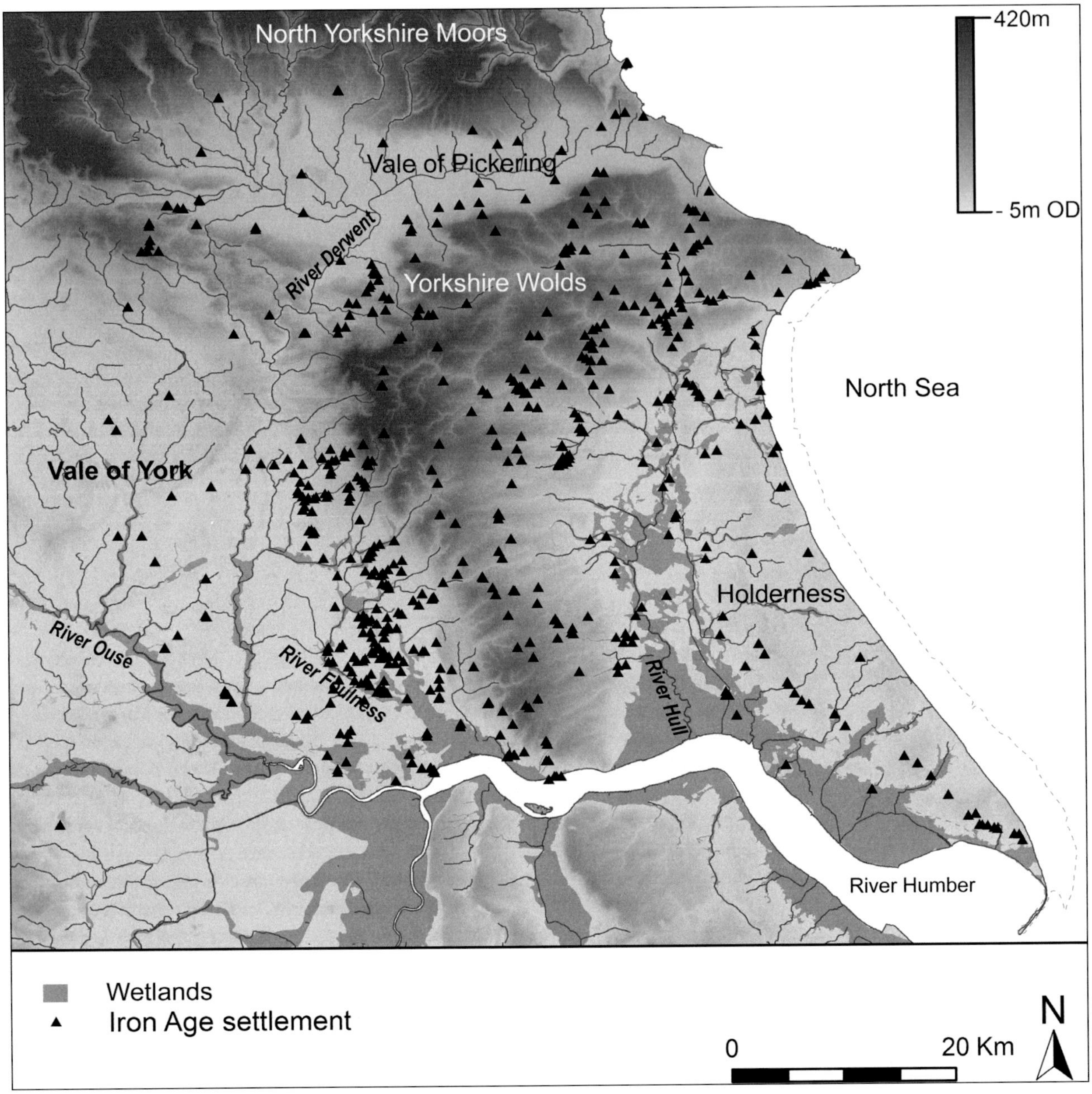

Figure 1: Iron Age settlements against the topography of Eastern Yorkshire. During most of the Iron Age the Wetland areas were inundated, the Walling Fen forming a tidal inlet. The dotted line marks the projected line of the North Sea Coast. (Graphics: P. Halkon and T. Sparrow).

the very large Neolithic burial mounds of Duggleby Howe and Willy Howe, the biggest concentration of Neolithic cursus monuments in Britain, the Rudston monolith, Britain's tallest standing stone and many Bronze Age round barrows (Manby *et al.* 2003). This remarkable concentration of monuments also includes Iron Age cemeteries and settlements no longer visible on the ground, but mapped by aerial survey (Stoertz 1997), some of which will be discussed below and most recently investigated by a team based at Cambridge University (Ferraby *et al.* 2017).

A ridge of Lower Lias and Jurassic geology lies immediately to the west of the Wolds escarpment, bordering the Vale of York. This comprises drift deposits of lacustrine clays, with relict dunes of sand and gravel forming higher points within the landscape. To the north of the Wolds escarpment is the lowlying Vale of Pickering, also formed through glacio-lacustrine activity, cut through by the River Derwent, which flows into the River Ouse south of York, which in turn joins the Humber estuary. Further drainage is supplied by the River Foulness which once emptied into what became known as the Walling Fen, crucial for understanding of Iron Age landscape change here (Catt 1990; Halkon 2008).

A major marine transgression between 800 and 500 BC, with sea levels reaching a Holocene maximum of about 0.7 m OD, transformed extensive low-lying woodland into a tidal estuarine inlet extending 12 km north of the present Humber coastline, about 8 km across where it joined the Humber estuary. The effects were also felt further to the east around the confluence of the rivers Hull and Humber, and a considerable distance upstream and up the North Sea coast (Long *et al.* 1998; Halkon & Innes 2005; Coles 2010). The 1991 and 2013 tidal surges, which caused large-scale inundation along the banks of the Humber, provide a reminder of the devastating potential of such events as much surrounding farmland was inundated despite modern flood defences. This early Iron Age transformation of the Humber coastline may not however have proven to have been totally without benefit, as it made the Yorkshire Wolds foothills more accessible to the trading networks provided by Humber, North Sea Basin and beyond. It is perhaps no coincidence that the Arras Iron Age cemetery itself lies at the top of Sancton Dale, a route way between the Yorkshire Wolds and Humber lowlands.

5.3 Iron Age settlement

5.3.1 Linear earthworks – the Yorkshire Wolds Dykes

Although there is some disagreement concerning climatic instability and its effect on Late Bronze Age and early Iron Age society (Brown 2008; Armit *et al.* 2014) at this time the Yorkshire Wolds was divided up by a network of linear earthworks known as the Wold Dykes or entrenchments (Mortimer 1905), some extending for many kilometres. There has been much debate about their precise function or who constructed them. Although most authorities agree that they are some form of land division, they have been perceived as communal enterprises (Giles 2007) or relating to occupants of the curvilinear hilltop enclosures that appear at around the same time *e.g.* Paddock Hill, Thwing (Manby 2007), which lies near a junction of the Great Wold Dyke. Grimthorpe hillfort (Stead 1968) may relate to a system of linear earthworks to the east, including one of the best preserved surviving examples at Huggate Dykes, where a system of five parallel banks and ditches lies along a ridge joining the heads of two major valleys. Recent geophysical survey (Fioccoprille 2015) confirms remodelling and elaboration at the entrances, in a similar style to the multi-vallate hillforts of southern England, such as Maiden Castle. Huggate Dykes probably controlled a route way across the Wolds between the Vale of York and Holderness. This system may also have controlled access to a valley containing many springs which feed Millington Beck, a valuable source of water in an otherwise relatively dry landscape. Grimthorpe hillfort also overlooks a valley containing many springs. A relationship between the earthworks, hillfort and the need to water livestock seems highly likely (Halkon 2013). Examination of the linear earthworks systems mapped from cropmarks recorded on aerial photographs (Stoertz 1997) and those surviving as upstanding earthworks recorded by the Ordnance Survey in successive map editions, suggests that re-planning took place on a number of occasions (Halkon 2008).

5.3.2 Hilltop enclosures

The corpus of large upstanding multivallate hillforts in East Yorkshire is small compared to those known on similar chalklands of southern Britain. Many of the largest hilltop enclosures on the Wolds have only been observed as cropmarks on aerial photographs, although geophysical survey has been undertaken at Greenlands hillfort, near Rudston (Payne 1989). The majority remain to be fully investigated, and most are now invisible on the ground surface, having been severely damaged by medieval and later ploughing. Although their construction began in the Later Bronze Age, in east Yorkshire it has been argued that by the Middle Iron Age they had fallen out of use (Millett 1990). Too few of these hillforts have been excavated to be sure of this, however.

In spring 2017, extensive geophysical survey was carried out by James Lyall, Clare Whiteley and the author on a large ovoid enclosure, 142 m long and at least 100 m across, near Middleton on the Wolds, which had been mapped by Stoertz (1997). The Stoertz plots only showed concentric inner and outer ditches, 30 m apart. The geophysical survey, however, revealed surprising results, for at the centre of the inner enclosure is a circular feature, 20 m in diameter, probably a large round house. At the centre of this structure is a 7 m diameter ring of post pits. The eastern entrance passage, flanked by large post holes, was aligned with similar entrance ways in both the inner and outer enclosure ditches. With its large central timber building and imposing entrances it most closely resembles the Late Bronze Age enclosures at Paddock Hill, Thwing, East Yorkshire (Manby 2007), and Springfield Lyons (Brown & Medlycott 2013) and Mucking (Bond 1988) in Essex, and therefore has the potential to be of national significance. Like Grimthorpe and Thwing it is situated in a conspicuous location visible from a considerable distance away and in turn overlooking a large territory. Its precise function and date however await further investigation.

Smaller in size is Staple Howe (Brewster 1963), an ovoid early Iron Age hilltop enclosure, once interpreted as a centre for Hallstatt invaders, constructed on a chalk outcrop which slid from the northern Wolds escarpment.

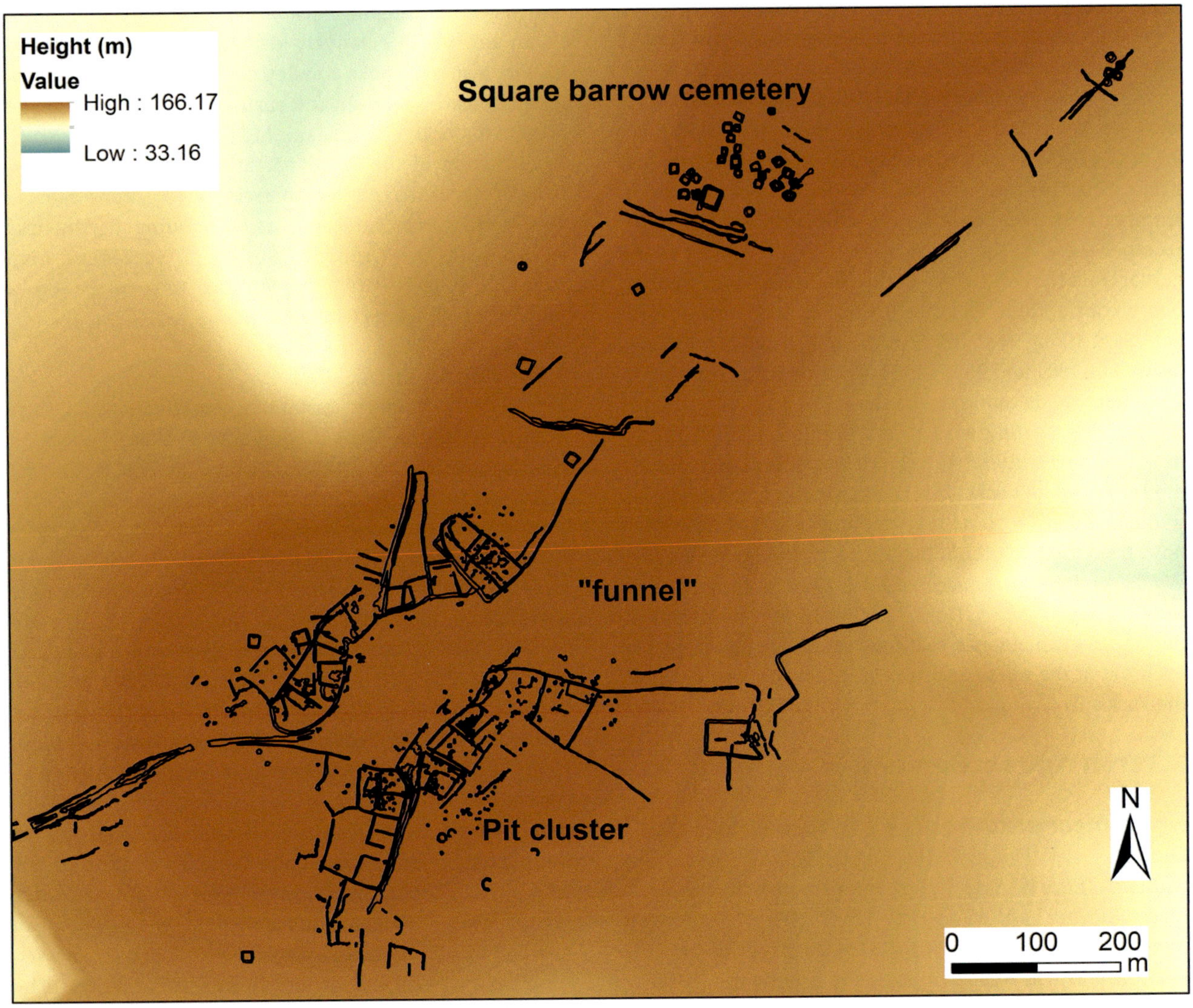

Figure 2: The Nunburnholme Wold site against topography. The ovoid enclosures lie on a plateau surrounded by valleys. Note the square barrow cemetery to the east of the 'funnel'. (Graphics: P. Halkon. Mapping by Clare Whiteley based on Geophysics by James Lyall).

Similar features have been recorded as cropmarks on the lower lying ground southwest of the Wolds escarpment at Londesborough Moor and Market Weighton Common, positioned on slightly raised ground near water courses (Halkon 2008).

It is clear that hilltops were significant in the early Iron Age East Yorkshire landscape as in previous eras. Although some of the hilltop enclosures referred to appeared *de novo* in the Late Bronze Age and Early Iron Age, others were positioned on pre-existing foci of activity, often relating to ritual, for example at Paddock Hill, Thwing, a late Neolithic Henge. Another such location is Nunburnholme Wold (Figure 2). Here a figure of eight shaped plateau at 160m OD on the western edge of the Wolds escarpment commands extensive views across the Vale of York and is also visible from a considerable distance. Although some features were plotted by Stoertz (1997) a 34 ha geophysical survey combined with selective excavation revealed much greater detail and many phases of activity (Halkon, Lyall & Lillie 2014; Halkon & Lyall 2015a; Halkon & Lyall 2016). On the eastern side of the plateau a probable Neolithic mortuary enclosure was followed by a hengiform feature, possibly of early to middle Bronze Age date as half a stone mace head was found in association. Other Bronze Age activity is demonstrated by the penannular ditch of what is likely to be a ploughed-out barrow, whose fill contained a rim sherd of a collared urn.

At the narrowest point of the Nunburnholme Wold plateau was a substantial double-ditched linear earthwork with a distinct kink at its mid-point, similar to the Great Wold Dyke at Paddock Hill, Thwing (Manby 2007), which may have had special significance. A major change at

Nunburnholme Wold is indicated by the digging of three parallel ditches cut straight through the hengiform structure, possibly a deliberate act designed to slight the monument. In contrast, linear earthworks elsewhere respected upstanding monuments such as round barrows, for example at Wetwang Slack, where the square barrow cemetery and linear earthwork respect a large round barrow (Dent 2010).

A possible reason for the slighting of the Nunburnholme hengiform may have been the construction of a 20 by 20 m square enclosure, respecting and aligned on the triple linear earthworks. This contained a central burial in a shallow disturbed grave. Marked as an upstanding tumulus on Ordnance Survey maps into the mid-twentieth century, it has now been ploughed flat. It may relate to a cemetery of square barrows, so characteristic of the Arras culture of Middle Iron Age eastern Yorkshire. These are square ditched enclosures, usually some 3 m to 10 m across, surrounding a central burial, which in the early period was placed on the ground surface, the spoil from the ditch forming a mound over the grave. Later square barrows are usually smaller, more regular in shape and have deeper central graves, making them more likely to be discovered as cropmarks during aerial survey.

The eastern half of the Nunburnholme Wold plateau may have been exclusively for ritual and burial, the double linear with the kink serving as a division with a western focus of more domestic-related activity. Possibly at the time of the construction of the double linear feature, a series of drove ways were constructed, leading through dry valleys from the lower lying land below the plateau, into a roughly oval space around 250 by 150 m containing very few geophysical anomalies, apart from a modern chalk quarry. Encircled by a palimpsest of rectilinear enclosures of varying sizes, the earliest phases contained pottery resembling that from Staple Howe and much animal bone. Two pits associated with the enclosures contained Iron Age pottery and animal bone, bone pins and needles and a miniature copper alloy axe very similar to one discovered at Arras (Stillingfleet 1846). To the southeast the enclosure opens out into a funnel 300 m across at its entrance.

One of a cluster of about 30 pits was excavated. The pit had been re-opened on a number of occasions in antiquity. It contained much Iron Age pottery, animal bone and unusual items including an iron ring headed pin, red and roe deer antler, the complete inverted cranium of a cow, and a piece of metalworking slag (Halkon & Lyall 2016a). The amount and character of the material suggests feasting activity. One of the enigmas of this site is the apparent absence of roundhouses revealed by geophysics or excavation. Although eaves-drip gullies may have been ploughed out, activity on this exposed hilltop site was perhaps seasonal, and shelters temporary. The drove ways, funnel and the animal bone present a picture of activities relating to herding livestock, complementing the palaeo-environmental evidence which shows that the immediate landscape consisted of open chalk grassland with some sparse woodland in surrounding valleys (Carrott *et al.* 2015). The evidence therefore points to this being a place of seasonal meeting and exchange, and given its size and prominence, perhaps for a whole region.

Many of the characteristics at Nunburnholme Wold are also evident at Market Weighton Wold (Halkon & Woodhouse 2010), where aerial photographs and geophysical survey have revealed features including two ovoid enclosures resembling Londesborough Moor, aligned on a triple linear earthwork and Bronze Age round barrows. Pottery in the ditch fills of the internal ovoid features resembled that from Staple Howe; animal bone comprising cattle, sheep and pig were perhaps the remnants of feasting. The curvilinear features were later enclosed in the Iron Age by a large enclosure some 90 m across. Overlooking the Vale of York, positioned between two shallow dry valleys, the re-planning here may be contemporary with the Nunburnholme Wold enclosure complex, and perhaps served a similar function.

5.3.3 Linear enclosure complexes or ladder settlements

Dominant features of the middle to later Iron Age of the Wolds are 'ladder settlements' consisting of a pair of ditches demarcating a drove way flanked by rectilinear enclosures, thus resembling the rungs of a ladder (Fenton-Thomas 2005; Dent 2010). In some cases these stretch for several kilometres. The Arras example extends for about 2 km (Stoertz 1997; Halkon 2008) (Figure 3). Ladder settlements, such as at Wharram (Hayfield 1987; 1988; Atha 2007) and Melton (Bishop 1999), began in the Iron Age and were occupied into and throughout the Roman period. During aerial survey and investigation of aerial photographs 46 ladder settlements were identified in the 30×20 km Foulness Valley study area (Halkon 2008, 79). Roundhouses were only present in five of these. Although the absence of roundhouses may due to visibility, as in general such timber structures are only visible in the very best conditions, many of the enclosures may have been paddocks or fields, rather than dwelling places. Enclosure palimpsests demonstrate replanning; the regularity of some such as Blealands Nook, Maiden's Grave Farm and Bell Slack, around the Great Wold Valley, contrasting with less structured agglomerations.

Ladder settlements tend to be restricted to the Wolds and immediate foothills, perhaps relating to topography, as the wide open plateaus allowed the laying out of long distance drove ways and enclosure systems. Their considerable length implies that landscape was cleared of woodland by the time of their construction. At lower elevations, they tend to be associated with streams or

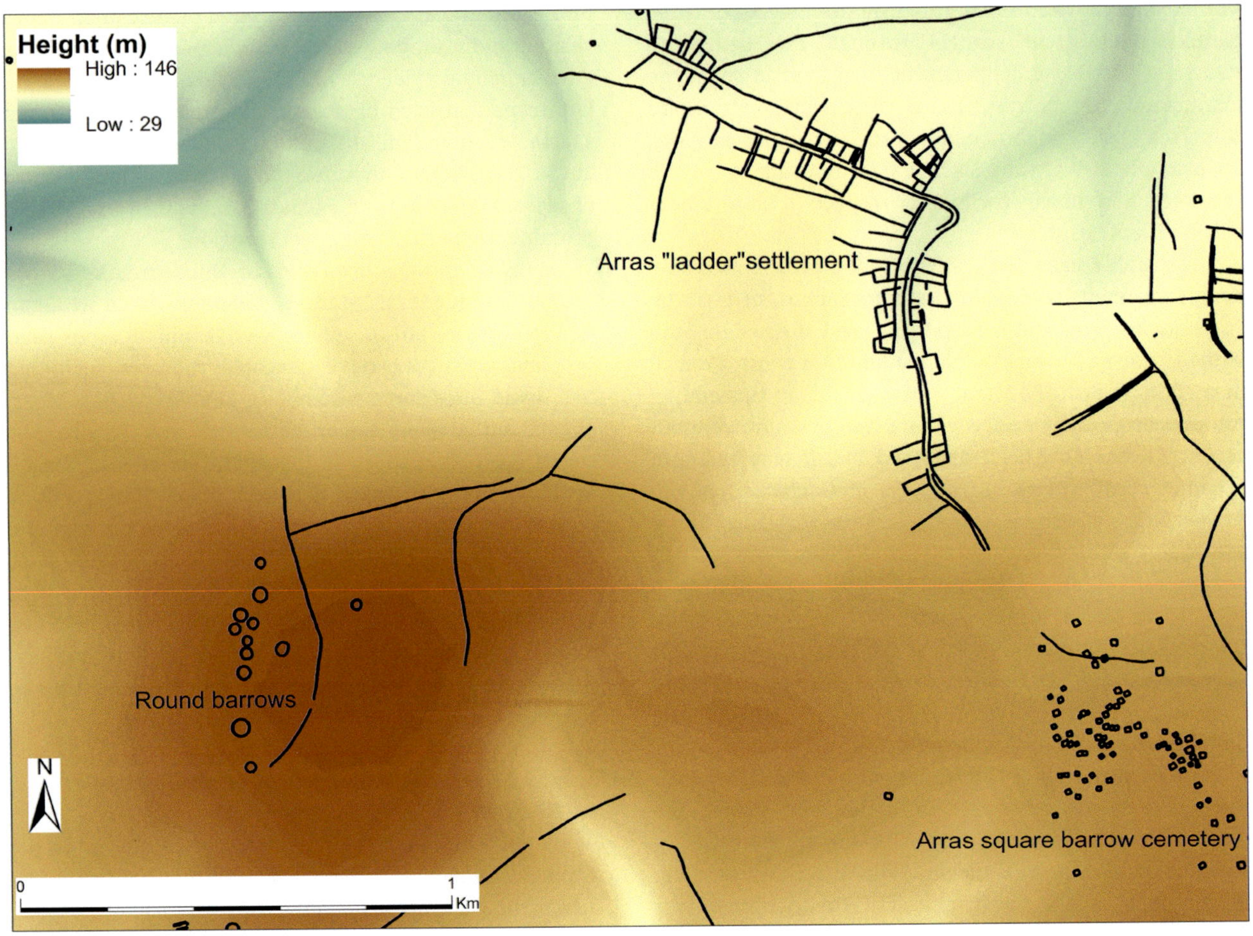

Figure 3: The 'ladder' settlement at Arras against topography. Note the position of the square barrow cemetery at the highest point of the wold. (Graphics: P. Halkon. Cropmark plots after Stoertz 1997).

rivers, for example at Arglam, Holme-on-Spalding Moor, where a series of enclosures flank a drove way which leads down to the rich summer grazing of the "carrs" (water meadows) (Halkon & Millett 1999). A string of enclosures was aligned on a stream running through the villages of Hayton and Burnby. A single ditch separates the wetlands close to the stream from the better drained gravel rises upon which most of the enclosures were situated (Halkon *et al.* 2015), perhaps designed for the management of animals. A similar explanation was given by Dent (2010) who argued that some enclosures were constructed to keep livestock away from growing crops rather than containing the animals themselves. The Hayton animal bone analysis showed a preponderance of sheep (Jaques 2015). Several of the enclosures here contained substantial roundhouses (Halkon *et al.* 2015).

Long-term landscape research around West Heslerton in the Vale of Pickering (Powlesland 2003) has revealed a linear enclosure complex that may have been occupied from around 500 BC to AD 500, running east-west for many kilometres along a ridge of slightly higher ground on the edges of a large wetland. Such a location, close to the chalk landscapes of the Yorkshire Wolds, provided the benefits of a range of ecosystems.

5.3.4 Lowland settlement types

In the lowland areas of East Yorkshire, particularly the Foulness Valley and Holderness, single rectilinear enclosures containing a roundhouse are more usual. Classic examples can be seen at Bursea Grange (Figure 4) Hasholme Hall (Halkon & Millett 1999; Halkon 2008), each within an area of around 3.6 ha demarcated by substantial ditches, strategically placed on sandy rises close to creeks.

Iron Age settlements in the Hull Valley were also designed to cope with poor drainage, their ring gullies widened by frequent recutting and cleaning out, for example (Figure 5) at Creyke Beck, Cottingham (Evans & Steedman 2001), Saltshouse Road, Hull (Didsbury 1990; Challis & Harding 1975) and Arram (Wilson *et al.* 2006). Not all ring gullies encircled roundhouses; those under 5m

Figure 4: Aerial photograph showing the cropmarks of the Iron Age enclosure containing a roundhouse at Bursea Grange, Holme-on-Spalding Moor. Note the cropmark of a former stream to the right. (P. Halkon).

in diameter forming complete circles rather than being penannular may have caught run-off water from haystacks. At Arram querns and palaeoenvironmental analysis imply that there was some arable agriculture in the vicinity, despite the relative wetness and clay soils there.

The variety in the ring ditch morphology has also been noted in Holderness, where the construction of gas pipelines has revealed an unexpected number of Iron Age settlements (Glover *et al.* 2016) in a region previously regarded as a blank area in terms of archaeology, due to its low-lying topography and areas of wetland. Although the settlements here may have been different in plan, their material culture, particularly the hand thrown pottery, was much the same as that found on Iron Age sites on the Yorkshire Wolds (Glover *et al.* 2016).

So far most of the settlements considered have been enclosed. Less easily detected through aerial survey and other forms of remote sensing are "open" settlements often only revealed through topsoil stripping during quarrying and other development, such as the extensive and most fully excavated site in the region at Garton and Wetwang Slack, where 80 round houses extended along the valley for over 1.3 km. The site comprised various activity zones for arable and pastoral agriculture and burial (Dent 2010).

Evidence for the presence of elites within middle Iron Age settlements such as Wetwang/Garton Slack has so far been elusive, as there appears to be little in terms of the material culture to differentiate the occupants. It is possible that status may have been expressed within settlements in other ways, for example the construction of larger or more impressive roundhouses, involving the procurement of more timber. This may have been the case on the Iron Age settlement excavated at Burnby Lane, Hayton, where one of the round houses was somewhat larger than an example in the neighbouring enclosure (Halkon *et al.* 2015).

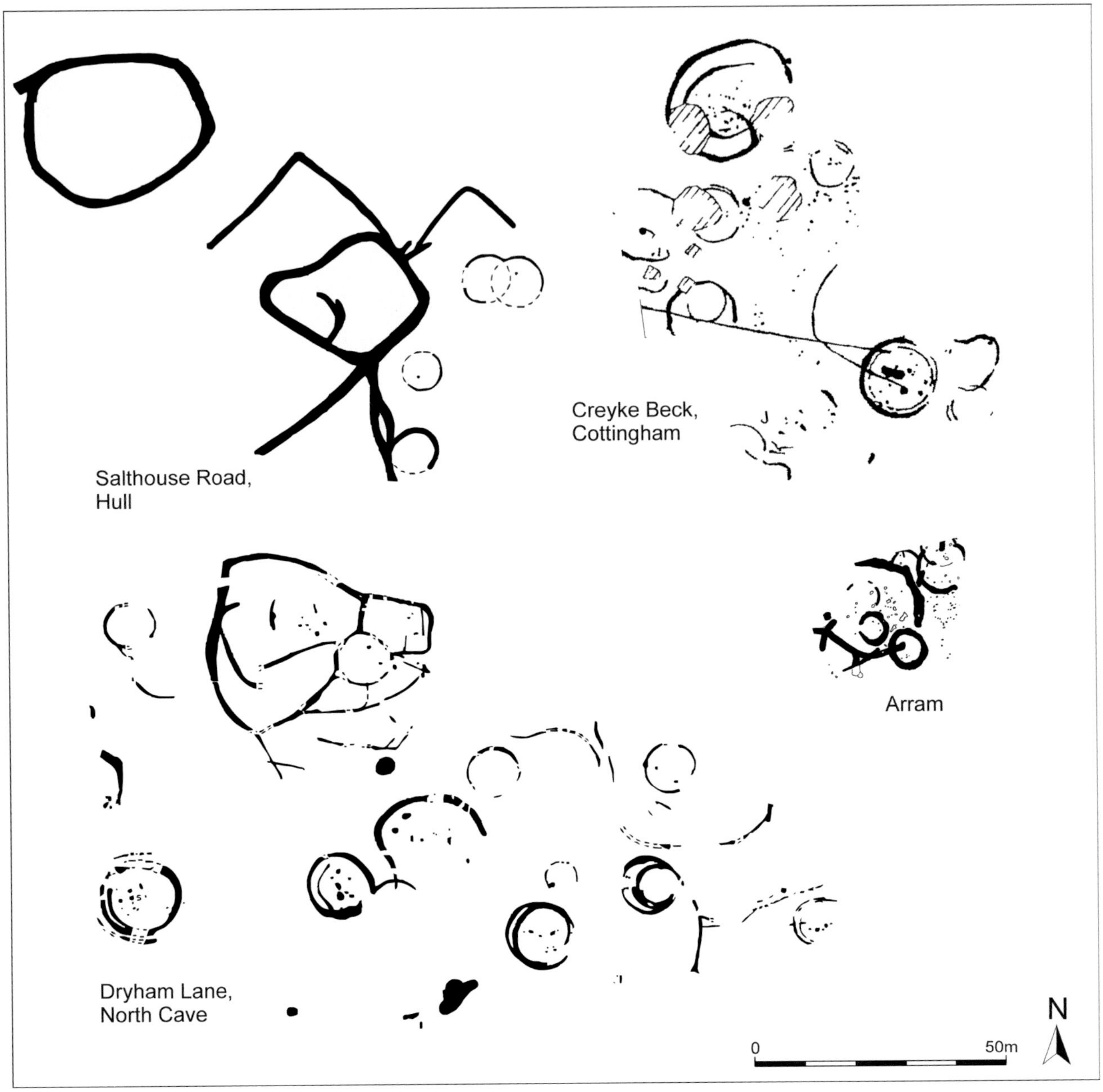

Figure 5: Iron Age lowland settlement types in eastern Yorkshire. (Graphics: P. Halkon and T. Sparrow).

5.4 The Burials of the Arras Culture

That there was some form of elite may be presumed from the concentration of chariot burials in eastern Yorkshire, as all but two of about 30 British examples have been discovered here, the majority contained within cemeteries of square barrows. An element of landscape control or ownership of some kind, whether by individual or community groups, may be implied from the positioning of these cemeteries, as many relate to route ways, particularly the dry valleys on the Wolds, or close to streams in the lower lying areas. The majority of larger cemeteries such as Arras itself are situated away from known major settlement complexes.

Square barrow cemeteries seem to appear suddenly around the fifth century BC. A square enclosure 10m across surrounded the burial of an elderly female in the usual crouched position with her head to the north, on a multiperiod site near Elloughton (Halkon & Lyall 2016b) close to the River Humber. This was radiocarbon dated to Cal BC 480 to 390 (Cal BP 2430 to 2340) (95% Probability; Beta-437590). This burial may relate to a cemetery of 43 square barrows excavated in autumn 2017 within the vicinity by Malton Archaeological Practice (pers. comm.

Paula Ware), including a most unexpected chariot burial. The skeleton itself was in the usual crouched position with its head the north, accompanied by pig bones, and harness fittings, some highly decorated. The two iron tyres were well preserved and the carriage, axle and pole visible as dark stains. A further remarkable burial in the cemetery was encircled by the complete skeletons of six goats and other animals (pers.comm. Paula Ware).

According to Bayesian modelling of the C14 dating the Wetwang chariot burials cluster around 200 BC (Hamilton *et al.* 2015; Jay *et al.* 2012) and the latest dates for burial in the Arras tradition extend into the early first century AD (Dent 2010).

Situated at the entrance to the extensive ladder settlement referred to above, the cemetery of around 200 square barrows at Arras (Stillingfleet 1847; Stead 1979; Halkon *et al.* 2019) was placed on a prominent ridge with extensive views south to the Humber and north to the Goodmanham gap, one of the major valleys running east-west through the Wolds. Consisting of both large sub-rectangular enclosures without visible central graves and smaller, more regular examples with a clear central grave, arranged in clusters, the cemetery extends for about 1.5 km and is almost as broad.

The largest Iron Age cemeteries mapped from aerial photographs on the Yorkshire Wolds (Stoertz 1997) are at Carnaby near Bridlington in the north-east of the region where over 300 burials are visible, and Dane's Graves with over 300. At Burton Fleming/Makeshift (Stead 1991) 346 square barrows were excavated and at Wetwang/Garton Slack there are about 450 (Dent 2010), separated from the main area of settlement in a discreet zone. A cemetery of 142 inhumations on the outskirts of Pocklington excavated in 2014-15 (Boughey & Ware 2016; Symonds 2017) was also separated from nearby settlement activity. The most spectacular discovery there was a chariot burial accompanied by two horses, although one of the iron tyres and most of the human occupant had been removed by ploughing. Other burials included a male with a sword, in a grave surrounded by a small circular ditch, with many spears, a phenomenon observed elsewhere in Arras culture burials (Stead 1991; Giles 2012; Halkon 2013), a female with a fine coral inlaid bow brooch and several with shields, their outlines picked out in decayed wood revealed through careful excavation (Boughey & Ware 2016; Symonds 2017).

5.5 Crafts and industry

The fact that there are more furnished burials in eastern Yorkshire than anywhere else in Iron Age Britain provides a large sample of grave goods for analysis. Of particular interest are those made of iron, including weapons, items of personal adornment, and fittings from chariots, including tyres and bridle fittings. Experimental archaeology has demonstrated that the production of iron was far more complex and time-consuming than hitherto supposed and it is estimated that a 1 kg of bar iron took eight to 25 person-days to produce, including ore extraction, transportation and preparation, charcoal production and furnace construction and operation (Crew 2013). If Crew is right, then the estimated amount of effort needed to produce the iron to furnish a chariot was 288 person days at the lowest estimate (Halkon 2012).

It has been suggested previously (Halkon 2012) that there was a strong connection between consumption of iron and status within society. It is perhaps no coincidence that the cemeteries of Garton/Wetwang Slack and Arras, which contain the most chariot burials in the region, were situated within relatively easy reach of the Hull and Foulness valleys respectively as these are the main eastern Yorkshire iron producing areas (Halkon 2012; Halkon & Millett 1999). One of the largest Iron Age slag heaps yet found in England at Moors Farm, Welhambridge, contained over five tonnes of slag and it has been estimated from this that the charcoal needed for the production of the iron from which this is the residue would have required around 47 ha of woodland. Pollen analysis and other environmental examination implies that the charcoal was produced within a system of managed woodland, rather than wholesale clearance, in a landscape of sandy rises close to wetland areas on the edges of the Walling Fen tidal inlet referred to above (Halkon & Millett 1999; Halkon 2012). A number of iron production sites have also been found at Arram (Wilson *et al.* 2006) and Thearne (Campbell 2008; Halkon 2012) in the Hull Valley. The grave goods found in the burials of the Arras culture provide evidence for highly skilled metalworking in copper alloy and the ability to combine different materials such as enamel to add a decorative effects to items such as swords and brooches. This is well illustrated by the spectacular sword from Kirkburn (Stead 1991; 2006), a tradition which the remarkable South Cave weapons cache, consisting of five swords in decorated sheaths bound up with 35 iron spearheads, demonstrates continued up to the time of the Roman conquest around AD 70.

5.6 The end of the Arras culture?

The high quality of the metalwork contrasts greatly with the relative crudity of the pottery of Middle Iron Age Eastern Yorkshire. This largely consists of straight sided jars in heavy calcite gritted and glacial erratic tempered wares (Rigby 2004) which paradoxically appears less competent than the decorated vessels, particularly those with slashed-rim decoration from the Early Iron Age site at Staple Howe. It was not until the latter part of the first century BC that wheel thrown vessels arrived in the region from Corieltauvian territory in what is now North Lincolnshire, across the River Humber, along with coinage. It is noticeable that wheel thrown pottery, particularly the cordoned Dragonby style vessels and hoards of Corieltauvian gold staters and single coin finds occur along the coastal regions and in the Hull and Foulness valleys closer to the Humber.

The appearance of these items may indicate a change in socio-political structure prior to the arrival of the Romans around about AD 70. The South Cave weapons cache (Evans 2006; Marchant & Halkon 2008) has been interpreted as a final act of structured deposition marking this transition, as the distinctive Iron Age traditions of eastern Yorkshire gave way to new influences from south of the Humber. One of the swords was around 150 years old before it was deposited, its decoration harking back to the art styles of earlier times. The hoard had been disposed of in a settlement ditch with some care, as it had been wrapped in leather or a fleece and covered by sherds of a Dressel 20 olive oil amphora from southern Spain. It may therefore have been deliberately hidden, perhaps to arm those planning to offer resistance against the invading forces.

Although aspects of material culture were changing, it is clear that occupation of the ladder settlements continued into the Roman period (Ferraby *et al.* 2017). It is interesting to note however that recent developer funded investigation along the Holderness pipelines has shown that round houses fell out of use by the late second or early third centuries AD (Glover *et al.* 2016). Even with the introduction of Romano British mass produced wheel thrown hard fired grey-ware pottery, many sites continue to use hand built coarse pottery jars which closely resembled Iron Age predecessors. Conversely wheel thrown greyware Romano-British pottery was found in the upper layers of the drove way feature at Nunburnholme Wold, and third and fourth century Roman coins also discovered there demonstrate continued activity on this key site within the East Yorkshire landscape.

5.7 Conclusion

The Arras Culture is a long-established construct, the significance of which was further enhanced in 2017 and 2018 when remarkable chariot burials, both containing horses, were found at Pocklington. A further chariot burial was excavated close to the River Humber on the margins of the Yorkshire Wolds. Furthermore, hitherto unknown cropmarks of settlements, burials and other features likely to be of Iron Age date were revealed by the summer drought of 2018. Although the full implications of these discoveries are yet to be assimilated, they provide an exciting reminder of the considerable potential of East Yorkshire to enhance our knowledge of Iron Age landscapes in Britian and beyond.

5.8 Bibliography

Armit, I., Swindles, G. T., Becker, K., Plunkett, G. & Blaauw, M. 2014. Rapid climate change did not cause population collapse at the end of the European Bronze Age. *Proceedings of the National Academy of Sciences* 111(48), 17045-9.

Atha, M. 2007. *Late Iron Age regionality and early Roman trajectories (100BC-200AD): A landscape perspective from East Yorkshire.* PhD Thesis, University of York.

Bishop, M. 1999. An Iron Age and Romano-British ladder settlement at Melton, East Yorkshire. *Yorkshire Archaeological Journal* 71, 23-63.

Bond, D. 1988. *Excavation at the North Ring, Mucking, Essex.* East Anglian Archaeology 43. Essex: East Anglian Archaeology.

Boughey, K. & Ware, P. 2016. Huge Iron Age cemetery discovered at Pocklington. *Prehistoric Yorkshire* 53, 109-10.

Brewster, T. C. M. 1963. *The excavation of Staple Howe.* Scarborough: East Riding Archaeological Research Trust.

Brown, N. & Medlycott, M. 2013. The Neolithic and Bronze Age Enclosures at Springfield Lyons, Essex: Excavations 1981-1991. *East Anglian Archaeology* 149.

Brown, T. 2008. The Bronze Age climate and environment of Britain. *Bronze Age Review – The international journal of research into the archaeology of the British and European Bronze Age* 1, 7-22.

Campbell, R. 2008. Manufacturing evidence of Romano-British glass bangles from Thearne, near Beverley, East Yorkshire. *Roman Antiquities Section Bulletin* 24. Leeds: Roman Antiquities Section, Yorkshire Archaeological Society, 12-7.

Carrott, J., Foster, A. & Jaques, D. 2015. *Assessment of sediment samples collected during the 2014 season of excavations at Nunburnholme Wold.* Palaeoecology Research Services PRS 2015/34.

Catt, J. A. 1990. Geology and Relief. In S. Ellis & D. Crowther (eds). *Humber Perspectives.* 13-28. Hull: Hull University Press.

Challis, A. J & Harding D. W. 1975. *Later Prehistory from the Trent to the Tyne.* Oxford: British Archaeological Reports 20.

Coles, A. 2010. *Palaeogeographical and relative sea-level changes at Hotham Carrs, East Yorkshire.* Unpublished BSc Dissertation, Department of Geography, University of Durham.

Crew, P. 2013 Twenty five years of bloomery experiments: perspectives and prospects. In D. Dungworth & R. Doonan (eds). *Accidental and Experimental Archaeometallurgy. Proceedings of the 2010 Conference.* 25-50. London: Historical Metallurgy Society.

Cunliffe, B. 2005. Iron Age communities in Britain. London and New York: Routledge (fourth edition).
De Boer, G. 1996. The coastal erosion of Holderness. In S. Neave & S. Ellis (eds). *An historical atlas of East Yorkshire*. 6-7. Hull: Hull University Press.
Dent, J. S. 2010. *The Iron Age in East Yorkshire*. Oxford: British Archaeological Reports British Series 508.
Didsbury, P. 1990. Exploitation of the alluvium in the Lower Hull Valley. In S. Ellis & D. Crowther (eds). *Humber Perspective*. 199-213. Hull: Hull University Press.
Evans, C. 2015. Wearing environment and making islands: Britain's Bronze Age inland North Sea. *Antiquity* 89, 1110-24.
Evans, D. H. & Steedman, K. 2001. Recent Archaeological work in the East Riding. *East Riding Archaeologist* 10, 116-71.
Evans, D. H. 2006. Celtic art revealed. The South Cave weapons hoard. *Current Archaeology* 203, 572-7.
Fenton-Thomas, C. 2005.*The Forgotten Landscapes of the Yorkshire Wolds*. Stroud: Tempus.
Ferraby, R., Johnson, P., Millett, M. & Wallace, L. 2017. *Thwing, Rudston and the Roman-period exploitation of the Yorkshire Wolds*. Leeds: Yorkshire Archaeological and Historical Society.
Fioccoprile, E. 2015. *Lines across the land: a biography of the linear earthwork landscapes of the later prehistoric Yorkshire Wolds*. Unpublished PhD thesis. University of Bradford.
Giles, M. 2007. Refiguring rights: later Bronze Age and early Iron Age landscapes of East Yorkshire. In C. Haselgrove, & R. Pope (eds). *The Earlier Iron Age in Britain and the near Continent*. 103-18. Oxford: Oxbow Books.
Giles, M. 2012. *A forged glamour: landscape, identity and material culture in the Iron Age*. Oxford: Windgather Press.
Glover, G. Flintoft, P., Moore, R. 2016. *'A mersshy contree called Holdernesse': Excavations on the Route of a National Grid Pipeline in Holderness, East Yorkshire*. Oxford: Archaeopress.
Halkon, P. 2008. *Archaeology and environment in a changing East Yorkshire landscape: the Foulness Valley c. 800 BC to c.AD 400*. BAR British Series 472. Oxford: Archaeopress.
Halkon, P. 2013. *The Parisi: Britons and Romans in Eastern Yorkshire*. Stroud: The History Press.
Halkon, P. 2017. Putting the iron back in the Iron Age – A case study from the UK. In I. Montero & A. Perea (eds). *Archaeometallurgy in Europe IV*. 203-12. Madrid: Bibliotheca Praehistorica Hispana, XXXIII. Editorial CSIC.
Halkon, P. & Innes, J. 2005. Settlement and economy in a changing Prehistoric lowland landscape – An East Yorkshire (UK) Case Study. *European Journal of Archaeology* 8(3), 225-59.
Halkon, P., Lillie, M. & Lyall, J. 2015. *The Archaeology of Nunburnholme Wold. An Interim Report*. University of Hull and Nunburnholme Community Heritage Project.
Halkon, P. & Lyall, J. 2014. *The Archaeology of Nunburnholme Wold. An Interim Report*. University of Hull and Nunburnholme Community Heritage Project.
Halkon, P. & Lyall, J. 2016a. *The Archaeology of Nunburnholme Wold. An Interim Report*. University of Hull and Nunburnholme Community Heritage Project.
Halkon, P. & Lyall, J. 2016b. Excavation of a multi-period site 'near Elloughton', East Yorkshire. *Royal Archaeological Institute Newsletter* 51, April 2016, 7.
Halkon, P., Lyall, J. Deverell, J., Hunt, T. & Fernández-Götz, M. 2019. Arras 200: revisiting Britain's most famous Iron Age cemetery. *Antiquity* 93 368, e11 (2019), 1–7.
Halkon, P. & Millett, M. 1999. *Rural Settlement and industry: Studies in the Iron Age and Roman archaeology of lowland East Yorkshire*. Leeds: Yorkshire Archaeological Report 4 Yorkshire Archaeological Society.
Halkon, P. Millett, M. & Woodhouse, H. 2015. *Hayton, East Yorkshire: Archaeological Studies of the Iron Age and Roman landscapes*. Yorkshire Archaeological Report 7. Leeds: Roman Antiquities Section, Yorkshire Archaeological Society.
Halkon, P. & Woodhouse, H. 2010. Market Weighton Wold Excavation Interim Report. *ERAS News* 73.
Hamilton, W. D., Haselgrove, C., & Gosden, C., 2015. The impact of Bayesian chronologies on the British Iron Age. *World Archaeology* 47 (4), 642-60.
Harding D. W. 2015. *Death and Burial in Iron Age Britain*. Oxford: Oxford University Press.
Hayfield, C. 1987. *An archaeological survey of the parish of Wharram Percy, East Yorkshire: 1.The evolution of the Roman landscape*. Oxford: British Archaeological Reports (British Series) 172.
Hayfield, C. 1988. The origins of the Roman landscape around Wharram Percy, East Yorkshire. In P. Wilson, J. Price S. Briggs & S. Hardman. *Recent research in Roman Yorkshire*. 99-123. Oxford: British Archaeological Reports 193.
Jacques, D. 2015. The animal bone. In P. Halkon, M. Millett, & H. Woodhouse. *Hayton, East Yorkshire: Archaeological Studies of the Iron Age and Roman landscapes*. Yorkshire Archaeological Report 7. Leeds: Roman Antiquities Section, Yorkshire Archaeological Society, 412.
Jay, M., Haselgrove, C., Hamilton, W., Hill, J. D. & Dent, J. 2012. Chariots and context: New radiocarbon dates

from Wetwang and the chronology of Iron Age burials and brooches in East Yorkshire. *Oxford Journal of Archaeology* 31.

Kent, P. 1980. *British Regional Geology: eastern England from the Tees to the Wash*. London: Her Majesty's Stationary Office.

Long A. J., Innes J. B., Kirby J. R., Lloyd J. M., Rutherford M. M., Shennan I. & Tooley, M. J. 1998. Holocene sea-level change and coastal evolution in the Humber estuary, eastern England: an assessment of rapid coastal change. *The Holocene* 8, 229-47.

Manby, T. G. 2007. Continuity of monument traditions into the Late Bronze age? Henges to ring-forts, and shrines. In C. Burgess, P. Topping & F. Lynch (eds). *Beyond Stonehenge. Essays on the Bronze Age in honour of Colin Burgess*. 403-24. Oxford: Oxbow.

Manby, T., King, A. & Vyner, B. 2003. The Neolithic and Bronze Age. In T. Manby, S. Moorhouse & P. Ottaway (eds). *The Archaeology of Yorkshire: An assessment at the beginning of the 21st Century.* 35-114.Leeds: Yorkshire Archaeological Society with English Heritage, CBA.

Marchant, D. & Halkon, P. 2008. *Heavy metal in the Iron Age: The South Cave weapons cache and other treasures*. Beverley: East Riding of Yorkshire Council.

Millett, M. 1990. Iron Age and Romano-British settlement in the southern Vale of York and beyond: some problems in perspective. In S. Ellis & D. Crowther (eds). *Humber Perspectives*. 347-57. Hull: Hull University Press.

Mortimer, J. R. 1905. *Forty years researches in the British and Saxon Burial Mounds of East Yorkshire*. London: A. Brown & Sons Ltd.

Payne, A. 1989. *Lower Caythorpe, Rudston Parish, North Humberside*. Report of Geophysical Survey Ancient Monuments Laboratory Report 94/91. London: Historic Buildings and Monuments Commission for England.

Powlesland, D. 2003. The Heslerton Parish Project: 20 years of research in the Vale of Pickering. In T. Manby, S. Moorhouse & P. Ottaway (eds). *The Archaeology of Yorkshire An Assessment at the Beginning of the 21st Century*. 275-93. Leeds: Yorkshire Archaeological Society with English Heritage, CBA.

Rigby, V. 2004. *Pots in Pits. The British Museum Yorkshire settlements project 1988-92*. Hull: East Riding Archaeologist 11.

Stead, I. M. 1968. An Iron Age hillfort at Grimthorpe, Yorkshire. *Proceedings of the Prehistoric Society* 34, 148-90.

Stead, I. M. 1979. *The Arras Culture*. York: Yorkshire Philosophical Society.

Stead, I. M. 2006. *British Iron Age Swords and Scabbards*. London: British Museum Press.

Stillingfleet, E. 1846. Account of the opening of some barrows on the Wolds of Yorkshire. *Proceedings of the Archaeological Institute held at York*, 26-32.

Stoertz, C. 1997. *Ancient Landscapes of the Yorkshire Wolds*. Swindon: Royal Commission on Historical Monuments of England.

Symonds, M. 2017. An Iron Age chariot burial: excavating a square barrow cemetery at Pocklington. *Current Archaeology* 327, 26-31.

Tipping, R., Bradley R., Sanders, J. McCulloch, R. & Wilson, R. 2012. Moments of crisis: climate change in Scottish prehistory. *Proceedings Society of Antiquaries of Scotland* 142, 9-25.

Van de Noort, R. & Ellis, S. 1995. *Wetland heritage of Holderness: an archaeological survey*. Hull: Humber Wetlands Project, University of Hull.

Wilson, F., Wilson I., Myers G. & Mackey, R. 2006. Excavations at Chapel Garth, Arram. *Prehistory Research Section Bulletin* 43. Leeds: Yorkshire Archaeological Society, 44-5.

Chapter 6

Settlement and landscape in the Iron Age of eastern Iberia

Ignasi Grau Mira

6.1 The Iberian *oppidum* and the local landscape

Recent research on the Iron Age in the eastern part of the Iberian Peninsula has improved our understanding of landscape organisation and the development of social dynamics during the period between the 6th to 1st centuries BC. A range of regions have been studied from the results of archaeological surveys, and the information offered by settlement patterns with varying spatial characteristics, chronology and morphology has supported reconstruction of the landscape dynamics of the period (Bonet *et al.* 2008; Bonet *et al.* 2015; Moratalla 2005). One of the regions in which the historical and socio-political evolution of settlement has been analysed is the Valley of Alcoi (Grau 2002; 2011), where eleven urban-type settlements have been identified (Figure 1). They are *oppida*, or urban settlements, such as La Covalta (Figure 2, A), El Xarpolar and El Puig d'Alcoi, expressed as fortified hilltop settlements of between 1.5 and 4 ha in area. They have large fortifications and dense well-defined urban layouts. One of them, La Serreta, developed during the 3rd century BC and came to dominate the rest of the *oppida* in the region (for a discussion of these historical processes in the Late Iberian Period see (Grau 2016)). Most of the sites are rural nuclei, settlements consisting of groups of houses with rural installations (Figure 2, B), or simple clusters of a few houses (farmsteads) distributed across the farming areas on the valley floor. The structure and morphology of these rural nuclei in the study area was completely unknown before the recent archaeological studies, and it is these that this paper focuses on.

The *oppida* are situated in prominent places in the landscape, generally on hilltops, from where they exercised a visual control of their respective surroundings. They were usually spaced some 8 to 10 kilometres apart to avoid competition for the control and exploitation of territory, and appear to have made use of valleys or landscape units to define the extents of their respective political spaces. These territories contained subordinate farming settlements, which were smaller and had few strategic or defensive characteristics. The visual connections between the fortified centre and the outlying rural settlements (Figure 1), together with the natural limits of each valley, clearly sketched out the local-scale population networks by means of which the community of each valley was organised.

In this way, the settlement model constituted a grid of small neighbouring territories, in which no particular settlement appears to have had primacy over another, at least until

In D.C. Cowley, M. Fernández-Götz, T. Romankiewicz & H. Wendling (eds). Rural Settlement. Relating buildings, landscape, and people in the European Iron Age (Leiden 2019: Sidestone Press) 69-77.

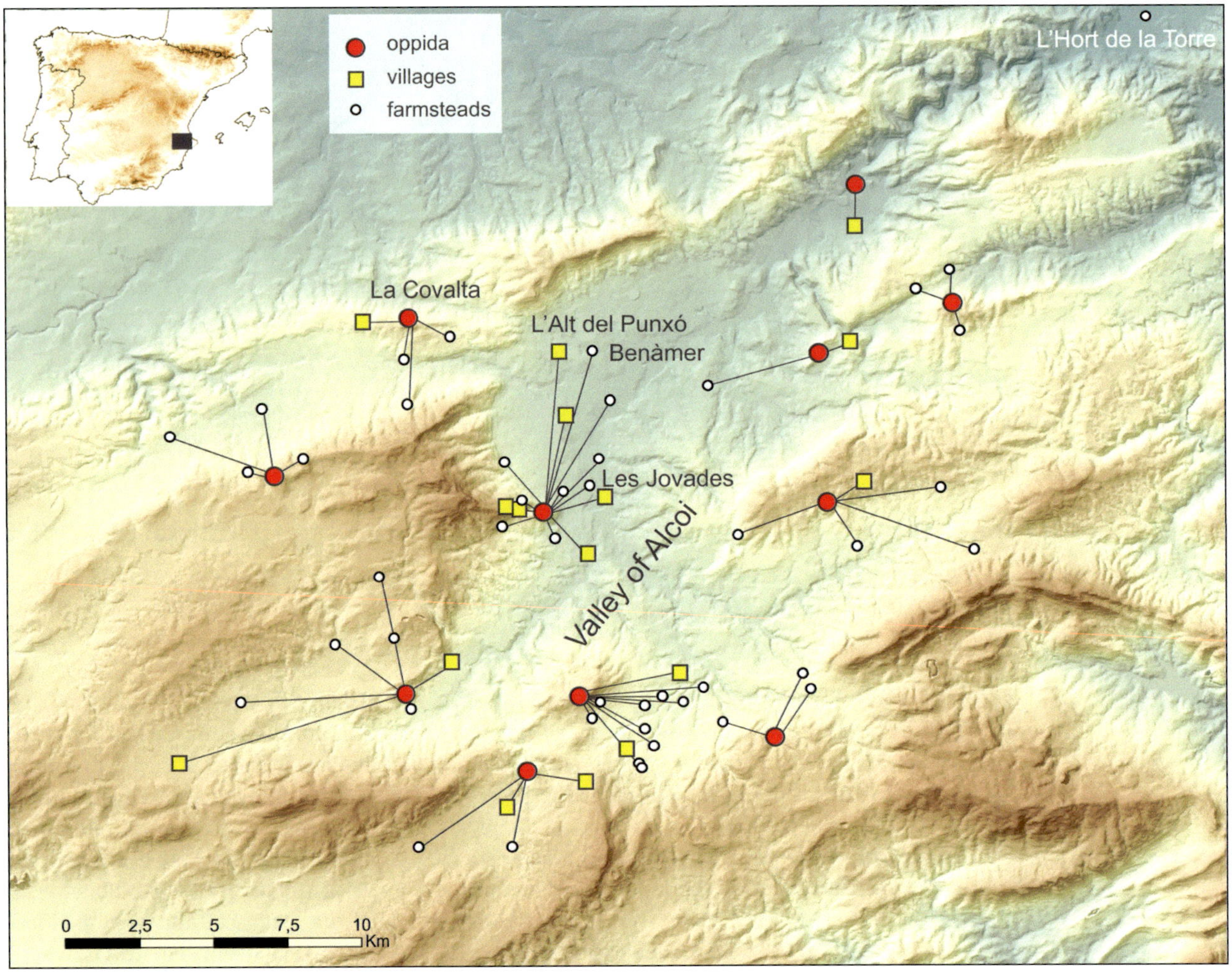

Figure 1: Iberian Iron Age settlement in the Valley of Alcoy with the sites analysed in the text. Lines indicate visual networks (Graphics: I. Grau Mira).

the 3rd century BC when the aforementioned *oppidum* of La Serreta emerged as capital of the territory. Although some differences in economic or territorial control can be seen, their establishment in the landscape suggests a certain equilibrium between the large nuclei of the settlement system.

6.2 Rural settlements: the evidence from archaeological survey

The evidence of Iberian rural occupation in the study area is based on documentation from archaeological surface surveys that has allowed us to identify the nature and distribution of this settlement, which can be characterised into two broad groups of farmsteads and villages.

6.2.1 Dispersed settlements: farmsteads

The term farmstead is used to refer to a series of small settlements of less than 0.5 hectare in area with a flat topography. These are always located near fields and often close to springs and streams. This indicates a clear agricultural vocation that sometimes includes the use of irrigated land near water courses (Grau 2002, 120-1).

There are 45 such known farmsteads, comprising just over 60% of the settlements detected, an indication of the frequency with which they occur. Dating evidence shows that they were common in the Early Iberian Period and then diminished considerably in number during the Middle Iberian Period, especially in the 4th century BC. During the 3rd century their numbers increased once more, reaching a peak in the Late Iberian Period (Grau 2002, 131).

6.2.2 Concentrated settlements: villages

The term village is used to refer to a group of unfortified settlements included among the medium-sized habitats with areas of between 0.5 and one hectare (Figure 2, B). They lie predominately on flat land or middle to low hillsides, with only two cases found on hills. They were agricultural settlements located near the farmlands and

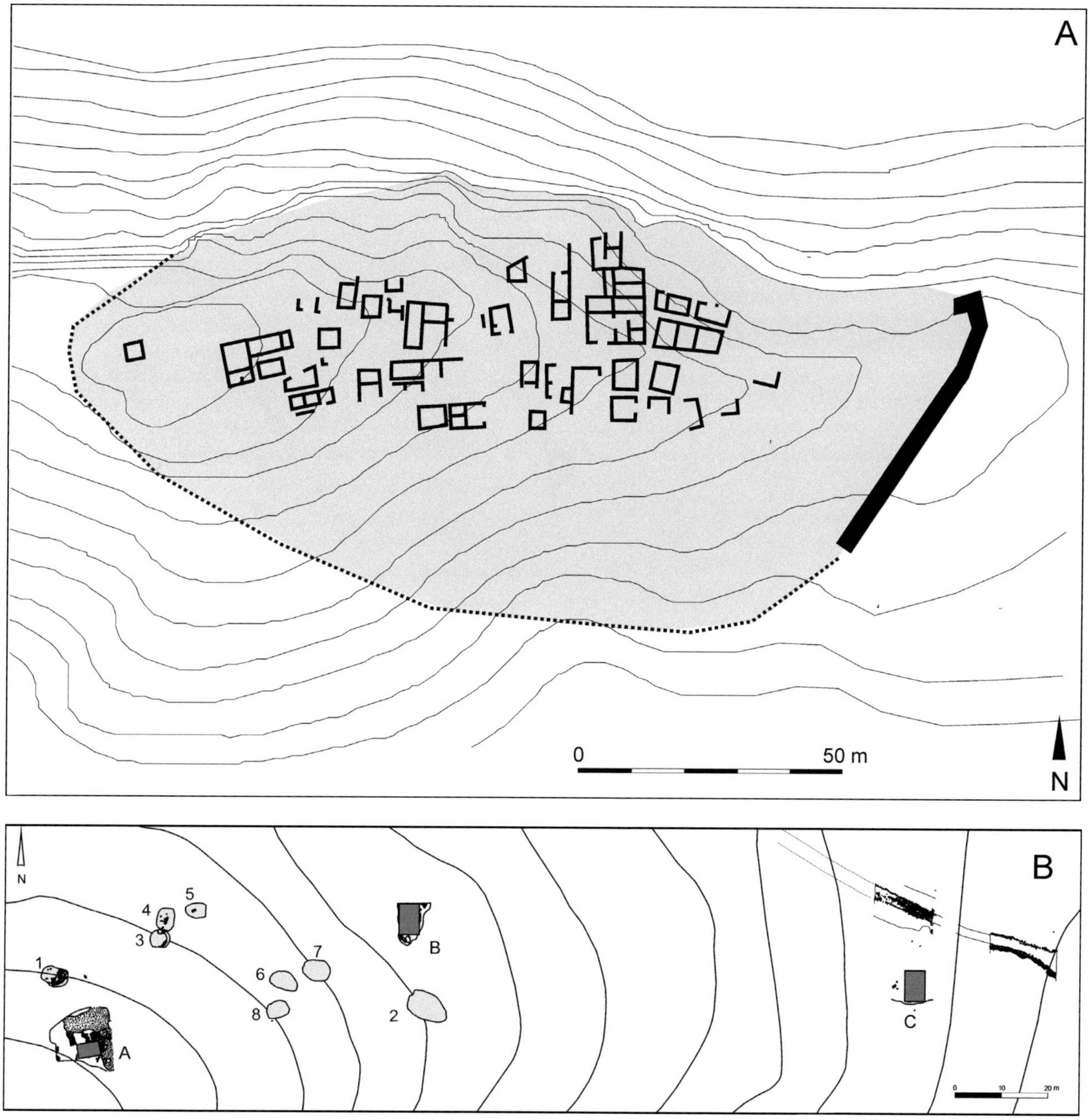

Figure 2: A) Oppidum of La Covalta; B) Village of L'Alt del Punxó (Graphics: I. Grau Mira).

with few defensive characteristics. They were stable settlements, as most were in use for more than two centuries, and their inhabitants possessed a certain social status, as can be seen from the finds of valuable items, such as imported vessels or prestige Iberian pottery. These prestige finds indicate the existence of a prominent social group among their inhabitants, who would have assumed the role of rulers of these enclaves (Grau 2002, 119-20).

The villages are poorly represented in the survey record, comprising only 11 known examples from a total of more than 70 settlements. However, they maintain a constant presence throughout the period under discussion and appear to have gained a certain importance from the Early Iberian period, reaching their peak development in the 4th century BC (Grau 2002, 131).

6.3 Rural settlements: the excavation evidence

Evidence from excavation provides further characterisation of the settlement forms that can be set alongside the survey

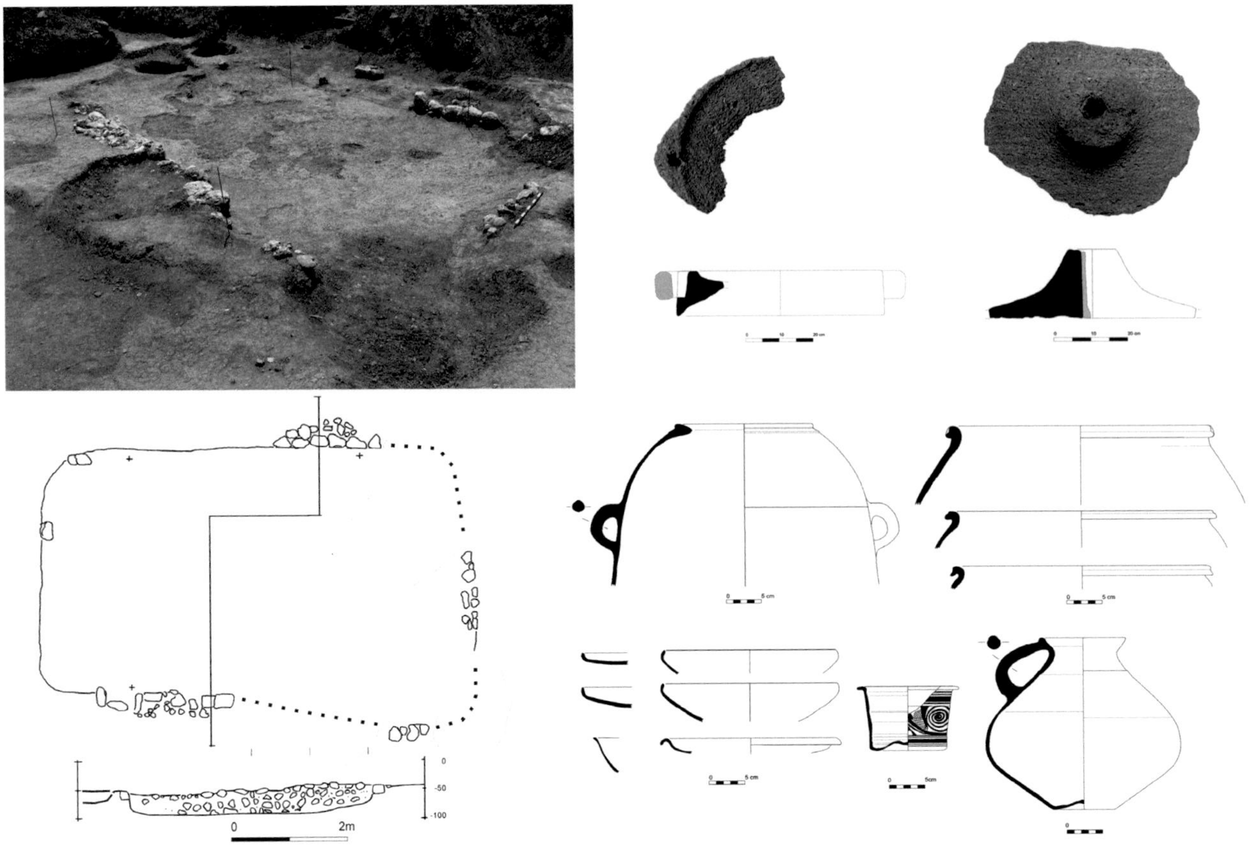

Figure 3: Farmstead at L'Hort de La Torre (Graphics: I. Grau Mira).

evidence, including information on building form, functions and activities that took place there.

6.3.1 *Dispersed settlements: farmsteads*

Recent excavations of farmsteads provide information to better define their morphology. A well-studied example is L'Hort de la Torre, where a rectangular building with rounded corners, measuring approximately 7.5 by 4.5 m and dated to the late 2nd century BC, has been excavated (Figure 3). Wooden posts and other perishable materials were used for the building, whose excavated remains comprised a heavily robbed stone foundation surmounted by mud walls. The domestic repertories consist of sets of fine tableware, cooking pots, food containers, transportation amphorae and some pieces of Iberian prestige pottery, judging by the symbolic-type decoration. Iron farming tools and a large stone mill for grinding the grain were also found (Roselló & Cloquell 2008-2009).

A second similar example close by is El Teular de Molla in Ontinyent (La Vall d'Albaida, Valencia). It is approximately 700 m^2 in area and the excavations revealed only the postholes of huts (Ribera 1990-91, 51-3.) The domestic finds consisted of storage and cooking items and tableware with plates and cups, with some noteworthy Iberian prestige vessels. Among the imported finds are Campanian A and Calena cups, as well as Italic wine amphorae. The pottery finds were accompanied by some iron objects, among which of particular note are farming implements, and the fragmentary remains of a domestic-type rotary mill (Ribera 1990-91, 51).

This evidence demonstrates that small rural settlements of huts carried out a range of activities that might be expected of a small, stable domestic group, possibly a nuclear family. Particularly interesting are the finds of Iberian prestige pottery and imported fine tableware, which tell us that they were families with a certain status and not servile groups, as might be assumed if comparing their flimsy constructions with the solid stone houses of the *oppida*.

6.3.2 *Concentrated settlements: villages*

Excavations in one of the villages in the study area, known as L'Alt del Punxó, has provided new clues for understanding this type of settlement (Figure 2, B; Espí *et al.* 2009), in particular indicating that they were heterogeneous settlement units composed of different

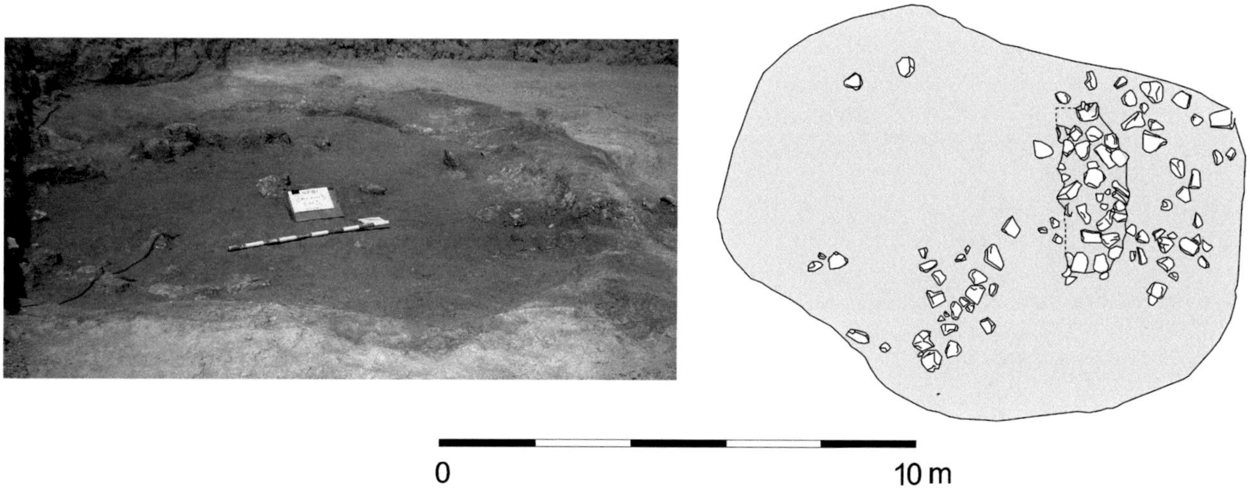

Figure 4: Hut at L'Alt del Punxó (Graphics: I. Grau Mira).

types of domestic units or households – at least partially expressed through both flimsy huts and stone built houses. The variability in composition is related to the different social groupings, which will be discussed below.

6.3.2.1 Huts

Eight huts have been excavated, although there must have been many more at the site. They constitute a very homogeneous group, despite the fact that their characteristics are obscured by the various post-depositional alterations to the structures. All the huts clearly preserve the cut made for them in the soil, which is always oval or circular and approximately 5 m diameter (Figure 4). Within the interior there are some building remains, including mud and stones that covered deposits of discarded domestic items. In some huts there is evidence of the remains of the walls, which were constructed of wattle and daub, and are preserved in cases where the structures must have burnt down. In some cases, the bases of some of the walls were founded on an irregular line of stones set around the edge of the hut. The existence of stones within the centre of the interior suggests that they were bases for setting load-bearing posts in place.

No hardened floors have been documented in the interiors of the huts, nor clear evidence of hearths, although there are abundant ash bearing strata that could be evidence of combustion areas. The domestic repertories are dominated by amphorae and large storage jars, found with domestic vessels, tableware, cooking pots and items associated with weaving. There is also evidence of long-distance Mediterranean trade, such as imported Phoenician-Punic amphorae and fine Attic tableware. These would have been very valuable items that were probably used for consumption in festive contexts at times of social aggregation.

In summary, this domestic equipment, including valuable items such as imported tableware from Mediterranean trade, make it difficult to interpret these flimsy hut structures as the residences of servile groups. Rather, they appear to have been lived in by domestic groups made up of nuclear families, judging by the size of the huts, who occupied them for more or less prolonged periods. A final noteworthy aspect of these huts is their chronology, which extends in total over the period between the 6th and the 4th centuries BC, but at the level of individual buildings has habitations of approximately one generation. It appears that in that span the huts came to the end of their cycle of occupation and were abandoned and destroyed, to be replaced by others. Some of these huts appear to have come to an abrupt end, destroyed by fire.

6.3.2.2 Stone houses

The huts of L'Alt del Punxó were accompanied by type of structure with a completely different form of construction, morphology, equipment and function to the huts described above. These were durable houses with masonry walls built of irregular, medium-sized stones laid in rows and bound together with soil. Although they are poorly preserved, these vestiges show us how the space was organised (Figure 5). The walls enclose rectangular areas approximately 5 m long and 2.5 m across, within which built structures include a circular setting of irregular stones 80 cm in diameter. This was probably a plinth to support a large sandstone rotary mill, the fragmented remains of which were found in the collapse level that sealed the interior. Plinths of this type are documented at other Iberian settlements, confirming their use to support large rotary mills (Bonet 1995, 359; Abad *et al.* 2001, 126-7).

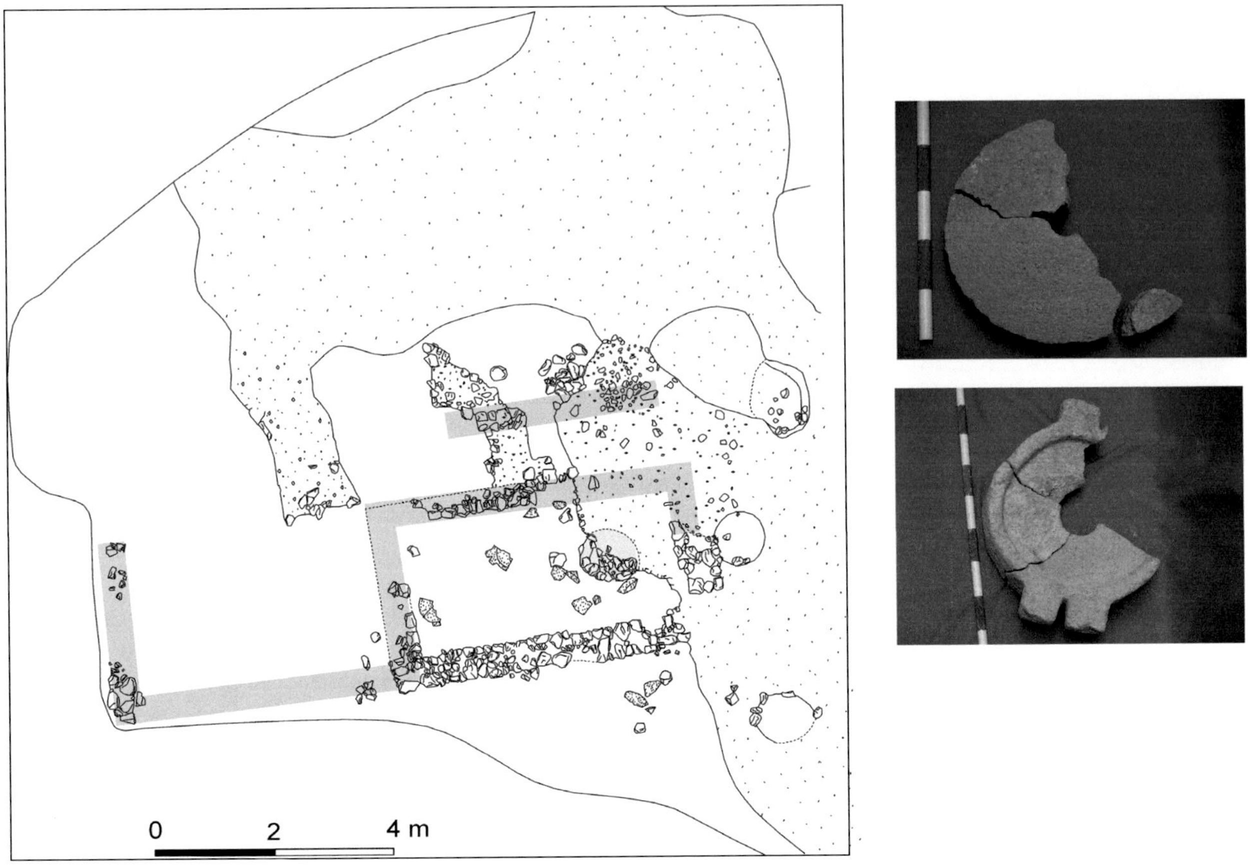

Figure 5: Stone house at L'Alt del Punxó (Graphics: I. Grau Mira).

Around this room and milling area there is a large area of a thick compacted earth floor at the natural soil level that covers both the interior of the building and the space around it. It extends up to 5 m to the north and 2 m to the east and west, where there are the remains of walls that may have formed part of other rooms organised around a courtyard. Areas of activity related to agricultural tasks are documented in this open area and there are abundant remains of ash and charcoal.

The material repertories consist of Iberian vessels, amphorae and imported fine tableware. There is an abundance of Iberian amphorae and large containers, with plates and cups from tableware sets and cooking pots in smaller proportions. Imported pottery is represented by Attic cups and amphorae from the Punic area of the Straits of Gibraltar and Ibiza.

We can conclude that this was a building consisting of quadrangular rooms organised around a courtyard and built with irregular stone masonry. The pottery repertories suggest a varied domestic functionality that is very similar to that of the huts. They have facilities for milling grain and the large courtyard, which was open or partially covered by a porch, would have provided space for processing grain and undertaking other farming activities. These same construction features and the grain processing facilities can be seen, at least in their main elements, in two more buildings in this village. In common with the building described above, there are large rotatory mills on circular platforms within quadrangular rooms. This milling space was located near open spaces in which a large hearth was found that may have been used to roast the grain. These rooms were built in the 4th century BC.

6.3.2.3 The cobbled road

The enduring buildings with mills and the simpler flimsier huts are accompanied by the remains of a cobbled road that was built and used at the same time as the Iberian village (Figure 2, B). This road follows a slightly ascending route approximately from east to west, with a southeast-northwest orientation, that would have crossed perpendicularly the top of the rise where the village was situated.

The road is constructed in a shallow U-shaped trench cut into the natural soil to a maximum width of 5 m within the two excavated sectors of approximately 15 m each. The base of the trench was filled with a levelling layer on which an edging of irregular stones was placed – designed to retain the slope next to the road. Between the edging walls there is a layer of pebbles and gravel that made up the rustic paving of the road, and while this was heavily disturbed very worn ruts of cart wheels can still be made out on it. In a later refurbishment, the original surface was covered with a fill of soil with pebbles and large quantities of ash and charcoal. The edging walls were also rebuilt and this surface is dated to the Middle Iberian Period, somewhere between the 5th and the 3rd centuries BC, coinciding with the dating of the village.

6.3.2.4 Other excavated examples

At present we do not know whether L'Alt del Punxó can be used as a model for the rural occupation of the area or whether there were other forms of sites. In principle, we believe that there was a wide variety of rural settlements, as has been borne out by diverse studies of the protohistoric rural world (Martín & Plana 2000; Rodríguez & Pavón 2007). Indeed, as we will see, the type of habitat analysed here is not unique and other excavated remains suggest similar forms of rural habitat, among which we can clearly differentiate the flimsy huts from the more solid constructions – an important point of commonality.

Some five kilometres south of L'Alt del Punxó is the rural settlement of Les Jovades, located in an area of fluvial terraces that are currently cultivated. Rescue excavations have revealed a village composed of huts dug into the geological substratum and the remains of walls and structures built with insubstantial materials that repeat the form identified at L'Alt del Punxó, although perhaps on a slightly larger scale. The chronology of these remains is centred on the Middle Iberian Period and possibly continuing into the Late Period, between the 3rd and the 1st centuries BC (Grau 2002, 285).

In other cases, the building remains consist of masonry walls and solid constructions that are similar to the stone house at L'Alt del Punxó. In the settlement of Benàmer, very close to L'Alt del Punxó, a series of very eroded building structures from the Middle Iberian Period has been documented. These consist of parallel transversal masonry walls bound by mud. The excavated length of 2.5 m is probably the remains of a rectangular building similar to those of the Punxó farmsteads. A similar range of remains of other buildings and work spaces, albeit very poorly preserved, has been documented in another sector of this same settlement. These are linked to various pits, which tend to be rectangular, and possible floors of flattened earth with the remains of lime (Torregrosa *et al.* 2011, 93-4).

In summary, the data from recent excavations have shown us how the morphology of the settlements is repeated in the association of insubstantial circular huts and more solid quadrangular houses that appear to be integrated in village units.

6.4 Discussion

The available data allow us to identify the variety of rural settlement forms that can be recognised beyond the confines of the fortified *oppida* that presided over the territories, and on which research has been concentrated until now. Based on the patterns described, we can make a series of observations about how the population and exploitation of the countryside was organised.

6.4.1 Integrated units

The first observation is the considerable difference between the forms of construction in the *oppida* and the rural nuclei. The dense construction of stone houses crammed together and organised around straight streets in the *oppida* contrasts with the rural occupations and their less regular groups of dispersed houses. Moreover, the types of house are very different, especially the compact, quadrangular houses of the urban nuclei and the oval huts of the countryside. However, in addition to these formal differences, we would like to look more deeply into the socioeconomic meanings revealed by these forms of occupation and organization of the countryside.

The rural settlements described above cannot be seen as independent units. Rather, they were components of complex settlement systems that integrated the community living in the same valley, a set of relationships that are indicated by the disposition of settlements within visual networks, as alluded to above. Those connections can be understood as a means of establishing contact with the fortified hilltop town that offered refuge to the dispersed communities, as well as the way in which the dominant groups established in the *oppidum* exercised control over the peasants in the countryside. Or, most likely, a combination of both factors.

The reading of the complex of concentrated rural settlements as a whole also allows us to deduce how the different households were integrated. There would have been dependency links between the stone houses, with a more solid construction and a series of facilities devoted to milling grain on a supra-domestic level, and the huts, which lacked these milling facilities and instruments. In other words, a large-scale agricultural processing appears to support the existence of means for organizing the production of surpluses on a scale beyond that of the basic household. This production model can be linked to the economic bases of increasing social complexity.

A second element that also supports this interpretation of an integrated system is the existence of the well-built paved track. Although only 30 m have been excavated and somewhat more than 150 m identified, this road implies connections beyond the local scale. The construction and maintenance of such infrastructure is a materialisation of an organised cooperative effort for the good of the community. Such a landscape constructed with major infrastructure and agricultural facilities "defines corporate hierarchies with overlapping relationships of people to resources" (Earle 2000, 46).

6.4.2 Different groups in the landscape

The existence of aggregated and dispersed rural population units indicates the different composition of the social units in each territory. They range from basic households to small corporative groups made up of a few families living together in villages. In the latter, we find groups of buildings belonging to nuclear family units, although they are very diverse in their forms. For example, the houses built with stone foundations and quadrangular rooms grouped around a courtyard are completely different to the oval huts built of wood and mud. The differences between the units open up certain interpretational possibilities for settlement frameworks, while allowing others to be ruled out.

Firstly, there may be differences between permanent and semi-permanent settlements, with permanent inhabitations of stone houses and less permanent settlements of huts normally belonging to households that had other residences, perhaps in the *oppidum*. This possibility must remain open, given the difficulty of confirming the temporality of the occupation with our current knowledge. However, some of the huts identified contain identical domestic equipment to the dwellings in the permanent settlements, which leads us to attribute the same temporality to both habitats.

A second consideration is that variation in wealth does not appear to relate directly to one type of dwelling or another. The structurally humble huts contain prestige elements, such as imported tableware and processed foodstuffs, that cannot be attributed to servile groups or persons excluded from conspicuous consumption. In contrast to what might be expected, their inhabitants had access to prestige goods in both types of settlement, which obliges us to reject a differentiation based on wealth.

A third factor to consider is control over the means of production, as one of the most important differences between the settlements analysed is the appropriation of the means of agricultural transformation. Most of the huts contain domestic equipment that makes them self-sufficient for daily subsistence, although they are dependent on other larger units for processing their agricultural production, as exemplified by the case of the mills, which are only found in the stone houses. The mills detected are larger than those of the basic domestic unit and would have been used for large-scale processing of harvested grain. This was mainly barley and wheat, judging by the local and regional archaeological records (Perez *et al.* 2013). This distinction between two forms of access to certain means of production, such as the grain processing facilities that were concentrated in them, suggests a dependency in the management of agricultural resources whereby some groups appropriated and retained the means to process cereal.

That same argument concerning the means of controlling production could be applied to access to property and use of the land. According to the forms of construction, there was a clear dichotomy between houses built to last on the land, with stone foundations and complex quadrangular forms, and the ephemeral huts built with perishable materials. To this can be added the clear differences in the duration of the periods the houses were occupied, as the stone house were built to last for many generational cycles that can be related to a differentiated access to the land. Those groups which had an assured ownership and/or use of the farmland were able to build stable, long-lasting dwellings. On the other hand, the huts made with flimsy materials, basically mud and plant matter, would have had to have been rebuilt regularly and were not designed to be long-lasting. This contrast tells us that there were groups that were not assured possession or use of agricultural land, although they had a degree of wealth similar to that of those who lived in the stone dwellings.

6.5 Concluding remarks

The social dynamics of the Iberian groups in the study area have traditionally been defined by the increase in social complexity and the formalisation of corporative groups or lineages controlled by families and leaders who monopolised power at the heart of the society (Grau 2011; Bonet *et al.* 2015). In the framework of this development of inequality, the appropriation of the means of production, especially the land, is a method of retaining power and controlling society for certain groups and families. The communities land was used by individual families, but the plots were controlled by the leaders. In other words, institutionally the land remained in the community, but its use was assigned to individuals (Ruiz 2008).

Our analyses of the rural settlement forms, in particular the village of L'Alt del Punxó, fits in well with this model of social organisation, in that it involved corporative groups with unequal forms of access to the land, which led to the formalisation of inequality. On the one hand, we have collective initiatives manifested in the construction, use and maintenance of agricultural plots and landscape infrastructure, such as the cobbled road or the collective use of grain mills. In other words, they demonstrate the formalisation of corporative groups or the union of households to jointly manage their basic economic activities, that is to say that they were "groups that functioned as individuals in relation to property" (Hayden & Cannon 1982, 134).

In summary, while the knowledge we have of the rural settlements of the Iberian groups in the study area is sparse, it supports a limited basic understanding of the economic and social foundations of these fundamentally agrarian communities. This paper has been able to outline hypotheses that certainly require study in greater depth, but even so, the analysis presented here does allow us to see into the fundamental operation of the societies represented by the archaeological remains. At the heart of these groups, we perceive the inherent inequality of these forms of organisation, in which certain families retained control of the land and other resources essential for the functioning of the group. They based their power on this differential access to the basic resources of the rural economy.

6.6 Bibliography

Abad, L., Sala, F., Grau, I., Moratalla, J., Pastor, A. & Tendero, M. (eds) 2001. Poblamiento ibérico en el Bajo Segura: El Oral (II) y La Escuera, Madrid: Real Academia de la Historia.

Bonet, H. 1995. *El Tossal de Sant Miquel de Llíria. La antigua Edeta y su territorio*. Valencia: Diputación de Valencia.

Bonet, H., Grau, I. & Vives-Ferrándiz, J. 2015. Estructura social y poder en las comunidades ibéricas de la franja central mediterránea. In M. C. Belarte, D. Garcia & J. Sanmartí (eds). *Les estructures socials protohistòriques a la Gàl·lia i a Ibèria*. 251-72. Barcelona/Tarragona: Universitat de Barcelona/Institut Català d'Arqueologia Clàssica.

Bonet, H., Mata, C. & Moreno, A. 2008. Iron Age Landscape and Rural Habitat in the Edetan Territory, Iberia (4th-3rd centuries BC). *Journal of Mediterranean Archaeology* 21.2, 165-89

Earle, T. 1997. *How chiefs come to power. The political economy in Prehistory*. Stanford: Stanford University Press.

Earle, T. 2000. Archaeology, Property and Prehistory. *Annual Reviews of Anthropology* 29, 39-60.

Espí, I., Grau, I., López, E., & Torregrosa, P. 2009. La aldea ibérica de L'Alt del Punxó: producción agrícola y asentamiento campesino en el área central de la Contestania. *Lucentum* XXVIII, 23-49.

Grau, I. 2002. *La organización del territorio en el área central de la Contestania Ibérica*. Alicante: University of Alicante.

Grau, I. 2007. Dinámica social, paisaje y teoría de la práctica. Propuestas sobre la evolución de la sociedad ibérica en el área central del oriente peninsular. *Trabajos de Prehistoria* 64.2, 119-42.

Grau, I. 2011. Landscape dynamics, political processes and social strategies in the Eastern Iberian Iron Age. In T. Moore & X-L. Armada (eds). *Atlantic Europe in the First Millenium: Crossing the divide*, 153-70. Oxford: Oxford University Press.

Grau, I. 2016. Forging communities: coalitions, identity symbols and ritual practices in Eastern Iberia Iron Age. *World Archaeology* 48.1, 110-24.

Hayden, B. & Cannon, A. 1982. The corporate group as an archaeological unit. *Journal of Anthropological Archaeology* 1.2, 132-58.

Martín, M. A. & Plana, R. (dirs.) 2001. *Territori polític i territori rural durant l'edat del Ferro a la Mediterrània Occidental*. Monografies d'Ullastret, 2. Girona: MAC-Ullastret.

Moratalla, J. 2005. El territorio meridional de la Contestania. In L. Abad, F. Sala & I. Grau (eds). *La Contestania Iberica, treinta años después*, 91-117. Alicante: University of Alicante.

Pérez, G., Carrión, Y. & Iborra, P. 2013. El registro paleoeconómico y la gestión de los recursos agrarios. In I. Grau & J. M. Segura. *El oppidum ibérico de El Puig d'Alcoi. Asentamiento y paisaje en las montañas de la Contestania*, 195-220. Alcoi: Museu d'Alcoi.

Ribera, A. 1990-91: El jaciment ibéric del Teular de Mollà (Ontinyent). L'excavació arqueològica de salvament de 1989. *Alba* 5-6, 29-54.

Rodríguez, A. & Pavón, I. (Coord.) 2007. *Arqueología de la tierra. Paisajes rurales de la protohistoria peninsular*. Cáceres: Universidad de Extremadura.

Roselló, P. & Cloquell, S. 2008-09. El jaciment ibèric de l'Hort de la Torre (Vilallonga, València). *Recerques* 17-18, 173-82.

Ruiz, A. 2008. Iberos, In F. Gracia (coord.), *De Iberia a Hispania*, 733-844. Madrid: Ed. Ariel.

Sanmartí, J. 2009. From the archaic states to romanization: a historical and evolutionary perspective on the Iberians. *Catalan Historical Review* 2, 9-32.

Torregrosa, P., Jover, J. & López, E. 2011. *Benàmer (Muro d'Alcoi, Alicante). Mesolíticos y neolíticos en las tierras meridionales valencianas*. Valencia: Diputación de Valencia.

Chapter 7

Approaching Late Iron Age rural landscapes

New ways of looking at the archaeological record in the southeast Iberian Peninsula

Leticia López-Mondéjar

7.1 Introduction

This paper discusses Late Iron Age settlements in the period between the 5th and the 3rd centuries BC (the so-called Iberian Period), in the present-day Region of Murcia, on Spain's Mediterranean coast (Figure 1). Beginning at the end of the 5th century and during the 4th century BC, local communities underwent a process of transformations that led to a new social framework defined by the displacement of earlier social relationships and the progressive development of client networks (Ruiz-Rodríguez & Molinos-Molinos 2007, 188-90). Moreover, this period was also characterised by geopolitical consolidation of the local elites, a process that was expressed through the landscape. As a result of this socio-political framework, the area is defined by a hierarchically organised landscape where fortified sites (known as *oppida*) emerge as key sites from the end of the 5th century. The *oppida* are located in strategic points of the landscape along the main valleys and, as dominant centres and the residences of social elites, would have controlled the territory. For example, the Segura River, the main watercourse in this region, was controlled by key sites such as Bolvax, Cabezo del Tío Pío, and the archaeological complex at Santa Catalina del Monte.

Taking this situation into account, it is easy to understand why these main centres, together with their cemeteries and sanctuaries, have attracted the majority of the attention of Iron Age research in the area. Studies of funerary areas and cult places associated with the *oppida* have revealed their richness and exceptional character, situating some of them amongst the most remarkable Iron Age sites in the Iberian Peninsula. However, the aim of this paper is to move beyond these centres, and to analyse the wider landscape, considering the little-known secondary rural centres. These are generally viewed as mainly agrarian and farming sites, occupied by families and small communities dedicated to growing crops and raising livestock. From this perspective, the rural world appears somewhat separate from the socio-political processes taking place in the *oppida*.

Fortunately, the archaeological richness of the region, the review of old data, and new finds are all helping to change this picture. A number of heterogeneous rural centres have been documented, producing remarkable finds which highlight the need to put these rural sites into a wider context, recognising that the landscape organisation and

In D.C. Cowley, M. Fernández-Götz, T. Romankiewicz & H. Wendling (eds). Rural Settlement. Relating buildings, landscape, and people in the European Iron Age (Leiden 2019: Sidestone Press) 79-88.

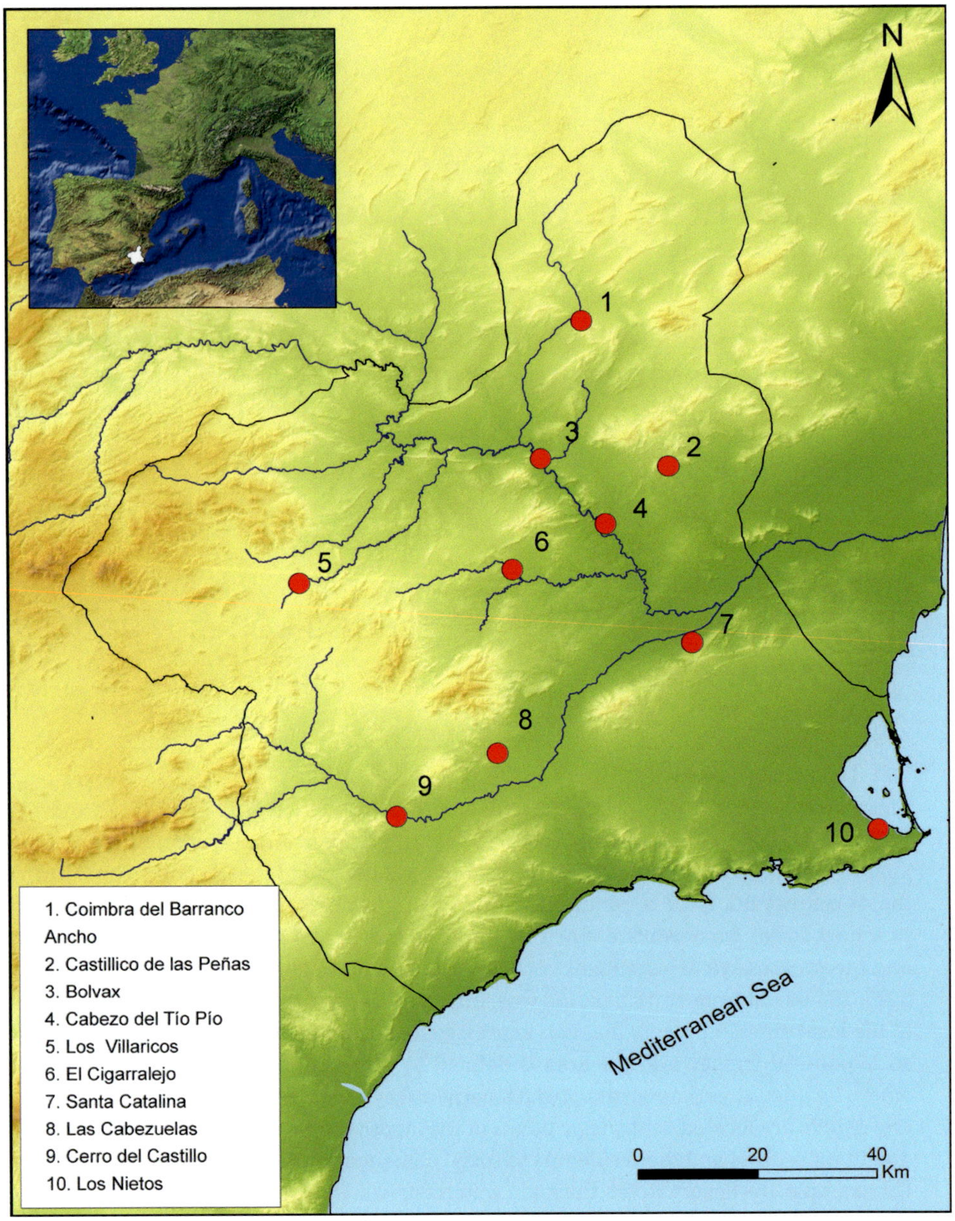

Figure 1: Study area and main fortified sites (Graphic: López-Mondéjar).

socio-political and economic context was more complex than was traditionally thought. The examination of the archaeological record for cemeteries, settlements, and sacred spaces (Figure 2) provides a different way of looking at these rural areas.

7.2 Rethinking data from rural cemeteries

The Late Iron Age funerary record probably provides the most direct insights as the arena where socio-political differences and relationships were expressed. The site of El Prado, in the north of Murcia, is a good example to start with. Here, a block of limestone with high relief human figures some 85-90 cm tall was discovered, with the remains of a stone pillar more than 2 m in height, both forming part of the same monument dating to the late 5th century BC. The pillar was reused in the 3rd century BC, by which time it had already lost its original funerary significance (Chapa-Brunet 1993, 189; Izquierdo-Peraile 2000, 69). There are a range of views about how to reconstruct the original funerary monument, but it seems likely that the sculpted figures were set at the top, based on analogy with similar examples (Izquierdo-Peraile 2000, 69; Lillo-Carpio 1990, 141-3). In any event, these remains suggest the presence in El Prado of a specific type of funerary monument, a pillar-stele type burial, that is characteristic of the Late Iron Age in the southeast Iberian Peninsula. These

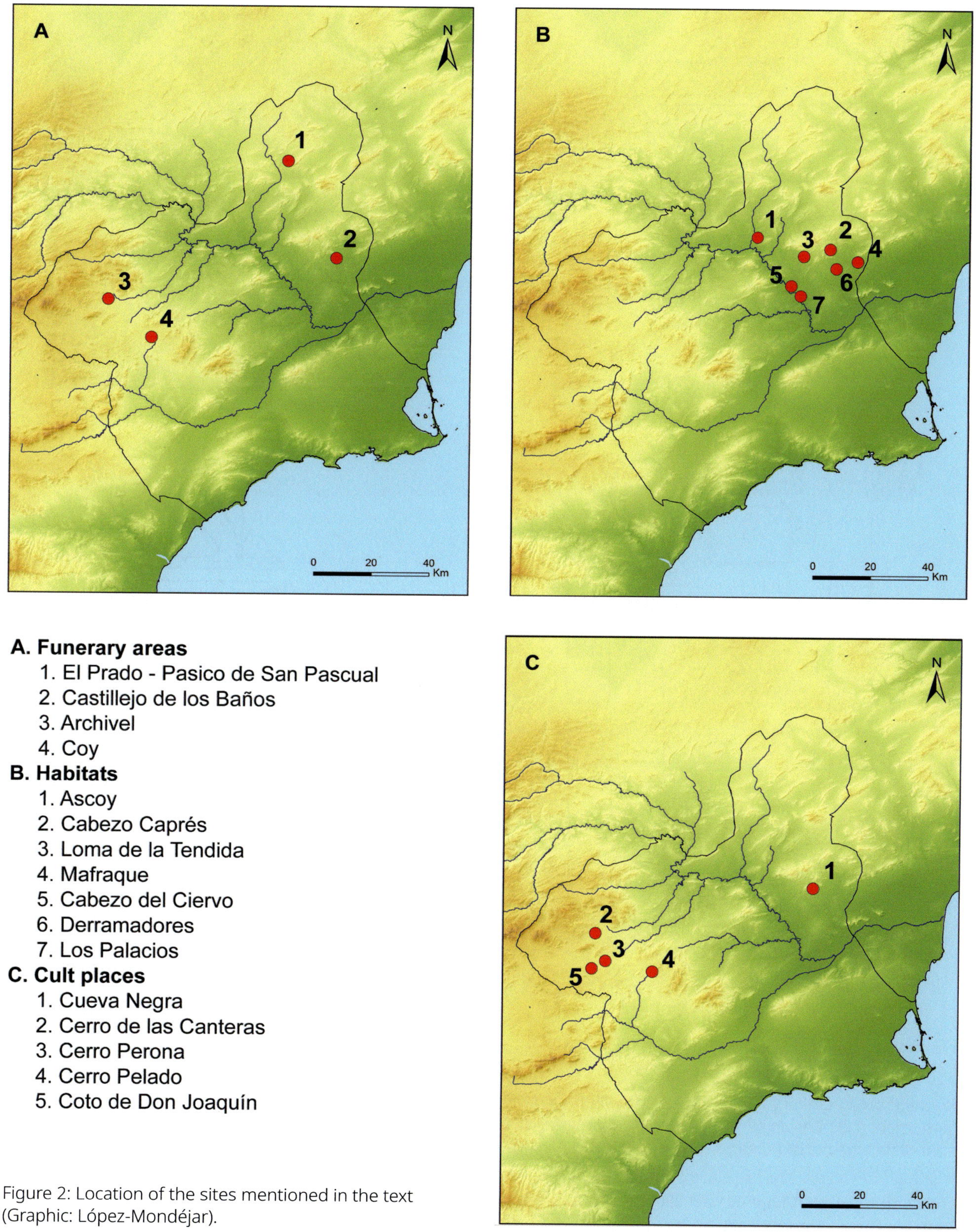

Figure 2: Location of the sites mentioned in the text (Graphic: López-Mondéjar).

monuments are usually associated with tombs of socially significant individuals. In fact, some of the stone figures on the top of these pillars seem to have had a symbolic and particular meaning within the Iberian communities of this period. In this sense, for example, the presence of certain animals such as lions or bulls has been related to

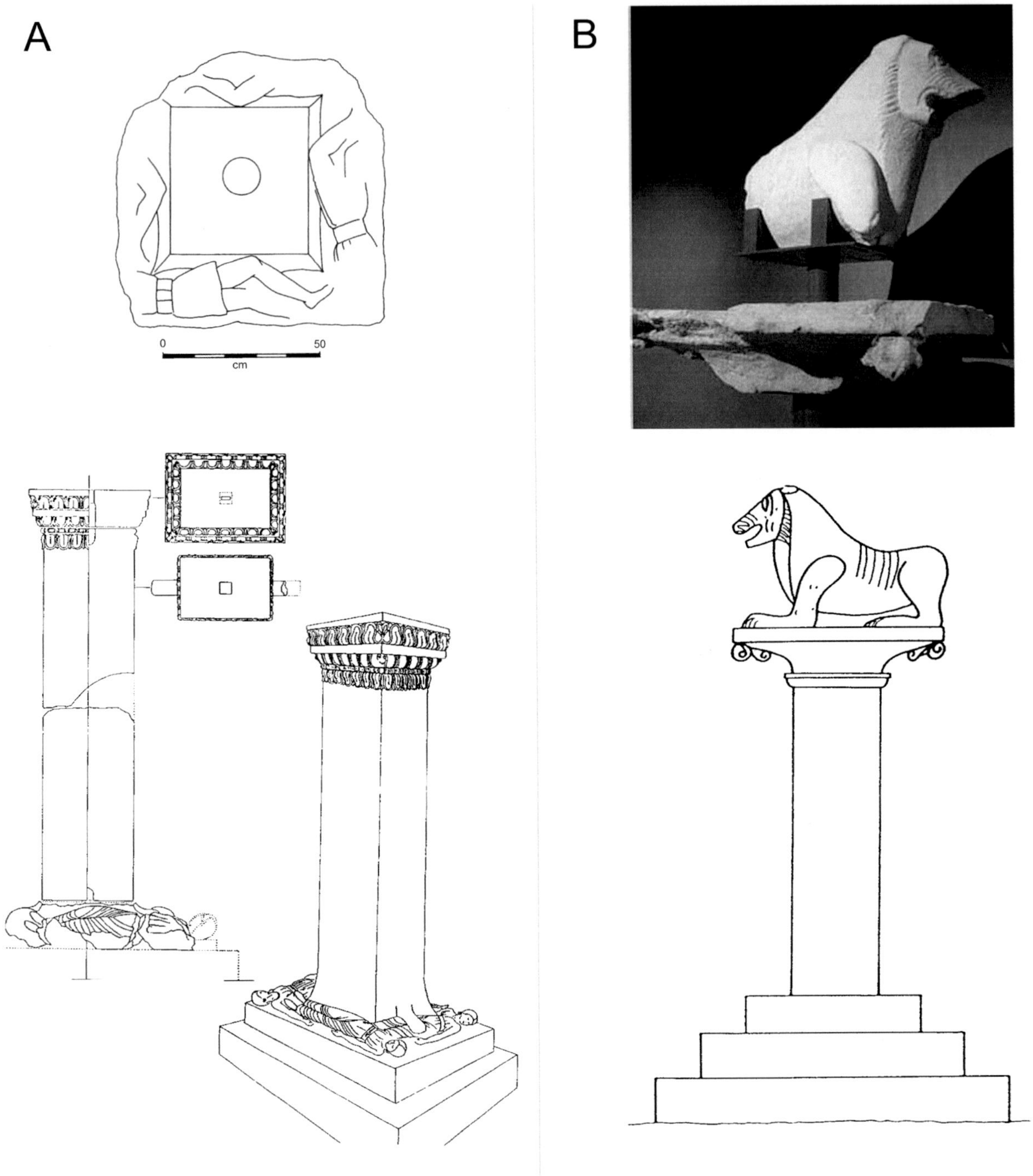

Figure 3: a) High relief carvings at El Prado (Muñoz-Amilibia 1987, fig. 4) and a hypothetical reconstruction of the monument (Lillo-Carpio 1990, figs 3-4); b) Monument at Coy (Prados-Martínez 2011, 196) and a reconstruction of the pillar-stele type burial (Almagro-Gorbea 1988, fig. 1).

aristocratic groups (Chapa-Brunet 2000, 202-3; Sala-Sellés 2007, 59; Olmos-Romera 2003, 27-30).

The four carved recumbent figures at El Prado are distributed around the base of a stone block (Figure 3a). While only two are well preserved, the figures wear short pleated tunics, which are belted at the waist (Muñoz-Amilibia 1987, 246), and find a few parallels in similar finds in Coimbra del Barranco Ancho, not far from El Prado, and Corral de Saus (Valencia) (Izquierdo-Peraile 2000, 75). The interest of all these reliefs lies in the way the figures are represented. Elements such as the belts and the tunics worn by these figures are reminiscent of the iconographic attributes of the Iberian elites, seen in other images, such as the sculptures from Cerrillo Blanco in Andalusia and a number of bronze votive offerings found in this area (Izquierdo-Peraile 2000, 255).

Both the iconography of the figures and the funerary monuments which they adorned, suggest they belong with the burial of an individual of a certain status. However, unlike other similar monuments documented in the cemeteries of the *oppida*, here there is no fortified centre connected with these finds. Only the nearby cemetery of Pasico de San Pascual may be associated with El Prado. Pasico de San Pascual dates to the 5th and 4th centuries BC, and has been associated with a secondary rural settlement located somewhere nearby. Despite the fact that the site has been largely destroyed, 23 tombs have been excavated containing locally produced artefacts and imported Greek pottery (Ramos-Martínez 2007), though no weapons or warrior grave goods were found.

The 5th century BC funerary monument at Coy, in southern Murcia, is a similar pillar-stele style burial monument, possibly linked with the necropolis of La Fuentecica del Tío Carrulo (Almagro-Gorbea 1988). In this case it was crowned by the figure of a lion (Figure 3b), and while again no *oppida* or main settlements have been identified in this area, the tomb could be related to the nearby rural site of Los Cantos. This is a large undefended site located on flat terrain characterised by arable lands, with a chronology extending from the Late Iron Age to the Roman period.

At both El Prado and Coy the presence of those monuments reveals the existence in these rural areas of elements that are traditionally associated with high social status individuals, and consequently with the principal sites of the territory. As these types of monuments clearly had a symbolic function in Late Iron Age Iberian society (Izquierdo-Peraile 2000), their appearance in rural necropolises allows us to extend the presence of these prestige elements of society to the regional rural areas.

Keeping these sites in mind, the village of Castillejo de los Baños also offers some interesting data. It lies on a small round hill close to the present-day city of Fortuna, not far from the Baño Mountains. It is not fortified, and with only stone walled houses visible on the surface it may be defined as a small village covering less than half a hectare, contrasting as it does with the seven hectares of some of the region's *oppida*. Works in its necropolis suggest that the settlement dates to the 5th and 4th centuries BC. Based on its size and location, this village cannot be properly included among the main *oppida* in the region, although the archaeological record from its necropolis compares with those at *oppida*. Even though no funerary monuments have been documented, it is remarkable for the large numbers of tombs with Greek pottery (almost 50% of tombs), weapons, and items such as a chariot wheel and bronze vessels that are usually associated with Iberian elites (Figure 4a; García-Cano & Page-del-Pozo 2001).

Somewhat later in date is the example of the necropolis at El Villar de Archivel. It is located on a plain, and has a broad chronology from the Iron Age to the Roman period, and illustrates the changes that took place following the arrival of the Romans. Although no settlement has so far been found in the surrounding area, the presence of a nearby religious site seems to point to the existence of a village in this area, possibly located beneath the current village of Archivel. Fieldwork in the necropolis has revealed the presence of tombs with Greek goods, weapons, and stone burial mounds (Inchaurrandieta-Ramallo 2005), features usually documented in the funerary areas of the region's *oppida* (Figure 4b). However, in Archivel the size of the mounds is significantly smaller than those observed in the necropolis of the fortified sites, ranging from 1.2 to 3.5 m across, in contrast to 7 m at El Cigarralejo. This said, both the richness of the grave goods and the existence of funerary structures demonstrate the importance of Archivel, whose archaeological record is not what would be expected for a rural centre. Consequently, their presence leads us to reconsider the character of this secondary site, once again suggesting that these elements were not exclusive to the regional *oppida* as previously thought.

7.3 The material record from rural settlements

In looking to the settlement record, it is unfortunate that most of them have been destroyed by being located in arable land. This is compounded by a lack of fieldwork, meaning that in many cases it is difficult to evaluate the nature and roles of these sites as few are known.

Bearing these difficulties in mind, a review of the material record from some centres in the central part of the Segura valley provides interesting information to rethink the current picture of these rural sites in Murcia. A number of these sites have been found to contain imported goods, which were of great importance in the Iberian communities of this period. These elements played a crucial socio-political role in the southeast Iberian Peninsula, and their arrival and redistribution seem to have been mainly controlled by local elites, who not only used these goods as symbols of prestige, but also as elements to create and maintain social ties.

One of these sites is that of Ascoy, a small farm occupied from the 5th to the 3^{r}d century BC, located in a completely flat area, close to a seasonal stream, and surrounded by farmland. Although it does not have a remarkable location and lacks defensive structures, the presence of Greek pottery at this site is significant (García-Cano 1982, 53-6). This includes a bell krater dated to the late 5th or early 4th century BC, painted with a female figure with a

Figure 4: a) Pottery from El Castillejo (Images: López-Mondéjar); b) Funerary structures from El Villar de Archivel (Brotóns-Yagüe 2008, fig. 4).

headband and earrings. A lekythos has also been found, decorated with red figures, in this case a lion, and of the same date. In addition, four plates and a bowl dating to the 4th century BC are known.

The site at Loma de la Tendida, located in an isolated, agricultural area, far from the main regional *oppida*, has some similar characteristics. Although not examined in detail, some structures are visible on the surface, and Greek pottery, as well as locally produced materials, is again noteworthy. Here, a kylix with red figures and a plate (Lamboglia 22), both dated to the first half of the 4th century BC, have been found (García-Cano 1982, 239).

Another example at Mafraque has produced two kylikes (42-A Lamboglia) and a kylix-skyphos with red figures, both dating from the early 4th century BC (García-Cano 1982, 240). Again, the site is located on an alluvial plain, and no remains of artificial defences are evident on the surface. Attic pottery dating from the late 5th century and early 4th century BC has also been found in the settlements of Los Palacios, Cabezo del Ciervo and Villareal (García-Cano 1982, 261), where a bell krater with red figures decorated with two young men wearing himatia and a Bacchic scene was found. Despite the lack of excavations, the locations of all these sites and the limited archaeological material on the surface would suggest they are villages or farms dedicated to raising livestock and agrarian activities. However, pottery indicates that these rural communities had access to imported goods from the Mediterranean coast. It is also interesting that some of these Greek vessels, such as certain kinds of cups and kraters, are usually associated with drinking wine and, consequently, with the Iberian elites, making their discovery in these rural areas even more interesting.

Finally, in the area of Fortuna, a recent review of surface finds in other rural settlements has revealed the presence of metal working. Sites at Cabezo Caprés and Derramadores have produced lead slag, alongside cooking ware and storage vessels which otherwise suggest a mainly farming-based economy. The lead working has not been documented at other sites, and this could point to a greater heterogeneity amongst regional rural settlements than previously thought.

In summary, the evidence from settlements shows a widespread occurrence of imported goods that has usually been associated with the presence of elites in *oppida* who controlled the arrival and redistribution of these Greek vessels. Similarly, metallurgy and craft activities are traditionally associated with the main centres, but not with secondary settlements. However, the examples above demonstrate that such characteristics were not exclusive to the *oppida*, suggesting that rural sites were part of exchanges due to their strategic position along communication routes, or that they formed a part in the social networks, which seems more likely. Either way, it is clear that certain individuals living in rural areas had access to these materials. Did they obtain them through their relationship as clients of the elites who controlled the distribution of the imported goods? Were they artisans (sculptors, metalworkers, potters, etc.) working for the aristocratic group? Or, instead, should we see them as members of the elite who lived either temporarily or permanently in rural areas?

In addressing these questions, studies in other Iberian regions close to Murcia provide key information. In the area of Valencia and the territories of the *oppida* at Edeta and Kelin (Mata-Parreño *et al.* 2009) analysis of the settlements shows different models of agrarian exploitation. At Edeta, cultivated fields were controlled by a part of the community with a high status, while at Kelin family groups exploited specialised crops that provided them with a surplus which was redistributed or exchanged, obtaining benefits, power, and status for the group, and consequently generating social inequality (Mata-Parreño *et al.* 2009, 140). In the Alicante area imported goods in some rural sites have been explained as 'social exchanges', ultimately being a reward for the peasants' loyalty given by the local elite (Espí-Pérez *et al.* 2009, 46). These examples demonstrate that social ties and power relationships were not only expressed in the *oppida*, but also in rural landscapes across a broad area. This indicates that such rural sites were integrated in both social and exchange networks, even though questions such as ownership of land and the character of dependence are difficult to characterise in detail (Pérez-Jordà *et al.* 2015, 68). So, while the situation in Murcia is not clear because of the lack of fieldwork on settlements, and the limited evidence from survey, the regional analogies from Valencia and Alicante suggest the development of a more diversified economy than traditionally thought. Evidence of metalwork, as well as imported goods, found in these small settlements point to their integration in economic and social networks within a socio-political landscape not limited to the *oppida* and their inhabitants.

7.4 Rural cult places and sacred spaces

A third source of insight into this period in Murcia is provided by the evidence for sacred spaces. During the Late Iron Age sanctuaries were established next to regional *oppida*. These symbolically defined their territorial domain and provided spaces to enhance the social position and prestige of the local elites. The votive offerings from these sanctuaries reveal an iconography associated with the Iberian elite, such as warriors, horses, and individuals wearing tunics, belts, and jewellery.

Although these main cult places are well-known in the southeast Iberian Peninsula, recent investigation supports the identification of a group of small and secondary sites with a sacred character. These could be related to cult practices based on their similarities with a number of sites located in the Granada (Andalusia) area. They have been well documented in the northwest area of Murcia, and their chronology is mainly focused in the Late Iron Age period, disappearing with the Roman conquest (López-Mondéjar 2010). Examples include Cerro de las Canteras, Coto Don Joaquín, Cerro Perona and Cerro Pelado, all of which lie on small hills close to main communication routes and to rural settlements (excepting Cerro Perona). Although they are not located in strategic positions, their location gave them a certain visual control of the surrounding countryside. They also appear to have a connection to the main cattle routes in this area, where livestock had become one of the main traditional economic activities.

Apart from their location, these cult places have other noticeable differences with those that are known to lie adjacent to the *oppida*. These rural sites have a locally produced homogeneous material record comprising only small bowls and pots (López-Mondéjar 2010), unlike the diverse range of imported goods, gold objects, votive offerings, and terracotta figurines known from the more remarkable sanctuaries close to *oppida*. Exceptionally, in the case of Cerro de las Canteras, a number of votive offerings representing swords in miniature have also been documented. This evidence indicates that the associated

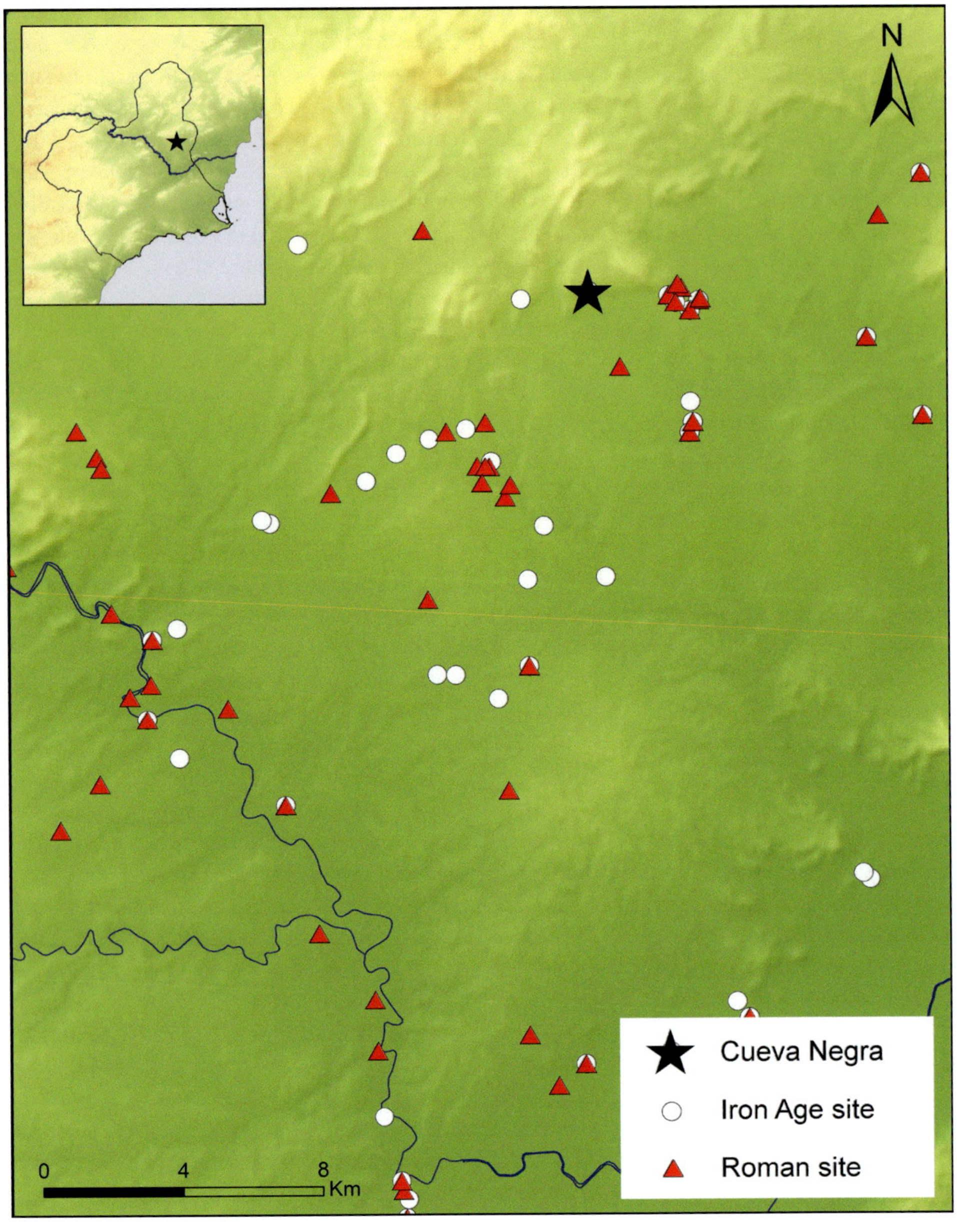

Figure 5: Known Late Iron Age and Roman sites around Cueva Negra (Graphic: López-Mondéjar).

rural settlements were much more dynamic than previously thought, incorporating cult practices that were apparently different to those taking place in the main regional sanctuaries.

Finally, another interesting site is Cueva Negra, a cave well known for the Roman graffiti written on its walls, dating to the second half of the 1st century (Stylow & Mayer 1996). The cave lies at a strategic point in the Baño Mountains, along the main routes through this area and has a natural spring. While studies have always focused on its Roman occupation, a recent review of the archaeological data from the cave has identified Late Iron Age local ware. Moreover, a preliminary review of this material shows parallels with that known from the rural sanctuaries discussed above. No other religious site has been documented in the area that may have been associated with the nearby main *oppida* or with other rural sites, and Cueva Negra may have been the only sacred space in this area at that date. Bearing in mind the importance that cult places had in the landscape of the southeast Iberian Peninsula during the Late Iron Age, it is not difficult to imagine that the cave served as a highly visible point of reference for all of the settlements in this area (Figure 5). Therefore, in the same way that Iberian sanctuaries adjacent to the main *oppida* played an important role as points for territorial integration of surrounding communities (López-Mondéjar 2014), Cueva Negra could have provided a similar function within the rural context.

7.5 Conclusions

The range of evidence articulated above provides new insights on regional settlement patterns, prompting a revision of the traditional archaeological view of these areas, the socio-political structure of the period, and its expression in the landscape in this part of the Iberian Peninsula. Beyond these insights, the evidence highlights five issues that could usefully be addressed by future studies in the region.

Firstly, the known sites point towards a diverse settlement pattern, suggesting a rural context that was much more complex in economic and social terms than has usually been thought. Social complexity is clearly expressed in these rural areas through prestige elements, although this differs in some ways from the ways that was expressed through the *oppida*. Within this framework, it is interesting that there are no remains of elements related to horses, such as harnesses or bits, in the necropolises that were analysed (only one piece has been documented in El Castillejo), but they are documented in the funerary areas of the regional fortified centres. Similarly, the funerary monuments are rarer in the rural necropolises, appearing as isolated examples, such as those of El Prado or Coy, or being smaller in size than those of the *oppida*, as has been indicated for the stone burial mounds of Archivel.

Secondly, these rural areas seem to have had a diversified economy. Alongside agriculture and livestock, metallurgical activities and exchange must have developed to a certain degree at some sites. From this perspective they can be seen as dynamic spaces whose inhabitants took part in other activities beyond those exclusively connected with agriculture and livestock.

Thirdly, these rural communities not only developed their own economic practices, but also their own cult practices. The sites located in the southern part of the region reveal the existence of specific rural sacred spaces, beyond those developed from the *oppida* and controlled by the urban elites.

Fourthly, as can be seen in the middle Segura valley, not only the *oppida* functioned as points of aggregation for these rural settlements. Some sacred sites, such as Cueva Negra, may have played a similar role, providing a focal point for the settlements scattered throughout the area, and bringing together a large and essentially rural territory. From this perspective, it is essential to take these types of sites into account in analysing both the territorial organisation and the ideological integration of rural communities within wider symbolic and socio-political landscapes, especially considering the key role that sacred spaces played during the period.

Finally, these aspects demand a reconsideration of the socio-political context of this area. Issues such as the development of client networks from the end of the 5th century BC, and how the exploitation of these rural territories was organised, are fundamental questions for future research, not only to help understand the main sites, but also the rural landscapes of this area. It is clear that socio-political ties operated beyond the walls of the *oppida*, and that socio-political processes are situated within a wider framework, in which the rural environment was a key factor. Rural settlements and communities appear as important agents in both the development of these processes and their consolidation, a factor that previous studies of the region have often failed to point this out – a weakness given the fact that society in the period was mainly rural.

7.6 Acknowledgments

This project has received funding from the European Union's Horizon 2020 research and innovation programme under the Marie Skłodowska-Curie grant agreement No 654906.

7.7 Bibliography

Almagro-Gorbea, M. 1988. El pilar-estela ibérico de Coy. In *Homenaje a Samuel de los Santos*, 125-9. Albacete: Instituto de estudios albacetenses.

Brotóns-Yagüe, F. 2008. La necrópolis tumular ibérica de El Villar. In *Actas del I Congreso Internacional de Arqueología Ibérica bastetana*, vol. 2, 23-42. Madrid: Universidad Autónoma de Madrid.

Chapa-Brunet, T. 1993. La destrucción de la escultura funeraria ibérica. *Archivo Español de Arqueología* 50, 185-95.

Chapa-Brunet, T. 2000. La utilització del llenguatge grec: homes, déus, monstres. In P. Cabrera-Bonet & C. Sánchez-Fernández (eds). *Els Grecs a Ibèria*, 197-207. Girona: Ministerio de Educación y Cultura.

Espí-Pérez, I., Grau-Mira, I., López--Seguí, E. & Torregrosa-Giménez, P. 2009. La aldea ibérica de L'Alt del Punxó: producción agrícola y asentamiento campesino en el área central de la Contestania. *Lvcentvm* XXVIII, 23-50.

García-Cano, J. M. 1982. *Cerámicas griegas de la Región de Murcia*. Murcia: Editora regional.

García-Cano, J. M. & Page-del-Pozo, V. 2001. El armamento de la necrópolis de Castillejo de los Baños. *Gladius* 21, 57-136.

Inchaurrandieta-Ramallo, A. 2015. Una aproximación a la necrópolis ibérica de El Villar. In A. Fernández-Díaz (ed.). *I Encuentro de jóvenes investigadores en arqueología de la Región de Murcia*, 195-226. Murcia: Editum.

Izquierdo-Peraile, I. 2000. *Monumentos funerarios ibéricos: los pilares-estela*. Valencia: Museo de Prehistoria de Valencia.

Lillo-Carpio, P. A. 1990. Los restos del monumento funerario ibérico de El Prado. In *Homenaje a Jerónimo Molina*, 135-61. Murcia: Academia Alfonso X.

López-Mondéjar, L. 2010. Los santuarios ibéricos del valle del Quípar. *Quaderns de prehistòria i arqueologia de Castelló* 28, 175-89.
López-Mondéjar, L. 2014. Santuarios y poder ideológico en el Sureste ibérico peninsular. *Munibe. Antropologia-Arkeologia* 65, 157-75.
Mata-Parreño, C., Moreno-Martín, A., Pérez-Jordà, G., Quixal-Santos, D. & Vives-Ferrándiz, J. 2009. Casas y cosas del campo: hábitat agrícola y estructura social en los territorios de Edeta y Kelin. In M. C. Belarte-Franco (ed.). *L'espai domèstic i l'organització de la societat a la protohistòria de la Mediterrània occidental.* Arqueomediterrània 11, 143-52.
Muñoz-Amilibia, A. M. 1987. La escultura funeraria de la necrópolis de Coimbra del Barranco Ancho. *Archivo de Prehistoria Levantina,* 229-55.
Olmos-Romera, R. 2003. Tiempo de la naturaleza y tiempo de la historia: una lectura ibérica en una perspectiva mediterránea. In D. Segarra-Crespo (ed.). *Transcurrir y recorrer.* 19-43. Madrid: CSIC.
Pérez-Jordà, G., Mata-Parreño, C., Moreno-Martín, A. & Quixal-Santos, D. 2015. Lagares de piedra y bodegas en el territorio ibérico de Kelin. In M. Contreras-Villaseñor & L. V. Elías-Pastor (eds). *Lagares rupestres.* 61-69. La Rioja: Adra.
Prados-Martínez, F. 2011. Iberia entre Atenas y Cartago. In ¿Hombres o dioses? Una nueva mirada a la escultura del mundo ibérico. 179-210. Alcalá de Henares: Museo Arqueológico Regional.
Ramos-Martínez, F. 2007. Intervención arqueológica en el Pasico de San Pascual. In *XVII Jornadas de Patrimonio Histórico y Arqueología Regional* 1, 79-82. Murcia: Servicio de Patrimonio Histórico.
Ruiz-Rodríguez, A. & Molinos-Molinos, M. 2007. *Iberos en Jaén.* Jaén: Universidad de Jaén.
Sala-Sellés, F. 2007. Algunas reflexiones a propósito de la escultura ibérica de la Contestania y su entorno. In L. Abad-Casal & J. A. Soler-Díaz (eds). *Actas del Congreso Arte Ibérico en la España Mediterránea.* 51-82. Alicante: Diputación Provincial de Alicante.
Stylow, A. U. & Mayer, M. 1996. Los Tituli de la Cueva Negra. *Antigüedad y Cristianismo* XIII, 367-406.

Chapter 8

From hut to factory

Models of rural occupation in the Lower Guadalquivir valley during the 1st millennium BC

Eduardo Ferrer-Albelda, Francisco José García-Fernández & José Luis Ramos-Soldado

In D.C. Cowley, M. Fernández-Götz, T. Romankiewicz & H. Wendling (eds). Rural Settlement. Relating buildings, landscape, and people in the European Iron Age (Leiden 2019: Sidestone Press) 89-99.

8.1 Introduction

The aim of this paper is to provide a preliminary diachronic perspective on rural settlement patterns in the Lower Guadalquivir Valley between the 9th and 3rd centuries BC, paying special attention to architectural, functional and spatial aspects. This is not straightforward as the evidence for this period is challenging: the archaeological record is unsystematic and dispersed; chronologies are not always reliable and the use of conventional periodisation (Late Bronze Age, Early Iron Age) is problematic; and the evidence is either poorly published or not published at all.

8.2 The beginning of 'ruralisation' in Lower Guadalquivir (9th-8th centuries BC)

The 9th century BC in the Guadalquivir Valley (Ferrer-Albelda 2017) marks the transition between the Late Bronze Age and the Early Iron Age, witnessing the first steps of a process which was to extend over a large region. From this date the emergence of a two level hierarchy of settlement can be seen, comprising hilltop settlements on the one hand and hamlets on the plains on the other. The naturally fortified hilltop settlements, which controlled a surrounding territory, lie near communication routes (Carmona, Montemolín, Setefilla, Osuna, Colina de los Quemados, Monturque), and were inhabited from the Late Bronze Age (Ferrer-Albelda *et al.* 2002; 2017). These settlements were inhabited by stock-keeping and warrior elites (Barceló 1992; 1995), and, during the Early Iron Age, they developed into *oppida*, assimilating urban concepts such as the rational organisation of space, construction of houses built with straight walls, and the specialisation in use of space (artisanal areas, meeting areas, sanctuaries, domestic areas, etc.). Secondly, there are hamlets of huts, or less well built structures, located on the plain, which emerged in the late 9th or early 8th century BC (Figure 1) at the same date as the beginning of the Phoenician colonisation of the Tarteside, the Greek name of Lower Gualquivir Valley (Ferrer-Albelda 2017). These were often, though not always, located in the vicinity of the *oppida*, and were strategically situated in order to exploit certain economic resources that were chiefly related to stock-keeping, but also to mining.

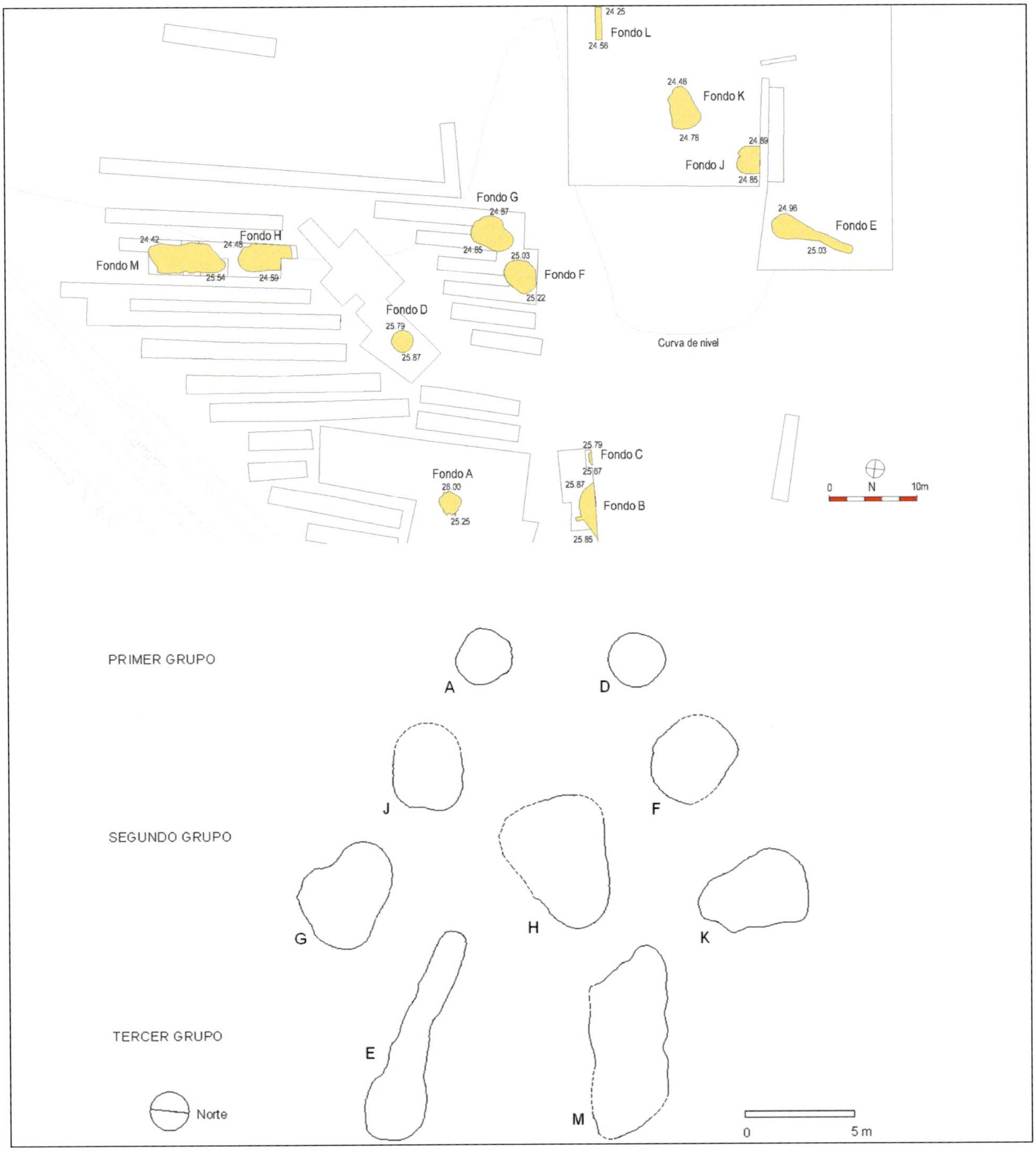

Figure 1: Jardín de Alá, Salteras, Seville (from Hunt & García Rivero 2017).

During the Late Bronze Age the hilltop sites played a role as central places at the regional level, to judge from the 'warrior stelae' found in some of them (Montemolín, Carmona, Setefilla) and their continuity into the following period. Stelae have been interpreted as displaying the importance of individuals, their military virtues and their connection with stock-keeping, as well as their relation to population movements in a lightly stratified society. The hierarchy of settlements also involved the formation of social spaces managed by peasant communities, which were the foundations of the future organisation of settlements in the Lower and Middle Guadalquivir Valley during the 1st millennium BC (Barceló 1992; 1995).

However, signs of incipient hierarchy must not be mistaken for complex forms of social organisation, as these were peasant communities that operated autarchic economic systems, in conditions of social equality and few formal institutions. In all events, the buildings present very different features, especially in terms of size, ranging from 2.6 m^2 (Vega de Santa Lucía) to 40/50 m^2 (Pocito Chico), even within the same settlements, and the settlements include very different models (isolated huts, multiple huts and possibly walled precincts). This diversity of size, complexity, location and internal form, could be early indicators of social hierarchy (Delgado Hervás 2005).

Not coincidentally, this phenomenon is contemporary with the foundation of Phoenician cities (Cádiz, Castillo de Doña Blanca), emporia (Onoba, Spal) and sanctuaries (El Carambolo), which acted as beacons for groups of settlers and which were at the centre of processes of synoecism, prompting the emergence of new settlements (Cerro de la Cabeza, Alcalá del Río, Cerro Macareno) and the concentration of hamlets and farmhouses in certain territories. Over the long term, these transformations brought about qualitative and quantitative changes to settlement patterns and a substantial increase in the number of settlements (Ferrer-Albelda *et al.* 2007; Ferrer-Albelda *et al.* 2008; Ferrer-Albelda 2017).

Between the 9th and 6th centuries BC, the hamlets on the plain were made up of clusters of huts of varying sizes, including some exceptionally large settlements such as San Bartolomé de Almonte (Huelva), which was approximately 40 ha in size (Ruiz Mata & Fernández Jurado 1986). These settlements were sometimes composed of a number of differentiated structures (22 in San Bartolomé, 13 in El Jardín de Alá: Hunt 2010; Hunt & García Rivero 2017), but isolated huts have also been attested. In any case, it is worth noting that none of these settlements has ever been fully excavated. In general, the huts are only recognised during excavation in the form of organic staining across a discrete area. These have traditionally, and by default, been described as 'hut floors', but are in fact the remains of features that served a variety of purposes including habitation, storage, workshop, kitchen, rubbish pits, and burial (Izquierdo 1998; Delgado 2005). The huts were circular or elliptical on plan and built of perishable materials, rammed-earth walls and a roof of organic material, though sometimes a stone foundation is present. In some cases, the conical roof was supported by timber posts. Sometimes, the inside of the walls is made impermeable with a lining made with clay, reeds and branches. Floors were made of beaten earth, and sometimes with layers of lime and schist slabs and stone paving in the entrance. On rare occasions, internal divisions and side benches have been attested (Izquierdo 1998). A number of different functions can be inferred from the archaeological record. Ceramic kitchen-, table- and storage-wares, hand querns and remains of fauna point to habitation, leisure and consumption; scoria and metal, especially silver, (Jardín de Alá, San Bartolomé de Almonte, La Coriana, Cerro de la Albina) seem to indicate use as workshops, while inhumations have also been attested in Vega de Santa Lucía (Murillo 1994) and El Jardín de Alá (Hunt 2010; Hunt & García Rivero 2017).

8.3 Agrarian colonisation and the occupation of the countryside

Some hilltop settlements (*tipo oppidum*) provide evidence for the coexistence of non-native and indigenous communities, and a transition between circular and rectangular buildings, which are sometimes found together, can be attested at *Acinipo* (Aguayos *et al.* 1991) and Montemolín (Chaves & Bandera 1991; Ferrer-Albelda & Bandera 2007). Similar processes of transition have been recognised in areas of Phoenician influence, such as Ratihnos, Portugal (Berrocal-Rangel & Silva 2010; Berrocal-Rangel *et al.* 2012; Gomes 2012, 49-59), Malaga (Melero 2008) and Alcorrín, Manilva, prov. Malaga (Suárez Padilla 2006; Marzoli *et al.* 2010, 153-82). No such transformation takes place in the hamlets on the plain, and these sites remained morphologically and functionally the same until at least the 6th century BC. Furthermore, the 7th and 6th centuries witnessed a widespread phenomenon in the Guadalquivir Valley and nearby farming regions with the proliferation of farmhouses and hamlets near waterways (Figure 2). These settlements were related to the extensive cultivation of cereal and vegetable gardens in better irrigated areas (Ferrer-Albelda *et al.* 2007). Such an agrarian colonisation has been attested near the Guadatín, in Córdoba (Murillo & Morena, 1992), the Corbones (Ferrer-Albelda & Bandera 2005; 2007) and the Guadajoz (Carrilero *et al.* 1993), in the hills around Ronda (Carrilero & Aguayo 1996), and the farmlands in the modern province of Cádiz (López Amador *et al.* 1996; López Rosendo 2007; 2013), Seville and Córdoba (González Acuña 2001; Ferrer *et al.* 2007).

These episodes of agrarian colonisation were directed by the great *oppida* – for example *Carmo* (Carmona, Seville), *Acinipo* (Ronda, Malaga) and Torreparedones, in Baena, Córdoba (Morena 1990) – the seats of powerful aristocracies (people who were probably the descendants of the old warrior elites). These people had originally based their economy on stock-breeding, especially cattle, but during the 7th and 6th centuries they began to base their status on the control of peasant-produced agricultural surplus, perhaps after the appropriation of communal land. This process of agrarian colonisation has been linked with demographic growth but, first and foremost, with the incorporation of these communities into a colonial economy and its needs (Ferrer *et al.* 2007).

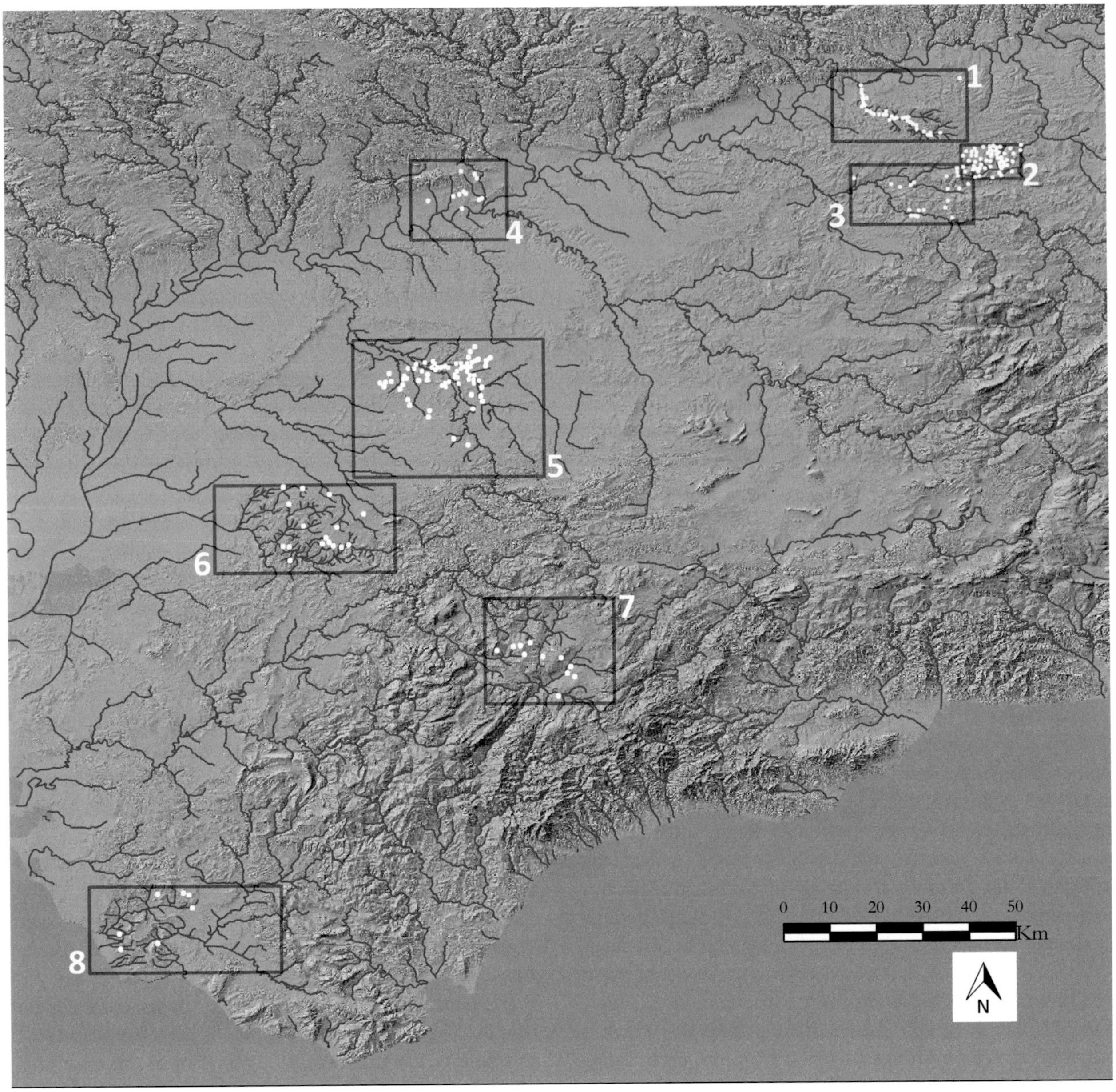

Figure 2: Cases of agrarian colonisation in Guadalquivir valley, 7th-6th centuries BC (from authors). 1. Arroyo Guadatín (Córdoba); 2. Baena (Córdoba); 3. Río Guadajoz (Castro del Río, Córdoba): 4. Peñaflor (Sevilla); 5. Río Corbones y arroyo Salado (Marchena, Sevilla); 6. El Coronil y Utrera (Sevilla); 7. Ronda (Málaga); 8. Vejer de la Frontera (Cádiz).

In addition to these dispersed farmhouses and agricultural hamlets, another kind of settlement emerged within the orbit of the main centres. Metallurgical activity, specifically the refining of silver, played a prominent role in this emergence. Examples include settlements Cerro de la Albina, near Coria del Río (Seville), ancient *Caura* (Escacena & Henares 1996; Escacena *et al.* 2010), and La Coriana, in the vicinity of Cerro de la Cabeza (Olivares, Seville), which was known as *Laelia* in the Roman period (Rodríguez Cuevas 2015).

8.4 New settlement patterns (6th-2nd century BC)

The situation began to change in the 6th century BC, when two phenomena occurred. The population became less dense throughout the Guadalquivir Valley, with the exception of the territory of Carmona (Seville), where a five-tier settlement structure persisted (city, second-rate *oppida*, towers and watchtowers, hamlets and farmhouses). The reason for this reduction in numbers of settlements may have been related to insecurity, and it resulted in a larger proportion of the population residing in large *oppida*. The exception posed by Carmona may be explained by the emergence of a powerful city-state, which was capable of defending its territory and the surrounding communities (García Fernández 2007; Ferrer-Albelda *et al.* 2011).

On the other hand, settlement also changed in terms of size, structure, construction techniques, and function – a process that resulted in the emergence of agricultural factories, dependent on pre-eminent centres and oriented towards the production of surplus. This did not involve a change in the *oppida* networks, which remained largely the same in the Lower Guadalquivir Valley between the First (8th -6th centuries BC) and the Second (5th-2nd centuries BC) Iron Ages (García-Fernández 2003; 2005; 2007; Ferrer-Albelda *et al.* 2008). In this case, the evidence concentrates chiefly on the north bank of the Guadalquivir River, which was less densely populated than the farmlands on the south margin. This area has been intensely explored following the mining project of Cobre Las Cruces (1996-2011) and the construction of the water reservoir of Melonares (2002-2007). These investigations resulted in the discovery of several agricultural settlements. One of these was located near the valley, whereas the rest are situated on the lower slopes of the Sierra Morena range, near the passes that lead to the central plateau.

8.4.1 SE-M (Cobre Las Cruces)

The first of these sites, known by the acronym SE-M, is located on a hilltop on the north bank of the Molinos stream, a tributary to the south of the Ribera del Huelva River (Vera Cruz 2012, 70-2). Excavations in June 2011 found the foundations of a building complex situated around an open area, enclosed by a wall and paved with pebbles. The construction technique is the same across the site: pebble masonry and blocks of limestone or granite, bound with an earth mortar, at the foundation level, and rammed-earth for the upper walls. The best-preserved building is 200 m^2 in area, with a longitudinal nave on the north-western side from which the transverse naves project (2 m across by 8.70 m long). Thus far, two of these transverse naves have been identified, but based on their dimensions, it is likely that there were six of them. In the courtyard, the remains of a pebble and limestone pavement have been found that may mark the location of a roofed veranda, probably built in timber. The north-eastern side of the building was occupied by a series of smaller rooms, which are only partially preserved. To the southeast of this complex there are two more buildings, one of which (that closest to the main complex) has a different orientation to the rest of the structures (Vera Cruz 2012, 71). The finds associated with these two buildings, as well those found in a refuse ditch nearby, including late Turdetanian and Italian wares, suggest that these buildings were built at a later date, probably in the Late Iron Age or the first centuries of Roman occupation.

The excavator interpreted these structures as a 'complex dedicated to the exploitation, production and storage of agricultural produce', which was built during the second half of the 6th century BC. This dating is based on the conventional chronology of the earliest variants of the Pellicer BC amphorae and the ring fibulae found sitting on top of the paving of the main structure (Vera Cruz 2012, 72). The best-preserved phase, however, seems to date to the 5th and 4th centuries BC, which are represented by other types of local amphorae, including imported (from *Gadir*/Cádiz) Ramón 11-type specimens and common wares such as locally-made plates, bowls, urns, *pithoi* and cooking pans. Some of these pieces present clear archaic features, as could be expected of productions situated in the transition between orientalizing and Turdetanian repertoires.

Both the construction techniques and the finds are reminiscent of post-orientalizing rural sites in Extremadura and Baixo Alentejo, such as Mata de Campanario (Rodríguez *et al.* 2004) and Fernão Vaz (Correia 1999; Calado *et al.* 1999), where we can find the same type of building – inspired by Levantine models – characterised by long and narrow rooms arranged around a transverse, elongated passage (a characteristic which should be linked to Phoenician models). This site, therefore, seems to represent an older phenomenon which dates back to the Early Iron Age. Another example would be that of El Palomar, Mérida (Jiménez Ávila & Ortega 2001). In some cases, this phenomenon may have survived in the Guadalquivir Valley both in rural settlements and in *oppida* (Alcalá del Río, Itálica) until well into the Middle Iron Age.

8.4.2 Los Provinciales

The construction of the Melonares Reservoir, on the Viar River, in the municipality of Castilblanco de los Arroyos (Seville), provided the opportunity to excavate several rural sites dating to the Middle Iron Age. The earliest of these sites, Los Provinciales, is located on a gentle slope, and intensive survey and test pits in 2007 documented a series of structures and two major occupation phases dating to the Early Iron Age and the beginnings of the Roman occupation. The first phase is characterised by the presence of both hand-made (pans, storage jars, bowls, etc.) and thrown (mostly *pithoi* and large vases) ceramic shapes, which are characteristic of the 7th-6th century BC. However, none of the structures can be dated to this period, perhaps because later occupation obliterated the earliest construction phases or because the oldest structures were built using perishable materials that have not survived.

The second phase is represented by a series of buildings that, between the 5th to the 3rd centuries BC, underwent successive modifications. There is no significant change in construction techniques, plan and, probably, function, which suggests continuity in occupation. In general, the buildings are oriented NE-SW, and are built with irregular masonry bound with earth mortar, set within simple foundation trenches. The buildings are rectangular on plan, but occasionally the central structure is abutted by semi-circular structures built on very substantial stone foundations. As noted, the differences in construction technique over time are minimal, with the exception of the arrangement of the stone blocks and the orientation of the walls. The remains of pavements are limited to some irregularly-shaped stone slabs placed to level out the floors. Some of the buildings are divided into two spaces by a longitudinal or a transverse partition.

Analysis of the stratigraphy indicates that the complex comprised at least eight construction phases, though poor preservation of the structures means that co-existence of some of these buildings cannot be ruled out. However, it is possible to isolate five building complexes, and develop a diachronic sequence divided into at least three phases from the 5th to the 3rd centuries BC. It seems likely that the structures were demolished in the 2nd-1st century BC.

8.4.3 Cerro de Las Niñas

The site of Cerro de Las Niñas is situated in the municipality of El Pedroso (Seville), to the south bank of the Viar River, on an oval-shaped rocky promontory. Investigations undertaken in 2007 revealed several structural complexes at different points on the promontory and a total of seven construction phases, five of which date to the Iron Age. Most of these phases were associated with the so-called Building Complex I, located on the south-southeast of the promontory, while the Building Complex II, situated along the south-western edge of the hill has a shorter life-span, between the 4th and the 3rd centuries BC. This latter complex, entirely built of irregular masonry blocks bound with earth mortar, comprises several discreet structures, including a double curved wall precinct constructed around the perimeter of the summit and a rectangular paved building, the function of which is unknown. Between the wall circuits there is a pebble pavement which suggests that the space between both walls was paved or, perhaps, the presence of a casemate.

Building Complex I, on the other hand, is the result of complex processes of occupation, transformation and abandonment of the structures situated in the south-southeast part of the hill between the 7th-6th century BC and the 1st century BC. The earliest phase dates to between the 7th-6th century BC and the 4th century BC. The structural remains from this phase comprise only a series of walls of a two-roomed building of uncertain dimensions, which was rectangular or trapezoidal in shape. The whole structure was built in sun-baked bricks, alternating courses of headers and stretchers, while the pavement was composed of irregular stone slabs and pebbles. The second phase involved a change in the wall orientations, perhaps after a short hiatus in occupation, and the laying down of another stone pavement of large masonry blocks. In this phase, which can be dated to between the 5th-4th century BC and the 3rd century BC, masonry is used for the first time in walls, which have a variable thickness, and became the predominant construction technique thereafter.

The third phase involves numerous changes to the site, including the digging of three large ditches which affected both building complexes, between the 3rd and the 2nd centuries BC. In the fourth phase, some of the old structures were reused, and some new buildings were erected. The latter include a trapezoidal building, 8.50 m long and 2 m across, with irregular masonry walls, no internal divisions and an entrance to the northeast. It is associated with different layers of pavement, some of it reused from the second phase, and some newly constructed. The abandonment levels suggest a date in the 2nd century BC for this phase. The last phase involved the reoccupation of the site after a hiatus in occupation between the 2nd and 1st centuries BC. The new constructions associated with the final phase are less solid and seem to be related to processing activities, including an oven made of sun-baked brick and two stone structures (one rectangular, one circular) interpreted as hearths, which are related to different clay pavements and other structural remains.

8.4.4 Dehesa de San Benito

Finally, Dehesa de San Benito, also situated in the municipality of Castilblanco de los Arroyos, in the right bank of the Viar River. The site takes in the entire summit of a small plateau, approximately 2500 m^2 in area. The site is elongated along a NE-SW axis, and it visually dominates most of the central sector of the valley below. Test pits dug in 2007 revealed a defensive wall around the perimeter and the partial remains of seven buildings. The structures comprised two walls of masonry bound with clay and gravel mortar, partially dressed on the exterior face and filled with rubble in the interior.

The buildings identified in the interior have not been excavated fully, but it is possible to see that the walls meet at right angles, and form rectangular rooms. Owing to the disturbed state of the stratigraphy no pavements have been identified, but one of the strata, which included a large ceramic assemblage, has been interpreted as a levelling deposit. Two mills have been identified in rooms 3 and 4, including two truncated cone-shaped rotating millstones and, possibly, their associated lower stones. The scarce finds are related to the abandonment level of the walls and the interior rooms, although some ceramic

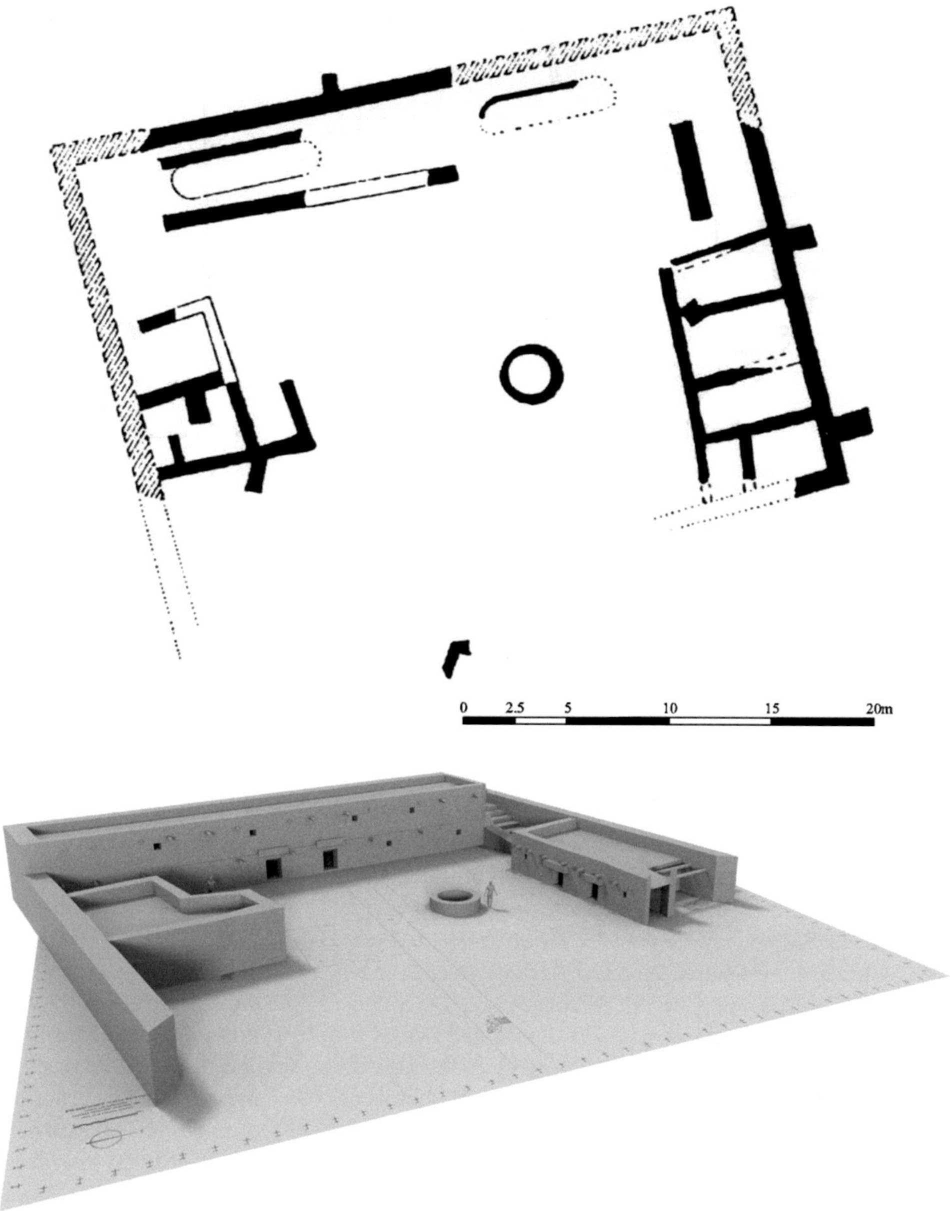

Figure 3: Cerro Naranja, Jerez de la Frontera, Cadix (from González Rodríguez 1987b , virtual reconstruction: F. Luengo).

fragments found in association with an occupation level and the levelling deposit can provide a more or less precise date for the foundation of the settlement. Most of these fragments correspond to thrown Turdetanian wares (bowls, large storage jars, cooking pots, etc.), and Italian and Phoenician imports (T-7.4.3.3 and Dressel 1 types amphorae, Campanian A table ware, fine walled wares and common kitchen and table wares). There is one Kuass-type fragment, probably an imitation, bearing the typical stamp on the base, which is the specimen of this Punic wares from Cádiz which has been found the farthest inland to date. These ceramic wares suggest a single occupation phase between the mid-2nd and the mid-1st centuries BC.

8.5 A new Phoenician-style exploitation model (3rd century BC)

These rural settlements, which we may classify as 'Turdetanian'[1] based on their geographical position and cultural features, stand in sharp contrast to a new type of settlement that becomes prevalent in the farmlands of Cádiz during the 3rd century BC. These settlements have been variously defined (*i.e.* villa, factory) but all opinions agree that their economic regime is no longer autarchic, but intensive, and we can even go so far as to consider

1 Turdetania is a region (the Lower Guadalquivir Valley in Roman Republic period) and Turdetanian is an archaeological culture (from Cultural Historicism) between 6th -2nd centuries BC.

it market-oriented. Based on their ground plans, they seem to play a dual role as both domestic and productive, with agricultural produce processed and packed in, and distributed from, the settlement itself. These settlements, for example Cerro Naranja (Jerez de la Frontera, Cádiz: González Rodríguez 1987a; 1987b), are a Mediterranean model, likely introduced in the Iberian Peninsula by the Carthaginians (Carretero 2007a; 2007b), whose influence in the region is significant from the late 4th century BC (Ferrer-Albelda & Pliego 2010a; 2010b; 2013; Ferrer *et al.* 2017).

Cerro Naranja presents a rectangular, almost fortified, layout, with thick walls and buttresses enclosing an area of approximately 1300 m^2 (Figure 3). The largest of the spaces identified to date in Cerro Naranja has been interpreted as an open courtyard, with a structure in the centre, perhaps the location of an olive or wine press. Around this courtyard there are several rooms, including storerooms that contain two large cisterns *a bagnarola* (7 x 1.80 m), water proofed and with a minimum combined capacity of 33 m^3. According to some estimates, up to 165 tonnes of olives would have been needed to fill these cisterns. C. Lozano (2011) estimates that this quantity of olives would have required approximately 2750 trees – that is, around 9 ha of land, at 300 trees per ha.

The architectural model for this settlement is paralleled in the Punic factories in Ibiza, Sardinia, Malta and North Africa (Pardo Barrionuevo 2015, 180-6). These are dispersed settlements in the hinterland of *Gadir* and *Asta Regia*, and were probably owned by large landowners dedicated to a single crop (*e.g.* olives, vines) for the market. The storage vessels found in Cerro Naranja suggest that the estate focused on the production of olive oil (Carretero 2004; García Fernández *et al.* 2016) distributed across a region that included *Gadir* and its hinterland, the Lower Guadalquivir Valley and the Portuguese Algarve – that is, what can be considered the economic area of influence of *Gadir* (Ferrer-Albelda *et al.* 2010).

8.6 Conclusions

In the early 1st millennium BC the Lower Guadalquivir River witnessed the proliferation of sites, or hamlets, formed by clusters of huts on the plain, as well as the emergence of the urban areas, which was related to Phoenician colonisation. Earlier, in the Late Bronze Age, a network of hilltop settlements, also formed by clusters of huts, had emerged, and over time, during the Iron Age, these settlements became *oppida*. These *oppida* proved to be a resilient model of settlement, as they largely survived in to the Roman period and, in some cases, even to the present. The rural population peaked between the 7th and early 6th centuries BC, when a twofold phenomenon took place: firstly the agrarian colonisation of the whole of the Guadalquivir Valley; and secondly the proliferation of small farmhouses and hamlets which were dedicated to agricultural or metallurgical activities and were satellites of the central *oppida*. Until this point, settlements had been formed by irregularly arranged circular or elliptical huts, accompanied by negative features such as burials, rubbish pits and kitchens.

However, throughout the 6th century BC, substantial changes occurred – the generalised contraction of the settlement pattern and the concentration of the population in larger sites (except in the territory of *Carmo*), perhaps a consequence of a period of social and political turmoil, and the transformation of the hut into an agricultural factory, formed by a single, straight-walled structure built of non-perishable materials (stone, adobe, rammed-earth, timber). This was to remain the predominant model until it was progressively replaced by the *villa* during the Roman period.

In parallel, during the 3rd century BC, a new model of agricultural building, which was clearly inspired by the Punic model and oriented towards market crops, especially wine and oil, emerged in the area surrounding Cádiz. The appearance of these centres may be attributed to the initiative of *Gadir*, perhaps prompted by the growing influence of Carthage in the area of the Strait of Gibraltar, as the products bottled in these areas were distributed throughout Cádiz's commercial dominions: the Lower Guadalquivir Valley, the Algarve and Alemtejo.

8.7 Bibliography

Aguayo de Hoyos, P., Carrilero, M. & Martínez, G. 1991. La presencia fenicia y el proceso de aculturación de las comunidades del Bronce Final de la depresión de Ronda (Malaga). *Atti del II Congresso Internazionale di Studi Fenici e Punici*, 559-71. Rome: Consiglio nazionale delle ricerche.

Barceló, J. A. 1992. Una interpretación socioeconómica del Bronce Final en el Sudoeste de la Península Ibérica. *Trabajos de Prehistoria* 49, 259-75.

Barceló, J. A. 1995. Sociedad y economía en el Bronce Final. In *Tartessos. 25 años después 1968-1993. Congreso Conmemorativo del V Symposium Internacional de Prehistoria Peninsular*, 561-89. Jerez de la Frontera: Biblioteca de Urbanismo y Cultura, Ayuntamiento de Jerez.

Berrocal-Rangel, L. & Silva, A. C. 2010. *O castro do Ratinhos (Barraquem do Alqueva, Moura). Excavaçoes num povoado proto-histórico do Guadiana, 2004-2007.* Lisbon: Museu Nacional de Arqueologia.

Berrocal-Rangel, L., Silva, A. C. & Prados Martínez, F. 2012. El Castro dos Ratinhos, un ejemplo de orientalización entre las jefaturas del Bronce Final del Suroeste. In J. Jiménez Ávila (ed.), SIDEREUM ANA II. *El río Guadiana en el Bronce Final. Anejos de Archivo Español de Arqueología* LXII, 167-83. Mérida: IAM-CSIC.

Calado, M. J. M., Barradas, M. P. & Mataloto, R. J. 1999. Povoamento proto-histórico no Alentejo central. *Revista*

Guimaraes, *volumen especial. Actas do Congreso de Proto-Historia Europeia*, 363-86.
Carretero Poblete, P. A. 2004. Difusión de ánforas tipo Tiñosa en Algarve (Portugal) y la comercialización de productos agrícolas púnico-turdetanos entre los siglos V y III a.C. *Xelb* 5, 305-16.
Carretero Poblete, P. A. 2007a. *Agricultura y comercio púnico-turdetano en el bajo Guadalquivir. El inicio delas explotaciones oleícolas peninsulares (siglos IV-II a.C.).* BAR International Series 1703. Oxford: Archaeopress.
Carretero Poblete, P. A. 2007b. Las villas agrícolas púnico-turdetanas de la campiña gaditana (Cádiz-España). In J. L. López Castro (ed.). *Las ciudades fenicio-púnicas en el Mediterráneo Occidental*, 187-208. Almería: Fuera de colección.
Carrilero, M. & Aguayo, P. 1996. Indígenas en el período orientalizante en Malaga (s. VIII-VI a.C.). In F. Wulff & G. Cruz Andreotti (eds). *Historia Antigua de Malaga*, 41-57. Malaga: Centro de Ediciones de la Diputación Provincial de Málaga.
Carrilero, M., Martínez, G. & Aguayo, P. 1993. Ocupación rural "tartésica" en el valle medio del Guadajoz (Córdoba). *Actas del I Coloquio de Historia Antigua de Andalucía* (I), 71-9. Córdoba: Cajasur.
Chaves Tristán, F. & Bandera, M. L. de la 1991. Aspectos de la urbanística en Andalucía occidental en los siglos VII-VI a.C. a la luz del yacimiento de Montemolín (Marchena, Seville). In *II Congresso Internazionale di Studi Fenici e Punici*, II, 691-714. Rome: Consiglio nazionale delle ricerche.
Correia, V. H. 1999. Fernão Vaz (Ourique, Beja). Balanco da investigação arqueológica. *Vipasca* 8, 23-31.
Delgado Hervás, A. 2005. La transformación de la arquitectura residencial en Andalucía occidental durante el Orientalizante: una lectura social. In S. Celestino & J. Jiménez Ávila (eds). *El período orientalizante. Actas del III Simposio Internacional de Arqueología de Mérida: Protohistoria del Mediterráneo Occidental. Anejos de Archivo Español de Arqueología* XXXV, I, 585-94. Mérida: IAM-CSIC.
Escacena Carrasco, J. L. 2000. *La Arqueología Protohistórica del sur de la Península Ibérica. Historia de un río revuelto.* Madrid: Editorial Síntesis.
Escacena, J. L., Feliú, M. J. & Izquierdo, R. 2010. El Cerro de la Albina y la metalurgia de la plata en Tartessos. *De Re Metallica* 14, 35-51.
Escacena, J.L. & Henares, M. T. 1996. Un fondo de cabaña de época tartésica en la Puebla del Río (Seville). Intervención arqueológica de urgencia. *Anuario Arqueológico de Andalucía 1994*, III, 504-10.
Ferrer-Albelda, E. 2017. La colonización fenicia de la Tartéside: estrategias y fases. In S. Celestino & E. Rodríguez (eds), *Territorios comparados: los valles del Guadalquivir, Guadiana y Tajo en época tartésica. Anejos de Archivo Español de Arqueología* LXXX, 11-46. Mérida: IAM-CSIC.
Ferrer-Albelda, E. & Bandera, M. L. de la 2005. El orto de Tartessos: La colonización agraria durante el período orientalizante. In S. Celestino & J. Jiménez Ávila (eds). *El período orientalizante. Actas del III Simposio Internacional de Arqueología de Mérida: Protohistoria del Mediterráneo Occidental. Anejos de Archivo Español de Arqueología XXXV, I*. 565-74. Mérida: IAM-CSIC.
Ferrer-Albelda, E. & Bandera, M. L. de la 2007. Santuarios, aldeas y granjas: El poblamiento durante el Bronce Final y el Período Orientalizante. In E. Ferrer Albelda (coord.). *Arqueología en Marchena. El poblamiento antiguo y medieval en el valle medio del río Corbones*. 45-87. Seville: Editorial Universidad de Sevilla-Secretariado de Publicaciones.
Ferrer-Albelda, E., Bandera, M. L. de la & García Fernández, F. J. 2007. El poblamiento rural protohistórico en el Bajo Guadalquivir. In A. Rodríguez & I. Pavón (eds). *Arqueología de la Tierra. Los paisajes rurales protohistóricos de la Protohistoria Peninsular*, 195-224. Cáceres: Universidad de Extremadura.
Ferrer-Albelda, E., García Fernández, F. J. & Escacena, J. L. 2010. El tráfico comercial de productos púnicos en el estuario del Guadalquivir. In E. Ferrer-Albelda (coord.). *Los púnicos de Iberia: Proyectos, revisiones, síntesis. Mainake* XXXII, 1, 61-89.
Ferrer-Albelda, E., García Fernández, F. J. & R. Pliego Vázquez 2017. Fuga a tres voces sobre la presencia cartaginesa prebárquida en la Península Ibérica. In *Alexander, Hannibal und Constantin. Drei historische Persönlichkeiten und ein Forscher, der sich ihnen widmet (Festschrift für Pedro Barceló)*. 337-58. Besançon: Presses Universitaires de Franche-Comté, Colección Institut des Sciences et Techniques de l'Antiquité (ISTA).
Ferrer-Albelda, E., García Fernández, F. J. & Sánchez Gómez, F. 2011. De la aldea al *oppidum*: el paisaje rural en el valle del Corbones durante el primer milenio a.C. In *Actas del VII Congreso de Historia de Carmona: 7000 años de historia rural*, 77-111. Carmona: Universidad de Sevilla.
Ferrer-Albelda, E., García Vargas, E. & García Fernández, F. J. 2008. *Inter Aestuaria Baetis.* Espacios naturales y territorios ciudadanos prerRomanos en el Bajo Guadalquivir. *Mainake* XXX, 217-46.
Ferrer-Albelda, E. & Pliego Vázquez, R. 2010a. Carthaginian Garrisons in Turdetania: the Monetary Evidence. In A. Dowler & E.R. Galvin. *Money, Trade and Trade Route in Pre-Islamic North Africa*, 33-41. London: British Museum Press.
Ferrer-Albelda, E. & Pliego Vázquez, R. 2010b. ...*Auxilium consanguineis Karthaginiensis misere*: un nuevo

marco interpretativo de las relaciones entre Cartago y las comunidades púnicas de Iberia. In E. Ferrer-Albelda (coord.). *Los púnicos de Iberia: Proyectos, revisiones, síntesis. Mainake XXXII, 1*, 525-57.

Ferrer-Albelda, E. & Pliego Vázquez, R. 2013. Cartago e Iberia antes de los Barca. In M. Bendala (ed.). *Fragor Hannibalis. Aníbal en Hispania*, 106-33. Madrid: Museo Arqueologioco Regional.

Ferrer-Albelda, E., Ruiz-Cecilia, J. I. & García-Fernández, F. J. 2002. Los orígenes de Osuna. Urso durante el Bronce Final y período orientalizante. In F. Chaves (ed). *Osuna. A la búsqueda de su pasado*, 99-147. Osuna: Ayuntamiento de Osuna, Fundación de Cultura García Blanco.

Ferrer-Albelda, E., Ruiz Cecilia, J. I. & García Fernández, F.J. 2017. Nuevos datos sobre el Bronce Final en Osuna. In S. Celestino & E. Rodríguez (eds). *Territorios comparados: los valles del Guadalquivir, Guadiana y Tajo en época tartésica. Anejos de Archivo Español de Arqueología* LXXX, 79-127. Mérida: IAM-CSIC.

García-Fernández, F. J. 2003. *El poblamiento turdetano en el Bajo Guadalquivir*. Unpublished thesis. Universidad de Sevilla.

García-Fernández, F. J. 2005. El poblamiento postorientalizante en el Bajo Guadalquivir. In S. Celestino & J. Jiménez Ávila (eds). *El período orientalizante. Actas del III Simposio Internacional de Arqueología de Mérida: Protohistoria del Mediterráneo Occidental. Anejos de Archivo Español de Arqueología XXXV, II*, 891-900. Mérida: IAM-CSIC.

García Fernández, F. J. 2007. El poblamiento turdetano en la comarca de Marchena. In E. Ferrer-Albelda (coord.). *Arqueología en Marchena. El poblamiento antiguo y medieval en el valle medio del río Corbones*, 89-142. Sevilla: Editorial Universidad de Sevilla – Secretariado de Publicaciones.

García Fernández, F.J., Ferrer Albelda, E., Álvarez Mateos, P. & Durán Barrientos, M. M. 2016. Análisis de residuos orgánicos y posibles contenidos en ánforas púnicas y turdetanas procedentes del valle del Guadalquivir. *Sagvntvm* 48, 50-87.

García Sanz, C. & Fernández Jurado, J. 2000. Peñalosa (Escacena del Campo, Huelva). Un poblado de cabañas del Bronce Final. *Huelva Arqueológica* 16, 5-87.

Gomes, F.B. 2012. *Aspectos do sagrado na colonização fenícia*. Cadernos de Uniarq 8. Lisbon: University of Lisbon.

González Acuña, D. 2001. Análisis de visibilidad y patrones de asentamiento protohistóricos. Los yacimientos del Bronce Final y período orientalizante en el sureste de la campiña Sevillena. *Archeologia e Calcolatori* 12, 123-42.

González Rodríguez, R. 1987a. Excavaciones de urgencia en el Cerro Naranja (Jerez de la Frontera, Cádiz), 1985. *Anuario Arqueológico de Andalucía 1985*, III, 90-6.

González Rodríguez, R. 1987b. Notas sobre las excavaciones de urgencia realizadas en el yacimiento prerromano de 'Cerro Naranja' (Finca de Los Garciagos, Jerez de la Frontera (Cádiz). *Cádiz en su Historia. VI Jornadas de Historia de Cádiz*, 27-44. Cádiz.

Hunt Ortiz, M. 2010. Intervención arqueológica en el yacimiento 'Jardín de Alá' (Término Municipal de Salteras, Seville). *Anuario Arqueológico de Andalucía 2006*, 4769-81.

Hunt Ortiz, M. & García Rivero, D. 2017. El asentamiento protohistórico de Jardín de Alá (Salteras, Sevilla). In S. Celestino & E. Rodríguez (eds). *Territorios comparados: los valles del Guadalquivir, Guadiana y Tajo en época tartésica. Anejos de Archivo Español de Arqueología* LXXX, 47-77. Mérida: IAM-CSIC.

Izquierdo de Montes, R. 1998. La cabaña circular en el mundo tartésico. Consideraciones sobre su uso como indicador étnico. *Zephyrus* 51, 277-88.

Jiménez Ávila, J. & Ortega Blanco, J. 2001. El poblado orientalizante de El Palomar (Oliva de Mérida, Badajoz). Nota preliminar. In D. Ruiz Mata & S. Celestino (eds). *Arquitectura oriental y orientalizante en la Península Ibérica*, 227-48. Madrid: CSIC.

López Amador, J. J., Bueno, P., Ruiz Gil, J. A. & de Prada, M. 1996. *Tartesios y fenicios en Campillo El Puerto de Santa María, Cádiz. Una aportación a la cronología del Bronce Final en el Occidente de Europa*. El Puerto de Santa María: Puertograf .

López Rosendo, E. 2007. El yacimiento arqueológico de Los Villares/Montealto y los orígenes tartésicos y Romanos de la población de Jerez. *Revista de Historia de Jerez* 13, 9-34.

López Rosendo, E. 2013. Fenicios e indígenas en la campiña gaditana: Los "fondos de cabaña" orientalizantes de Los Villares (Jerez de la Frontera, Cádiz). In *VI Congresso Internacional de Estudos Fenícios Púnicos*, 1, 428-35. Lisbon: Faculdade de Letras da Univesidade de Lisboa.

Lozano Rubio, C. 2011. *Cerro Naranja. Un estudio sobre el poblamiento rural púnico en la campiña gaditana*. Unpublished Trabajo Fin de Máster. Universidad de Sevilla.

Marzoli, D., López Pardo, F., Suárez Padilla, J., Mielke, D.P., León Martín, C., Ruiz Cabrero, L., Thiemeyer, H. & Torres Ortiz, M. 2010. Los inicios del urbanismo en las sociedades autóctonas localizadas en el entorno del Estrecho de Gibraltar: Investigaciones en los Castillejos de Alcorrín y su territorio (Manilva, Malaga). *Menga* 1, 153-82.

Melero García, F. 2008. Nuevas aportaciones para el estudio del poblado del Bronce Final de San Pablo (Malaga). La secuencia de c/ Tiro 9-11, esquina Zamorano. *Mainake* XXX, 355-77.

Morena López, J. A. 1990. Asentamientos rurales de época tartésica en Baena. *Hespérides. VIII Congreso de Profesores-Investigadores*, 471-504. Baena.

Murillo Redondo, J. F. 1994. *La cultura tartésica en el Guadalquivir Medio. Ariadna* 13-4. Palma del Río.

Murillo, J. F. & Morena, J. A. 1992. El poblamiento rural en el arroyo de Guadatín: un modelo de ocupación del territorio durante el Bronce Final y el período orientalizante en el valle medio del Guadalquivir. *Anales de Arqueología Cordobesa* 3, 37-50.

Pardo Barrionuevo, C A. 2015. *Economía y sociedad rural fenicia en el Mediterráneo occidental.* Seville: Editorial Universidad de Sevilla – Secretariado de Publicaciones.

Rodríguez Cuevas, P.D. 2015. *La Coriana: Análisis arqueológico y contextualización histórica de un yacimiento orientalizante en la cuenca del Guadiamar*, Unpublished Trabajo Fin de Máster. Universidad de Sevilla.

Rodríguez Díaz, A., Pavón, I. & Duque, D. M. 2004. 'La Mata' y su territorio. In *El edificio protohistórico de "La Mata" (Campanario, Badajoz) y su estudio territorial* (II), 497-569. Badajoz: Universidad de Extremadura.

Ruiz Mata, D. & Fernández Jurado, J. 1986. El yacimiento metalúrgico de época tartésica de San Bartolomé de Almonte (Huelva). *Huelva Arqueológica* VIII. Huelva.

Ruiz Mata, D. & González Rodríguez, R. 1994. Consideraciones sobre asentamientos rurales y cerámicas orientalizantes en la campiña gaditana. *Spal* 3, 209-56.

Suárez Padilla, J. 2006. Indígenas y fenicios en el extremo occidental de la costa de Malaga. Siglos IX-VI a.C. *Mainake* XVIII, 361-82.

Vera Cruz, E. 2012. El yacimiento púnico-turdetano SE-M. In M. A. Hunt Ortiz, (coord.). *Intervenciones arqueológicas en el área del Proyecto Minero Cobre Las Cruces (1996-2011). De la Prehistoria a la época Contemporánea (Provincia de Seville, España)*, 70-2. Seville: Fundación Cobre las Cruces.

Chapter 9

Space and place in the Early Iron Age in eastern Burgundy

Régis Labeaune

9.1 Introduction: Geographical context and research history of the study area

This paper is concerned for the most part with the eastern zone of the Côte d'Or during the 8th to 5th century BC, focusing on the region around Dijon and the Saône plain (Figure 1). In this area the network of rivers plays an important role in how settlements are distributed and their organization and is also significant for transport. The Saône River is an important commercial route between the Mediterranean and the North Sea via the Rhône and the Rhine. It is located 80 km to the south of the site of Vix where imported objects from the Mediterranean have been found. These were transported along commercial routes via eastern Burgundy, using the Saône River and its tributaries to gain access to the Seine Valley further to the north. With this developed exchange system in place, the number of settlements increased in this area.

Up until the 1980s, the excavations of tumuli, cemeteries and hilltop settlements were the main source of data for the Early Iron Age (Figure 2 A). These sites, which are still visible in the landscape today, gave the incorrect impression of a higher density of occupation on the plateau than in the valleys during Late Prehistory. Work on settlements located on the plains was under-represented and based mainly on incidental discoveries (Figure 2 B).

However, over the last 20 years, the rise in the number of preventive archaeology excavation projects has provided the opportunity to investigate large areas, and this has had a major impact on our knowledge of settlement patterns on the plain (Figure 2 C). With the expansion of the urban area of Dijon, over a thousand hectares have been archaeologically investigated through evaluation and full area excavation. These areas are mainly to the east and the southeast of the town, where the landscape is more suitable to large-scale development. This mosaic of interventions supports a new approach to the Hallstattian occupation of this area which has completely overturned the schema established before the 1980s. In contrast, during the last 30 years or so there have been no excavations of hilltop sites and tumuli.

In D.C. Cowley, M. Fernández-Götz, T. Romankiewicz & H. Wendling (eds). Rural Settlement. Relating buildings, landscape, and people in the European Iron Age (Leiden 2019: Sidestone Press) 101-112.

9.2 Problems in understanding the spatial organisation of settlements

The excavation of large areas within the framework of preventive archaeology has shed new light on the spatial occupation of sites even though investigation is restricted to the actual surface area of the project. This limitation can be frustrating in the case of linear developments, such as roads, where the area investigated is rarely more than 50 m across and it is impossible to explore the full extent of archaeological sites. Thus, it is only after multiple excavations in adjoining areas over several years that a complete picture is possible. This is not a problem for largescale investigation in quarries or with the development of large commercial zones.

The methods used for evaluation can also limit understanding of the spatial occupation of a site. Evaluation trenches cover about 10% of the surface area on a random sampling, and the results of these interventions inform the decision by the Ministry of Culture whether an excavation takes place or not. The number and the concentrations of features in the trenches need to be sufficiently important to trigger an excavation. However, the density of features on small rural settlements is generally low which does not encourage the excavation of these types of sites.

The second factor that can alter our perception of occupation patterns concerns their state of preservation, which is dependent on the type of agriculture practiced on the land. In the second half of the 20th century, ploughing to depths of 35 cm was particularly damaging for archaeological sites. With the exception of the site of Talant "La Peute Combe" (which we will discuss further on) where occupation levels have been preserved, all other sites have been heavily truncated and important information has been lost. To give an idea to the extent of this erosion, the plans of three buildings from Talant can be used to simulate the impact on our knowledge of the site of truncation to depths of 10 cm, 20 cm and 30 cm (Figure 3). In building 1 truncation to 10 cm depth would remove the layer of burnt flooring, leaving only two postholes about 15 cm in depth and a third about 30 cm deep.

The second example (Figure 3, number 4) is apsidal on plan with an earth floor delimited by a partition defined by stake holes. With truncation to a depth of 30 cm, only the postholes and the principal structure of the building

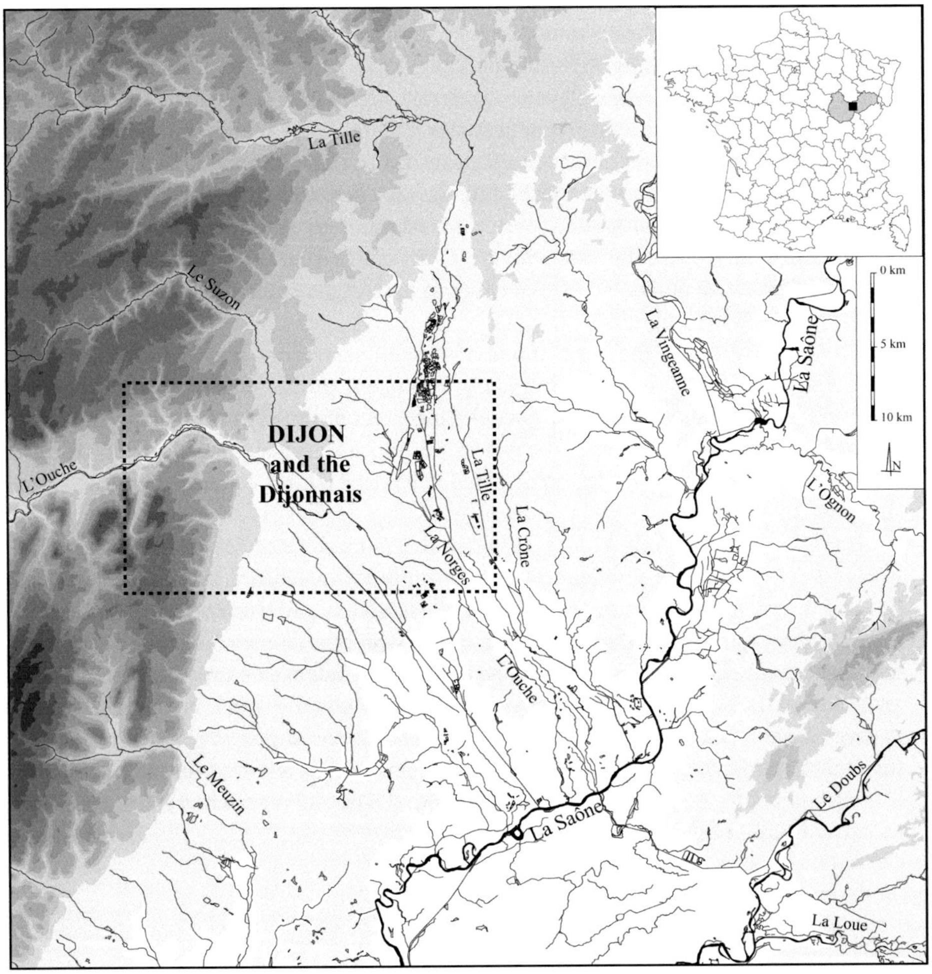

Figure 1: Presentation of the geographical context.

and several pits remain, making it look more like a six post hole granary. The third example (Figure 3, number 5) is divided into two parts, one with a sunken floor, which seems to have been a forge workshop. At a depth of 30 cm only this sunken area is still visible under the level of the forge, while the other part of the building has totally disappeared.

These examples are presented to illustrate the potential impact of truncation on our knowledge-base. If this site had been discovered in an area subjected to heavy ploughing these three buildings would appear as a granary, a few isolated post holes and a refuse pit showing metalworking activity. However, even when two thirds of the information on the spatial organization of the buildings might have disappeared, the artisan activity on the site might still be identified.

9.3 The evidence for the Early Iron Age

The combination of past work, and the growth in the evidence base over the last two decades provides us with a range of evidence for the Early Iron Age occupation of the study area. This ranges across both settlement and funerary evidence, which will be reviewed briefly before turning to a more general synthesis of occupation during this period.

9.3.1 Hilltop sites

From the beginning of the 20th century, local scholars compiled the first inventories and made the first site plans of hilltop dwellings that survived as earthworks visible on the surface. On many sites, trenches were also dug in order to understand the architecture of the ramparts. In the 1960s these settlements became the focus of research

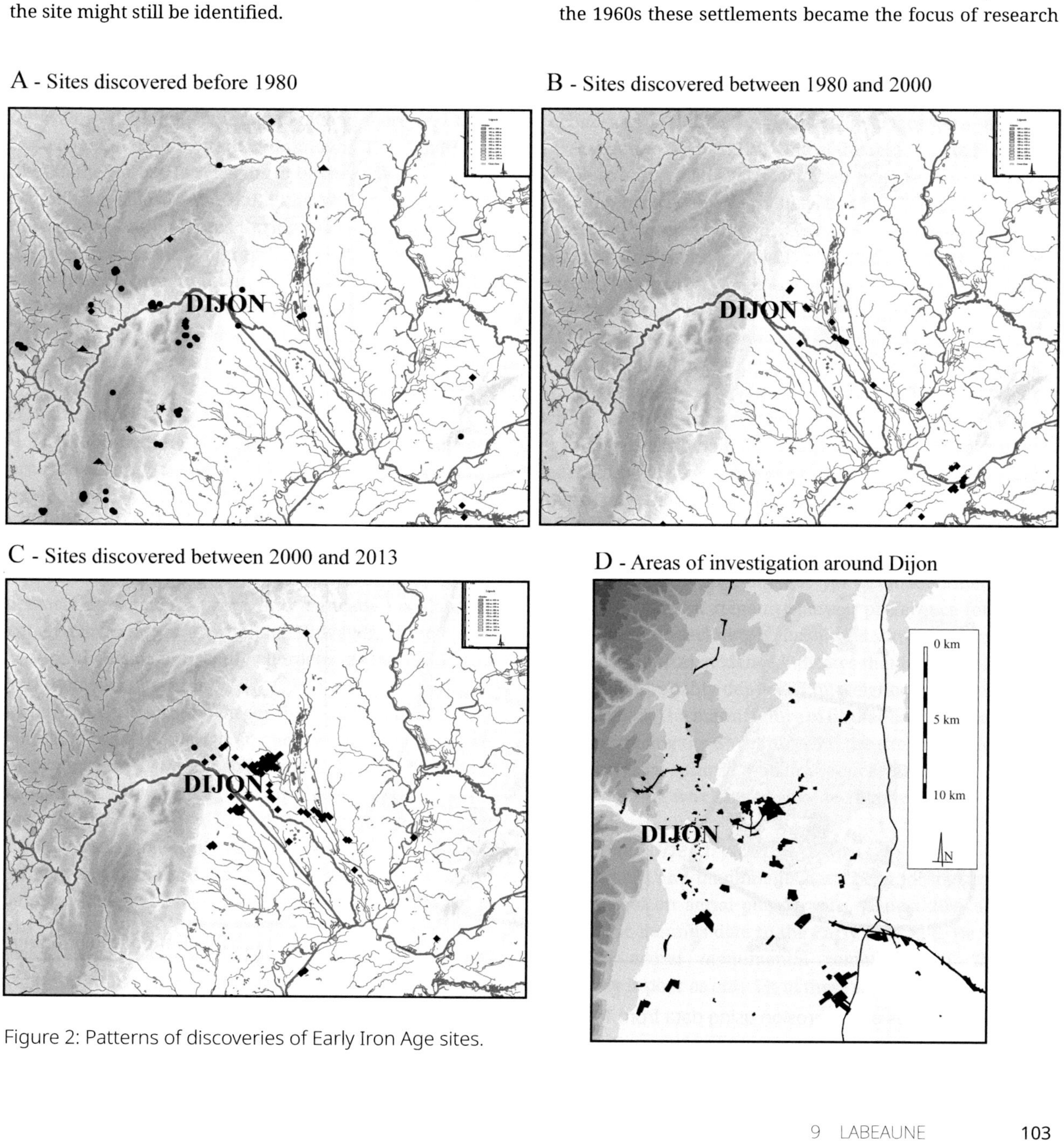

Figure 2: Patterns of discoveries of Early Iron Age sites.

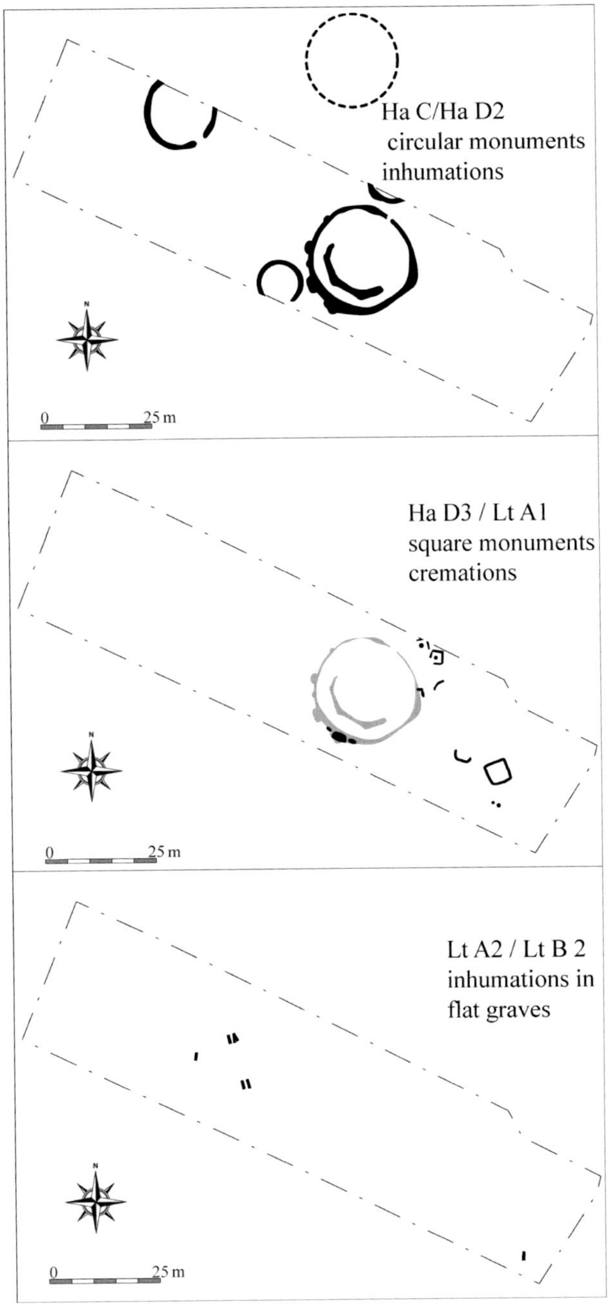

Figure 6: Evolution of the Genlis cemetery illustrating the continuity of funerary sites.

The development of aerial reconnaissance and photography has transformed our archaeological knowledge of the Saône plain and its tributaries. One of the most studied cemeteries in the area is Genlis discovered during aerial reconnaissance and excavated during construction of the railway line to the east of Dijon (Figure 6). It comprises three circular ditches and six small quadrangular enclosures with six inhumations and two cremation burials located around the monuments. Two of the smaller circular ditches with diameters of 6 and 10 m have gaps in the ditches on the south-east. Four supplementary burials were discovered in the ditch of the largest monument confirming that the funerary space was extended. A burial sealing the ditch fill contained small iron toiletry objects dating to the Ha D3/LT A1. In the 5th century, funerary monuments change as the circular ditches with inhumations are replaced by quadrangular ditched monuments measuring less than 5.5 m across and containing cremation burials. More recent burials that date to the LT A2 and LT B, are found around these monuments showing a continuity in the use of the cemetery. As is the case for the tumuli, these cemeteries remained in use for around three centuries.

9.4 A synthesis of land occupation

Most of the archaeological data from Eastern Burgundy comes from the area around Dijon and the synthesis of occupation from the 9th to the 3rd century BC is mainly focused on this area. The interpretations are based on work carried out during the last 30 years within the framework of preventive archaeology, taking account also of older discoveries.

In the second half of the 9th century, the density of sites in the area seems to be low and only a few can be dated to the Ha B3 (Figure 7a). The two known settlements in the Dijon area are characterised by post-hole buildings, large extraction pits, granaries and storage pits, though the excavations were not extensive enough to show how the sites were organised. However, the series of features that extend over an area of more than 10 hectares indicate a dispersed organisation of settlements, the question being whether these features belong to several smaller settlements or to one large settlement equivalent to the lakeside dwellings (Billaud *et al.* 1993). The finds from Varanges provide an excellent reference for regional pottery production of the Ha B3 similar to pottery from the east of France or from the west of Switzerland. Cemeteries are rare and only two areas have produced burials of this period. The first is the Longvic cemetery (Goguey 1984) and the second is an isolated cremation burial in a simple pit (Bressey-sur-Tille). The date of the latter burial is based on the pottery used to cover the cremation which dates to the end of the 11th century BC. It is impossible to propose any kind of spatial organisation for these discoveries, but they indicate that settlements were mainly located in the valleys of the river Tilles and the river Ouche.

During the Hallstatt C1, the area of the Ouche plain appears to be completely abandoned. However, the northeast of the Dijon agglomeration is heavily occupied with the presence of at least six settlements (Figure 7b). These contain small units located at regular distances over the area. Their surface areas are less than 2000m^2 and in most cases they are characterised by the presence of large

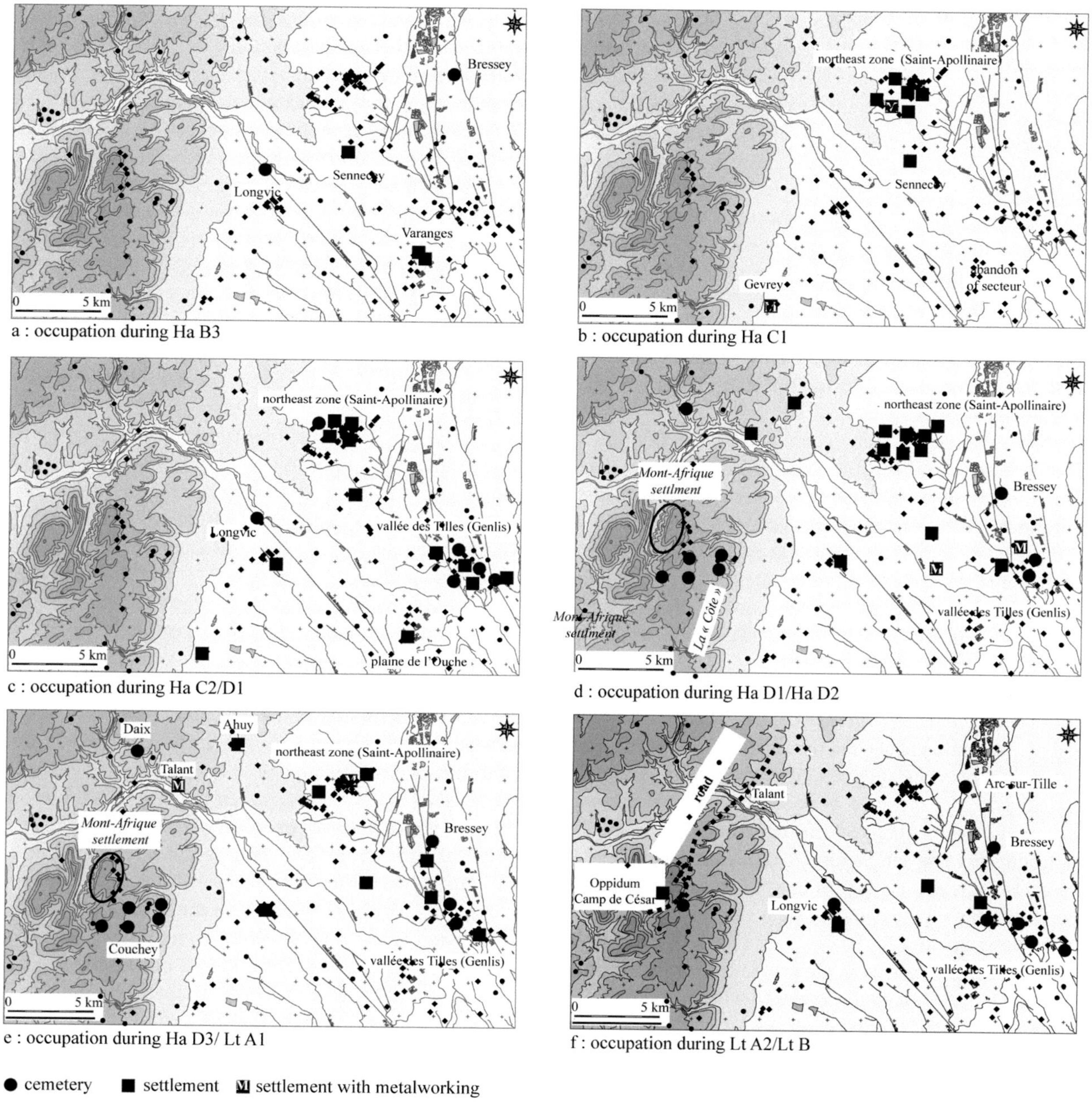

Figure 7: Proposed development of spatial occupation in the Dijon area.

extraction pits used for building materials (then refilled with refuse that contains many pottery sherds). Storage areas are located on the eastern periphery of these farms. Two other settlements have been identified in the Dijon area at Sennecey-les-Dijon, a small farmstead which seems to correspond to the relocation of an earlier Ha B3 farm located 300 m away. The second was discovered at Gevrey-Chambertin during an evaluation, but investigations did not go far enough to better characterise the site. The identification of bronze metalworking in one of the pits indicated the proximity of a building, perhaps a workshop. Evidence of metalworking dating to this period is rare and was not observed on the Saint Appolinaire site even though a clay mould fragment was found in a pit. Archaeobotanical study indicates that these settlements are mainly agricultural installations. No cemeteries have been discovered that are directly linked to these settlements.

During the Hallstatt C2 the density of land occupation increases (Figure 7c). To the northeast of the area, settlements are displaced towards the east to form a new concentration of buildings that extends over 1 km². This seems to be the result of regrouping several small farmsteads along a river. The distance between the settlements is too great to be able to define this organisation as a village. Other settlements gradually colonise the Tilles valley. They are most often made up of a main building with silos and granaries and can cover an area smaller than 2500m². As is the case for settlements, the number of cemeteries also increases, as six funerary sites have been identified in the area. Only one inhumation with a bronze sword discovered in the Longvic cemetery was already in use during the Ha B3 (two circular monuments), and can be dated to the Hallstatt C2. This cemetery does not seem to have been used during the Hallstatt C1, but this chronological hiatus could be the result of the lack of extensive excavation around the cemetery. In total eight circular ditched monuments have been identified from aerial photographs and only three have been excavated. Monuments with several ditches have also been identified at three sites in the Tilles valley. It is not sure when the monuments were built but the ditches were filled in during the Hallstatt D2. By comparison the doubled ditched monuments of the middle Tille valley are built during this period.

In the late 7th century and early 6th century BC (early Hallstatt D1) land occupation of the plain becomes denser with the founding of several new settlements (Figure 7c). As in the previous periods, the principal activity is agriculture. The distance between the farmsteads and the cemeteries is about 500 m, which could mean that each funerary site can be directly linked to a settlement. Unfortunately, archaeological investigation on the linear developments only gave an insight into a small area of these funerary sites. To the north-east the settlements are located in the same area as the previous period. The only funerary feature is a double cremation burial dated to Ha C2/D1 by radiocarbon analysis. The Tille valley and the northeast of Dijon are the areas that are the most densely occupied during the first half of the Hallstatt DA. The rest of the Dijon area has a lower density of occupation and the Ouche valley is reoccupied after being abandoned for over two centuries. This hiatus could be linked to flooding of the area.

During the second half of the Hallstatt D1 is easier attribute chronology to excavated remains even though pottery forms evolve slowly. In addition, the fibulae start to appear on settlements during this period and are good chronological markers. However, it is still necessary to group together Ha D1 and D2 as this is a short period difficult to identify in settlement contexts. The north-eastern area of Dijon is still densely occupied by at least seven settlements (Figure 7d). These farmsteads double in size to an area of about 5000m². There are higher numbers of four post granaries and silos, as storing cereals remains a major activity. Settlements in this area are located about 1 km apart. In the Tilles plain the monumental cemeteries are still in use as long term funerary sites that extend over several generations. Settlements move around but stay close to the cemeteries. The Bressey-sur-Tille tumulus is somewhat different with 114 inhumations and six cremations – a large cemetery founded in the 6th century and remaining in use for two centuries. Several cemeteries containing stone tumuli located on the 'Côte' are founded during this period. They occupy this area and the plateau at the foot of the '*Mont-Afrique*', which were not occupied until this period.

Many fibulae have been discovered in Corcelles-les-Monts, which indicate the presence of a large settlement over eight hectares. This could be a hilltop clustered settlement that dominated the Dijon area. During the Ha D2 metalworking appears in several small settlements (Figure 7d). On these sites bronze (*e.g.* crucibles, clay moulds, cast metal) and iron (slag, shafts and bars) are worked together in the same installations. This remains still a rare activity in the Dijon area.

In Hallstatt D3 the tumuli founded during the previous period remain in use (Figure 7e). This is the case at Couchey, at Bressey-sur-Tille and at Daix where surrounding burials have been identified. However, in the Tilles plain funerary practices change and inhumation is replaced by cremation. The large circular ditched monuments are abandoned for smaller quadrangular monuments built to enclose simple cremation burials. These changes were in progress since the Ha C2/D1 on funerary sites in use for long periods. The number of settlements decreases but they are larger with a greater storage capacity (*e.g.* Ahuy where the storage pits are the main features found on the site). The number of granaries also increases and these are located on the outskirts of the farmsteads. Finds of timbal shaped fibulae on the '*Mont Afrique*' indicate that the site was still in use during this period. Metalworking has been identified at Saint Apollinaire but with its three forges, Talant has been identified as the main metalworking site of the area.

From the second half of the 5th century (La Tène A) occupation in the Dijon area is mainly represented by cemeteries and isolated inhumations (Figure 7f). The Bressey-sur-Tille tumulus is still in use and Dux type fibulae are found in the most recent tombs. At Genlis the flat graves are located between earlier circular and quadrangular monuments. Cremation is again replaced by inhumation but older cemeteries continue to be used. The inhumations are often at the centre of large quadrangular ditched monuments such as at Longvic or circular monuments such as at Arc-sur-Tille. These clan or family cemeteries are abandoned during the La Tène B.

The organisation of settlements is not easily observed as sites become rarer. Only three settlements dating to this later period have been excavated. These farmsteads have large storage areas (granaries and silos). The disposition of cemeteries can provide indications of occupation patterns but again it is difficult with so little information to propose a coherent model. The cemeteries are located in the valleys along the rivers. At Talant a road dating to the first half of the 5th century overlies the settlement dated by La Tène B fibulae. The first occupations on the '*Mont-Afrique*' appear during this period. The Talant road could provide the means of transport between the '*Mont Afrique*' and the plain via the river valleys. From the end of La Tène B indications of occupation become rarer and seem to finally disappear. This absence could however be linked to a change in the forms of sites or a change in the type of remains, with a reduced visibility in the archaeological record.

9.5 Conclusion

This first comparative approach drawing together recent evidence from preventive archaeology projects shows the diversity of occupation mainly at the end of the 6th and the beginning of the 5th century BC, a period during which princely or high status seats develop (Milcent 2012). One of the criteria that characterises this trend is the founding of a hilltop settlement or a centralised seat of power. However, in the Dijon area, most of the excavated settlements are small farmsteads. The increase in the number of sites during the Early Iron Age is linked to the multiplication of farming communities in the area. The scarceness of Mediterranean imports on these sites indicates that they did not engage in long distance exchange in order to support their communities.

Talant « *la Peute Combe* » does not however fall into this category of sites. This suburb of artisans is exclusively given over to the manufacture of small bronze and iron objects. The high degree of specialisation means that the site relied on at least one or two other settlements to distribute its products. The number of fibulae in the Dijon area is high and indicates that the consumer sites have not yet been discovered and that they could be located near to the workshops. A similar organisation is found in Bourges where the workshops are located about 2 km from the princely settlement (Augier *et al.* 2012). The same organisation appears in Lyon (Ramponi 2009; Carrara 2009) and the Heuneburg where the artisan quarters are on the outskirts of the fortified settlement (Kurtz 2012).

Comparing the Dijon sector with neighbouring areas during the Early Iron Age leads us to believe that there was a major site in this area located on the hilltops near to Talant (Labeaune 2016). This secondary economic power base probably administered the increasing number of small agricultural settlements that gravitated around the Dijon area during this period.

9.6 Acknowledgments

I am grateful to my colleague Rebecca Peake for translating my French text into English.

9.7 Bibliography

Augier, L., Buchsenschutz, O., Durand, R., Filippini, A., Germinet, D., Macon, P., Pauly, S., Pescher, B., Ralston, I., Roure, R., Salin, M., Tichit, A. & Vanniere, B. 2009. *Un complexe princier de l'âge du Fer : le quartier de Port Sec sud à Bourges (Cher)*, volume 1: Analyse des structures et du mobilier, BITURIGA, Monographie 2012-1. Bourges/Tours: Bourges Plus, Service d'archéologie préventive et FERAC.

Billaud, Y., Marguet, A. & Simonin, O. 1993. Chindrieux, Châtillon (lac du Bourget, Savoie): ultime occupation des lacs alpins français à l'Age du Bronze? *Actes du 116e Congrès national des Société savantes, Chambéry, 1991*. 277-310. Paris: Comité des travaux historiques et Scientifiques.

Carrara, S., with Maza, G. & Rottier, S. 2009. L'agglomération urbaine de Lyon-Vaise (Rhône) à la fin du VIe siècle et au Ve siècle avant J.-C.: bilan des découvertes. In Buchsenschutz, O. (dir.). *L'âge du Fer dans la boucle de la Loire. Les gaulois sont dans la ville*. Paris-Tours: Actes du XXXIIe colloque AFEAF.

Goguey, R. 1984. Les enclos protohistoriques de Longvic-les-Dijon. *In Transition Bronze final-Hallstatt ancien : problèmes chronologiques et culturels*. In actes du 109e Congrès national des Société Savantes, Dijon 1984. Paris: Comité des travaux historiques et scientifiques, 1984, 59-66 (Section archéologie et d'histoire de l'art ; tome 2).

Kurtz, S. 2012. La Heuburg. Etat des dernières recherches. In Sievers, S. & Schönfelder, M. *La question de la proto-urbanisation à l'âge du Fer*, Actes du 34e colloque international de l'Afeaf, 13-16 mai 2010, *R.G.Z.M.* 2012, 15-27.

Labeaune, R. & Wiethold, J. 2007. L'habitat du Premier Âge du Fer dans le Dijonnais, d'après les fouilles récentes: résultats archéologiques et carpologiques. In *L'âge du fer dans l'arc jurassien et ses marges (est de la France Suisse, sud de l'Allemagne), dépôts, lieux sacrés et territorialité à l'âge du Fer*. Actes du 29e colloque international de l'A.F.E.A.F. (Bienne, 5-8 mai 2005), Annales littéraires, Série « Environnement, sociétés et archéologie, Besançon » Presses Universitaires de Franche-Comté, 2 vol., 2007, 73-100 (Supplément *A.L.U.B.* ; 11).

Labeaune, L. & Alix, S. 2014. *Découvertes d'un établissement rural gallo-romain et d'un hameau à vocation artisanale du Ve siècle avant J.-C., rapport d'opération de fouille archéologique*. Inrap, 5 volumes.

Labeaune, R., Berranger, M., Dubreucq, E. & Dunikowski, C. 2017. *Les chaînes opératoires de production dans les forges hallstattiennes de Talant « La Peute Combe »*

(Côte d'Or). Dans actes du XXXIX° colloque de l'Afeaf de Nancy, production et proto-industrialisation aux âges du Fer, 2015, 383-402.

Labeaune, R. 2016. *Céramique, habitat et territoires au premier âge du Fer en Bourgogne orientale (du VIIIe au Ve siècle avant J.-C.)*. Thèse de doctorat, Ecole Pratique des Hautes Etudes.

Milcent, J.Y., 2012. Résidence aristocratiques et expérience urbaine hallstattiennes en France (VIe -Ve siècle av. J. -C.). In Sievers, S. & Schönfelder, M. (eds). *La question de la proto-urbanisation à l'âge du Fer*. 91-113. Actes du 34e colloque internationnal de l'Afeaf, 13-16 mai 2010, *R.G.Z.M.* 2012.

Malrain, F., Matterne, V., Meniel, P. & Pinard, E. 2005. *De l'intérêt des grands décapages. Les fermes des VIe et Ve siècles avant notre ère de Verberie (Oise)*. R.A.P. Numéro spécial 22, 2005. 175-82.

Nicolardot, J.-P. 2003. *L'habitat fortifié pré-et-protohistorique en Côte d'Or. Les camps de Myard à Vitteaux et du Châtelet d'Etaules dans le contexte archéologique régional (du Ve millénaire au IVe siècle avant J.-C.)*. Dijon: R.A.E., 2003 (Supplément R.A.E. 19).

Ramponi, C. 2009. L'occupation du sol dans l'est lyonnais de la fin de l'âge du Bronze à la fin de l'âge du Fer. In *La moyenne vallée du Rhône aux âges du Fer*, actes du XXXe colloque international de l'AFEAF, co-organisé avec l'APRAB (Saint-Romain-en-Gal ; 26-29 mai 2006). 143-64.

Ratel, R. 1977. *Un tumulus de l'Age du Fer à Bressey-sur-Tille (Côte d'Or), Dijon, 1977*. (supplément R.A.E. 2).

PART 2

SETTLEMENT UNITS AND BUILDINGS

Chapter 10

The chronology of wetland settlement and its impact on Iron Age settlement dynamics in southwest Scotland

Graeme Cavers & Anne Crone

10.1 Introduction

The limited capacity of radiocarbon dating to resolve intra-site chronologies to a level where individual building durations can be defined from typically multi-phase settlements of the Scottish earlier Iron Age has severely hampered discussion of settlement dynamics. These settlements typically comprise enclosed and unenclosed round houses in a variety of forms, recognised in a range of contexts from earthworks surviving in uplands, to plough-truncated sites in improved ground and often well-preserved monuments in wetlands (Harding 2004). Even where sufficient suitable radiocarbon samples might be obtained from excavated contexts uncertainty over sample provenance and a general lack of clear stratigraphy on dryland sites means that even on sites with numerous superimposed roundhouses (*e.g.* Banks 2000; Ellis 2007), chronology is poorly defined across the later 1st millennium BC. Progress is being made through the application of Bayesian statistics to dryland datasets (*i.e.* Hamilton 2016) but wetland sites still offer the best prospect of chronological resolution.

Archaeological sites located in wetlands have long held out the promise of precise chronological resolution because the wood with which they were constructed, so well-preserved by the waterlogged conditions, could potentially be dated by dendrochronology. The value of multiple precisely dated sites in understanding settlement dynamics has been ably demonstrated by the multi-disciplinary work on the Neolithic and Bronze Age lake dwellings of the circum-Alpine region of central Europe where it now appears possible to track individual communities across the landscape (Menotti 2012, 151-4).

In Scotland, the crannog is the archetypal wetland site; commonly defined as an artificially constructed island with a settlement on top, they can be found scattered throughout Scotland wherever there were suitable lochs, although there appears to be a distinct western distribution, perhaps enhanced by research foci in southwest Scotland, Argyll and Perthshire (see *e.g.* Cavers 2010, 36; Stratigos 2016).

Although very few crannogs have been extensively excavated, a sizeable dataset of radiocarbon dates has been assembled which indicates that from the 1st millennium BC to at least the 16th century AD there were intermittent episodes of crannog building activity (Crone 2012; Stratigos & Noble 2017). The later prehistoric period saw the most intensive use of crannogs, with 71% of all the dated sites falling within the period 850 BC-AD 200

In D.C. Cowley, M. Fernández-Götz, T. Romankiewicz & H. Wendling (eds). Rural Settlement. Relating buildings, landscape, and people in the European Iron Age (Leiden 2019: Sidestone Press) 115-124.

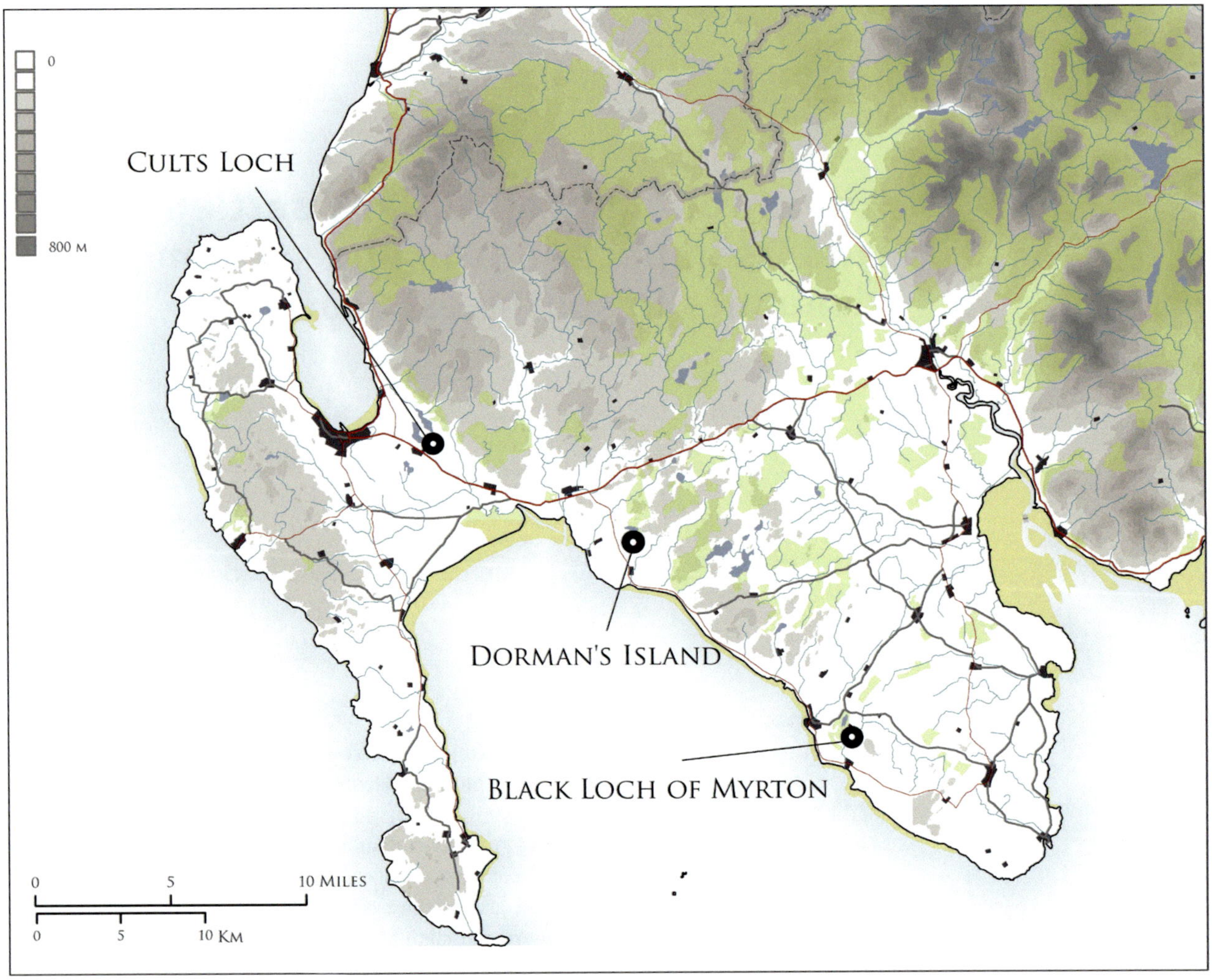

Figure 1: Map of southwest Scotland showing the location of wetland sites mentioned in the text.

(Crone 2012, 152-3). In Loch Tay, Perthshire, for example, nine of the 13 dated crannogs in the loch were in use during the period 800-400 BC; such a cluster immediately raises a query about the relationship between the crannogs (and ultimately the sites around the shores of the loch), and with this query comes issues of contemporaneity, settlement duration, why they were built and why they were eventually abandoned. However, without further chronological resolution these questions and therefore the settlement dynamics of the area cannot be adequately addressed (these issues are now being tackled by the *Living on Water* project – www.livingonwater.scot and Stratigos *et al.* 2018). Previous syntheses of crannog data have made inroads into identifying regional and national patterns but have suffered from the imprecision of C14 dates in the Halstatt plateau, which act to spread what may be related episodes of short-lived activity over several centuries.

In southwest Scotland, however, a decade of excavation of later prehistoric wetland sites is beginning to pay dividends in terms of chronological resolution. Three sites have now been excavated as part of the Scottish Wetland Archaeology Programme (Figure 1) and the growing dendrochronological evidence is beginning to suggest that, rather than a spread of crannog-building activity across the 1st millennium BC, there were very specific times during the millennium when wetland living was favoured. In this paper we present the chronological evidence and look at its implications for settlement dynamics at the national and regional but also human scales.

10.2 The chronological evidence

10.2.1 Cults Loch 3 (Stranraer, Galloway)

Cults Loch 3 is a low artificial island which lies only 18 m from the shore of the small loch within which it is located (Cavers & Crone 2017). It was initially connected to the shore by a timber causeway; over time sediments built up around the causeway and were also added to it, so that the

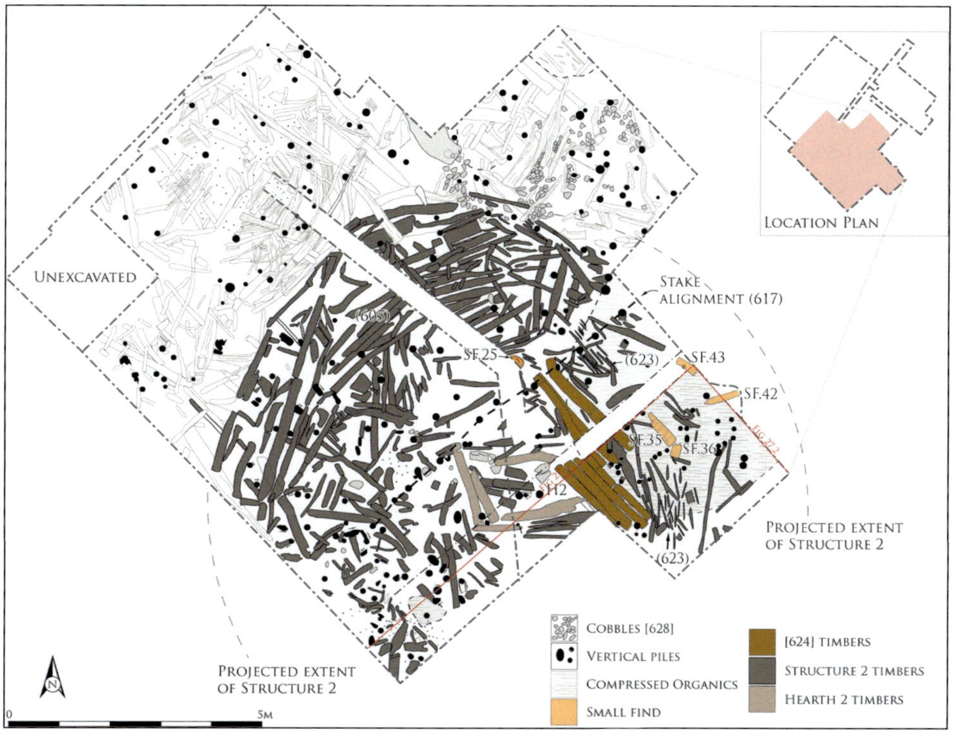

Figure 2: Structure 2 at Cults Loch 3; plan (top) and image during excavation (bottom).

site now survives as a small promontory projecting into the loch. The poorly-preserved remains of three structures, at least two of which were roundhouses (Figure 2), were found on the crannog; these had been occupied sequentially, the footprint of each house overlapping the other. The evidence for a defensive perimeter around the settlement is ambiguous; a thick deposit of carbonised hazel and willow roundwood near the edge of the crannog may have been the remains of a light wattle fence, while oak planks found to either side of the junction between causeway and crannog may represent the collapsed remains of walling flanking the entrance onto the crannog.

The excavation yielded a small assemblage of structural oak timbers from various phases in the development of the crannog, of which nine were incorporated into a dated site chronology. None of the dated timbers retained the bark edge and therefore an absolute felling date could not be obtained, but several retained some sapwood and a felling range between 438 BC and 412 BC was calculated (Figure 3). Bayesian analysis of wiggle-match dates from sampled timbers indicates that there was only about 30 years between the construction of the two roundhouses (Jacobsson *et al.* 2018), a duration also supported by dendrochronological analysis of alder timbers from the structures. Thus, we have identified building activity in the latter half of the 5th century BC which comprised at least two phases of house building and occupation which probably lasted for no more than half a century. A single oak pile from the causeway was also dendrochronologically dated to 193 BC. The third structure did not yield any datable timbers but a radiocarbon date from floor deposits in the structure spans the 4th to 2nd centuries BC and may therefore be associated with the early 2nd century BC causeway construction.

10.2.2 Dorman's Island (Glenluce, Galloway)

Dorman's Island is also artificial but lies further out in the water than Cults Loch 3; the modern shoreline has encroached on it but the rough causeway or 'ford' of large boulders which connected it to the shore was some 45 m long (Cavers *et al.* 2011, Figure 2). High water levels prevented extensive excavation but in a small trench in the middle of the island, floors of clay, compacted plant litter and cleft oak timbers, piles and small alignments of stakes indicated the presence of a building – the trench probably lay within the interior of the building so its overall structure remains unknown. A site chronology of seven timbers, six from the oak floor and a pile, was constructed. The timbers in the floor had been felled sometime between 153 BC and 121 BC; the pile (Figure 3 – T1), with a *tpq* of 144 BC, could also belong to the same phase of construction but it had been heavily trimmed so it remains possible that it might have been inserted at a slightly later date. Radiocarbon dates from the piles, stakes and floor deposits span the 4th to 1st centuries BC while glass beads and a shard of Roman glass found in the topsoil indicate later activity on the crannog, probably in the 1st/2nd century AD.

10.2.3 Black Loch of Myrton (Port William, Galloway)

The settlement at Black Loch of Myrton is a somewhat different type of site, previously unknown or unrecognised in Scotland (Crone & Cavers 2016). It sits on a low island of peat within what would probably have been a fen marsh surrounding a small, shallow loch at the time of occupation, joined to the shore by a short natural causeway. There is no evidence for an artificial or even partially modified substructure to the island so it is not a crannog in the strict sense; it has variously been referred to as a loch village or island settlement. The site is highly stratified and the deposits and structures well-preserved; consequently, after four seasons of excavation, a substantial dataset of dendrochronological- and radiocarbon-dated material exists.

The current phasing for the site, based on the chronological and stratigraphic evidence, suggests that there were at least two, possibly three major episodes of construction and occupation on the island. In Episode 1 a cluster of three roundhouses were constructed in the northern half of the island, defended by a palisade of closely-set alder posts. The chronological evidence for this episode is the most detailed. Structure 2, the best-preserved of the roundhouses so far excavated, was constructed using oak posts to support the roof and massive oak planks forming a double-skinned facade on either side of a monumental entranceway (Figure 4). These oaks have yielded a 363-year chronology which demonstrates that most of the oaks cleft to make the planks were felled in 435 BC. A few trees were felled a year to 18 months earlier over the winter of 437/436 BC, indicating a degree of planning and stockpiling in advance of construction (Figure 3). None of the oaks used in neighbouring Structure 1 had retained the bark edge but a felling range of 461-429 BC straddles the exact felling year for Structure 2, while analysis of the hazel, ash and alder assemblages from both structures shows that they were all felled in the same year, so the two buildings are almost certainly contemporary.

There is no physical evidence in Structure 2 that any of the superstructure, *i.e.* the double-skinned outer wall and the inner post-rings, was ever replaced or refurbished – there are no duplicate posts or stakes along either circuit, for instance. However, inside the roundhouse, the floor surfaces, the central hearths and the entrance structure had all been replaced three times. A sequence of 22 radiocarbon dates was obtained from the sequence of floors and hearth deposits and, together with the dendrochronological evidence, this assemblage has been subject to Bayesian analysis. This suggests that Structure 2 was occupied for 40 years at most (D. Hamilton pers comm.). Thus, we have evidence at Black Loch of Myrton for an episode of settlement beginning in 435 BC and lasting until about 400 BC.

The later episodes are currently defined primarily by radiocarbon dates and cannot yet be separated into discrete phases. In Episode 2, the settlement moved into the southern half of the island, with at least one roundhouse built over the disused Episode 1 palisade. In the later episodes multiple concentric palisades were built around the southern edge of the island and several structures containing ovens and associated deposits were built just inside the defences. The palisades and

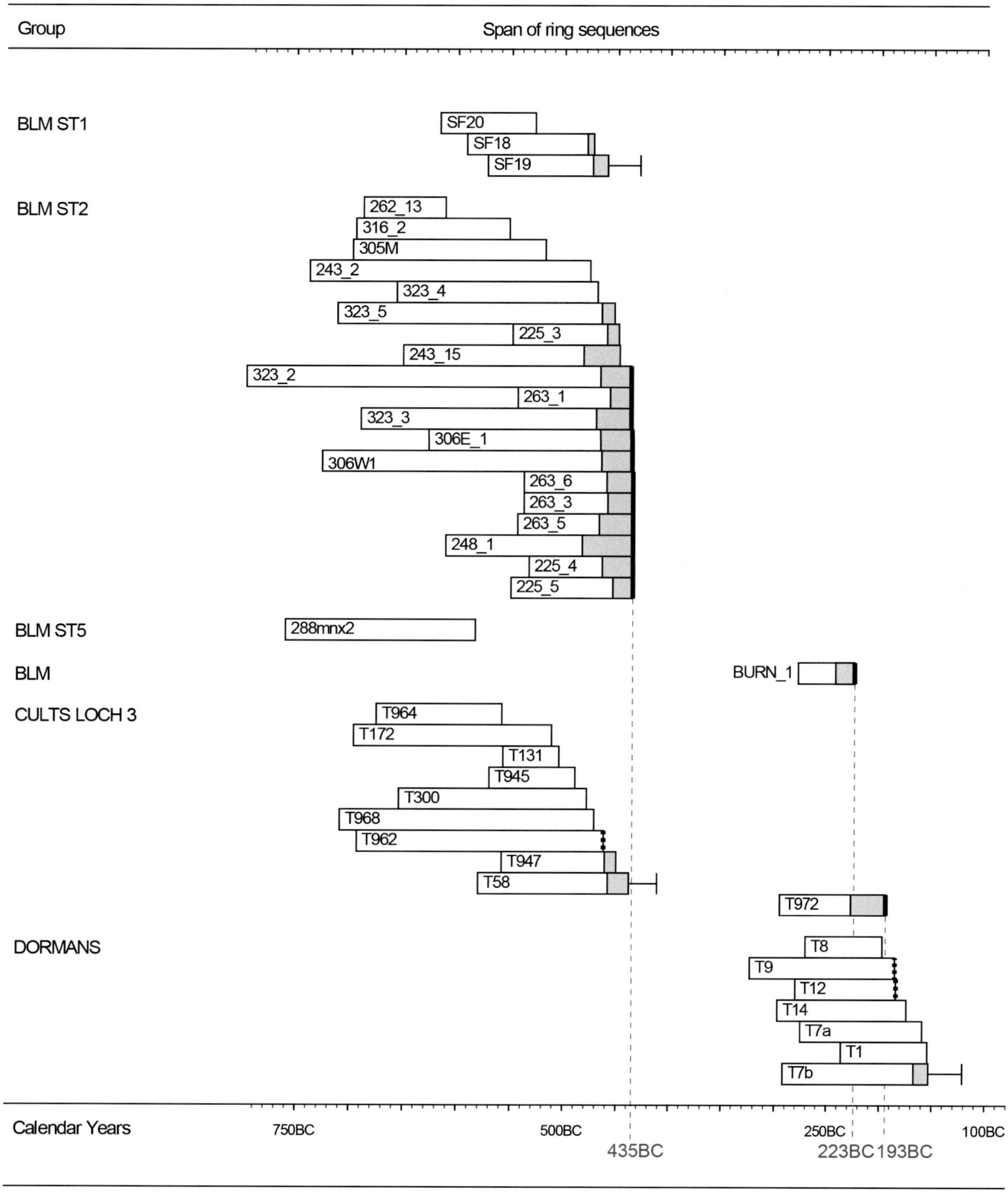

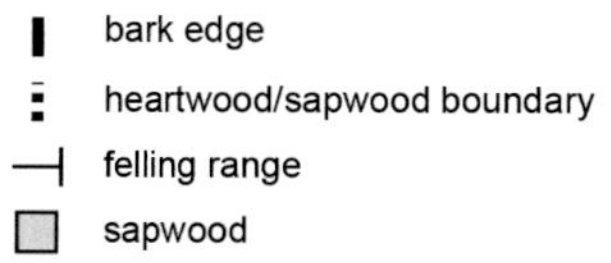

Figure 3: Bar diagram showing the chronological relationships between the dendro-dated timbers from the excavated sites.

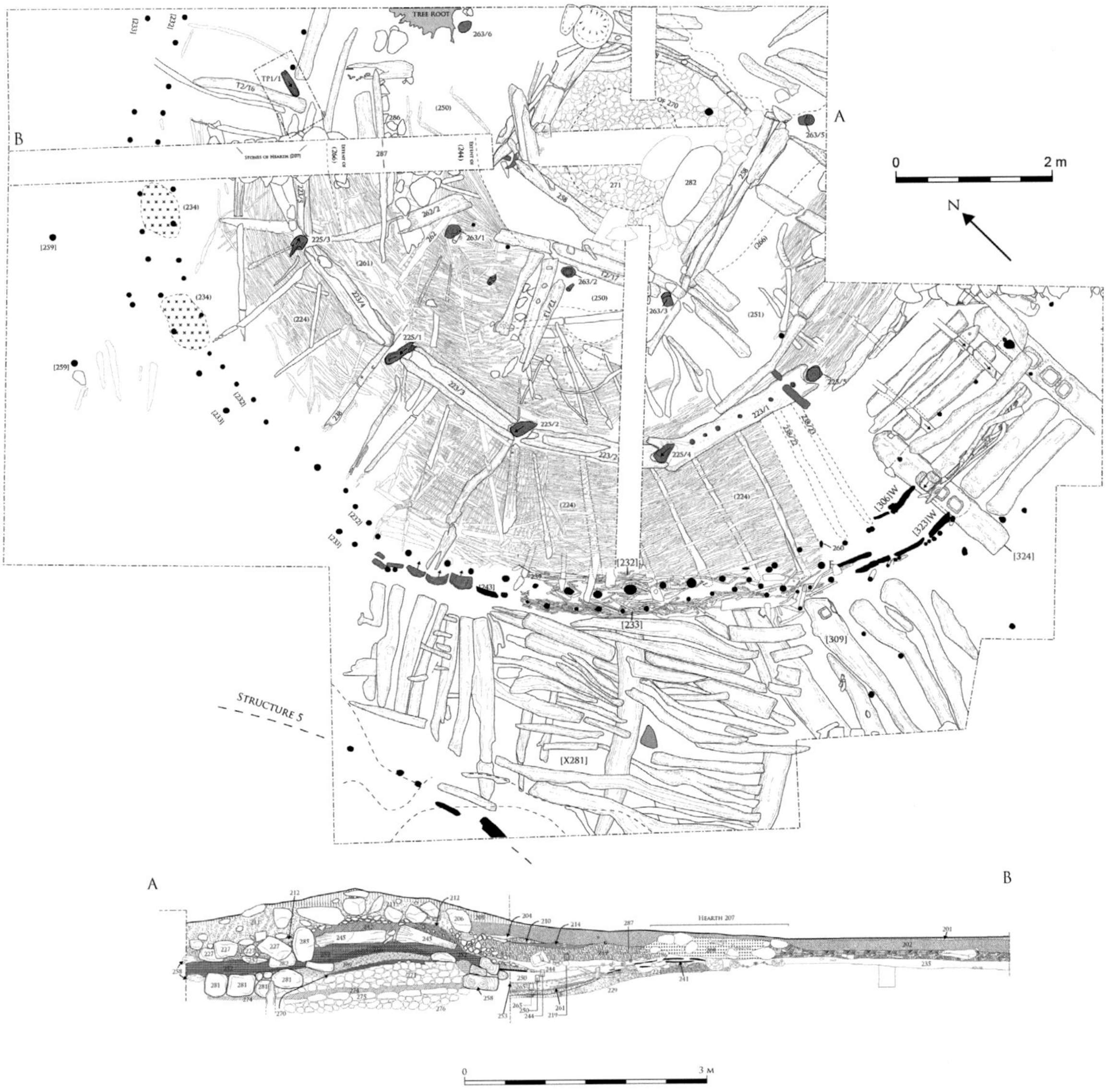

Figure 4: Structure 2 at the Black Loch of Myrton; plan (above) and section through the hearth sequence (below).

structures have all produced radiocarbon dates spanning the late 5th to early 2nd centuries BC, including the outermost palisade which consists of a line of massive oak planks. These timbers, which have not yet been analysed, promise to deliver dendrochronological dates for this episode which may help to resolve the issue of continuity of settlement on the island. A large oak post found in isolation on the southern periphery of the island has produced a dendrochronological date of 223 BC, so it is feasible that all the chronological evidence will cluster around this date. Currently we do not know whether the island was abandoned between Episodes 1 and 2, or whether settlement moved southwards immediately upon abandonment of the northern cluster of houses.

10.3 Wetland sites as part of wider changes in Scottish Iron Age settlement patterns

The dendrochronology dates from these three wetland sites mean that we can now move from the very general statement made earlier that 'the later prehistoric period saw the most intensive use of crannogs…' to identifying spikes or horizons of crannog-building activity in southwest Scotland. These concentrate in the latter half of the 5th century BC at Cults Loch 3 and Black Loch of Myrton, and in the late 3rd/2nd century BC at all three sites. Other crannogs in southwest Scotland with radiocarbon dates which could place them in one or other of these embryonic horizons include the White Loch of Myrton,

Barhapple, Loch Arthur, Loch Heron I and II, Milton Loch 1 and 2 (Crone 2012, Table 1). In other words, the data is beginning to suggest that the overall chronology of wetland settlements in the wider area may not be uniform through time. If these horizons are indeed real (and the database is still admittedly small) then they suggest that in certain specific periods in later prehistory settlements were built in wetlands and lochs across Scotland (including the Western and Northern Isles) perhaps in relation to changing environmental or socio-political circumstances (Crone 2012, 163-4). As such, the decision to relocate settlement to a new environment seems strikingly coterminous with other major changes in the settlement record. Recent modelling of radiocarbon chronologies has indicated that many defended settlements enter newly monumental phases in the 5th/4th century BC (*e.g.* Armit & McKenzie 2013, 496), while in the north and west, the origins of broch construction may yet be pushed back to a similar horizon (and are already known to be in the range 390-200 BC at Scatness, Dockrill *et al.* 2015, 45) The precise date and duration of this horizon cannot yet be reliably placed, given the low number of closely dated sites, but it may yet be found to be restricted to a very short calendar range as more high precision dates are applied to suitably stratified sites. Nonetheless, the overriding impression is that the proliferation of wetland settlement in the Early Iron Age can be tied to a much wider pattern where new emphasis is placed on the impression of defence and display in settlement architecture, albeit that the causes of this pattern may be complex. Whether driven by economic, political or religious motivation, however, the impression of the 5th/4th century BC in southern Scotland is one of insecurity, instability and change; investigation of the causes and effects of this instability must be a major new priority for Iron Age research. It may not be coincidental that Bayesian modelling of radiocarbon data from settlement sites in the Tyne-Forth region has identified a horizon of rectilinear enclosure which begins at the end of the 3rd century BC (Hamilton 2016, 237), at exactly the same time that wetland settlement appears to become popular again in southwest Scotland (Crone 2012). Rectilinear enclosures are also a component of the settlement record of southwest Scotland; the only excavated example at Rispain Camp (Haggarty & Haggarty 1983, 40) is poorly dated but could conceivably be related to fundamental stylistic changes in settlement character which saw the resurgence of crannog use after an apparent hiatus.

10.4 Wetland sites as part of Iron Age settlement at the local scale

The dendrochronological dates mean we can now examine 'real-time' chronological relationships locally between sites for the first time. Cults Loch 3 and Black Loch of Myrton are near-contemporary; if they were not constructed in the same year then Cults Loch 3 was constructed within a decade or so after Black Loch of Myrton. The significance of this is that, rather than representing evolving site types, as they might hitherto have been interpreted, the crannog and the island settlement, which lie only 30 km apart, can be seen as different architectural expressions of the same society. What this suggests is that it was all-important for some section of society to live out in the wetlands, in whatever type of settlement they could build, be it on a natural island or on a man-made island.

The other significant issue that is emerging with greater clarity is that of duration and the intermittent, discontinuous nature of settlement. At both Cults Loch 3 and Black Loch of Myrton we have been able to demonstrate that the houses had lifespans of little more than a single generation. And even within that lifespan the houses may not have been continuously occupied; there is evidence for abandonment between phases at Cults Loch 3 and at both sites the repeated cleaning and resurfacing of the floors observed in all the structures may represent a form of spring-cleaning when returning to the crannog on an episodic basis (Cavers & Crone 2018, 92). When the occupant group was not living on their wetland settlements, where were they living instead? At Cults Loch, Bayesian analysis of the chronological evidence from the excavated sites around the loch suggests that occupation of the sites could have been sequential, occupants from the palisaded enclosure on the shore moving out onto the crannog and then back to the enclosure (Cavers & Crone 2018, 241). The roundhouses within the palisaded enclosure displayed no evidence of repair or refurbishment so they may also have been occupied for a similarly short duration. At Black Loch of Myrton, it is clear that the initial settlement was short-lived but until we have dendrochronological dates for the second episode of occupation, we can only speculate that the occupant community moved off the island and into one of the numerous settlements in the area, before returning onto the island at a later date.

The integrated chronology from Cults Loch (Hamilton & Krus 2018), together with the increasing evidence for short duration and discontinuity of settlement in one particular locus suggests the more fluid movement of communities across the landscape. Around the Alpine lakes the concept of the *Siedlungskammer* (defined as a settlement area) has been employed to model Neolithic and Bronze Age settlement dynamics (Ebersbach 2013, 294-5), and it is a concept that might usefully be applied to Iron Age southwest Scotland. Within the *Siedlungskammer* settlements are highly dynamic but the definition of the settlement area, or territory, remains durable over long periods of time. The implication for the settlement record is of fewer people moving more frequently within defined territories. Patterns of short occupation durations for dryland sites in northern England and southeast Scotland have also been suggested

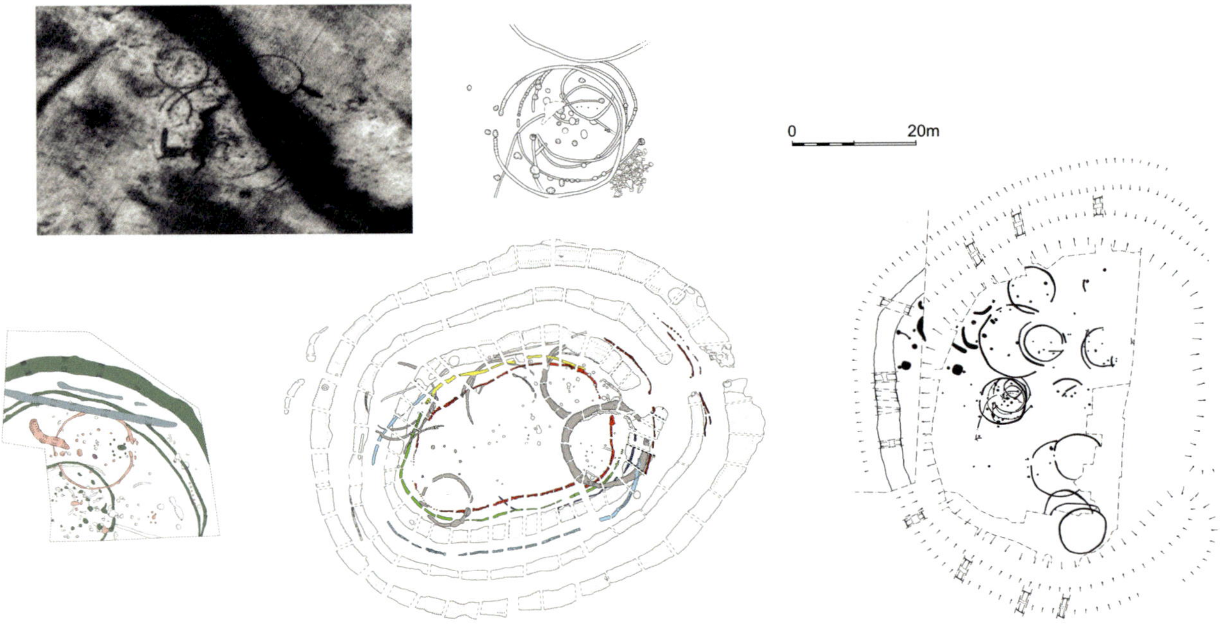

Figure 5: Typical later prehistoric enclosures of the 1st millennium BC in southwest Scotland; clockwise from top: Garphar (after Cowley & Brophy 2001), superimposed ring groove houses at Woodend (after Banks 2000), the enclosure at Woodend, Braehead (after Ellis 2007) and Cults Loch 5 (Cavers & Crone 2018).

by Hamilton (2010), and more generally by Halliday (2007) and Cowley (2003). This has fascinating implications for how we view the structure of society and for the numbers of people who may have occupied a landscape.

10.5 Iron Age settlement on a human scale

The superimposed floors and hearths encountered within the Black Loch of Myrton houses indicate repeated phases of refurbishment, but within the generational lifespan of the major structural timbers. Identification of later phases of enclosure, perhaps coupled with expansion of the settlement at Black Loch echo the familiar pattern of abandonment and reoccupation seen on dryland sites, but now recognisable on a generational scale. With the identification of similar patterns on other wetland settlements in the region, southwest Scotland could offer the opportunity to investigate the causes of these dramatic changes in settlement location and design, with ever-improving short chronologies offering the prospect of recognising the correlates of those changes on a regional or national scale. In this sense, wetland sites 'flesh out' prehistory, not just in the provision of the otherwise missing organic component of the record, but by providing an insight into patterns of construction, abandonment and reoccupation of Iron Age settlement that is otherwise beyond the reach of archaeology.

It may never prove possible to demonstrate complete abandonment of Iron Age settlements, since gaps in chronology may be attributable to survival bias, but the prospect becomes much more realistic if patterns are repeated across other crannogs and related sites in Scotland. At Cults Loch and Black Loch of Myrton, little in the way of material culture has been recovered and the otherwise extremely well-preserved occupation surfaces have produced very few artefacts. In this sense, the site is very different to the snapshot offered by other exceptional survivals like the Late Bronze Age settlement at Must Farm, Cambridgeshire[1]: far from a chance survival, Black Loch of Myrton is the product of patterns occurring on a national scale in the second half of the 1st millennium BC. It may be the unexceptional nature of the Black Loch of Myrton settlement that proves of most value to our understanding of Iron Age settlement in Scotland.

10.6 The wetland/dryland continuum?

The chronological evidence thus requires that wetland settlements be seen an integral part of the settled landscape. The excavations at Black Loch of Myrton are also serving to blur the oft-perceived distinction between the wetland settlements of Iron Age Scotland and the

1 http://www.mustfarm.com/bronze-age-settlement/

contemporary forts and enclosed settlements that make up the dryland component (see *e.g.* Cavers & Crone 2018, 237-41). Structure 2 at Black Loch of Myrton is effectively a 'ring-groove house' (to use 'dryland' terminology), comfortably within the typical diametrical range for early Iron Age roundhouses and sharing several features familiar from mid-1st millennium BC dryland settlements (Figure 5), such as a heavy doorframe structure and sill beams (*e.g.* House A at Broxmouth – Armit & McKenzie 2013, 30-1; House 2, Dryburn Bridge – Dunwell 2007, 54-60; House A at Cults 5 – Cavers & Crone 2018, 159-62; Structures 3, 5 and 6 at Braehead – Ellis 2007). Coupled with the emerging picture of repeated refurbishment and elaboration of the enclosing palisades and banks at Black Loch of Myrton, the format of the settlement becomes increasingly familiar to the extent that, if the footprint of the earthfast components were all that survived, the Black Loch of Myrton settlement would not look out of place anywhere in the aerial photographic cropmark record of the Scottish lowlands (*e.g.* Cowley 2000; Cowley & Brophy 2001).

This interpretation implies that the choice of living in a wetland environment was not made arbitrarily, nor as a wholesale break with the *status quo*, but rather that the decision to occupy lochs and bogs can be thought of as a direct translation of the existing settlement format into a new environment. As outlined above, Cults Loch 3 potentially fills a gap in the settlement sequence of the surrounding area, thus drawing the site into the wider settlement continuum of Iron Age Scotland: based on our current understanding there is little to distinguish the site from its near-contemporaries on architectural or artefactual grounds. The dendrochronological results have demonstrated that Cults Loch 3, a crannog and Black Loch of Myrton, a settlement built on a natural island are near-contemporary, emphasising that it was their location (in a wetland environment), not the nature of their foundations which was important. This lends weight to the growing impression that it is the domestic architecture of the settlement that should be a uniting factor in considering the role of crannogs in Iron Age archaeology (see Harding 2000; Cavers 2010, 36), rather than the issue of whether the site has artificial foundations. These observations are important to the incorporation of wetland archaeology into mainstream narratives (see ScARF 2012, 53), and to ensure that the significance of the insights afforded by sites like Cults Loch and Black Loch of Myrton are not neglected.

10.7 Bibliography

Armit, I. & MacKenzie, J. 2013. *An inherited place. Broxmouth hillfort and the southeast Scottish Iron Age.* Edinburgh: Society of Antiquaries of Scotland.

Banks, I. 2000. Excavation of an Iron Age and Romano-British enclosure at Woodend Farm, Johnstonebridge, Annandale, 1994 and 1997. *Proceedings Society Antiquaries Scotland* 130, 223-81.

Cavers, G. & Crone, A. 2018. *A lake dwelling in its landscape: Iron Age settlement at Cults loch, Castle Kennedy, Dumfries and Galloway.* Oxford: Oxbow.

Cavers, G., Crone, A., Engl, R., Fouracre, L., Hunter, F., Robertson, J. & Thoms, J. 2011. Excavations at Dorman's Island, Whitefield Loch: an Iron Age crannog in SW Scotland. *Journal Wetland Archaeology* 10, 71-108.

Cowley, D. 2000. Site morphology and regional variation in the later prehistoric settlement of Southwest Scotland. In J. Harding & R. Johnston (eds). *Northern pasts: interpretations of the Later Prehistory of Northern England and Southern Scotland.* 167-76. Oxford: British Archaeological Reports.

Cowley, D. 2003. Changing places – building life-spans and settlement continuity in northern Scotland. In J. Downes & A. Ritchie (eds). *Sea change: Orkney and Northern Europe in the later Iron Age AD 300-800.* 75-81. Balngavies: The Pinkfoot Press.

Cowley, D.C. & Brophy, K. 2001. The impact of aerial photography across the lowlands of south-west Scotland. *Trans Dumf. Gall. Nat. Hist. Ant. Soc.* 3rd series Vol 75, 47-72.

Crone, A. 2012. Forging a chronological framework for Scottish crannogs; the radiocarbon and dendrochronological evidence. In M. Midgley & J. Sanders (eds). *Lake-dwellings after Robert Munro*, 139-68. Leiden: Sidestone Press.

Crone, A. & Cavers, G. 2016. Black Loch of Myrton. An Iron Age village. *British Archaeology* 151, 36-41.

Dockrill, S.J. Bond, J.M., Turner, V.E., Brown, L.D., Bashford, D.J., Cussans, J.E.M. & Nicholson, R.A. 2015. *Excavations at Old Scatness, Shetland, Volume 2: the broch and Iron Age village.* Lerwick: Shetland Heritage Publications.

Dunwell, A. 2007. *Cist burials and an Iron Age settlement at Dryburn Bridge, Innerwick, East Lothian.* Scottish Archaeological Internet Reports 24.

Ebersbach, R. 2013. Houses, households, and settlements. Architecture and living spaces. In F. Menotti & A. O'Sullivan (eds). *The Oxford handbook of wetland archaeology.* 283-301. Oxford: OUP.

Ellis, C. 2007. Total excavation of a later prehistoric enclosure at Braehead, Glasgow. *Proceedings Society Antiquaries Scotland* 137, 179-264.

Halliday, S.P. 2007. Unenclosed round-houses in Scotland: occupation, abandonment, and the character of settlement. In C. Burgess, P. Topping & F. Lynch (eds).

Beyond Stonehenge: Essays on the Bronze Age in honour of Colin Burgess. 49-56. Oxford: Oxbow.

Hamilton, W. D. 2010. *The use of radiocarbon and Bayesian modelling to (re)write later Iron Age settlement histories in East-central Britain*. Univ Leicester; unpubl Phd thesis.

Hamilton, D. 2016. Timing transformation: the application of radiocarbon dating and Bayesian modelling to produce refined chronologies for Later Prehistoric settlements from the Tees to the Forth. In R. Crellin, C. Fowler & R. Tipping (eds). *Prehistory without borders. The prehistory of the Tyne-Forth region*. 224-43. Oxford: Oxbow.

Hamilton, D. & Krus, T. 2018. Radiocarbon dating and Bayesian modelling of Cults Loch 3, 4 and 5. In Cavers, G. & Crone, A. *A lake dwelling in its landscape: Iron Age settlement at Cults loch, Castle Kennedy, Dumfries and Galloway*. 187-94. Oxford: Oxbow.

Harding, D.W. 2000. Crannogs and island duns: classification, dating and function. *Oxford Journal of Archaeology* 19.3, 307-17.

Harding, D.W. 2004. *The Iron Age in Northern Britain: Celts and Romans, natives and invaders*. London: Routledge.

Haggarty, A. & Haggarty, G. 1983. Excavations at Rispain Camp, Whithorn, 1978 – 81. *Transactions Dumfries & Galloway Natural Heritage & Antiquarian Society* 58, 21-51.

Jacobsson, P., Hamilton, D. & Cook, G. 2018. ^{14}C wiggle-match dating and the structural sequence at Cults Loch 3. In Cavers, G. & Crone, A, *A lake dwelling in its landscape: Iron Age settlement at Cults loch, Castle Kennedy, Dumfries and Galloway*. 50-5. Oxford: Oxbow.

Menotti, F. 2012. *Wetland archaeology and beyond. Theory and practice*. Oxford. OUP.

ScARF 2012. The settlement and exploitation of inland waters. In D. Atkinson & A. Hale (eds). *Scottish Archaeological Research Framework: Marine and Maritime Report*, 52-8.

Stratigos, M.J. 2016. A reconsideration of the distribution of crannogs in Scotland. In G. Erskine, P. Jacobsson, P. Miller & S. Stetkiewicz (eds). *14th Iron Age Research Student Symposium, Edinburgh 29th May-1st June 2014*. 95-106. Oxford: Archaeopress.

Stratigos, M. & Noble, G. 2017 'A new chronology for crannogs in north-east Scotland' *Proceedings Society Antiquaries Scotland* 147, 147-73.

Stratigos, M., Cook, G., Hamilton, D. & Jacobsson, P. 2018 Living on water. The early Iron Age crannog-dwellers of Loch Tay. *History Scotland*, 12-3.

Chapter 11

Settlement nucleation and farmstead stabilisation in the Netherlands

Karen M. de Vries

In D.C. Cowley, M. Fernández-Götz, T. Romankiewicz & H. Wendling (eds). Rural Settlement. Relating buildings, landscape, and people in the European Iron Age (Leiden 2019: Sidestone Press) 125-134.

11.1 Introduction

One of the most profound social changes in the later prehistory of what is now the Netherlands is the transition in settlement structure from mobile patterns of 'wandering' farmsteads to stable settlements or hamlets (Arnoldussen & Jansen 2010, 381-2; Gerritsen 2003, 181-9). This phenomenon of settlement stabilisation and nucleation fits within a broader process of the development of large agglomerations and early urbanism that occurs in northwest and central Europe during the last millennium BC (Kristiansen 1998, 307-12; Cunliffe 2009, 347-406; Fernández-Götz & Ralston 2017). For Dutch prehistory, this transition becomes most evident in the Late Iron Age (250-12 BC) and at the start of the Early Roman (12 BC-AD 70) period (Waterbolk 1995, 14-20), but it has been suggested that its roots lie earlier in the Iron Age (Arnoldussen & Jansen 2010; Gerritsen 2003, 104). In general terms, it is thought that the process of settlement nucleation started first at the level of the farmstead, whereby an earlier pattern of intermittent farmstead relocation over relatively large areas was modified as distance between relocations decreased (stabilisation), followed by the addition of new houses to existing settlements (nucleation) and, finally, the enclosure of the settlement area by ditches or fences (demarcation). Even though the broad trajectory of these changes is well established, the process of change itself is still poorly understood (Arnoldussen & Jansen 2010, 379; Gerritsen 2007, 158-62).

Several factors impede our understanding of this process. Firstly, a pattern of wandering farmsteads is difficult to divide into different phases, as the archaeological evidence is often a palimpsest in which it is hard to establish whether four building floor plans at the same location, for example, represent four contemporaneously inhabited structures or successive phases of just one farmstead (cf. Gerritsen 2003, 70; Fokkens 1996, 204). As a result, the moment at which farmsteads started to cluster into stable settlements is hard to pinpoint. Secondly, the relationship between farmstead and subsistence is still poorly understood. Often, the relationship between arable fields and farmstead is seen as the major factor in the way settlements were structured. For the Iron Age, the formation and use of Celtic fields are thought to be the major reason for the relocation of farmsteads. Only a small part of the field system was taken into cultivation, while the larger part lay fallow. After some time, when fields were given up, the farmstead relocated within the fields and other parts were taken into cultivation (*e.g.* Gerritsen 2003, 172-3; Harsema 2005, 548). At the end of the Iron Age, subsistence is thought to change. The Celtic fields

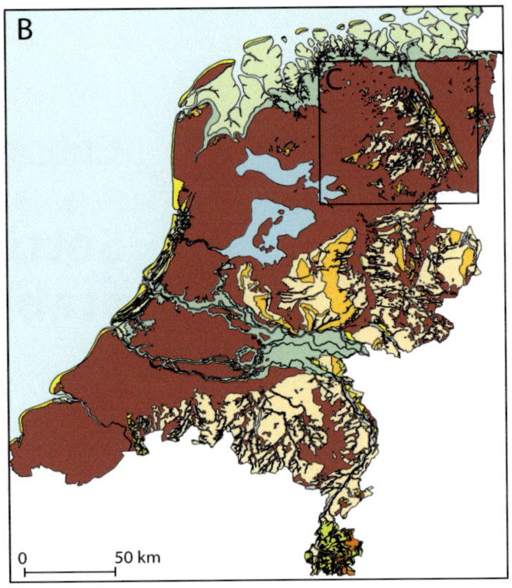

Figure 1: (A) The location of the Netherlands (B) within northwest Europe. (B) Palaeogeographical map of the Netherlands around 500 BC, with the Fries-Drents plateau indicated within the frame (C). (Palaeogeographical map based on Vos & De Vries 2013).

are thought to be abandoned and new methods of land use introduced. For the Late Iron Age and Early Roman period, land tenure and stable settlements are seen as interlinked phenomena – settlements became more or less fixed in the landscape and families became landholding units, the two processes positively reinforcing each other (Gerritsen 2003, 250-4). The relationship between farmstead and arable land does not fully explain the change in settlement structure. Specifically the relationship between farmsteads and Celtic fields is complex, as houses and fields do not neatly relate one to another (Arnoldussen & De Vries 2017, 79-82). Moreover, new investigations indicate that Celtic fields were in use much longer than previously thought, well into the Roman period (cf. Arnoldussen 2018, 317-8, 321-4), indicating the continuity of this form of agricultural practice in a period showing evidence for stable settlements.

A third factor in the process of settlement stabilisation and nucleation is the durability of the house itself. Because house construction techniques supposedly improved in the course of the Iron Age, houses are thought to have become more durable and to have had a longer lifespan at the start of the Common Era (Gerritsen 2003, 104; Gerritsen 2007). This line of argumentation continues, that as a result, farmstead mobility declined and settlements became stable focal points in the landscape and could be inhabited over multiple generations. Though mentioned as a cause for settlement stability, little structural research has been undertaken so far into actual modifications of prehistoric house constructions in the Netherlands (but see Kooi 2005; Gerritsen 2003, 75-9). These results have not yet been reviewed in relation to the model of settlement stabilisation. In this paper, I will discuss the processes of later prehistoric settlement stabilisation and nucleation in the Netherlands with reference to evidence of building construction, with a special focus on the Fries-Drents plateau, a boulder clay area in the north of the Netherlands covered with aeolian sand deposits (Figure 1). The central questions are whether there is evidence for constructional changes at house level, *i.e.* were houses renovated, extended, or rebuilt, and what this structural evidence means for models of settlement stabilisation in the Netherlands as outlined above?

11.2 A model for settlement nucleation and house modification

Within the general process of settlement nucleation outlined above, two connected factors are considered, firstly the degree of mobility of buildings and secondly the durability of house constructions. In the early phases of the Iron Age (800-250 BC) characterised by wandering farmsteads there is an expectation of high mobility and short-lived buildings (*i.e.* low durability). As a result, predominantly single-phased farmsteads are expected, with few modifications, if any, since there was no need to renovate when habitation was assumed to be relatively short, roughly a generation (Kooi 2005, 115, Gerritsen 2003, 172-3).

If indeed the duration of habitation did increase in the course of the Iron Age, alongside a process of nucleation, we would expect mobility to decrease and excavated houses to produce evidence of use over a longer period. Furthermore, if the durability of the houses only improved at the very end of the Iron Age and at the transition to the Roman period (Gerritsen 2003, 104, 350-4), a tension might emerge between the desire for

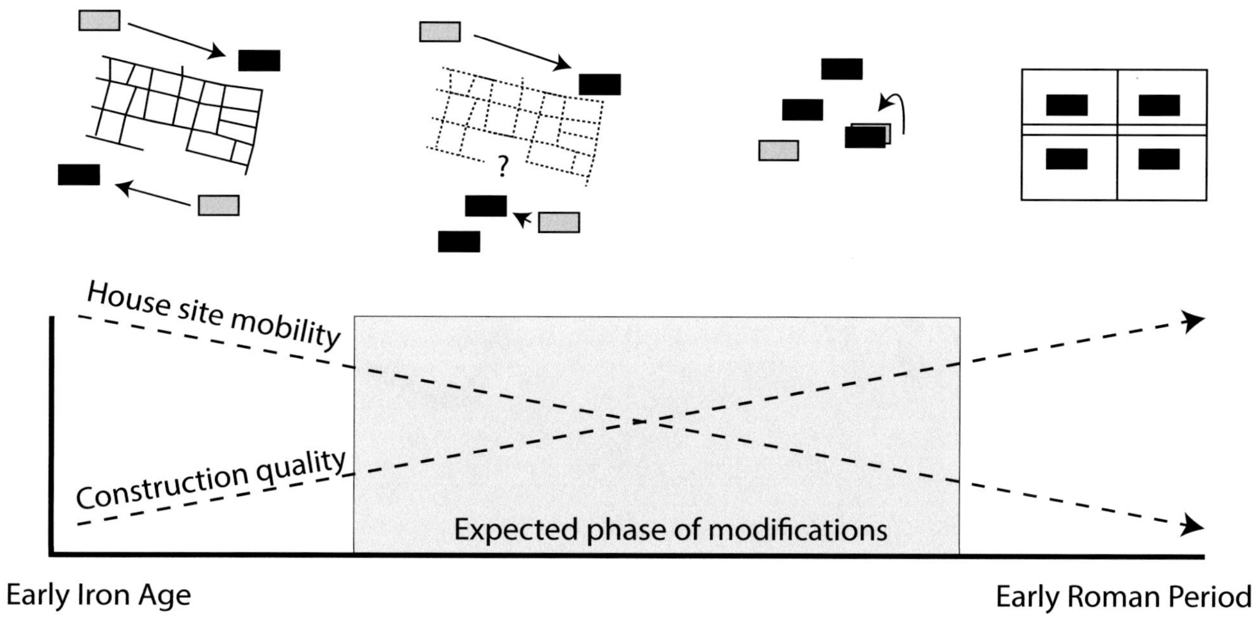

Figure 2: Schematic model of settlement stabilisation and house modifications. (Image by K. M. de Vries).

fixed or settled inhabitation of a specific location and the actual durability of the initial house construction. In such a framework, most house modifications, as indications of longevity of the structure, would be expected to appear towards the end of the Iron Age (Figure 2).

The preservation of unburnt organic material in the sandy soils is often poor, with implications for loss of detail in the archaeological record (*e.g.* Gerritsen 2003, 19, 38, 64). Thus, the remains of all later prehistoric houses in the sandy soils of the Netherlands are the deepest features cut into the subsoil, the upright posts that supported the load of the roof and the walls (Huijts 1992, 15). As a consequence, it is likely that much evidence for modifications has been lost, especially those above ground (*e.g.* repair of a roof). However, this may not be the problem it might appear. Of all the modifications that could have been made to a house, those that have left traces in the archaeological record likely relate to the support of the roof load. Such archaeologically visible modifications are labour intensive and, rather than indicating simple maintenance, signal fundamental changes in the house construction. They indicate a desire to prolong the lifespan of a building, signalling of the wish to stay in a given location over a wish to leave (cf. Gerritsen 1999, 86-7; 2003, 75-9)

In this study, three different kinds of house modifications are considered: (1) renovations; (2) extensions; and (3) rebuilds. Renovations are evident when extra posts are added to an otherwise regularly spaced row of posts or in the occurrence of doubled posts, and are modifications to the structure that do not change its dimensions. Extensions are additions to an existing structure, roughly along the longitudinal axis of the original building (thoug often a slight skew in alignment is evident). It is often impossible to establish when renovations or extensions took place, but contexts might include improvements to the layout after construction or repair of damage or decay after a longer period of use. The third type of modification occurs when a house is demolished and reconstructed on (nearly) the same location – the house is rebuilt. This differs from a gradual replacement of all posts (a total refurbishment), as walls are replaced as well. Continuity of the house on the same general footprint is evident through similarities in dimensions and execution of the new building, though orientation may slightly vary. In these cases, it is clear that the house was reconstructed on the same footprint deliberately. Here, there is a difference between houses that are rebuilt and those that are overbuilt, which is more likely the result of chance than of intentionality. This can be seen in clear differences in dating, construction type and/or major deviations in orientation (Figure 3).

11.2.1 The dataset

For this study, 182 house plans were studied from 38 sites on the Fries-Drents plateau (Figure 1C). Because of the sandy soils, features are here only evident as surface discolourations. The houses date between the Late Bronze Age (1100-800 BC) and the Middle Roman period (AD 70-270), noting that it is not always possible to closely date later prehistoric houses. Ceramics, for example, may only be datable to the Late Bronze Age or Early Iron Age or to the Late Iron Age or Early Roman period (Taayke 1996, 182, fig. 10d). Absolute dates also yield broad ranges because of the plateau in the calibration curve between approximately 800 and 400 BC and a wiggle between

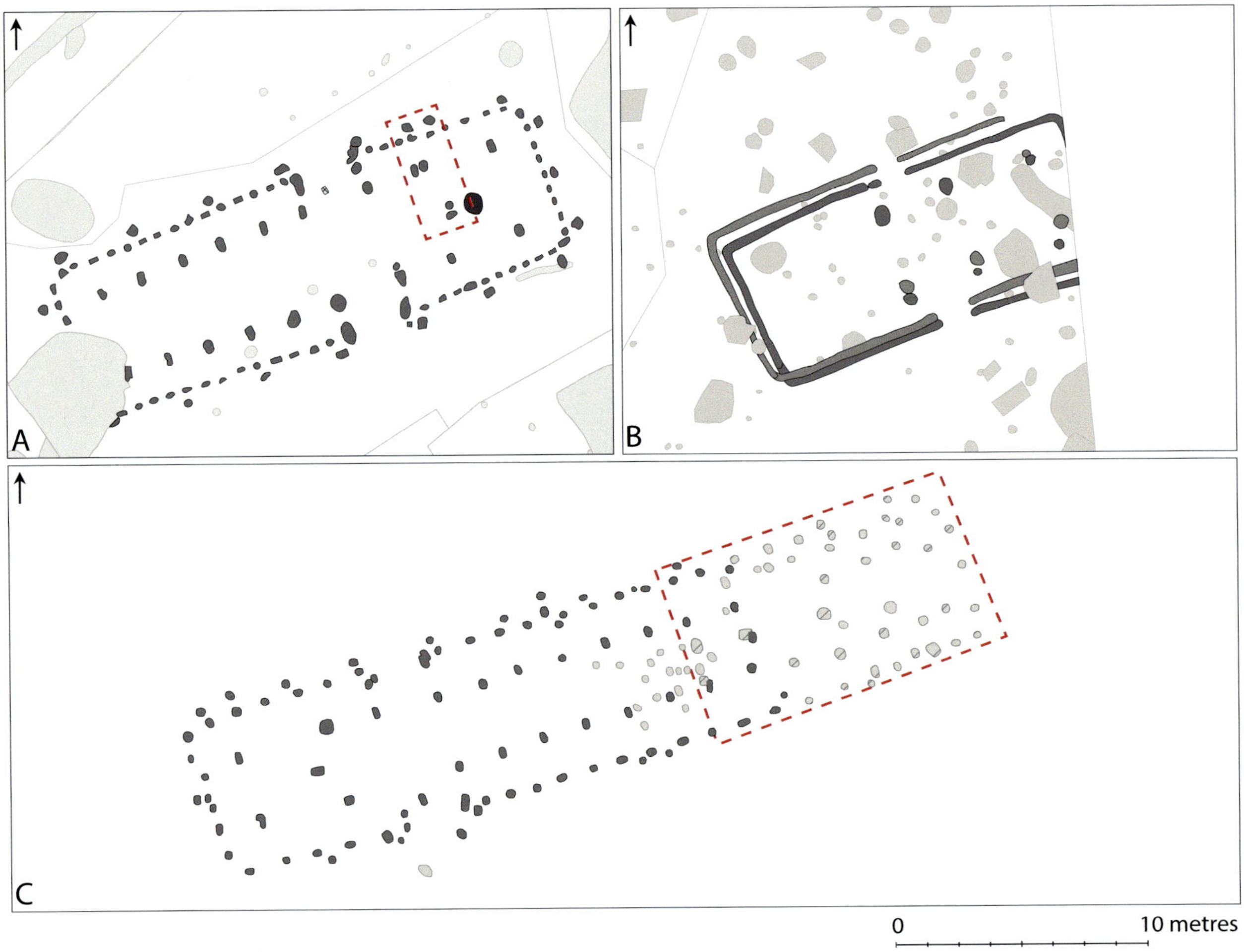

Figure 3: Examples of different types of house modifications. A: Renovation at Ruinen-Oldhave Bos (Koopstra & Lenting 2016); B: Rebuild at Gieten-OV knooppunt (Loopik 2010); C: Extension at Peelo-Es (Kooi 1994). For Peelo-Es only the house is depicted, not the adjacent features. (Images adapted by K. M. de Vries).

approximately 400 and 200 BC (for similar problems see Lanting & Van der Plicht 2006, 269).

For more than half of the houses in the dataset (n=100), it is not possible to establish whether modifications had taken place. The main reason for this is the long-term use of some sites which resulted in many overlapping structures. Because of this overlap, it is difficult to attribute features to individual house plans. As a result, renovations may be obscured (*e.g.* Wijster: Van Es 1967; Midlaren-De Bloemert: Nicolay 2008). Another problem proved to be the lack of detail available in publications (*e.g.* old excavations such as Zeijen I: Waterbolk 1976, 638-9). However, in 82 cases it could be established whether the house was modified or not, and these are analysed below. In 38 cases, parts of the house were repaired or renovated, in 16 cases the house was extended, and in eight examples a house was rebuilt (a total of 16 houses involved in the rebuilding). In two associated cases, the houses underwent some change, but these could not be assigned to the three different classes. In six cases, houses could be classified as a combination of two types of modifications and were counted in each category (leading to a total of more than 82). Only in 16 cases was it evident that no profound repairs or renovations had taken place, as there were no evident changes in the postholes. The incidence of modifications was plotted on a graph, arranging them per century and correcting numbers as percentages of the total number of known houses per century. Both the incidences of modifications and total number of known houses per century are calculated as a weighted average. If a house dates between 800 and 600 BC, it will count as 0.5 for 800-700 and 0.5 for 700-600. If a house dates between 800 and 500 BC, it will count as 0.33 for 800-700, 0.33 for 700-600 and 0.33 for 600-500. Per century, numbers are added. The weighted average of renovations, extensions

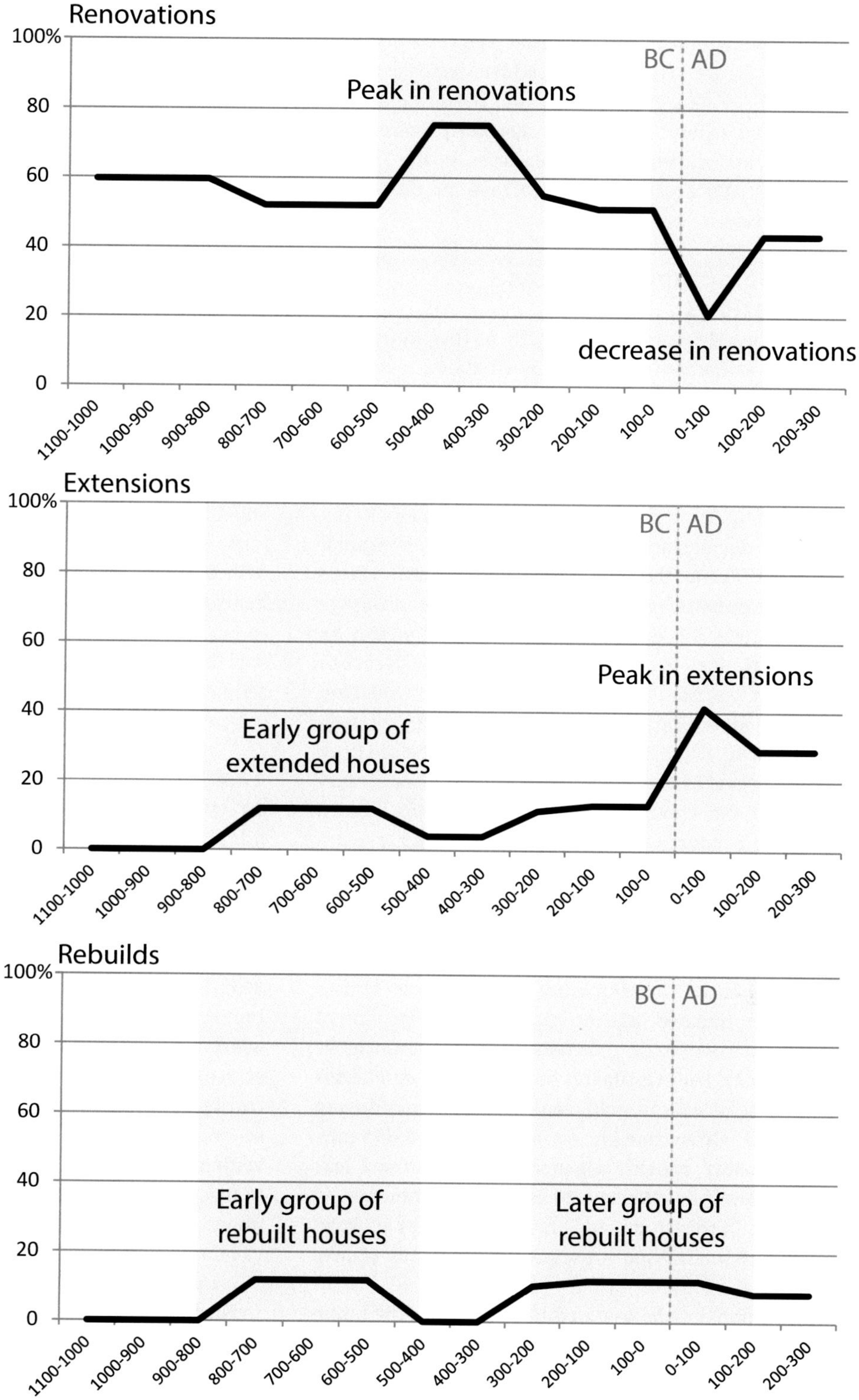

Figure 4: Percentages of houses that show modifications corrected for the number of houses known per century. Top: house renovations; Middle: house extensions; Bottom: house rebuilds. (Images by K. M. de Vries).

and rebuilds is calculated as a percentage of the weighted average of all houses (Figure 4).

A comparison between the different types of house modification (*i.e.* renovations, extensions and rebuilds) shows that there is a chronological difference between renovations on the one hand and extensions and rebuilds on the other. Although all three types of house modifications have early examples, renovations seem to start earlier (already in the Late Bronze Age) and have a prominence earlier on than extensions and rebuilds.

Renovations are more prominent in the Middle Iron Age and at the transition to the Late Iron Age (between 500 and 100 BC; Figure 4) and show a sudden decrease at the very end of the Late Iron Age and the beginning of the Roman period. Extensions however, become prominent at the start of, and during the first centuries, of the Roman period (12 BC-AD 270). Rebuilds are rare for the whole research period.

11.3 Developments in house modifications

Assessing the relevance of the results of this analysis to the general settlement model discussed above, it is clear that the patterns are not as expected. Renovations, for example, are common for the whole research period. This is counter to what is thought, as mobile short lived patterns supposedly dominated in the earlier periods (*e.g.* Kooi 2005, 115). Even if the results are not in line with the model, they do not stand on their own, as they correspond to findings from the southern Netherlands, where renovations are also evident for the whole of the Iron Age (Gerritsen 2003, 77, table 3.6). Still, information can be found in variations in house modification, as the degree of renovations was not uniform over the course of the Iron Age. A peak in renovations (Figure 4) can be seen between 600 and 300 BC. From 300 to 100 BC, renovations are back to the same level as before 600 BC. In the centuries around the start of the Common Era (100 BC-AD 200), a steep decrease in renovations is visible. Even though repairs generally remain common, this suggests a changing attitude towards the house at this point.

The frequency of pervasive renovations is important, as this may be relevant to the expected lifespan of the individual house. The durability of prehistoric houses is still much debated, and estimates of the lifespans of wooden constructions range between a few years and more than a century. These estimates depend on soil conditions and the type of wood used (see discussion: Arnoldussen 2008, 88-90). Often though, an average of 25-35 years, or, conveniently, roughly a generation, is assumed (*e.g.* Gerritsen 2003, 39; Webley 2008, 40). The number of renovations in this study may argue for a longer lifespan of renovated houses and consequently habitation phases of multiple generations.

Renovations can be seen in different parts of the house plan, such as the wall, posts around the entrance and interior roof supporting posts. Often, these renovations appear to be ad-hoc repairs particular to individual house plans. Some types of renovations reoccur, and are common to houses of the same type, perhaps suggesting recurrent problems or motivations for the work. These renovations can be seen in houses of the Hijken-Zwinderen type (Waterbolk 2009, 55, 62, fig. 38). This type stands out from houses of the contemporary Hijken-Hijken type because of the inward placement of the first set of posts in the byre section. Frequently, duplication of posts is visible on both sides of the entrance. Possibly, the dislocation from the wall line of the posts flanking the entrance creates instability around the entrance, as house plans show repairs around the entrance area. These repairs may indicate a weakness in the construction of this particular type (Figure 5).

As with renovations, house extensions are known from the entire Iron Age, though in smaller numbers than renovations. A remarkable inversion in this pattern is evident in the centuries around the start of the Common Era (100 BC-AD 200) when the number of renovations strongly decreases and the number of extensions dramatically increases throughout the research area. This pattern coincides with the dating proposed for nucleated settlements. The number of rebuilds is low for the whole period, but there are examples in both the Early Iron Age and in the Late Iron Age/Early Roman period. It would make sense that the rebuilding of houses was associated with a clearly defined area for inhabitation within the hamlet. Nonetheless, the evidence does not support this association, as rebuilds are found as early as 800 – 600 BC, well before the phase of stable settlements or hamlets. Neither can the presence or absence of rebuilds be related to sturdier house constructions.

11.4 'Sedentary' farmsteads and the origins of nucleated settlements

It is proposed here that the development of aggregated or nucleated settlement sites was a process that has its origins in processes seen at the level of individual houses. The earliest stable settlements or hamlets can be dated in the centuries around the start of the Common Era (100 BC-AD 200). Prior to this, we see an increase in renovations of buildings (Figure 4), indicating a wish or need to prolong the use of houses. Other indicators for farmstead stabilisation, such as the rebuilding of a building on the same footprint, can be interpreted as evidence for extended occupation of individual buildings as a process that preceded settlement site stabilisation. However, the wider context of these individual modifications in buildings has yet to be analysed to see if there is a coincidence of the eight cases of house rebuilds with later stable settlements or hamlets.

A comparison of the settlement contexts immediately indicates that rebuilds are not straightforward predecessors of stable settlements or hamlets. The two Early Iron Age rebuilds at the settlement site of Angelsloo-Emmerhout are the earliest examples of farmstead stability in this study (house 6 and house 75: Kooi 2008, 336, 356), with both rebuilt on exactly the same location. They are perfect examples of rebuilds as the new houses have the same dimensions, almost similar orientation and the same construction technique as the previous houses, leaving no room for an interpretation of overbuild

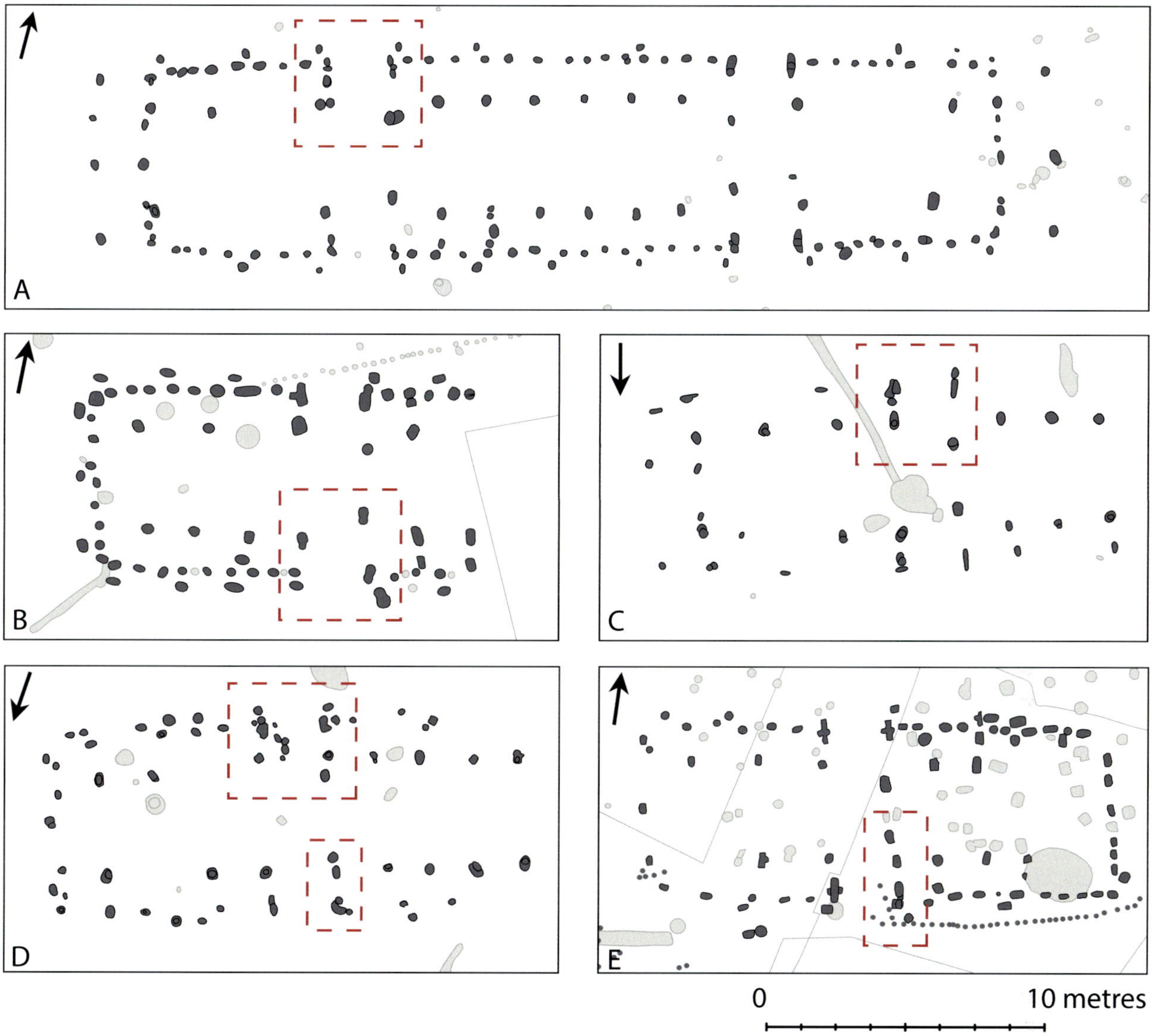

Figure 5: Houses of the Hijken-Zwinderen type with renovations around the entrances. All houses are displayed with the inward placement of the first posts to the right. Renovations are indicated by red pecked frames. A: Borger-Daalkampen II (phase 2) house 4 (Van der Meij 2010); B: Noordbarge-Hoge Loo house 11 (Arnoldussen & Albers 2015); C: Holsloot-Holingerveld house 2 (Van der Velde et al. 2003); D: Holsloot-Holingerveld house 3 (Van der Velde et al. 2003); E: Hijken-Hijkerveld house 2 (Arnoldussen & De Vries 2014). (Images adapted by K. M. de Vries).

by chance. Because of this clear evidence of farmstead continuity (the immediate rebuilding of the house on the same footprint), it is all the more remarkable that these houses belong not to the first, but to the final phases of a long period of habitation on this settlement site. The site of Angelsloo-Emmerhout was inhabited from the Middle Bronze Age to the end of the Early Iron Age (Kooi 2008; Arnoldussen & Scheele 2012). Later habitation is known in the adjacent area, in the form of an enclosed and nucleated settlement, but this particular settlement is located at some distance, a few kilometres to the west (the site of Emmen-Frieslandweg: De Wit 2003).

Two other rebuilds, from Groningen-Helpermaar (House 2: Huis in 't Veld *et al.* 2010, 29-31) and Gieten-OV knooppunt (Loopik 2010, 16-21), date respectively to the transition from the Late Iron Age to the Early Roman period and the Early Roman period. The Groningen-Helpermaar house was both rebuilt and extended, whereas the Gieten house was rebuilt in a similar fashion to the houses from Angelsloo-Emmerhout with respect to previous dimensions, orientation and construction. Neither settlements, though, hold any indications for a long period of habitation after the houses were rebuilt, as there is no evidence of later human presence in the area in the form of ceramics (*e.g.* Groningen-Helpermaar: Helfrich 2010, 37-49). Nor do these rebuilds indicate the start of any stabilisation, nucleation or demarcation of the whole settlement. As holds for Angelsloo-Emmerhout, house rebuilds in Groningen and Gieten do not seem to predict any settlement stabilisation at a later point in time.

In this study, the only case in which a phase of rebuilt houses precedes a phase of settlement nucleation and demarcation is at Noordbarge-Hoge Loo (Harsema 1976; Arnoldussen & Albers 2015). Here, a Late Iron Age to Early Roman period phase with a number of rebuilds precedes a later phase in which the settlement site consisted of a number of nucleated and extended houses clearly demarcated by a ditch. In contrast to the examples of Angelsloo-Emmerhout, Groningen-Helpermaar and Gieten-OV Knooppunt, the rebuilds of Noordbarge-Hoge Loo are not perfect rebuilds, as there are small deviations in footprint and construction techniques (Arnoldussen & Albers 2015, 159-63, especially fig. 9).

If house rebuilds do not signal the onset of the nucleation of settlements, do house extensions provide a better root for the process of nucleation? Once again, the pattern in the data is complex and certainly not all sites with extended houses developed into nucleated and clearly demarcated settlements. Some house extensions belong to earlier phases of settlement sites that develop into hamlets. Again, the case of Noordbarge-Hoge Loo confirms that house modifications can precede a phase of nucleated and demarcated settlements (Harsema 1976; Arnoldussen & Albers 2015). The later, Early Roman period, habitation phase of Noordbarge-Hoge Loo can be characterised by its many extensions, for which the site and the eponymous house type are known (Waterbolk 2009, 72, 78, fig. 50). At the site of Peelo-Es, house extensions were visible in two phases of the habitation, with house 27 dating to between the Middle Iron Age and Early Roman period and house 21 dating to the Early to Middle Roman period (Kooi 1994, 178, 182). The site of Peelo-Es proved to be an enduring settlement location continuously inhabited up to the Early Medieval period, with phases of habitation with nucleated houses demarcated by ditches (Kooi 1994, 265-71).

Other house extensions, however, do not mark the start of settlement stabilisation. An extended Late Iron Age to Early Roman period house at Zwinderen-Kleine Esch (Erf 3: Van der Velde *et al.* 1999, 67-71) appears to be isolated with no signs of settlement nucleation or demarcation, despite extensive archaeological evaluation of the area. Another example, again from Angelsloo-Emmerhout (House 64: Kooi 2008, 353), dates to the Early Iron Age and evidences the end of a long period of habitation rather than the start of one.

In the context of this discussion, house extensions are complex phenomena because they might not just signal an investment in the durability of the farmstead. The majority of extensions in this study comprise the addition of a larger byre section to an existing smaller byre section. This raises the question of whether all house extensions should be considered a prolonging of the lifespan of the building. In general, Iron Age houses are said to be relatively small as they are part of an agricultural economy and only need to contain a small number of animals (Kooi 2005, 115). Thus, while some extensions may represent a prolonging of the lifespan of the building, some may also signal a change in subsistence whereby extensions, especially when they relate to the byre section, could also indicate an increase in livestock.

11.5 Conclusion

Modifications in buildings at a farmstead level have been assessed for evidence of settlement nucleation. This is based on the premise that house modifications are an early phase in a long process of settlement stabilisation, demarcation and nucleation. All three categories of house modifications (renovations, extensions and rebuilds) have examples that date from the earlier phases of the Iron Age. At the scale of the house, activities to prolong the lifespan of the house and farmstead occurred centuries before the first hamlets came into being.

However, a direct spatial relationship between early evidence for settlement stabilisation and the emergence of nucleation is not always evident. House extensions are found as often in settlements that do not develop into hamlets as in settlements that later become nucleated. For house rebuilds, the association between the two is even less evident as most rebuilds are seen in contexts that are not nucleated. This does not only hold for the Early Iron Age examples of Angelsloo-Emmerhout, but also for the Late Iron Age and Early Roman period rebuilds. These do not mark a trajectory towards formation of hamlets. Indeed, considering Angelsloo-Emmerhout and Emmen-Frieslandweg raises the possibility that knowledge developed in one location does not necessarily find practical expression there at a later time. Indeed, such knowledge, or intent, may move around and find expression elsewhere in the landscape through the relocation of the settlement.

A positive result of this analysis of house modifications is the improved insight into house maintenance practices and house construction techniques. The research into house modifications has shown that repairs are a much more common element of prehistoric houses, even in contexts where mobility is expected to be high and the lifespans of houses relatively low. This raises questions about expectations of the lifespans of houses. In addition, a remarkable similarity in types of repairs in the Hijken-Zwinderen type indicates not only the recurrence of the particular construction, including its flawed building technique, but also the apparent acceptance of it by its different inhabitants who repaired and renovated this particular form of building at different locations.

11.6 Bibliography

Arnoldussen, S. 2008. *A living landscape. Bronze Age settlement sites in the Dutch river area (c. 2000-800 BC).* Leiden: Sidestone Press.

Arnoldussen, S. 2018. The fields that outlived the Celts: the use-histories of Later Prehistoric field systems (Celtic fields or *raatakkers*) in the Netherlands. *Proceedings of the Prehistoric Society* 84, 303-27.

Arnoldussen, S. & Albers, P.C.H. 2015. When urnfields lose their meaning... The case of the Middle and Late Iron Age habitation amidst the Noordbarge Urnfield. In E.A.G. Ball & S. Arnoldussen (eds). *Metaaltijden 2. Bijdragen in de studie van de metaaltijden.* 149-69. Leiden: Sidestone Press.

Arnoldussen, S. & Jansen, R. 2010. Iron Age habitation patterns on the southern and northern Dutch Pleistocene coversand soils: The process of settlement nucleation. In M. Meyer (ed.). *Haus – Gehöft – Weiler – Dorf. Berliner Archäologische Forschungen 8.* 379-97. Rahden: Verlag Marie Leidorf GmbH.

Arnoldussen, S. & Scheele, E.E. 2012. The ancestors nearby. In H.M. Velde, N.L. van der, Jaspers, E. Drenth, & H.B.G. Scholte Lubberink (eds). *Van graven in de prehistorie en dingen die voorbij gaan.* 153-86. Leiden: Sidestone Press.

Arnoldussen, S. & Vries, K.M. de 2014. Of farms and fields. The Bronze Age and Iron Age settlement and Celtic field at Hijken-Hijkerveld. *Palaeohistoria* 54/55, 85-104.

Arnoldussen, S. & Vries, K.M. de 2017. A plan in place? Celtic field habitation at Westeinde (prov. Drenthe, The Netherlands). *Lunula Archaeologia protohistorica* XXV, 79-89.

Cunliffe, B. 2009. *Iron Age communities in Britain. An Account of England, Scotland and Wales from the seventh century BC until the Roman conquest.* London: Routledge & Francis Ltd.

Es, W.A. van 1967. *Wijster. A native village beyond the imperial frontier.* Groningen: J.B. Wolters.

Fernández-Götz, M.A. & Ralston, I. 2017. The complexity and fragility of Early Iron Age urbanism in West-Central temperate Europe. *Journal of World Prehistory* 30, 259-79.

Fokkens, H. 1996. The Maaskant project. Continuity and change of a regional research project. *Archaeological Dialogues* 3(2), 196-215.

Gerritsen, F.A. 1999. To build and to abandon. *Archaeological Dialogues* 6(2), 78-97.

Gerritsen, F.A. 2003. *Local identities. Landscape and community in the late prehistoric Meuse-Demer-Scheldt region*, Amsterdam: Amsterdam University Press.

Gerritsen, F.A. 2007. Relocating the house. Social transformations in late prehistoric Northern Europe. In R.A. Beck (ed.). *The Durable House. House Society Models in Archaeology.* 154-74. Carbondale: Center for Archaeological Investigations, Southern Illinois University.

Harsema, O.H. 1976. Noordbarge. *Bulletin van de Koninklijke Nederlandse Oudheidkundige Bond* 75, 52-5.

Harsema, O.H. 2005. Farms amongst Celtic fields. Settlements on the northern sands. In L.P. Louwe Kooijmans, P.W. van den Broeke, H. Fokkens, & A. van Gijn (eds). *The prehistory of the Netherlands. Vol. 2.* 543-55. Amsterdam: Amsterdam University Press.

Helfrich, K. 2010. Aardewerk. In J. Y. Huis in 't Veld (ed.). *Helpermaar-Eiland: een ijzertijd-vindplaats op de westelijke flank van de Hondsrug. Een opgraving in het plangebied Helpermaar, gemeente Groningen. Stadse fratsen 24.* 37-49. Groningen: Dienst Ruimtelijke Ordening en Economische Zaken van de Gemeente Groningen.

Huijts, C.S.T.J. 1992. *De voor-historische boerderijbouw in Drenthe. Reconstructiemodellen van 1300 vóór tot 1300 na Chr.*, Arnhem: Stichting Historisch Boerderij-onderzoek.

Huis in 't Veld, J.Y. 2010. *Helpermaar-Eiland: een ijzertijd-vindplaats op de westelijke flank van de Hondsrug. Een opgraving in het plangebied Helpermaar, gemeente Groningen. Stadse fratsen 24.* Groningen: Dienst Ruimtelijke Ordening en Economische Zaken van de Gemeente Groningen.

Kooi, P.B. 1994. Project Peelo: Het onderzoek in de jaren 1977, 1978 en 1979 op de es. *Palaeohistoria* 33/34, 165-285.

Kooi, P.B. 2005. Reparaties en verbouwingen vanaf de bronstijd tot en met de middeleeuwen. *Nieuwe Drentsche Volksalmanak* 122, 113-30.

Kooi, P. B. 2008. Nederzettingen uit de bronstijd en ijzertijd in Angelslo-Emmerhout. *Palaeohistoria* 49/50, 327-73.

Koopstra, C. G. & Lenting, J. J. 2016. *Hof van Ruinen; archeologische resten uit de IJzertijd, Middeleeuwen en Nieuwe tijd. Een archeologische begeleiding, IVO-P en een opgraving in plangebied Oldehave-Bos te Ruinen. Archeodienst rapport 824.* Zevenaar: Archeodienst BV.

Kristiansen, K. 1998. *Europe before history.* Cambridge: Cambridge University Press.

Lanting, J.N. & Plicht, J. van der 2006. De 14C-chronologie van de Nederlandse pre- en protohistorie V: de midden- en late ijzertijd. *Palaeohistoria* 45/46, 241-427.

Loopik, J. 2010. *Een Aa-typische begeleiding in Gieten. ADC rapport 2300.* Amersfoort: ADC archeoprojecten.

Meij, L. van der 2010. *Project bestemmingsplan Daalkampen II te Borger. Locatie: Klokbeker. ADC rapport 2065*, Amersfoort: ADC archeoprojecten.

Nicolay, J. A. W. 2008. *Opgravingen bij Midlaren. 5000 jaar wonen tussen Hondsrug en Hunzedal.* Groningen: Groningen Insitute of Archaeology.

Taayke, E. 1996. Die einheimische Keramik der nördlichen Niederlande, 600 v.Chr. bis 300 n.Chr., Teil v: Übersicht und Schlußfolgerungen. *Berichten van de Rijksdienst voor Oudheidkundig Bodemonderzoek*, 42, 163-208.

Velde, H.M. van der, Haaster, H. van, Kars, E.A.K., Kenemans, M.C., Rijn, P. van, Spek, Th., Smits, L & Taayke, E. 2003. *Archeologisch onderzoek langs de snelweg. Opgravingen in het kader van de aanleg van de Rijksweg 37: Het Hoolingerveld bij Knooppunt Holsloot. ADC rapport 156*. Bunschoten: ADC archeoprojecten.

Velde, H.M. van der, Haaster, H. van, Spek, Th. & Taayke, E. 1999. *Archeologisch onderzoek langs de snelweg. Opgraving in het kader van de aanleg van de Rijksweg 37: de essen van Wachtum en Zwinderen. ADC-rapport 11*. Bunschoten: Archeologisch Diensten Centrum.

Vos, P. & Vries, S. de 2013. *2e generatie palaeogeografische kaarten van Nederland (versie 2.0)*. Utrecht: Deltares.

Webley, L. 2008. *Iron Age households. Structure and practice in Western Denmark, 500 BC-AD 200*. Aarhus: Aarhus University Press.

Waterbolk, H.T. 1976. De "versterking naar Romeins patroon" bij Zeijen opnieuw bekeken. In J.S. Boersma (ed.). *Festoen. Opgedragen aan A.N. Zadoks-Josephus Jitta bij haar zeventigste verjaardag*. 637-52. Bussum: Fibula-Van Dishoeck.

Waterbolk, H. T. 1995. Patterns of the peasant landscape. *Proceedings of the Prehistoric society* 61, 1-36.

Waterbolk, H.T. 2009. *Getimmerd verleden. Sporen van voor- en vroeghistorische houtbouw op de zand- en kleigronden tussen Eems en Ijssel*. Eelde: Barkhuis Publishing.

Wit, M.J. M. de 2003. *Een Definitief Archeologisch Onderzoek langs de Frieslandweg in Emmen, gemeente Emmen (Dr.). ARC-publicaties 64*, Groningen: ARCbv.

Chapter 12

Turf worlds

Towards understanding an understudied building material in rural Iron Age architecture – some thoughts in a Scottish context

Tanja Romankiewicz

In D.C. Cowley, M. Fernández-Götz, T. Romankiewicz & H. Wendling (eds). Rural Settlement. Relating buildings, landscape, and people in the European Iron Age (Leiden 2019: Sidestone Press) 135-142.

12.1 Introduction

Most later prehistoric houses in Britain and Ireland were built in the round (see Bradley 2012). From the postholes that survive, we conclude that they were built with timber posts and reconstruct timber roofs and organic thatching material for their roofing (Harding 2009, plates 14-6; Reynolds 1993). The typical plan consists of a ring of substantial timbers that directly supported the roof structure. These main structural uprights were placed inside the building and divided the interior into a central and peripheral space (Romankiewicz 2011, 97). Within these reconstructions, the rafters extend about one third of their length beyond the postring. Towards the outer end of the rafters, a wall is assumed to have encased the house and to have supported the rafter ends (Figure 1; Musson 1970). As the main load of the roof was carried by the internal posts in this model, the outer wall is often of a lighter construction. In some instances, excavation has revealed a groove or line of stakeholes in this area. This has been interpreted as demarcating an outer wall of a wattle-screen, typically reconstructed as covered with daub (Reynolds 1993, 95).

Detailed study of the architectural features of roundhouses, such as the cuts for outer wall lines, postholes, and associated pits, can recognise further evidence for the construction of outer roundhouse walls and their related building materials. Webley (2007, 136-7), for example, identified burnt remains of structural daub deposited within posthole fills associated with the decommissioning of roundhouses in southern England. Comparable results from detailed architectural analyses of later prehistoric houses across Scotland, England, the Netherlands, and Denmark highlight how individual fills of architectural features and their materials relate to individual actions during house construction or deconstruction. This has also suggested alternative wall constructions to the standard wattle-and-daub and the use of other soil-based building materials (Romankiewicz 2016a; 2017; 2018). Because of their soil component, these can be more difficult to detect in an archaeological fieldwork setting.

12.2 Identifying lost building materials in Iron Age Scotland

The use of wattle-and-daub as the typical wall construction method during Scottish later prehistory still requires systematic testing. For many excavated roundhouses no

Figure 1: Reconstructed roundhouse at Whithorn, Galloway, Scotland. 2018. (Photograph: Tanja Romankiewicz).

direct evidence of daub survives. Unfired, this material disintegrates over time and becomes difficult to detect macroscopically in archaeological excavations. Indeed, only when fired are fragments of daub recognisable, and it is rare for any more than a few pieces to be recovered. The general lack of large quantities of daub raises questions about whether this material was widely used on wattle walls during the Scottish Iron Age. The framework impressions and tightly curving surfaces found on many of those burnt daub fragments that are preserved often suggest that they are derived from installations used for firing processes such as ovens of furnaces, rather than from vertical wattle walls (Hunter 2011, 27).

For medieval and later periods, few upstanding timber structures remain. The typical timber-framed buildings with wattle-and-daub infilling between the large structural timbers, common in medieval and post-medieval England, the Netherlands, or Germany, are rare in Scotland (Stell 1980; compare Murray 1982, 227). While an ethnographic analogy in the former regions could plausibly inform rural prehistoric house reconstructions with the medieval and later evidence, this cannot readily be transferred onto Scottish rural prehistory. However, excavations in the medieval towns of Perth and Aberdeen, for example, have recovered evidence of 12th to 14th century buildings using two general types of construction, either on sill-beams or as light wattle-walls (Murray 1982). The former is less frequent and associated with stretches of wattling and earthfast timber uprights, which implies a different construction than the typical sill-and-post frameworks common in England or Germany (see above). The light wattle screens could not have supported a heavy superstructure without additional support of planks or potentially a turf, mud, or manure backing (Murray 1982, 225; compare Perry *et al.* 2010, 132-4). Although in an urban medieval setting, the latter might lend itself as a possible analogy for rural building in the Iron Age, this will require further testing. The evidence for clay-covering of the medieval walls is also tentative as it would be expected to survive in the good preservation conditions, but only occasional evidence is known (see Murray 1982, 225). Few Scottish rural buildings in use today predate the early 18th century, and these later ones are generally constructed entirely in stone (Murray 1980, 227-8). They were built during a period of large-scale and comprehensive social and economic changes in the 18th and 19th centuries, replacing houses and other structures that more commonly employed turf as the principal material for their walls, especially in rural areas (*e.g.* RCAHMS 1994, 116-9; compare Colls & Hunter 2015, 110-1).

The use of turf – sods cut into strips or blocks with the surface vegetation and the root mat holding together soil and sediments – is widely documented in Scottish historical records for rural areas, and widely implied in

Figure 2: Reconstructed turf houses at the Highland Folk Museum, Newtonmore, Highland, Scotland. 2016. (Photograph: Tanja Romankiewicz).

the observations of archaeological survey throughout the country. This ranges from the stone footings of medieval and post-medieval buildings in deserted rural settlements, to the decayed banks of small, seasonally occupied structures, the so-called shieling huts in more marginal areas (Walker & McGregor 1996; Walker 2006; Colls & Hunter 2015). Turf building also has a long history in rural early medieval contexts, from longhouses in the Perthshire and Angus uplands (Carver *et al.* 2012) to Norse houses in the Northern and Western Isles (*e.g.* Bornais Mound 3, Sharples 2005). In the post-medieval period, such materials were often associated with lower-status dwelling, overall acquiring negative associations of unhygienic living conditions (Mackie 2014). These were repeatedly implied by the descriptions of 18th- and 19th-century travellers and writers reviewing agricultural practices at the end of the 18th century. However, these accounts could be coloured by the authors' social standing and external perspective (*e.g.* Pennant 1769, 144; see Romankiewicz 2010; compare Mackie 2014, 326). In contrast, historical documents show that some of the lower strata of landed clan-aristocracy, and the officials managing larger 18th-century estates, may also have lived in turf houses, albeit much more substantial in construction and size than those of the general rural population. One of the larger rebuilt houses in the Highland Folk Museum at Kingussie, Highlands, presents such a substantial turf house (Figure 2; Noble 1985, 69; see Romankiewicz 2010). Similarly, the two cottages of Old Leanach and King's Stable preserved on the Culloden battlefield near Inverness, Highlands, and associated with the battle's history, were at least in parts built of turf and used as homes for estate administrators (Addyman & Kay 1999; Romankiewicz 2009).

In comparison of this widespread evidence for turf building in rural areas of medieval and later Scotland, this material has seen little discussion for later prehistoric construction in a rural domestic or farming context. Among the few exceptions are the palynological analyses of samples from the wall, postholes, and floor layers of a roundhouse at Cùl a'Bhaile that survived as an unploughed earthwork on the island of Jura. Here, Whittington's work suggests that the stone and earthen house wall had been built, repaired, and remodelled with turves first cut from nearby, then, in a later phase, with turves cut from material not found elsewhere on the site (Whittington 1985, 155-6). Only recently have interpretations of excavated evidence from often plough-truncated sites in the north and northeast of Scotland suggested that turf was used more widely as a wall material for prehistoric roundhouses, though the evidence itself is not always conclusive. Cut from an area on or near the settlement, it is often difficult to distinguish sediments derived from imported turf from other sediments on site, especially for sites where later ploughing has removed most of the upstanding evidence for walls. The proposition that many of those roundhouses were provided with turf walls is often not demonstrated, but inferred from either the lack of any surviving evidence of an outer wall, or the insubstantial nature of what remains visible as cut features of outer wall constructions (compare Cook & Dunbar 2008, Fig. 195; Cressey & Anderson 2011, 8, 10, 35).

12.3 The archaeological evidence for turf building in Scottish later prehistory

While detection is difficult in many Scottish contexts, turf is easily recognisable in the highly stratified volcanic ashy sediments prevalent in Iceland, where turf construction was abundant until the early 20th century (Milek 2012). Similarly, excellent evidence of turf construction can be seen in the so-called terp farmsteads or Wurten of early medieval Friesland in the northern parts of the Netherlands and Germany (Nieuwhof & Schepers 2016; Schmid 1994) or in the later prehistoric settlement mounds of northern Jutland (Bech *et al.* 2018). In these areas, artificial settlement mounds have developed, incorporating superimposed turf house remains with still partially upstanding wall stumps. These turf walls are sometimes associated with wattle screens as revetments (see *e.g.* Schmid 1994, 243), comparable to the medieval evidence from Aberdeen discussed above. An archaeological and architectural study to test the wider applicability of such wattle-and-turf wall constructions for later prehistory is currently underway and suggests that this method of walling may have been employed also in areas with poorer archaeological preservation (see Romankiewicz 2016a for outline; compare prehistoric evidence *e.g.* in Louwe Kooijmans 1985, 104).

In Iron Age Scotland building with turf is typically associated with defensive works of Iron Age hill forts or for the Roman military installations, particularly the Antonine Wall (Breeze 2006). In Scotland's northeast, however, the sites of Birnie and Clarkly Hill, Moray, currently being prepared for publication (compare Hunter 2000-2011) are amongst the few sites truncated by modern agriculture where evidence of walls seemingly built solely of small turf blocks has been identified. These were recognised during excavation because they had been cut from layered sediments visually different in character and colour from the surrounding soil (Romankiewicz 2010, 24-5). Elsewhere, such detailed identifications are often obscured in the homogenous peaty soils, tills, and gravels characteristic of most of Scotland's superficial deposits (compare Huisman & Milek 2017).

Where turf blocks are difficult to recognise during excavation, other proxy indicators may exist for the use of turf in house construction, for example the presence of residual artefacts from earlier occupations. For the earliest Neolithic buildings in Scotland, such as Knap of Howar on Papa Westray, Orkney Islands, Loveday suggests that their wall cores were not formed of midden material as assumed by the excavator, but of turves cut from an area of earlier occupation (Loveday 2006; compare Ritchie 1983, 42, 43). He argued that the midden was not intended as the main wall fill, but was simply redeposited accidentally together with the turf blocks as a consequence of the turves having been cut from an area of earlier midden (Loveday 2006, 89). This practice, therefore, may not only introduce earlier cultural materials into stratified contexts, but also carbonised macrofossils and other environmental data samples from the site where they were cut (compare Nieuwhof & Schepers 2016, 59). Redeposited cultural or environmental material within a homogenous, humic soil layer on the floor of a house or within the topfill of its cut or worn features is therefore often a good proxy indicator for a collapsed turf wall.

A reassessment of later prehistoric roundhouses in Scotland with this in mind helps to identify further examples with a probability of original turf walls. For example, the 'problem' of the chronologically inverted sequence produced by Neolithic flints found in the upper fills of a Middle Bronze Age roundhouse at Deer's Den, near Kintore in Aberdeenshire (Alexander 2000, 22), can easily be explained if these flints were imported within turf blocks for a turf wall. This wall then seemingly collapsed and part of its material became trapped in the worn hollows within the roundhouse footprint, escaping later truncation. Similar evidence is known from Iron Age sites, such as Seafield West, Inverness, where a concentration of flints overlay a roundhouse settlement. Some roundhouses on this site are clearly of Iron Age date, but the Middle to Late Bronze Age material found in the posthole fills of others may not date those houses as other associated features also contained Iron Age material culture (Cressey & Anderson 2011, 5, 10-1). The earlier material may only indicate that the turf for the walls had been cut from the locations of other Bronze Age activities on or near the site.

In the case of the Deer's Den structure, the flints within the Middle Bronze Age house were similar in type to those found in pits immediately to the south of the roundhouse (Finlayson 2000). Radiocarbon dating suggests these flints were deposited within those pits shortly after their usage in the Neolithic period (Alexander 2000, 16-7, 63, 66). Here at least, it seems plausible to interpret the area of the Neolithic pits as the site for later turf-cutting to construct a new house, suggesting that the turf was sourced in the immediate vicinity of the house construction site. In the case of Deer's Den, this provides an insight into construction logistics.

The best evidence for the use of turf as a building material is of course to employ geoarchaeological methods for scientific analysis. Micromorphology has recently proven very useful for identifying and describing turf material (Huisman & Milek 2017). Recent work at the stone-walled roundhouses at Old Kinord, Aberdeenshire, employed such methods, which substantiated the macro evidence visible during excavation of an upper turf wall on top of the stone base. The results also indicated the environmental conditions of the area from which the turves were cut (Bradley *et al.* 2017; compare Banerjea 2017 and 2018). The results of such geoarchaeological analyses, including pollen and non-pollen palynomorphs, demonstrate the potential to identify turf constructions archaeologically, especially when combined with proxy evidence as described above. The routine adoption of such techniques will allow the prevalence of turf to be tested. On the basis of the evidence above, it is likely that the use of turf for prehistoric house wall construction may emerge much more widely in Scotland and elsewhere.

12.4 Embedding turf as a building material into wider agricultural cycles

If, as is suggested by the evidence articulated above, turf was a relatively commonly used building material, the sourcing of turf for house construction can also help the understanding of wider landscape management strategies and agricultural practices. Ethnographic evidence, for example, attests the bringing of turf sods into byres and byrehouses as bedding materials, especially for overwintering animals (Holden 2004, 45). The turf material soaks up the animal manure and can then be spread onto the fields in the spring. This well-known plaggen-economy (also known as Plaggenwirtschaft) of the medieval and pre-industrial periods is known from many northern landscapes across Europe, and also recorded for Scotland (Mackie 2014, 320, 324-5; compare Guttman *et al.* 2004). The stalling of animals and periodic emptying of the accumulated manure is understood to lie behind the formation of the annular-dished hollows found around the periphery of many later prehistoric roundhouse interiors in Scotland. This so-called 'ring-ditch' resulted from a series of interlocking hollows, especially in the examples in southern Scotland and Northumberland for which this interpretation was first proposed (Jobey & Tait 1966, 14-5; Reynolds 1982). Detailed stratigraphic analysis of ring-ditch roundhouse morphologies at Kintore, Aberdeenshire, confirms this evidence and suggests that these hollows did not necessarily result from erosion caused by stalling animals (Romankiewicz 2018). The depth of some ring-ditches indicates that they were cut features, presumably created by shovelling out accumulated manure and bedding material and imply several cutting actions and different activity areas (Figure 3). From this evidence, relative sequences of formation can be reconstructed. While these actions could be in theory all part of a single and substantial episode, the overall depth and complexity of intercutting features implies a series of excavations and re-excavations within the lifetime of the building (Romankiewicz 2017; 2018).

Other evidence indicates that the remains of some turf-walled houses were ploughed over in prehistory and seemingly cultivated *in situ*. Plough marks over walls have been recorded in a Bronze Age context, for example at Lairg, Sutherland, north Scotland (McCullagh & Tipping 1998), and at Deer's Den, Aberdeenshire (see above, Alexander 2000). Similar evidence at the Iron Age sites of Ironshill, Angus, eastern Scotland, and Seafield West mentioned above, suggests that this practice also occurred in later periods (Pollock 1997, 349; Cressey & Anderson 2011, 33). In these cases, it would seem that the nutrient transfer from house to field as suggested by the ring-ditch cutting was at some point reversed by bringing the field to the house site. The turf walls of these houses then provided the rich compost to be ploughed and cultivated *in situ*. In the areas on the Atlantic coast in the far north and west of Scotland, where stone-walled roundhouses are predominant, middens were not accumulated inside these houses, but in their immediate vicinity. These middens, for example at the site of Old Scatness in southern Shetland or Hornish Point, South Uist in the Western Isles, were directly cultivated, close to where they were generated rather than spread further out onto fields (Guttman *et al.* 2004, 61-2; Dockrill & Bond 2009, 45; see Romankiewicz 2016b, 7). The Atlantic evidence therefore suggests a similar practice as for the turf-walled houses, here bringing the fields to the midden close to the house.

An ongoing systematic analysis suggests that such practices were probably quite widespread across Scotland and possibly further afield (for preliminary results see Romankiewicz 2017; 2018). It is likely that practices reflected specific environments and cultural contexts, presenting a range of complex and interconnected agricultural and architectural cycles that closely linked house spots and farmsteads, their building materials, and agricultural subsistence strategies in a very direct way (Romankiewicz 2017). The next step of this research will look at these aspects from an architectural-conceptual perspective beyond the individual house evidence and examine how building and dwelling fitted into the wider prehistoric agricultural cycles beyond the immediate settlement site. This requires consideration of larger-scale land use and resource management, but also an in-depth analysis of how these practices were interlinked at different scales from house, farmstead, hamlet, or village to the wider landscape (Romankiewicz 2018). This brief regional analysis of turf as an understudied, but likely more prevalent, building material provides a new

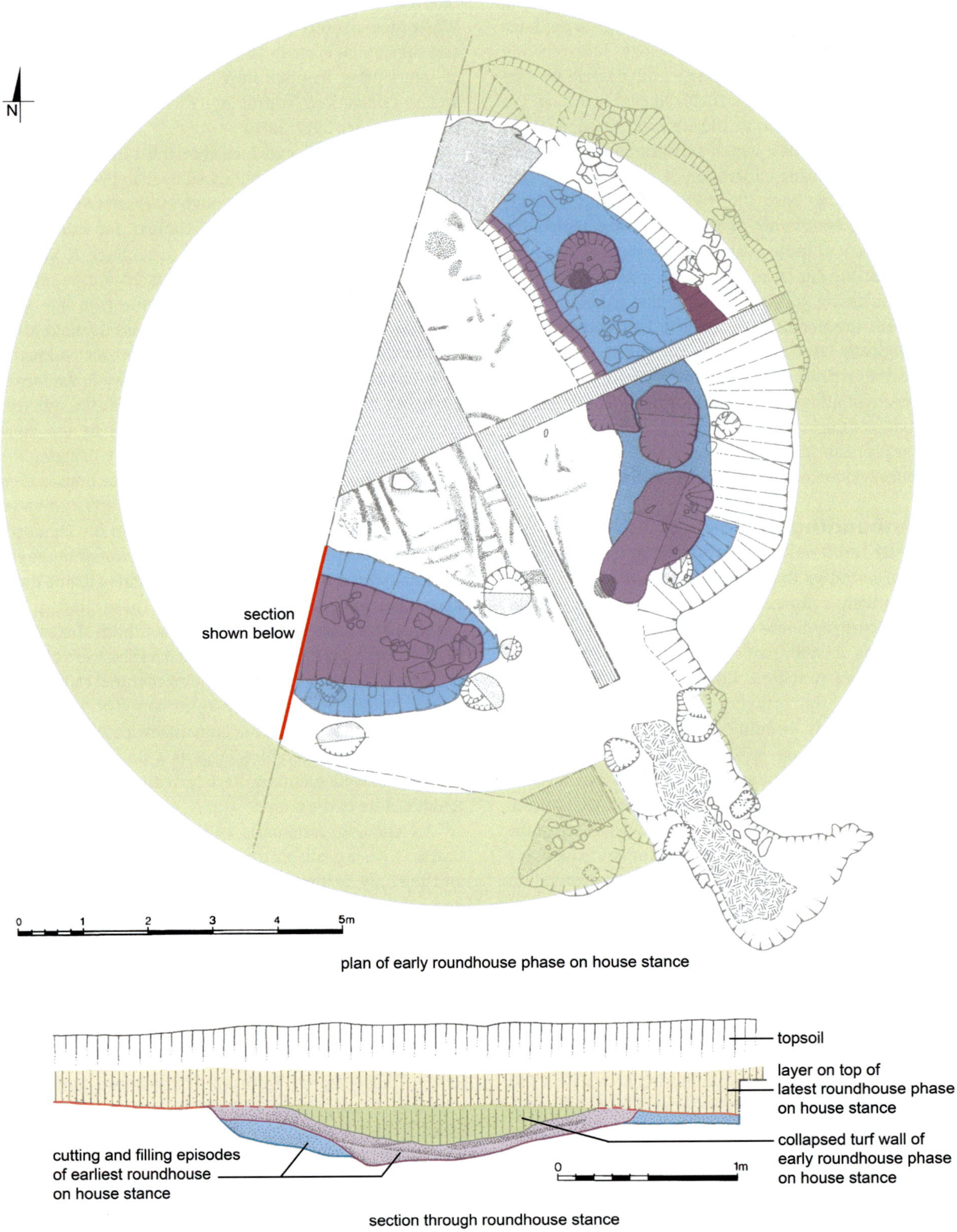

Figure 3: Intercutting ring-ditch sequences: Structure 3, Deer's Den, Kintore, Aberdeenshire. (Drawing: Tanja Romankiewicz after Alexander 2000, Illus 8-9, courtesy D Alexander and Society of Antiquaries of Scotland).

perspective on how such ephemeral evidence can feed into wider questions of rural settlement strategies. Such an approach can offer fuller understandings of how the construction, maintenance, deconstruction, and reuse of buildings, and the resourcing of their materials, was interwoven into the rural subsistence practices in the European Iron Age.

12.5 Acknowledgements

The author would like to thank The Leverhulme Trust (Early Career Fellowship ECF-2014-424) and Aberdeenshire Council for their financial support of the research on which this paper is based. The author is grateful to Derek Alexander and the Society of Antiquaries of Scotland for allowing the reproduction of the plan and section drawings in Figure 3. Helpful comments from a number of reviewers were gratefully received. All errors and omissions remain with the author.

12.6 Bibliography

Addyman, T. & Kay, W. 1999. *King's Stable Cottage, Culloden, Inverness-shire: An Architectural record: Final Report*. Unpublished report: Addyman Archaeology.

Alexander, D. 2000. Excavation of Neolithic pits, later prehistoric structures and a Roman temporary camp along the line of the A96 Kintore and Blackburn Bypass, Aberdeenshire. *Proceedings of the Society of Antiquaries of Scotland* 130, 11-75.

Banerjea, R.Y. 2017. *Old Kinord, Aberdeenshire, Scotland. Micromorphology and phytolith report*. Unpublished report: Quest Quaternary Scientific and University of Reading.

Banerjea, R.Y. 2018. *Old Kinord, Aberdeenshire, Scotland. Micromorphology and non-pollen palynomophrs report*. Unpublished report: Quest Quaternary Scientific and University of Reading.

Bech, J.-H., Eriksen, B.V. & Kristiansen, K. 2018. *Bronze Age Settlement and Land-Use in Thy, Northwest Denmark. Vol. 1-2*. Hølbjerg: Jutland Archaeological Society Publications/Museum Thy.

Bradley, R. 2012. *The idea of order: the circular archetype in prehistoric Europe*. Oxford: Oxford University Press.

Bradley, R., Romankiewicz, T. & Clarke, A. 2017. Old Kinord, Dinnet. *Discovery and Excavation in Scotland* 18 (new series), 19.

Breeze, D.J. 2006. *The Antonine Wall*. Edinburgh: John Donald Ltd.

Carver, M., Barrett, J., Downes, J. & Hooper, J. 2012. Pictish Byre-houses at Pitcarmick and their landscape: investigations 1993-5. *Proceedings of the Society of Antiquaries of Scotland* 142, 145-99.

Colls, K. & Hunter, J. 2015. Archaeological Signatures of Landscape and Settlement Change on the Isle of Harris. *Journal of the North Atlantic* 2015: 901, 108-24.

Cook, M. & Dunbar, L. 2008. *Ritual, roundhouses and Romans. Excavations at Kintore, Aberdeenshire 2000-2006, vol. 1 Forest Road*. Monograph 8. Edinburgh: Scottish Trust for Archaeological Research.

Cressey, M. & Anderson, S. 2011. *A later prehistoric settlement and metalworking site at Seafield West, near Inverness, Highland*. Scottish Archaeological Internet Report (SAIR) 47. Edinburgh: Society of Antiquaries of Scotland with Historic Scotland and the Council for British Archaeology.

Dockrill S.J. & Bond J.M. 2009. Sustainability and resilience in prehistoric North Atlantic Britain: the importance of a mixed paleoeconomic system. *Journal of the North Atlantic* 2(1), 33-50.

Guttman, E.B.A., Dockrill, S.J. & Simpson, I.A. 2004. Arable agriculture in prehistory: new evidence from soils in the Northern Isles. *Proceedings of the Society of Antiquaries of Scotland* 134, 53-64.

Harding, D.W. 2009. *The Iron Age round-house. Later prehistoric building in Britain and beyond*. Oxford: Oxford University Press.

Holden, T. 2004. *The blackhouses of Arnol*. Research report. Edinburgh: Historic Scotland.

Huisman, D.J. & Milek, K. 2017. Turf as constructional material. In C. Nicosia & G. Stoops (eds). *Archaeological soil and sediment micromorphology*. 113-9. Chichester: John Wiley & Sons Ltd.

Hunter, F. 2000-2011. *Excavations at Birnie, Moray*. Unpublished excavation reports. Edinburgh: National Museums Scotland.

Hunter, F. 2011. Fired clay. In M. Cressey & S. Anderson. *A later prehistoric settlement and metalworking site at Seafield West, near Inverness, Highland*. Scottish Archaeological Internet Report (SAIR) 47. Edinburgh: Society of Antiquaries of Scotland with Historic Scotland and the Council for British Archaeology, 27.

Jobey, G. & Tait, J. 1966.Excavations on palisaded settlement and cairnfields at Alnam, Northumberland. *Archaeologia Aeliana*, (4)44, 5-48.

Loveday, R. 2006. Where Have all the Neolithic Houses Gone? Turf – an Invisible Component. *Scottish Archaeological Journal* 28(2), 81-104.

Finlayson, B. 2000. Chipped stone. In D. Alexander. Excavation of Neolithic pits, later prehistoric structures and a Roman temporary camp along the line of the A96 Kintore and Blackburn Bypass, Aberdeenshire. *Proceedings of the Society of Antiquaries of Scotland* 130, 53-8.

Louwe Kooijmans, L.B. 1985. *Sporen in het land. The Nederlandse delta in de prehistorie*. Amsterdam: Meulenhof Informatief.

Mackie, C. 2014. Crossing the threshold: negotiating space in the vernacular houses of the Isle of Lewis. *Archaeological Journal* 171(1), 312-39.

McCullagh, R.P.J. & Tipping, R. 1998. *The Lairg project 1988-1996*. STAR Monograph no. 3, Edinburgh: AOC Archaeology.

Milek, K.B. 2012. Floor formation processes and the interpretation of site activity areas: An ethnoarchaeological study of turf buildings at Thverá, northeast Iceland. *Journal of Anthropological Archaeology* 31, 119-37.

Murray, H.C. 1982. The excavated secular buildings. In J. C. Murray (ed.). *Excavations in the Medieval Burgh of Aberdeen, 1973-81*. 224-8. Society of Antiquaries of Scotland Monograph No. 2, Edinburgh: Society of Antiquaries of Scotland.

Musson, C. 1970. House-plans and Prehistory. *Current Archaeology* 21, 267-75.

Nieuwhof, A. & Schepers, M. 2016. Living on the edge: synanthropic salt marshes in the coastal areas of the northern Netherlands from around 600 BC. *Archaeological Review from Cambridge* 31(2), 48-74.

Noble, R.R. 1985. Turf-Walled Houses of the Central Highlands. An Experiment in Reconstruction. *Folk Life, A Journal of Ethnological Studies* 22 (1983-84), 68-83.

Pennant, T. 1769. *A Tour of Scotland in 1769*. Knight, B. (ed.), republ. 1979. Perth: Melven Press.

Perry. D., Murray, H., Beaumont, T., Bogdan, J. & Bogdan, N.Q. 2010. *Perth High Street: archaeological excavation 1975-77. Fascicule 1: the excavations at 75-95 High Street and 5-10 Mill Street, Perth*. Perth: Tayside and Fife Archaeological Committee.

Pollock, D. 1997. The excavation of Iron Age buildings at Ironshill, Inverkeillor, Angus. *Proceedings of the Society of Antiquaries of Scotland* 127, 339-58.

RCAHMS (Royal Commission on the Ancient and Historical Monuments of Scotland). 1994. *South-east Perth: an archaeological landscape*. Edinburgh: HMSO.

Reynolds, D.M. 1982. Aspects of later prehistoric timber construction in south-east Scotland. In D.W. Harding (ed.). *Later prehistoric settlement in south-east Scotland*. 44-56. Department of Archaeology Occasional Paper No. 8. Edinburgh: University of Edinburgh.

Reynolds, P.J. 1993. Experimental Reconstruction. In D.W. Harding, I.M. Blake & P.J. Reynolds. *An Iron Age Settlement in Dorset: Excavation and Reconstruction*. 93-122. Edinburgh: University of Edinburgh, Department of Archaeology, Monograph Series No. 1.

Ritchie, A. 1983. Excavation of a Neolithic farmstead at Knap of Howar, Papa Westray, Orkney. *Proceedings of the Society of Antiquaries* of Scotland 113, 40-121.

Romankiewicz, T. 2009. Overview of traditional building methods. In A. Gow. *Old Leanach Cottage, Culloden, Inverness-shire*. 27-30. Unpublished report: Addyman Archaeology.

Romankiewicz, T. 2010. Around the Roundhouses. In J. Trythall & B. Dalgarno (eds). *Beakers, Bones & Birnie – Archaeological works in progress associated with Elgin Museum*. 17-26. Elgin: Elgin Museum.

Romankiewicz, T. 2011. *The Complex Roundhouses of the Scottish Iron Age. Volume 1: Text and Illustrations*. British Archaeological Reports British Series 550 (i). Oxford: Archaeopress.

Romankiewicz, T. 2016a. Building (Ancient) Lives: new perspectives on the past for a sustainable future. *The European Archaeologist* 48, 25-30.

Romankiewicz, T. 2016b. Land, stone, trees, identity ambition: the building blocks of brochs. *Archaeological Journal* 173(1), 1-29.

Romankiewicz, T. 2017. Turf. In R. Harkness (ed.). *Knowing from the inside. An unfinished compendium of materials*. 196-201. Aberdeen: University of Aberdeen.

Romankiewicz, T. 2018. Pour une nouvelle conception de l'architecture domestique protohistorique métamorphosable dans le nord de la Grande Bretagne. In A. Villard-Le Tiec (ed.), Y. Menez & P. Maguer (collabs). *Architectures de l'age du Fer en Europe occidentale et central. Actes du 40e colloque international de l'AFEAF*. 619-23. Rennes: Presses Universitaires de Rennes.

Schmid, P. 1994. Oldorf – eine frühmittelalterliche friesische Wurtsiedlung. *Germania* 72, 231-67.

Sharples, N.M. 2005. *A Norse Farmstead in the Outer Hebrides: Excavations at Mound 3, Bornais, South Uist*. Oxford: Oxbow.

Stell, G. 1980. Scottish burgh houses 1560-1707. In A. Turner Simpson & S. Stevenson (eds). *Town houses and structures in medieval Scotland: a seminar*. 1-31. Glasgow: Scottish Burgh Survey.

Walker, B. & McGregor, C. with Little, R. 1996. *Earth structures and construction in Scotland. A guide to the recognition and conservation of earth technology in Scottish buildings*. Technical Advice Note 6. Edinburgh: Historic Scotland.

Walker, B. 2006. *Scottish turf construction*. Technical Advice Note 30. Edinburgh: Historic Scotland.

Webley, L. 2007. Using and abandoning roundhouses: a reinterpretation of the evidence from Late Bronze Age-Early Iron Age southern England. *Oxford Journal of Archaeology* 26(2), 127-44.

Whittington, G. 1985. Report on the pollen analyses. In J.B. Stevenson. The excavation of a hut circle at Cúl a'Bhaile, Jura. *Proceedings of the Society of Antiquaries of Scotland* 114, 147-57.

Chapter 13

The concept of 'house' and 'settlement' in the Iron Age of the middle Tisza region

Péter F. Kovács

13.1 Introduction

The Middle Tisza region is situated in East Hungary and roughly covers the centre of the Great Hungarian Plain (Figure 1). This is basically a flat area, which, until the regulation of rivers in the 19th century was a rather damp and watery region (Kovács 2016, pl. 1.2). This is visible in the schematic hydrogeological reconstructions and is demonstrated in the range of alluvial soil (Stefanovits 1992, fig. 1). Although alluvial soil types dominate the area, the percentage of loess soils is also quite high. In certain areas the presence of sand and quicksand is also characteristic, for example at Jászság (Kovács 2015, 33-5). The region is quite heterogeneous and includes different morphological, hydrographical characteristics, and various types of soil and vegetation (Dövényi 2010, 151-86).

From a chronological point of view, the general east Hungarian system characterizes the region: pre-Scythian, Scythian, and La Tène periods. Still, there are few pre-Scythian finds in the region (Kovács 2018, 22-3). In connection with the Scythian finds, we have somewhat more information at our disposal, but still rather sporadic. The Late Iron Age La Tène culture seems to be the richest in sources, based upon which we can interpret the settlements on a wider scale. The Dacian archaeological and historical evidence dating back to the latest period of the Iron Age is not known in the region. Based upon the above mentioned considerations, we can only talk about the Late Iron Age in detail, however, the basic characteristics of settlements of the Middle Iron Age will also be presented.

Archaeological studies in the region started in the second half of the 19th century; mainly amateur historians started to collect archaeological objects and carried out small-scale excavations apart from the experts of the Hungarian National Museum engaged in excavations at a few locations. In 1954, the archaeological collection was established at the Szolnok Museum, then systematic archaeological studies began: mainly rescue excavations. Until the 1980s the documentation of these excavations is rather incomplete and fragmented. In the 1990s systematic archaeological survey of the Tiszazug region took place and large-scale commercial excavations as well as regular rescue excavations were increasingly launched (Kovács 2017, 14-6). Up to date, there are in total 90 sites from the Middle Iron Age, and 132 from the Late Iron Age, including 21 sites from the Vekerzug culture and archaeological excavations carried out at sites of the La Tène culture, mainly rescue excavations. Altogether approximately 12 Scythian settlements have been unearthed, and more than double this figure from the Celtic period.

In D.C. Cowley, M. Fernández-Götz, T. Romankiewicz & H. Wendling (eds). Rural Settlement. Relating buildings, landscape, and people in the European Iron Age (Leiden 2019: Sidestone Press) 143-152.

Figure 1: Sites mentioned in the text.

13.2 Survey of the Tiszazug region

Since systematic site surveys have only been carried out in the Tiszazug area (approximately 248 square km), it is difficult to draw reliable conclusions on the number of sites located in other areas of the Middle Tisza region. However, a certain tendency can be observed in the location of sites. The sketch map of the county suggests that the sites tend to appear in greater numbers near big streaming waters both during the Scythian and La Tène periods (Kovács 2017, 87). In Tiszazug, due to the regular site survey, the sampling seems to be more reliable (Csányi-Tárnoki 2011), so this area is probably more suitable for drawing conclusions about medium term trends (Figure 2).

Altogether 35 Early and Middle Iron Age sites have been localized in the Tiszazug region. These clearly follow the course of the two major rivers Tisza and Körös. These sites are normally small in size, on average a few hundred, occasionally a few thousand square metres. These sites appear to fit into regular groups with each group consisting of four to five sites, in the close vicinity of one another, and these groups can clearly be separated. Apart from these site clusters, we know a few individual sites as well. A question that arises in case of clusters is how they relate to one another chronologically. Whether they were used at the same time, or belonged to a community that moved in space and time.

During the La Tène period, the number of sites increases to 63. Not only is this a quantitative increase, but also the size of the sites is larger by two or even three times. At the same time, it is still evident that the sites were basically organized in clusters forming a larger and loosely structured unit. These clusters can be classified into further greater units, such as in the Csépa Szelevény or Mesterszállás areas. Apart from the above mentioned clusters and units, the individual/single settlement type is still the most characteristic; these lone settlements are usually located further away from the interrelated clusters. The separated settlements still characterize the region somewhat further away from the interrelated clusters. Discrete single sites are still usual, but these are located a bit further from the bigger groups. A comparison between the different periods of the Iron Age in the study area shows a few remarkable characteristics of habitation patterns. Namely, the settlement clusters did not disappear at transition periods, but rather persisted and grew in size. It may be justifiably assumed that as a result of the

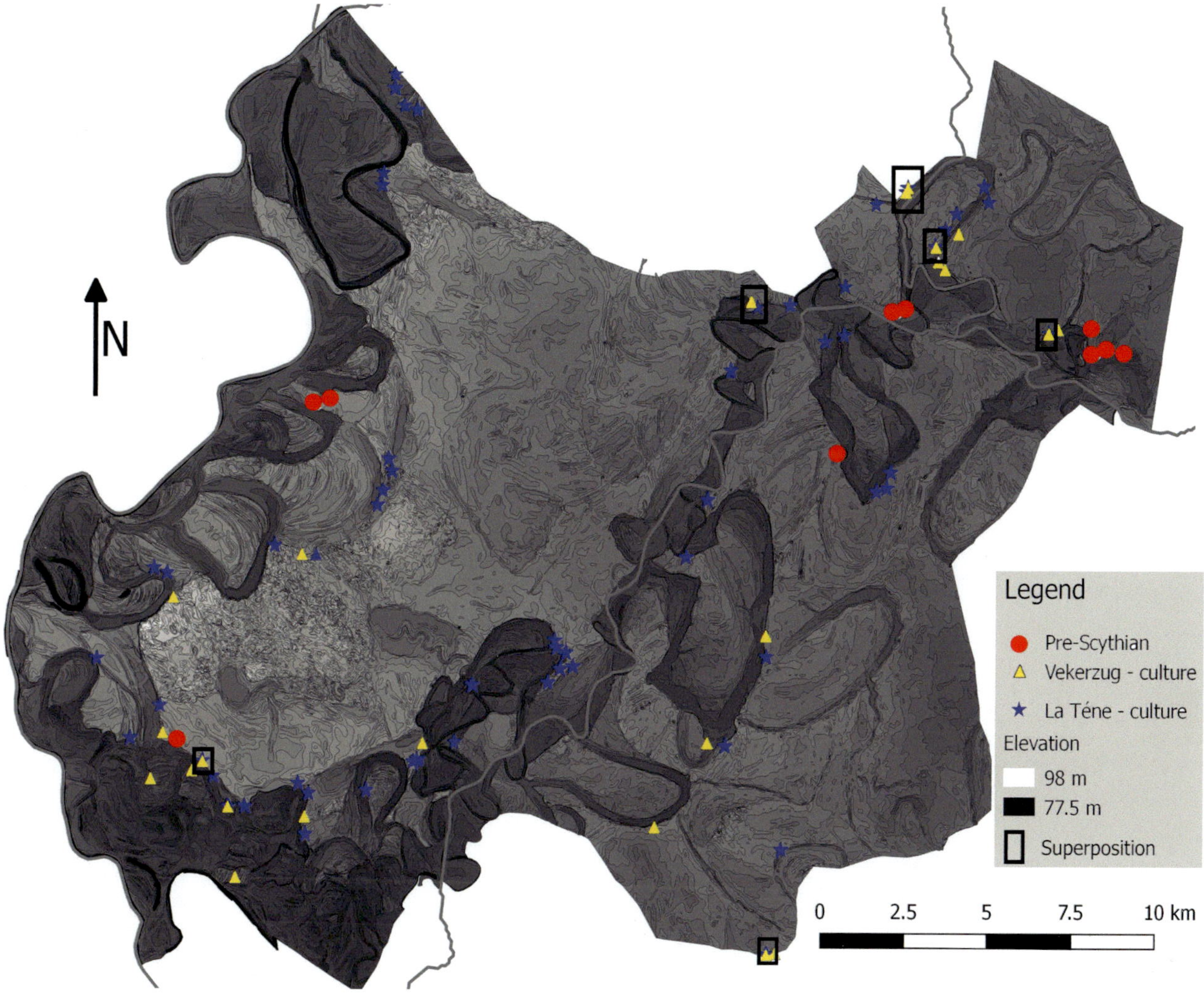

Figure 2: The distribution of Iron Age sites in the Tiszazug region (Map by Péter Mali).

negative economic and demographic developments in case of an aggressive, militant expansion, the previous structure of settlements would have been completely destroyed and probably re-arranged. Furthermore, in such cases we would not see the increase in the number of sites, but rather a sharp decrease. It is also important to take into account that there is no archaeological evidence of any conflict between the freshly arrived colonists and the locals in either the smaller nor in the broader region (e.g. Hellebrandt 1999, 233-6) – unlike in the second half of the 7th century BC when archaeological traces of conflict(s) can be detected. (Szabó *et al.* 2014, 5-6). These considerations allow us to conclude that a basically peaceful and rapid amalgamation process must have taken place. The sites of the newcomers fit into the previous network of sites of the indigenous community, therefore a peaceful integration process must have been implemented. On the other hand, Gergely Bóka suggests that the La Tène and Vekerzug cultures applied slightly different settling strategies (Bóka 2014, 25-6), which he attributes to climatic and other environmental reasons (Bóka 2008, 150-8; 2012a, 27; 2012b, 64). At the same time, he points out that while small differences can be detected, the trends characterizing the settling seem to be the same as in Tiszazug (Bóka 2013, 285-6). Yet, the Körös-region and Tiszazug sub-region show different morphological, hydrographical and environmental characteristics, so that they cannot be compared because of their different sizes. Furthermore, different environmental conditions might have required different solutions that could have varied from region to region.

In the Tiszazug micro-region, the results of two excavations could help to observe the cultural mixture in rural settlements, and the resulting co-existence in these communities. In 2017 a small part of an Iron Age settlement was unearthed at Kunszentmárton – Nagy-

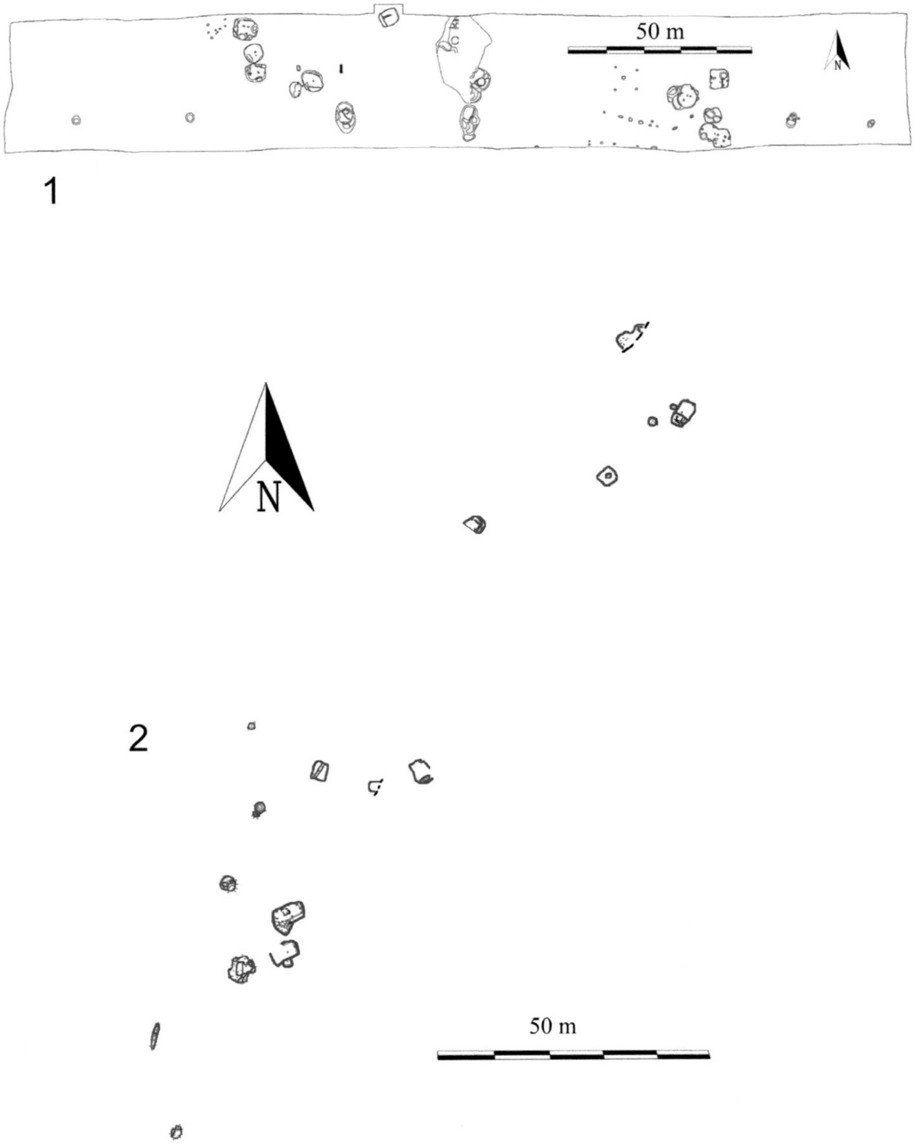

Figure 3: (1) Layout of the Jászberény-Almási tanya site and (2) Rákóczifalva-Bagi-föld.

Éri-Főcsatorna-Keleti Part I. In the fill of the semi-sunken dwellings ceramic fragments from the Middle and Late La Tène period were found. Because of the recent discovery of these finds, it is now not possible to publish and comment of these developments. In 1986 and 1987, János Cseh excavated a building where some Late Iron Age pottery came to light (Cseh 2013, fig. 12.). Similar amalgamation tendencies can be observed in the northern edge of the Great Hungarian Plain and in the connecting zones in the North Hungarian Mountains at Polgár (Szabó *et al.* 2008, 205) and at Sajópetri (Szabó *et al.* 2007, 251; Szabó & Tankó 2007, 173-4). Recently, Károly Tankó has demonstrated the presence of the ceramics of the Vekerzug culture in a Late Iron Age context in a comparative typological study (Tankó 2016, 172-3).

The study of cemeteries does not bring us closer to understanding of the cultural process either. Two cemeteries have been unearthed. At Öcsöd-Rédai kert nine graves of La Tène culture came to light. Unfortunately, a great part of the finds is not available and cannot be used for further analysis (Kovács 2017, 16). Due to the lack of reliable data, the very dating of the cemetery is rather uncertain, but based upon a sword in grave 9 a dating to LT B2/C1 (late 4th to early 3rd centuries BC) is well-founded (Kovács 2017, 64). Most of the finds from an excavation carried out by Gábor Csallány at Kunszentmártok-Telekpart have disappeared. Based upon the description of graves from the original documentation we know that there were two contracted skeletons in the cemetery (Hunyadi 1957, 120). In the case of La Tène assorted rite cemeteries, a cultural mixture of the locals and newcomers' communities is usually assumed, with similar cases known in north-east Hungary and north-west Romania (Rustoiu-Berecki 2016). In case of the Tiszazug Iron Age finds a few comprehensive studies have been published (Cseh 2006, 19-23; Kemenczei 2009; Kovács 2017). It is thus rather difficult to draw far-reaching conclusions. The basic problem is that there are neither fully excavated settlements, nor remote sensing data at our disposal.

13.3 The internal structure of settlements

From the Middle Iron Age we know of only one part of a settlement that is suitable for the study of internal settlement organisation, and this was unearthed at Jászberény 'Almási' in 2004 prior to road-construction works. Some eleven buildings were identified (Figure 3). Based upon their arrangements, we can draw limited conclusions of the settlement structure. Inside the basically loose structure, there are two nuclei of five and six buildings set very close to one another. In the other half of the site, a settlement section of the La Tène culture is also located (Kovács 2013; 2016). The aggregated ground plan clearly shows that in the La Tène settlement section an area twice the size contains a quarter fewer buildings than in the Middle Iron Age settlement section. The distance between individual buildings can be up to 100 metres. One interesting characteristic of the settlement is the massive size of the ditches (Kovács 2016, fig. 3; Pl. 2.1), which might have been used to channel away water as well as for defensive functions. However, it is difficult to interpret a multitude of small branches inside the ditches. If we suppose that the ditches enclose a circular area it may have extended to 8 ha. Another La Tène period settlement came to light in 2006/07 near Rákóczifalva close to Szolnok. Sporadic settlement structures can also be observed there. The buildings belong to two distinct groups (Figure 3).

Since only a few sections of the settlements are known, far-reaching conclusions cannot be drawn about their structure. It may be established, though, that the fundamentally sporadic structure might have been dominant, with some smaller groups signalling households, or other functional units. The main difference between the Middle and Late Iron Age can be established that in case of the Vekerzug culture building groups or households are more conceivable. This concentration can be seen in case of Jászberény Almási Tanya, where the archaeological features of the Vekerzug culture form two distinct groups, whereas it does not apply to the settlement area of the La Tène culture. The La Tène period settlement of Rákóczifalva reveals rather dispersed structures, however, one can detect two groups.

13.4 Buildings and function

A question that always arises in case of buildings is the correlation of function and form. Scythian buildings have four basic plans:

- circular house: simple circle with central post hole, the pit is usually shallow (Figure 4.1).
- amorphous building: amorphous outline with irregular posts, with pit(s) of variable depth (Figure 4.2).
- generic pit house: rounded square in shape, with a single post hole on the long axis, frequent interior pits and wall-seats, the building pit is clearly detectable (Figure 4.3).
- quadratic house: square-shaped building, with supporting posts on the long axis, small irregular posts, shallow building pit (Figure 4.4).

In the case of Celtic buildings, there are only two variants: rectangular and square houses (Figure 4). These are normally similar in size and almost seem to be standardized, but differ in details (Tímár 2011, 300). These differences include rounded corners, the location of posts or the shape of the wall-seats (Kovács 2013).

The finds unearthed in the buildings usually provide very few hints to their function or use. In most cases only simple fragments of ceramics come to light, which also makes precise dating rather difficult. Apart from the meagre inventories of finds, in most cases they are rather fragmented to smaller than 5 cm (Kovács 2016, Figure 4.2). In a few cases, however, it is possible to suggest the function of individual buildings. At the Vekerzug settlement of the Jászberény-Almási tanya site, feature number 37 is a roughly regular building, with traces of a probable weaving frame identified in the interior (Figures 4.4 & 5.1). Spindle whorls and a bone awl were also found in the building.

In Szolnok County, iron slag has been found in the infill of building structures. At Jászfelsőszentgyörgy – Túróczi-tanya site a pie-shaped iron object has been unearthed from a Scythian building which might be interpreted as a semi-final product. The excavation documentation reports on a few lumps of iron slag found in a La Tène age building at Kengyel-Kis-tanya (Cseh 2011, 26; 1993; 2001). At the La Tène settlement at Jászberény-Almási tanya, iron slag weighing approximately 1 kg was excavated (Kovács 2016, 193), and is regarded as similar to La Tène period samples of slag found at Ordacsehi. It is probable that these few lumps of iron slag might indicate household-level metalworking activities.

Other finds and phenomena are related to the archaeologically more detectable range of grain processing activities. Nearly all Vekerzug and La Tène period sites produce millstones and grindstones in

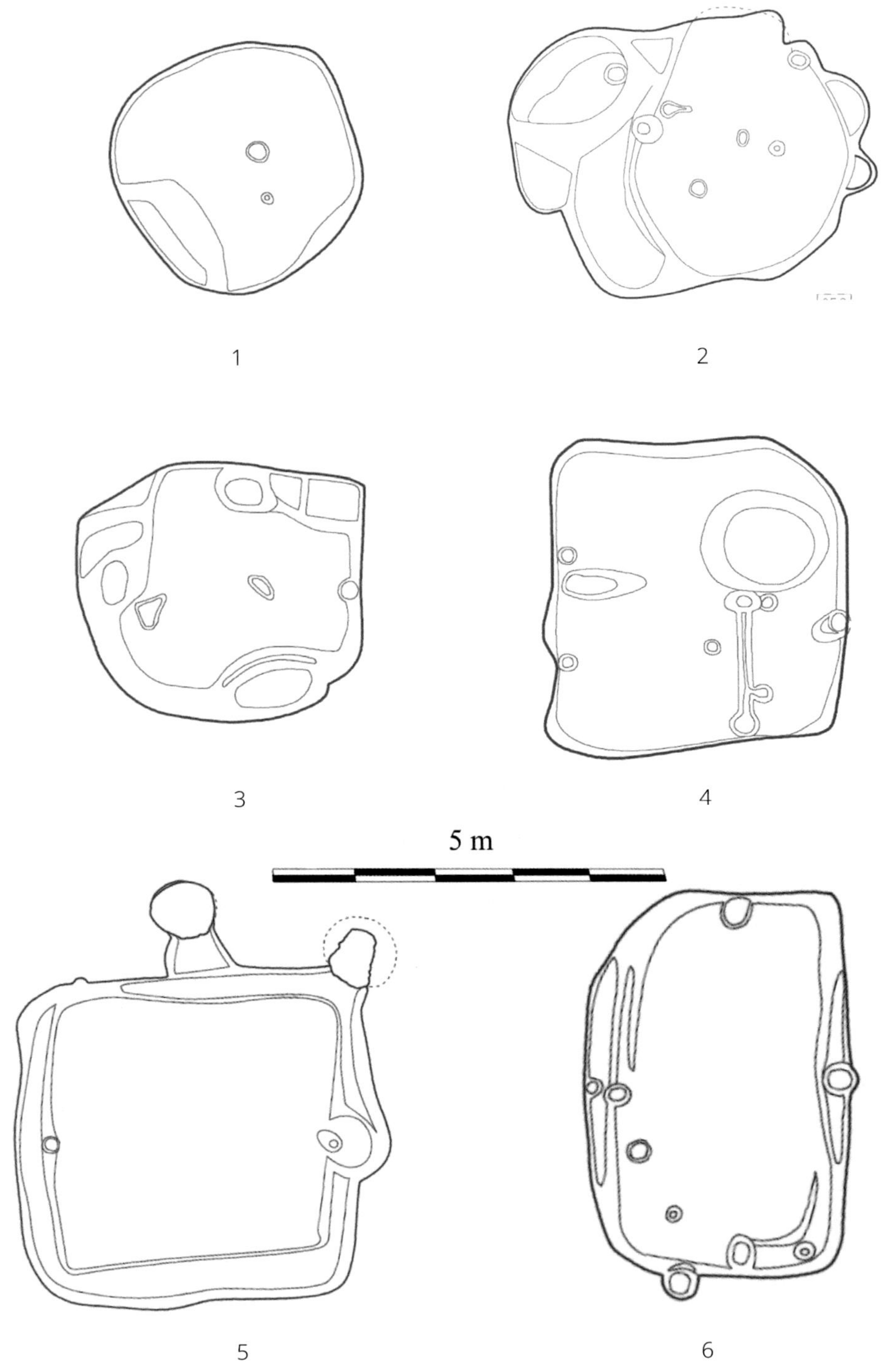

Figure 4: Main types of sunken floor houses.

smaller or bigger fragments (Cseh 1990a, fig. 11; 1990b, 74; 1992, Pl. III.17; 2005, 16.). Probably one of the most spectacular ones is the Jászberény stone tablet, which was placed on the floor inside the building, and it is highly likely that hand milling and chopping was carried out on its surface. Another example is from Tiszagyenda, where nearly intact millstones were placed on a burnt patch inside a building (Figure 5.2). It is generally characteristic in the region that fragments of millstones come to light in buildings or in other features. Small-scale tool finds are fairly scarce, though there is a scythe ring from Kengyel-Kis-tanya (Cseh 2011, 14).

Direct evidence of agricultural activities is represented by implements and tools from Tiszafüred (Kriveczky 1991,

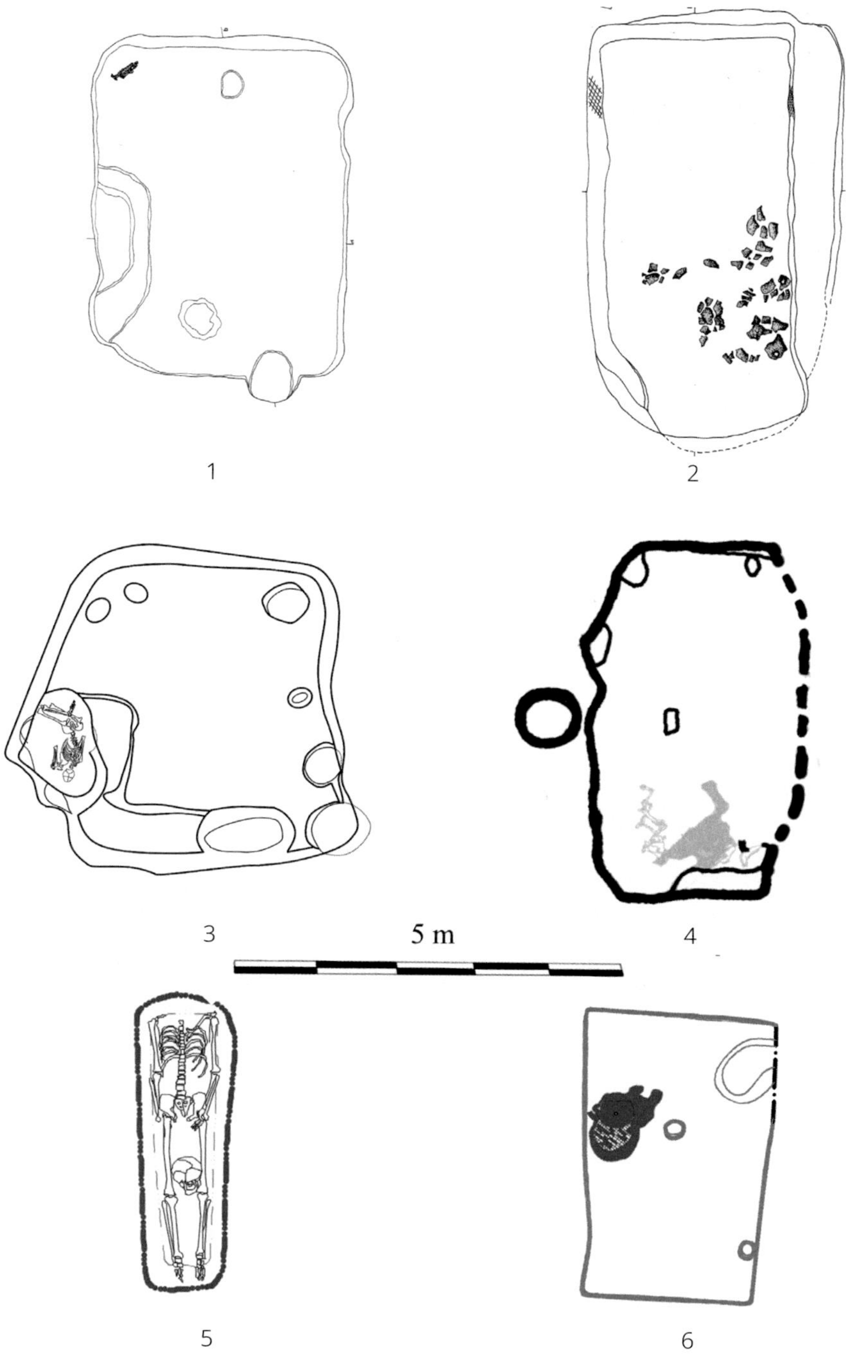

Figure 5: Traces of different activities on the settlements.

73-5), where three iron ploughshares and three sickles were found placed on top of each other in a corner of the building. The tools do not appear to have been worn through use and may have been a ritual deposition. Other ritual features were unearthed at the site (e. g. pseudo-kernos).

More cult features come from Rákóczifalva, where the skeleton of a horse was placed on the floor of a La Tène culture building (Figure 5.3). The skeleton was deposited in anatomical order with no signs of post-mortem manipulation. Similar phenomena were reported from Tihany-Óvár (Regenye 2004, 189; Bartosiewitz 2004, 201-22) and Sopron Krautacker" (Jerem *et al.* 1985, 12). In the Middle Iron Age part of a settlement described above (Jászberény-Almási tanya), there was a decapitated individual buried between the buildings. No other signs of injuries can be identified on the skeleton of the 30/40 year-old man, but his third and fourth vertebrae were missing and these might have been destroyed during the removal of the skull (Figure 5.4). The skeleton of a 30/40 year-old woman was lying under the floor of a La Tène period building in Túrkeve. From the position of the skeleton (legs curved backwards, arms crossed in front of the chest), it seems as if the victim had been tied and after the assumed execution the body was thrown into the pit (Figure 5.5). The anthropological examinations revealed no traces of other trauma on the skeleton. In both periods unusual or irregular position of skeletons suggest some unusual events or acts behind these burials, such as homicide or sacrifice.

The most interesting phenomenon of a votive nature is the pseudo-kernos pot unearthed in building number 9 at Tiszafüred-Morotvapart. Fragments were lying on the floor of the building, on top of a slightly burnt red patch (Laszlovszky-Kriveczky-Cseh 1985, 4-8; Kriveczky 1991, 72). We can assume that the pot was destroyed after ritual feasting. Due to the inadequacy of the documentation, we do not know what animal bones were found in the building, the composition of which might provide hints about the event.

Another significant aspect of the buildings is the role they played in culture contact and exchange. In the study area there are no burials where the interaction between the La Tène culture and the Vekerzug culture can be discerned. However, there are buildings where the material items of the two cultures are mixed. One possible example is a number of archaeological features at Jászberény-Almási tanya (Kovács 2017, 194-5). A similar situation is at Tiszapüspöki-Holt-Tisza-part, where a vessel from the Vekerzug culture was found lying on the floor of a Late Iron Age house. Excavation documentation reports that fragments of Vekerzug pots and fragments of a La Tène graphite *situla* came to light in one of the wells at the Middle Iron Age Vekerzug-culture Jászkisér-Ludas-oldal site (Csányi 2010, 231-2). In 2017, a part of a settlement was unearthed, presumably dating from the 4th century BC, at Kunszentmárton – Nagy-Éri Főcsatorna-Keleti Part I, where material culture exhibits approximately equal characteristics of both the Vekerzug and the La Tène cultures.

13.5 Conclusion

In the Middle Tisza Region, the location of settlements was largely determined by environmental conditions. The primary factor seems to be the closeness to waters. The surveys in the Tiszazug region indicate that the sites were situated on the high banks, but never too far from the watercourse. During the Middle Iron Age Vekerzug culture and the Late Iron Age La Tène culture, there are no traces of any rearrangement of settlement structure during transitional periods. It is more likely that the settlement structure developed on the basis of Early- (Pre-Scythian) and Middle Iron Age (Vekerzug culture) foundations, and that the number and size of sites increases, with the new sites integrated into previously established patterns. It seems that during these processes, settlement clusters formed in certain parts of the region.

Although any functional determination of building structures is difficult, it is quite apparent that the various types of buildings of the Middle Iron Age were replaced by more uniform and regular building structures. Sometimes, the economic function and sacral role of settlements and buildings can be established. Iron working tools, implements for grain processing, and agricultural tools, and weaving and spinning accessories provide evidence of economic diversity. Ritual activities are illustrated by the presence of human and animal skeletons, but there are signs of ritual feasting as well. Although the structures of settlements and buildings do not show great variability, a wide spectrum of activities can be observed. Phenomena reflecting sacral activity exist alongside purely economic functions, the central sphere of which is the house and the settlement.

As one of the most significant aspects of settlement history, the phenomena hinting at cultural exchange and assimilation must be emphasized. Although the settlements and the highly fragmented ceramic finds allow for precise dating, mixed pottery assemblages of the Vekerzug and La Tène cultures suggest that in certain cases we can suppose contemporary coexistence. While Iron Age settlement studies sometimes suggest simple rural communities operating on a low economic level, this is an over-simplification that fails to address the complexity indicated by the archaeological evidence. The examples discussed above indicate a considerable complexity with ritual, economic, environmental, social, and political aspects expressed through the settlement record.

13.6 Acknowledgements

Péter Mali kindly granted access to the finds from the excavation at Kunszentmárton – Nagy-Éri-Főcsatorna-Keleti. The examination of the slags was evaluated by Béla Török, the head of the ARGUM archaeometallurgic work-group of the University of Miskolc. The anthropological examinations were carried out by Tamás Hajdu and Tamás Szeniczey (Eötvös Loránd University).

13.7 Bibliography

Bartosiewitz, L. 2004. A Tihany-Óváron feltárt szarvascsontváz előzetes vizsgálata. The Preliminary Study of a Red Deer (Cervuselaphus) Skeleton from Tihany-Óváron, Hungary. In E. Gy. Nagy, J. Dani & Zs. Hajdú (eds). *ΜΩΜΟΣ II Őskoros Kutatók II. Összejövetelének konferenciakötete, Debrecen, 2000. november 6-8.* 201-8. Debrecen: Hajdú-Bihar Megyei Múzeumok Igazgatósága.

Bóka, G. 2008. A körös-vidéken zajló településtörténeti változások paleoökológiai háttere a késő bronzkor-végén és a kora vaskorban. Egy hipotézis. In G. Bóka & E. Martyin (eds). *Körös-menti évezredek. Régészeti ökológiai és településtörténeti kutatások a Körös-vidéken. Gyulai Katalógusok 13,* Gyula, 149-69.

Bóka, G. 2012a. Changes in the Settlement History of the Late Bronze and Iron Age Körös Region Hydrology, Relief and Settlements. In L. Marta (ed.). *Die Gáva-Kultur In Der Theißebene Und Siebenbürgen Symposium Satu Mare 17-18 June 2011 Satu Mares Sudii Şi Comunicări seria Arheologie.* 23-34. Satu Mare: Muzeul Judeţean Satu Mare.

Bóka, G. 2012b. Településtörténeti változások a Körös-vidéken a késő bronzkorban és a vaskorban. In A. Kreiter, Á. Pető & B. Tugya (eds). *Vízrajz, térszínek és települések. Környezet – Ember – Kultúra. A természettudományok és a régészet párbeszéde. Environment – Human – Culture Dialogue between applied sciences and archaeology Proceedings of the Conference Held Between 6 th and 8th of October 2010 by the National Heritage Protection Centre of the Hungarian National Museum.* 57-66. Budapest: Magyar Nemzeti Múzeum.

Bóka, G. 2013. Településtörténeti változások a Körös-vidéken a késő bronzkorban és a vaskorban II. Paleoökológiai elemzés. Talajtípusok és településrendszer. In L. Marta (ed.). *Peregrinări Arheologice Între Estul Şi Vestul Europei Archäologische Wanderungen Zwischen Ost- Und Westeuropa. Studii În Onoarea Lui Tiberius Bader La Aniversarea De 75 De Ani. Studien Für Tiberius Bader Zum 75. Geburtstag. Satu Mare Studii Şi Comunicări Seria Arheologie XXIX/I 2013.* 269-312. Satu Mare: Muzeul Judetean Satu Mare.

Bóka, G. 2014. Településtörténeti változások a Körös-vidéki késő bronzkorban és vaskorban. Settlement historical transformations in the Late Bronze Age and the Iron Age Körös Region. In V. Kiss, G. Kulcsár, G. V. Szabó & G. Váczi (eds). *State of the Hungarian Bronze Age Research. Abstracts of the conference papers held between 17th and 18th of December 2014.* 25-6. Budapest.

Csányi, M. 2010. Jászkisér, Ludas-oldal I. In J. Kisfaludi (ed.). *Régészeti Kutatások Magyarországon 2009. Archaeological Investigation in Hungary 2009.* 231-2. Budapest:Kulturális Örökség Igazgatósága és Magyar Nemzeti Múzeum.

Csányi, M. & Tárnoki, J. 2011. Településrégészeti kutatások a Tiszazugban. Életjel – Tanulmányok az ezredvégi Tiszazug Népéletéből. In J. Bartha, Cs. Benedek & A. Gecse (eds). *Szolnok.* 7-36. Szolnok: Damjanich János Múzeum.

Cseh, J. 1990a. Egy szkíta ház Szolnok-Zagyvapartról. In I. Turóczy & I. T. Bereczki (eds). *Múzeumi Levelek 63-64.* 3-16. Szolnok: Damjanich János Múzeum.

Cseh, J. 1990b. Egy kelta lakóház a Közép-Tisza-vidékéről. *Jászkunság 36/6.* 58-74.

Cseh, J. 1992. Kelta, szarmata, gepida és avar település maradványai egy nagykunsági lelőhelyen (Kuncsorba – XIV. dűlő). *A Nyíregyházi Jósa András Múzeum évkönyve 30-32. – 1987-1989.* Nyíregyháza, 145-60.

Cseh, J. 1993. Kengyel-Kiss-tanya. *Tisicum – A Jász-Nagykun-Szolnok Megyei Múzeumok Évkönyve VIII,* Szolnok. 137-58.

Cseh, J. 2001. Egy késő vaskori ház Kengyel határából (Adalékok a kelta telepépítmények ismeretéhez). *ΜΩΜΟΣ I. „Fiatal Őskoros Kutatok" I. Összejövetelének konferenciakötete.* 249-62.

Cseh, J. 2005. Szkíta telepobjektum Besenyszög-Szórópusztán. *Múzeumi Levelek* 80-81. Szolnok, 2005. 5-23.

Cseh, J. 2006. Archaeologia Scythica. Adalékok a Közép-Tisza mente vaskori történetéhez. Archaeologia Scythica. Additamenta to History of the Middle Tisza Region in The Iron Age. *Tisicum – Jász-Nagykun-Szolnok Megyei Múzeumok Évkönyve 15.* (2006), 13-37.

Cseh, J. 2013. Kelta ház Szelevény mellett (1986-1987). Celtic House Near Szelevény Village (1986-1987). *Tisicum – Jász-Nagykun-Szolnok Megyei Múzeumok Évkönyve 13.* (2003), 47-67.

Hunyadi, I. 1957. Kelták a Kárpát-medencében. Leletanyag. *Régészeti Füzetek 2.* Budapest: Magyar Nemzeti Múzeum.

Jerem, E., Facsar, G., Kordos, L., Krolopp, E. & Vörös, I. 1985. A Sopron-Krautackeren feltárt vaskori telep régészeti és környezetrekonstrukciós vizsgálata. II. *Archaeológiai Értesítő 112.* 3-24.

Kemenczei, T. 2009. Studien zu den denkmälern skythisch geprägter alföld gruppe. *Inventarta Praehistorica Hungariae 12;* Budapest: Magyar Nemzeti Múzeum.

Kovács, P. F. 2013. Egy késő vaskori teleprészlet a Jászságból – Jászberény-Almási-tanya 5. lelőhely. A késő vaskori telepek kutatásának helyzete és kutatástörténeti áttekintése. *TISICUM, Jász – Nagykun – Szolnok Megyei Múzeumok Évkönyve,* XXII. Szolnok, 65-78.

Kovács, P. F. 2016. Chronological and Typological Problems of a La Tène Settlement Section from the Great Hungarian Plain. In S. Berecki (ed.). Iron Age Chronology in the Carpathian Basin Proceedings of the International Colloquium from Târgu Mureş 8-10 October 2015. *Biblotheca Musei Marisiensis Series Archaeologica XIII.* 191-202. Târgu Mureş 2016.

Kovács, P. F. 2017. Szkíták és kelták öröksége. A vaskor régészete Jász-Nagykun-Szolnok megyében. Legacy of Scythians and Celts. The Archaeology of the Iron Age in Jász-Nagykun-Szolnok County. *Szolnoki Régészeti Tanulmányok 1. Archaeological Papers of Szolnok 1.* Szolnok: Damjanich János Múzeum.

Kriveczky, B. 1991. A késő vaskori (kelta) telep. Régészeti ásatások Tiszafüred-Morotvaparton. In L. Tálas & L. Madaras (eds). *Szolnok Megyei Múzeumi Adattár, 32,* Szolnok: Damjanich János Múzeum 65-96.

Laszlovszky, J., Kriveczky, B. & Cseh, J. 1985. Településnyomok és temetkezések az őskortól a későközépkorig a tiszafüredi Morotvaparton. *Múzeumi Levelek 47-48.* Szolnok, 1985. 3-27.

Regenye, J. 2004. Előzetes jelentés a Tihany-Óvárban folytatott feltárásról. *ΜΩΜΟΣ* II Őskoros Kutatók II. Összejövetelének konferenciakötete Debrecen, 2000. 187-200.

Rustoiu, A. & Berecki, S. 2016. Cultural Encounters and Fluid Identities in the Eastern Carpathian Basin in the 4th-3rd Centuries BC. In I. Armit, H. Potrebica, M.Č. Rešnar, P. Mason & L. Büster (eds). Cultural Encounters In Iron Age Europe. *Archaeolingua Series Minor 38.* 285-304. Budapest: Archeolingua.

Szabó, M., (dir) Czajlik, Z., Bödőcs, A., Guillaumet, J-P., Szabó, D., Tankó, K., Tímár, L., Bartosiewitz, L., Mohai, R. & Molnár, F. 2007. *L' habitat de l' époque de La Tène à Sajópetri-Hosszú-dűlő.* Budapest: L'Harmattan.

Szabó, M., Czajlik, Z., Tankó, K. & Timár, L. 2008 Polgár: L'habitat du Second Age du Fer (IIIe Siecle Av. J.-Chr.). *Acta Archaeologica Academiae Scientiarum Hungaricae 59,* 183-223.

Szabó, D. & Tankó, K. 2007. Présentation du système de gestion de céramique de Sajópetri (Hongrie). A Sajópetriben feltárt La Tène-kori kerámialeletek feldolgozási rendszere. Ősrégészeti Levelek 8-9, 2007, 168-77.

Szabó, G. V., Czajlik, Z. & Reményi, L. 2014. Traces of an Iron Age Armed Conflict. *Hungarian Archeology*, 2014, Winter, 1-7.

Tankó, K. 2016. Chronological Aspects of Ceramic Types from Recently Investigated La Tène Settlements in Hungary. In S. Berecki (ed.). Iron Age Chronology in the Carpathian Basin Proceedings of the International Colloquium from Târgu Mureş 8-10 October 2015. *Biblotheca Musei Marisiensis Series Archaeologica XIII.* Târgu Mureş. 165-90.

Tímár, L. 2011. Késő vaskori veremházak maradványainak értelmezése. Interpretation of the sunken houses of the Late Iron Age. Ősrégészeti Levelek, *Prehistoric Newsletter*, ΜΩΜΟΣ, Őskoros Kutatók VII. Összejövetele, 2011. március 16-18. Százhalombatta, Matrica Múzeum, Budapest 2013. 290-302.

Török, B., Kovács, Á., Barkóczy, P. & Kristáy, F. 2012. Complex Archaeometrical Examination of Iron Tools and Slag from a Celtic Settlement in the Carpathian Basin; *Proceedings of the 39th International Symposium for Archaeometry*, Leuven (2012) 2014. 125-34.

Török, B.,Kovács Á., Barkóczy, P. & Kristáy, F. 2013. Ordacsehi-Csereföld kelta településéről származó vassalak és vastárgyak anyagvizsgálata és készítés-technológiai vonatkozásai. *Archeometriai Műhely 2013/X./1.* 23-32.

Chapter 14

House or workshop?

A case study of two pit-houses at the Iron Age settlement site of Michałowice, Kazimierza Wielka county (Poland)

Jan Bulas, Michał Kasiński & Gabriela Juźwińska

14.1 Introduction

The settlement site of Michałowice is located in the southern part of Poland, in Świętokrzyskie Voiw, Kazimierza Wielka county (Poland). The site, excavated between 2012 and 2014, revealed only two settlement horizons, both dated to the Iron Age (Bulas *et al.* 2015, 196). The earlier comprised finds of the La Tène culture, and the later one remains of the Przeworsk culture. While the excavations, which covered approximately 500 m^2, did not recover any habitation features of La Tène culture, many Przeworsk culture features were uncovered, including two pit-houses.

The Przeworsk culture is an archaeological complex known largely from excavations of cemeteries that dates from 3rd century BC to the 5th century AD, and is spread across large areas of what is now central and southern Poland (Andrzejowski 2010, 59-60). It is considered to be heavily influenced by La Tène culture, which can be seen in both the material culture and funeral customs (Andrzejowski 2010, 59). The other possible La Tène influence may be the adaptation of pit-houses/dwellings. Before the 21st century, only small scale excavation had been undertaken on settlement sites, and this limited the possibility to study a full range of structures present on Przeworsk culture sites. As a result of wide scale excavations conducted in the last decade, it has become possible to look at the subject with fresh eyes with recent archaeological work at Michałowice shedding new light on this topic.

14.2 Przeworsk pit-houses

In D.C. Cowley, M. Fernández-Götz, T. Romankiewicz & H. Wendling (eds). Rural Settlement. Relating buildings, landscape, and people in the European Iron Age (Leiden 2019: Sidestone Press) 153-156.

The pit-houses of the Przeworsk culture, comprising the remains of buildings characterised by a sunken-floor, used to be considered "ordinary" or standard habitations of the period (Godłowski 1981, 105; Jadczykowa 1983, 190-4). This position was due to a lack of evidence for long, above ground, post-built structures that are typical of some other areas of Barbaricum (Schuster 2012, 429-30). However, this position is being undermined by a number of factors. Firstly, large area excavations during highway construction projects have revealed post-built structures similar to those known from elsewhere in Barbaricum (Schuster 2012; Naglik *et al.* 2014, 79-278; Kot & Piotrowska 2016, 107-22). Moreover reappraisals of the published results of older excavations have provided widespread

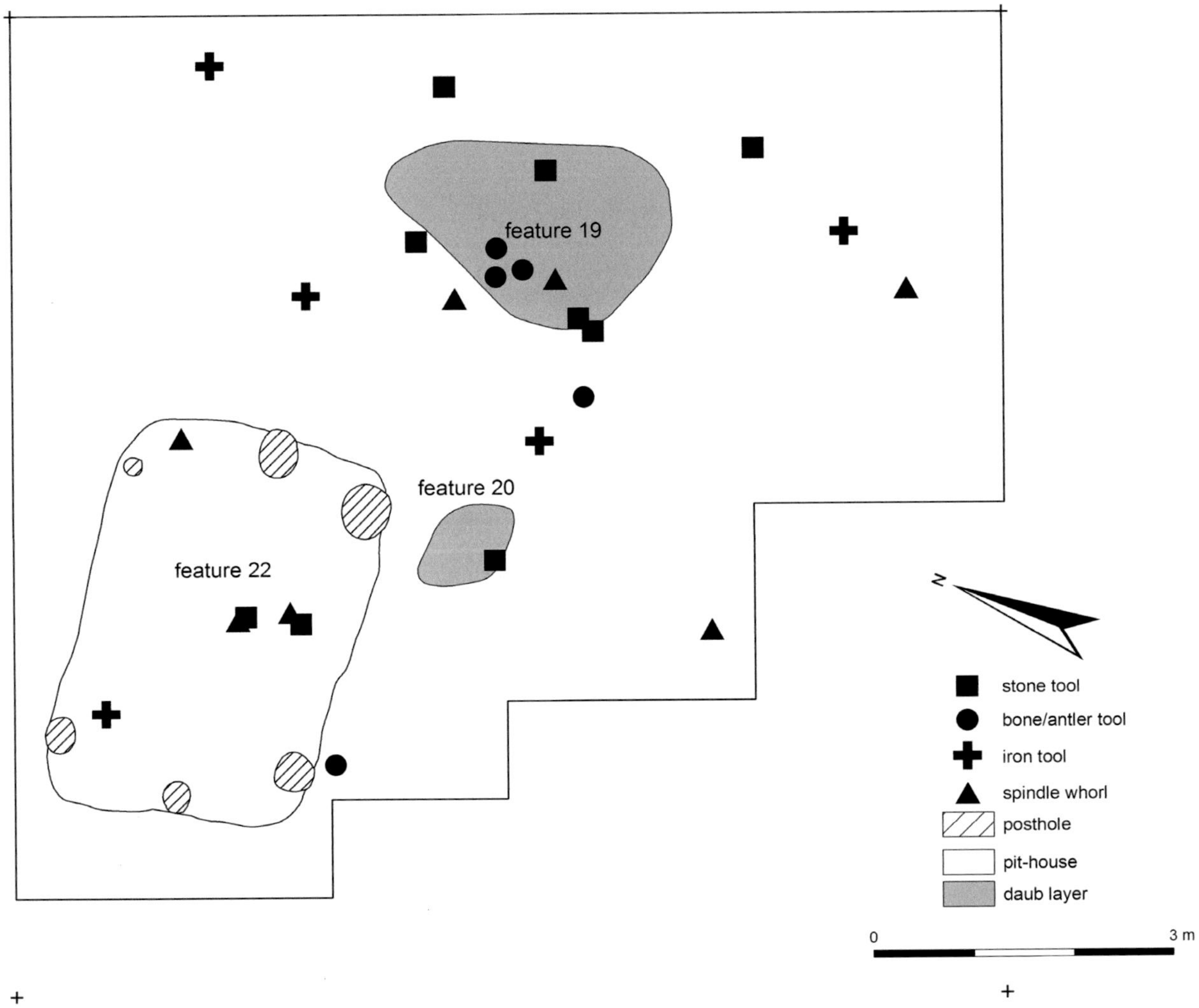

Figure 1: Pit-house I.

evidence of Przeworsk culture long-houses (Schuster 2012, 427-60). Secondly, new studies are shedding light on the range of possible functions of structures of La Tène and Przeworsk culture date, such as storage, production of bone/antler, metal tools and textile or pottery (Danielisová 2006, 294; Pazda & Tomczak 2008, 253-66; Michałowski 2011, 164). Thus, there are a few factors that now seem to indicate that pit-houses were not residential in purpose, including that they are small in area (*i.e.* approx. 9-15m²) and maybe more importantly a lack of hearths in most of the excavated examples. In exploring this issue two excavated pit-houses at Michałowice are described here.

14.2.1 Feature 22 (Pit-house I)

The first of the excavated pit-houses comprised a subrectangular pit 11 m² in area, and up to 80 cm in depth below the present-day surface level. Three posts are ranged along both of the shorter sides, presumably providing support for the walls and roof (Figure 1). In the filling of the feature typical settlement material was found, including pottery fragments and small iron tools, possibly used for fine carving. There was no evidence, such as fragments of daub, which would suggest insulation of the walls. Numerous fragments of half-worked antler were discovered along with iron and stone tools such as chisels and smoothing planes around the feature. Most of the finds were located in a layer covered by daub, interpreted as the remains of a collapsed light wall construction. It is suggested that it separated the working space related to the function of the pit-house.

14.2.2 Feature 28 (Pit- House II)

The interpretation of this feature, which comprises an oblong pit about 9 m² in area and up to 1m in depth, rather depends on whether a hearth situated next to the eastern side of the pit is associated with it or not (Figure 2).

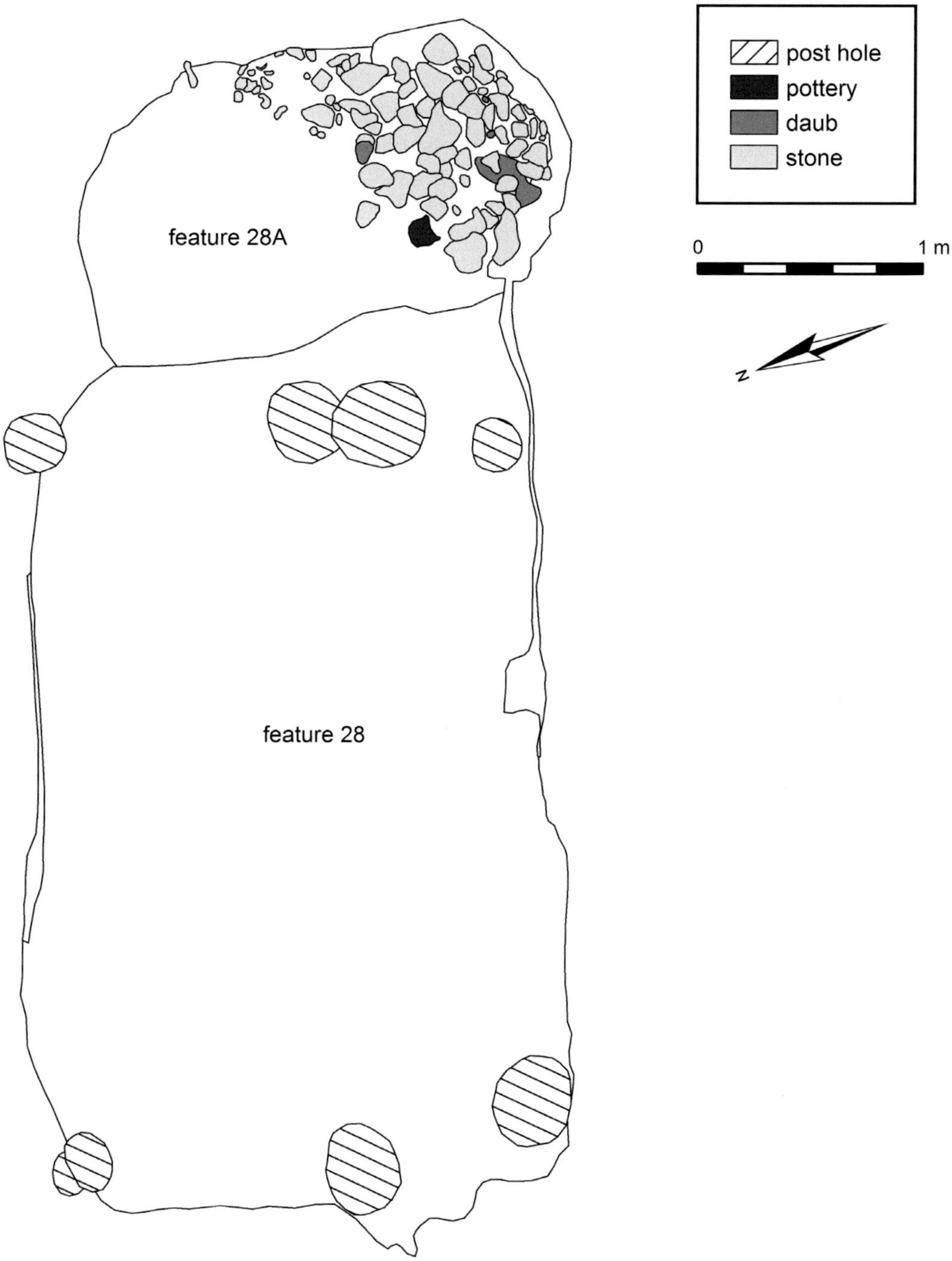

Figure 2 : Pit-house II.

Unfortunately the stratigraphic relationship of the pit and the hearth is unclear, but if it was an integral part of the building then the size of the whole structure was about 11 m^2. Like feature 22, three posts are ranged along both ends. The fill of the pits contained pottery fragments, and like feature 22, artefacts were discovered in the surrounding area, including grinding tools, a quern, and bone tool, probably for hide working. The presence of the hearth and the ceramics bearing evidence of metalworking suggest activities connected with metallurgy.

14.3 Conclusions

Recent excavations at the settlement site in Michałowice have explored two structures interpreted as pit-houses. The good preservation of both features and the recovery of a wide range of artefacts invites alternative interpretations of the structures, which have previously been regarded as domestic habitations. Rather, the new evidence supports interpretation of the use of the buildings in various production activities. The finds from around feature 22 suggest bone and antler working.

While it is difficult to specify the type of activities that took place around feature 28, hide or metal working are probable.

It is also worth noting that there is no evidence that these small structures were used for habitation, and that such remains have previously invited interpretation as domestic buildings in the absence of other suitable buildings. However, this is no longer the case, and traces of a larger post-built structure were also found at site 20 in Michałowice. Indeed, other excavations of settlements discovered during highway construction projects illustrate that pit-houses are often located between other usually larger post structures (Naglik *et al.* 2014, 79-278; Kot & Piotrowska 2016, 107-22). Like other examples known from other parts of Barbaricum these were laid out in clusters. The fuller understanding of the functions of the structures commonly called pit-houses requires further work, including excavation, and the analysis of forms of construction and of finds. Previous studies (Jadczykowa 1981; Michałowski 2011) of Przeworsk settlement have not been able to explore the role of the sunken features within settlements, but the excavations and analysis reported here provide some foundation for a fuller understanding of building morphology and function, which includes indications of specialisation in building function and differentiation between domestic and workshop spaces.

14.4 Bibliography

Andrzejowski, J. 2010. The Przeworsk Culture. A Brief Story. In U. Lund Hansen & A. Bitner-Wróblewska (eds). *Worlds Apart? Contacts across the Baltic Sea in the Iron Age.* 59-110. København-Warszawa: Det Kongelige Nordiske Oldkriftselskab.

Bulas, J. & Zagórska-Telega J. & Wroniecki, P. 2015. Non-invasive prospection of two Iron Age sites in Michałowice, southern Poland. In A. Rzeszotarska-Nowakiewicz (ed.). *Archeologia Polona* 53, 194-8.

Danielisová, A. 2006. To the architecture of oppida. Reconstruction of one part settlement pattern behind the ramparts. In B. Gediga & W. Piotrowski (eds). *Architektur und Bauwesen in der Bronze- und den frühen Perioden der Eisenzeit. Probleme der Rekonstruktion.* 269-302. Prace Komisji Archeologicznej Nr. 16. Biskupin-Wrocław: Universität Leipzig.

Godłowski, K. 1981. Kultura przeworska. Budownictwo. In J. Wielowiejski (ed.). *Prahistoria ziem polskich 5, Późny okres lateński i okres wpływów rzymskich.* 105-6. Wrocław: Zakład Narodowy im. Ossolińskich.

Jadczykowa, I. 1981. Budownictwo mieszkalne ludności kultury przeworskiej na obszarze Polski. *Prace i Materiały Muzeum Archeologicznego i Etnograficznego w Łodzi, Seria Archeologiczna* 28, 109-247.

Kot, K. & Piotrowska, M. 2016. Mąkolice, stan. 15, gm. Głowno. Przyczynek do badań nad zagospodarowaniem przestrzennym osad ludności kultury przeworskiej. In S. Kadrow (ed.). *Raport* 11. 107-22.

Michałowski, A. 2011. *Budownictwo kultury przeworskiej.* Poznań: Wydawnictwo Poznańskie.

Naglik, R., Roczkalski, B. & Kosik-Roczkalska, A. 2014. Materiały z okresu wpływów rzymskich. In R. Naglik & P. Włodarczak (eds). *Wyniki badań na wielokulturowym stanowisku 4 w Łysokaniach, gm. Kłaj, pow. Wielicki.* 79-278. Kraków: Via Archeologica.

Pazda, S. & Tomczak, E. 2008. Pracownia garncarska na osadzie w Dobrzeniu Małym, woj. Opolskie. In. A. Błażejewski (ed.). *Ceramika warsztatowa w środkowoeuropejskim Barbaricum.* 253-66. Wrocław: Instytut Archeologii Uniwersytetu Wrocławskiego.

Schuster, J. 2012. Długie domy na późnorzymskiej osadzie w Konarzewie koło Poznania. Przyczynek do badań nad budownictwem kultury przeworskiej w okresie rzymskim. In A. Jaszewska (ed.). *Z najdawniejszych dziejów. Grzegorzowi Domańskiemu na pięćdziesięciolecie pracy naukowej.* 427-60. Zielona Góra: Wydawnictwo Fundacji Archeologicznej.

Chapter 15

Late Iron Age settlements in Hungary

Károly Tankó & Lőrinc Timár

15.1 Introduction

In Central Europe the Late Iron Age period between the 5th century BC and the beginning of the Calendar Era is characterized mostly by La Tène material culture. This paper reviews the current state of knowledge for the unfortified settlements of this period in the area of what is today Hungary (see Szabó 2005; 2015 for an exhaustive bibliography on this topic).

Our knowledge of the Iron Age settlement structure and historical landscape of Hungary is largely based on a series of conventional excavations on the Great Hungarian Plain and in western Transdanubia undertaken since the 1990s. Until recently, our knowledge of the Late Iron Age in the Carpathian Basin, the La Tène period, was based on unevenly distributed assemblages. From the Early and Middle La Tène period, burial assemblages dominate, while Late La Tène finds originate mainly from small-scale excavations of fortified settlements. Any information on the settlements of the Early and Middle La Tène periods and the related finds was scarce until recently. This imbalance is illustrated in I. Hunyady's monograph on Celtic finds excavated in the Carpathian Basin, where her typology is based entirely on burial assemblages (Hunyady 1942-1944). The situation changed in the second half of the 1990s, when the Institute for Archaeological Sciences of the Eötvös Loránd University began to explore the Late Iron Age settlement structure on the Great Hungarian Plain in collaboration with French archaeologists, in a programme of work that has since developed independently (Szabó 1995, 36; Goguey *et al.* 2003; Czajlik 2010). This work has revealed that La Tène period villages excavated near Sajópetri and Polgár were established in the earliest stage of Celtic occupation on the Great Hungarian Plain, during the late 4th and early 3rd centuries BC (Guillaumet *et al.* 1999; Szabó 2007; Szabó *et al.* 2008). These assemblages show the traditions of the immigrant Celts as well as the local so-called Scythian communities. The recent rescue excavations in advance of the construction of motorways and a number of small scale investigations have provided new information regarding the extents of the La Tène Culture in Hungary in the 3rd and 2nd centuries BC (*e.g.* at the site of Mátraszőlős: Tankó & Vaday 2010).

This paper presents summaries of the excavation results at four sites (Figure 1 A), which represent three different geographical areas, dating to the Early and Middle La Tène. Sajópetri – Hosszú-dűlő and Polgár – Királyérpart are Late Iron Age settlements on the north-eastern perimeter of Great Hungarian Plain (Alföld). The site of Ménfőcsanak is situated in the western part of Hungary on the Small Hungarian Plain (Kisalföld),

In: D. Cowley, M. Fernández-Götz, T. Romankiewicz, & H. Wendling (eds), Rural Settlement. Relating buildings, landscape, and people in the European Iron Age (Leiden 2019: Sidestone Press) 157-166.

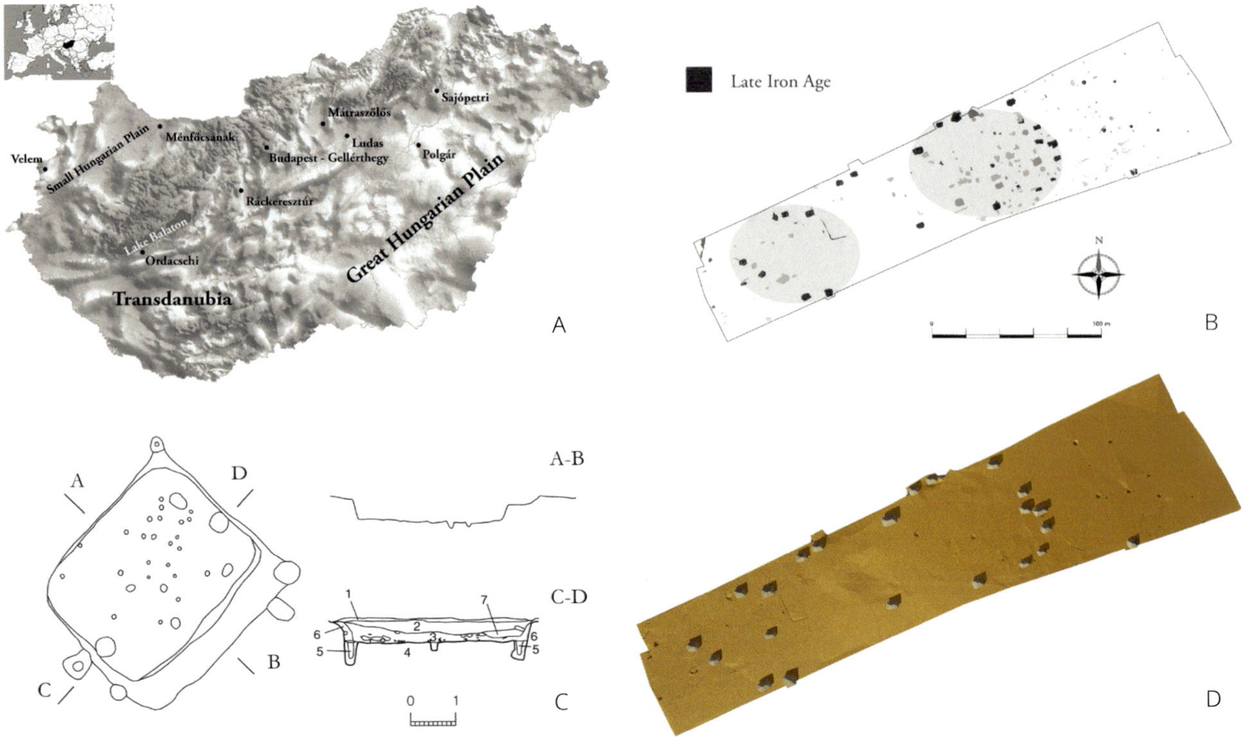

Figure 1: A) Map of Hungary with the sites mentioned in the text. B) Plan of the Late Iron Age site at Ordacsehi-Csereföld. Note the arrangement of the buildings. C) A typical Late Iron Age sunken-featured building (nr. 98.7) at Sajópetri. D) Reconstructed 3D view of the excavated site at Ordacsehi-Csereföld (D) near Lake Balaton (after Gallina et al. 2007). (Figure credits: L. Timár).

while Ráckeresztúr is located Transdanubia (Dunántúl). The common feature of these settlements is the almost exclusive presence of sunken-featured buildings (see Figure 1 C for a typical example) arranged in loose circular groups. The arrangement of the buildings suggests that they were grouped around a clearing or central area, but without any strict order in their disposition (Figure 1 B & D). Comparison of their plans to sites of the same period excavated in Austria is instructive. Although Ménfőcsanak in Hungary and Prellenkirchen in Austria lie only 70 kilometres apart, the settlement structures are rather different. In the Austrian example post built houses arranged in a different manner are the predominant form in the Middle La Tène period (Timár 2016, 192). Buildings from present-day Hungary are relatively small and have a simple floor-plan. Unfortunately there are not too many surviving structural elements which could decisively demonstrate their architectural form and finds related to their functions are also rare, though in some cases we can identify building types with specific uses (for workshop-type buildings see Timár 2016, 199-201). The nature of the evidence changes in the Late La Tène period, where we see the emergence of fortified oppida, suggesting significant changes in society at this time.

15.2 Four Early and Middle La Tène settlements in Hungary

15.2.1 Sajópetri – Hosszú-dűlő and Polgár – Királyérpart, north-eastern Hungary

The site at Sajópetri – Hosszú-dűlő is a Late Iron Age settlement in north-eastern Hungary, located on the alluvial plain in between the Sajó valley and the Bükkalja, at the boundary between the Great Hungarian Plain and the mountains. This large Celtic settlement (Figure 2 A), of which about 41000 m^2 has been excavated and published under the direction M. Szabó, is perhaps the most extensively researched and published Late Iron Age settlement in the Carpathian Basin to date (Szabó 2007). Furthermore, the wide repertoire of pottery from the site has supported the development of a technological and typological classification which provides a reference for interpretation at other archaeological sites (Szabó & Tankó 2007). The work at Sajópetri – Hosszú-dűlő was interdisciplinary in character, with special attention paid to architecture, archaeometallurgy, archaeozoology and petrography.

The settlement, following the bend of the small river Sajó, consisted of three main zones. More than 30 buildings

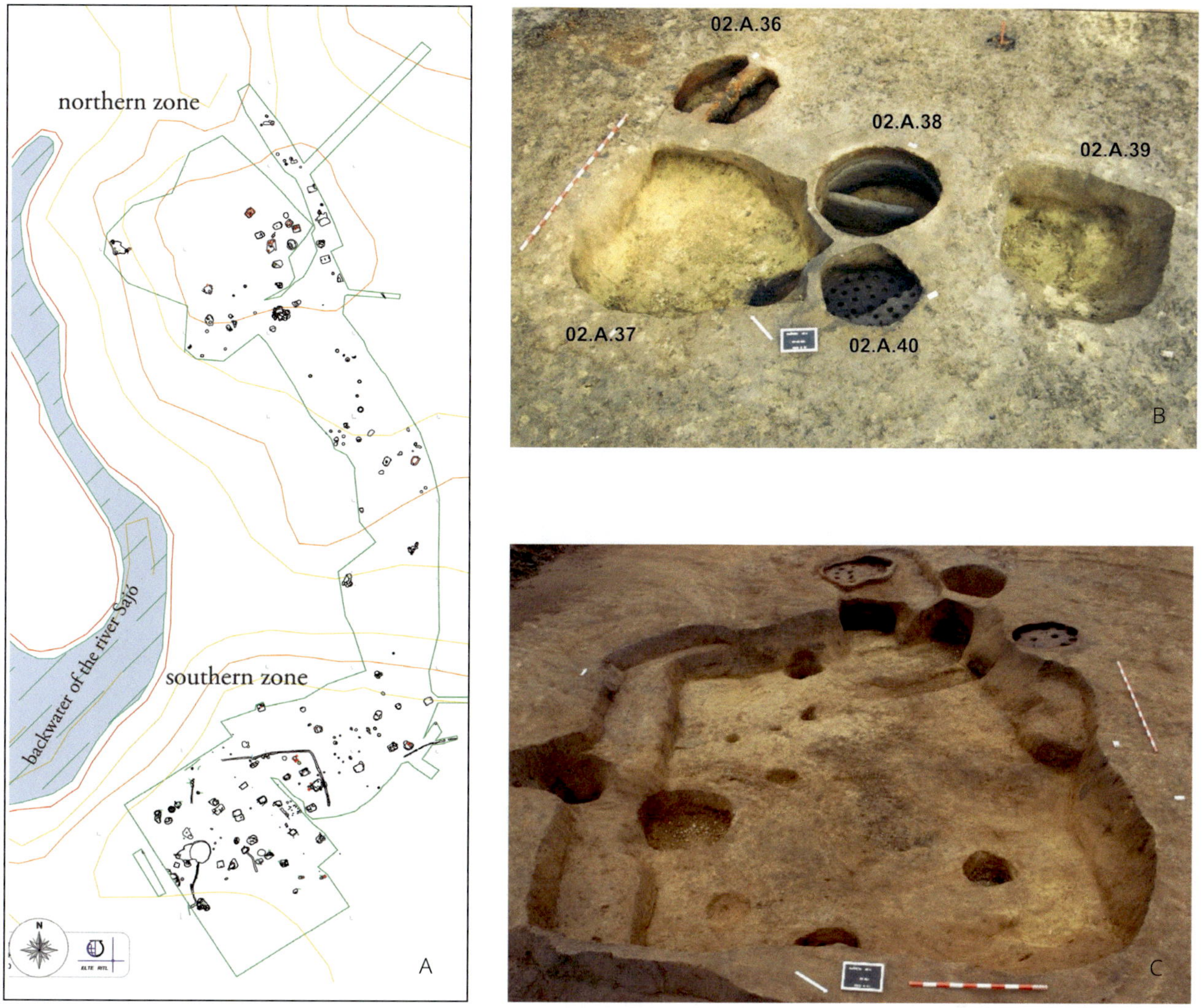

Figure 2: A) Map of the site at Sajópetri. B) A complex pottery kiln nr. 02.A.36-40. C) The large workshop nr. 02.A.93 with attached kilns in the central zone of the settlement. One of the special features of the large workshop is the step or bank on its longitudinal southern side, which seems to be a common attribute among the workshops (Timár 2016, 200, fig. 11). (Figure credits: L. Timár, C – Z. Czajlik, D – K. Tankó).

stood around an open central area in the southern zone, forming a rather densely built-up village (Figure 2 A). The northern zone was similar to the southern one but distinctly smaller. While the central area was almost devoid of structures which could be identified as houses, most of the wells were located there. Pits related to various activities (*e.g.* storage, clay extraction, but also votive offerings) seem more common in the west of the site, while pottery kilns were recovered in the south-eastern part of the investigated area (Figure 2 B & C; Timár 2007, 216-9). It seems likely that artisanal activities had their definite places within the settlement.

The multi-period site at Polgár – Királyérpart was the first Late Iron Age settlement excavated to modern standards in 1993-94 (Figure 3 A), and is located in the Tisza valley on the northern periphery of the Great Hungarian Plain. It lies on the bank of a palaeochannel of the Tisza river, on the north side of the Sajó-Tisza confluence. The Late Iron Age is represented by sunken featured buildings (see house nr. 100 in Figure 5 B) and a series of pits. Polgár is an important site for research on Late Iron Age pottery, with the publication of its ceramic assemblages based on the technological and typological framework previously developed at the Sajópetri site. At Polgár, quern stones were found on the floor of one building, with an iron sickle in another building. Beside the agrarian character, demonstrated by finds like the quern stones and sickle, metalworking also played an important role attested by a burnt crucible and slag remains found in the buildings.

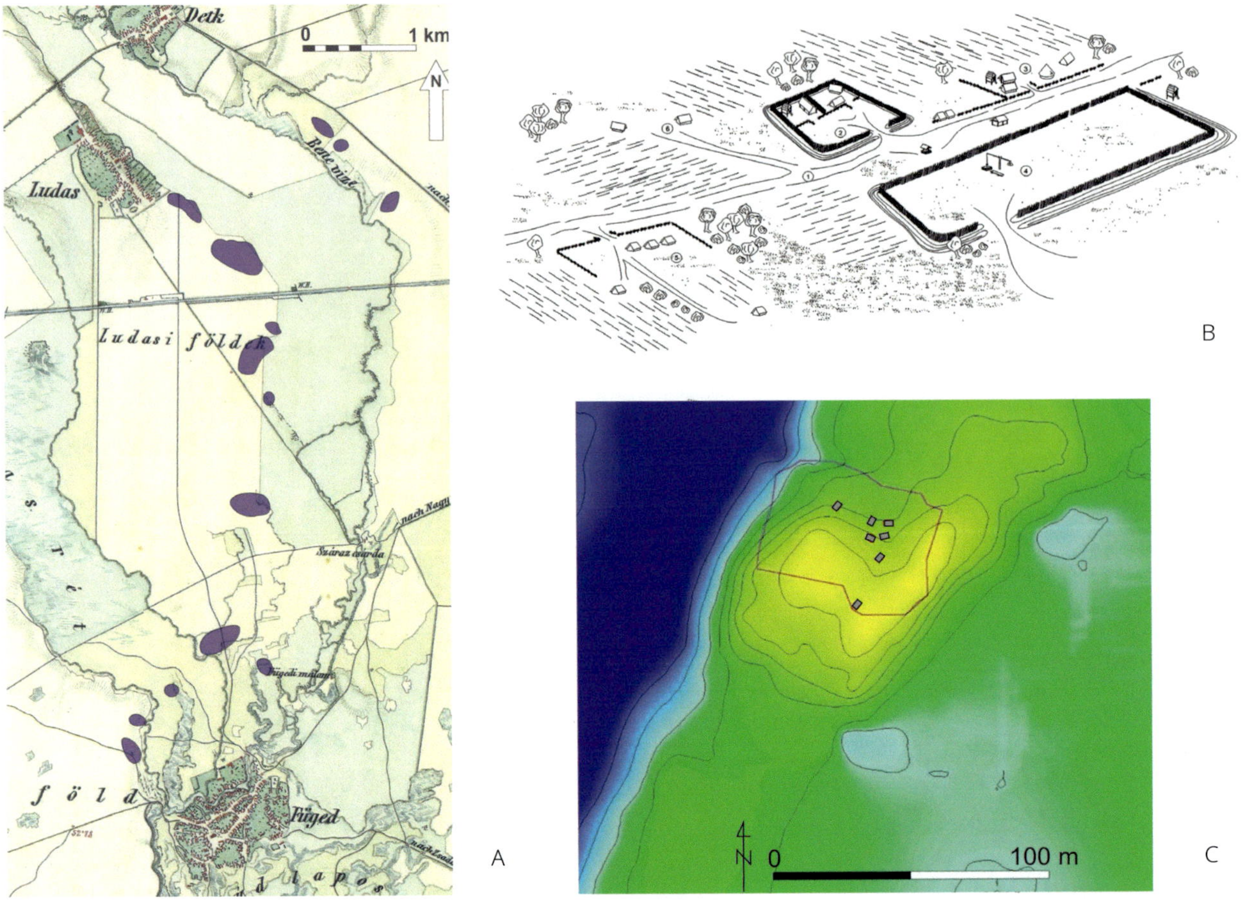

Figure 3: A) A chain of small settlements along a stream at Ludas. B) Graphic reconstruction of the site at Ménfőcsanak. Note the ditches and fences around the habitations. C) Map of the site Polgár 1, showing the arrangement of the sunken-featured houses. (Figure credits: A & B – K. Tankó, C – B. Holl).

The finds from Polgár reflect the dominance of the La Tène culture, but besides these Celtic finds, a number of artefacts refer to a different local tradition. The hand-built pottery types, as well as a range of metal and bone artefacts, illustrate the survival of local Scythian cultural traditions and also denote some continuity in the population. According to the chronologically "sensitive" finds, this settlement was established at the turn of the 4th-3rd centuries BC and did not survive beyond the first half of the 2nd century BC (Szabó *et al.* 1997, 81-90; Szabó *et al.* 2008).

In summary, the vessel types present at Sajópetri and at other sites in northeast Hungary in the 3rd-2nd centuries BC are uniform, with both Scythian (Vekerzug Culture) and Celtic (La Tène Culture) traditions represented in the pottery forms. This suggests that the Celtic occupation in the 3rd century BC saw the peaceful assimilation of the local indigenous population, indicating the cohabitation and ultimately the blending of the Celtic and Scythian communities. Some caution is needed at this point, as we must beware of drawing direct conclusions regarding the ethnicity of these communities because the archaeological finds do not provide precise evidence on this aspect (Szabó & Tankó 2007; Szabó *et al.* 2007). Besides the dominance of finds of the La Tène and Scythian cultural traditions, relations pointing towards the Transylvanian and Transcarpathian regions can be also demonstrated, although only in the case of a few, unique objects. In other words, the pottery manufacturing techniques and the statistical distribution of vessel types suggest that the heterogeneous cultural traditions and their mixing led to the establishment of an independent pottery manufacturing custom on the fringes of the Great Hungarian Plain and the surrounding mountainous zone (Tankó 2010b; 2016).

The sites at Sajópetri – Hosszú-dűlő and that at Polgár – Királyérpart are typical, but rare, examples of the many unfortified settlements beside rivers that were typical in the Carpathian Basin in the Iron Age. These villages are generally interpreted as primarily agricultural in character, although there is also abundant evidence for local artisanship. The piles of slag and limestone (used as flux) provide evidence for iron smelting and the number of tools among the finds is also remarkable (Szabó & Czajlik 2006, 513-20; Czajlik 2014, 141-2). These phenomena offer some explanation as to why the settlements were established at their respective places – an important motive behind the eastward expansion of the Celts was the need to access iron and copper resources which were processed locally. The quantity of metal artefacts, such as tools and semi-finished products (Guillaumet 2007, 253-62), confirms this observation.

Beyond the evidence provided by these two sites, micro-regional research has played a significant role in the mapping of Late Iron Age settlement patterns in northeast Hungary, including intensive field surveys along the Sajó and Zagyva rivers and in the valley of the Bene stream. Besides the field research, aerial reconnaissance has led to the discovery and recording of sites (Czajlik & Tankó 2007, 321-4; Czajlik *et al.* 2012, 171-80; Tankó & Vaday 2010, 151-3). The investigated areas are at the foot of Mátra and Bükk mountains and covered by soil, rock or dissolved material eroded from the mountains. The alluvial top soils in the valleys are rich in minerals and suitable for agricultural use. The aim of field surveys in these areas was to identify the Late Iron Age archaeological sites in this contact zone of the Great Hungarian Plan and the northern mountainous region of Hungary. The results, for example in the surroundings of the Ludas necropolis in the valley of the Bene stream, have shown that the valleys, running mainly north-south, were densely populated during the La Tène period (Figure 3 A). The general map of discoveries in the vicinity of Ludas indicates that the Celtic rural settlements follow the wide valley of Bene stream on its lower banks alongside the plain. This is particularly noticeable on the right bank where 12 La Tène culture villages were found in an approximately 7 km long section. This density is significant even though they may not all be contemporaneous (Czajlik & Tankó 2012, 174-80).

15.2.2 Ménfőcsanak, Transdanubia, western Hungary

The Late Iron Age settlement at Ménfőcsanak is located on the gentle slope of a hill rising above a bend on the Marcal River, surrounded by marshy meadows beside a stream. The orientation and structure of the settlement was defined by hydro-geological, topographic, environmental and agricultural factors. Easy access to water and the topography could have been the key factors in location, considering that the main concentrations of Late Iron Age features are generally located on the higher ground separated by 50-200 m empty spaces with no archaeological features (Tankó 2010a, 249-52).

The north-eastern part of the site is the most complex, containing evidence for sunken-featured houses, post in ground structures and wells. Ditches, which can be interpreted as the remains of fences, subdivide the site. At the south-eastern edge of the site a 70 m by 150 m rectangular area surrounded by a ditch broken by an entrance on the south can be interpreted as a paddock or an enclosure for animals, since it contains only two wells. Another rectangular area, similarly bounded by a ditch enclosing an area of about 40 by 50 m, lies to the northwest and is set parallel to the first enclosure, in this case with an entrance to the southeast. This enclosure is subdivided, with two buildings and a storage pit to the northeast and numerous postholes to the southwest (Figure 3 B). As one of the buildings has the same orientation as the enclosure ditch one may assume they were contemporary.

While it is difficult to reconstruct the main prehistoric transport routes because of scarce archaeological evidence, it is clear that the existence of roads both within and between settlements can be inferred. At Ménfőcsanak the two rectangular boundary ditches and the similar alignment of the buildings suggest the presence of an Iron Age road aligned northeast-southwest which was reused in the Roman period. The evidence from the Celtic cemetery of Ménfőcsanak suggests this settlement was established in LT B1 during the second half of the 4th century BC, and abandoned during the LT B2/C1 transition period at the latest, in the second half of the 3rd century BC (Tankó 2010a).

15.2.3 Ráckeresztúr, Transdanubia, Dunántúl

The development of aerial reconnaissance for archaeology in Hungary has proved indispensable for exploring settlement patterns. Combined with field and magnetometer surveys this approach has provided data about the Late Iron Age settlement network in Transdanubia, with some sites further investigated by small-scale excavations with the aim of obtaining dating evidence. In a research project led by Z. Czajlik, three Celtic settlements were investigated at Harc (Czajlik *et al.* 2010), Báta (Czajlik 2010) and Ráckeresztúr (Czajlik *et al.* 2015) – the latter of which will be described in some detail here.

The outlines of the buildings and pits at Ráckeresztúr are easily observed on aerial photographs taken while the site was covered by growing winter wheat (Figure 4 A). Magnetometry surveys showed not only the archaeological structures but also a great number of geomorphological features and stray metal objects in the plough soil, creating a more confusing picture than the aerial photographs. The aerial photographs show a number of pits, and nine large and five small buildings, three of which were subsequently excavated. One of these buildings produced a relatively large number of Late Iron Age finds, mostly pottery fragments. In general, the pottery from Ráckeresztúr corresponds to the ceramic assemblages from other contemporaneous sites of the La Tène Culture. In view of the currently known relative chronology, the excavated

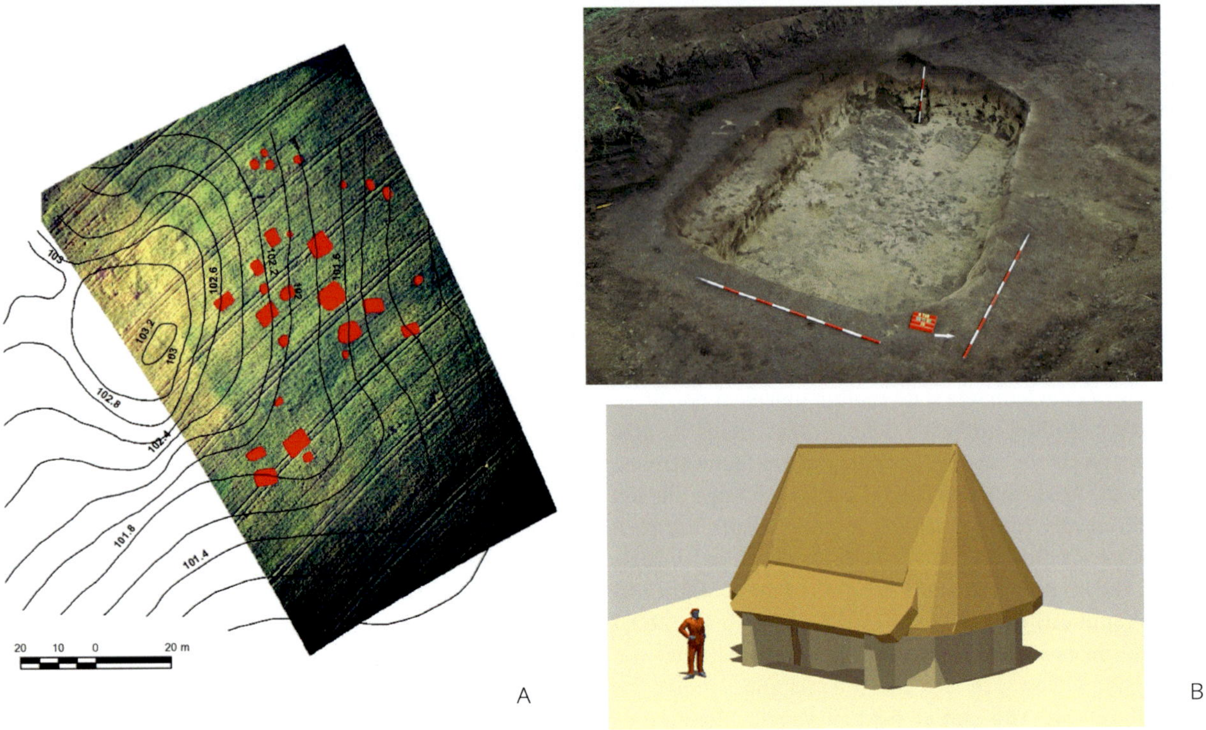

Figure 4: A) Aerial photographic based mapping of the site at Ráckeresztúr, after Czajlik et al. 2015. B) Excavation view (top) and reconstruction (below) of the sunken-featured building nr. 10 at Ráckeresztúr (Photo: Z. Czajlik; Reconstruction: L. Timár).

building was used between the LT B2 and C1 phases (Czajlik *et al.* 2015).

15.3 Late Iron Age Buildings

The excavations described above provide opportunities to understand and reconstruct the form of Late Iron Age buildings. There are challenges since structural evidence is scarce, comprising only postholes, hollows and any other negative features, and it is often impossible to ascertain the functions of buildings. These issues, the building types and their theoretical reconstructions are comprehensively discussed in previous papers (see Timár 2016), and are presented here in summary form only.

Those in the central part of the Carpathian Basin in present-day Hungary exhibit a fairly uniform construction comprising a rectangular pit measuring between 2m or 3m across by between 3m and 5m in length with postholes on the shorter sides (building 10 at Ráckeresztúr is a good example of this type, Figure 4 B).

The traditional reconstruction of the sunken-featured buildings is based on a modern shepherd's hut with the roof resting upon the ground (see Tankó 2004, 105, Abb. 3/1-2; Timár 2007, 204-7). This model carries undesirable implications, since it implies the subordinate function of such buildings, and that the population was living in other types of houses. However, we have already seen regional differences in the settlement patterns and there are only a few traces of buildings built on the surface in the settlements in Hungary, contrary to those excavated in Austria where such features are common. An assumption that the sunken-featured buildings were destined to fulfil subordinate functions only creates a problem imagining what kind of structure these settlements had. Therefore, the understanding of the remains is very important, and for a variety of reasons the old theoretical reconstruction cannot be accepted anymore (for a critical review see Timár 2007, 205; 2016). Among others, a section across a La Tène period building at Ménfőcsanak demonstrated clear evidence of a sunken-featured building with low standing walls.

Available raw materials should have played a decisive role in the structure of these buildings. It can be suggested that the Celts of Liptovska Mara in present-day Slovakia (Pieta 2008, 91) would have faced the greatest difficulties if they had tried to build sunken-featured house types of the plains due to the rock under the thin soil layer, while the soils at Sajópetri are conducive to constructing an alpine-type sunken-featured house. Sunken-featured houses proved to be very cheap, slightly impractical and highly unhealthy in modern times (they

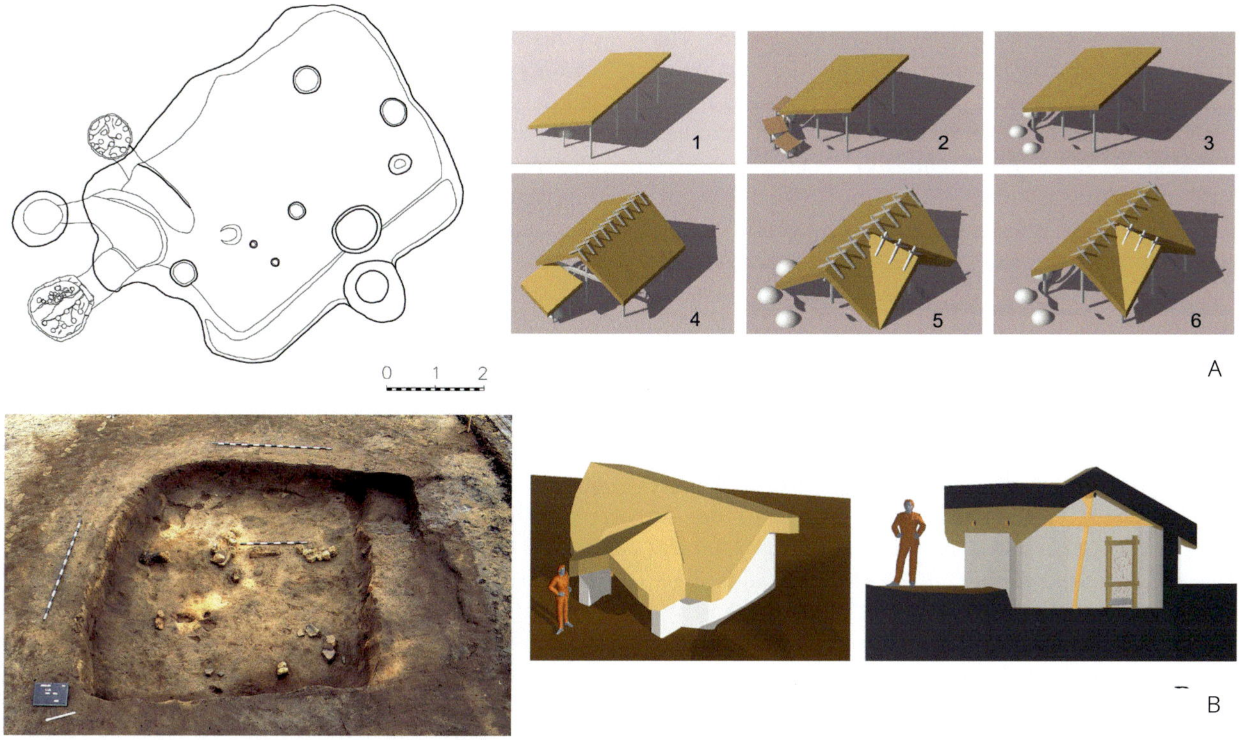

Figure 5: A) Building 02.A.93 from Sajópetri with attached pottery kilns. The small 3D sketches show all the possible roof shapes. B) Building nr. 100 from Polgár with loom weights on its floor. The reconstructed cross-section shows the minimal ceiling height that would allow the use of the loom inside the house, while the axonometric reconstruction shows the minimal exterior volume of the house. (Figure credits: L. Timár).

existed in Hungary until the 1960s, Timár 2013, 299) and there must be no doubt that they were always built when timber was scarce.

We know little about the general structural evolution of Late Iron Age houses, and it is also possible that the various Celtic tribes had their own architecture which makes the classification of the buildings more difficult. The presence or absence of the postholes was often used as a criterion for the respective typological categories, but according to our opinion, all the sunken-featured buildings belonged to the same structural type (see Timár 2016, 197-8; Buchsenschutz 2005, 56, fig. 4) and other features like size or proportions are more important.

In some houses at Sajópetri the finds indicate blacksmithing activity, which is almost impossible without raising of hands above the head, thus an adequate ceiling height would have been vital in their case. As the number of the possible reconstruction variants is relatively low, with such a single consideration one could reduce the six variants to one in the case of building 02.A.93 (Figure 5 B, see also Timár 2007, 219). Building number 100 at Polgár housed a warp-weighed loom which must have had a frame as tall as its user (Figure 5 B). Therefore, it could be assumed that buildings of the workshop-type had upright, vertical walls above the ground surface instead of roofs placed on the surface. It is also important to mention that computer technology allows the precise 3D modelling of even difficult structures which is very useful for reconstructing a particular building (Timár 2007, 216-9; 2011, 400-4; 2013, 291-300; Czajlik *et al.* 2015, 88-90).

15.4 The Late La Tène period: emergence of fortified *oppida*

The study area suffers from an assumption that there is a clear connection between archaeological finds and historical events in the Late Iron Age of Central Europe. Thus, the term 'La Tène culture' refers to the finds only, while designations like La Tène B period and Middle La Tène period refer to different archaeological contexts. Furthermore, chronologically sensitive information is restricted to cemeteries. It is not easy to reconstruct a timeline from the overlap of the burials of three or four generations, using refined chronologies of brooches, weapons and similar objects which had changed over time, and it is more difficult to transpose such a relative chronology to the settlements, where such finds are extremely rare. There is therefore a heavy reliance on proportions of pottery assemblages which provide only an approximate date in a relative chronology, which is restricted to a certain region of Central Europe. The abandonment of the Sajópetri site was presumably at the end of the La Tène C1 period, but the cause of this is unknown. While the settlement may have been relocated to the nearby hill of Bükkszentlászló – Nagysánc, where there is a fortified hilltop *oppidum* (Szabó 2007, 310-9), and this appears to be a general tendency in Central Europe, the processes whereby unfortified settlements were replaced by *oppida* from the La Tène C2 period onwards remain unclear.

Besides the investigations of unenclosed Early and Middle La Tène settlements described above, there have also been significant excavations at fortified settlements of the Late La Tène period. Hungarian-French work focused first on the *oppida* of Transdanubia (Guillaumet 2000), and test excavations have been carried out on Szent Vid at Velem and Gellérthegy in Budapest (Barral *et al.* 1996; Guillaumet *et al.* 1999). These excavations have furnished important information on the later phases of the La Tène period, providing a Hungarian perspective on the general European research trends of the culture of the *oppida*. Nevertheless, since these excavations have concentrated on the fortified settlements there is little known about potential satellite settlements. Thus, there is a notable distinction between the evidence for dispersed open settlement in the Early and Middle La Tène periods, while in the Late La Tène period our knowledge is rather restricted to fortified settlements of proto-urban character.

It is a fact that towards the end of the Middle La Tène period, considerable changes took place in Transdanubia and in the Carpathian Basin as a whole. The use of cemeteries established in the early phases ceased by the La Tène C1, a phenomenon which can also be observed in east and northwest Hungary (Szabó & Tankó 2006, 331). Recently excavated Iron Age settlements show a similar pattern and it appears that the Early La Tène unfortified settlements were abandoned by the end of the Middle La Tène phase. Thus, the 3rd century BC can be considered as a transitional period, when early urbanization in this region had begun (Szabó 2007, 331).

The first constructions of the later *oppida* were laid down during this transitional phase, along with the establishment of a network of secondary settlements linked to these centres. The close relationship between unfortified and fortified settlements is evident from the similarities in their ceramic assemblages. However, it is still an open question why the La Tène cemeteries and settlements in the Carpathian Basin ceased being used by the first half of the La Tène C period. Since no destruction layers were discovered at Polgár, Sajópetri and Ménfőcsanak, one has to assume that the Celtic inhabitants must have abandoned these sites peacefully. It is tempting to link this phenomenon to the establishment of the *oppida*, but unfortunately there is, at present, no supporting evidence of this from the Carpathian Basin. This aspect of the Late La Tène period of the Great Hungarian Plain is still difficult to interpret from an archaeological perspective, while the further fate of this Celtic population in eastern Hungary is also obscure. Remnants of the La Téne traditions refer to surviving Celtic populations at least until the arrival of the Germanic groups to northeast Hungary.

In western Hungary the situation was more straightforward, since under Roman rule the Celtic population was Romanised. The conversion was rapid in the frontier zone and along major roads, but was significantly slower and partial in the hinterland (Bíró 2017, 249-71). Here many of the *vici* maintained their indigenous character with sunken-featured houses and irregular plans (Bíró 2017, 142-50), often similar to the unfortified settlements of the Middle La Tène period instead of following the densely urbanized patterns of the Late La Tène *oppida*.

15.5 Acknowledgments

This research was supported by János Bolyai Research Scholarship of the Hungarian Academy of Sciences and the MTA-ELTE Research Group for Interdisciplinary Archaeology.

15.6 Bibliography

Barral, Ph., Guillaumet, J.-P., Parette, Cl. A. & Szabó, M. 1996. Recherches récentes sur les Oppida Celtiques en Pannonie (Fouilles franco-hongroises á Velem-Szent-vid et á Budapest Gellérthegy). In E. Jerem, A. Krenn-Leeb, J.-W. Neugebauer & O. Urban (eds). *Die Kelten in den Alpen und an der Donau. Akten des Internationalen Symposions St. Pölten, 14.-18. Oktober 1992.* 415-31. Budapest-Wien: Archaeolingua.

Bíró, Sz. 2017. *Die zivilen Vici in Pannonien.* Mainz: RGZM Verlag.

Buchsenschutz, O. 2005. Les survivances des constructions sur poteaux plantés: éléments modernes de comparaison. In O. Buchsenschutz & Cl. Mordant (eds). *Architectures protohistoriques en Europe occidentale du Néolithique final à l'âge du Fer.* 543-7. Paris: Editions du CTHS.

Czajlik, Z. 2010. Les possibilités de la prospection aérienne conventionelle en Hongrie. In L. Borhy (dir.). *Studia Celtica Classica et Romana Nicolae Szabó Septuagesimo Dedicata.* 79-96. Budapest: Pytheas.

Czajlik, Z. 2014. Traces of Prehistoric smelting workshops in the Carpathian Basin. In S. Berecki (ed.). *Iron Age crafts and craftmen in the Carpathian Basin. Proceedings of the International Colloquium from Târgu Mureş.* 139-46. Cluj-Napoca: Editura Mega.

Czajlik, Z., Czövek, A., Csippán, P., Holl, B., Magyari, E., Szöllősi, Sz., Rupnik, L. & Timár, L. 2010. Archaeological and palaeoenvironmental data on Late Iron Age settlements in South-Eastern Transdanubia (Tolna County). In S. Berecki (ed.). *Iron Age Communities in the Carpathian Basin. Proceedings of the International Colloquium from Târgu Mureş.* 149-70.Cluj-Napoca: Editura Mega.

Czajlik, Z. & Tankó, K. 2007. Les sites celtiques de la micro-région. In M. Szabó (dir.). *L'habitat de l'époque de La Tène á Sajópetri – Hosszú-dűlő.* 321-4. Budapest: L'Harmattan.

Czajlik, Z. & Tankó, K. & Gherdán, K. 2012. Recherches microrégionales dans les environs de Ludas. In M. Szabó (dir.), K. Tankó & Z. Czajlik (eds). *La nécropole celtique à Ludas-Varjú-dűlő.* 171-80. Budapest: L'Harmattan.

Czajlik, Z., Tankó, K., Timár, L. & Holl, B. 2015. Remains of a Celtic settlement at Ráckeresztúr. In L. Borhy, K. Tankó & K. Dévai (eds). *Studia archaeologica Nicolae Szabó LXXV annos nato dedicata.* 77-94. Budapest: L'Harmattan.

Hunyady, I. 1942-1944. *Kelták a Kárpátmedencében. Die Kelten im Karpatenbecken.* Dissertationes Pannonicae II. 18. Budapest: Királyi Magyar Pázmány Péter Tudományegyetem Érem- és Régiségtani Intézete.

Gallina Zs., Molnár I. & Somogyi K. 2007. Ordacsehi-Csereföld. In Belényesy K., Honti Sz. & Kiss V. (eds). *Gördülő idő. Régészeti feltárások az M7-es autópálya Somogy megyei szakaszán Zamárdi és Ordacsehi között. Rolling time. Excavations on the M7 Motorway in County Somogy between Zamárdi and Ordacsehi.* 197-206. Budapest-Zalaegerszeg: SMMI-MTA RI.

Goguey, R., Czajlik, Z. & Bödőcs A. 2003. Magyar-francia légi régészeti kutatások Magyarországon 2000 – Recherches franco-hongroises d'archéologie aérienne en Hongrie en 2000. *Régészeti kutatások Magyarországon – Archaeological Invetigation in Hungary* 2000 (2003), 75-86.

Guillaumet, J.-P. (dir.) 2000. *Dix ans coopération franco-hongroise en archéologie 1988-1998.* Budapest: Collegium Budapest.

Guillaumet, J-P. 2007. La mobilier métallique. In M. Szabó (dir.). *L'habitat de l'époque de La Tène á Sajópetri – Hosszú-dűlő.* 253-62. Budapest: L'Harmattan.

Guillaumet, J-P., Szabó, M. & Czajlik, Z. 1999. Bilan des recherches franco-hongroises à Velem-Szentvid, 1988-1994. A velem-szentvidi francia-magyar ásatások mérlege, 1988-1994. *Savaria – A Vas Megyei Múzeumok értesítője* 24/3 (1998-1999) 383-408.

Hunyady, I. 1942-1944. *Kelták a Kárpátmedencében. Die Kelten im Karpatenbecken*, Dissertationes Pannoniae II.18. Budapest: Pázmány Péter Tudományegyetem Érem- és Régiségtani Intézete.

Malrain, F. 1994. Les établissements ruraux du second âge du Fer dans les régions picarde et ardennaise, d'après les fouilles et les prospections aériennes. In O. Buchsenschutz & P. Méniel (eds). *Les installations agricoles de l'âge du Fer en Îl-de-France. Actes du Colloque de Paris, 1993.* 185-203. Études d'Histoire et Archéologie 6. Paris: École normale supérieure.

Pieta, K. 2010. *Die keltische Besiedlung des Slowakei. Jüngere Latènezeit,* Nitra: Archeologický ústav SAV.

Szabó, M. 1995. Régészet és légi fényképezés Magyarországon. In R. Goguey & M. Szabó. *A történelem madártávlatból – L'Histoire vue du ciel,* 95-7.

Szabó, M. 2005. *A keleti kelták. A késő vaskor a Kárpát-medencében.* Budapest: L'Harmattan.

Szabó, M. 2015. A kelták Magyarországon. In M. Szabó & L. Borhy. *Magyarország története az ókorban.* 13-82. Budapest: L'Harmattan.

Szabó, M. (dir.) 2007. *L'habitat de l'époque de La Tène á Sajópetri – Hosszú-dűlő.* Budapest: L'Harmattan.

Szabó, M. & Czajlik, Z. 2006. La sidérurgie dans le Nord-Est de la Hongrie au IIIe s. avant J-C., Sajópetri-Hosszú-dűlő. In L. Baray (ed.). *Artisanats, sociétés et civilisations: hommage à Jean-Paul Tevenot: actes du colloque organisé par l'UMR 5594, Dijon et le Centre de Recherche et d'Étude du Patrimoine (CEREP), Sens, 2-3 avril 2003.* 513-21. 24ème suppl. à la Revue Archéologiede l'Est. Dijon: Societé Archéologique de l'Est de la France.

Szabó, D. & Tankó, K. 2007. Présentation du systeme de gestion de céramique de Sajópetri (Hongrie). Őségészeti Levelek 8-9, 168-77.

Szabó, M. & Tankó, K. 2006. Nécropole laténienne à Ludas – Varjú-dűlő. *Acta Archaeologica Scientiarum Hungaricae* 57, 325-43.

Szabó, M., Guillaumet, J.-G. & Kriveczky, B. 1997. Polgár – Király-érpart. in *Utak a múltba. Az M3-as autópálya régészeti leletmentései – Path into the past. Rescue excavations on the M3 motorway.* 81-90. Budapest: Pytheas.

Szabó, M., Tankó, K. & Szabó, D. 2007. Le mobilier céramique. In M. Szabó (ed.). *L'habitat de l'époque de La Tène à Sajópetri – Hosszú-dűlő.* 229-52. Budapest: L'Harmattan.

Szabó, M. Tankó, K. & Czajlik, Z. 2012. *La nécropole celtique à Ludas-Varjú-dűlő.* Budapest: L'Harmattan.

Szabó, M., Czajlik, Z., Tankó, K. & Timár, L. 2008. Polgár 1: l'habitat du second Age du Fer (IIIe siecle av. J-Chr.), *Acta Archaeologica Academiae Scientiarum Hungaricae* 59, 183-223.

Tankó, K. 2004. Rekonstruktion eines latènezeitlichen Grubenhauses aus Ménfőcsanak-Szeles. *Communicationes Archaeologiae Hungariae* 2004, 105-12.

Tankó, K. 2010a. Late Iron Age settlement in the vicinity of Ménfőcsanak (Road no. 83 and Bevásárlóközpont). In L. Borhy (ed.). *Studia celtica classica et romana Nicolae Szabó septuagesimo dedicata.* 249-60. Budapest: L'Harmattan.

Tankó, K. 2010b. La Tène ceramic technology and typology of settlement assemblages in Northeast Hungary. In S. Berecki (ed.). *Iron Age Communities in the Carpathian Basin: Proceedings of the International Colloquium from Târgu Mureş*. 321-32. Cluj-Napoca: Editura Mega.

Tankó, K. 2016. Chronological aspects of ceramic types from recently investigated La Tène settlements in Hungary. In S. Berecki (ed.). *Iron Age chronology in the Carpathian Basin. Proceedings of the international colloquium from Târgu Mureş*. 165-90. Cluj-Napoca: Editura Mega.

Tankó, K. & Egry, I. 2009. Kelta település Győr – Ménfőcsanak-Bevásárlóközpont területén. Celtic settlement excavations at Győr-Ménfőcsanak-Bevásárlóközpont between 1995 and 2006. Az 1995. és 2006. évi ásatás. In G. Ilon (ed.). *MΩMOΣ, Őskoros Kutatók VI. Összejövetele, Kőszeg 2009. március 19-21. Nyersanyagok és kereskedelem*. 401-16. Szombathely: Kulturális Örökségvédelmi Szakszolgálat & Vas Megyei Múzeumok Igazgatósága.

Tankó, K. & Vaday, A. 2010. Késő bronzkori és késő vaskori telepleletek Mátraszőlős-Királydombról – Spätbronzezeitliche und früheisenzeitliche Siedlungsfunde aus Mátraszőlős-Királydomb. In Sz. Guba & K. Tankó (eds). *Régről kell kezdenünk..." Studia Archaeologica in honorem Pauli Patay – Régészeti tanulmányok Nógrád megyéből Patay Pál tiszteletére*. 133-90. Szécsény: Gaál István Egyesület.

Timár, L. 2007. Structure d'habitat, formes de maison. In M. Szabó (dir.). *L'habitat de l'époque de La Tène á Sajópetri – Hosszú-dűlő*. 201-19. Budapest: L'Harmattan.

Timár, L. 2010. Les reconstitutions possibles des constructions de l'âge du Fer, découvertes à Ráckeresztúr. In L. Borhy (dir.). *Studia Celtica Classica et Romana Nicolae Szabó Septuagesimo Dedicata*. 261-72. Budapest: Pytheas.

Timár, L. 2011. A brief analysis of Late Iron Age buildings. In E. Jerem, F. Redő & V. Szeverényi (eds). *CAA 2008 – On the Road to Reconstructing the Past. Proceedings of the 36th Annual Conference on Computer Applications and Quantitative Methods in Archaeology*. 399-405. Budapest: Archaeolingua.

Timár, L. 2013. Késő vaskori veremházak maradványainak értelmezése. Interpretation of the sunken featured houses of the Late Iron Age. Ősrégészeti Levelek 13, 290-302.

Timár, L. 2016. The Sunken-Featured Buildings of the Middle La Tène Period: Problems and Reconstructions. In M. Karwowski & P. C. Ramsl (eds). *Boii – Taurisci: Proceedings of the International Seminar, Oberleis-Klement, June 14th-15th, 2012*. 191-206. Mitteilungen der Prähistorischen Kommission 85. Wien: Österreichische Akademie der Wissenschaften.

Chapter 16

At the fringes of the La Tène world

The Late Iron Age rural occupation of the Banat region, Romania

Andrei Georgescu

16.1 Introduction

The historical region of the Banat has traditionally integrated influences from the Balkans and Central Europe. During the Late Iron Age these characteristics are evident mainly through the funerary archaeological record. Until recently, the La Tène period occupation of this region was virtually unknown (Georgescu & Floca 2015). However, recent rescue excavations have brought to light several structures that allow some preliminary hypotheses concerning the everyday life of the early and middle La Tène period to be sketched out. This paper focuses on the period from the end of the 4th century BC to the middle of the 2nd century BC – the time of the so-called *Celtic horizon* of the Carpathian Basin. The settlement record of this period is characterised by small sites amongst which no evident social hierarchy can be distinguished. The grouping of some structures might however indicate certain familial or clan structures.

16.2 The landscape

From a geographical perspective, the historical province of Banat is composed of two major units, namely a mountain area in the east, and lowlands in the west. The La Tène culture, with its Central European traits, seems to have spread only in the plain area, while the mountainous zone remained orientated towards the Balkan culture (Rustoiu & Ursuțiu 2013, 325). However, the lack of finds and features from the 4th and 2nd centuries BC in the western area prevents any further conclusions.

The Mureș River and the Danube are the two main communication routes that border the region. Other secondary rivers, like the Timiș and the Bega followed meandering and shifting courses before the major drainage works of the modern era. Their numerous tributary creeks constantly flooded the lowlands, leaving little land suitable for settling. In this landscape, the communities of the Late Iron Age occupied low hills, formed as a result of alluvial depositions. For example, the settlement at Moșnița Veche-Dealul Sălaș was located on a hillock rising only 6 m above the surrounding plain, surrounded by the course of an old stream creek (Georgescu & Floca 2015). A similar situation can be noticed in the recently excavated settlement from Timișoara-Freidorf (Figures 1 & 2). Although the landscape has been significantly transformed by modern industrial works, the 18th and 19th century topographic maps seem to show that a small stream enclosed the area

In D.C. Cowley, M. Fernández-Götz, T. Romankiewicz & H. Wendling (eds). Rural Settlement. Relating buildings, landscape, and people in the European Iron Age (Leiden 2019: Sidestone Press) 167-171.

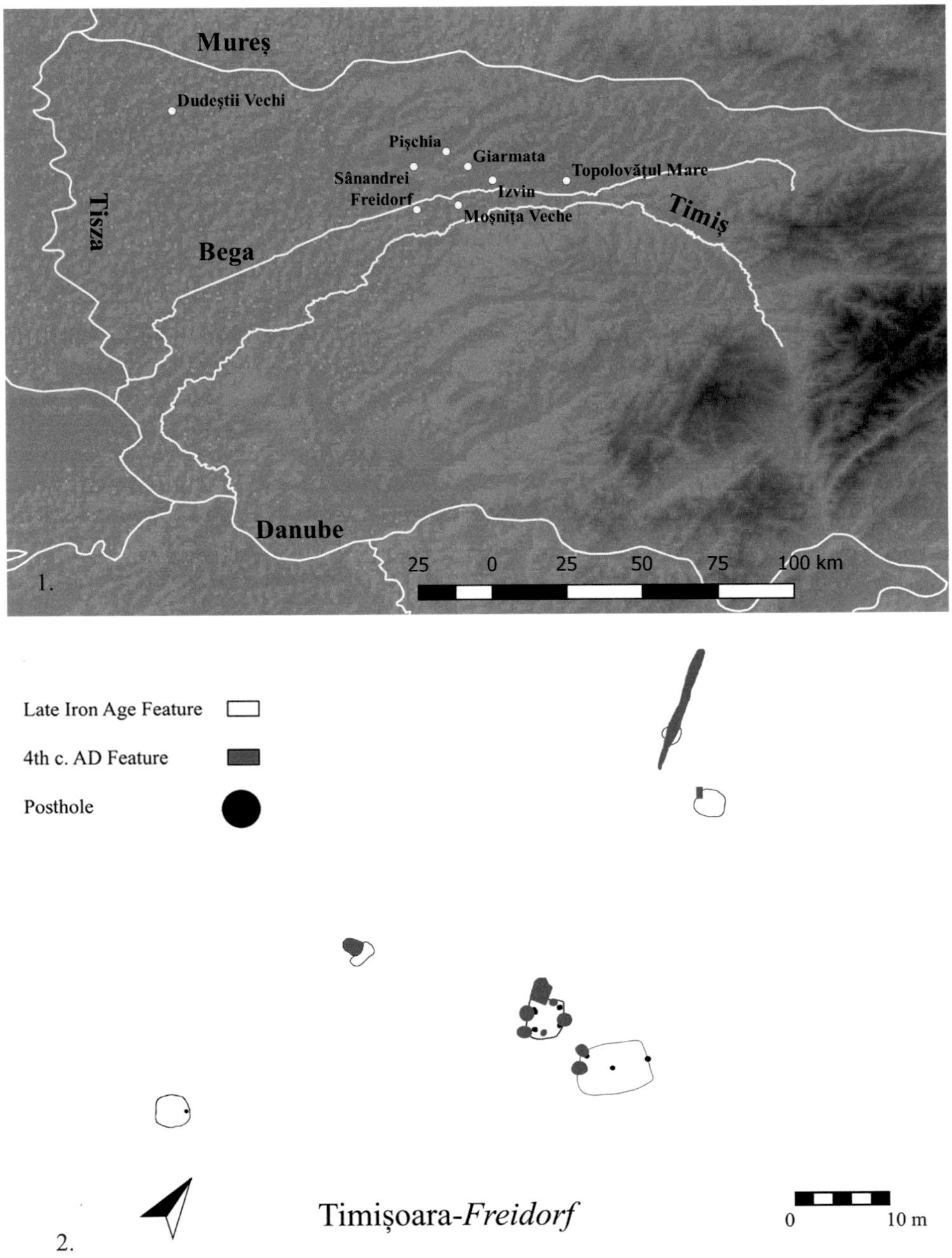

Figure 1: Top – Map of early and middle La Tène settlements in the Banat region; Bottom – plan of the settlement of Timişoara-Freidorf.

of the site. This type of landscape was preferred by the Early and Middle La Tène period communities throughout the Carpathian Basin (Berecki 2009, 9). The sandy loess soils and proximity to water were vital for those agrarian communities (Jerem 2003, 197).

16.3 Settlement structures

Although not many archaeological features have been unearthed and none of the known settlements have been excavated completely, some valuable information concerning the architecture and organization of buildings is available. Most of the data comes from the recently excavated settlement at Timişoara-Freidorf. Here, six Late Iron Age building structures have been excavated. The largest, feature number 17 (Figure 2, 4), is rectangular with rounded corners and extends to about 46 m^2. Structures of similar size are not uncommon in the Carpathian Basin, with similar buildings in the settlement of Szeged-Kiskundoroszma, in the vicinity of the Banat region (Piling & Ujvári 2012, 218). The building at Timişoara-Freidorf had a northeast-southwest orientation and a large posthole in the centre of the northeast end. There may have been a corresponding post at the opposite end, but unfortunately part of the building was destroyed by two pits in the

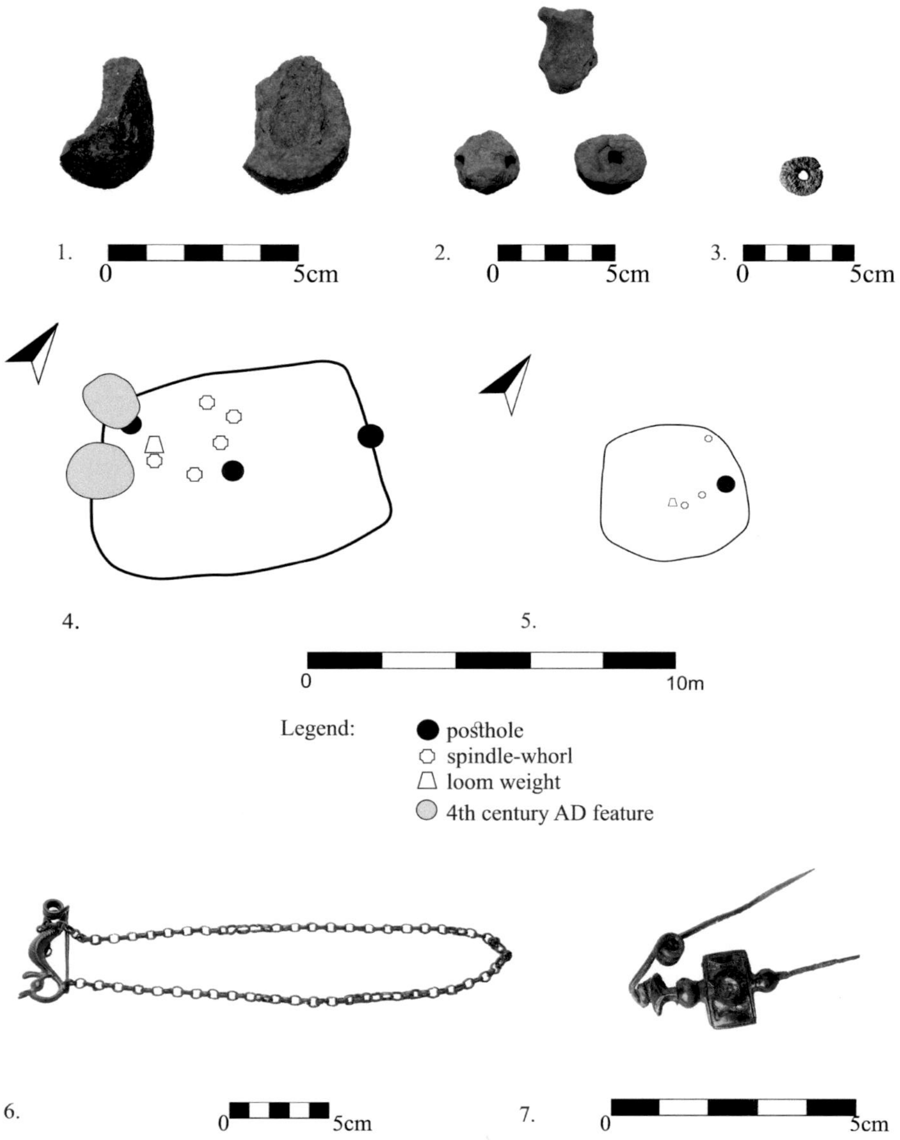

Figure 2: Crucible (1) and Bellow pipe (2) from Moșnița Veche; Bellow pipe (3), Feature 17 (4), Feature 308 (5), Zoomorphic brooch (6) and Rectangular plated brooch (7) from Timișoara-Freidorf.

4th century AD. A similar construction, with two postholes at either end, was discovered in a settlement at Moșnița Veche, and is a type of building that is quite common in the Carpathian Basin (Georgescu & Floca 2015, 302).

Adjacent to structure number 17 at Timișoara-Freidorf, there was a smaller rectangular building which had a posthole in each corner. The positioning, size, and structure of this building might indicate that it served as an ancillary building for the larger structure near it.

Most of the structures unearthed so far in this region are shallow in depth. However one sunken feature, number 308 (Figure 2, 5), was discovered in the settlement at Timișoara-Freidorf. It is rectangular on plan and 1.1 m deep. The fill of all such sunken features discovered so far in the Banat region comprises post-abandonment waste. Therefore the functions of the building, or any internal organization of the dwellings, are very difficult to discern. Indeed, possible floor surfaces have been identified only in some cases, and so far, no surface structures have been identified. Such constructions are most often found in the western Carpathian Basin, in contrast to the eastern part of this region where sunken dwellings are predominant (Timár 2015, 192).

16.4 Craft activities

Although, the precise function of the buildings discussed above cannot be identified, some objects found in secondary contexts document craft activities that took place in these settlements. Spindle-whorls are a common item of textile working. In feature number 14 at Moșnița Veche, several spindle-whorls alongside fragmentary loom-weights were found in the southern part of the building. The layer they were found in was composed of ash and charcoal from burnt waste, so it is likely that the weaving tools were found in secondary positions (Georgescu & Floca, 309). In structure number 17 at Freidorf, seven spindle-whorls were found. Most of them were concentrated in the northwest of the building, where a fragmentary loom-weight was also found. One spindle-whorl was found at the bottom of a posthole, suggesting a possible structured ritual deposit. In the sunken structure 308 at the same settlement, three spindle-whorls and a fragmentary loom-weight were discovered in the eastern part of the feature.

Metal working is documented by a range of tools. In feature number 14 at Moșnița Veche, a bellow pipe (Figure 2, 2), a crucible (Figure 2, 1) and a fragment from an ore reduction furnace were found (Georgescu & Floca 2015, 323; pl. 27-8). A pipe fragment from Freidorf also indicates metalworking (Figure 2, 3). The ore, wood and water supply required for iron production in a small community might have been produced with little impact on the surrounding environment (Venclová & Dreslerová 2013, 296). Ceramic production could also have been carried out at both settlements discussed here. Although no clear proof of a ceramic workshop exists so far, the presence of mica schist could be indicative of production, as it is not local and is often used as temper for fine wheel-made pottery.

16.5 Cultural connections

The most significant category of artefacts in settlement contexts is ceramics. Although not many archaeological contexts have been recorded so far, handmade pottery is predominant with less wheel-made ceramics. The handmade pottery has been considered to be specific to the autochthonous population (whoever they were) as opposed to the wheel-made ceramic that was considered a trait specific for the Celtic 'newcomers' (see for instance Pupeză 2012, 325). However, the handmade ceramic found in the settlements from the Banat is similar to that found in other regions like south Pannonia, southeast Slovakia or southwest Transylvania. This indicates that the typology of the pottery is not relevant to assumptions about the ethnicity of the communities. The stamped wheel-made pottery from Freidorf shows cultural connections with the rest of the Carpathian Basin. The 'double-lyre' motif found on a fragmentary bi-truncated pot is a characteristic feature of the eastern Celtic art (Megaw & Megaw 2006, 382).

Although not many garment accessories have been found in settlements so far, two brooches from Timișoara-Freidorf illuminate the ideological and cultural interactions of the communities from the Banat region. At the base layer of structure number 17 a bronze zoomorphic ring brooch and a bronze chain were found (Figure 2, 6). These fibulae are most commonly found in female graves and were worn in pairs (Szabó 1974; Rustoiu 2012). The 'dress code' that accompanies these brooches is encountered throughout the Carpathian Basin and might be a reflection of a shared ideology. Another fibula, made of bronze with a rectangular plate decorated with enamel inlay, was found in the above mentioned settlement (Figure 2, 7). This brooch belongs to 5a type in Rustoiu`s typology (Rustoiu 1997, 38). The recent analysis of this kind of jewellery, and the creation of a specific typology with distribution maps (Dizdar 2014), allows the Freidorf brooch to be placed in the context of a group with a central depression surrounded by curvilinear depressions, found in an area centred on the Tisza Basin (Dizdar 2014, 102, fig.4).

16.6 Conclusions

Although information is scant, some valuable conclusions can be drawn concerning the early and middle La Tène period occupation of the Banat region. One important observation is that all of the settlements researched so far are not on the major communication routes of the Mureș and Danube rivers. Even so, the communities of the Banat plains are connected to the wider cultural and economic zone of the Carpathian Basin. Moreover, some influences from the outer Carpathian regions and from the Balkan Peninsula can be traced. These traits confirm the information provided so far by funerary data.

16.7 Acknowledgements

This work was supported by a grant from the Ministry of Research and Innovation, CNCS – UEFISCDI, project number PN-III-P4-ID-PCE-2016-0353, within PNCDI III

16.8 Bibliography

Berecki, S. 2009. The Enviroment and Landscape of the Celtic Settlements and Cemeteries from Transylvani. In V. Sîrbu & V. Ciobanu (eds). *Mousaios, XIV, The Necropolises and Enviroment (1st mill. BC)*. 9-24. Buzău: Editura Istros.

Dizdar, M. 2014. Bronze Fibulae with Enamel Inlay from Scordiscan Sites. In S. Berecki (ed.). *Iron Age Craft and Craftsmen in the Carpathian Basin*. 97-114.Târgu Mureş: Mega Publishing House.

Georgescu, A. & Floca. C. 2015, Habitat Structures in the Early and Middle La Tène Period from the Banat Region. Feature No. 14 discovered at Moșnița Veche-*Dealul Sălaș*. In S. Froțiu & A. Stavilă (eds). *Arheovest*, III, JATE Press, Szeged, 299-330.

Jerem, E. 2003. The Late Iron Age. The Celts of the La Tène Period. In Z. Visy & M. Nagy (eds). *Hungarian Archaeology at the Turn of the Millenium*. 192-200. Budapest: Ministry of National Cultural Heritage.

Megaw, J.V.S. & Megaw, M.R. 2006. Stryke the Lyre: Notes on an Eastern Celtic Motif. *Acta Archaeologica Academiae Scientarium Hung. (57)*, 367-93.

Piling, Z. & Ujvári, F. 2012. Iron Age Settlement and Cemetery from Szeged-Kiskundorozsma. Some new Data on Iron Age Burial Rite in the Southern Part of the Great Hungarian Plain. In S. Berecki (ed.). *Iron Age Rites and Rituals in the Carpathian Basin.* 217-48. Târgu Mureş: Mega Publishing House.

Pupeză, P. 2012. The Local Tradition Pottery from the Eastern Carpathian Basin Celtic Graves. In S. Berecki (ed.). *Iron Age Rites and Rituals in the Carpathian Basin.* 317-42. Târgu Mureş: Mega Publishing House.

Rustoiu, A. 1997. *Fibulele din Dacia Preromană (sec. II î.e.n.-I e.n.)*, București: Institutul Român de Tracologie.

Rustoiu, A. 2012. The Celts and Indigenous Populations from the Southern Carpathian Basin. Intercommunity Communication Strategies. In S. Berecki (ed.). *Iron Age Rites and Rituals in the Carpathian Basin.* 357-90. Târgu Mureş: Mega Publishing House.

Rustoiu, A. & Ursuțiu, A. 2013. Celtic Colonization in Banat. Comments Regarding the Funerary Discoveries. In V. Sîrbu & R. Ștefănescu (eds). *The Thracians and Their Neighbours in the Bronze and Iron Ages* II. 323-45. Brăila: Editura Istros.

Szabó, M. 1974. Contribution à l'étude de l'art et de la chronologie de La Tène ancienne en Hongrie, *Folia Archaeologica(XXV)*, 71-86.

Timár, L. 2015. The Sunken-Featured Buildings of the Middle La Tène Period. In P. Ramsl & M. Karwowski (eds). *Boii-Taurisci.* 191-203. Wien: Verlag der Österreichischen Akademie der Wiessenschaft.

Venclová, N. & Dreslerová, D. 2013. Iron Production, Settlement and Enviroment: a Regional Approach. In S. Krausz, A. Colin, K. Gruel, I. Ralston & T. Dechezleprêtre (eds). *L'âge du Fer en Europe. Mélanges offerts à Olivier Buchsenschutz.* 291-303. Bordeaux: Ausonius Èditions.

Chapter 17

Late Iron Age rural settlements in southern Pannonia

Ivan Drnić

17.1 Cultural and chronological context

In contrast to urban landscapes, which are, in their essence and development, anthropogenic, rural landscapes are composed of two mutually intertwined components: the cultural/anthropogenic and the natural. Although the level of archaeological knowledge about the south-Pannonian Iron Age landscape is rather poor, it is possible, using available data, to deduce that the entire landscape, dominated by the rivers Sava, Drava and Danube and some hilly regions in the central and western parts, can be defined as rural. Only few settlements point to certain urban characteristics (organisation of space, fortifications, production, regional/long-distance contacts, etc.) in particular chronological phases, such as the Late Hallstatt and the Late La Tène periods.

One of these settlements is located on the confluence of the Kupa and Sava Rivers in the modern-day town of Sisak in central Croatia. It shows a continuous development with complex settlement dynamics from the Late Bronze Age (Ha B) to the end of the Late Iron Age. After the siege and conquest of the indigenous settlement in 35 BC, the Romans established a military stronghold as the key point for advance into the Pannonian plain and, in the second half of the 1st century AD, it was transformed into civilian city or colony (*Colonia Flavia Sisci*a). As recent excavations and geophysical surveys reveal, in the late Hallstatt period (6th-4th centuries BC) a structured settlement with densely packed houses organised in a grid system that covered an area of 3-4 ha existed (Drnić & Groh 2018). A number of attributes, such as settlement structure and its central position in the local network, evidence of metal, pottery and textile production, regional and long-distance contacts, as well as the existence of warrior elites, could indicate an urban character of the settlement, in accordance with several proposed models used in research on early urbanisation (Fernández-Götz *et al.* 2014). Settlement complexity increased in the Late Iron Age (3rd-1st century BC) with a slightly different internal organisation, covering an area of 5-10 ha on both banks of the river Kupa. The introduction of urban concepts in southern Pannonia, certainly with a minor temporal delay, correlates with the emergence of the first complex communities in temperate Europe in the period between the later 7th and the 5th centuries BC, as suggested by several authors (Fernández-Götz *et al.* 2014; Fernández-Götz 2018; Fernández-Götz & Krausse 2017). Thus, the case of the Sisak late Hallstatt settlement could be interpreted as a result of an internal socio-political development of an indigenous community, with a probable influence from central

In D.C. Cowley, M. Fernández-Götz, T. Romankiewicz & H. Wendling (eds). Rural Settlement. Relating buildings, landscape, and people in the European Iron Age (Leiden 2019: Sidestone Press) 173-178.

Europe. Another possible region of influence could be the Po valley, which witnessed intense Etruscan colonization and establishment of several urban centres, such as Spina and Adria at the north Adriatic coast, in the course of the 6th century BC. These urban impulses could spread to the east, with a good example provided by the Late Hallstatt settlement at Most na Soči in the Isonzo valley (Svoljšak & Dular 2016; Dular & Tecco Hvala 2018).

Similar processes took place in the Late La Tène period, mostly in south-eastern Pannonia, the area of the historically attested Scordisci communities. Resting on a solid regional basis, the emergence of fortified settlements undoubtedly reflects central European political, economic, and cultural processes that led to the formation of what is called 'the *oppida* civilisation'. For example, most of these settlements are situated at prominent 'tell' sites with thick occupation layers from previous and later periods. Several fortified centres are known from the region, including Gomolava near Hrtkovci (SR) in the lower Sava valley. Having been extensively excavated and analysed, this site serves as a model for this type of settlement (Jovanović & Jovanović 1988). In the Croatian part of the middle Danube region two prominent fortified Late La Tène centres are situated in Vinkovci and in Osijek. Both extended over large areas, yielded evidence of intense metal and pottery production, and, in the case of Osijek, included a ritual area or sanctuary (Šimić & Filipović 1997; Dizdar 2001; Filipović 2010).

17.2 Rural settlements

By way of contrast to the larger fortified centres, a large number of smaller unenclosed settlements have been

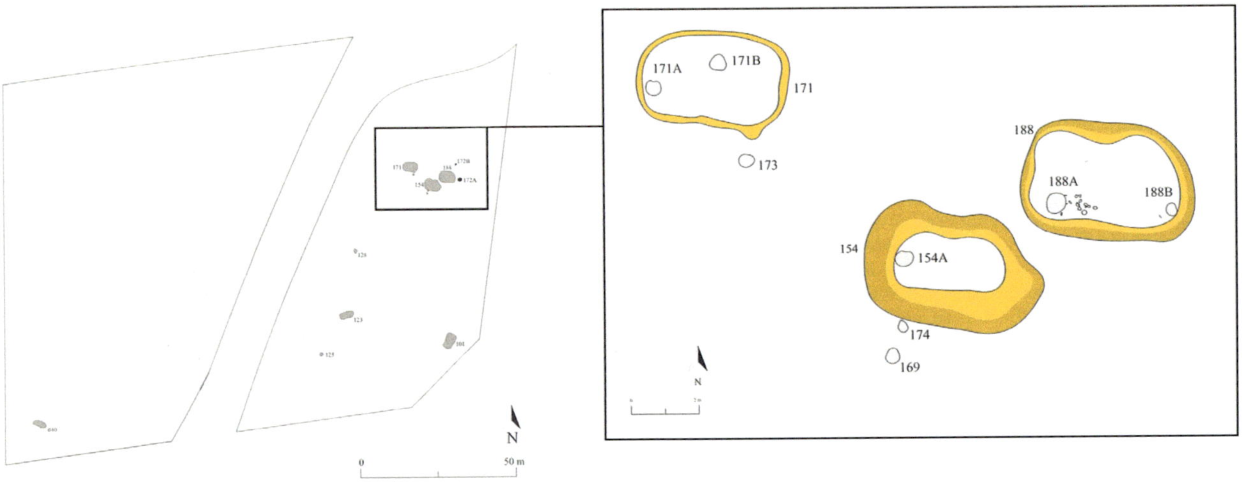

A

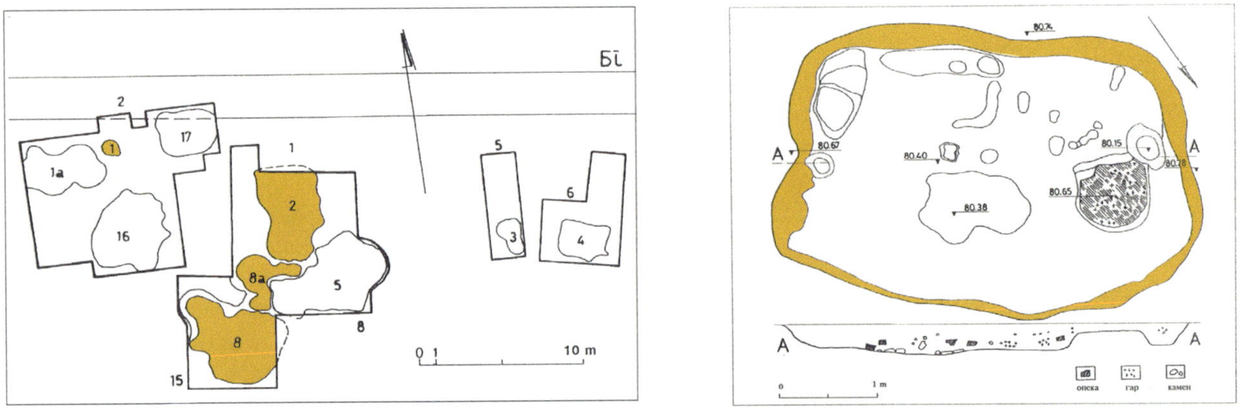

B

Figure 1: a) Late La Tène farmstead at the Murska Sobota-Nova Tabla site (after Pavlovič 2011). b) Late La Tène and early Roman period structures at the Atovac-Bregovi site near Kuzmin, Republic of Serbia (marked ochre) ; Semi-dugout structure of Grubenhaus-type from the Atovac-Bregovi site near Kuzmin (after Brukner 1995).

detected during the 1970s and 1980s, together offering a dichotomous framework for interpreting the Late La Tène cultural landscape (Brukner 1995; Jovanović 2009). However, as a result of recent discoveries, a much more complex pattern has started to emerge, including some new settlement categories that indicate a complex settlement network that is yet to be reconstructed. For example, at the Blato site near Vinkovci, a large open settlement provides evidence of metal production, coin circulation and long-distance contacts suggesting it is the south-eastern Pannonian equivalent of the Němčice-Roseldorf type of settlements in central Europe (Salač 2012). Fine chronological resolution suggests a slightly later date for the Blato settlement between LT C2 and LT D2 phases, with a *floruit* in LT D1, in comparison with the Němčice-Roseldorf centres which roughly cover LT B2-LT C (Dizdar 2016). Blato was contemporary to the nearby fortified settlement of Vinkovci-Ervenica. Recent geophysical survey at the Turski Šanac site near Bačka Palanka has revealed a settlement with a complex system of ramparts and ditches, interpreted as a heavily fortified centre of the late La Tène warrior elite (Wendling, this volume).

The most numerous category of Late La Tène settlements in southern Pannonia includes small unenclosed open settlements in a rural environment. Research on these settlements faces several methodological problems. In older excavations, usually smaller areas were investigated, yielding only a few features, hampering a comprehensive reconstruction of the layouts of the settlements including internal structures, settlement dynamics, and the like. On the other hand, in recent, mostly rescue excavations, a considerable number of similar Late La Tène sites have been discovered. Unfortunately, most of these are still unpublished and therefore unavailable to inform further landscape studies.

However, research on currently available data allows the identification of two sub-categories of rural settlements. The first includes sites with a limited number of features, which are best described as hamlets or farmsteads and were occupied by a single nuclear or extended family. A good example of this type is the Late La Tène settlement of Murska Sobota-Nova Tabla in south-western Pannonia that yielded eight semi-sunken features situated on the bank of an ancient river bed (Figure 1a) (Pavlovič 2011). A similar situation was also registered in the Syrmia region at the Atovac-Bregovi site near the village of Kuzmin, were remains of two Late La Tène hamlets were excavated some 480 m apart (Brukner 1995). The hamlets comprised a few semi-dugout structures, accompanied with several pits and fireplaces (Figure 1b).

A

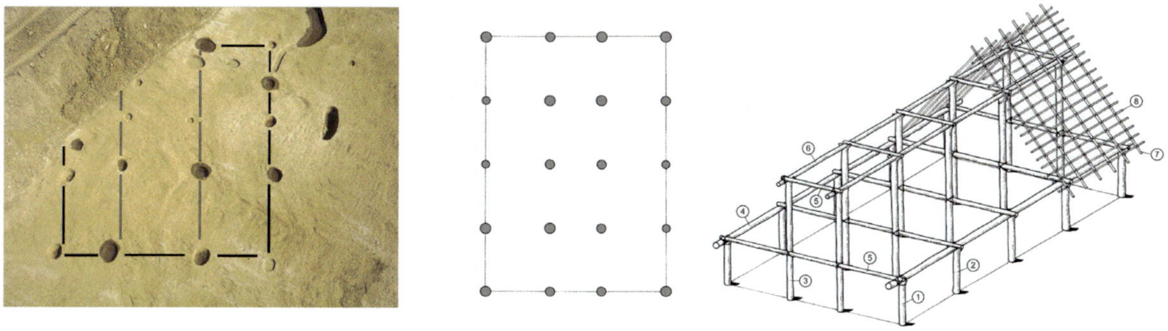

B

Figure 2: a) Post-built structure from the Virovitica-Kiškorija north site (after Dizdar 2006), and reconstruction (Dular 2008); b) Semi-sunken structure and its reconstruction from the Josipovac-Selište site (after Filipec *et al.* 2009).

Figure 3: Late La Tène village at the Virovitica-Kiškorija site (Dizdar 2007).

Larger rural settlements, covering an area of several thousand square metres with numerous different features, such as rectangular storage pits above-ground post-built houses, semi-dugout working places of *Grubenhaus*-type, kilns, fireplaces, wells, storage pits, and ditches, can probably be termed villages. Simple post-built structures with two rows of post holes occur at several sites, but larger ones, with three or four rows of post holes have also been found, suggesting a more complex roof construction for some buildings (Figure 2a). Some dugout structures with post-holes suggest the existence of houses with underground storage places or cellars, for example in the case of a structure at Josipovac-Selište (Figure 2b; Filipec *et al.* 2009). A settlement that fits this description, with all listed features and an internal structure comprised of smaller units separated by shallow ditches or fences, was excavated over an area greater than 15000 m^2, and is dated to the Late La Tène period (Figure 3; Dizdar 2006; 2007). Several larger rural settlements, or villages, came to light in the central Sava River valley in recent rescue excavations. One of the largest is at the site of Stružani near Slavonski Brod, and yielded more than 15 post-built houses, as well as numerous dugout features (Miklik-Lozuk 2012). A larger rural settlement, dating from LT D to the beginning of the Roman period, was partially excavated at the Pećinci site in Syrmia, with 19 dugout structures, including kilns (Brukner 1995).

Although these rural Late La Tène settlements are generally classified as open or unenclosed, some evidence suggests that some of them were enclosed by a basic system of defence in the form of a ditch, such as at the Bukovica-Sjenjak site in the Podravina region (Kovačević 2017). Similarly, sometimes multiple ditches have been identified in other regions, for instance the La Tène settlements at Södinberg and Lebing in Austrian Styria (Tiefengraber 2009). Besides a basic defensive purpose, these ditches, just like the walls in larger fortified settlements, could also have symbolic meaning, marking the limits of the community or inside and outside space (von Nicolai 2014).

Low intensity production is attested in these rural settlements, although on a much more restricted level in comparison to larger fortified centres. For example, several sites yielded remains of vertical pottery kilns with double fire chambers and grids, with production probably directed at the level of the local community. Additionally, several *in situ* remains of vertical looms in the form of linear arrangements of pyramidal weights are known from Late Iron Age sites, as are finds of numerous spindle whorls used in household textile production (Sekelj Ivančan & Karavidović 2016).

17.3 Conclusion

The Late Iron Age landscape of southern Pannonia fits into a general central European context. Certain regional particularities result from its peripheral position between the La Tène cultural complex and autochthonous Balkan/Lower Danube communities influenced by the Hellenistic world. Although the state of research is significantly less developed by comparison to some other European regions, it is possible to reconstruct to a certain degree social dynamics in the period between the late 4th century and the end of the 1st century BC. In the LT B2/C1 phases, sometimes labelled 'the Celtic migration period', there is virtually no data on settlements. This could, on one hand, indicate a lack of methodological tools allowing for a better insight into this transitional period that is heavily influenced by data from graves. On the other hand, the absence of settlement data could to some extent be a reflection of the historical reality of the late 4th and 3rd centuries BC, wherein specific settlement and subsistence strategies of the local communities resulted in a lower population density. From the 2nd century BC (LT C2/D1), there is a significant increase of settlements in the archaeological record, including numerous smaller and larger rural settlements, but also fortified *oppida*, open production and distribution centres in southeastern Pannonia, and hillforts in the southwest, for example Kuzelin near Zagreb (Sokol 2001; 2006). As a result, a complex cultural landscape emerged in the final stage of the proto-historic development of southern Pannonia, reflecting a specific socio-political structure. At the end of the 1st century BC, this structure was partially deconstructed and integrated into the Roman provincial system. Due to their strategic importance, some of the larger Late Iron Age settlements became important Roman centres, like Segestica/Siscia (Sisak), Cibalae (Vinkovci), or Mursa (Osijek). There is also significant evidence for continued occupation of some rural settlements, especially in the Syrmia region. Here examples like the Šimanovci-Vrtlozi and Pećinci-Tromeđa sites (Brukner 1995) might imply not only the survival, but also integration, of local communities in the new social context, most likely as peregrines (*civitates peregrinae*), for example *civitas Scordiscorum*.

17.4 Bibliography

Brukner, O. 1995. Domorodačka naselja (Native settlements), In *Arheološka istraživanja duž autoputa kroz Srem (Archaeological investigations along the highway route in Srem)*, 92-136. Novi Sad: Pokrajinski Zavod za zaštitu spomenika kulture.

Dizdar, M. 2001. *Latenska naselja na vinkovačkom području (La Tène Settlements in the Vinkovci Region)*. Zagreb: Department of Archaeology, Faculty of Arts, University of Zagreb.

Dizdar, M. 2006. Zaštitna istraživanja naselja latenske kulture na nalazištu Virovitica-Kiškorija sjever (Rescue Excavations of La Tène Settlement at the Virovitica-Kiškorija sjever Site). *Annales Instituti Archaeologici* 2, 55-60.

Dizdar, M. 2007. Naselje mlađeg željeznog doba Virovitica-Kiškorija sjever, In *Zapadna virovitička obilaznica. Zaštitna arheološka istraživanja 2005./2006. godine.* Virovitica: Gradski muzej Virovitica.

Dizdar, M. 2016. Late La Tène settlements in the Vinkovci region (Eastern Slavonia, Croatia): centres of trade and exchange. In M. Karwowski & P. C. Ramsl (eds). *Boii – Taurisci*, 31-48. Wien: Verlag der Österreichischen Akademie der Wissenschaften.

Drnić, I. & Groh, S. 2018. Iskopavanja i geofizička prospekcija željeznodobnog i rimskog nalazišta na poziciji Sisak-Pogorelac. *Vjesnik Arheološkog muzeja u Zagrebu* 51, 37-140.

Dular, J. 2008. Prazgodovinske lesne gradbene tehnike in njihova terminologija (Prehistoric building techniques and their terminology). *Annales. Series historia et sociologia* 18/2, 2008, 337-48.

Fernández-Götz, M. 2018. Urbanization in Iron Age Europe: Trajectories, Patterns, and Social Dynamics. *Journal of Archaeological Research* 26, 117-62.

Fernández-Götz, M., Wendling, H. & Winger, K. 2014. Introduction: New Perspectives on Iron Age Urbanisation. In M. Fernández-Götz, H. Wendling & K. Winger (eds). *Paths to Complexity: Centralisation and Urbanisation in Iron Age Europe*, 2-14. Oxford: Oxbow.

Fernández-Götz, M. & Krausse, D. 2017, Urbanization process and cultural change in the Early Iron Age of Central Europe, In M. Fernández-Götz & D. Krausse (eds). *Eurasia at the Dawn of History: Urbanization and Social Change*, 319-35. New York: Cambridge University Press.

Filipec, K. , Roksandić, D., Šiša Vivek & M., Karneluti, M. (eds) 2009. Josipovac-Selište (AN 14). In *Arheološke slike Slavonije*. Zagreb: Odsjek za arheologiju Filozofskog fakulteta Sveučilišta u Zagrebu.

Filipović, S. 2010. Lokalitet Osijek (Mursa)-Vojarna (Učiteljski fakultet). *Hrvatski arheološki godišnjak* 6, 37-41.

Jovanović, B. 2009. Late La Tène unfortified settlements in the surroundings of Gomolava / Lower Srem, *Rad Muzeja Vojvodine* 51, 91-102.

Jovanović, B. & Jovanović, M. 1988. *Gomolava. Naselje mlađeg gvozdenog doba (Gomolava. Late La Tène settlement)*, Gomolava 2, Novi Sad – Beograd: Vojvođanski muzej & Arheološki institut.

Kovačević, S. 2017. Nova Bukovica-Sjenjak 2016. *Annales Instituti Archaeologici* 13, 50-3.

Miklik-Lozuk, L. 2012. *Stružani, život naselja kroz stoljeća*. Slavonski Brod: Muzej Brodskog Posavlja.

Pavlovič, D. 2011. La Tène farmsteads near Murska Sobota. In M. Guštin & M. Jevtić (eds). *The Eastern Celts.The Communities between the Alps and the Black Sea*, 83-90. Beograd-Koper: Univerza na Primorskem, Znanstveno-raziskovalno središće Koper, Založba Annales.

Salač, V. 2012. Les oppida et les processus d'urbanisation en Europe centrale. In S. Sievers & M. Schönfelder (eds). *Die Frage der Protourbanisation in der Eisenzeit*, 319-45. Bonn: Habelt.

Sekelj Ivančan, T. & Karavidović, T. 2016. Tkalački stan iz Virja (A loom from Virje). *Prilozi Instituta za arheologiju u Zagrebu* 33, 171-235.

Sokol, V. 2001, Neue Latènfunde aus der Umgebung von Zagreb (Croatia). Instrumentum 14, 16.

Sokol, V. 2001, Kuzelin. In A. Durman (ed), Stotinu hrvatskih arheoloških nalazišta, Zagreb, Leksikografski zavod Miroslav Krleža, 154-155.

Svoljšak, D. & Dular, J. 2016. *Most na Soči. Settlement structures and Small Finds*. Opera Instituti Archaeologici Sloveniae 33. Ljubljana: Založba ZRC SAZU, ZRC SAZU, Inštitut za arheologijo.

Šimić, J. 1997. Kelti. In J. Šimić & S. Filipović, *Kelti i Rimljani na području Osijeka*, 3-49. Osijek: Muzej Slavonije.

Tecco Hvala, S. & Dular, J. (eds). 2018, *Most na Soči. Treatises*. Opera Instituti Archaeologici Sloveniae 34. Ljubljana: Založba ZRC SAZU, ZRC SAZU, Inštitut za arheologijo.

Tiefengraber, G. 2009. Befestigte mittel- und spätlatènezeitliche Flachlandsiedlungen im Südostalpenraum. In G. Tiefengraber, B. Kavur & A. Gaspari (eds). *Keltske študije II. Studies in Celtic Archaeology. Papers in honour of Mitja Guštin*. 259-82. Montagnac: Mergoil.

von Nicolai, C. 2014. Symbolic Meanings of Iron Age Hillfort Defences in Continental Europe. In M. Fernández-Götz, H. Wendling & K. Winger (eds). *Paths to Complexity: Centralisation and Urbanisation in Iron Age Europe*. 111-20. Oxford: Oxbow.

Chapter 18

Meillionydd

A Late Bronze and Iron Age double ringwork enclosure in northwest Wales

Katharina Möller & Raimund Karl

18.1 Introduction

Since 2010, Prifysgol Bangor University has been conducting excavations at Meillionydd, a Late Bronze and Iron Age double ringwork enclosure on the Llŷn peninsula in northwest Wales, UK. A cross-section of the site has been excavated, including the east-facing entrance, numerous roundhouses and other buildings, and the two enclosing banks on its western side. While in general fitting a pattern characteristic for enclosed Late Bronze Age and Iron Age settlements in much of Britain, Meillionydd is one of the best-preserved, and by now the most comprehensively excavated, representatives of a local sub-type of British settlement architecture, a so-called narrow double ringwork enclosure. Settlements of this type can be found mainly on the Llŷn peninsula, with two additional sites on Anglesey.

Meillionydd was densely occupied over a period of about half a millennium, with 12 distinct phases of occupation currently distinguishable. The development of the site demonstrates that it was not a double ringwork over the whole period of its occupation. Rather, it started out as an open Late Bronze Age settlement of timber roundhouses. The period during which it was a bi-vallate enclosure with an impressive in-turned inner gate passage, which gave it the form that survives in the surface topography today, was probably quite short, perhaps less than 100 years roughly around the middle of its overall period of occupation. The development of the site shows the first emergence of a distinct settlement hierarchy in this corner of Britain, which appears to have more in common with Ireland (which is visible from the site in good weather) than with much of the rest of the British mainland. In addition, finds in some features could indicate burials, which are rare in Iron Age contexts in Wales.

18.2 The site

Meillionydd is a double ringwork enclosure near Rhiw in northwest Wales (Figure 1; for site identification and selection methodology for this map, see Waddington 2013, 5-6). The site lies on the crest of a ridge jutting out from the lower slopes of Mynydd Rhiw at about 190 m above sea level and covers an area of 0.8 ha (Waddington 2013, 216). Classed as a 'weak double ringwork' by the Royal Commission on the Ancient and Historical Monuments of Wales (RCAHMW 1964, lxxvi-lxxviii), it belongs to a local sub-type of so-called narrow

In D.C. Cowley, M. Fernández-Götz, T. Romankiewicz & H. Wendling (eds). Rural Settlement. Relating buildings, landscape, and people in the European Iron Age (Leiden 2019: Sidestone Press) 179-190.

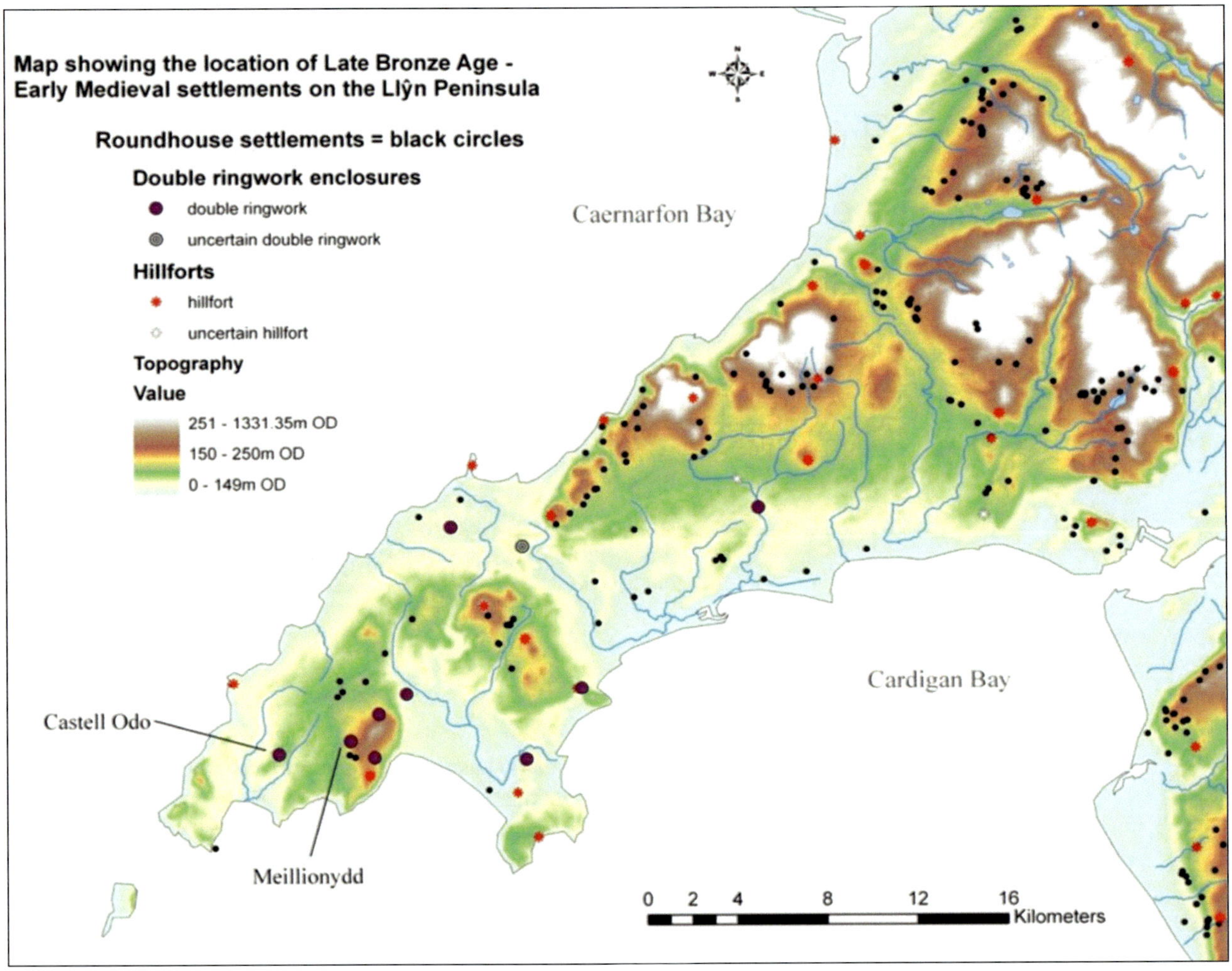

Figure 1: The distribution of known 1st millennium BC and AD settlements on the Llŷn peninsula, northwest Wales (Image: K. Waddington).

double ringwork enclosures. While similar to sites in other areas of the UK, this enclosed settlement type is defined by the narrow distance between the outer and inner banks, which on average is less than 10 m. Of the eleven currently known examples of this sub-type, nine are located on the Llŷn peninsula, with the other two on Anglesey, which is visible from the Llŷn across Caernarfon Bay. Meillionydd (Figure 2) was one of six sites of this type that were surveyed in 2007 by G. H. Smith and D. Hopewell from the Gwynedd Archaeological Trust (Smith & Hopewell 2007). Despite the only remains visible in the surface topography, the two circular banks, being slighted, a magnetometer survey indicated that the archaeology on site was well preserved. Besides the banks and a possible entrance in the east of the settlement, at least three roundhouses could be identified (Smith & Hopewell 2007, 15).

The results from the geophysical survey indicated that the site was similar to Castell Odo, another narrow double ringwork on the Penllŷn (Breese 1932; Alcock 1960), just under 5 km away and visible from Meillionydd. Alcock, who excavated part of Castell Odo in 1958 and 1959, found evidence of timber and stone-built roundhouses, as well as an earlier wooden palisade beneath the outer bank. He identified five main building phases, with phase 1a comprising an unenclosed settlement of timber roundhouses, which was later enclosed by a wooden palisade (phase 1b). The change from phase 1 to phase 2 was marked by the use of stone rather than timber as building material. During phases 2 to 5 the settlement was enclosed by two earth and rubble banks (Alcock 1960, 84-103).

A similar stratigraphy was expected at Meillionydd when the site was chosen for excavation, and the initial excavations (Waddington & Karl 2010) focussed on the banks and an area inside the inner bank where an obvious anomaly in the magnetometer survey indicated the presence of a roundhouse. These excavations produced evidence for timber and stone-built roundhouses and a U-shaped ditch predating the banks.

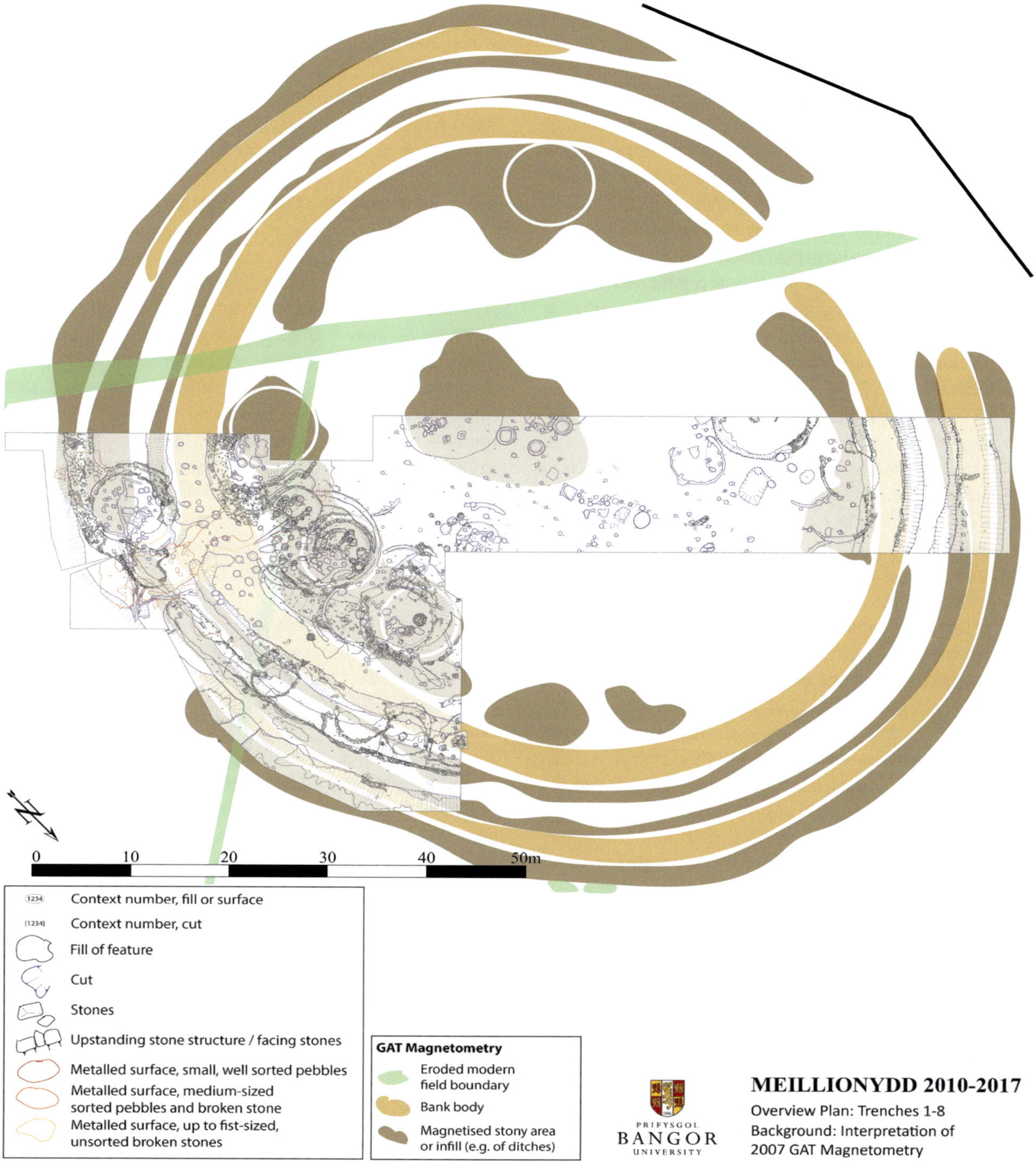

Figure 2 : Plan of all trenches excavated at Meillionydd between 2010 and 2017, superimposed on the interpretation of the 2007 magnetometer survey (Smith & Hopewell 2007) (Image: R. Karl).

Subsequent excavations (2011-2013) extended the excavated area (Waddington & Karl 2015a; 2015b; 2016), with a GPR survey carried out 2012 by the Zentralanstalt für Meteorologie und Geodynamik (ZAMG). The results showed that the site was much more densely occupied than previously assumed (Löcker *et al.* 2013), and in total about 100 roundhouses have been identified (Higgins 2014, 2). By the end of the 2013 season, evidence for an earlier enclosed phase with a U-shaped ditch and a wooden palisade, which was later replaced by the banks, and a total of 4-5 building phases had been uncovered. Despite the large number of roundhouses discovered through the

GPR survey, the overall occupation sequence seemed to be very similar to that at Castell Odo.

In 2014 excavation focused on the entrance through the inner bank (Möller *et al.* 2016), where, amongst other things, three layers of a metalled road surface were discovered. Further excavations in the inner entrance area during 2015 produced evidence of an even more complex occupation sequence than anticipated. Due to various intersecting features in this particular area, at least 12 building phases were identified (Karl *et al.* 2016, 20-39).

Once the excavations of the entrance area were completed, the trench was extended towards the northwest to create a half-section of the site, which was finished in 2016. The results indicate that the building activity was concentrated along the inside of the banks, while the middle of the enclosure was only sparingly occupied. Furthermore, evidence of a repair phase of the inner bank and a second ditch was found. In 2017 a further trench to the north of the eastern entrance into the enclosure was excavated, bringing the total area excavated to about 2125 m^2. Mainly concentrating on the area between the outer and inner banks in this area, remains of a number of smaller (c. 4 m internal diameter) huts alongside the inner side of the outer bank were discovered.

Despite the large numbers of well-preserved features excavated, the range of finds is limited. Due to the acidic soils, organic material is only preserved under specific circumstances, as was the case with shell deposits found in a loosely infilled stone layer in 2014. Iron finds also corrode badly due to the soil conditions, to the point where they cannot be extracted from the ground. Nevertheless, a number of iron objects were found in the inner ditch. Two postholes belonging to the gate through the inner bank produced a decorated glass bead and a piece of a jet bracelet. Three additional glass beads were discovered in the fill of a storage pit and a number of spindle whorls were found in house contexts. However, by far the most common type of find are stone tools, including hammer stones, smoothing stones, whetstones, grinding stones and quern stones.

The finds from Meillionydd are very similar to those of Castell Odo, where stone tools and saddle querns (Breese 1932, 385; Alcock 1960, 133) and a piece of a jet bracelet were found (Alcock 1960, 132). In addition, a large (for the region) assemblage of pottery was found on the western side of Castell Odo in a midden under the outer bank (Alcock 1960, 130).

Pottery is rare in Late Bronze and Iron Age Wales (Davies & Lynch 2000, 199) and a midden has not yet been found at Meillionydd. The more common finds like stone tools and spindle whorls give no indication for dating the site, which rather relies on two radiocarbon samples taken from an area with at least four building phases. This produced dates between 753-410 cal. BC for the earliest and 384-203 cal. BC for the latest building phase in this area (Waddington 2013, 218-20). Further 14C samples from other areas of the site are currently being analysed. While the post-excavation work is still ongoing, a preliminary interpretation of the complex stratigraphy and the distribution of finds will be presented in this paper.

18.3 The occupation sequence

The occupation sequence has recently been discussed in detail by R. Karl (2017) and is only summarized here. The earliest building phase (phase 1) represents an open settlement of timber houses (Figure 3). The houses vary in size with diameters of up to 14 m and some seem to have been replaced – more or less on the same footprint – over time. Hence, phase 1 has been divided into two sub-phases (phase 1a and 1b). At the beginning of phase 2 (Figure 3), the site is enclosed with two ditches with a U-shaped profile and a wooden palisade. This first enclosed phase consists of three sub-phases (phase 2a, 2b and 2c), the latter of which is marked by the construction of a metalled road surface leading up to the palisade gate. This metalled surface partially overlies the northern terminal of the inner ditch.

Phase 3 (Figure 4) marks a major re-modelling of the site, which includes a change in building material from timber to stone. The timber houses are consequently replaced by smaller stone-built houses (max. 10 m diameter) and the palisade and the two ditches are replaced by a more monumental enclosure consisting of two earth and stone banks (phase 3a). In the in-turned entrance through the inner bank there was a wooden gate structure, which was replaced in phase 3b. In the same phase, part of the inner bank on the western side of the enclosure was repaired.

Despite the creation of such an elaborate entrance, it does not seem to have been in use for long. In phase 4 (Figure 4) the entrance is blocked by a roundhouse, which is replaced by another in phase 5. The lack of evidence for a second entrance suggests that at the start of phase 4 the inner bank was no longer maintained and had eroded to the point that an entrance was no longer necessary to reach the inside of the enclosure. The remains of the inner entrance are further degraded by the construction of three roundhouses replacing one another in phases 6 to 8 (Figure 5). In addition, a new metalled road surface, which partially covers the southern terminals of both banks, indicates that at the latest by phase 6 the outer bank was not (fully) maintained anymore either. This sequence highlights the change from an unenclosed settlement to a lightly and later a monumental enclosed one, which then becomes open again during the final stages of its existence. This fits well with an interpretative narrative of a settlement development and subsequent decline in status and social hierarchy.

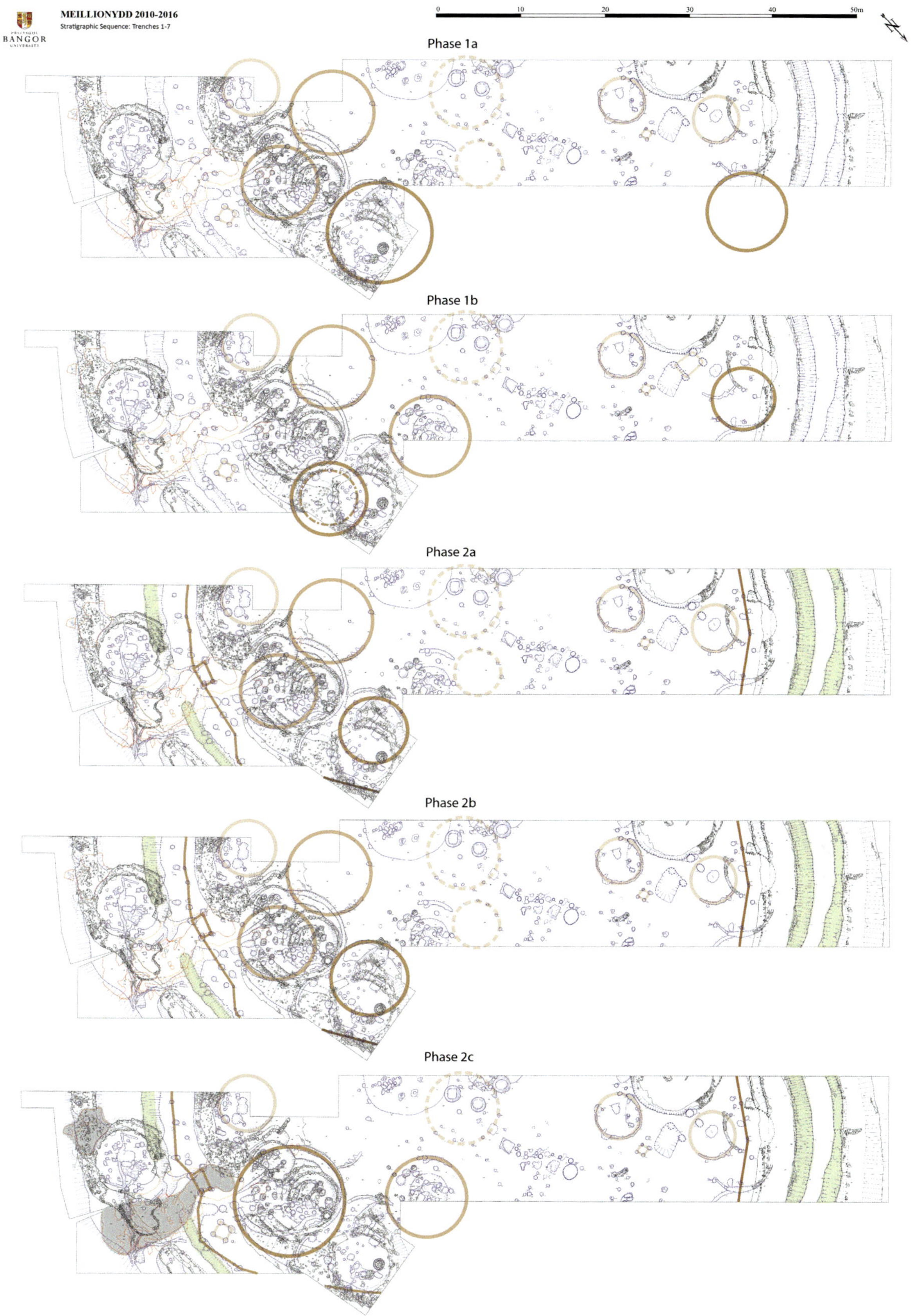

Figure 3: Phases 1 a, b and 2 a, b, c of the occupation sequence at Meillionydd (excavations 2010-16; Image: R. Karl).

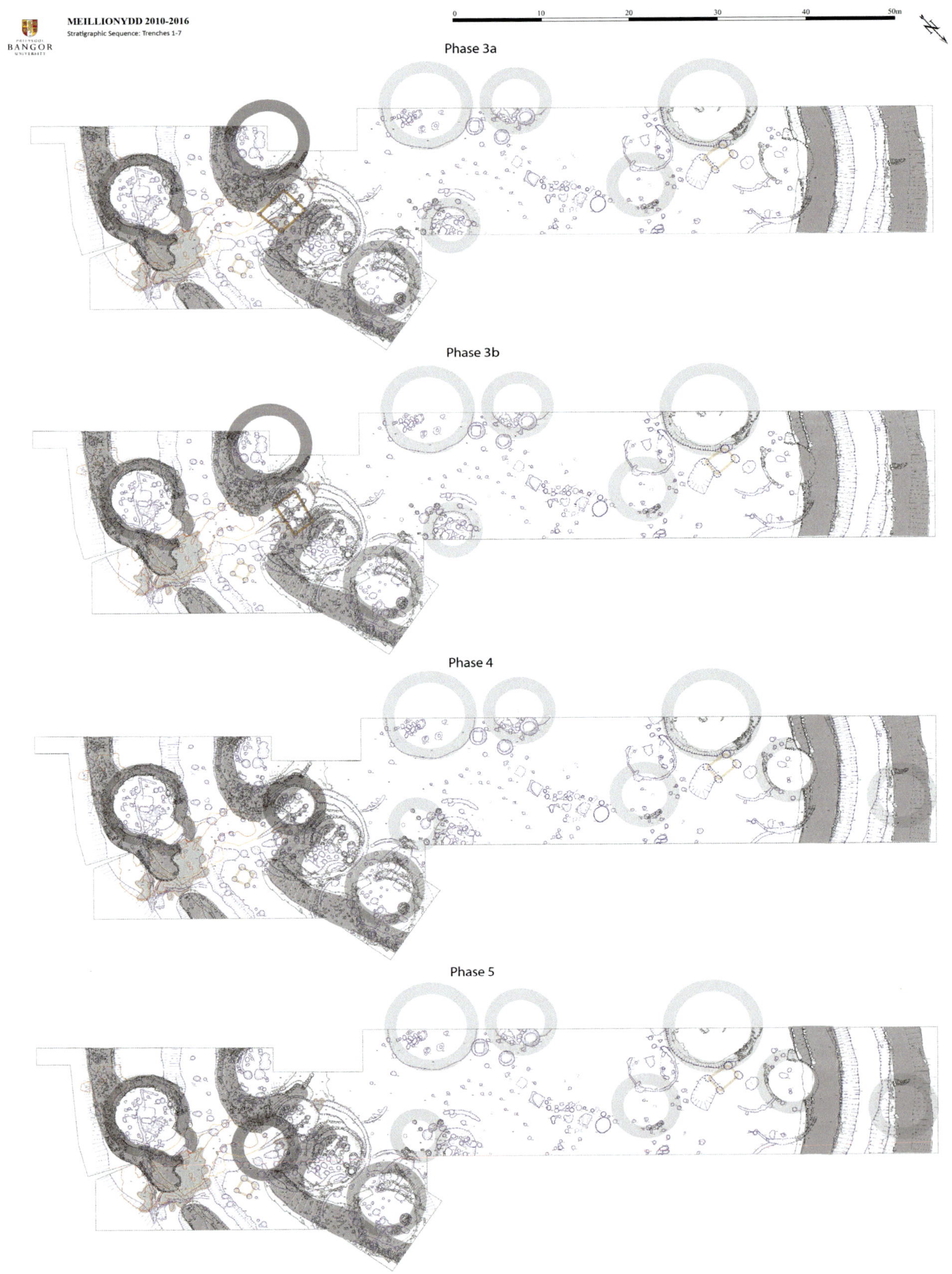

Figure 4: Phases 3 a, b, 4 and 5 of the occupation sequence at Meillionydd (excavations 2010-16; Image: R. Karl).

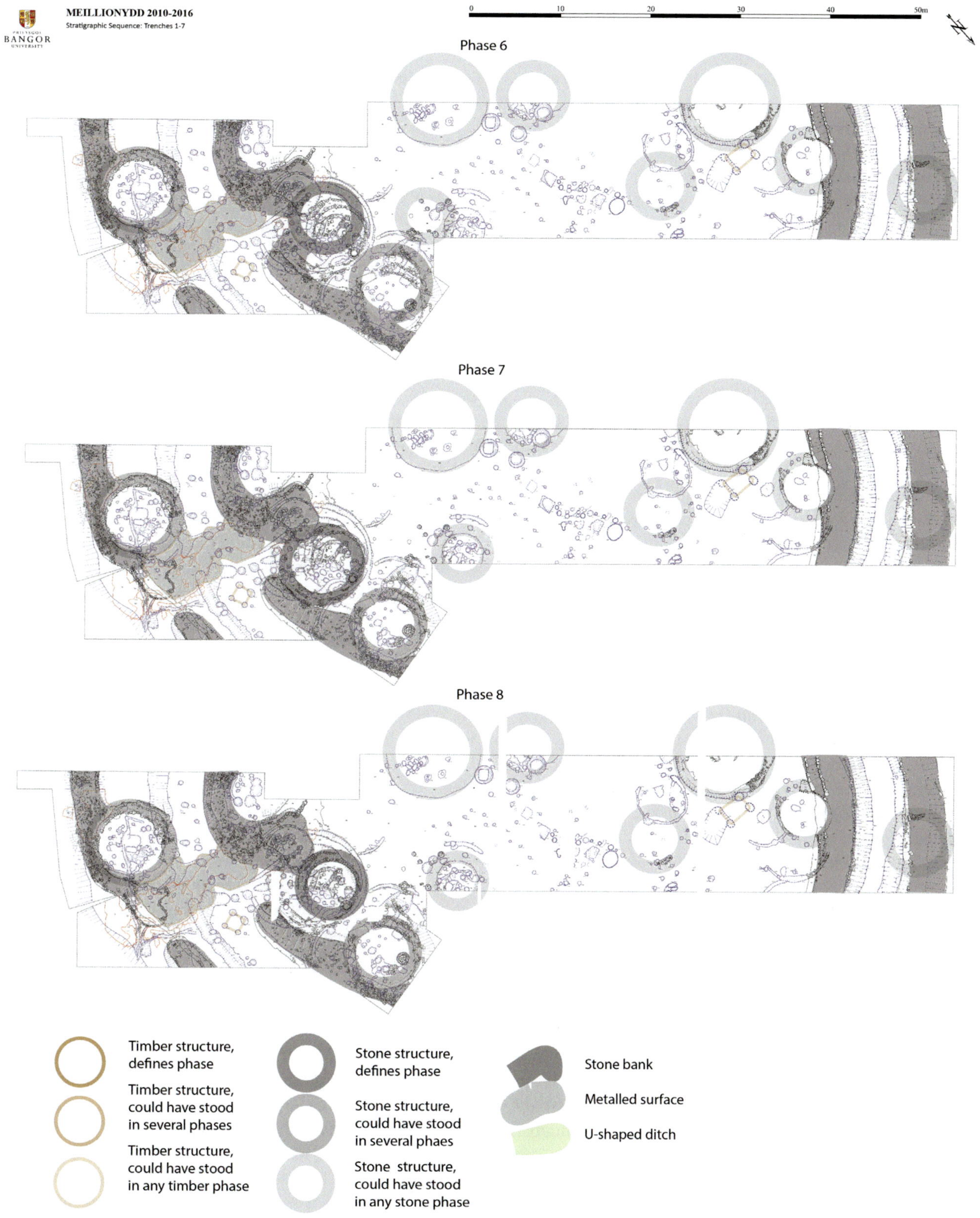

Figure 5: Phases 6, 7 and 8 of the occupation sequence at Meillionydd (excavations 2010-16; image R. Karl).

This interpretation is based on the fact that building enclosures is a labour intensive task, which takes away from other important activities such as, for example, food production. As such, it requires a surplus of human resource, which in turn is an indicator for social significance. Depending on the degree of monumentalisation, the community building the enclosure might have to source materials and human resource from outside the settlement (Karl 2007, 66-8; Sharples 2007, 179-80), which indicates control over a larger area than the immediate settlement. In the Iron Age this conspicuous consumption of labour in the display of status and wealth through lavish expenditure, is often associated with feasts (Ralston 2006, 100) or a more general distribution of food in exchange for labour (Sharples 2007, 180).

That the consumption of labour can be classed as conspicuous becomes obvious when looking at particularly elaborate entrances and banks that serve no defensive purpose. A good example is the univalate enclosure Woodside Camp in southwest Wales (Williams 1998). A 75 m long approach leading to two gate-towers was flanked by ditches as well as a bank on the northern side and two on the southern side (Williams 1998, 17-8), thus creating an impressive entrance. While a narrow entrance passage can generally be seen as a defensive feature, the one at Woodside Camps seems unnecessarily long for a purely defensive purpose (see Ralston 2006, 66-8). Furthermore, the out-turned outer defences of the passage way do not surround the settlement fully, but terminate some 50 m beyond the entrance passage. In a later phase two short concentric sections of banks and ditches were added to the northwest of the settlement, partially overlaying the earlier banks and ditches, which were no longer maintained and had been deliberately infilled. However, these new features had no defensive value either, because they also did not enclose the settlement and could easily have been circumvented. While not strictly necessary or completely unsuitable for defensive purposes, both the elaborate entrance way and the later banks and ditches attest to an investment of labour (Karl 2014, 146) for no other discernible purpose than conspicuous consumption.

Following this narrative, one possible interpretation of the occupation sequence at Meillionydd could be that the inhabitants' status increased slowly, allowing them to invest labour to enclose the site with ditches and a palisade (phase 2), which were later replaced with the double ringwork (phase 3) when their status reached its peak. The subsequent decline in status starts in phase 4, when the inner bank is no longer maintained and decreases until the site reverts to an unenclosed state, which highlights a lack of influence.

However, while this explanation might fit for sites like Meillionydd, it does not explain the labour investment in the deliberate backfilling of the ditches and construction of partial banks shortly afterwards at Woodsite Camp. After all, maintaining existing banks and ditches is less labour intensive than constructing new enclosures, and would therefore require less investment. As such, it would seem more sensible to maintain the existing structures if the available resources do not allow the building of new ones.

That eroding banks are not necessarily linked to a decline in status, as assumed in the above explanation, can clearly be seen at other sites like Collfryn (Britnell 1989). This site is enclosed by three banks in the Middle Iron Age with an elaborate entrance between the outer and the middle bank and a simpler gate through the inner bank. During the Late Iron Age only the inner bank was maintained while the outer and middle bank were left to erode. However, a new bank was added between the middle and the inner bank, thus turning the site into a bivallate enclosure. Finally, in the Romano-British period, the inner and medial banks were reused and a new, elaborate entrance passage was built through them. This example shows that instead of maintaining the existing banks, the occupants of this settlement choose to remodel the enclosure by constructing new banks, while the old ones were left to erode. This was a deliberate choice, because the construction of new banks shows that they would have been able to invest resources in the maintenance of the existing banks had they wanted to. After all, this would have required less labour than constructing new banks.

While the defences at Collfryn were remodelled twice with new banks being built during each phase, defensive structures at other sites were left to decay rapidly (Ralston 2006, 91), as can also be seen at Meillionydd, where the entrance through the inner bank was already blocked in the following construction phase. However, sites like Collfryn, where old banks were left to slowly erode while new banks where being constructed, lend themselves to explanations other than social decline, which would also explain why some defences might not have been in use for long.

Caesar attests that social status was inheritable in Gaul during the Iron Age (*Bellum Gallicum*, 6.15). Assuming that the same was true for Britain at the time, eroding banks could have been seen as a sign of pedigree rather than social decline (Karl 2017, 87-8) and as such might have been more desirable than well-maintained banks. So while the original enclosure (phase 2) at Meillionydd and the monumental banks of phase 3 might indeed have been a sign of increasing social status, the decay of the banks does not necessarily need to be a sign of decline in status. Rather, it could be a sign of an established elite that no longer required banks to show social status, much like the eroding banks at Collfryn which might rather have demonstrated the long-lasting importance of a settlement and its inhabitants.

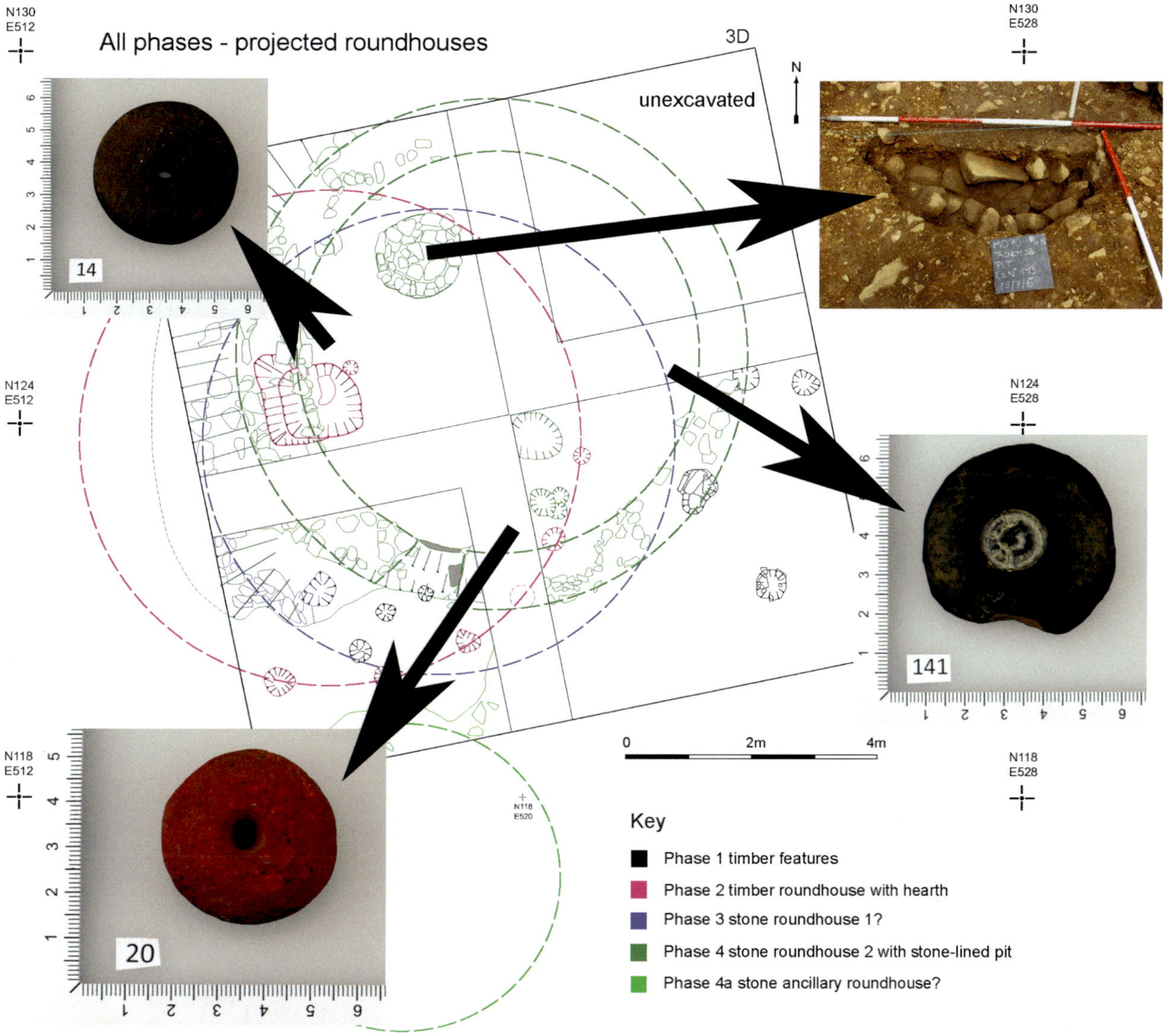

Figure 6: Find accumulation around stone lined pit no. 210 (Image: K. Waddington & K. Möller).

18.4 The finds distribution

Another interesting aspect at Meillionydd was the distribution of finds. While the most common type of find, the stone tools, were found all over the site, other types of finds are limited to specific features. While iron finds are rare and usually very badly corroded, a hewing knife, two armrings, a bent sword and a spear head have been found. All were found in the inner ditch, with the hewing knife and the spear head from the northern terminal and the other finds found close to the southern terminal. Furthermore, two of the most spectacular finds, the decorated glass bead and a piece of a jet bracelet, were found in postholes that were part of the gate through the inner bank.

Aside from the inner ditch and the gate structure, there were two other features associated with a comparably high number of finds – two stone lined pits (nos 210 and 1238). One (no. 210) lay inside a roundhouse that had been deliberately infilled with a layer of mostly burnt stones (Figure 6). Among these stones were structured deposits, comprising three spindle whorls, distributed in the east, the south and the west of the house. The stone lined pit was located in the north of the roundhouse, and it had been infilled with large stones and covered with a saddle quern.

The second stone lined pit (no. 1238; Figure 7) was also located in the north of a roundhouse and had been covered with a layer of large stones that was only loosely infilled with soil. As a result, there were pockets of air between the stones in which deposits of shells survived despite the acidic soil. In addition, two spindle whorls were found in the same layer. When the pit was excavated two small blue

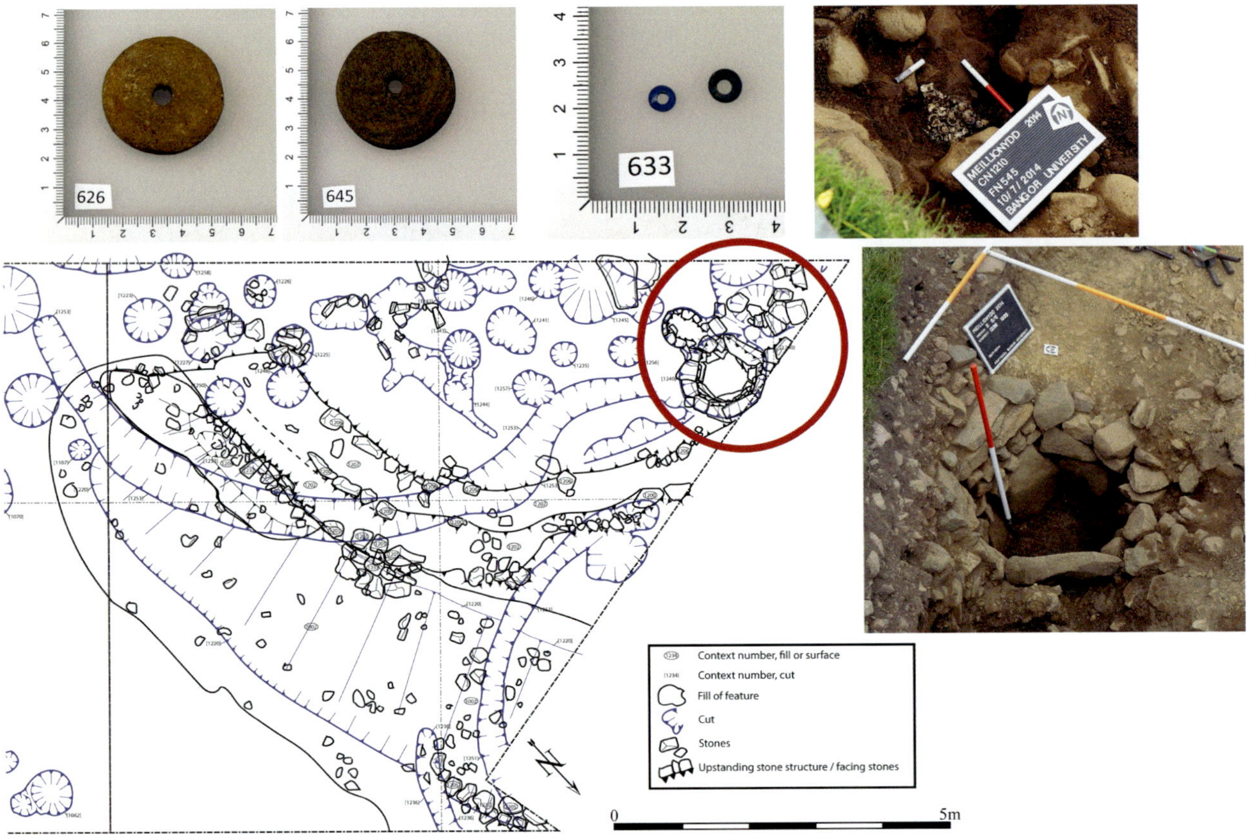

Figure 7: Find accumulation around stone lined pit no. 1238 (Image: R. Karl & K. Möller).

glass beads were found, with a third discovered during post-excavation wet sieving of soil samples from the pit. Furthermore, one of the stones used to build the pit had previously been used as a mortar bowl.

Considering the overall scarcity of finds on site and the fact that other particularly notable finds were found mainly in the enclosure, which is a symbol of status and pedigree as established above, one has to wonder why so many finds have been found in these two pits.

While the objects from the postholes of the inner gate are clearly foundation deposits and the same could be true for the finds from the ditch, the objects from the stone lined pits were found in the fill or the overlying layer rather than at the bottom of the features. Therefore, there must be another explanation for their deposition. Of particular interest in this context is that objects like spindle whorls, jewellery and weapons are typical grave goods in the Iron Age.

However, Iron Age burials are rare in Wales. Pollock (2006, 128-31, tab. 1) identified a total of 50 to 55 burials from this period, of which only three are in northwest Wales. It is noticeable that most graves were found in or around Iron Age settlements. Nevertheless, this does not necessarily mean that settlement burials were the most common form of burial. As part of the transition from the Late Bronze Age to the Iron Age there is a distinctive change in burial practice. Graves are no longer covered by large mounds and, therefore, leave no traces above the ground. As a result Iron Age burials are chance finds and as such are often found during excavations at more noticeable sites such as settlements (Möller 2017, 69). Furthermore, Pollock (2006, 14) suggests that burials in settlement contexts might also be better preserved due to the fact that most of these were found in hillforts, which due to their location in the uplands might be less likely to be destroyed by ploughing or development. In the context of Meillionydd it is noteworthy that settlement burials were often found in storage pits or the enclosures (Pollock 2006, 13). Therefore, one possible explanation for the accumulation of finds in the ditch and the storage pits could be that these were grave goods. The fact that no human remains were found does not necessarily refute this thesis, as bone would not survive in the acidic soil. It would, however, leave chemical traces.

As part of a recently submitted MA thesis (George 2017), a phosphate analysis of soil samples was carried out. Amongst the samples were those from the storage pit 1238 (sample no. 639), which contained high levels of phosphorus (George 2017, 50). In addition, manganese and copper levels were also examined and, as in the case of phosphorus, the samples from the stone lined pit contained higher levels than control samples from other areas of the site (George 2017, 51). In combination these results could indicate that the pits were used for burials as high levels of phosphorus, manganese and copper have also been found in other burials (Keeley *et al.* 1977).

18.5 Summary

Excavations at the Late Bronze Age and Iron Age double ringwork enclosure of Meillionydd have revealed a complex stratigraphy with 12 building phases. These show the development from an unenclosed settlement with timber buildings to a lightly enclosed one surrounded by two ditches and a wooden palisade. At a later phase the timber buildings are replaced by stone-built roundhouses and the enclosure is transformed into a double ringwork consisting of two earth and rubble banks with an elaborate in-turned entrance through the inner bank. This type of monumentalisation is commonly associated with a rise in social status and wealth. However, while the inner bank does not seem to have been in use for long as the entrance is blocked by a roundhouse in the following phase, this does not necessarily indicate a decline in status. Defensive features have been left to decay at other sites like Collfryn while new enclosures were being built. Hence, there must be another explanation for why the previous structures were no longer maintained. Assuming that social status was inheritable in Britain, as it was in Gaul, eroding banks could be interpreted as a sign of pedigree that indicated the long-lasting importance of a settlement.

Another interesting pattern can be seen in the distribution of finds at Meillionydd. While stone tools are found all over the site, other types of finds are rarer and found solely in specific contexts. Of particular interest are the iron objects from the inner ditch and the concentrations of finds around two stone lined (storage) pits. The objects found in these contexts are common grave goods in the Iron Age period. In addition, graves in settlement contexts are often found in enclosures and storage pits. However, since the soil on site is very acidic organic matter does not usually survive, though analysis of soil chemistry suggests that the concentrations of finds around the pits could indeed indicate the presence of burials.

18.6 Bibliography

Alcock, L. 1960. Castell Odo: An embanked settlement on Mynydd Ystum, near Aberdaron, Caernarvonshire. *Archaeologia Cambrensis* 109, 78-135.

Breese, C. E. 1932. Castell Odo. *Archaeologia Cambrensis* 87, 372-85.

Britnell, W. J. 1989. The Collfryn hillslope enclosure, Llansantfffraid Deuddwr, Powys: excavations 1980-82. *Proceedings of the Prehistoric Society* 55, 89-134.

Davies, J. L. & Lynch, F. 2000. The Late Bronze Age and Iron Age. In F. Lynch, S. Aldhouse-Green & L. J. Davies 2000. *Prehistoric Wales.* 139-219. Stroud: Sutton Publishing Limited.

George, N. 2017. *The living and the dead of Meillionydd: A soil phosphorus study.* Unpublished thesis, Bangor University.

Higgins, M. 2014. *The prehistoric buildings of Meillionydd. An interpretation based upon ground-penetrating radar (GPR) data.* Saarbrücken: LAP LAMBERT Academic Publishing.

Karl, R. 2007. Der Haushalt des „Landesherrn" – zum Verhältnis von *tegesākos und *mrogirīgs im eisenzeitlichen Wales. In P. Trebsche, I. Balzer, C. Eggl, J. K. Koch, H. Nortmann & J. Wiethold (eds). *Die unteren Zehntausend – auf der Suche nach den Unterschichten der Eisenzeit.* 57-70. Beiträge zur Ur- und Frühgeschichte Mitteleuropas 47, Langenweissbach: Beier & Beran. Archäologische Fachliteratur.

Karl, R. 2014. Viel Arbeit, kein Geld? Arbeitskraftbeschaffung in der vormodernen Keltiké. *Mitteilungen der Anthropologischen Gesellschaft in Wien* 144, 123-48.

Karl, R. 2017. In charge since time immemorial? Disused monumental features as markers of inherited social status. In R. Karl & J. Leskovar (eds). *Interpretierte Eisenzeiten Fallstudien, Methoden, Theorie. Tagungsbeiträge der 7. Linzer Gespräche zur interpretativen Eisenzeitarchäologie.* 75-89. Studien zur Kulturgeschichte von Oberösterreich 47. Linz: Oberösterreichisches Landesmuseum.

Karl, R., Möller, K. & Waddington, K. 2016. *Characterising the double ringwork enclosures of Gwynedd: Meillionydd excavations, June and July 2015. Interim report.* Bangor Studies in Archaeology, Report No. 14. Bangor: Bangor University School of History, Welsh History and Archaeology.

Keeley, H. C. M., Hudson, G. E. & Evans, J. 1977. Trace element content of human bones in various states of preservation. I. The soil silhouette. *Journal of Archaeological Science* 4, 19-24.

Löcker, K., Trausmuth, T. & Wallner, M. 2013. *Archäologisch-Geophysikalische Prospektion Meillionydd / Wales. Endbericht.* Unpublished report, Wien: Zentralanstalt für Meteorologie und Geodynamik.

Möller, K. 2017. „Dead men walking" – Zum weitgehenden Fehlen eisenzeitlicher Bestattungen in Nordwest-Wales. In R. Karl & J. Leskovar (eds). *Interpretierte Eisenzeiten Fallstudien, Methoden, Theorie. Tagungsbeiträge der 7. Linzer Gespräche zur interpretativen Eisenzeitarchäologie.* 67-74. Studien zur Kulturgeschichte von Oberösterreich 47. Linz: Oberösterreichisches Landesmuseum.

Möller, K., Waddington, K. & Karl, R. 2016. *Characterising the double ringwork enclosures of Gwynedd: Meillionydd excavations, June and July 2014. Interim report.* Bangor Studies in Archaeology, Report No.13. Bangor: Bangor University School of History, Welsh History and Archaeology.

Pollock, K. J. 2006. The *evolution and role of burial practice in Roman Wales.* BAR British Series 426. Oxford: John and Erica Hedges Ltd.

Ralston, I. 2006. *Celtic fortifications.* Stroud: Tempus Publishing Limited.

RCAHMW 1964. *An inventory of ancient monuments in Caernarvonshire, Vol. 3, West.* The Royal Commission on Ancient and Historical Monuments in Wales and Monmouthshire, London: HMSO.

Sharples, N. 2007. Building communities and creating identities in the first millennium BC. In C. Haselgrove & R. Pope (eds). *The Early Iron Age in Britain and the near continent.* 174-84. Oxford: Oxbow.

Smith, G. H. & Hopewell, D. 2007. *Survey of prehistoric defended enclosures in North-West Wales: Assessment of some possibly early multivallate enclosures in Llyn and Anglesey 2006-7.* Unpublished report no. 664. Bangor: Gwynedd Archaeological Trust.

Waddington, K. 2013. *The settlements of northwest Wales. From the Late Bronze Age to the Early Medieval Period.* Cardiff: University of Wales Press.

Waddington, K. & Karl, R. 2010. *The Meillionydd Project: Characterising the double ringwork enclosures in Gwynedd. Preliminary excavation report.* Bangor Studies in Archaeology, Report No. 4. Bangor: Bangor University School of History, Welsh History and Archaeology.

Waddington, K. & Karl, R. 2015a. *Characterising the double ringwork enclosures of Gwynedd: Meillionydd excavations, July 2011. Stratigraphic report.* Bangor Studies in Archaeology, Report No. 10. Bangor: Bangor University School of History, Welsh History and Archaeology.

Waddington, K. & Karl, R. 2015b. *Characterising the double ringwork enclosures of Gwynedd: Meillionydd excavations, July 2012. Interim report.* Bangor Studies in Archaeology, Report No. 11. Bangor: Bangor University School of History, Welsh History and Archaeology.

Waddington, K. & Karl, R. 2016. *Characterising the double ringwork enclosures of Gwynedd: Meillionydd excavations, July and August 2013. Interim report.* Bangor Studies in Archaeology, Report No. 12. Bangor: Bangor University School of History, Welsh History and Archaeology.

Williams, G. 1998. Woodside camp. In G. Williams & H. Mytum. *Llawhaden, Dyfed. Excavations on a group of small defended enclosures, 1980-4.* 16-29. BAR British Series 275. Oxford: Archaeopress.

Chapter 19

The changing patterns of La Tène farmsteads in Central and Continental Western Europe

Angelika Mecking

19.1 Introduction

There are large numbers of Late Iron Age farmstead settlements known across Central and Continental Western Europe (Figure 1). These undergo a series of transformations over the period between about 500 BC and the early centuries AD – and this broad sequence of settlement is the subject of this paper. The sequence of settlements begins at the end of the Hallstatt period with some open settlements, as well as rectangular and oval enclosures with fences or palisades (Berg-Hobohm 2010, 99). Some of the Hallstatt period enclosures continue into the early La Tène period (*e.g.* Kirchheim-Osterholz, Baden-Württemberg: Krause 2014, 32-4). In turn, middle La Tène period rectangular enclosures bounded by palisades have been found under the ramparts of late La Tène rectangular farmsteads – so-called *Viereckschanzen*. The variations in settlement trajectories between areas include those characterised by continuity and those where relocations within a specific area are indicated (Wendling 2010, 364). Despite similar starting points and similarities in their initial phases, in Central Europe the rectangular farmsteads enclosed by a rampart marked an end of a trajectory or transition, while to the west some farmsteads were subsequently transformed into Pre-Roman *villae* with a *"pars urbana"* and a *"pars rustica"* (Fichtl 2013a; 2013b; 2013c, 20-4). This paper sets out aspects of the morphology of these settlements and discusses the different processes of transformations that they underwent in the La Tène period and the abandonment of farmsteads in Central Europe after LT D1.

19.2 The morphology of La Tène farmsteads in Central and Western Europe

There is extensive archaeological evidence from the many large-scale excavations and evaluations of La Tène farmsteads in northern France (*e.g.* Blancquaert & Malrain 2016; Fichtl 2013a; 2013b; Malrain 2013; Touquet Laporte-Cassagne 2018). Alexandra Cony's typology of multiple farmsteads based on this large corpus classifies the sites into 'accolée' (accreted), 'emboîtée' (nested) and 'partitionnée' (subdivided) (Cony 2016). In this typology (Figure 2) rectangular farmstead plans are not differentiated from round ones (Malrain 2013, 179 fig. 117; Cony 2011, 20-1, figs 6-7) and Stephan Fichtl already proposed a similar classification for the high-status farmsteads of France, like Batilly-en-Gâtinais (see Fichtl, this volume), which has been slightly modified by Cony. This classification is

In D.C. Cowley, M. Fernández-Götz, T. Romankiewicz & H. Wendling (eds). Rural Settlement. Relating buildings, landscape, and people in the European Iron Age (Leiden 2019: Sidestone Press) 191-199.

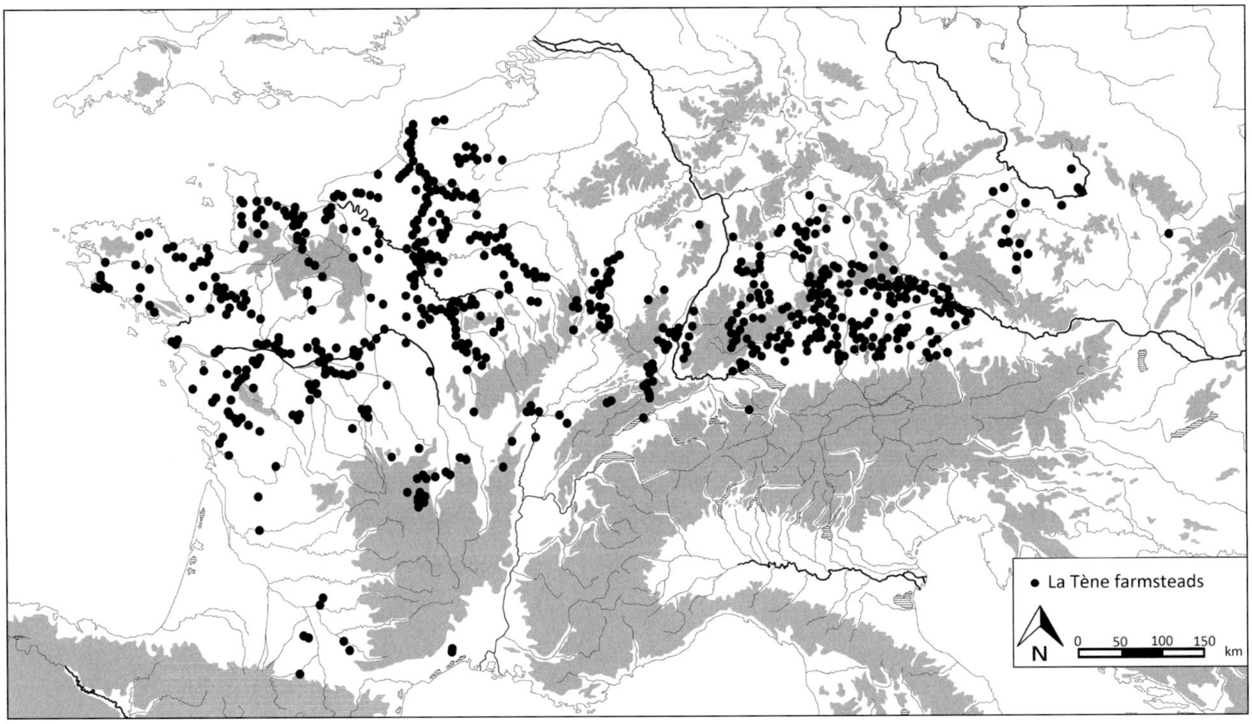

Figure 1: Distribution of La Tène farmsteads in Central and Continental Western Europe (after httpagedufer.inrap.frindex and Mecking, based on stumme Karte Tübingen).

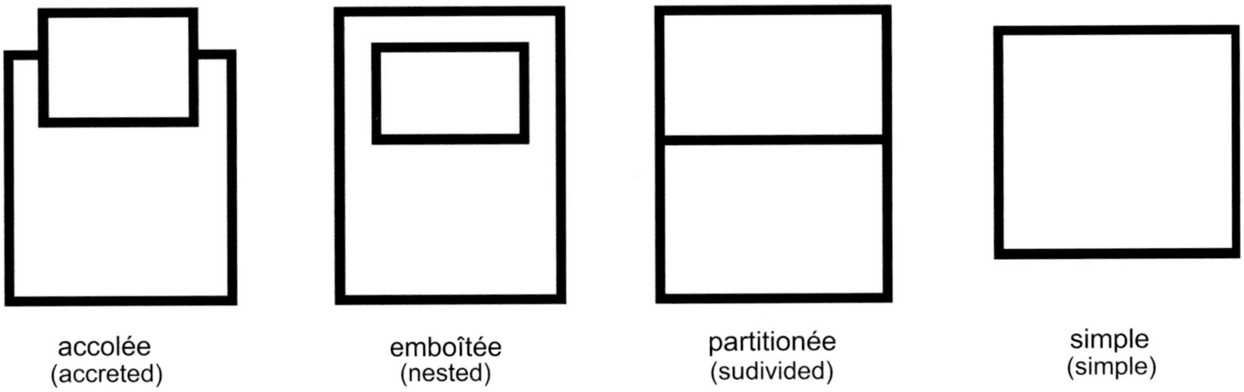

Figure 2: Typology of La Tène farmsteads in Central and Continental Western Europe (Graphic: Mecking, after Cony 2011 for the multiple types).

useful to explore a wide range of farmsteads, not only the 'high-status' enclosures (Fichtl 2013b; 2013c). To complete the classification, of course, simple farmsteads also need to be considered.

Recurrent features of the farmsteads include rectangular enclosures defined by ramparts and ditches with notable variation in the layout of additional 'annex' enclosures or fence systems. Caroline von Nicolai investigated Late Iron Age farmsteads in Central and Western Europe, focussing on the function of farmsteads and the differences between previous interpretations of sanctuaries and settlements (von Nicolai 2006, 1-21). By comparing morphology, size, architecture, and the lifespan of settlements and sanctuaries in Germany and France, she has demonstrated how different the farmsteads of southern Germany and northern France are, but also found some similarities (von Nicolai 2009, 245-80). Günther Wieland has also analyzed the morphology, function, construction, and Roman re-use of the farmsteads of southern Germany (Wieland 2017). To summarise, each of Cony's types, with perhaps one exception, is present across Europe. It appears that farmsteads with an inner transverse division by an additional rampart or ditch (*i.e.* Cony's 'subdivided' type) known in Central Europe (*e.g.* Mšecké Žehrovice Rakovník, Czech Republic: Venclová 1998; Kirchheim-Osterholz, Baden-Württemberg: von der Osten Woldenburg 2002), do not exist in Continental Western Europe. In Central Europe, and mostly in southern Germany, farmsteads are generally of the simple type. Nested types such as Sallach, Bavaria, (Müller 2008), subdivided types Osterholz, Kirchheim (Figure 2), or accreted types such as Nordheim "Bruchhöhe", Baden-Württemberg, (Auer *et al.* 2018) are present, but rare. At the farmstead of Riedlingen, Baden-Württemberg, there is a small conjoined fenced enclosure, but it is not really comparable to the adjoining fence systems in France (Bollacher 2009, fig. 6, 7, 23, 25).

19.3 Multiphase La Tène farmsteads: a few examples

Rectangular palisaded enclosures are a common feature of the initial phases of La Tène period farmsteads. Holzhausen in Bavaria is a good example, with three palisaded lines of enclosure beneath the late La Tène D1 ditch and rampart enclosure system that represents the simple type (Figure 3, 2 fence numbers 1, 2, 4). A fourth palisade (Figure 3, 2: fence number 3) is contemporary with the LT D1 phase rampart and ditch (Schwarz & Wieland 2005, 78-82; Wieland 1999, 195-8). A similar pattern is evident at Blaufelden in Baden-Württemberg (Figure 3, 1), where there are palisades underneath the rampart. In contrast to the other farmsteads in southern Germany, where LT D2 finds are usually absent, a pit with LT D2 "Kammgrübchenware" ceramics was found there (Stork 1997; 1999a fig. 76, 120; 1999b).

One of the best examples is the farmstead of Bopfingen-Flochberg, where Bronze Age remains were built over by an unenclosed early La Tène A/B1 phase settlement (Friederich 2017, 207-22). In turn a LT B1 oval palisaded enclosure was built and thereafter a middle La Tène palisade farmstead of the simple type developed (Figure 4; Friederich 2017, 233-42). Continuous use of the area is assumed, uninterrupted from the early La Tène period to the middle La Tène period, following which the late La Tène fortified farmstead with rampart was built. Other examples of multiphase La Tène farmsteads include Markdorf "Riedwiesen", Baden-Württemberg (Klein 2016, 162 fig. 116). Here, a palisaded enclosure 0.26 ha in extent was expanded to 0.37 ha in area, amongst other modifications, and was finally replaced by a late La Tène farmstead 0.6 ha in area enclosed by a ditch and rampart (Figure 3, 3).

Similar sequences are known at La Tène period sites in Continental Western Europe. At Brebières, Pas-de-Calais (Lacalmontie 2016, 133-46), a group of La Tène farmsteads develop into just one farmstead, which continues into the Roman period (Figure 3, 5). At Mondeville "L'Etoile" (Caen) the sequences of developmental phases are evident in some farmsteads in a small area. These lie only about 250 m apart and project a similar situation to Bopfingen-Flochberg, but in a larger area (Besnard-Vauterin *et al.* 2016, 73-5), and are thus considered an example of a moving settlement (Figure 3, 6).

This complexity is also evident at Paule (Figure 3, 4 phase IV), where the late Hallstatt and early La Tène (550-300 BC) settlement phase comprises an enclosure some 9000 m^2 in area, within which there is a large building 410 m^2 in area together with other smaller annex buildings (Menez 2016, 139 fig. 1). A restructuring at about 300 BC saw the creation of two quadrangular fenced enclosures, one forming a domestic space (Menez 2016, 139-40 fig. 2). At about 250 BC, the ramparts were expanded giving the site a fortified character, although the internal organization remained unchanged. At about 175 BC, a considerable part of the settlement was destroyed by fire, following which three enclosures with ramparts and one with an added palisade were built in the period 150-50 BC, ultimately enclosing an area of about 10 ha with distinct residential and production areas. The final phase is a transitional one, with a Roman occupation starting at about 10 BC (Menez 2016, 142 fig. 6).

19.4 The idea of transformation

The examples described above demonstrate that some La Tène farmsteads underwent similar transformations during the Late Iron Age, with both phases of change and periods of continuity such as from about the 2nd century BC. These different forms of transformation include alterations within a settlement, changes within a shifting settlement, and extensive expansion of the settlement. In these processes of transformations, the similarity between Central and Continental Western Europe is notable until the farmsteads with ramparts and ditches emerged. So, a general pattern can be seen in both areas, whereby an initial phase of open settlements is followed by round, oval or amorphous enclosures most often bounded by a palisade. Then the farmsteads with wall and ditch emerged. In some regions, several farmsteads coalesced to form a larger single unit during the transformation process, as is the case at Brebières (Lacalmontie 2016, 133-46). In later phases, larger fences are added, which can sometimes be compared morphologically to the precursor of a *pars urbana* and *pars rustica* setting (Fichtl 2013c). It is important to note that among the Western European farmsteads different sites had differing histories, some remaining in occupation at the same time others were abandoned. The steps of transformation, where farmsteads aggregated into one big farmstead and farmstead groups coalesce into an extended settlement area with fortifications (*e.g.* Paule) is, at present, only a feature of Western Europe.

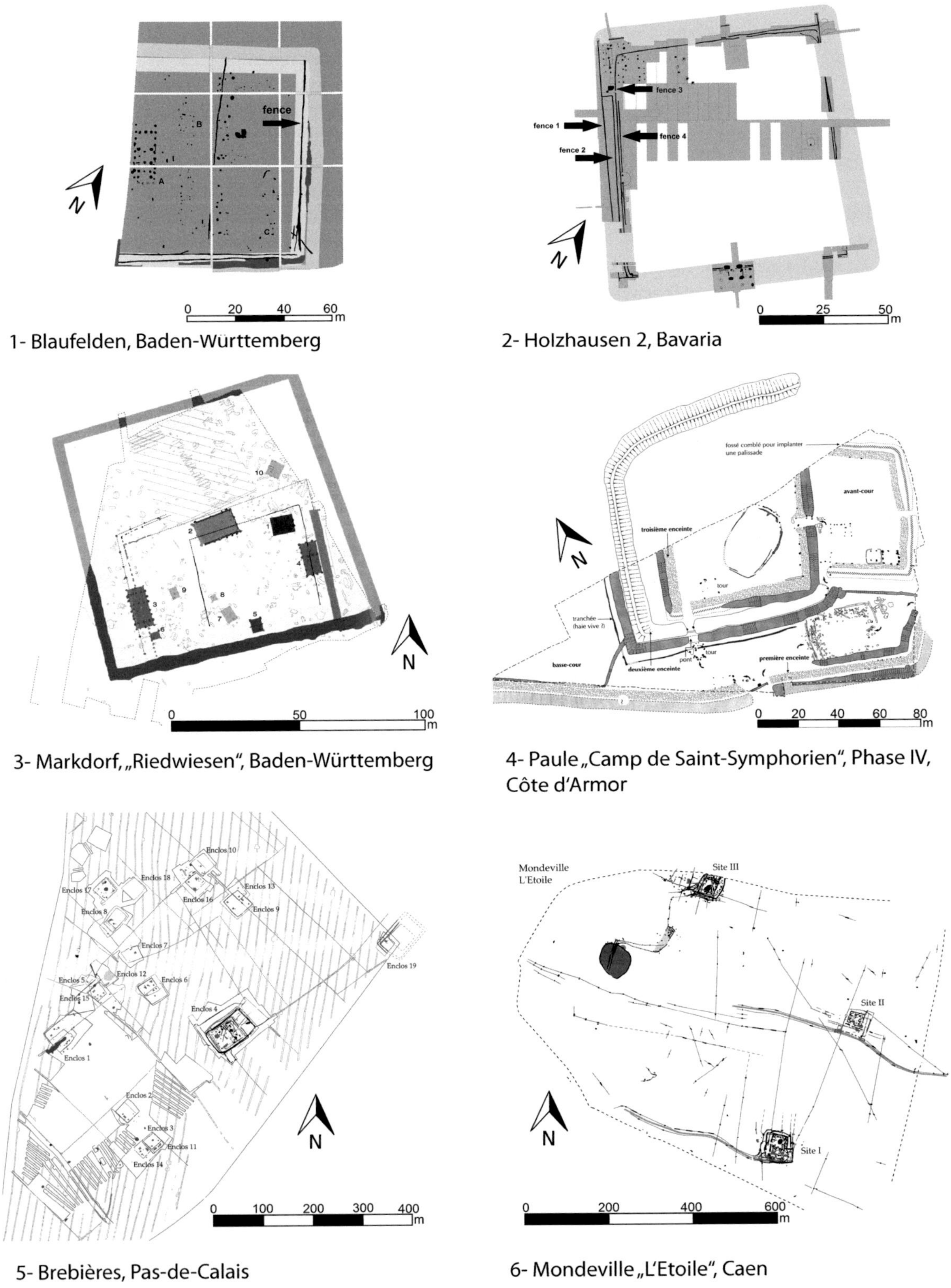

Figure 3: Multi-phase La Tène farmsteads (Graphic: Mecking. 1 – Blaufelden after Stork 1999a, Figure 74; 2 – Holzhausen after Schwarz &Wieland 2005, supplement 1; 3 – Markdorf 'Riedwiesen' after Klein 2017, Fig. 116; 4 – Paule after Menez & Arramond 1998, Fig. 29; 5 – Brebières after Lacalmontie 2016, Fig. 3; 6 – Mondeville 'L'Etoile' after Besnard-Vauterin et al. 2016, Fig.14).

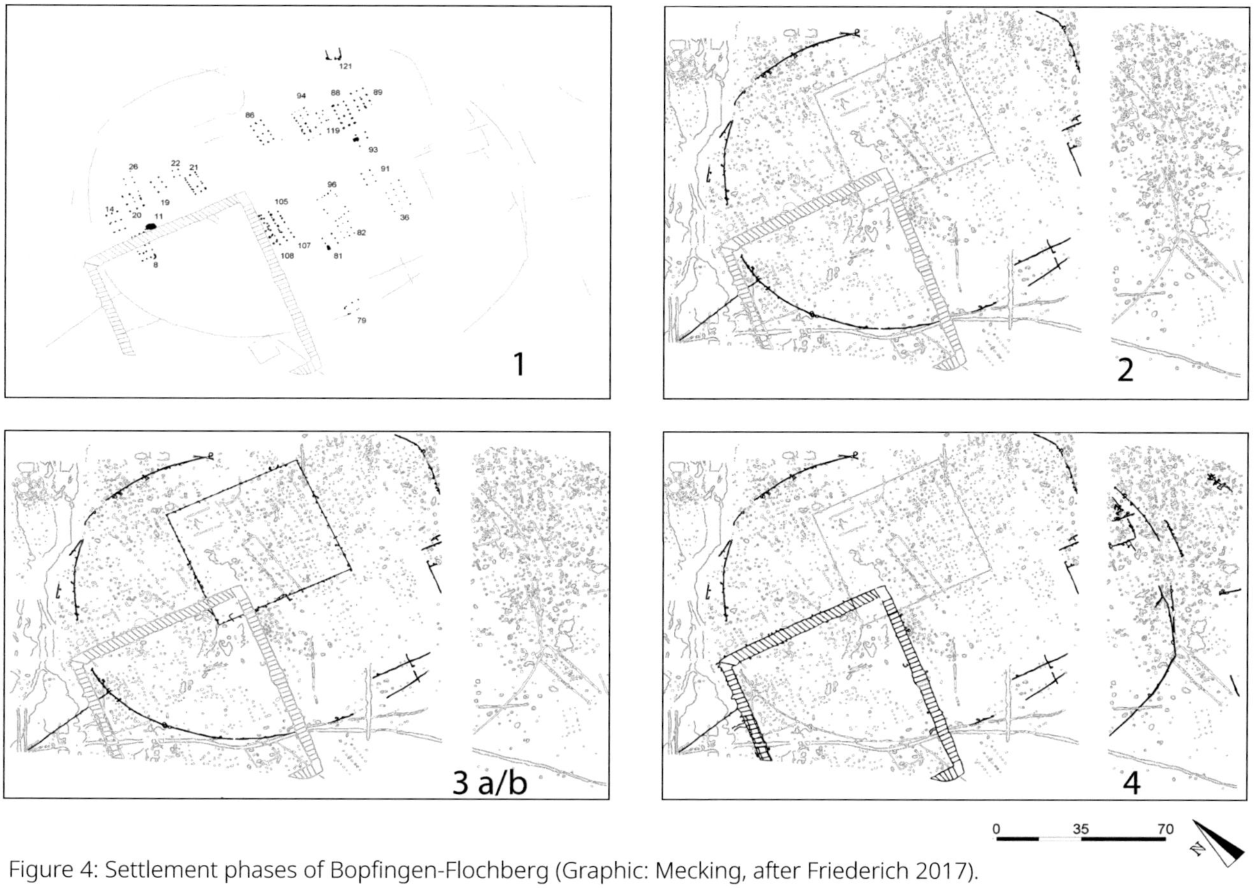

Figure 4: Settlement phases of Bopfingen-Flochberg (Graphic: Mecking, after Friederich 2017).

19.5 Hiatus and continuity – Roman finds in Late La Tène farmsteads

While occasional Roman objects in Late La Tène farmsteads (Table 1) are often interpreted as evidence of Roman re-use of the site, it is clear that many Roman finds occur in La Tène farmsteads (*e.g.* Zanier 2005, 205-36). Günther Wieland investigated the connections of La Tène farmsteads and Roman settlements, like the farmstead of Mengen-Ennetach (von der Osten Woldenburg *et al.* 1999, 125-3) and Hardheim-Gerichtstetten (Wieland 2009, 22-6). Stephan Fichtl also investigated the connection of La Tène farmsteads and "Roman *villae* of axial type", noting that there is a time-span of approximately 100 years between those types (Fichtl 2013c, 20-4). Sabine Rieckhoff has interpreted the cessation of occupation of farmsteads in southern Germany as a product of emigration, because there are no phases of decline before abandonment, nor continuity to the Roman period (Rieckhoff 2002, 367).

Besides this older evidence, recent excavations have produced new Roman finds in Central Europe, which will be briefly summarised. The farmstead of Ludwigsburg "Römerhügel" is a good example where many Roman objects were found above the La Tène cultural layer mixed in with medieval finds (Bollacher & Piros 2017, 165). In addition, there are some Roman settlement features in the farmstead, including a pit house, some storage pits, a cellar and a brick-lined well shaft (Bollacher & Piros 2017, 168). The date of the excavated Roman remains ranges in most cases from the 2nd century AD to the 3rd century AD (Bollacher & Piros 2017, fig. 118, 167). This is a time-span of more than 200 years between the La Tène farmstead which produced some ceramics and a Nauheim type fibula and the Roman population (Bollacher & Piros 2017, 167).

At Beuren "Pfaffenhofen" Stefan Reuter examined the Roman finds from the farmstead, including one fragment of a late Republican italic vine amphora found in the late La Tène layer, and interpreted them as evidence of a trade route (Reuter 2011, fig. 164, 151). All the other Roman finds are not associated with La Tène material and include a *Terra Sigillata* vessel (Type Drag. 37) dated to the early 2nd century AD and some coarse middle Roman empire period pottery (Reuter 2011, 152).

As discussed above for Continental Western Europe, some farmsteads like Brebières (Pas-de-Calais) illustrate the transformation process whereby a group of farmsteads merge into one big farmstead. In LT C there are many farmsteads, which are abandoned and merge together in one large farmstead that continues into the Roman period (Lacalmontie 2016, 133-46). The same transformations

La Téne farmstead	Roman finds	Dating of Roman finds	References
Hardheim-Gerichtstetten	Kreuzaxt, ceramics	Kreuzaxt = late Roman empire to early middle ages, ceramics = 1st c. AD to early Roman empire	Zanier 2005, 208-10. Wieland 2009, 222-6.
Nordheim „Kupferschmied"	ceramics, fences	Roman, 2nd c. and 3rd c. AD	Zanier 2005, 210. Auer *et. al* 2018, 113-8.
Nordheim „Bruchhöhe"	Terra Sigillata, fragmented bowl	fragmented bowl = 2nd c. AD	Zanier 2005, 210. Auer *et al.* 2018, 113-8.
Fellbach-Schmiden	Roman plate (2 fragments)	plate = 2nd c. AD	Zanier 2005, 211.
Leinfelden-Echterdingen	foundation of stone	Roman	Zanier 2005, 211.
Ehningen	ceramics, sandstone blocks, scaled column, Terra Sigillata (Drag. 37), jupiter column, bricks	ceramics = end of 1st c. AD beginning of the 2nd c., Terra Sigillata =2 1/2 2nd c. AD to 1 1/2 3rd c. AD	Zanier 2005, 212.
Pliezhausen-Rübgarten	ceramics	ceramics = 2nd c. AD	Zanier 2005, 213.
Mengen-Ennetach	two fibula	fibula = Augustan to Claudian	Zanier 2005, 2013.
Altheim-Heiligenkreuztal	brick	undated	Zanier 2005, 214.
Riedlingen	bronze fibula,	bronze fibula = end of 1st c. AD	Zanier 2005, 214.
Heidenheim-Schnaithaim	two Sigillata fragments	undated, untraceable	Zanier 2005, 215.
Neresheim-Kösingen	Terra Sigillata	Terra Sigillata = 2 1/2 2nd c. AD	Zanier 2005, 215.
Bopfingen-Flochberg	collar edge bowl	collar edge bowl = 2 1/2 1st c. AD	Zanier 2005, 216.
Kirchhaslach-Olgishofen	coin hoard in vessel	coin hoard in vessel = latest coin 258/259 AD	Zanier 2005, 216.
Pfaffenhofen-Beuren	ceramics, Terra Sigillata (Drag. 37)	ceramics = middle Roman empire, Terra Sigillata (Drag 37.) = late 1st to 2nd c. AD	Reuter 2011, 151-2. Zanier 2005, 216.
Türkheim-Poenburg	coin, ceramic, brick	coin = 114/117 AD, ceramic and brick= Roman	Zanier 2005, 216.
Holzhausen	Carinated cup, Phase 5 of the excavation	Carinated cup = 1st or 2nd c. AD ?, Phase 5 = maybe Roman	Zanier 2005, 217.
Schelldorf	brick	undated	Zanier 2005, 217.
Plattling-Pankhofen	Terra Sigillata splinter	Terra Sigillata splinter = middle Roman empire	Zanier 2005, 217.
Pocking-Hartkirchen	Terra Sigillata, Reibschale	Terra Sigillata = 2nd/3rd c. AD, Reibschale = middle Roman empire	Zanier 2005, 217.
Römerhügel, Ludwigsburg	ceramics, Gürtelverteiler, pit house, storage pits,	Roman period	Bollacher& Réka Piros 2017, 167-169.
Markdorf „Riedwiesen"	not specified	not specified	Klein 2016, 164.

Table 1: Roman finds in La Tène farmsteads in southern Germany (Mecking).

are evident from the La Tène to the Augustan period in a microregional analysis by Célia Basset and Fanny Trouvé in the Val-d'Oise (Basset & Trouvé 2018, 252-62).

At the farmstead of Reinach-Mausacker (Basel-Land, Switzerland) Debora C. Tretola Martinez investigated a La Tène farmstead which is overbuilt by a Roman villa with several different interpretations. One scenario is that the late La Tène farmstead, abandoned in the 1st century BC, was replaced by a new settlement in the northern area, which itself continued into the Roman period as a *villa* (Tretola Martinez 2014, 267; 2016, 441-5).

To summarise, it is clear that the interpretation of Roman finds in La Tène farmsteads should differentiate between sites occupied until the Roman period and those farmsteads which include later Roman finds post-dating the La Tène period occupation. There are some farmsteads in Central and Continental Western Europe which continue into the Roman period (*e.g.* Reinach-Mausacker or Brebières), some of which may have been repopulated in the Roman period (*e.g.* Ludwigsburg "Römerhügel"), and other farmsteads which have just occasional Roman finds dating to the 1st-3rd centuries AD (*e.g.* Beuren or Mengen-Ennetach). Thus, there is no evidence to suggest continuity of habitation to the Roman period just because of the incidence of occasional Roman finds. In addition, it is possible to recognise that some farmsteads end in late La Tène and are subsequently repopulated after the 1st century AD. Here, there is an issue of how these patterns are expressed – often as continuity with a hiatus. However, there is a question of how long a hiatus can last before it effectively no longer represents continuity – certainly 100 years, but also presumably much shorter periods of abandonment. In Western Europe there are a range of transformation processes and also continuity to the Roman period, while in southern Germany it appears that most of the farmsteads were abandoned after LT D1. This is the biggest disparity in the transformation processes between Central and Western Europe after the date at which the development of farmsteads with ramparts occurs.

19.6 Conclusion

The processes of transformation in the La Tène farmsteads that have been discussed above are complex and never linear – they do not follow just one system, scheme or pattern, even if similarities can be identified. Indeed, the fortified enclosed La Tène farmsteads have precursors that are distinguished in different ways. Most common are examples, generally built of palisades, that directly underlie the later rampart and ditch systems. Farmsteads which expanded through the accretion of additional enclosures are also evident, together with elements that aggregate to form large units. Furthermore, earlier settlements with somewhat amorphous layout are reorganized with palisaded boundaries which developed into ditched square enclosures with ramparts, in a pattern evident in Central and Continental Western Europe. However, the processes of transformation of farmstead connections, in which they turned into one big farmstead, and farmstead groups, which coalesced into an extended settlement area with fortifications, are present only in Continental Western Europe. It is also notable that in Central Europe most farmsteads end during LT D1, and the earliest Roman finds are from after the 1st century AD. Thus, there is no evidence for continuity directly into a Roman-La Tène mixed material culture, such as can be seen in Continental Western Europe. While variations on these general themes are expressed through individual site histories, the common trajectory across large areas is striking, reflected also in different patterns of settlement abandonment and continuity.

19.7 Acknowledgments

I would like to thank Thomas Pabst and Ralph Ucheh for comments on my text.

19.8 Bibliography

Auer, I, Martin, H., Stephan, E. & Steppan, K. 2018. Die Viereckschanzen von Nordheim. Zwei spätkeltische Gutshöfe im Neckarland. *Denkmalpflege in Baden-Württemberg* 47(2), 113-8.

Basset, C. & Trouvé, F. 2018. Occupation et strucuration de l'espace au cours du second âge du fer dans le bassin versant du Crould (Val-D'Oise): de l'angle archéologique à l'approche archéogéographique. In C. Touquet Laporte-Cassagne (ed.). *Les site ruraux du second âge du fer dans le Bassin versant du crould en Val-D'Oise et ses marges.* 525-67. Revue archèologique D'Île-de-France 5e supplement. Paris: Raif.

Berg-Hobohm, St. 2010. Herrenhöfe in Bayern – Maganates' farms in Bavaria – Rectangular enclosures of Early Iron Age. In Niedersächsisches Institut für Küstenforschung (ed.). *Herrenhöfe and the Hierarchy of Power in the Region to the South and East of the North Sea from the Pre-Roman Iron Age until the Early Middle Ages and the Viking Age.* 96-106. Memorial Colloqium to Werner Haarnagel (1907-1984) 11.-13. Oktober 2007. Settlement and Coastal Research in the Southern North Sea Region 33. Rahden-Westf.: Verlag Maria Leidorf.

Besnard-Vauterin. Ch.-C, Giraud, P., Lepaumier, H. & Giazzon, D. 2016. Genèse d'un reseau de fermes du second âge du Fer en plaine de Caen. In G. Blancquaert & F. Malrain (eds). *Actes du 38e colloque de l'AFEAF – Amiens du 29 mai au 1er juin – Èvolution des sociètès gauloises du Second âge du Fer, entre mutations internes et influences externe.* 61-82. Revue archèologique de Picardie RAP – n° spècial 30. Amiens: AFEAF.

Blancquaert, G. & Malrain, F. 2016 (eds). *Actes du 38e colloque de l'AFEAF – Amiens du 29 mai au 1er juin – Èvolution des sociètès gauloises du Second âge du Fer, entre mutations internes et influences externe.* Revue archèologique de Picardie RAP – n° spècial 30. Amiens: AFEAF.

Bollacher, Chr. 2009. *Die keltische Viereckschanze auf der "Klinge" bei Riedlingen.* Materialhefte zur Archäologie in Baden-Würrtemberg 88. Stuttgart: Konrad Theiss Verlag.

Bollacher, Chr. & Piros, R. 2017. Kelten und Römer am Römerhügel in Ludwigsburg. *Archäologische Ausgrabungen in Baden-Württemberg.* 165-9. Stuttgart: Theiss.

Cony, A. 2011. *Les habitats ruraux à cours multiple* (mèmoire de Master 2 soutenue en juin 2009 sous la direction de Stephan Fichtl à l'Universitè de Tours) Volume 1. Unpublished thesis, University Tours.

Cony, A. 2016. Les habitats ruraux enclos à cours multiples dans le nord de la France: rèflexions sur leur morphologie et leur chronologie. In G. Blancquaert & F. Malrain (eds). *Actes du 38e colloque de l'AFEAF – Amiens du 29 mai au 1er juin – Èvolution des sociètès gauloises du Second âge du Fer, entre mutations internes et influences externe.* 435-9. Revue archèologique de Picardie RAP – n° spècial 30. Amiens: AFEAF.

Fichtl, S. 2013a. Les « sites à banquets »: un mythe de l'archéologie celtique? In C. Grandjean, Chr. Hugoniot & B. Lion (eds). *Le banquet du monarque dans le monde antique.* Actes du colloque international tenu à Tours les 25-27 mars 2010, PUR/PUFR, Rennes-Tours 2013.

425-51. Rennes: Presses universitaires de Rennes / Presses universitaires François-Rabelais de Tours.
Fichtl, S. 2013b. Les agglomèrations gauloises de la fin de l'âge du Fer en Europe celtique (IIIe-Ier siècles av. J.-C.). In D. Garcia (ed.). *L'habitat en Europe celtique et en Mèditerranèe prèclassique: domaines urbain*. 19-45. Paris: Editions Errance.
Fichtl, S. 2013c. Die gallische villa von Batilly-en-Gâtinais (Loiret) und die Frage nach dem Ursprung der großen villae „à pavillons multiples alignès". *Alemannisches Jahrbuch 2011/2012, Jahrgang 59/60*. Kolloquium Juli 2012, 9-26.
Friederich, J. 2017. *Die keltische Viereckschanze von Bopfingen-Flochberg am Nördlinger Ries*. Frankfurter Archaeological Studies 32. Ipf Forschungen 2. Bonn: Habelt Verlag.
Klein, F. 2016. Die spätkeltische Viereckschanze in den „Riedwiesen" bei Markdorf. *Archäologische Ausgrabungen Baden-Württemberg* 2016, 160-4.
Krause, R. 2014. Zum Stand der Forschung auf dem Ipf und den Perspektiven aus dem Schwerpunktprogramm der Deutschen Forschungsgemeinschaft 2004-2010. In R. Krause (ed.). *Neue Forschungen zum frühkeltischen Fürstensitz auf dem Ipf*. 1-49. Bonn: Frankfurter Archäologische Schriften 24.
Lacalmontie, A. 2016. L'occupation du second âge du fer á Brebières (Pas-de-Calais). In G. Blancquaert & F. Malrain (eds). Actes du 38e colloque de l'AFEAF – Amiens du 29 mai au 1er juin – Èvolution des sociètès gauloises du Second âge du Fer, entre mutations internes et influences externe. 133-46. Revue archèologique de Picardie RAP – n° spècial 30. Amiens: AFEAF.
Malrain, F., Blancquaert, G. & Lorho, T. 2013. *L'habitat rural du second âge du Fer. Rythmes de creation et d'abandon au nord de la Loire*. Recherche Archéologiques 7. Paris: Inrap/CNRS Éditions.
Menez, Y. 2016. De la rèsidence rurale à l'agglomèration. In St. Fichtl, E. Le Goff & A. Mathiaut-Legros (eds). *Les premières villes de l'ouest. Agglomèrations gauloises de Bretagne et Pays de la Loire*. 139-46. Jublains: Musée archéologique de Jublains.
Müller, S. 2008. *Die Viereckschanzen von Sallach, Gde. Geiselhöring, Lkr. Straubing-Bogen, Niederbayern im Spiegel keltischer Besiedlung des kleinen Labertals*. Regensburger Beiträge zur prähistorischen Archäologie 18. Regensburg: Universitätsverlag Regensburg.
Reuter, S. 2011. Römische Keramik aus der Viereckschanze. In R. Ambs. *Die keltische Viereckschanze bei Beuren*. 151-2. Martgemeinde Pfaffenhofen an der Roth, Landkreis Neu-Ulm, Bayern. Berichte zur Archäologie im Landkreis Neu-Ulm und den angrenzenden Gebieten 4. Ulm: Ziegler.
Rieckhoff, S. 2002. Der Untergang der Städte: Der Zusammenbruch des keltischen Wirtschafts- und Gesellschaftssystems. In C. Dobiat, S. Sievers & T. Stöllner (eds). *Dürrnberg und Manching: Wirtschaftsarchäologie im ostkeltischen Raum*. 359-79. Bonn: Habelt.
Schwarz, K. & Wieland, G. 2005. *Die Ausgrabungen in der Viereckschanze 2 von Holzhausen. Grabungsberichte von Klaus Schwarz zusammengestellt und kommentiert von Günther Wieland*. Veröffentlichung der Kommission zur vergleichenden Archäologie römischer Alpen- und Donauländer der bayerischen Akademie der Wissenschaften. Rahden/Westf: Verlag maria Leidorf.
Stork, I. 1997. *Eine neuentdeckte Viereckschanze bei Blaufelden, Kreis Schwäbisch Hall*. Archäologische Ausgrabungen 1996, 87-91.
Stork, I. 1999a. *Zum Abschluss der Ausgrabungen in der Viereckschanze von Blaufelden, Kreis Schwäbisch Hall*. Archäologische Ausgrabungen. Baden-Württemberg 1998, 115-20.
Stork, I. 1999b. *12. Blaufelden, Kr. Schwäbisch-Hall*. In Wieland, G. 1999. *Viereckschanzen. Einem Rätsel auf der Spur*. 162-6. Stuttgart: Konrad Theiss.
Touquet Laporte-Cassagne, C. 2018. *Les site ruraux du second âge du fer dans le Bassin versant du crould en Val-D'Oise et ses marges*. Revue archèologique D'Île-de-France 5e supplement. Paris: Raif.
Tretola Martinez, D.C. 2014. Reinach-Mausacker (BL) – Ein spätkeltisches Gehöft im Wandel der Zeit. In S. Hornung (ed.) *Produktion – Distribution – Ökonimie. Siedlungs- und Wirtschaftsmuster der Latènezeit*. 257-71. Akten des internationalen Kolloquiums in Otzenhausen, 28.-30. Oktober 2001.
Tretola Martinez, D.C. 2016. Reinach-Nord (BL, Suisse): Une ferme gauloise à l'aube de l'époque romaine. In G. Blancquaert & F. Malrain (eds). Évolution des sociétés gauloises du Second âge du Fer, entre mutations internes et influences externes. 441-5. RAP – n° spécial 30-2016 – Actes du 38e colloque de l'AFEAF.
Venclová, N. 1998. *Mšecke Žehrovice in Boheimia. Archaeological background to a celtic hero 3rd – 2nd cent. B.C.* Sceaux: Kronos Editions.
von der Osten Woldenburg, H. 2002. Eine keltische Doppelschanze bei Osterholz, Gde. Kirchheim am Ries, Ostalbkreis. *Archäologische Ausgrabungen in Baden-Württemberg 2001*, 79.
von der Osten Woldenburg, H., Wieland, G. & Wahl, J. 1999. Untersuchungen in der spätkeltischen

Viereckschanze „Am Scheerer Weg" bei Mengen-Ennetach, Kreis Sigmaringen. *Archäologische Ausgrabungen in Baden-Württemberg*, 125-33.

von Nicolai, C. 2006. Sakral oder profan? Späteisenzeitliche Einfriedungen in Nordfrankreich und Süddeutschland. *Leipziger online-Beiträge zur Ur- und Frühgeschichtlichen Archäologie 22*, 1-21.

von Nicolai, C. 2009. La question des Viereckschanzen d'Allemagne du Sud revisitèe. In I. Bertrand, A. Duval, J. Gomez de Soto & P. Maguer. *Habitat et paysages ruraux en Gaule et regards sur d'autres règions du monde celtique*. Actes du XXXIe colloque international de l'Association Française pour l'Ètude de l'Âge du Fer 17.-20 Mai 2007, 245-80. Chauvigny.

Wendling, H. 2010. Landbesitz und Erbfolge -Ein ethnographisches Modell zur Sozialstruktur und Raumgliederung der mitteleuropäischen Latènezeit. In P. Trebsche, N. Müller-Scheeßel & S. Reinhold (eds). *Der gebaute Raum. Bausteine einer Architektursoziologie vormoderner Gesellschaften*. 325-54. Münster/New York/München/Berlin: Tübinger Archäologische Taschenbücher 7.

Wieland, G. 1999. *Viereckschanzen. Einem Rätsel auf der Spur*. Stuttgart: Theiss.

Wieland, G. 2009. Die keltische Viereckschanze von Hardheim-Gerichtstetten, Neckar-Odenwald-Kreis. Ein Meilenstein in der Erforschung einer archäologischen Denkmälergruppe. *Denkmalpflege in Baden-Württemberg 38/4*, 222-6.

Wieland, G. 2017. The rural contribution to urbanism: late La Tène Viereckschanzen in southwest Germany. In S. Stoddart (ed.). *Delicate urbanism in context: Settlement nucleation in pre-Roman Germany*. 51-9. Cambridge: The DAAD Cambridge Symposium.

Zanier, W. 2005. Ende der Viereckschanzen in früher römischer Kaiserzeit? *Fundberichte Baden-Württemberg 28/1*, 207-36.

Chapter 20

Rural settlement patterns in urbanised areas

The *oppidum* of Manching

Thimo J. Brestel

In D.C. Cowley, M. Fernández-Götz, T. Romankiewicz & H. Wendling (eds). Rural Settlement. Relating buildings, landscape, and people in the European Iron Age (Leiden 2019: Sidestone Press) 201-206.

20.1 Introduction

An increasing concentration of people and economic power led to a phase of urbanisation in the Central European Iron Age, the first time a non-rural lifestyle developed in this area. The division between 'rural' and 'urban' spaces became important for Iron Age societies and was perceptible through different markers. Only some markers, such as different settlement patterns or architectural boundaries, are recognisable in the archaeological record.

The urbanisation process took place in two different steps. The Hallstatt period saw the appearance of the *Fürstensitze*, developing further during the La Tène period (LT) with the emergence of *oppida* and other major settlements (Fernández-Götz 2018). However, a closer look at the 'first cities' reveals that they were not completely urbanised, as sites still show rural settlement patterns within the urban environment. This observation of the mix of urban and rural is essential for understanding the characteristics of Iron Age urbanism, and will be explored here through the example of the *oppidum* of Manching in Bavaria.

The site of Manching is located in the Ingolstadt basin on the Danube and was inhabited from the 4th to the first half of the 1st century BC. To date more than 30 ha of the 380-ha settlement area (Figure 1) have been excavated, providing a representative sample of the settlement layout. The occupation of the site has a non-urbanised phase during LT B2-LT C1 (ca. 330-220 BC), followed by a phase of extensive urbanization during LT C2 (ca. 220-120 BC). During this phase the settlement was bounded by a ditch-system enclosing a large circular area (Brestel 2015, 47-8). The rampart surrounding the *oppidum* was built later, probably at the end of LT C2, and maintained until the abandonment of the settlement at the end of LT D1 (80/50 BC). During LT C2 and D1 Manching shows great diversity in the patterning of occupation within the boundary of the rampart.

20.2 Rural settlement patterns in Manching

While the urban character of Manching has been extensively discussed (Eller *et al.* 2012), the rural character of elements of the occupation of the site has received less attention.

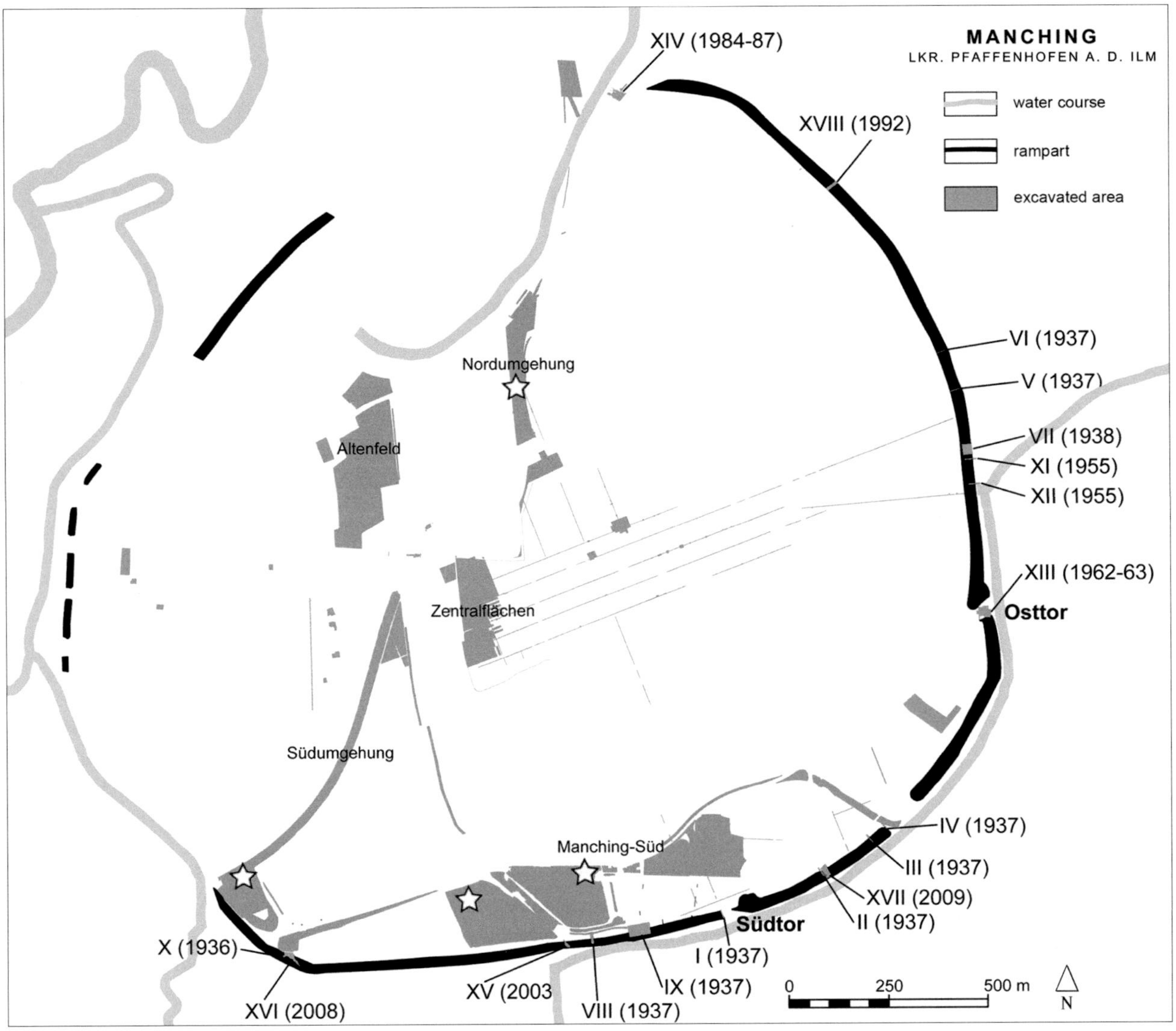

Figure 1: Plan of the *oppidum* of Manching. The stars mark the farmsteads discussed in the text (Image: T.J. Brestel & Römisch-Germanische Kommission).

Thus, the very densely settled areas at the centre of the *oppidum* are well-known, with large houses grouped alongside roads, sometimes forming compounds. While these may remotely reflect former rural settlement patterns (Sievers 2012, 118; Wendling 2013, 470), nevertheless, the density of construction, the diversity of building ground plans, and the finds illustrate the urban characteristics of the area.

On the other hand, the areas in the southern and northern periphery of the site show a much looser settlement plan (Figure 2). These areas are dominated by smaller buildings set amongst ditch systems and open spaces, which were probably meadows or fields. Four- and six-post granaries make up a large proportion of the buildings in this part of the settlement close to the rampart, while houses larger than 80 m^2 in area are absent. High occupation densities can be seen as one parameter for the degree of urbanisation (Fröhlich & Wendling 2013, 41), and these peripheral areas of the site present a considerable contrast to the centre of the *oppidum*, rather sharing more of the characteristics of small settlements and farmsteads in rural areas beyond the *oppidum* boundary.

In these peripheral areas of Manching, the arrangement of buildings inside compounds delimited by a ditched boundary has a strong resemblance to the *établissement rural* in France and southwest Germany. One

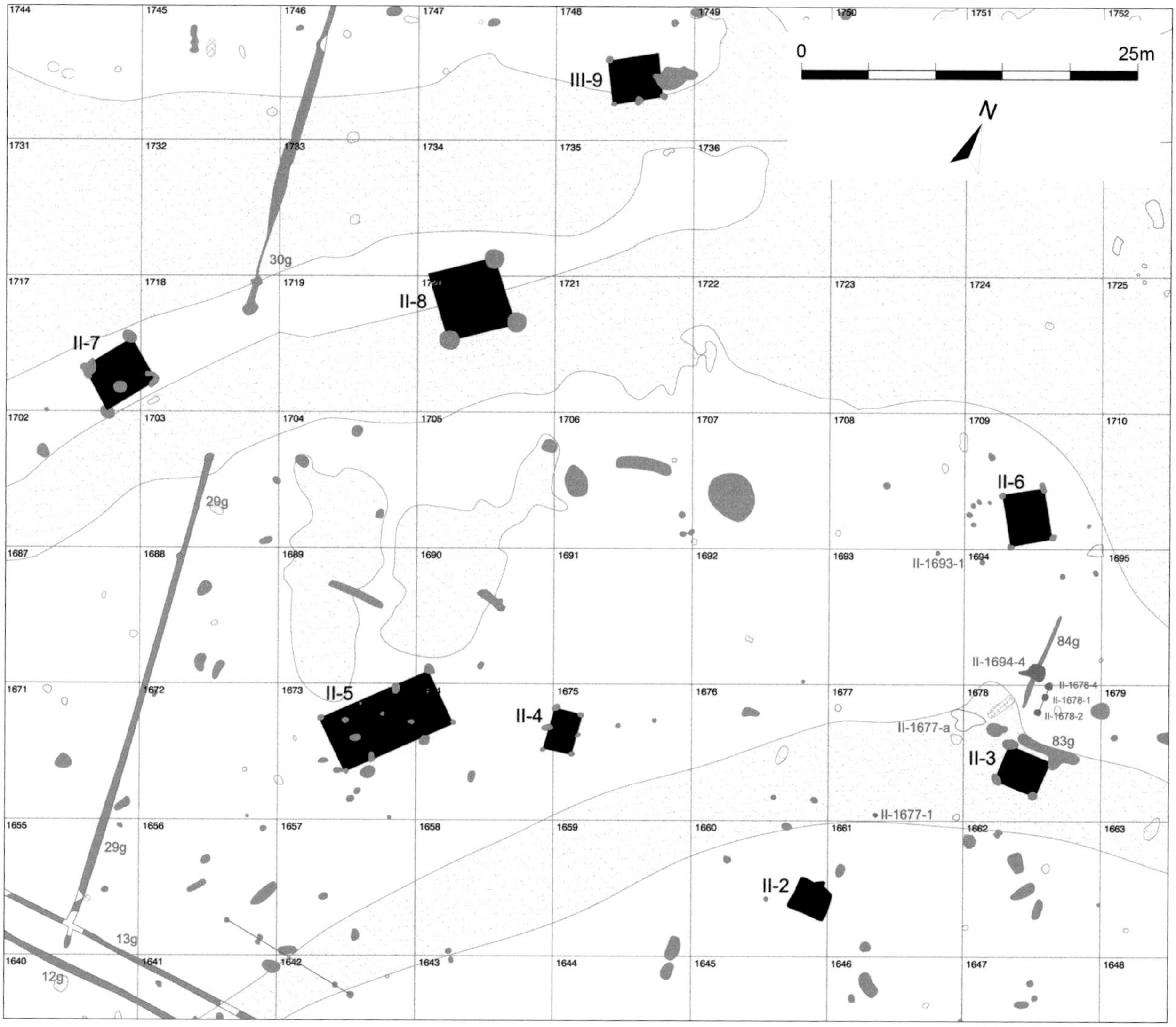

Figure 2: The 'loose' settlement plan of 'Manching-Süd' (Image: T.J. Brestel & Römisch-Germanische Kommission).

such enclosed farmstead has been partially excavated in the southwest of the *oppidum* ('Südumgehung', Figure 3). This extended to an area of approximately 0.25 ha and to date three buildings have been excavated, including a granary. The finds indicate that the compound was built in LT C2 (Winger 2016, 64).

Another farmstead (Figure 4) has been found in the so-called 'Manching-Süd' area, with three granaries, probably dating in LT C2 or D1, discovered in the small excavated area. The adjoining areas in the south and west were mostly open with drainage ditches and scattered small buildings. In the north of Manching ('Nordumgehung') three enclosed empty spaces have been excavated. The archaeobotanical analyses of these areas indicate that they were used as fields (Küster 1987, 451-2; Sievers 2007, 55-6), while an adjacent group of buildings (with a large number of granaries) forming a farmstead was found to the south (Sievers 1987, 334).

20.3 Conclusion

These examples illustrate the diversity in the pattering of occupation and activity in Manching. While the centre of the *oppidum* is characterized by a high density of buildings, large prestigious buildings, religious spaces and a large number of finds connected to crafting activities, most of the areas at the outskirts of the settlement present a marked contrast, with scattered farmsteads set amongst large areas of fields and open ground.

Figure 3: Enclosed farmstead in the 'Südumgehung' area (Image: T.J. Brestel after Winger 2016).

This pattern can be interpreted as a result of the development of Manching out of several hamlets during LT B2/C1, but it also tells us about a key characteristic of Late Iron Age urbanism whereby essentially rural settlement patterns were transferred into the enclosed area of the *oppidum* (Fernández-Götz 2018, 141). The resemblance of some of the compounds presented in this paper with *Viereckschanzen* and *établissement rural* is not only based on a common rural heritage but also a result of the economic situation. The contrasts between low and high density construction and habitation inside the *oppidum* of Manching most likely resulted from the mode of production, which, although mainly based on craft production and trade (Wendling 2013, 460), was still partly reliant on autonomous agricultural production.

The large-scale excavations in Manching have revealed a long-lasting process of urbanisation, which resulted in a large open settlement and then a 'lowland *oppidum*', both with significant evidence for rural settlement patterns. These rural elements have even led some researchers to

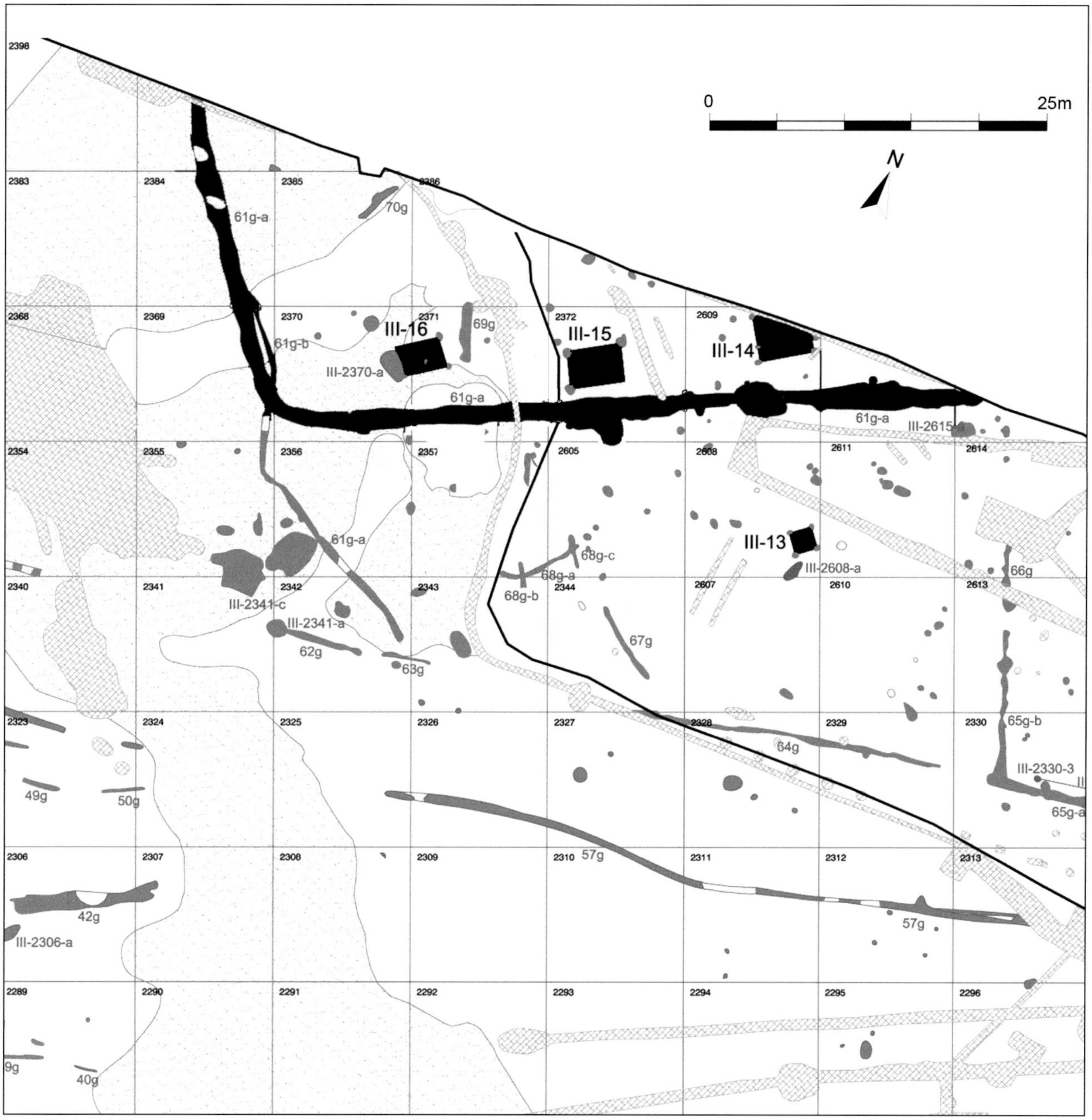

Figure 4: Enclosed farmstead in 'Manching-Süd' (Image: T.J. Brestel & Römisch-Germanische Kommission).

classify Manching as a primarily rural settlement (Lorenz & Gerdsen 2004, 130-1; Küster 2013, 742), a position that emphasises the difficulties of applying an oppositional or dualistic 'urban vs rural' classification to Manching. While this broad dichotomy may be helpful to describe the general social development in the La Tène Period, at a local scale Manching shows us that it can be too restrictive to describe the complexities of a settlement structure. It is important, therefore, to emphasise that urbanism in the Late Iron Age was primarily a process of centralisation, which included longstanding, common, rural structures (Sievers 2010, 33).

20.4 Bibliography

Eller, M., Sievers, S., Wendling, H. & Winger, K. 2012. Zentralisierung und Urbanisierung – Manchings Entwicklung zur spätkeltischen Stadt. In S. Sievers, & M. Schönfelder (eds). *Die Frage der Protourbanisation in der Eisenzeit. La Question de la Proto-Urbanisation à l'Âge du Fer. Akten des 34. internationalen Kolloquiums der AFEAF Vom 13.-16. Mai 2010 in Aschaffenburg*. 303-18. Bonn: Habelt Verlag.

Fernández-Götz, M. 2018. Urbanization in Iron Age Europe: Trajectories, Patterns, and Social Dynamics. *Journal of Archaeological Research* 26, 117-62.

Küster, H. 2013. Neue botanische Analysen an Fundgut aus dem latènezeitlichen Manching. In S. Sievers, M. Leicht, & B. Ziegaus (eds). *Ergebnisse der Ausgrabungen in Manching Altenfeld 1996-1999*. 737-44. Die Ausgrabungen in Manching 18. Wiesbaden: Reichert Verlag.

Küster, H. 1992. Vegetationsgeschichtliche Untersuchungen. In F. Maier, U. Geilenbrügge, E. Hahn, H.J. Köhler & S. Sievers (eds). *Ergebnisse der Ausgrabungen 1984-1987 in Manching*. 433-76. Die Ausgrabungen in Manching 15. Stuttgart: Franz Steiner Verlag.

Lorenz, H. & Gerdsen, H. 2004. *Chorologische Untersuchungen in dem spätkeltischen Oppidum bei Manching am Beispiel der Grabungsflächen der Jahre 1965-1967 und 1971. Fundstellenübersicht der Grabungsjahre 1961-1974*, Ausgrabungen in Manching 16. Stuttgart: Franz Steiner Verlag.

Sievers, S. 2012. Manching – Ein Oppidum nach Plan? In W. Raeck & D. Steuernagel (eds). *Das Gebaute und das Gedachte. Siedlungsform, Architektur und Gesellschaft in prähistorischen und antiken Kulturen*. 115-23. Bonn: Habelt Verlag.

Sievers, S. 2010. Vom Fürstensitz zum Oppidum. In D. Krausse (ed.). *"Fürstensitze" und Zentralorte der frühen Kelten. Abschlusskolloquium des DFG-Schwerpunktprogrammes 1171 in Stuttgart, 12.-15. Oktober 2009*. 31-4. Forschungen und Berichte zur Archäologie in Baden-Württemberg 120. Stuttgart: Theiss.

Sievers, S. 1992. Die Siedlungsstruktur unter chronologischen und funktionalen Aspekten. In F. Maier, U. Geilenbrügge, E. Hahn, H.J. Köhler & S. Sievers (eds). *Ergebnisse der Ausgrabungen 1984-1987 in Manching*. 326-35. Die Ausgrabungen in Manching 15. Stuttgart: Franz Steiner Verlag.

Wendling, H. 2013. Manching Reconsidered. *European Journal of Archaeology* 16, 459-90.

Winger, K. 2016. *Baubefunde und Siedlungsentwicklung der Südumgehung im Oppidum von Manching*, Die Ausgrabungen in Manching 19. Wiesbaden: Reichert Verlag.

PART 3

STATUS AND SETTLEMENT HIERARCHY

Chapter 21

Rural residential places?

Rethinking the *Fürstensitze*-elites correlation

Manuel Fernández-Götz & Ian Ralston

21.1 Introduction

This paper aims to challenge the enduring assumption that Late Hallstatt elites in Central Europe necessarily had their principal residences in the so-called 'princely seats' (*Fürstensitze*). While some elite members or families may have settled permanently inside the large fortified centres, there is ample evidence that this arrangement was often not the case (cf. also Adam & Fichtl 2014). The positions of some high status farmsteads, as well as the distribution patterns of numerous sumptuous burials that were located at varying, but often considerable, distances from the central settlements, suggest that in many cases high-status individuals may have lived for much of their time at their country estates, where they were also eventually buried. Bettina Arnold already highlighted the fact that there are many 'princely graves' (*Fürstengräber*) not associated with *Fürstensitze*, which she argues implies that members of the Early Iron Age social elites were dispersed across landscapes in which such status markers were not complemented by significant enclosed places (Arnold 1995, 47). It follows that members of the elite may have inhabited such rural locations, rather than necessarily having been resident year-round at the fortified centres. Key rural places are indicated by major wealthy barrows set at a distance, up to several hours of horseback travel, from the 'princely seats', and less usually by the discovery of elite farmsteads similarly located. We will present four case-studies from southern Germany and central France which contribute to this perspective: these consider respectively the 6th and 5th centuries BC evidence from the Heuneburg, Hohenasperg and Ipf in southern Germany; and from Bourges and its hinterland in Berry, central France (cf. Krausse 2008; Krausse 2010 for a summary of the archaeological evidence on the *Fürstensitze*). But before we start with the Late Hallstatt and Early La Tène evidence, it is worth having a brief look for comparative purposes at the situation during the Late La Tène period.

In D.C. Cowley, M. Fernández-Götz, T. Romankiewicz & H. Wendling (eds). Rural Settlement. Relating buildings, landscape, and people in the European Iron Age (Leiden 2019: Sidestone Press) 209-218.

21.2 Rural elite residences: The Late La Tène evidence

In the area around the Titelberg *oppidum* in the Grand Duchy of Luxembourg, both the famous elite grave of Clemency (Metzler *et al.* 1991) and the slightly later aristocratic cemetery at Goeblingen-Nospelt (Metzler & Gaeng 2009) are situated at considerable distances from the *oppidum*, at 5 and 17 km respectively. The rich La Tène D graves of Pétange are rather nearer to it, lying some 3 km away, but all the evidence indicates that they too were first and foremost associated with a rural settlement which

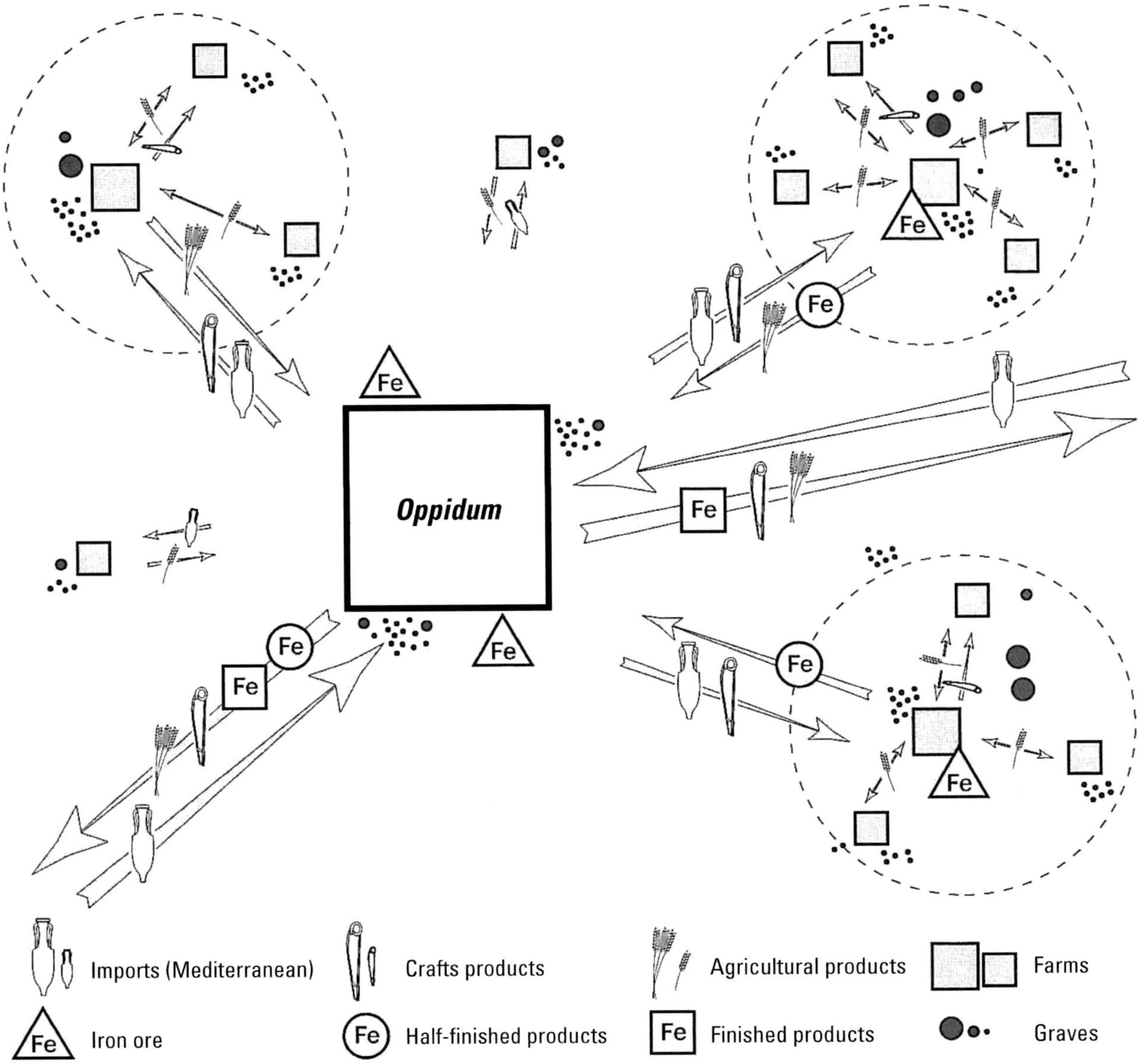

Figure 1: Theoretical diagram of relations between the *oppidum* and its surrounding rural territory, based on the data of the Titelberg area during La Tène D (after Fichtl 2005, based on Metzler 1995).

subsequently became a Gallo-Roman *villa rustica*, and not directly with the *oppidum* (Metzler 1995, 535). On the other hand, the cemeteries in the immediate vicinity of the *oppidum* of Titelberg, both on its east and its west sides, are characterised by the marked absence of aristocratic burials amongst those interred there. This contrast, between the relatively modestly furnished graves at Lamadeleine (Metzler-Zens *et al.* 1999) and in the eastern cemetery on the one hand and the wealthier examples represented at Clemency, Goeblingen-Nospelt and Pétange on the other, points to a separation between the *oppidani* interred at the former and the more distant burial places of the *nobiles* (Krausse 2006, 350).

Both the distribution of the burials and the still poorly documented remains of rural settlements around Titelberg suggest that the choice of localities for the elite graves was determined with reference to the locations of the major farms with which they were connected (Metzler 1995, 535-41, 568; Metzler & Gaeng 2009, 16-9). A similar situation can also be observed around the important *oppidum* of Château-Porcien in the territory of the Remi (Lambot *et al.* 1994). For its part, in Berry the rich graves of the Bituriges in La Tène D and the beginning of the Gallo-Roman period such as Fléré-la-Rivière (Batardy *et al.* 2001, 102; Ferdière & Villard 1993) are again not directly linked to their *oppida* but are scattered across the countryside, again probably near the rural residences that housed the individuals who were subsequently buried in these tombs. In all three cases mentioned above (Titelberg, Château-Porcien and Berry), the location of the sumptuous burials suggests that the aristocrats they held had not lived in the *oppida* permanently, but rather spent considerable portions of their lives on their country estates (Buchsenschutz & Ralston 2012; Krausse 2006, 347; Metzler *et al.* 1991, 171-2). In western Berry, two small rectilinear enclosed settlements at Luant and Meunet-Planches (both in Indre; and respectively c. 1 ha and c. 2 ha in extent, see Batardy *et al.* 2001, 59-61), offer one model for the characteristics of such estate settlements. The former is entered through a small *Zangentor* and both possess *muri gallici* – in these regards effectively miniaturised *oppida* in their emulation of the appropriate architecture, but are distinct from the network of Biturigan *oppida* because of their smaller enclosed areas. Based on the data just rehearsed from Luxembourg, Jeannot Metzler proposed a model for the western Treveran territory in which the *oppidum* would have represented the political, religious, craft and commercial centre for that region, whilst not necessarily being the place where the powerful aristocratic families lived permanently (Figure 1).

Major residential structures such as those found in some cases rebuilt in ever-grander formats as at the *Parc aux Chevaux* (Maison 1: Paunier & Luginbühl 2004) within *the oppidum* of Bibracte (Mont Beuvray, Nièvre) suggest that some of the elite may have lived – even if not permanently – in the *oppidum* itself. In many other places, however, the Late La Tène land-owning aristocracy would have continued to live by preference on their country domains, from which their fundamental wealth may have derived and where their key clients and retainers may also have lived. In exceptional cases, of which Paule in Brittany is the best-examined, such an upscale rural residence (Menez 2009; 2012) may have accreted extra functions to it – increasing elaboration marking successive reconstructions until the final stage of Paule represented the development of a full-blown *oppidum* at its cross-roads location. The evidence from such settlement trajectories indicates that living in the countryside would thus not have impeded such members of the aristocracy from also actively participating in the political, economic and religious activities that took place in the large fortified centres. The apparent friction of distance resulting from rural living would have been much reduced by the increasing available of wheeled vehicles and, perhaps even more, of the ridden horse.

It is possible that some Gallic aristocratic families had houses in the *oppida* that were used during their temporary visits, but that they resided most of the year in the countryside, matching a pattern not uncommon in European aristocracies of more recent centuries. In such cases, the rural domains would have represented the main source of primary wealth through the exploitation of the agricultural, livestock and mineral resources of these estates. Even after the Roman conquest, when Gaul became part successively of the Roman, Frankish and Carolingian Empires, much of the economic, political and social power remained firmly anchored in the rural world (Crumley 1995, 28). As Olivier Buchsenschutz has also pointed out, we can imagine, *mutatis mutandis*, a situation that was rather similar to that of the nobility of the Île-de-France during the *Ancien Régime*, who held office in the Paris parliament or at the court of Versailles, but who lived several dozen kilometres away in their castles for much of the year (Buchsenschutz 2006, 61).

21.3 Moving back: The Late Hallstatt and Early La Tène evidence

The examples presented above are obviously more recent in date by some centuries than the cases we now wish to consider, but there are reasons to assume that a situation similar to that described above for La Tène D can also be identified in the Late Hallstatt and Early La Tène periods. The distribution pattern of barrows covering elite graves attributable to the period around 500 BC is particularly interesting. While from a regional and macro-regional perspective there are significant concentrations of major barrows apparent in the general neighbourhood of the so-called *Fürstensitze*, if we focus in at a detailed, local scale, we observe that many of these elite burials are located several kilometres away from the fortified centres, rather than being set in their immediate vicinities. The most striking example is perhaps the 'princely' grave of Hochdorf (Biel 1985), situated about 10 km away from the Hohenasperg plateau, the setting of the *Fürstensitz* candidate nearest to it. Although the important open settlement of Eberdingen-Hochdorf (Biel 2015), located close to this rich barrow, was occupied between the 5th and 4th centuries BC and is therefore later than the date of this famous elite grave, it is tempting to postulate that the main residence of the illustrious deceased man buried at Hochdorf was also to be found somewhere in this locality, although it was not set within this village of artisans when that was in use. In fact, some isolated Hallstatt D finds from this unenclosed settlement hint at the possibility of an earlier occupation of that site which might have coincided with the lifetime of the leader buried at Hochdorf.

But Hochdorf is not the only example in the Middle Neckar region; the former existence of the residences of important elite members outside the fortified centres is also supported by other evidence (Balzer 2010; Bolay *et al.* 2010) (Figure 2). The famous anthropomorphic stone sculpture of Hirschlanden, as well as other sumptuous graves such as those of Stuttgart-Bad Cannstatt or Esslingen-Sirnau are located equally or even further

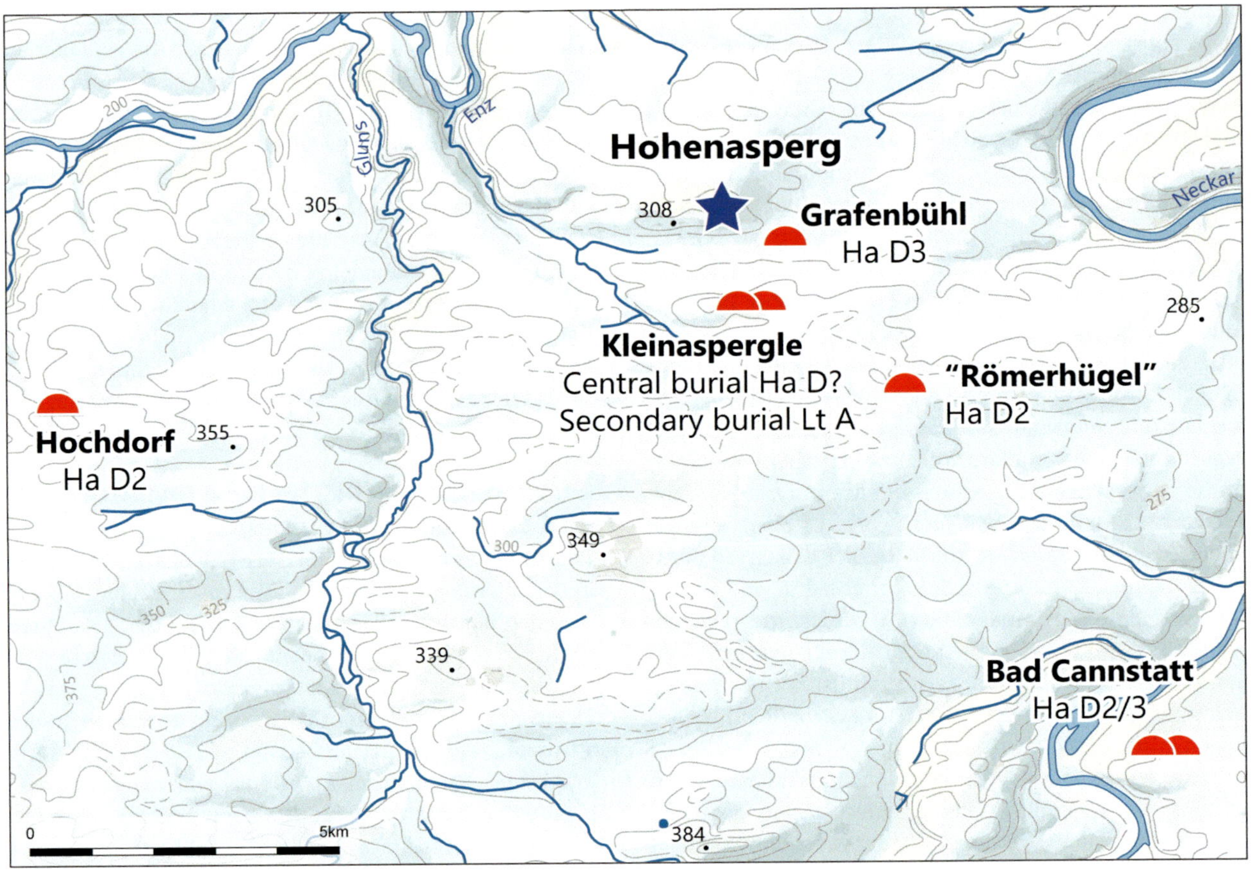

Figure 2: Some of the main Hallstatt D and La Tène A sumptuous graves in the surroundings of the Hohenasperg (redrawn after Krausse et al. 2016; design: C. Nübold. © Landesamt für Denkmalpflege im RP Stuttgart).

away from the nearest supposed *Fürstensitz,* that on the Hohenasperg. It is unlikely that the individuals buried in the central chambers of the latter elite barrows had their main residences in that rather distant hillfort, with which there is no direct line of sight.

A similar scenario can be proposed to account for the distribution of some of the elite graves in the landscape surrounding the Heuneburg on the upper Danube (Krausse *et al.* 2016, 113-38; Kurz & Schiek 2002). Using some of these burial mounds, situated several kilometres from the Heuneburg, as proxy indications of their rural landholdings allows the proposition that at least some sections of the ruling cohort did not live year-round on that hilltop above the Danube, or even in the outer settlement surrounding it, during the decades when the latter was in existence (Figure 3). It is certainly worthy of note that the major barrows of the earliest phases of the period of intense use of this landscape (corresponding to building periods IVc-IVa of the Heuneburg itself), such as the Hohmichele-Speckhau group, were almost always constructed at a distance of several kilometres from the hillfort. Moreover, the central graves from Tumuli 17 and 18 of the Speckhau group testify to the existence of elites in the environs of the Heuneburg already during the preceding Hallstatt C period, thus predating the foundation of the *Fürstensitz* agglomeration itself around 630/620 BC (Arnold & Murray 2016; forthcoming). It can thus be proposed that the emergence of elite rural locales or even estates, with their associated burials, in some cases preceded the development of the main fortified centres, rather than simply being satellites of them (Fernández-Götz & Arnold 2017; Kurz 2007). It is also conceivable that a central settlement focus never subsequently developed within some such groupings.

In terms of distance to the settlement core, it is particularly noticeable that the impressive tumulus of Rauhe Lehen is situated no less than 5 km as the crow flies from the Heuneburg and that, significantly, it lies across the Danube on the other side of its valley (Figure 4). While, given the recovery of timbers intimating that a bridge spanned the inner ditch at the foot of the Heuneburg plateau (Bofinger & Goldner-Bofinger 2008), it is possible that the river was also bridged at that time, this would have required more sophisticated engineering and there

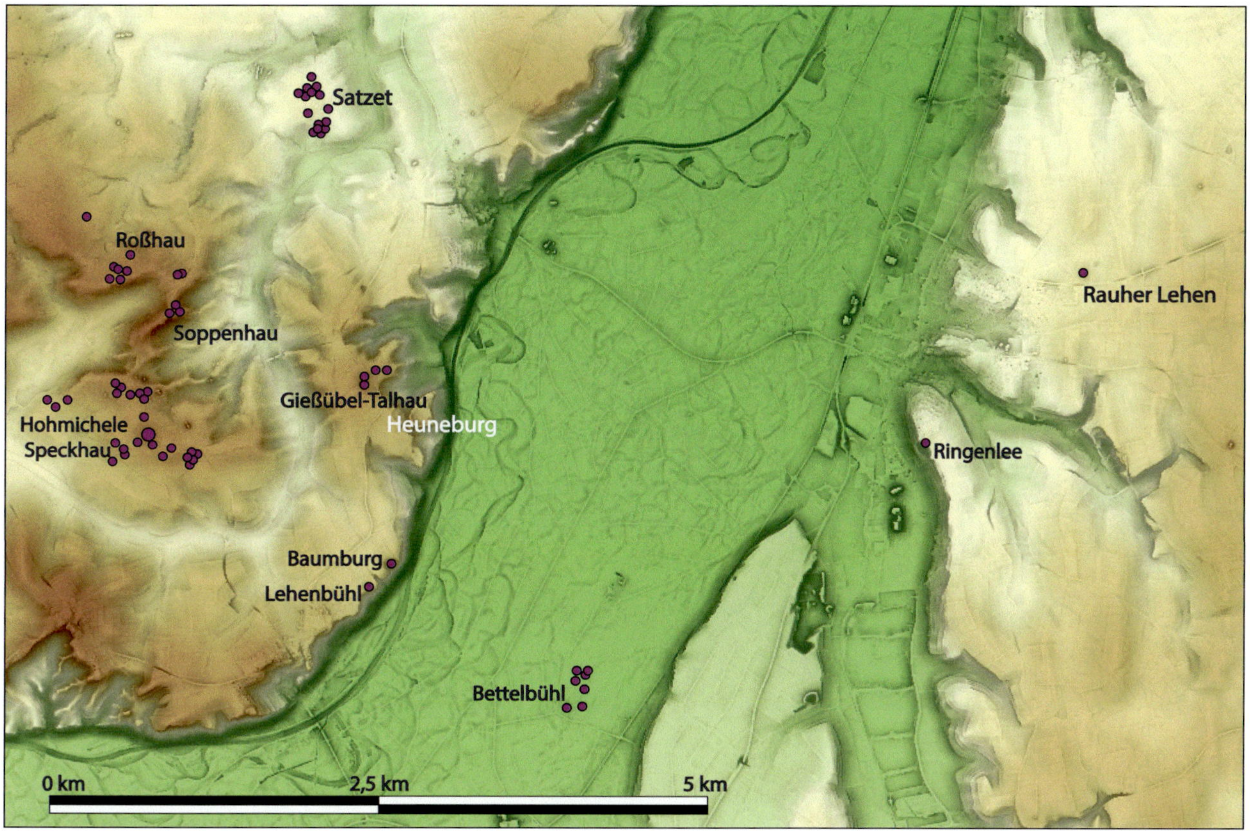

Figure 3: Numerous Hallstatt period barrow cemeteries are known within several kilometres of the Heuneburg (after Krausse et al. 2016; design: I. Kretschmer/C. Steffen. © Landesamt für Denkmalpflege im RP Stuttgart).

is meantime no evidence for such a construction. It is more likely that the Danube had to be forded here and this requirement – even on horseback – suggests the need for greater effort and inconvenience to access the Heuneburg than the straight-line distance of 5 km mentioned above intimates.

Even more distant is the recently discovered elite cemetery at Unlingen, set about 11 km from the Heuneburg, which was in use from Hallstatt C to Hallstatt D3 (Meyer & König 2016). The chronological range of the Early Iron Age burial mounds at Unlingen thus provides further archaeological testimony for the presence of elites in the Heuneburg region in the decades before the foundation of the agglomeration itself (Fernández-Götz & Arnold 2017).

In the areas surrounding the Heuneburg and the Hohenasperg, we still lack direct archaeological evidence for elite rural farmsteads contemporary with the 'princely seats' themselves, so that assumptions as to the residential places of the members of the elite away from the hillforts themselves must be drawn indirectly from the proxy evidence provided by the locations of their burial monuments. Investigations in the environs of the Ipf have however produced a more complete set of evidence. Various rectilinear enclosures have been identified in the surroundings of this prominent hilltop (Krause 2004; Krause 2014; Krause *et al.* 2010). These structures can be convincingly interpreted as the residences of members of the socio-political elite. Excavations in the rectangular farmsteads at the foot of the Ipf have produced numerous high quality finds such as items of glass, amber, metal and ceramics, including wheel-thrown pottery, in addition to Greek amphorae, sherds of Attic red-figure drinking bowls and a bronze Greek coin. One feature of the rectangular enclosure at Bugfeld bei Osterholz is particularly unusual. Here a substantial building some 15 by 15 m in size was demolished after 500 BC and then carefully covered with 50 tonnes of stones (Figure 5). Parallels for this practice from the Mediterranean world indicate that this action should be interpreted as the ritual covering of a significant cult building, and this again emphasises the important of these sectors of the landscape in the proximity of the major enclosed places.

In Berry, circumstances are rendered more complicated by the fact that the central settlement, the present-day city of Bourges, has had a long occupation history such that the accretion of subsequent deposits

Figure 4: The Rauhe Lehen tumulus near Ertingen with dense tree cover (after Krausse et al. 2016; photo: M. Friemelt. © Landesamt für Denkmalpflege im RP Stuttgart).

Figure 5: Rectangular farmstead at Bugfeld bei Osterholz near the Ipf: stone covering of a large building in the northeast corner of the enclosure (Photo: O. Braasch. © Landesamt für Denkmalpflege im RP Stuttgart).

makes the identification of the characteristics of its centre about 500 BC problematic. Fragmentary structural remains identified at depth in rescue projects, for example from the rue Littré, indicate elite occupation, here represented by successive layers with imported Attic black and then red-figure pottery as well as locally wheel-finished pottery and evidence of a diet in which hunted species are well-represented (Augier *et al.* 2007; Yvinec 1992). The presence of foodstuffs taken from the wild is again significant in allowing us to focus on another dimension of the interplay between rural pursuits and the 'princely seats' themselves. Littré, like the nearby Hôtel-Dieu, is positioned towards the apex of the promontory on which the core of Bourges is set, and in the absence of any clear indication of where the mid-first-millennium BC enceinte was located, it is not possible to be definitive as to whether these sites were within the enclosure or set very close by but outside it. Here too, however, major barrows are located in the immediate surroundings, within a few kilometres of the core of the site, as at Les Carrières à Bachon at Lazenay and very probably the massive barrow now crowned by modern housing at the Butte d'Archelet, set in the suburbs across the Yèvre valley to the north of town.

Recent models proposed by Milcent (2012) on the one hand, and Augier and Krausz (2012) on the other, remarked on the rich mid-first millennium BC barrows extending out from the core of Bourges, more particularly in the direction of the better agricultural land of the *Champagne berrichonne* to the south-west and to the south. Milcent (2004) in particular already noted in his doctoral study of this material that some patterning was apparent in the relative wealth of these graves, and in the known sizes of the barrows. In general, once beyond the zone constituted of the immediate surroundings within a few kilometres of Bourges, there seems to be a sector extending out to about 30 km where elite burials are seemingly less richly accompanied, before richer graves and bigger barrows are encountered anew further away from the inner core formed by Bourges itself. Whether and to what degree elites at this distance from the central place were still related to it socially, politically, and economically is perhaps open to question – there is for example the possibility of a lesser central place at Issoudun to which some of the other individuals who ended up buried in these barrows may have related. Whichever model is preferred, this does not change the fundamental point that – particularly on the better land of the limestone plain of the *Champagne berrichonne* and the valleys of the tributaries, ultimately of the Loire – if we use the proxy evidence furnished by their burial places, members of the elites lived and died in the countryside; and we may assume at rural places that were significant to them and which they may well have owned.

The accumulating evidence from Bourges and its surroundings can thus be accommodated in the model of peripatetic elites exercising power in the centres but residing much of their time on their rural estates, with the added proviso that, around the core of Bourges, sites such as Saint-Martin-des-Champs and Port-Sec, up to 4 km from the centre of the site as the crow flies, indicate that imports – notably red-figure Attic pottery at Port Sec (Augier *et al.* 2012), could end up deposited in craftworking areas, and not simply in the wealthier residential portions of the 'princely seats'. This pattern too challenges the normal association between such material and elite inhabitants, at least extending the range of types of locations which have produced such material.

21.4 Conclusion: Rethinking the *Fürstensitze*

Just as is known to have been the case at the La Tène D *oppidum* at the Titelberg in Luxembourg, so too at the Hallstatt D 'princely seats' a considerable proportion of the members of the socio-political elites may have lived much of their time on their country estates. Primary resources, such as those drawn from agriculture and livestock farming on such landholdings, whatever the mechanisms by which they were distributed, will have formed the basis of their power. The recurrent, cyclical nature of such primary production may well have served to underpin their more speculative endeavours, whether economic or political – endeavours which could of course be practised elsewhere. To assert the likely rural foundation of much elite power and status at this time, however, is not to deny that this was complemented by other activities undertaken by the elites in other places, not least in the new social and political arenas offered by the developing 'princely seats' themselves. It is equally likely that, in other cases, elite members did indeed take the decision to live permanently within the new fortified citadels. The Hallstatt D2-D3 *Herrenhäuser* on the Heuneburg plateau (Gersbach 1996, 68-72; Krausse *et al.* 2016, 92-5), and at least some of the monumental apsidal buildings at Mont Lassois (Chaume *et al.* 2013), may have served as aristocratic or even royal residences, although alternative interpretations for these substantial constructions, such as communal assembly spaces, are also possible.

Overall, however, in such pre-monetary economies, the key elements which underscored elite status and power would have included the ability to obtain or extract key commodities and services – notably practical requirements such as foodstuffs but extending to, for example, the rights to make demands on others for military service (Karl 2015; Gosden 1985). The different settlement and developmental trajectories of the 'princely seats' tend to emphasize, as we have asserted elsewhere, the relative fragility and weakness of political arrangements within their polities (cf. Fernández-Götz & Ralston 2017). For well over a generation, since at least the writings of Frankenstein and Rowlands (1978), archaeologists have frequently pointed to the apparent interplay between the highest echelons of society considered to be resident in the 'princely seats' and there surrounded by their master craftsmen, and subsidiary elites located elsewhere within the polities. There are also indications of interplays and familiarities across the *Fürstensitze* system, in what is sometimes characterised as peer-polity interaction.

It may be suggested that – as in other circumstances such as early Medieval Scotland (*e.g.* Alcock 2003, chapter 5) or the extension of Norman power – the establishment of elites in the countryside is a key component required to make such systems function. In a world where the bulk transport of perishable goods over any distance must have been difficult, while food renders or simply the products of one's own rural property could be moved to central places for consumption, in many cases it must have been easier for the elite to move to the food supplies than the contrary. At its simplest, such purposes would serve to distribute the elites to key places in the landscape, here suggested as the foci of their rural estates. Once there, they would not only have been able to consume and redistribute food as necessary, but they would be able to show themselves in their finery and high-quality jewellery and, for example and as necessary, making direct demands for military service from their retinues on their estates in a manner which would not have been so readily possible if they had been based remotely in a 'princely seat' some tens of kilometres away. We might therefore argue on purely hypothetical grounds – such as the requirement to show themselves and be seen, to consume food renders, to enforce military obligations and doubtlessly, physically to remind their retinues of a range of other requirements – that the elites of the Late Hallstatt period needed to make themselves visible and be present in the rural world that quantitatively dominated this, and indeed all, periods of the pre-Roman European Iron Age. It remains the case, despite strides in the recognition and examination of Hallstatt-period rural settlements over recent decades, that the best archaeological correlate for an elite dispersed in the countryside at this time is the pattern of elite burials beneath barrows of lesser or greater impressiveness.

In any case, what we need to do is to rethink the nature of the *Fürstensitze* in particular in regard to the relationships between their inhabitants and those settled within their vicinities, here taken to mean those portions of the landscape from which the 'princely seat' could be accessed within say two days of relatively easy riding. In the case of the Hohenasperg, for example, Stéphane Verger (2006, 38) has suggested that the plateau-top of the hill should not be considered to have been a 'princely' residence but rather as the main seat of the polity, the location for particular assemblies and collective ceremonies which required to be held at a neutral location, but external to the estates of the major elite families who controlled the plains below this conspicuous hill. Even admitting that direct evidence from the hill itself is not recoverable, and without trying to establish this perspective as a general model, reflections such as Verger's can open new avenues for future interpretations of the lives of the elite members of Late Hallstatt societies in and around the so-called *Fürstensitze*.

21.5 Bibliography

Adam, A.-M. & Fichtl, S. 2014. L'aristocrate des villes et l'aristocrate des champs. In S. Bourdin, J. Dubouloz & E. Rosso (eds). *Peupler et habiter l'Italie et le monde romain. Etudes d'histoire et d'archéologie offertes à Xavier Lafon*. 43-52. Aix-en-Provence: Presses universitaires de Provence.

Alcock, L. 2003. *Kings and warriors, craftsmen and priests in northern Britain AD 550-850*. Edinburgh: Society of Antiquaries of Scotland.

Arnold, B. 1995. The material culture of social structure: rank and status in early Iron Age Europe. In B. Arnold & D. B. Gibson (eds). *Celtic Chiefdom, Celtic State: The Evolution of Complex Social Systems in Prehistoric Europe*. 43-52. Cambridge: Cambridge University Press.

Arnold, B. & Murray, M. L. 2016. Two Hallstatt burial mounds in the Hohmichele group in the 'Speckhau'. In D. Krausse, M. Fernández-Götz, L. Hansen & I. Kretschmer (eds). *The Heuneburg and the Early Iron Age Princely Seats: First Towns North of the Alps*. 121-7. Budapest: Archaeolingua.

Arnold, B. & Murray, M. L. Forthcoming. *A Landscape of Ancestors. Archaeological Investigations of Two Iron Age Burial Mounds in the Hohmichele Group, Baden-Württemberg*. Forschungen und Berichte zur Vor- und Frühgeschichte in Baden-Württemberg. Darmstadt: Theiss.

Augier, L., Buchsenschutz, O. & Ralston, I. (eds) 2007. *Un complexe princier de l'âge du Fer. L'habitat du promontoire de Bourges (Cher) (VIe-IVe s. av. J.-C.)*. Bourges/Tours: Bituriga.

Augier, L., Buchsenschutz, O., Durand, R., Filippini, A., Germinet, D., Levéry, M., Maçon, P., Pescher, B., Ralston, I. Salin, M. & Troadec, J. 2012. *Un complexe princier de l'âge du Fer: le quartier artisanal de Port Sec sud à Bourges (Cher)*. Tours/Bourges: Revue Archéologique Centre France Suppl. 41.

Augier, L. & Krausz, S. 2012. Du complexe princier a l'oppidum : les modèles du Berry. In S. Sievers & M. Schönfelder (eds). *Die Frage der Protourbanisation in der Eisenzeit. La question de la proto-urbanisation à l'âge du Fer. Akten des 34. internationalen Kolloquiums der AFEAF vom 13.-16. Mai 2010 in Aschaffenburg.* 167-92. Bonn: Habelt.

Balzer, I. 2010. Neue Forschungen zu alten Fragen. Der früheisenzeitliche „Fürstensitz“ Hohenasperg (Kr. Ludwigsburg) und sein Umland. In D. Krausse (ed.). *„Fürstensitze“ und Zentralorte der frühen Kelten. Abschlußkolloquium des DFG-Schwerpunktprogramms 1171 in Stuttgart, 12.-15. Oktober 2009. Teil I.* 209-38. Forschungen und Berichte zur Vor- und Frühgeschichte in Baden-Württemberg 120/1. Stuttgart: Theiss.

Batardy, C, Buchsenschutz, O. & Dumasy, F. (eds) 2001. *Le Berry antique: Atlas 2000.* Tours: Revue Archéologique Centre France Suppl. 21.

Biel, J. 1985. *Der Keltenfürst von Hochdorf.* Stuttgart: Theiss.

Biel, J. 2015. *Hochdorf IX. Die eisenzeitliche Siedlung in der Flur Reps und andere vorgeschichtliche Fundstellen von Eberdingen-Hochdorf (Kreis Ludwigsburg).* Forschungen und Berichte zur Vor- und Frühgeschichte in Baden-Württemberg 111. Stuttgart: Theiss.

Bofinger, J. & Goldner-Bofinger, A. 2008. Terrassen und Gräben – Siedlungsstrukturen und Befestigungssysteme der Heuneburg-Vorburg. In D. Krausse (ed.). *Frühe Zentralisierungs- und Urbanisierungsprozesse. Zur Genese und Entwicklung frühkeltischer Fürstensitze und ihres territorialen Umlandes. Kolloquium des DFG-Schwerpunktprogramms 1171 in Blaubeuren, 9.-11. Oktober 2006.* 209-27. Forschungen und Berichte zur Vor- und Frühgeschichte in Baden-Württemberg 101. Stuttgart: Theiss.

Bolay, G., Krüger, A., Müller, F. O. & Paul, H. (eds) 2010. *Kelten am Hohenasperg.* Asperg: Keltenfürst-Verlag.

Buchsenschutz, O. 2006. Le monde rural et ses productions (IIe-Ier s. av. J.-C.). In C. Haselgrove (ed.). *Celtes et Gaulois, l'Archéologie face à l'Histoire. 4: Les mutations de la fin de l'âge du Fer.* 55-65. Collection Bibracte 12/4. Glux-en-Glenne: Centre Archéologique Européen.

Buchsenschutz, O. & Ralston, I. 2012. Urbanisation et aristocratie celtiques. In S. Sievers & M. Schönfelder (eds). *Die Frage der Protourbanisation in der Eisenzeit. La question de la proto-urbanisation à l'âge du Fer. Akten des 34. internationalen Kolloquiums der AFEAF vom 13.-16. Mai 2010 in Aschaffenburg.* 347-64. Bonn: Habelt.

Chaume, B., Nieszery, N. & Reinhard, W. 2013. L'enclos des grands bâtiments absidiaux du plateau du mont Saint-Marcel. *Bulletin archéologique et historique du Châtillonnais 7ème série,* n° 4, 13-9.

Crumley, C. L. 1995. Building an historical ecology of Gaulish polities. In B. Arnold & D. B. Gibson (eds). *Celtic Chiefdom, Celtic State: The Evolution of Complex Social Systems in Prehistoric Europe.* 26-33. Cambridge: Cambridge University Press.

Ferdière, A & Villard, A. 1993. *La tombe augustéenne de Fléré-la-Rivière (Indre) et les sépultures aristicratiques de la cité des Bituriges.* Saint Marcel, Indre: Mémoire 2 du Musée d'Argentomagus.

Fernández-Götz, M. & Arnold, B. 2017. Elites before the Fürstensitze: Hallstatt C Sumptuous Graves between Main and Danube. In R. Schumann & S. van der Vaart-Verschoof (eds). *Connecting Elites and Regions. Perspectives on contacts, relations and differentiation during the Early Iron Age Hallstatt C period in Northwest and Central Europe.* 183-99. Leiden: Sidestone Press.

Fernández-Götz, M. & Ralston, I. 2017. The Complexity and Fragility of Early Iron Age Urbanism in West-Central Temperate Europe. *Journal of World Prehistory* 30 (3), 259-79.

Frankenstein, S. & Rowlands, M.J. 1978. The Internal Structure and Regional Context of Early Iron Age Society in South-Western Germany. *Bulletin of the Institute of Archaeology* 15, 73-112.

Gersbach, E. 1996. *Baubefunde der Perioden IIIb-Ia der Heuneburg.* Heuneburgstudien 10. Römisch-Germanische Forschungen 56. Mainz: Philipp von Zabern.

Gosden, C. 1985. Gifts and Kin in Early Iron Age Europe. *Man* 20, 475-93.

Karl, R. 2015. Labour Procurement in Pre-Monetary Europe. In B. Danielisova & M. Fernández-Götz (eds). *Persistent Economic Ways of Living. Production, Distribution, and Consumption in Late Prehistory and Early History.* 21-36. Budapest: Archaeolingua.

Krause, R. 2004. *Der Ipf. Frühkeltischer Fürstensitz und Zentrum keltischer Besiedlung am Nördlinger Ries.* Esslingen: Archäologische Informationen aus Baden-Württemberg 47.

Krause, R. (ed.) 2014. *Neue Forschungen zum frühkeltischen Fürstensitz auf dem Ipf.* Frankfurter Archäologische Schriften 24. Bonn: Habelt.

Krause, R., Stobbe, A., Euler, D. & Fuhrmann, K. 2010. Zur Genese und Entwicklung des frühkeltischen Fürstensitzes auf dem Ipf bei Bopfingen (Ostalbkreis, Baden-Württemberg) und seines Umlandes im Nördlinger Ries. In D. Krausse (ed.). *„Fürstensitze“ und Zentralorte der frühen Kelten. Abschlußkolloquium des DFG-Schwerpunktprogramms 1171 in Stuttgart, 12.-15. Oktober 2009. Teil I.* 169-207. Forschungen und Berichte zur Vor- und Frühgeschichte in Baden-Württemberg 120/1. Stuttgart: Theiss.

Krausse, D. 2006. *Eisenzeitlicher Kulturwandel und Romanisierung im Mosel-Eifel-Raum.* Römisch-Germanische Forschungen 63. Mainz: Philipp von Zabern.

Krausse, D. (ed.) 2008. *Frühe Zentralisierungs- und Urbanisierungsprozesse. Zur Genese und Entwicklung frühkeltischer Fürstensitze und ihres territorialen Umlandes. Kolloquium des DFG-Schwerpunkt-*

programms 1171 in Blaubeuren, 9.-11. Oktober 2006. Forschungen und Berichte zur Vor- und Frühgeschichte in Baden-Württemberg 101. Stuttgart: Theiss.
Krausse, D. (ed.) 2010. *„Fürstensitze" und Zentralorte der frühen Kelten. Abschlußkolloquium des DFG-Schwerpunktprogramms 1171 in Stuttgart, 12.-15. Oktober 2009. Teil I und II*. Forschungen und Berichte zur Vor- und Frühgeschichte in Baden-Württemberg 120. Stuttgart: Theiss.
Krausse, D., Fernández-Götz, M., Hansen, L. & Kretschmer, I. 2016. *The Heuneburg and the Early Iron Age Princely Seats: First Towns North of the Alps*. Budapest: Archaeolingua.
Kurz, S. 2007. *Untersuchungen zur Entstehung der Heuneburg in der späten Hallstattzeit*. Forschungen und Berichte zur Vor- und Frühgeschichte in Baden-Württemberg 105. Stuttgart: Theiss.
Kurz, S. & Schiek, S. 2002. *Bestattungsplätze im Umfeld der Heuneburg*. Forschungen und Berichte zur Vor- und Frühgeschichte in Baden-Württemberg 87. Stuttgart: Theiss.
Lambot, B., Friboulet, M. & Méniel, P. 1994. *Le site protohistorique d'Acy-Romance (Ardennes). II: Les nécropoles dans leur contexte régional*. Reims: Mémoire de la Société Archéologique Champenoise 8.
Menez, Y. 2009. *Le Camp de Saint-Symphorien à Paule (Côtes d'Armor) et les résidences de l'aristocratie du second âge du Fer en France septentrionale*. Paris 1: unpublished PhD thesis.
Menez, Y. 2012. Die Entshehung städtischer Siedlungen bei befestigten Adelssitzen des jüngeren Eisenzeit in Gallien: das Beispeil von Paule. In S. Sievers & M. Schönfelder (eds). *Die Frage der Protourbanisation in der Eisenzeit. La question de la proto-urbanisation à l'âge du Fer. Akten des 34. internationalen Kolloquiums der AFEAF vom 13.-16. Mai 2010 in Aschaffenburg*. 289-301. Bonn: Habelt.
Metzler, J. 1995. *Das treverische Oppidum auf dem Titelberg (G.-H. Luxemburg). Zur Kontinuität zwischen der spätkeltischen und der frührömischen Zeit in Nord-Gallien*. Luxembourg: Dossiers d'Archéologie du Musée National d'Histoire et d'Art 3.
Metzler, J. & Gaeng, C. 2009. *Goeblange-Nospelt: une nécropole aristocratique trévire*. Luxembourg: Dossiers d'Archéologie du Musée National d'Histoire et d'Art 13.
Metzler, J., Waringo, R., Bis, R. & Metzler-Zens, N. 1991. *Clemency et les tombes de l'aristocratie en Gaule Belgique*. Luxembourg: Dossiers d'Archéologie du Musée National d'Histoire et d'Art 1.
Metzler-Zens, N., Metzler, J., Méniel, P., Bis, R., Gaeng, C. & Villemeur, I. 1999. *Lamadelaine: une nécropole de l'oppidum du Titelberg*. Luxembourg: Dossiers d'Archéologie du Musée National d'Histoire et d'Art 6.
Meyer, M. & König, J. 2016. Mit Reiter und Wagen ins Jenseits – außergewöhnliche Grabfunde aus keltischen Grabhügeln bei Unlingen. *Archäologische Ausgrabungen in Baden-Württemberg* 2016, 120-3.
Milcent, P.-Y. 2004. *Le premier âge du Fer en France centrale*. Paris: Mémoire de la Société Préhistorique Française 34.
Milcent, P.-Y. 2012. Résidences aristocratiques et expérience urbaine hallstattiennes en France (VIe-Ve siècles av. J.-C.). In S. Sievers & M. Schönfelder (eds). *Die Frage der Protourbanisation in der Eisenzeit. La question de la proto-urbanisation à l'âge du Fer. Akten des 34. internationalen Kolloquiums der AFEAF vom 13.-16. Mai 2010 in Aschaffenburg*. 91-114. Bonn: Habelt.
Paunier, D. & Luginbühl, T. (eds) 2004. *Bibracte: le site de la Maison 1 du Parc aux Chevaux (PC 1) des origines de l'oppidum au règne de Tibère*. Collection Bibracte 8. Glux-en-Glenne: Centre Archéologique Européen.
Verger, S. 2006. La grande tombe de Hochdorf, mise en scène funéraire d'un cursus honorum tribal hors pair. *Siris* 7, 5-44.
Yvinec, J-H. 1992. Etude comparative de deux faunes, datées du Hallstatt, provenant de Bourges (Cher). In D. Vuaillat (ed.). *Le Berry et le Limousin à l'âge du Fer. Actes du XIIIe Colloque de l'A.F.E.A.F.*. 253-66. Guéret: Editions VERSO.

Chapter 22

Middle and Late La Tène rural aristocratic establishments in Gaul

Plans and organisation

Stephan Fichtl

22.1 Introduction

This article presents an assessment of high status establishments that are equated to aristocratic settlements. Rescue excavations and research projects in France over the last twenty years have led to the identification of sites with special characteristics dating to the end of the Iron Age (2nd-1st century BC) that might correspond to the domains of grand aristocrats known from the antique written sources.

22.2 Concerning the Gaulish *equites*...

Julius Caesar provides us with insights on Gaulish society, identifying the importance of the druids and the knights (*equites*). For the latter Caesar especially emphasizes the military aspect, with their power attested in the number of attendants and clients (Brunaux 1995, 146). In the passage known as 'the ethnographic excursus', Caesar refers to earlier authors, particularly Posidonios of Apameia, and so reflects an image of 2nd century BC society when Gaul was primarily an agrarian territory. The *equites* clearly owned large estates, and amongst the wealthiest of them were the members of the senate and the chief magistrates of each people. However, there is relatively little information about the senates of the *civitates* of Gaul (Fichtl 2012, 118-9). Caesar explicitly mentions eight *civitates* presided over by a senate, but their number may have been more extensive. As to the number of senators, the only reliable information concerns the senate of the Nervians which comprised 600 senators (Caesar BG II 28, 2). Beyond these details, certain rules for the formation of the senate are known, including among the Haedui, for example, that it was forbidden for two members of the same family to have a seat in the senate concurrently (Caesar BG VII 33, 3).

Another important issue for the Gaulish *equites* was the significance of their ancestry. Caesar regularly mentions the glorious ancestors or illustrious origin of one or other dignitary. But this is not the case for the Haeduan Dumnorix, who despite his tremendous wealth clearly felt it important to link himself to the major established Gaulish families by marriage of different members of his own family. He himself was married to the daughter of the Helvetian Orgetorix, "the first by birth and by his riches" (Caesar BG I 2, 1). He urged his mother to remarry a Biturigan person of rank, "one of the most noble and most powerful personages among the Biturigans" (Caesar BG I 18, 6). This demonstrates that

In D.C. Cowley, M. Fernández-Götz, T. Romankiewicz & H. Wendling (eds). Rural Settlement. Relating buildings, landscape, and people in the European Iron Age (Leiden 2019: Sidestone Press) 219-231.

there were two types of nobles in 1st century BC Gaulish society, one group depending on trade and tenure, as in the case of Dumnorix, and the other drawing on a long line of succession. The latter are the grand squires, a group that invites parallels with Republican Rome. Here we see the distinction between patricians on the one hand, belonging to the ancient and traditional superior class by birth, and on the other hand the order of the *equites* who aspire to high offices, as in the case of Cicero. In Gaul, it appears that the *senatores* formed a class of rich landowners, while the *equites* represented a class of military-magistrates and rich merchants.

22.3 The archaeological evidence for rural aristocratic settlements

In France, archaeological excavations over the last twenty years have led to a better understanding of the residences of the grand Gaulish families discussed above (Adam & Fichtl 2014). This archaeological evidence shows that even though part of the Gaulish elite established itself in *oppida*, it still retained control of its land in a similar manner to the senators of the Roman Republic, who possessed one or several *villae* on their estates besides their *domus* in Rome. The archaeological criteria by which the aristocratic status of a rural site might be established have been reviewed by François Malrain and Yves Menez (Malrain *et al.* 2002; Menez 2009; Adam & Fichtl 2014).

22.3.1 Dimension of the sites

One of the main markers for the identification of an aristocratic site is the size of the enclosure (Menez 2009), though he qualifies this by emphasizing an essential problem in using this criteria – that the sites are actually "composed of several enclosures which are fitted into each other or joined together. And moreover, around these, often allotments develop". Thus they differ from the majority of fortified sites, even from the German *Viereckschanzen*, which have a distinct demarcation. Menez therefore proposes "to limit oneself to the densely built-up areas which more often than not represent the living quarters complemented by one or two attached courts" (Menez 2009, 431).

However, it is difficult to test this criteria against the excavation record, as often only on the central part of a site has been excavated. While additional enclosures are known from aerial photography or geomagnetic prospection, neither method provides detailed information about the density of the occupation in these areas. Besides, certain sites present an astonishingly regular structure, as in the case of Batilly-en-Gâtinais (Loiret (Figure 1): Liégard & Fichtl 2015; Liégard & Fourvel 2017) or Génâts (Vendée (Figure 2): Nillesse 2007c). In order to assess their area the extent within the outermost enclosure delimiting these sites is used, even when extensive areas of the interior are unoccupied. At Batilly, for example, an esplanade of nearly 10 ha was left open at the centre of the site, but it is difficult to ignore it when establishing the total area of the site. In contrast, certain enclosures are surrounded by a large number of external buildings, clearly indicating a considerable extension beyond the main ditch system. Natteries (Maine et Loire (Figure 2): Maguer 2007) provides a good example. While the enclosure is only 1.2 ha in area, excavation revealed a dense spread of constructions beyond the enclosure extending over an area of at least 3.4 ha.

There is also evidence for considerable regional variability. In Picardie, the areas of high status establishments average about one hectare (Malrain & Pinard 2006), while in the southern Paris basin, an area extensively covered by aerial survey, sites regularly exceed 3 or 4 ha. Many of them, like Batilly (19.8 ha), Manchecourt (9.9 ha) and Marsainvilliers (15 ha), are exceptionally large and typically consist of two joined or interlinked enclosures. In order to fully understand these sites, it is necessary to consider the entire area, though this makes regional comparisons impossible. However, even if only the central enclosure is taken into consideration, these three sites are still among the largest (Batilly: 1.8 ha; Manchecourt: 1.4 ha; Marsainvilliers: 2.5 ha).

22.3.2 A clear division of space

The division of space is the principal criterion in Malrain´s four level classification of rural establishments (Malrain *et al.* 2002). This classification is predominantly functional, separating one enclosure used for aristocratic dwelling from a smaller enclosure housing agricultural facilities. Malrain compares this arrangement with the division of the large Roman *villae* of Gaul into *pars urbana* and *pars rustica*. The excavations at Batilly have since established that this organization is not of Roman origin, but can be clearly identified in Gaul since the 2nd century BC.

Batilly is typical of a group of nearly 20 similar sites that have been identified so far (Figure 1). It comprises a central enclosure 1.8 ha in area, set within a larger trapezoidal enclosure of nearly 20 ha. The buildings in the latter enclosure lie in a row along the longitudinal sides flanked by two palisades, with an esplanade in the middle which is nearly void of any construction. A second model of spatial arrangement for which over 66 examples can be identified comprises a square enclosure to which is attached a second, even larger enclosure of rectangular or trapezoidal form. One of the most prominent examples is the site of Aubigny (Vendée (Figure 3): Pétorin 2013) which comprises a quadrangular enclosure 80 m square, preceded by a rectangular enclosure almost 2 ha in extent. Agricultural buildings form long alignments parallel to the long sides of this enclosure.

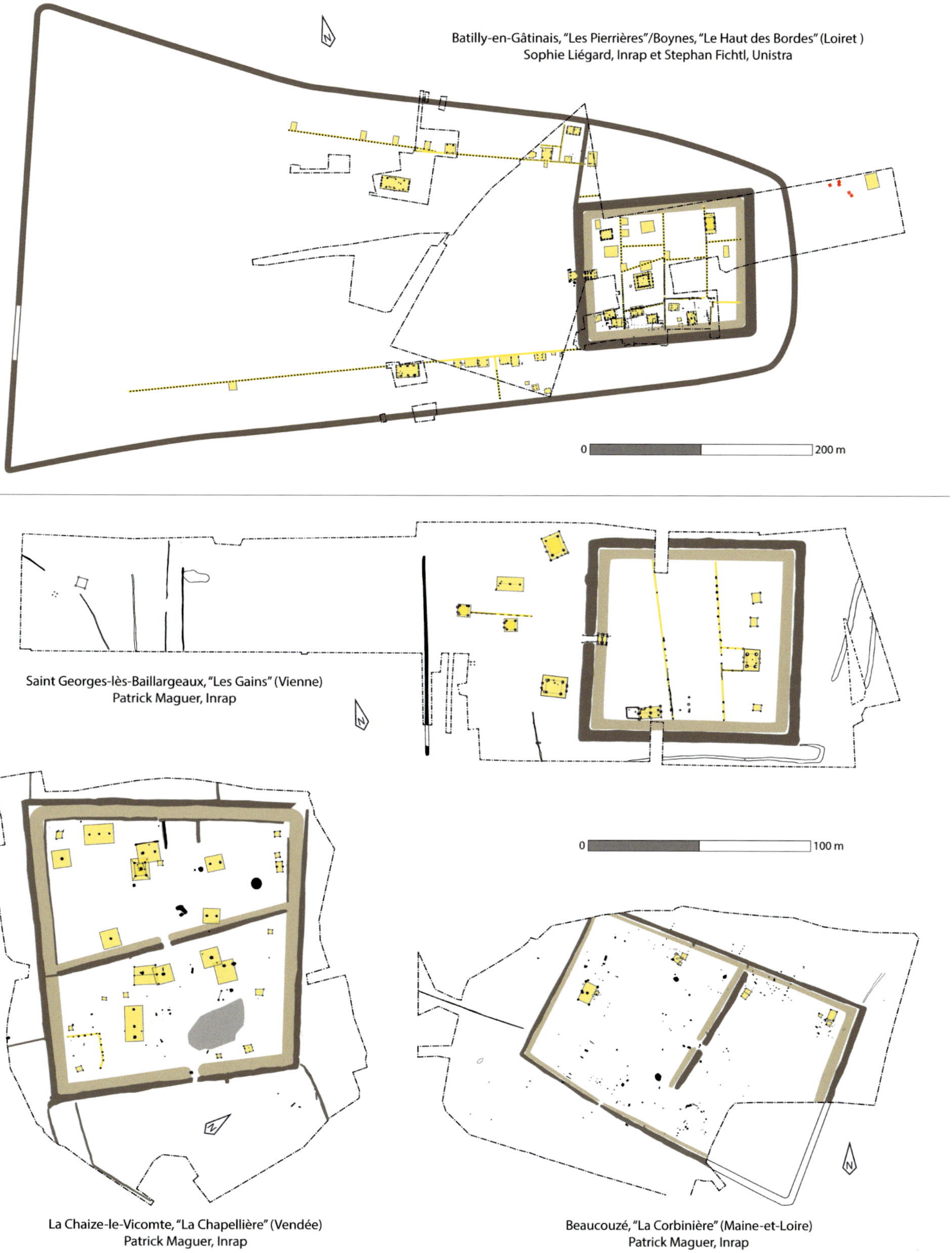

Figure 1: Plans of the rural establishments at Batilly-en-Gâtinais, Saint Georges-lès-Baillargeaux, La Chaize-le-Vicomte and Beaucouzé (Graphics: S. Fichtl).

Figure 2: Plans of the rural establishments at Natteries and Génâts (Graphics: S. Fichtl).

Figure 3: Plans of the rural establishments with attached courtyard at Aubigny, Varennes-sur-Seine, Savigny-le-Temple and Herblay (Graphics: S. Fichtl).

The region with the best representation of these complex sites is in the southern Paris basin. But the same layout is also found in other regions as illustrated by the sites of Aubigny and Grand Paisillier (Vendée: Nillesse 2007a), Douains in Normandy, and those at Baud and Crédin in Brittany. The size of these complex sites varies greatly between examples over 10 ha in extent and much smaller sites of only one hectare like Herblay (Val d'Oise, 0.9 ha (Figure 3): Valais 1994). Other examples, like Savigny-le-Temple and Varennes-sur-Seine (Seine-et-Marne (Figure 3)), hardly exceed this extent. The surroundings of Batilly, where numerous sites are documented on aerial photographs, illustrate this variety of size. Establishments like Barville-en-Gâtinais or Boynes, which are only some hundred metres away from Batilly are 5.5 ha and 4.3 ha in area respectively (Fichtl 2013a). In all other regions of Gaul these sites would be considered as of high status but seem rather modest in the immediate periphery of Batilly. Undoubtedly, these minor sites represent 'satellite establishments' constructed with reference to the principal site.

The enclosures of certain sites reveal an internal division in the form of a ditch or palisade separating residential and agricultural zones. Several examples reveal an exceptionally large building situated on the axis of the two entrances, clearly expressing an intentional layout. This central building is considered to have been the residence of the proprietor (Saint Georges-lès-Baillargeaux (Figure 1): Maguer *et al.* 2015; La Chaize-le-Vicomte (Figure 1): Maguer *et al.* 2005; Beaucouzé (Figure 1): Maguer & Lusson 2009). Although this characteristic is evident at certain sites interpreted as high status establishments, an internal division also exists at some more modest sites which do not show any aristocratic characteristics. This clearly indicates that subdivision and specialization of different spaces is not restricted to high status sites (for example, La Chaize-le-Vicomte and Beaucouzé).

22.3.3 Dimensions of the ditches

The size of the ditches, which is highly variable, is another element used for the definition of the sites. While the average depth is around 1.30 m, the range extends from only a few decimetres in depth to over 3 m (Menez 2009). In Gaul there are about thirty sites with ditches over 2 m or even 3 m in depth. These include Paule (Côtes d'Armor (Figure 4): Menez 2009; 2012) at 4.50 m deep and 11 m across, Bourguébus (Calvados) where part of the ditch is 4.50 m deep and 6.20 m across, Batilly-en-Gâtinais at 3.50 m deep and some 7 to 8 m across, Natteries at 3.40 m deep and 8 m across, and Coulon (Deux-Sèvres) where the principal enclosure ditch is 3 m deep and 7 m across. The digging of such large ditches demands a certain organization and a lot of human resource, and it may have been the privilege of rich proprietors who were able to undertake such works. Menez identifies that for ditches greater than 2.5 m in depth the evacuation of the material dug out becomes a veritable problem (Menez 2009; 2012). The dimensions of some of these ditches indicates a defensive function – especially when a rampart of comparable dimensions is added to the picture. At Batilly, the base of this rampart could be observed in the excavation and was more than 8 m across. We can therefore assume a defensive system of rampart and ditch with a footprint of more than 16 m and an overall height from the base of the ditch to the top of rampart (including a wooden parapet) of nearly 7 m.

The large sites of more than 3 ha are generally delimited by massive ditches (depths of more than 2 m), but these may also be evident at smaller sites. In some cases the largest ditches may enclose only one part of the site – for example at Batilly where the 3.50 m deep ditch surrounds the inner enclosure of 1.8 ha, while at Natteries the 1.1 ha enclosure is defended by a ditch 3.40 m in depth. At these two examples the large ditch only constitutes one part of the site, and the rest is delimited by a more modest construction (at Batilly the outer ditch measures 1.70 in depth). In some cases outer defences cannot be identified archaeologically at all.

22.3.4 A monumental entrance

The form of the entrances is closely linked to the ditch and the rampart, and usually the ditch is interrupted at the entrance through the rampart bank. However, in numerous cases there is no interruption in the course of the ditch at the entrance, clearly indicating a bridge or similar structure across the ditch.

At the monumental sites, the entrance is flanked by two big posts suggesting a substantial porch or gate. The posts are situated on the inside of the ditch at a distance that indicates the extent of the former rampart. This arrangement occasionally contains four posts forming a rectangular building behind the rampart, as is the case at Saran (Maguer & Robert 2013) or at Villavard (Maguer & Lusson 2009).

In rare cases the entrance construction is monumental, as at Inguiniel (Figure 4; Tanguy 2000), Saint-Georges (Figure 1) or Batilly (Figure 1), with the monumentality clearly linked to the status of the site. The principal entrance at Batilly shows several building phases identifiable through two series of posts that hold back the mass of the rampart on both sides. The latter is closed by a large twelve-post gatehouse. In a later phase a second gatehouse is built outside the ditch. At Saint-Georges the gatehouse is built on six posts closing the access to the enclosure. Two balustrades protected the passage between the two wings of the ditch in front of this gate.

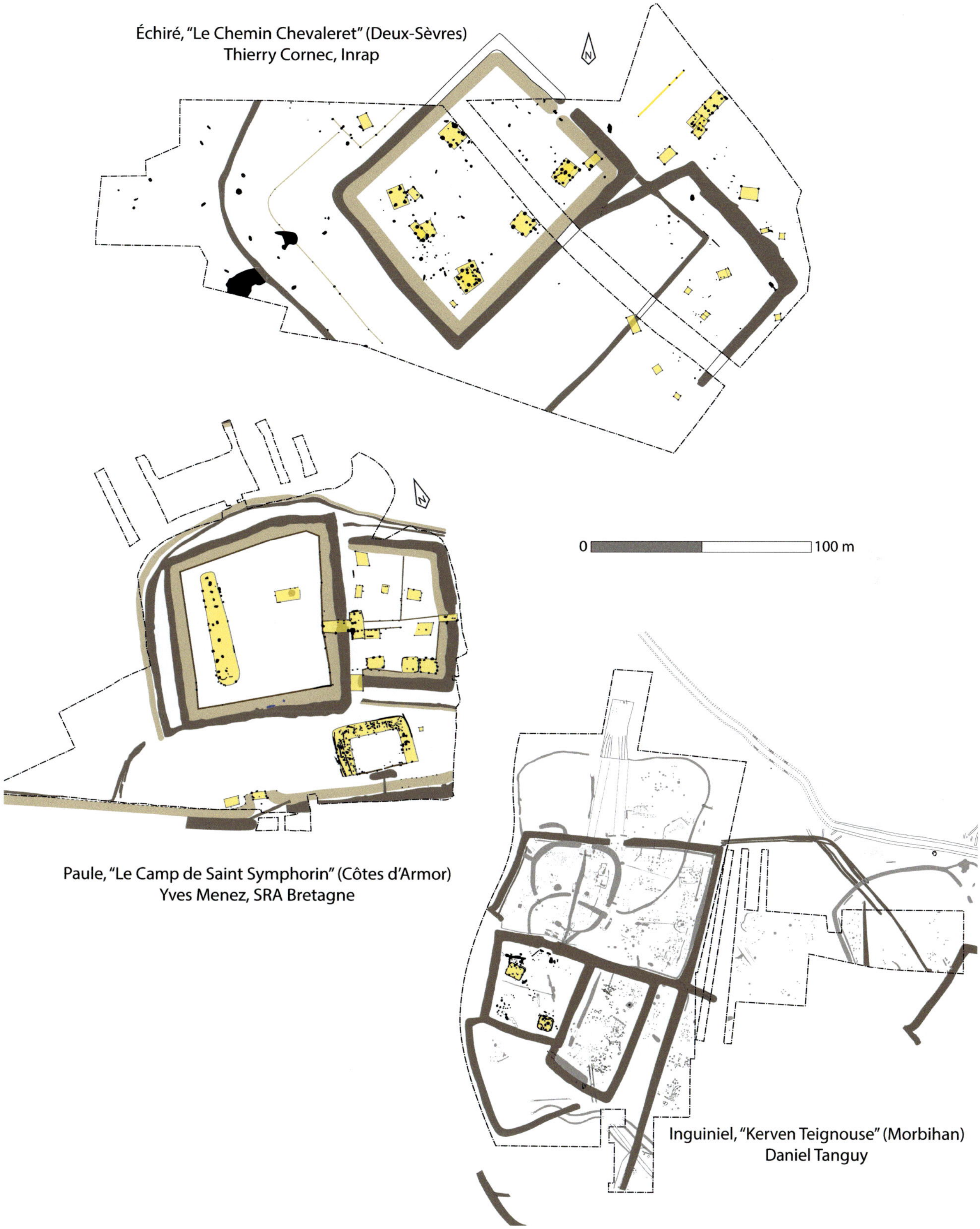

Figure 4: Plans of the rural establishments at Chemin Chevaleret, Paule and Inguiniel (Graphics: S. Fichtl).

22.3.5 *Quality of architecture*

Architecture may be characterised according to building plans as well as to the layout of structures, and from the materials used and/or the degree of decoration. At Batilly, several buildings have ground plans of more than 200 m^2 and even 300 m^2. Their layout consists of six big posts surrounded by a wooden wall, thus creating a spacious area in the centre. This elaborate construction, which relies only on outer posts, clearly proves Celtic architectural mastery (Fichtl in press a). The central building of Saint-Georges is more modest than many examples, but has a forecourt that suggests that it might have been a formal building. At Les Natteries a notably sumptuous building is flanked by buildings that together form an open courtyard. This resembles a structure found at Paule which was used for housing animals, and may have been a stables, according to chemical analysis.

At Batilly, remains of painting on daub in geometric patterns and rosette decoration made with a compass have been documented. One of the pigments is Egyptian blue, the first synthetically composed silicate of copper and calcium. Known in Egypt since the middle of the 3rd millennium BC, it was produced at Pozuolli at least since the 1st century BC according to Vitruvius (Cavassa *et al.* 2010). The pigment used at Batilly must have been imported from Campania, if not from Egypt.

Architectural influences from Italy are attested at some settlements, including tiles (*tegulae* and *imbrices*) dating to the 2nd century BC (LT D1) at Lyon-Vaise (Rhône) and Sennecé-lès-Mâcon (Saône-et-Loire: Clément 2015). The clay and comparisons with local dolia suggests local production, probably from a single workshop between Vienne and Mâcon. The site of Lyon-Vaise exhibits further architectural elements of Mediterranean origin in the roof of the entrance tower. This was made from limestone slabs (*opus pavonaceum*), the stone coming from the region of Saint-Rémy-de-Provence, more than 200 km to the south. Another building had tiled roofing and walls decorated in stucco, with a further monumental building incorporating an open portico over a walkway which was built on posts, the walls being made of wattle and daub. The walls were decorated with paintings in the first Pompeian style, comprising a relief or incised decoration accentuated by polychrome painting in red, black and yellow, forming panels of rhombs or bands. This building is also roofed in tiles. Lyon-Vaise has been the subject to numerous interpretations – banquet hall, sanctuary, emporium or aristocratic residence. The latter hypothesis is favoured by the researchers from Lyon especially in comparison with the site of Batilly as both share certain similarities in their general organization (Maza & Clément 2016).

A final example at Arnac-la-Poste exhibits peculiar architectural details. The trapezoidal enclosure of 1.5 ha, is bounded by ditch 4 m across and 1.85 m deep, and is notable for two reasons. Firstly, there are the fragmented remains of almost 840 wine amphorae and, secondly, its buildings show special architectural features (Poux 2004; Toledo i Mur 1999). The two main buildings are constructed in the Mediterranean tradition with adobe walls resting on a stone foundation and a tiled roof. Ceramic cattle head figures were initially interpreted as antefixes, though more recent studies suggest *bucrania* forming a mural decoration (Clément 2013). There are numerous hypotheses concerning the function of the site. The excavator, Assumpció Toledo i Mur, proposed an *emporium*, the storage facility of an Italian merchant or a strongly Romanised Gallic wine merchant, while Matthieu Poux proposed a 'banqueting hall'. But in the light of the new perceptions of rural Gaulish habitation and especially the analysis of Batilly and Lyon-Vaise, the idea of an aristocratic Gaulish residence seems to be the most likely interpretation (Fichtl 2013b).

22.3.6 *Sanctuaries and/or cemeteries*

Recent excavations have shown that rural settlements were regularly connected with small cemeteries that can be related to the proprietors and their families. These burials indicate the social status of the owners of the establishments. They can be rather modest and without important furnishing as at Oject'Ifs Sud near Caen (Le Goff 2009) or at Jaux (Malrain *et al.* 1996). However, other graves such as at Chevilly (Josset 2015) and even more distinctly the wagon grave at Orval (Figure 5; Lepaumier *et al.* 2010) reveal distinct aristocratic traits.

The presence of a small sanctuary is also an important element indicating the high grade of a rural site. At present, Génâts is the only site definitely associated with a small sanctuary. A small rectangular palisaded enclosure 17 m across was detected approximately 50 m south of the settlement enclosure, at which amphora fragments, pottery sherds, and a bent spearhead (as an explicit sign of sacrifice) were found. Moreover, the skeleton of a sheep had been deposited in the northern ditch. This ensemble could also represent the scattered remains of a funerary monument, but an interpretation as a small cult enclosure belonging to the adjacent settlement is rather more probable (Poux & Nillesse 2003). Lacking any associated finds, a small square enclosure measuring 9.2 m across at Teuilles has the same orientation and some similarities to the sanctuary at Génâts (Figure 2; Bouvet *et al.* 2003).

Moreover, crouched inhumations are an obvious sign of cult practice. This type of inhumation is attested in a large part of Gaul, for instance at Acy-Romance or in sanctuaries like Saint-Just-en-Chaussée. Similar features are known at Batilly (Figure 1, Liégard & Pecqueur 2014), where five small quadrangular pits (0.70 to 0.90 m in length) containing the remains of individuals buried in a sitting position have been excavated east of the main

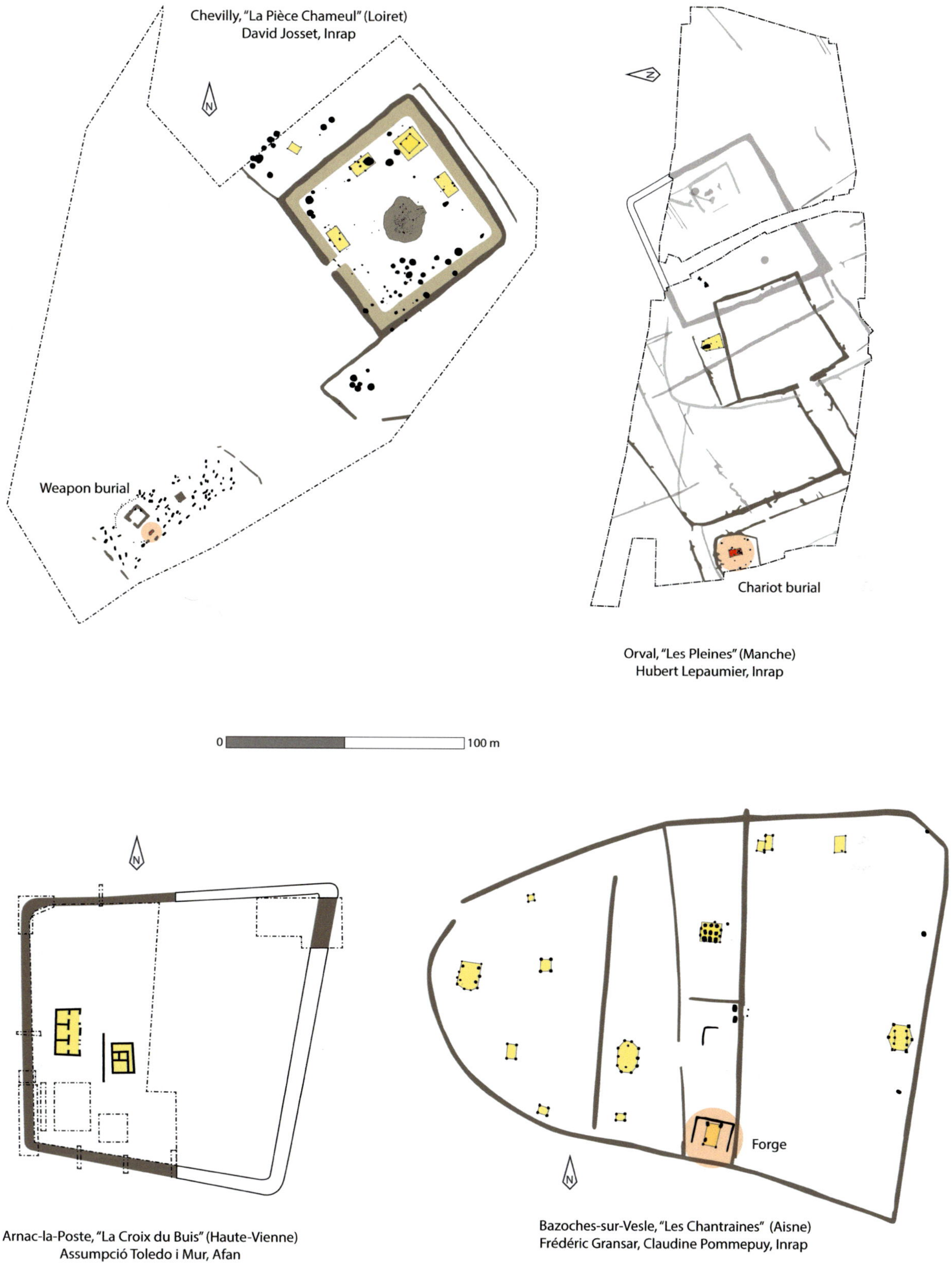

Figure 5: Plans of the rural establishments at Chevilly, Orval, Arnac-la-Poste and Bazoches-sur-Vesle (Graphics: S. Fichtl).

enclosure. They were positioned on their left ankle so that the right knee was elevated. No finds could be associated with the burials, but not far away the complete skeleton of a cow lay in a pit and a small ditched enclosure some 10 to 12 m across was also documented. These features represent a particular funerary and/or cultic character which is distant from the idea of a cemetery linked to the inhabitants of the site.

22.3.7 *Quality of finds*

Reflection on the potential role of finds in defining the status of a site demands a short preamble, in particular to address the question of how the finds found at a site really mirror its status? For example, at Batilly, one of those sites best meeting other criteria of an aristocratic residence, the quality of finds is rather poor. However, this does not reflect the status of the site, but is rather a result of a waste management regime which saw refuse transported outside of the enclosure, at best thrown into the peripheral ditches, but more often deposited much further away. In the larger estates, for example at Paule, there were many hands available for these tasks (Menez 2009, 439).

Objects made from precious materials or imports, like amphorae and Campanian pottery, directly reflect the wealth of the proprietor. However, there is considerable regional variability in the distribution of such objects. In certain regions like the Saône valley, amphorae are abundant on nearly all sites, while, by contrast, in Belgian Gaul or in the West amphorae are generally infrequent and the presence of even single objects is extraordinary. Thus, the site of Chemin Chevaleret is classified as particularly rich with 3135 fragments of approximately 134 amphorae (Nillesse 2007b).

Weaponry, armament or harnesses are linked with a military elite. Complete arms are rare finds, more often only fragments occur, indicating the presence of warriors in some of these settlements.

Traces of feasting also reflect aristocratic activities as Matthieu Poux has shown (Poux 2004). It is not only the presence of amphorae which can sometimes be found in larger numbers on rural sites, but also assemblages which indicate special activities. The site of Sarrewerden (Bas-Rhin) with a ditch 1.40 m deep and 2 m across was not extensively excavated but provided more than 400 amphorae (6044 sherds). This amount greatly exceeds the number of amphorae in any of the contemporary rural sites in Alsace. These amphorae show traces of damage, which is generally seen in relation with banquets, such as chipped bottlenecks, severed handles or cut off bases (Féliu & Olmer 2013). Feasting is also suggested at Batilly, where more than 200 amphorae (3000 sherds) were found in the principal ditch, some of which showed cutmarks on the necks (Liégard & Fourvel 2017).

Works of art are only exceptionally found in rural settlements. In Gaul, the sites of Paule and Batilly are worth mentioning. At Paule, four stone sculptures depicting humans were found, one of these carrying a torque and a lyre. This is interpreted as an example of genealogical memory (Menez *et al.* 1999). A comparable human representation is the sculptured limestone head from Mšecké Žehrovice, Bohemia (Venclová 1998), found at a double quadrangular enclosure which can also be considered as an aristocratic residence. At Batilly, a small bronze statue of a griffin might point to similar concepts (Liégard & Fourvel 2017). The statue is hollow and open at the back – a rotatable hook at the front is attached to an axe which is held by the claws of the bird. In the absence of any comparable items, the function of this object remains obscure but its quality makes it an exceptional find. The rarity of these objects in habitation contexts, and even more so in a rural context, stresses their importance.

Three sites in Gaul have produced remarkable examples of coin hoards. In 1992, a hoard of 242 staters of the 'globules à la croix' type dating to around 70-60 BC was found in a post hole at Saint-Denis-lès-Sens (Barrandon *et al.* 1993). Certainly, the site does not correspond to any of the other aristocratic criteria. Yet, the weight of gold represented by this treasure cannot easily be correlated with a modest landowner. It rather constitutes a deposition related to a special event without reference to the status of the site. A hoard of 545 electrum coins (58 staters, 487 quarters of staters) was found at the rural site of Laniscat in 2007 (Nieto-Pelletier *et al.* 2013). Even if the first phase-size of the site, dating to the mid-3rd century BC, exceeds the surrounding estates, it is still mainly associated with agricultural activities like grain storage and milling. The hoard dating to the mid-1st century BC is linked to a period of transition between this grand enclosure and a more modest one established in the second half of the 1st century BC. The importance of this hoard once again increases the problem of its association with the rural site. Can it be connected with agricultural activities or is it linked to the military elements of the Gaulish war where coin hoards are often seen in connection with the guerdon of troops engaged against Caesar?

Finally, a hoard of 1111 Gaulish *quinarii* was found at the rural settlement of Bassing in 2010 (Guihard *et al.* 2013). This three phase site initially comprised a farm bounded by a ditch 2-3 m across dating to 80-30 BC. This farm is succeeded by a palisaded enclosure of Augustan date and then transformed into a Roman villa in the 1st century AD. The hoard is connected with the Augustan phase where the site seems to be the least monumental. It might represent the pay of Celtic auxiliary forces under the command of the proprietor of this domain.

None of these three examples shows any evident connection between the status of the site and wealth of the respective high value finds. In this case, it seems to be the military aspect and more precisely the funding of the troops that best explains the finds rather than the inherent status of the site. Thus, finds of monetary treasures do not appear to be useful criteria to prove any aristocratic quality of a rural Gaulish establishment.

22.4 Conclusion

Various criteria allow for an attribution of aristocratic status to rural domains, but these are rarely found together on a single site. While on the one hand certain sites like Batilly or Paule demonstrate a significant number of criteria, others only present one or two.

The residences of the Gaulish aristocracy reveal a great diversity, directly reflecting the hierarchy and the social and economic status of the proprietors. Indeed, the rural settlements reflect the pyramidal structure of Gaulish society with some eminent families at the top providing senators, magistrates or even kings. At a subordinate level, there are the clients of more modest lineage or lesser wealth, in turn without doubt representing still further levels inside this social class. The diversity of the residences perfectly mirrors the heterogeneity of this group which includes families of very divergent condition and status.

While in western Gaul, in Normandy, and Brittany enclosed sites are frequent in the 5th century BC, in the rest of northern Gaul this phenomenon – with a multiplication of rural establishments – is attested only from the 3rd century BC onwards. The 2nd century BC seems to be the period when the most important rural sites are established, like Batilly, founded around 150 BC, Lyon-Vaise around 140/130 BC, Saint-Georges-lès-Baillargeaux around 125 BC, or Génats at the end of the 2nd century BC. There are further sites as examples of this phase of monumentalisation, for example Natteries, where the last rearrangement takes place in the second half of the 2nd century BC, and also phase IV at Paule when a rampart surrounding an area of 10 ha is constructed. These dates roughly correspond with the foundation of the *oppida* in the last quarter of the 2nd century BC. If the first phase of the site of Aubigny dates to the beginning of the 2nd century BC then its embellishment with two courts has to be placed rather at the end of the 2nd century BC. This raises the question of whether the two phenomena emerged in parallel as interlinked developments, despite a slight lag in the process of monumentalisation in the rural world?

22.5 Acknowledgements

My thanks to the Archaeological Society of the Puiseaux region, in particular Dominique Godefroy and Christophe Devilliers, who provided unpublished inventories of aerial photographs. Thanks also to Andrea Zeeb-Lanz (Speyer) who translated the text.

22.6 Bibliography

Adam, A.-M. & Fichtl, S. 2014. L'aristocrate des villes et l'aristocrate des champs : où les élites celtiques habitaient-elles ? In S. Bourdin, J. Dubouloz & E. Rosso (eds). *Peupler et habiter l'Italie et le monde romain.* 43-52. Aix-en-Provence: Presses de L'Université de Provence.

Barrandon, J.-N., Dhenin, M., Fischer, B. & Pradat, R. 1993. Le trésor de Saint-Denis- Lès-Sens, le point sur une étude en cours. *Bulletin de la Société Française de Numismatique* 48, 637-44.

Bouvet, J.-P., Daire, M.-Y., Le Bihan, J.-P., Nillesse, O., Villard-Le Tiec, A., Batt, M. & Bizien-Jaglin, C. 2003. La France de l'Ouest (Bretagne, Pays de la Loire). *Gallia* 60, 75-105.

Brunaux, J.-L. 1995. Religion gauloise et religion romaine. La leçon des sanctuaires de Picardie. *Cahiers du Centre Gustave Glotz* 6, 139-61.

Cavassa, L., Delamarre, F. & Repoux, M. 2010. La fabrication du bleu égyptien dans les champs phlégréens (Campante, Italie) durant le Ier siècle de notre ère. In P. Chardron-Picault (ed.). *Aspects de l'artisanat en milieu urbain: Gaule et occident romain.* 235-49. Dijon: Revue archéologique de l'Est.

Clément, B. 2013. *Les couvertures en tuiles de terre cuite en Gaule du Centre-Est (IIe s. av. -IIIe s. ap. J.-C.).* Montagnac: Éditions Monique Mergoil.

Clément, B. 2015. Approvisionnement et organisation de la production de terre cuite architecturale en Gaule. L'exemple de la colonie de Lugdunum (Lyon). *Archeologia dell'Architettura* 20, 158-67.

Féliu, C. & Olmer, F. 2013. Un enclos fossoyé à Sarrewerden (Bas-Rhin). *Bulletin de l'AFEAF* 31, 45-8.

Fichtl, S. 2012. *Les peuples gaulois. IIIe-Ier s. av. J.-C.* Paris: Editions Errance.

Fichtl, S. 2013a. À propos des résidences aristocratiques de la fin de l'âge du Fer : l'exemple de quelques sites du Loiret. In S. Krausz, A. Colin, K. Gruel, I. Ralston & T. Dechezleprêtre (eds). *L'âge du Fer en Europe.* 329-43. Bordeaux: Ausonius.

Fichtl, S. 2013b. Les « sites à banquets » : un mythe de l'archéologie celtique ? In C. Grandjean, C. Hugoniot & B. Lion (eds). *Le banquet du monarque dans le monde antique.* 425-51. Rennes-Tours.

Fichtl, S 2014. Dumnorix, un nouveau riche ? Portrait d'un aristocrate gaulois In G. Alberti, C. Féliu & G. Pierrevelcin (eds). *Transalpinare.* 171-80.

Guihard, P.-M., Laffite, J.-D. & Thomashausen, L. 2013. De l'argent pour la guerre. Le trésor monétaire de Bassing (Moselle). *L'Archéologue* 124, 33-7.

Josset, D. 2015. Chevilly, La Pièce Chameul. In A. Ferdière & T. Guiot (eds). *Les sites archéologiques de l'autoroute A19 (Loiret)*. 111-6. Tours: FERACF.

Le Goff, E. 2009. Habitats, terroir et paysage rural: aménagement et structuration du territoire et de la campagne gauloise Ifs, ZAC "Object'Ifs Sud" (Calvados). In I. Bertrand, A. Duval, J. Gomez de Soto & P. Maguer (eds). *Habitats et paysages ruraux en Gaule et regard sur d'autres régions du monde celtique*. 93-107. Chauvigny: Association des Publications Chauvinoises.

Lepaumier, H., Giazzon, D, & Chanson, K. 2010. Orval, « Les Pleines » (Manche). Habitats enclos et tombe à char en Cotentin. In P. Barral, B. Dedet, F. Delrieu, P. Giraud, I. Le Goff, S. Marion & A. Villard-Le Tiec (eds). *L'âge du Fer en Basse-Normandie*. 315-33. Besançon: Presses Universitaires de Franche-Comté.

Liegard, S. & Pecqueur, L. 2014. Les inhumés assis laténiens de Batilly-en-Gâtinais (Loiret), *Gallia* 71-2, 89-101.

Liégard, S., & Fichtl, S. 2015. Batilly-en-Gâtinais, « Les Pierrières », Établissement aristocratique de la fin de l'âge du Fer (IIe s. av. n. è. au déb. Ier s. de n. è.). In A. Ferdière & T. Guiot (eds). *Les sites archéologiques de l'autoroute A19 (Loiret)*. 187-94. Tours: FERACF.

Liégard, S. & Fourvel A. 2017. « Les Pierrières » à Batilly-en-Gâtinais (Loiret). Présentation d'un site gaulois hors norme, *Revue Archéologique du Loiret* 38, 34-54.

Maguer, P. 2007. Le site aristocratique des Natteries, Le Puy-Saint-Bonnet (Maine-et-Loire). In I. Bertand & P. Maguer. *De pierre et de terre. Les Gaulois entre Loire et Dordogne, catalogue d'exposition*. 78-80. Chauvigny: Association des Publications Chauvinoises.

Maguer, P., Arthuis, R. & Hiernard, J. 2005. L'établissement rural de la Chapellière à la Chaize-le-Vicomte (Vendée): une ferme gauloise de la fin du deuxième âge du Fer (IIe siècle-Ier siècle a. C.). *Aquitania* 21, 21-72.

Maguer, P., Linlaud, M. & Bertrand, I. 2015. Parure, éléments de serrure et autre mobilier métallique de l'établissement rural des Gains à Saint-Georges-lès-Baillargeaux (LT D1b-LT D2b) (Vienne, F): morceaux choisis. In S. Raux, I. Bertrand & M. Feugère. *Actualité de la recherche sur les mobiliers non céramiques de l'Antiquité et du haut Moyen Âge*. 181-209. Montagnac/ Chauvigny: Publi Chauvinoi.

Maguer, P. & Lusson, D. 2009. Fermes, hameaux et résidences aristocratiques entre Loire et Dordogne. In I. Bertrand, A. Duval, J. Gomez De Soto & P. Maguer (eds). *Habitats et paysages ruraux en Gaule et regard sur d'autres régions du monde celtique*. 423-59. Chauvigny: Association des Publications Chauvinoises.

Maguer, P. & Robert, G. 2013. La maison gauloise dans l'Ouest et le Centre de la France. In S. Krausz, A. Colin, K. Gruel, I. Ralston & T. Dechezleprêtre (eds). *L'âge du Fer en Europe*. 247-58. Bordeaux: Ausonius.

Malrain, F. & Pinard, E. 2006. Les sites laténiens de la moyenne vallée de l'Oise du Ve au Ier s. avant notre ère. Amiens: *Revue archéologique de Picardie*. N° sp. 23.

Malrain, F., Matterne, V. & Méniel, P. 2002. *Les paysans gaulois, IIIe siècle – 52 avant J.-C.* Paris: Errance.

Malrain, F., Gransar, F., Matterne V. & Le Goff, I. 1996. Une ferme de La Tène D1 et sa nécropole : Jaux «Le Camp du Roi» (Oise). In La chronologie du second âge du fer en Gaule du Nord, *Revue archéologique de Picardie* 3-4, 245-306.

Maza, G. & Clément, B. 2016. Les processus de romanisation à Lyon à la fin du Second âge du Fer. Entre traditions indigènes et influences méditerranéennes. In G. Blancquaert & F. Malrain (eds). Évolution des sociétés gauloises du Second âge du Fer, entre mutations internes et influences externes, 531-54. Amiens: Revue Archéologique de Picardie.

Menez, Y. 2009. *Le Camp de Saint Symphorien à Paule (Côtes d'Armor) et les résidences de l'aristocratie du second âge du Fer en France septentrionale*, Thèse de doctorat, Université de Paris 1, Panthéon-Sorbonne.

Menez Y. 2012. Die Entstehung städtischer Siedlungen bei befestigten Adelssitzen der jüngeren Eisenzeit in Gallien: Das Beispiel von Paule (Côtes d'Armor). In S. Siervers & M. Schönfelder (eds). *Die Frage der Protourbanisation in der Eisenzeit. La question de la proto-urbanisation à l'âge du Fer*. 289-301. Bonn: AFEAF.

Menez, Y., Giot, P.-R., Laubenheimer, F., Le Goff, E. & Vendries, C. 1999. Les sculptures gauloises de Paule (Côtes-d'Armor). *Gallia* 56, 357-414.

Nieto-Pelletier, S., Gratuze, B. & Aubin, G. 2013. Le dépôt monétaire Gaulois de Laniscat (Côtes-d'Armor): 547 monnaies de bas titre ; étude préliminaire. *International Numismatic Congress Proceedings of the XIVth International Numismatic Congress* 2, 1217-26.

Nillesse, O. 2007a. L'établissement rural du Grand Paisilier à Pouillé (Vendée). In I. Bertand & P. Maguer. *De pierre et de terre. Les Gaulois entre Loire et Dordogne, catalogue d'exposition*. 72-4. Chauvigny: Association des Publications Chauvinoises.

Nillesse, O. 2007b. La résidence aristocratique de Chemin Chevaleret à Échiré (Deux-Sèvres). In I. Bertand & P. Maguer. *De pierre et de terre. Les Gaulois entre Loire et Dordogne*, catalogue d'exposition. 81-2. Chauvigny: Association des Publications Chauvinoises.

Pétorin, N. 2013. *Aubigny, Vendée, la Pâquerie. Établissement rural La Tène finale – Ier s. AD* Rapport final d'opération. Nantes: SRA Pays de la Loire.

Poux, M. 2004. *L'âge du vin. Rites de boisson, festins et libations en Gaule indépendante*. Montagnac: Editions Mergoil.

Poux, M. & Nillesse, O. 2003. Le vin, le sang et le fer: un passage de Polybe (II, 19) et le rôle du vin importé dans les cultes indigènes de la fin de l'âge du Fer. In B. Mandy & A. de Saulce (eds). *Les marges de l'Armorique à l'âge du Fer: archéologie et histoire: culture matérielle et sources écrites*. 293-308. Rennes: AFEAF.

Tanguy, D. 2000. Le Site d'habitat de l'âge du Fer de Kerven-Teigouse à Inguiniel (Morbihan). *Revue archéologique de l'Ouest* 17, 143-73.

Toledo i Mur, A. 1999. La Croix du Buis (Arnac-la-Poste, Haute-Vienne). Un entrepôt du Ier siècle av. J.-C., *Aquitania* 15, 109-40.

Valais, A. 1994. La ferme des Fontaines. Herblay (Val-d'Oise). In O. Buchsenschutz & P. Méniel (eds). *Les Installations agricoles de l'âge du Fer en Île-de-France*. 113-24. Paris: Rue d'Ulm.

Venclová, N. 1998. *Mšecké Žehrovice in Bohemia. Archaeological background to a Celtic hero, 3rd-2nd cent. B. C.* Sceaux: Kronos.

Chapter 23

Scordiscan stronghold

A Late Iron Age multiple fortification at Bačka Palanka in northern Serbia

Holger Wendling

In D.C. Cowley, M. Fernández-Götz, T. Romankiewicz & H. Wendling (eds). Rural Settlement. Relating buildings, landscape, and people in the European Iron Age (Leiden 2019: Sidestone Press) 233-243.

23.1 A Late La Tène enclosure at Bačka Palanka

Flat sandy plains with large tracts of fertile, cultivated land on both banks of the Danube are a constituent component of the landscape in Serbian Vojvodina and Croatian Slavonia. Lying some 30 km west of Novi Sad, the modern town of Bačka Palanka is situated on the northern river bank. Some 5.5 km further north, in an area called "Turski Sanač" (*i.e.* "Turkish entrenchment"), aerial photographs have documented a soil mark revealing a bank or rampart which describes a square enclosure measuring some 150 m across internally (Figure 1). The photographs also show traces of ancient riverbeds which indicate that the site is situated on the northern edge of a formerly highly structured flood plain at approximately 84 m a.s.l. The northern side is disturbed by a cart track but is exceedingly well preserved at its western side where it still survives up to 1.8 m in height (peak elevation at c. 86.9 m a.s.l.). However, more precise dimensions for the structure are difficult to establish due to the erosion of the sandy body of the rampart. This has also caused the external ditch to be evident only as a very flat depression along all four sides of the enclosure. The view towards the slightly higher southern flank shows a rise in the centre of the rampart which might suggest the existence of some additional defensive work there. Recent rescue excavations some 150 m to the south revealed building structures as evidence of a Late La Tène *extra-muros* occupation. Previous excavations of the western part of the wall have revealed a Late La Tène period ceramic assemblage which correlates with the chronological phase Gomolava VIb (Brukner 1978, 10-2; Dizdar 2001, 125; Jovanović & Jovanović 1988, 193, 198; Jovanović 2012, 74-5; Lexikon 2012, 1883-4). This phase approximately covers the 1st century BC.

23.2 Hidden traces of a monumental fortress

In cooperation with the University of Belgrade, the Serbian Institute of Archaeology and the Museum of Vojvodina, the Romano-Germanic Commission (German Archaeological Institute) conducted large-scale geophysical survey in 2012, making a significant contribution to the understanding of the Late Iron Age settlement record of north-western Serbia and north-eastern Croatia (Rummel *et al.* 2012). The survey at Bačka Palanka was conducted using a vehicle-drawn system of 16 geomagnetic sensors (FMG

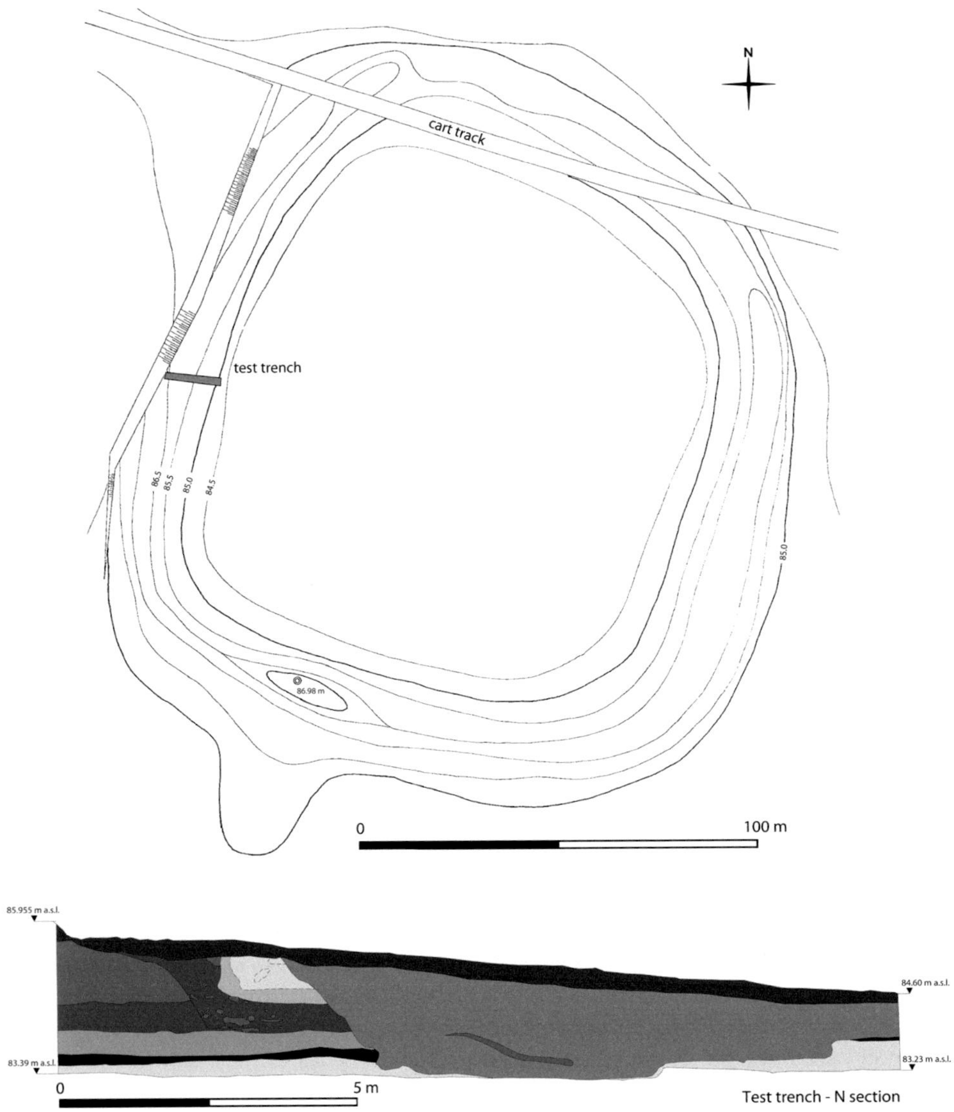

Figure 1: Bačka Palanka "Turski Šanac". Elevation plan and location of test trench excavated in the 1970s (After Brukner 1978, plan 1).

650 B; 0.25 m sensor distance, 1 s impulse frequency). Whereas the aerial photographs show only a general white substructure on the lines of both the rampart and the ditch, the geomagnetic mapping reveals a complex arrangement of positive and negative anomalies (Figure 2). These indicate a sequence of dug features (darker values) and upstanding supposedly stone-built remains (light grey or white values).

The width of the external ditch ranges from 12 m on the north to some 6 to 7 m on the south (Figure 3), though it is not clear if this difference reflects the original form or is due to later erosion of either ditch. Certainly, the geomagnetic data does not help to assess this issue, nor the ditch fill. The proximity to the Danube, which might have meandered further north in prehistory, and a high groundwater level might suggest a moat as an effective defensive measure.

The rampart is contiguous to the ditch without any evidence of a berm between them, though such a feature could have been obscured by slumping. This arrangement is nearly identical to the fortification at the slightly smaller site at Čarnok near Vrbas, some 30 km to the north. At this Late La Tène site, a 1.4 m broad bank of natural soil ran parallel to the rampart, possibly to prevent the earthen rampart from eroding into the ditch. Additionally, traces of a wooden framework with horizontal beams were identified in a cross section of the Čarnok rampart (Jovanović 2008, 71). Unfortunately, at Bačka Palanka, the section of the interior part of the western rampart does not substantially contribute to an understanding of the construction of the defensive works. However, the geomagnetic survey allows details of rampart construction to be detected. In the south and north there are linear positive anomalies within the line of the rampart, which might represent a stabilizing

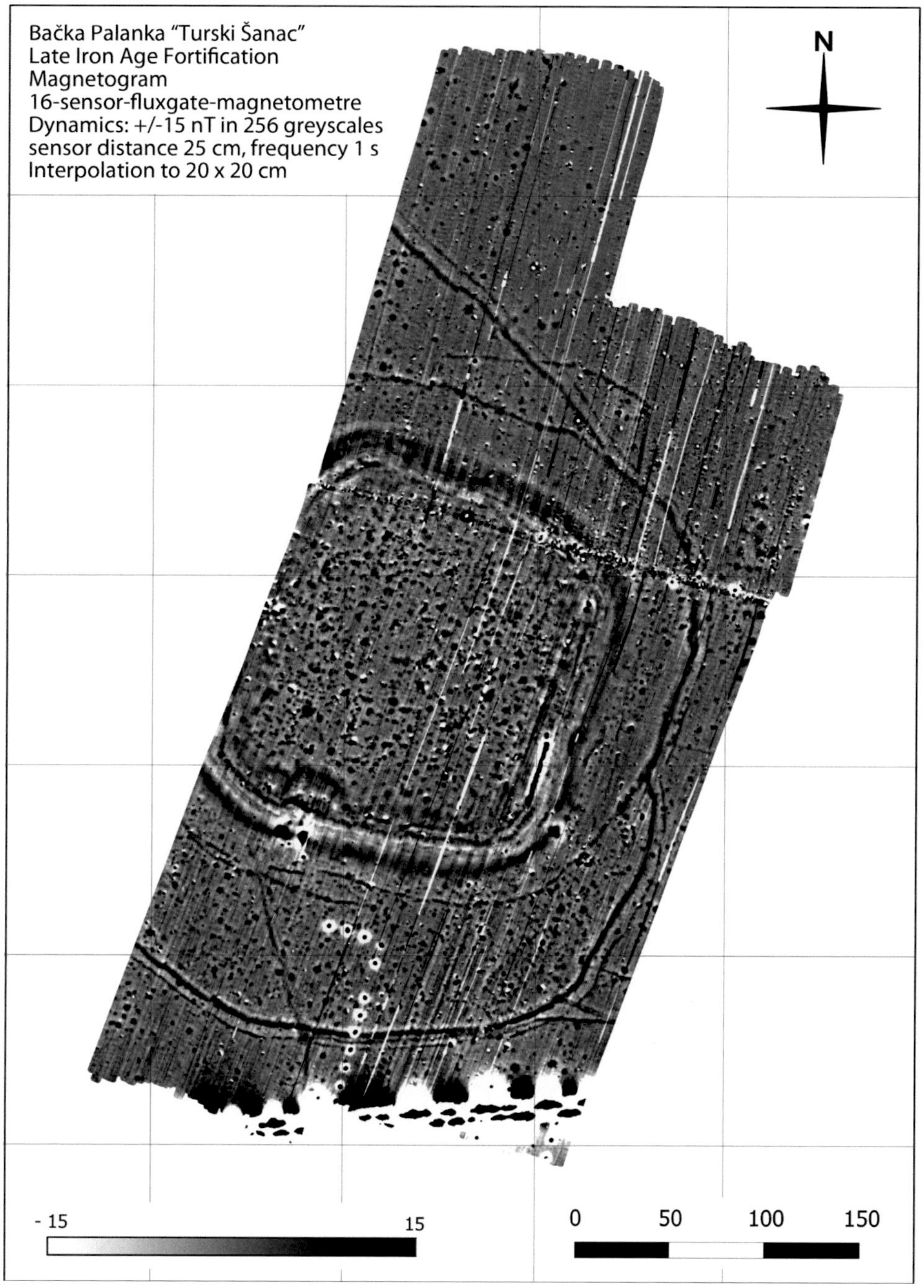

Figure 2: Bačka Palanka "Turski Šanac". Magnetogram of Late Iron Age fortification (Graphics: Römisch-Germanische Kommission and H. Wendling).

internal wooden structure set in small foundation ditches. Then again, they could also represent foundation ditches of a supplementary palisade on top of the earthen rampart. Alternatively, the parallel ditches could be traces of two-phase external wooden revetments of the wall. The negative anomalies on the external side of these ditches might thus be interpreted as stone debris, caused by the collapse of the rampart and its putative external facing – with an intentional reinforcement as a sort of drystone revetment a further possibility (Dizdar 2001, 115; Lexikon 2012, 1884).

Another parallel ditch with additional circular dug features runs at the internal face of the 4-5 m or 7-8 m thick rampart. Set at a distance of 2-3 m from each other, these circular anomalies seem to be large and might have been postholes for internal vertical beams. The vertical posts of *Pfostenschlitzmauern* or "Kelheim-type-ramparts" reinforce the faces of many eastern Celtic fortifications, for example in phases 2 and 3 at Manching (DE) (Sievers 2010; Wendling 2010). At Turski Šanac they might have supported an internal or upper wooden part of the fortification. Similar parapet walks or backward

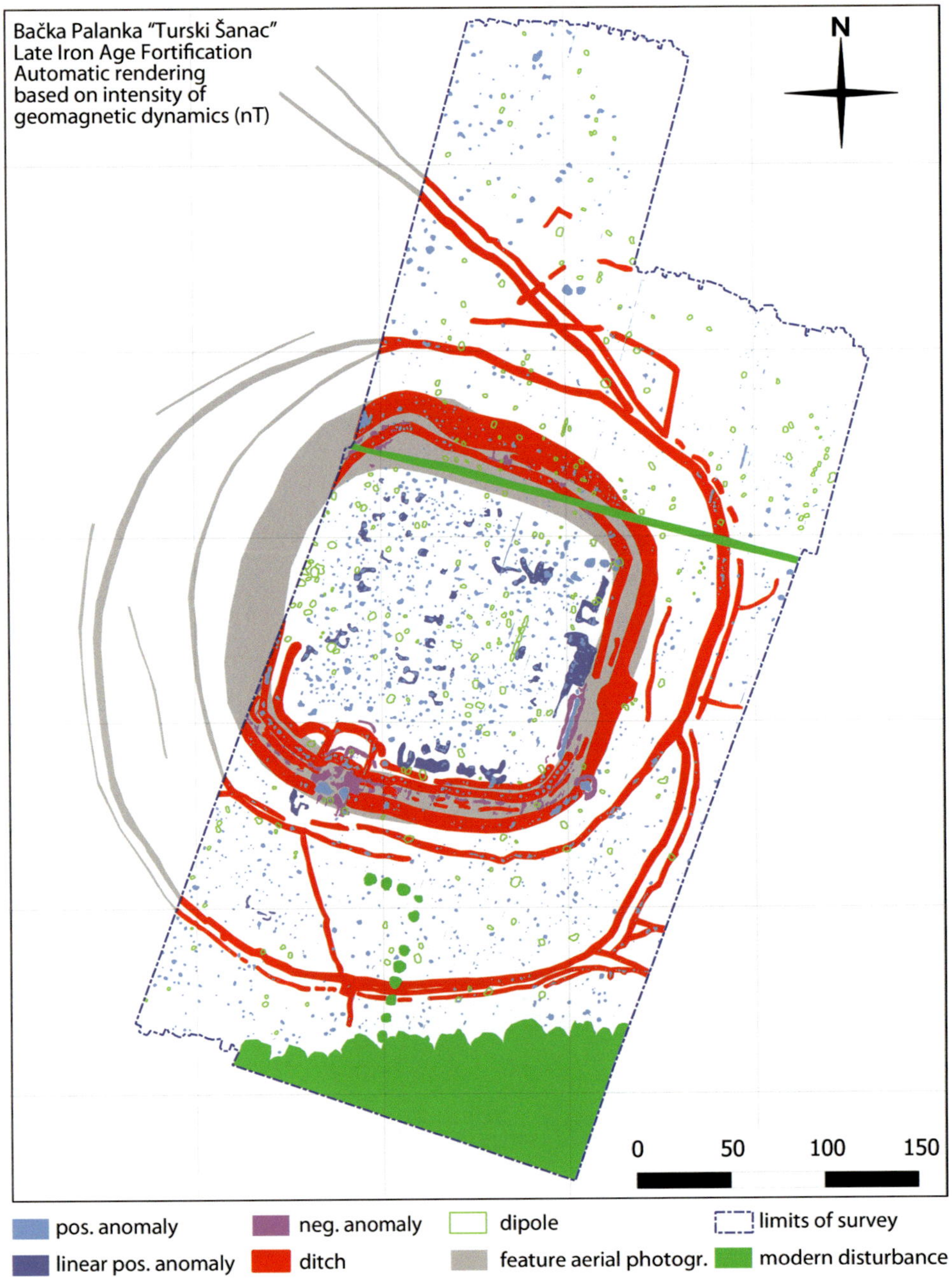

Figure 3: Bačka Palanka "Turski Šanac". Interpretation of the magnetic survey and aerial photographies of the Late Iron Age fortification (Graphics: Römisch-Germanische Kommission and H. Wendling).

reinforcements are attested in Roman legionary camps, and also at large Late Iron Age fortified sites, for example Gomolava (Jovanović & Jovanović 1988, 190).

The walls of the northern Balkan Late Iron Age fortifications, however difficult to date precisely, are frequently built of earthen material excavated from the ditch and local soil, sometimes including previous constructions into the rampart (Dizdar 2001, 128). At Bačka Palanka, the slightly dark zone that extends for up to 15 m behind the rampart might indicate a slight depression which can be traced in the cross section filled with dark earth of the cultural layer (Brukner 1978, plan 2). Soil for rampart construction had probably been stripped from this area. However, the broad negative anomaly of the rampart suggests the use of magnetic susceptible material like stone for wall construction. There is only evidence of a drystone wall at Stari Slankamen, whereas at Čardak near Mošorin turf divots from a nearby bog were used to build the fortification (Dimitrijević 1971, 571-2; Todorović 1971, 562-4). Test trenches at Turski Šanac suggest the existence of drystone foundations in the rampart. Complex rampart architecture is documented at Privlaka, Plavna, and Stari Mikanovci, while at Ravna there are vertical beams set between 0.2 and 0.5 m apart forming the external face of a drystone and soil rampart. The rear of the rampart consisted of vertical beams placed in 1 m steps with a wattle infill (Lexikon 2012, 1493, 1535-6). Traces of intense burning at several sites demonstrate a catastrophic end of the rampart rather than a deliberate measure to stabilize the construction, as has been occasionally suggested (Jovanović 1988/89; Majnarić-Pandžić 1996, 260). Similar traces of extreme heat are visible as a linear dipole near the south-eastern corner. Further traces of fire are visible at the gate and especially at the two-post bridge across the ditch. Together with the gatehouse in the wall it was destroyed by fire. The geomagnetic features of the monumental gate apparently reveal some characteristics at the inner side of the rampart – here a ditch encloses a square measuring 15 by 25 m that is attached to the gateway like an inner bailey. To the exterior some 12-15 m beyond the ditch, there is an additional palisade trench which blocked direct access to the bridge in a similar way to a Roman *titulum* gate system.

23.3 Dwelling, storage, and production

Beyond the gateway there are no traces of a road crossing the interior of the fort (Figures 2 & 3). Strong positive anomalies are scattered across much of the interior, though no patterning that indicates a planned layout of buildings can be recognised. There is however an oval area that is relatively free of anomalies in the centre of the interior (market place or place used for gatherings?), and an area free of anomalies in a band some 10-15 m across along the inner face of the rampart.

The overall size and number of anomalies strongly resembles the situation at Gomolava (Lexikon 2012, 665-6) and indicates a dense pattern of occupation and extended activity at Turski Šanac. A large number of the anomalies are in the size range that would be expected of rectangular semi-sunken dwellings of *Grubenhaus*-type. Indeed, test excavations at the inner western flank of the fortification revealed traces of such dwellings beneath a cultural layer of between 0.6 and 1.9 m in depth (Brukner 1978, 7). These buildings are frequently interpreted as economic constructions and workshops and thus might indicate an intense and diversified craftsmanship. However, corresponding houses at other sites in the eastern Celtic sphere and ethnographic evidence suggest that they were also regularly used for dwelling. They frequently occur in rural settlements, but are also a feature of fortified sites of the region (*e.g.* at Čarnok; Jovanović 2012, 74; Lexikon 2012, 300-1) and in urbanised central places, like at Manching (Leicht 2013, 78-93; Wendling 2018).

Other, smaller anomalies of dug features might represent storage pits and would thus fit well into a predominant agricultural and rural environmental setting. The 1970s test trench contained remains of pits possibly similar to those at Osijek or Sremska Mitrovica/Livade, for example (Brukner 1978, 7; Popović 1987, 113; Drnić & Skelac 2008). At Čarnok, some pits filled with settlement debris have been unearthed which were supposedly used for grain storage (Jovanović 2008, 78). However, a relatively high water table would compromise sub-surface storage of perishable goods, and this factor might support the interpretation of most of the smaller features as wells used for water-supply of a considerable population. There are a vast number of wells with wood-lined shafts at Manching, for example, which is situated in a similar natural environment (Leicht 2013, 110). The soil conditions might also explain other strategies like grain storage in baskets or above-ground wooden chests which have been excavated at Čarnok (Jovanović 2008, 78; 2011).

At Turski Šanac potential traces of above-ground buildings, like postholes or shallow ditches, cannot be identified amongst the large numbers of features in the geomagnetic record, which obscure smaller features in a similar way to geomagnetics at Manching. However, given the damp subsurface conditions, raised constructions like four-post granaries are likely. Moreover, the known buildings south of the external enclosure indicate the likelihood of similar structures in other parts of the settlement. Indeed, post-built structures are attested inside of the main fortification at Čarnok and at various other sites in the region (Dizdar 2001, 116; Jovanović 1994, 124; 2012, 74-5). Some of these have an elaborate, multi-purpose layout with special rooms or annex buildings (Jovanović 2012, 74-5), though at Turski Šanac, such remains have not yet been identified. Fragments of wall plaster illustrate construction details of both residential and estate buildings (Brukner 1978, 7; Jovanović & Jovanović 1988, 193). Some dipoles and other very intense anomalies might indicate remains of different sizes of ovens or hearths of the types that have been excavated in the interior of the Čarnok fortress – those were used as grain drying-kilns (Jovanović 2008, 78). At Turski Šanac such anomalies might also include pottery kilns and smithing hearths such as have been found at Gomolava and Osijek, for example (Jovanović & Jovanović 1988, 67-77; Majnarić-Pandžić 1996, 258-9).

23.4 Super size me! – monumentalising a site

Around the principal fortification, an area of 35 m is delimited by a narrow ditch, which becomes quite substantial around its northern course (Figures 2 & 3). In front of the gate the ditches overlap considerably to form a staggered gap. This, and the scarcity of features in this *intervallum* suggest a strategic purpose. Furthermore, there is a double or triple ditch system that forms an additional circuit around the south and east of the internal fortification. The strategic significance of the arrangement of the ditches with one or two small ditches (presumably holding palisades) running parallel to quite a substantial, 3 m broad ditch is not entirely clear. Indeed, there are several gaps in the external palisade ditch which indicate the presence of smaller gateways into the interior, and in these areas quite a few anomalies indicate dense occupation similar to that in the central area. The combination of the geomagnetic data and aerial photographic evidence shows a complex layout of ditches and palisades around the main fortification, raising a question of how big the overall size of the site was. While the inner fortification encloses an area of 2.3 ha, the medial system of ditches encloses more than 5.7 ha, while the outer ditch system takes in more than 8.5 ha. A further double ditch system protruding from the northern segment of the main ditch to the northwest was not tracked along its entire course, but considerably increases the structural extent of the settlement. Moreover, quite a few anomalies outside the outer ditch system indicate a considerable occupation beyond the fortification, confirmed by excavation of several post-built houses south of the external multiple-ditch system (pers. comm. M. Jevtic) and indicating that the extent of the site may not be defined by the ditches.

At present, the complex ditch system at Bačka Palanka appears to be a unique feature in Late Iron Age fortifications of the north-western Balkans. However, at several sites including Čarnok, there is evidence for occupation in the surroundings of the central fortification (Lexikon 2012, 302). However, it is difficult to establish whether this is contemporary to the fortification or not, especially as the extents of external dwelling zones are difficult to detect only by means of excavation. This challenges an assumption of unfortified settlements in the Late Iron Age, and the differentiation of unfortified or fortified phases at Čarnok needs to be reconsidered (Jovanović 1991, 124; 2012, 73-4). Moreover, speculations about a fortification in or around seemingly unenclosed settlements, for example at Osijek, have to be reviewed in the light of the evidence from Bačka Palanka, as the outer palisades and ditches here represent a substantial defensive system even though they are small in comparison with the monumental inner wall and ditch. In this case it is the additional evidence from survey that has revealed this monumentalisation, and for those sites without such evidence their form is now open to question.

23.5 Time and history

The ceramic assemblage at Bačka Palanka "Turski Šanac" is contemporary with the second fortified phase of Čarnok where two silver fibulae date to an advanced LT D1 or LT D2 (*i.e.* the last century BC). At Čarnok, too, a non-fortified phase is attested by Late La Tène pits beneath the rampart (Dizdar 2001, 119; Jovanović 2011, 130; 2012, 74-5; Lexikon 2012, 300-1). At Bačka Palanka, evidence of a multi-phase construction is limited to the stratigraphic sequence of external ditches and their layout (*e.g.* not strictly symmetrical arrangements of ditches and bifurcating lines of defence). The arrangement of the different ditch systems clearly indicates a phased process of settlement growth. The stratigraphy of the interior rampart section is blurred by the post-occupation erosion of the wall. At the most, the nearby coin hoard of Bački Obrovac is dated to LT D1 and might be related to an earlier phase at Turski Šanac (Lexikon 2012, 100) (Figure 4). The absence of Augustan ceramics indicates an end of occupation towards the turn of millennia, while the Čarnok fort might have continued a little later (Jovanović 2012, 75). The dating evidence shows that the establishment and development of the Bačka Palanka stronghold is framed by the complex political history documented by ancient sources, and in time this may support robust interpretations of settlement history and functional and strategic foundations (Dizdar 2001; Jovanović & Popović 1991; Popović 1992).

This background begins towards the end of the 4th century BC, when presumably "Celtic" groups spread into the area around the middle Danube and together with indigenous groups gradually transformed into the ethnic community of the *Scordisci* in a complex process of cultural adaptation, appropriation and amalgamation (Džino 2007). These groups were the principal part of the military power that tried to sack the Greek sanctuary at Delphi in 279 BC. After their defeat they retreated to their area of origin, the territory around the Danube and Sava rivers. Archaeological traces of characteristic features of La Tène art and material culture attest to the consolidation of Celtic communities in an area stretching some 350 km along the course of the middle Danube, from the rivers Bosna and Drava in the west to the Morava in the east. Thereafter from this central Balkan power base, we see them as a dominant power in conflicts between Hellenistic states like Macedonia in the south, with Roman influence from the west, and Celtic and Dacian communities to the east and north. After the Roman conquest of Macedonia between 168 and 148 BC, indigenous, presumably Celtic, people later named *Scordisci* repeatedly figure in successful and unsuccessful assaults on Roman territory after a first encounter in 156 BC. The Scordiscans mounted another assault on Delphi in 84 BC, but were defeated by Scipio Asiagenus in the same year. While they were able to repel the Cimbri towards the end of the 2nd century BC, Strabo reports an increasing decline and their subjugation by the Dacian king Burebista around 50 BC. Finally, the Roman advance during the Illyrian wars of Octavian spelled the end of Scordiscan independence in the last third of the 1st century BC.

This short historical account may give a strong hint to the strategic role of Bačka Palanka and similar strongholds like Čarnok, Plavna or Zabalj (Figure 4). After their defeat in 84 BC, the *Scordisci* were driven back to the left bank

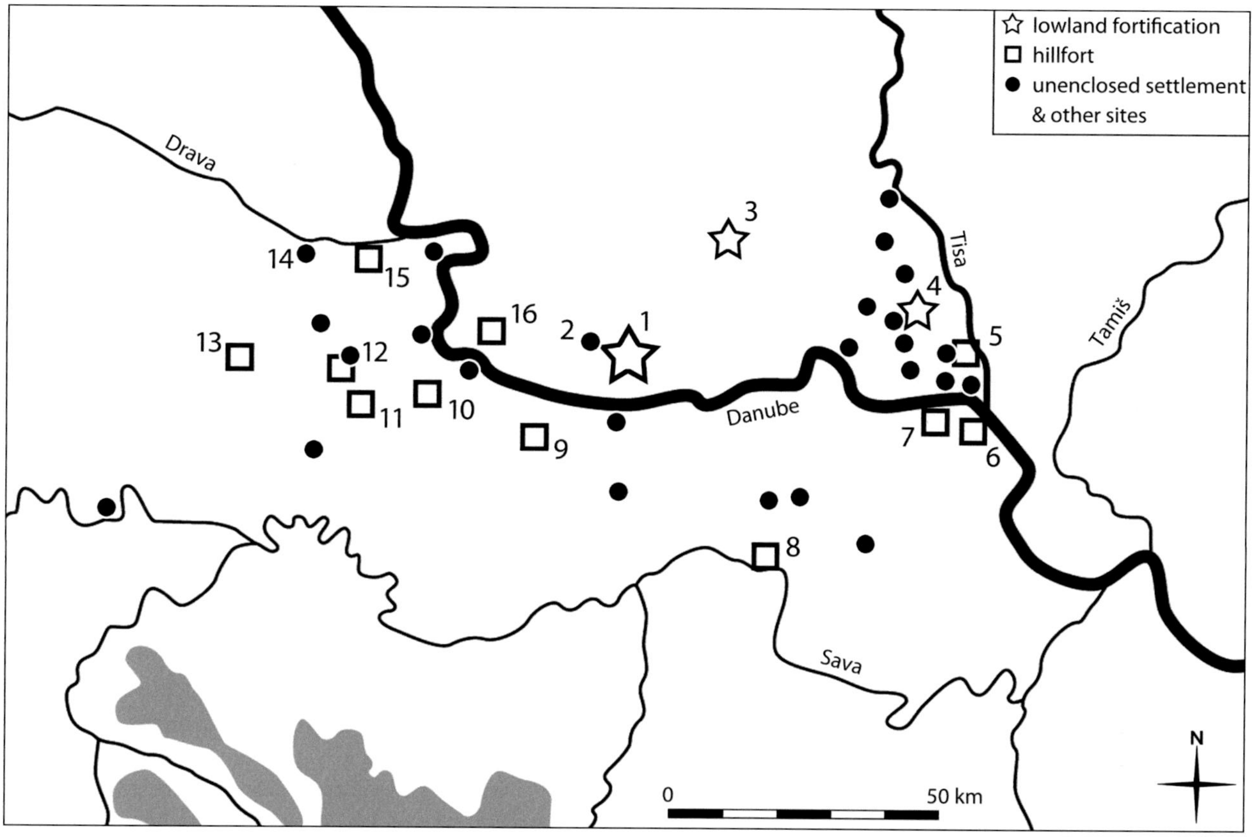

Figure 4: Late Iron Age lowland fortifications, hillforts, unenclosed settlements and other sites around the middle Danube in the area between the Drava, Sava, and Tiša Rivers. 1 Bačka Palanka "Turski Šanac" – 2 Bački Obrovac – 3 Čarnok – 4 Zabalj – 5 Mosorin – 6 Stari Slankamen – 7 Gardinovci – 8 Gomolava – 9 Sid "Gradina na Boštu" – 10 Orolik – 11 Privlaka – 12 Vinkovci "Dirov Brijeg" & "Borut" – 13 Stari Mikanovci – 14 Osijek – 15 Sarvaš – 16 Plavna (Graphics: H. Wendling after Dizdar 2016 and other sources).

of the Danube, and such fortresses might have guarded the new frontier against Roman advance. Then again, the forts might also have served as bridgeheads of Roman advance and interests in the hands of indigenous allies. Special finds, like the well-known helmet from the Sava River near Stara Gradiška might represent members of these Celtic elites on Roman duty (Mihaljević & Dizdar 2007; *cf.* Wendling 2009; 2013). Highly burnt features at the ramparts and gates of some fortifications, such as Bačka Palanka or Čarnok (phase II), are interpreted as traces of catastrophic events and military action (Jovanović 2012, 74-5; Majnarić-Pandžić 1996; Dizdar 2001, 114-5, 125, 129).

23.6 The settlement system – urban growth in a rural setting

The large multiple fortification at Bačka Palanka is part of a complex settlement system which evolved around the middle Danube in the territory of the *Scordisci* from the 4th century BC (Figure 4). In its western part (*i.e.* eastern Slavonia), there are two basic categories of sites (Dizdar 2001, 113-6). The first category includes a range of fortified settlements distributed equidistantly across the landscape. The known concentration of unfortified settlements in the east (*i.e.* western Syrmia) is a result of recent intensive field survey. Detailed survey has also revealed a similar pattern and an increase of unenclosed sites in the west (Dizdar 2016). However, as discussed above, the presence or apparent absence of enclosure might to some degree be misleading and does not unequivocally apply to local settlement structures. As to the situation in the west, there is a considerable concentration of both fortified and unenclosed settlements south of the Danube, with only some fortifications on its left bank.

Fortified sites can be subdivided into two categories. A number of fortifications were established on traditional settlement sites, some of which were occupied since the Neolithic. Frequently, they are situated on natural and artificial elevations on the banks of rivers, as for example the site at Gomolava, the Gradina at the river Bosut near Šid, or the Dirov Brijeg at the confluence of the Nevkoš and Bosut Rivers (Dizdar 2001, 113-5; 2016, 32). On the other hand, in addition to these tell-like sites, there are a number of fortifications which seem to lack any earlier occupation and might thus represent foundations of the initial Celtic occupation in the 4th or 3rd centuries BC, or establishments at the end of the 2nd century BC. Some fortifications exhibit a dense *extra muros* occupation. As a *suburbium*, this evokes an urban character of the settlement.

Following Caesar's concept of Gallic fortified centres and a notion of underlying urban characteristics of this ancient classification, some Late Iron Age fortified sites in the Balkans have generally been termed *oppida*. As consequence, the status of these settlements was considered to be urban, with exchange, crafts and production as well as political control of the hinterland (Dimitrijević 1971; Todorović 1971; cf. Dizdar 2016, 32-3). This assumption is confirmed by Gomolava which has some 40 pottery kilns producing high quality wheel turned and painted pottery. Crucibles attest metalworking while architectural structures in the centre of the site are interpreted as buildings intended to serve public or military functions (Dizdar 2001, 116; Jovanović 2009a). However, a re-evaluation of the south-eastern situation is appropriate with regard to recent reconsiderations of the urban character of both fortified and unfortified Late Iron Age sites in Central and Western Europe. A number of studies suggest a complex pattern of multi-purpose settlement types with different structural and functional characteristics including economic, religious, and social parameters, but also varying structural elements, such as (non-)fortification, layout, and architecture (Fernandez-Götz *et al.* 2014; Fichtl 2005; Salač 2014; Sievers & Schönfelder 2012).

The wider reassessment of settlement diversity in other parts of Europe may thus be relevant to the southeastern "Celtic" communities as well. Recent fieldwork has confirmed the existence of at least one large unenclosed site dating to LT C2/D1 at Blato in northern Vinkovci (Dizdar 2016). The quality and quantity of finds, including a large assemblage of fibulae, glass jewellery, and fine ware pottery, suggest a very complex economic structure including diversified production facilities and a broad network of communication and exchange. Other open settlements have been identified in the same region and beyond (Dizdar 2001, 115-6). Horse gear, weaponry and imported bronze vessels indicate the presence of martial warrior elites in or around these settlements (Dizdar 2016, 40-2). In other parts of Celtic Europe, similar sites have been identified as "centres of production and distribution" or, with an even more complex economic differentiation, as "Němčice-Roseldorf type centres" (Salač 2005; 2014; Wendling 2005). Small lowland sites in the surroundings of Gomolava and elsewhere are interpreted as farmsteads or hamlets which represent the basic units of the settlement hierarchy (Dizdar 2001, 127; Jovanović 2009b).

It is quite difficult to establish the position and functions of the monumental lowland fortifications in this settlement system. Their foundation as an apparently unenclosed settlement took place no earlier than in LT D1, towards the end of the 2nd century BC. The monumental development, together with the establishment or extension of a complex system of enclosure, at least at Bačka Palanka, followed during the course of the 1st century BC. Towards the turn of the era, traces of intense burning indicate a catastrophic end with no evidence of Roman presence at the sites so far.

Further functional interpretation of this distinct type of Scordiscan settlement must consider structural similarities to other fortified sites in Celtic Europe. A Late Iron Age fortified site at Niederzier-Hambach near Cologne (DE) reveals some corresponding features (Joachim 2007) (Figure 5 B). In the last phase the settlement is enclosed by a double ditch and wall describing an oval plan (210 x 160 m), which corresponds to the size of the central fortification at Bačka Palanka, though it does not have any additional internal complexity. Several compounds of post-built houses of moderate size and storage pits roughly resemble the occupation at the Balkan sites. A deposit of gold coins and torques, and a large amount of iron ingots, indicate both elaborate cult activities and a wealthy and dominant population. However, other traces of social differentiation are missing and the settlement is interpreted as a fortified rural village (Gechter-Jones 2007).

Massive walls and V-shaped ditches are also a feature of a small number of central European rectangular enclosures which have a very standardized internal occupation. The size and layout of these *Viereckschanzen*-type fortified farmsteads are generally standardized. However, a number of sites exhibit additional complex internal and external systems of ditches and walls, which suggests economic and social differentiation (Figure 5 C). These multiple enclosures lies at the pinnacle of a hierarchy of strongly fortified enclosures, which are interpreted as elite residences of owners of large estates (Müller 2008, 129-60). However, a comparison of the fortification and the internal settlement of the Scordiscan fortresses quite obviously shows the differences in size and intensity of occupation. In contrast to the *Viereckschanzen* farmsteads, the very few Balkan strongholds exhibit a far more exclusive and powerful scale of the defences, which might indicate that they occupied a more exalted level in a settlement hierarchy.

Further west, in Gaul, a large number of enclosed farmsteads has been detected and excavated in recent years. While highly variable in size and structure, some common features allow for the definition of distinct types of estates. Monumental architecture, quality of finds, and size, unequivocally confirm their outstanding position as residences of the higher nobility of pre-Roman Gaul (Fichtl 2013 and this volume). The aristocratic residence at Paule (F) is one of the most prominent examples (Figure 5 D), where the final phases of a sequence of construction

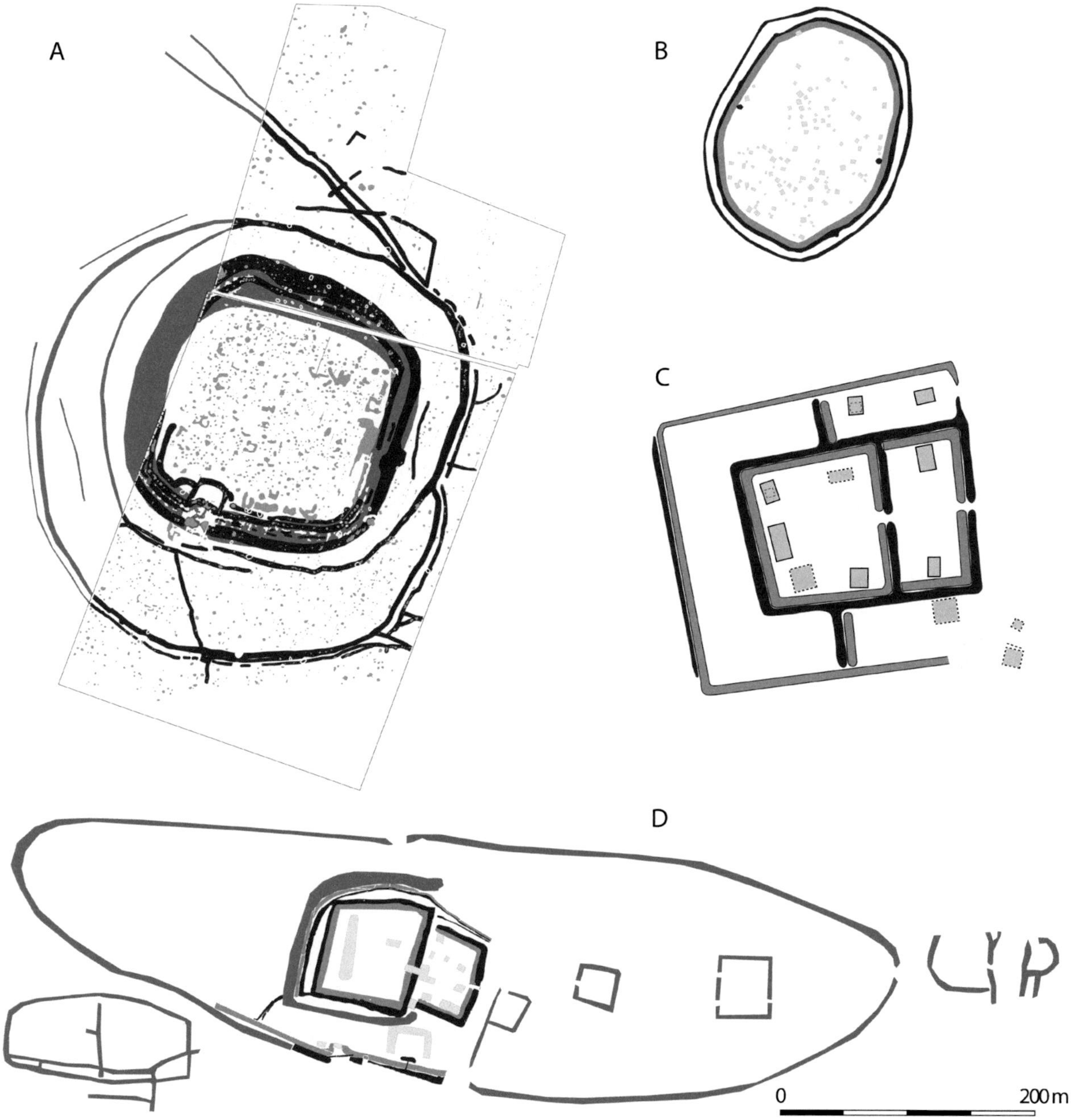

Figure 5: Schematic plans of selected Late Iron Age multiple enclosures and fortifications: A Bačka Palanka "Turski Šanac" (SRB); B Niederzier-Hambach (DE); C Sallach (DE); D Paule "St. Symphorien" (F; different phases) (Graphics: H. Wendling after different sources).

see it construed as a multi-vallate fortification housing an aristocratic residence, with a densely settled locality, that acted as a rural core in a process of urbanisation (Menez 2012). In a similar manner to Bačka Palanka, the defences contain monumental gateways, massive ramparts and multiple ditch systems. Correspondingly, the Scordiscan Late La Tène fortresses at Bačka Palanka, Čarnok and Zabalj are interpreted as predominantly rural elite residences, which played a role in a similar development towards urban growth. The ostentatious display of wealth and power through monumental architecture and defences illustrates economic and social claims, and military initiative. The social and economic role of the settlements can be characterised by evidence from excavation at Čarnok and applied to the other sites. High quality objects like silver fibulae indicate the presence of members of the elite. Burials or depositions of horses and dogs suggest cult and religious activity as a prerogative tool of elite social control (Jovanović 2012, 74). However, as large facilities for processing and storing grain at Čarnok show, the economy was deeply embedded in an agricultural environment and possibly had to counteract military threats. Thus, the lowland strongholds complemented a settlement system undergoing a process of urbanisation as manifested in the unenclosed industrial centre at Blato. An assumed temporal sequence of those sites indicates fundamental dynamics in settlement history.

As centres of a martial elite preoccupied with agriculture, the Scordiscan fortresses resemble some large-scale aristocratic residences in Late Iron Age Gaul. Correspondingly, during the 1st century BC powerful aristocrats might have dominated their territory as warlords against or in the service of Rome. Such indirect rule by indigenous forces is recognised as a means of exercising Roman power in other parts of Celtic Europe (cf. Caesar BG 1,47,4-6; 5,25,1-2; Harmand 1971/72, 103-5; Goudineau 1989; Wightman 1977).

23.7 Acknowledgements

I am most grateful to Milos Jevtic (University of Belgrade) who shared his experience and suggested undertaking the geomagnetic survey at Bačka Palanka. Many thanks to him and to Gordana Milosevic for their assistance and friendship. Jovan Koledin, Curator at the Museum of Vojvodina, hosted us at Novi Sad and actively supported our project at Turski Šanac. Teamwork and friendship of Christoph and Jana Rummel, née Škundrić (FU Berlin), and her family in Belgrade made RGK's survey campaign in 2012 a great experience! This project was generously enabled by a grant from the Cluster-research of the German Archeological Institute. Kathrin Schreiner (University of Frankfurt/M.) kindly assisted in data processing and GIS-rendering and Ivan Drnić (Archaeological Museum Zagreb) gave valuable comments and suggestions.

23.8 Bibliography

Brukner, O. 1978. The Celtic Oppidum near Bačka Palanka. *Grada za proučavanje spomenika culture Vojvodine* 8/9, 5-12.

Dimitrijević, D. 1971. Spätlatènezeitliche Oppida in Jugoslawien. *Archeologické rozhledy* 23, 567-84.

Dizdar, M. 2001. *Latenska naselja na vinkovačkom području. Tipološko-statistička obrada keramičkih nalaza. – La Tène Settlements in the Vinkovci Region. A typological and statistical analysis of the settlement pottery.* Dissertationes et Monographiae (Zagreb) 3. Zagreb: Arheološki Zavod Filozofskog Fakulteta Sveučilišta u Zagrebu.

Dizdar, M. 2016. Late La Tène Settlements in the Vinkovci Region (Eastern Slavonia, Croatia): Centres of Trade and Exchange. In M. Karwowski & P. C. Ramsl (eds). *Boii – Taurisci. Proceedings of the International Seminar, Oberleis-Klement, June 14th–15th, 2012.* 31-48. Mitteilungen der Prähistorischen Kommission 85. Wien: Verlag der ÖAW.

Drnić, I. & Skelac, G. 2008. La Tène Finds from the Site of Ciglana – Zeleno Polje in Osijek. *Vjesnik Arheološkog Muzeja u Zagrebu* 41, 385-415.

Džino, D. 2007. The Celts in Illyricum – whoever they may be: the hybridization and construction of identities in Southeastern Europe in the fourth and third centuries BC. *Opuscula Archaeologica* 31, 49-68.

Fernandez-Götz, M., Wendling, H. & Winger, K. (eds) 2014. *Paths to Complexity. Centralisation and Urbanisation in Iron Age Europe.* Oxford: Oxbow.

Fichtl, S. 2005. *La ville celtique. Les oppida de 150 av. J.-C. à 15 ap. J.-C.* 2nd ed. Paris: Errance.

Fichtl, S. 2013. À propos des résidences aristocratiques de la fin de l'âge du Fer: l'exemple de quelques sites du Loiret. In S. Krausz, A. Colin, K. Gruel, I. Ralston & T. Dechezleprêtre (eds). *L'âge du Fer en Europe. Mélanges offerts à Olivier Buchsenschutz.* 329-43. Ausonius Éditions, Mémoirs 32. Bordeaux: Ausonius.

Gechter-Jones, J. 2007. Die befestigte spätlatènezeitliche Siedlung Niederzier, Kreis Düren. In *Krieg und Frieden. Kelten – Römer – Germanen. Katalog der Ausstellung im Rheinischen Landesmuseum Bonn, 21.6.07-6.1.08.* 163-5. Bonn & Darmstadt: Landschaftsverband Rheinland & Rheinisches Landesmuseum Bonn, Primus Verlag.

Goudineau, C. 1989. A propos de C. Valerius Procillus, un prince helvien qui parlait ... gaulois. Études celtiques 26, 61-2.

Harmand, J. 1971/72. Des Gaulois autour de César. *Rivista storica dell'Antichità* 1, 99-107; 2, 131-67.

Joachim, H.-E. 2007. Die Datierung der jüngerlatènezeitlichen Siedlung von Niederzier-Hambach im Kreis Düren. *Bonner Jahrbücher* 207, 33-74.

Jovanović, M. 1988/89. Plavna – keltische Befestigung. *Rad vojvodanskih muzeja* 31, 59-74.

Jovanović, M. 1994. Die keltische Festung Čarnok bei Vrbas. In N. Tasić (ed.). *The Iron Age Cultures in the Yugoslav Danube Bassin.* 119-30. Beograd: Balkanoloski Institut, SANU.

Jovanović, M. 2008. The late La Tène fortified settlement of Čarnok in the vicinity of Vrbas (A review of excavations from 1984 to 2007). *Rad vojvodanskih muzeja* 50, 61-78.

Jovanović, M. 2009a. Gomolava – Handicraft Center Skordiska. *Rad vojvodanskih muzeja* 51, 117-35.

Jovanović, B. 2009b. Late La Téne unfortified settlements in the surrounding of Gomolava (Lower Srem). *Rad vojvodanskih muzeja* 51, 91-102.

Jovanović, M. 2011. Secrets of the baskets from Čarnok of Vrbas. *Rad vojvodanskih muzeja* 53, 127-32.

Jovanović, M. 2012. Stratigraphy of the Celtic settlement of Čarnok in Bačka (Vrbas, Vojvodina, Srbija). *Rad vojvodanskih muzeja* 54, 63-75.

Jovanović, B. & Jovanović, M. 1988. *Gomolava. Late La Tène Settlement*. Beograd & Novi Sad: Arheoloski Institut & Vojvodanski muzej.

Jovanović B. & Popović, P. 1991. The Scordisci. In S. Moscati (ed.). *The Celts*. 337-47. Milano: Bompiani.

Leicht, M. 2013. Siedlungsbefunde und Bebauungsrekonstruktion. In S. Sievers, M. Leicht & B. Ziegaus (eds). *Ergebnisse der Ausgrabungen in Manching-Altenfeld 1996-1999*. 17-117. Die Ausgrabungen in Manching 18. Wiesbaden: Reichelt.

Lexikon 2012. Lemmata "Backi Obrovac, Serbien"; "Čarnok, Serbien"; "Gomolava, Serbien"; "Plavna, Serbien"; "Čarnok, Serbien"; "Privlaka-Gradina, Kroatien"; "Turski Šanac, Serbien". In S. Sievers, O. H. Urban & P. C. Ramsl (eds). *Lexikon zur keltischen Archäologie*. Mitteilungen der prähistorischen Kommission 73, 100; 300-2; 665-70; 1493-4; 1535-6; 1883-4. Wien: Verlag der ÖAW.

Majnarić-Pandžić, N. 1996. Einige Beispiele der spätlatènezeitlichen Siedlungen in Nordkroatien und ihre Beziehungen zu den Zentren der frühen Romanisation. *Arheološki Vestnik* 47, 257-65.

Menez, Y. 2012. Die Entstehung befestigter Siedlungen bei befestigten Adelssitzen der jüngeren Eisenzeit in Gallien: Das Beispiel von Paule (Côtes d'Armor). In S. Sievers & M. Schönfelder (eds). *Die Frage der Protourbanisation in der Eisenzeit. La question de la proto-urbanisation à l'âge du Fer. Akten des 34. internationalen Kolloquiums der AFEAF vom 13.-16. Mai 2010 in Aschaffenburg*. 289-301. Kolloquien zur Vor- und Frühgeschichte 16. Bonn: Habelt.

Mihaljević M. & Dizdar, M. 2007. The late La Tène bronze helmet from the Sava at Stara Gradiška. *Vjesnik Arheološkog Muzeja u Zagrebu* 40, 117-46.

Müller, S. 2008. *Die Viereckschanzen von Sallach, Gde. Geiselhöring, Lkr. Straubing-Bogen, Niederbayern im Spiegel keltischer Besiedlung des Kleinen Labertales*. Regensburger Beiträge zur Prähistorischen Archäologie 18. Regensburg: Universitätsverlag.

Popović, P. 1987. Sremska Mitrovica/Livade. Late La Tene Settlement, Roman Cemetery and Mausoleum. *Arheološki Pregled* 28, 113-8.

Popović, P. 1992. The Scordisci from the Fall of Macedonia to the Roman Conquest. In N. Tasić (ed.). *Scordisci and the native Population in the Middle Danube Region*. 35-52. Beograd: SASA Institute for Balkan Studies.

Rummel, C., Schafferer, G. & Wendling, H. 2012. Geomagnetik Balkan. *Berichte der Römisch-Germanischen Kommission* 93, 368-71.

Salač, V. 2005. Vom Oppidum zum Einzelgehöft und zurück – zur Geschichte und dem heutigen Stand der Latèneforschung in Böhmen und Mitteleuropa. *Alt-Thüringen* 38, 279-300.

Salač, V. 2014. Oppida and Urbanisation Processes in Central Europe. In M. Fernández-Götz, H. Wendling & K. Winger (eds). *Paths to Complexity. Centralisation and Urbanisation in Iron Age Europe*. 64-75. Oxford: Oxbow.

Sievers, S. 2010. Die Wallgrabungen von Manching im Vergleich. In S. Fichtl (ed.) *Murus celticus. Architecture et fonctions des remparts de l'âge du Fer. Table ronde internationale, 11, 12 octobre* 2006, Glux-en-Glenne. Collection Bibracte 19, 176-86. Glux-en-Glenne: Centre archéologique européen.

Sievers, S. & Schönfelder, M. (eds) 2012. *Die Frage der Protourbanisation in der Eisenzeit. La question de la proto-urbanisation à l'âge du Fer. Akten des 34. internationalen Kolloquiums der AFEAF vom 13.-16. Mai 2010 in Aschaffenburg*. Kolloquien zur Vor- und Frühgeschichte 16. Bonn: Habelt.

Todorović, J. 1971. Die Oppida der Skordisker im jugoslawischen Donaugebiet. *Archeologické rozhledy* 23, 559-66.

Wendling, H. 2005. Offene "Städte" – befestigte Höhen. Ein Sonderfall der Siedlungsstruktur im Oberrheingebiet. In A. Bräuning (ed.). *Kelten an Hoch- und Oberrhein*. 19-24. Führer zu archäologischen Denkmälern in Baden-Württemberg 24. Stuttgart: Theiss.

Wendling, H. 2009. Zur spätkeltischen Sozial- und Siedlungsstruktur im südlichen Oberrheingebiet – Herrschaft im Wandel. In S. Zimmer (ed.). *Kelten am Rhein. Proceedings of the Thirteenth International Congress of Celtic Studies. 23.-27. Juli 2007 in Bonn. 1. Archäologie. Ethnizität und Romanisierung*. Beihefte Bonner Jahrbücher 58(1), 57-70. Mainz: Zabern.

Wendling, H. 2010. *Opus deforme non est*... Neue Erkenntnisse zur Konstruktion des Manchinger murus, Landkreis Pfaffenhofen a. d. Ilm, Oberbayern. *Das archäologische Jahr in Bayern* 2009, 75-8.

Wendling, H. 2013. Monnaies et monnayage celtiques au "Münsterberg" de Breisach. Le temps des "chefs de guerre" au Rhin supérieur. *Cahiers alsaciens d'archéologie, d'art et d'histoire* 56, 91-104.

Wendling, H. 2018. Dynamiques locales et influences externes – Architecture et organisation spatiale à Manching en regard des oppida celtiques. In A. Villard-Le Tiec (ed.). *Architectures de l'âge du Fer en Europe occidentale et centrale. Actes du 40e colloque international de l'AFEAF, Rennes, 4-7 mai 2016*. 159-76. Collection Archéologie et Culture. Rennes: Presses universitaires de Rennes.

Wightman, E. M. 1977. Soldier and Civilian in Early Roman Gaul. In J. Fitz (ed.). *Limes. 11th International Congress of Roman Frontier Studies, Székesfehérvár 1976*. 75-86. Budapest: Akadémiai Kiadó.

Chapter 24

The emergence of *oppida* in Celtiberia

The case study of Los Rodiles (Guadalajara, Spain)

Marta Chordá, Álvaro Sánchez-Climent,
Emilio Gamo & María Luisa Cerdeño

24.1 Introduction

The *Celtiberian* were the most genuinely Celtic pre-Roman culture in the Iberian Peninsula, with a well-known cultural development from the late 8th century BC to the Roman period (Cerdeño & Sagardoy 2014, 17). Written sources and archaeological evidence from several recent archaeological excavations indicate that they inhabited the highest central areas of the peninsula, an area of extreme climate conditions (Burillo 2007). This fact contributed to maintaining a rural character to settlement for this period. From the Early Iron Age, the settlement pattern was based on small fortified hillforts, the fixed points within a territorial, social and economic network adapted to a rather hostile environment. This settlement pattern experienced substantial transformations in the Late Iron Age, when the population was concentrated in larger fortified settlements called *oppida*. These sites played a key role as regional centres in resistance to the Roman campaigns.

24.2 Settlement patterns

The earlier model of settlement consisted of small fortified hillforts with approximately 30-50 inhabitants. These were located in strategic places controlling agricultural areas, mineral resources, salt, hunting grounds, pasture and water, and appear to have been occupied for long periods. The likelihood that overall population numbers in the area were low because of the harsh climate and the enduring character of the settlement pattern suggests that the hillforts necessarily formed part of a network (Cerdeño & Sagardoy 2010, 312). In some cases there is solid archaeological evidence from cemeteries related to hillforts which proves that the inhabitants occupied the same territory for a long time. For example, the hillfort of El Ceremeño (Herrería, Guadalajara) dates to the same period as Herrería III phase cemetery (Cerdeño & Juez 2002), the demographic study of which revealed that the estimation of the population for both archaeological sites are approximately the same (Cerdeño & Sagardoy 2010, 330). This ancient pattern persisted until the final period of the Celtiberian Culture.

In the last decades of the 3rd century BC, the settlement pattern of the *Celtiberian* underwent a process of settlement amalgamation, developing into a model based on

In D.C. Cowley, M. Fernández-Götz, T. Romankiewicz & H. Wendling (eds). Rural Settlement. Relating buildings, landscape, and people in the European Iron Age (Leiden 2019: Sidestone Press) 245-248.

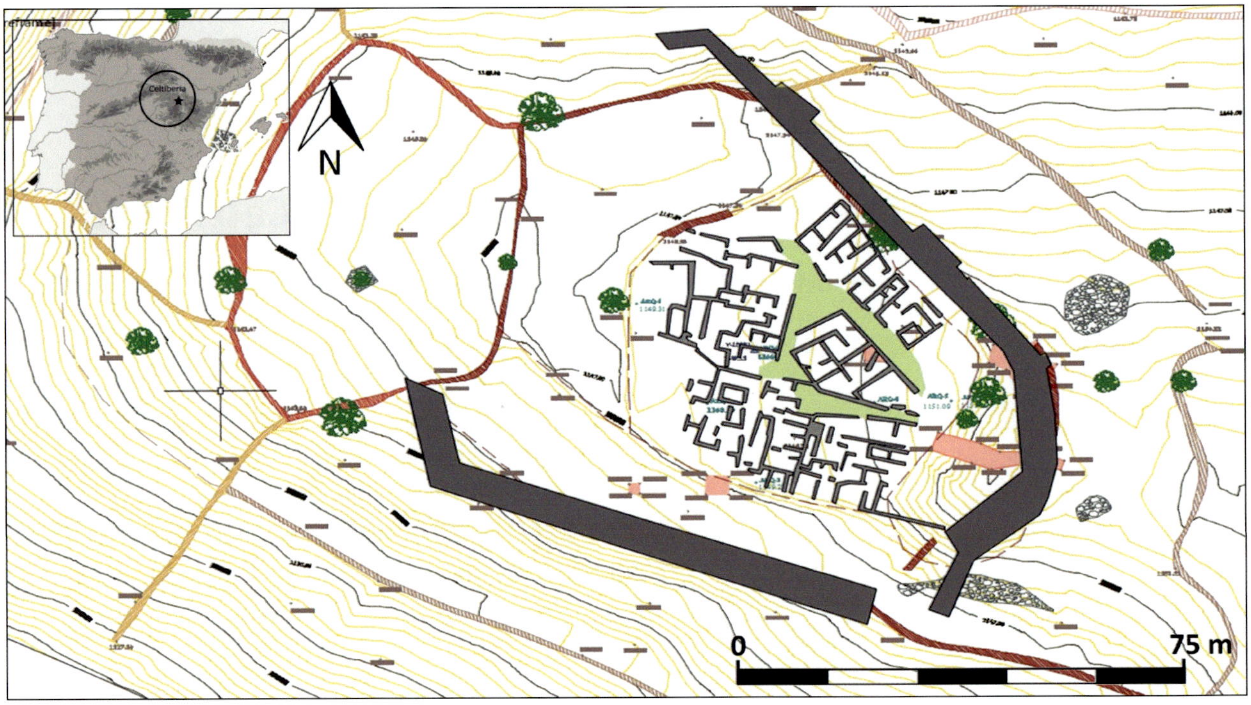

Figure 1: Location and urban structure of the archaeological site.

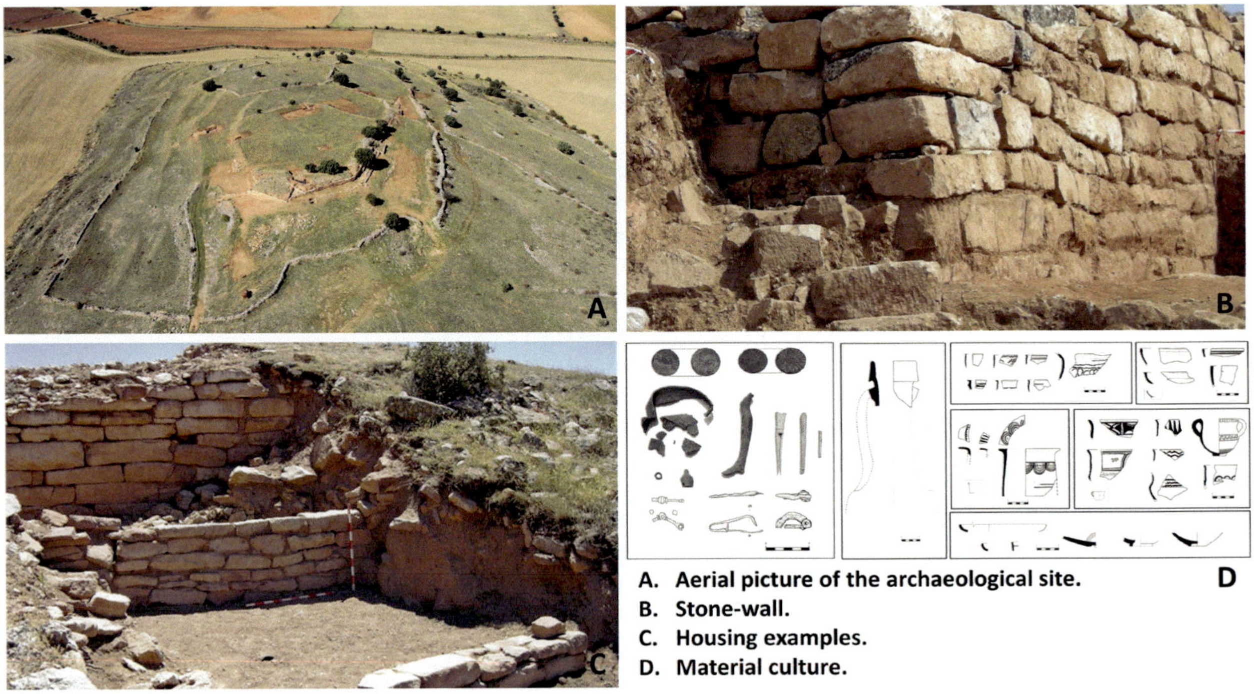

Figure 2: Aerial view, stone-built wall, examples of houses and material culture.

larger settlements with different strategic considerations and a heavier defensive emphasis – the *oppida* of the *Celtiberian*. While these *oppida* are not comparable in size to other contemporary examples elsewhere in Europe, they played a key role as focal centres in their territory. Their inter-visibility, apparently controlling important economic or strategic points, such as communication routes, indicates that they formed a network of sites.

The Roman conquest promoted the emergence of the Celtiberian social elites, also stimulating the development of territorial and hierarchical organisation of the *oppida* and subsidiary hillforts. The urbanisation of Celtiberia was organised by the strengthening of the aristocratic elites called *nobile* and *princeps* by the Classical written sources. In these sources the elites appear to play a key role in the urban formative process (principally due to their military role) and were linked also with the kinship organization of the *Celtiberian*. However, the base of their privilege resided in the control of landscape and its economic resources, including agriculture, livestock and mining (González 1999, 134).

The *oppida* became the foci of political units in the last stages of the Celtiberian culture, in an equivalent way to the Mediterranean city-states. Some of the *oppida* were mints with their city names on the coins. They developed new commercial relationships with other sites, reflected in imported pottery, iconography and exotic bronze artefacts. This is the evidence that supports the interpretation of these sites as *oppida*, due to the role they played in relationship to smaller neighbouring settlements as providers of prestige objects for the elites.

24.3 Los Rodiles case study

One of the most important *oppida* in Celtiberia is Los Rodiles (Cubillejo de la Sierra, Guadalajara), a typical fortified hillfort dating to the 3rd to 1st centuries BC. It is located on the top of a large hill and is about five hectares in extent. Due to its size and importance this *oppidum* is interpreted as a regional centre, controlling important key elements of the landscape, including cereal production on the adjacent plain, the iron and copper mines in the Caldereros mountain range and a very important communication route across the plateau to the Jalon and Ebro valleys. Los Rodiles was probably a regional centre controlling a territory including smaller hillforts, a privileged position that may have stimulated an increase in its population at the expense of nearby hillforts. This period also saw the refortification of its defences for both defensive purposes and ostentation. Indeed, the importance of Los Rodiles was such that it was attacked during the Roman invasion in the first half of the 2nd century BC, although the site remained occupied for another hundred years more.

Around 200 m^2 of the site has been excavated (Figure 1). The excavation of the site reveals two occupational levels. The earlier hillfort from the first occupation (3rd century BC) was laid out around a central 'street', which was superseded by a north-south orientated grid of walls which delimited large spaces in the latest years of the site (1st century BC). In some of these spaces lime-rich soils have been identified, as well as reddish-coloured household slabs made of sand-clay and post supports, indicating the presence of limestone-walled buildings (Figure 2). Other walls of red sandstone slabs set perpendicular to the main walls define large rectangular or quadrangular blocks bounded by streets cut into the bedrock or made up of layers of small and medium stones, sand and household waste (for example very fragmented pottery and rubbish). Some ditches in the defensive system have been excavated and demonstrate a growing complexity of the system through the articulation of several elements (three wall facings, pits, etc.) as well as its construction system.

24.4 Conclusions

Archaeological evidence provides insights on the Iron Age *oppida* in Celtiberia, in a pattern of settlement that persisted some decades after the siege of *Numantia* (133 BC) and the destruction due to the Sertorius civil conflict (82-72 BC). Indeed, these *oppida* increased their economic and social activity under the Roman administration because all these regions became stipendiary areas. This required the maintenance of its indigenous social and economic structures, although under the protection and the rules of the conquerors (Abascal & Espinosa 1989, 21), with the indigenous elites accepting the rule of Rome.

The imposition of Roman authority eventually modified the settlement model, even creating new *oppida*, mixing the population and controlling the processes of settlement amalgamation. Indeed, the building of new cities without Roman supervision was forbidden (*i.e.* the treaty of Sempronius Gracchus (*Apianus*, 43)). The organisation of *oppida* and their integration into Imperial territorial policy was the culmination of a long-lasting trend with origins in the early 1st millennium BC by which urban nodes, which articulated large territories, were created.

24.5 Bibliography

Abascal, J.M. & Espinosa, U. 1989. *La ciudad hispanorromana: privilegio y poder*. Logroño: Logroño: Colegio Oficial de Aparejadores y Arquitectos Técnicos de La Rioja.

Apiano. 1993. *Sobre Iberia y Anibal*. Madrid: Alianza.

Burillo, F. 2007. *Los Celtíberos. Etnias y Estados*. Barcelona: Crítica.

Cerdeño, M. L. & Juez. P. 2002. *El Castro Celtibérico de El Cerameño (Herrería, Guadalajara)*. Teruel: Monografías del S.A.E.T.

Cedeño, M. L. & Sagardoy, T.2010. Sobre demografía celtibérica: nuevos datos arqueológicos. *Arqueología Espacial, 28*. Teruel, 311-34.

Cedeño, M. L. & Sagardoy, T. 2014. Relaciones continentales durante la genesis del mundo celtibérico: nuevas evidencias en el periodo protoceltibérico, VII Simposio sobre Celtíberos, Estudios Celtibéricos, 7. *Teruel*, 13-20.

Cerdeño, M.L. Chordá, M. & Gamo, E. 2014. Huellas arqueológicas de la conquista romana en Celtiberia. El *oppidum* de Los Rodiles (Guadalajara, España). F. Cadiou & M. Navarro (eds). *La guerre et ses traces: conflits et sociétés en Hispanie à l'époque de la conquête romaine (IIIe-Ier s.a.C.)*. 297-318. Bourdeaux: Ausonius.

González, C. 1999. *El trabajo de la agricultura en la Hispania romana. El trabajo en la Hispania romana.* 119-216. Granada: Sílex.

PART 4

NEW TOOLS AND PERSPECTIVES

Chapter 25

Microtopographies of Dacian upland settlement strategies and community aggregation trends in the Orăştie Mountains, Romania

Ioana A. Oltean & João Fonte

In D.C. Cowley, M. Fernández-Götz, T. Romankiewicz & H. Wendling (eds). Rural Settlement. Relating buildings, landscape, and people in the European Iron Age (Leiden 2019: Sidestone Press) 251-261.

25.1 Introduction

The core of the Dacian realm before its conquest by Rome has long been acknowledged to be in the Orăştie Mountains, part of the Southern Carpathians (Figure 1). The area is densely occupied by hillforts, tower-houses and open settlement of round houses and ancillary buildings scattered across the mountains and valleys, broadly dated between 1st century BC and the 1st century AD. The best known of these stone-walled hillforts, constructed using the so-called *murus Dacicus* technique, is Sarmizegetusa Regia. Located on the Grădiştea Muncelului hill, since 1999 this is part of the *Dacian Citadels in the Orăştie Mountains UNESCO World Heritage Site,* alongside a series of other citadels located either around the mountain periphery (Costeşti-Cetăţuie, Costeşti-Blidaru, Băniţa, and Căpâlna) or Piatra Roşie, and Vârfu lui Hulpe in the interior (Figure 1). These elite residences are part of a vast archaeological landscape, many of them also being surrounded by open settlement. Unfortunately, only in the case of Sarmizegetusa Regia do we know of a more densely built habitation. According to previous estimates (Luca 2008, 82-3) this extended over at least 100 man-made terraces (Oltean 2007, 89-90 with bibliography). In amongst numerous timber-built round houses, the settlement includes a series of stone-built sanctuaries and extensive metallurgical workshops, and is usually thought to have fulfilled at least a proto-urban function. Tower-houses, sometimes associated with, but often structurally distinct from the citadels, have been identified (see Oltean 2007, 76-80 with bibliography), mostly located in and around the two hillforts at Costeşti.

The study area is one of the most intensely surveyed archaeological landscapes in Romania. Fieldwalking surveys to various extents have taken place there in association with excavations since the 1960s and are largely responsible for the identification of at least 61 separate locations recorded in the county gazetteer (Luca 2008, 82-3, with bibliography). A few of these have been excavated subsequently, mostly at Sarmizegetusa Regia and on the surrounding hills, including Muncelu (Feţele Albe, Şesul cu Brânză), Gerosu, Meleia and Rudele, providing a broadly homogenous and contemporaneous material culture. Focusing primarily on cropmark identification, the first systematic programme of aerial reconnaissance in Western Transylvania (1998-2004) led by Bill Hanson (Glasgow

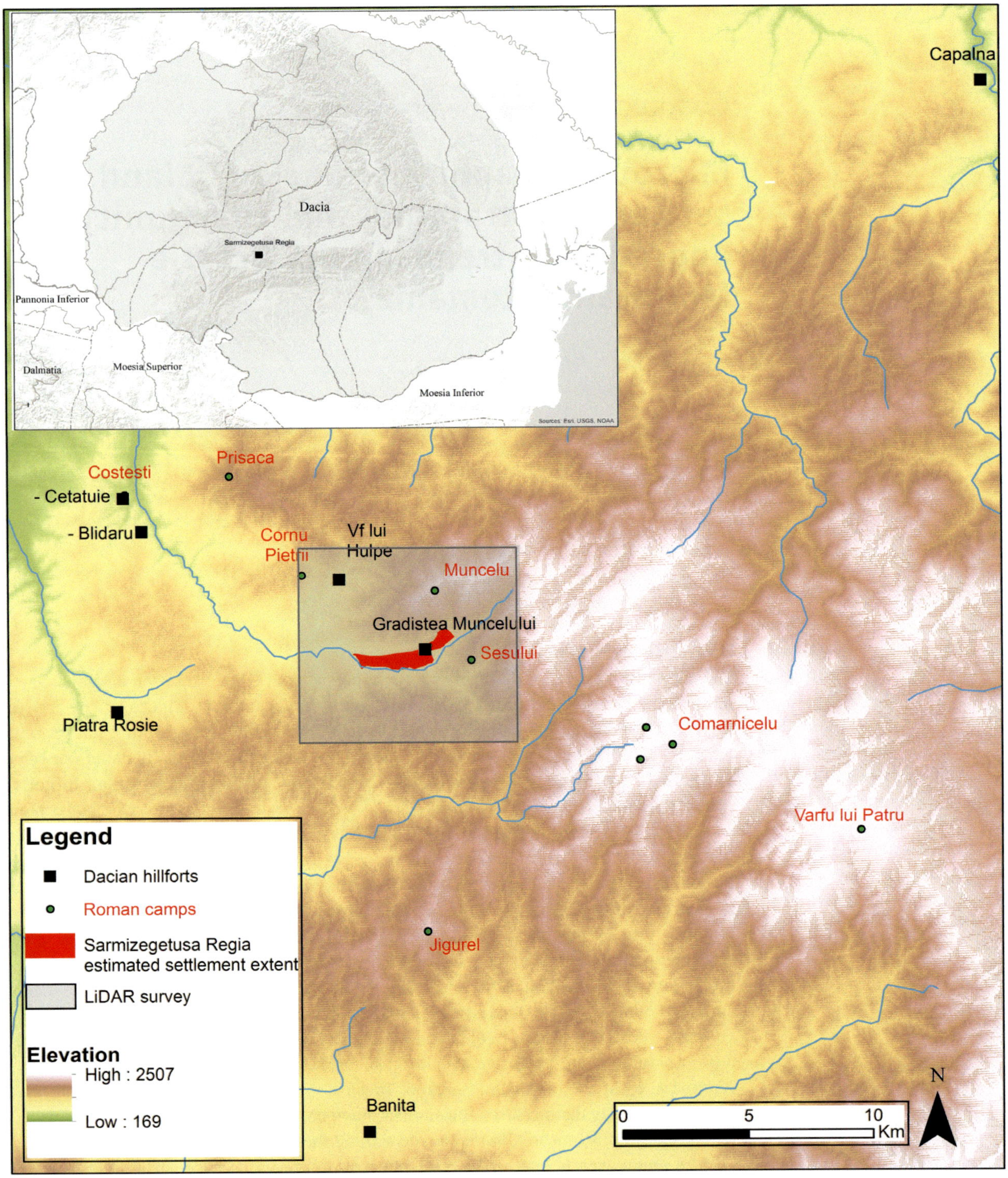

Figure 1: Location map of the study area (Elevation data based on Shuttle Radar Topography Mission (SRTM) 1 Arc Second ~30 m DEM developed by NASA).

University) in conjunction with the first-named author also extended into the Orăştie Mountains area. Though this research facilitated the documentation from the air, and analysis within their wider context of a large number of mostly unknown archaeological sites, and opened the way for landscape archaeology in Romania (Hanson & Oltean 2002; 2004; 2007), it had more limited success in and around Sarmizegetusa Regia due to extensive forest coverage

Figure 2: Oblique aerial photograph of the ***area sacra*** at Sarmizegetusa Regia (B. Hanson).

(Figure 2). As a result, the subsequent landscape analysis remained reliant on previous discoveries on the ground and did not support in-depth assessment of settlement extent, structure, topographic distribution and adaptability strategies, nor of community aggregation trends (Oltean 2007, 12-6; Oltean & Hanson 2017, 430).

Community aggregation trends are particularly important, given the presumed proto-urban, core status of Sarmizegetusa Regia within Iron Age Dacia, and the uniquely centralised character of this realm before the Roman conquest. Communities imply the presence of more direct and intimate connections between people than states or other similarly impersonal social entities, with space sharing allowing for the creation of places where people can meaningfully interact and dwell together (Harris 2014, 77-80 with bibliography). However, it becomes more difficult to estimate the original extent of ancient communities in upland areas, which are traditionally dominated by scattered, non-aggregated settlement. There, meaningful interaction is less obviously facilitated by spatial proximity or by the provision of defined formal spaces. Nevertheless, aggregation trends apparent in the spatial distribution of settlement can be strengthened further by assessing affordances, including the potential for and the ease of networking across space and topography, through bodily movement and/or visual connection (see *e.g.* Gillings 2012; Verhagen 2012 with bibliography). Unfortunately, visual and physical communication between scattered settlement locations in the area have not been extensively explored, with previous attempts to understand movement across the Orăştie Mountains based exclusively on modern practice with historic and ethnographic parallels (Daicoviciu *et al.* 1989, 86-120). In the Eastern Carpathians, more recently slope analysis of elevation data have been employed to enhance empirical observation (*e.g.* Kavruk *et al.* 2017; Ştefan *et al.* 2015). Unfortunately this model is compromised by the poor resolution of the original dataset as the 30 m intervals in the EU-DEM height data effectively masks significant topographic variation. On the other hand, an airborne laser scanning (ALS/airborne LiDAR) derived height dataset, may achieve values well below 1 m, providing a dataset that allows detailed exploration of archaeological topography. Also, it supports the identification and mapping of archaeological features under forest canopy (*e.g.* Doneus & Briese 2006; 2011; Risbøl 2013, 53) which was the main limiting factor of previous research within the study area.

25.2 Data and analysis

25.2.1 LiDAR Data

A high-resolution airborne LiDAR dataset, acquired in November 2011 (about 12 points per m^2 in all returns and 8 in last return only, with 5 returns in total) and covering approximately 100 km^2, became available in the area of Sarmizegetusa Regia World Heritage Site (WHS) and its surrounding landscape (Figure 1). This has allowed a re-assessment of the archaeological landscape with potentially profound implications for further understanding of the impact of the Roman conquest of Dacia (Oltean & Hanson 2017). LAStools was used for processing the LiDAR data and obtaining a Digital Terrain Model (DTM) with 0.25 cm spatial resolution (LAStools n.d.). Further analysis to identify archaeological features was undertaken using different visualisations of the DTM, from basic hillshading and slope visualizations to more complex ones, like local relief model (Hesse 2010) and sky view factor (Kokalj *et al.* 2011; Kokalj & Hesse 2017). As a result, over 2000 features of potential archaeological significance have been identified, most of them within forest cover. By far the most numerous are artificial terraces of variable size and shape, lying across the slope to form a stance for buildings. A number of circular house platforms of a type known from excavation, and of enclosures, defined by ditches, ramparts or both, have also been identified. The visualizations were sufficiently detailed to allow the identification in a few cases of slight traces of round houses on such terraces or platforms (Figure 3).

This high resolution LiDAR dataset allowed us to generate our own data for the natural setting of the study area, independent from conventional maps, consisting of detailed ground elevation data (as surfaces or contour lines), watercourses and watersheds. These were obtained using ArcGIS surface contour generation of triangulated surfaces and its hydrological tools. For the latter, in order to avoid unnecessary noise in the results due to the high detail of the DTM, we first applied a low pass filter and then resampled the model to a spatial resolution of 1 m.

25.2.2 Spatial Analyses

Movement and perception are primary mechanisms of human inhabitation of landscape and their study are major subjects in the analysis of any archaeological

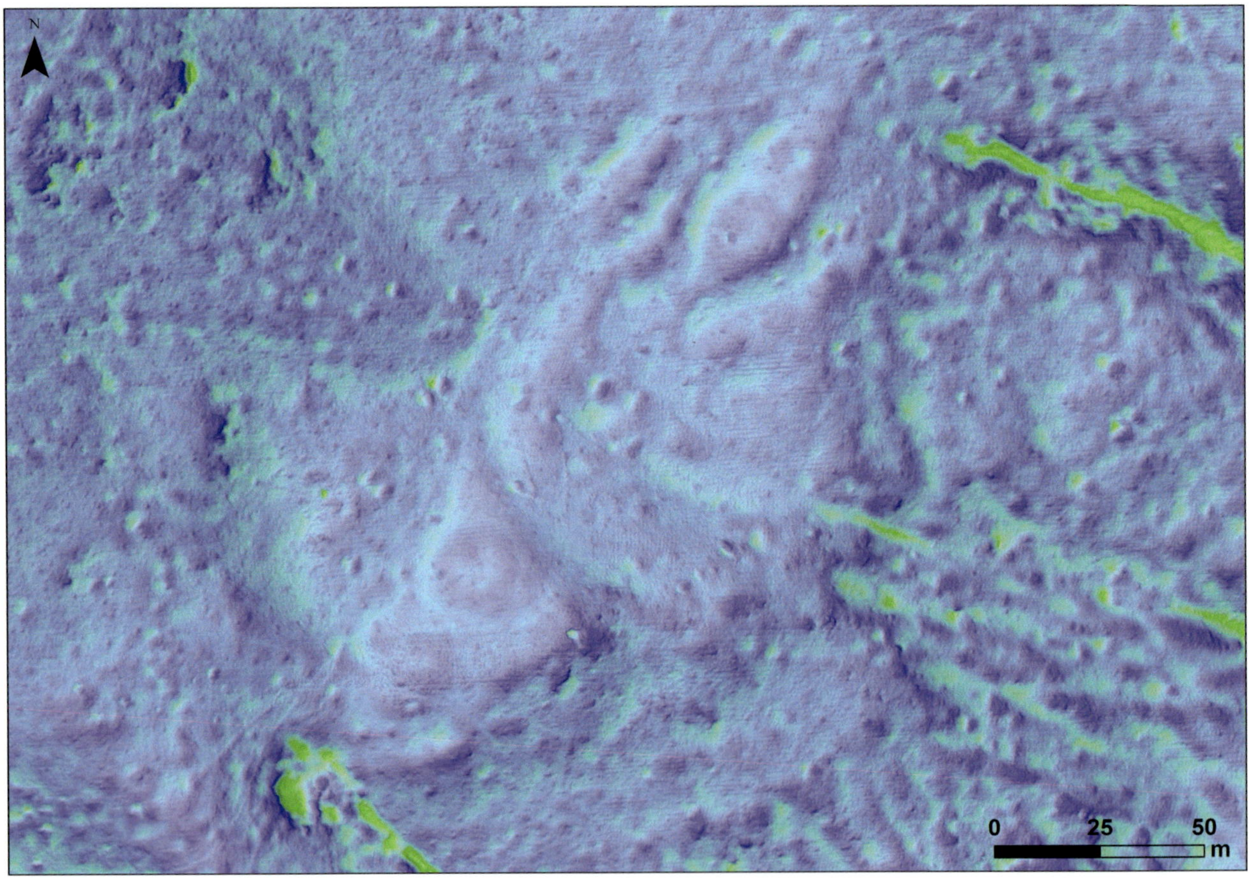

Figure 3: Dacian terraces and house platforms visible on LiDAR-generated Local Relief Model.

context (Verhagen 2018). In order to model the spatial relationships between the identified archaeological sites and the surrounding landscape, we used GIS-based spatial analysis in ArcGIS 10.5.1 software based on the LiDAR-derived DTM as a way to formalise and test hypotheses and as an integral part of interdisciplinary archaeological research (Verhagen 2018). We have used the same DTM for the hydrological modelling to avoid as much as possible the influence of limited modern infrastructure while maintaining a high-resolution DTM (Herzog 2014; Verhagen & Jeneson 2012). To verify the effective visual control that sites could have had over the surrounding landscape, individual viewsheds were obtained using the Viewshed tool in the ArcGIS Spatial Analyst extension. In addition, to assess the prominence of the sites regarding the wider landscape and their visual connections, total and cumulative viewsheds were also calculated (Llobera *et al.* 2010; Wheatley 1995).

In order to study mobility patterns between the settlements and their potential inter-relationships, two analyses were carried out. Firstly, based on an accumulated cost model, we have calculated least cost paths between the sites, using the Path Distance and Cost Path tools also in the ArcGIS Spatial Analyst extension. This allowed us to calculate the potentially most efficient route between the two hillforts within the study area. Secondly, we have used a focal mobility network analysis, MADO (*Modelo de Acumulación de Desplazamiento Óptimo*; Fábrega Álvarez 2006), which is based on a given cost model and hydrological tools (Flow Direction and Flow Accumulation in ArcGIS Spatial Analyst Tools). This allows us to calculate optimal paths without a specific destination and to define potential networks of natural mobility over the landscape (Llobera *et al.* 2011). In this way, the viability of certain routes can be analysed with greater precision by connecting the different sites under analysis. An anisotropic cost model is used that considers that the cost of displacement depends on the direction of movement, taking into account how slope influences movement effort in biomechanical terms (metabolic energy expenditure; Llobera & Sluckin 2007). For the calculation of the cost model, a friction model was used in which the watercourses (previously extracted using ArcGIS hydrological tools) were penalized as areas not suitable for movement (Fábrega-Álvarez & Parcero-Oubiña, 2007; for historical and ethnographic observations in the study area see also Apolzan 1987; Floca 1957). Being a mountainous area, we have assigned to the rivers a value equivalent to a slope of 60 degrees according to the cost function of Llobera and Sluckin (2007). We have also extracted time isochrones from the reclassification of the cost model, divided in 15 minutes intervals. An average speed of 5 km/h has been applied for human movement.

A kernel density analysis using a standard function available in ArcGIS which estimates density probability was performed in order to highlight the density aggregation trends within the spatial distribution of Dacian settlement terraces (Figure 4).

25.3 Discussion

The data analyses support greater understanding of our knowledge of the extent and intensity of ancient settlement, providing an explicit assessment of some of the factors which may have facilitated ancient community aggregation within the study area. Typologically, the new evidence supports previous assumptions that the overwhelming majority of Late Iron Age settlement in this area is unenclosed (see Oltean 2007, 66-76 with discussion and bibliography). A lack of pre-Roman enclosures remains marked, with the notable exceptions of two hillforts. Both are small (Sarmizegetusa Regia: 1.66 ha; Vârfu lui Hulpe: 0.2 ha) with ramparts laid out along contour lines. Both are very poorly preserved and may have been destroyed during the Roman conquest (see also Oltean & Hanson 2017, 432, 440-5).

25.3.1 The form of open settlement

All open settlement is readily identifiable as artificial terraces and platforms (Figure 3). Dug into the slope, the terraces are elongated and range from under 20 m to over 100 m in length. Many are quite narrow, sometimes even less than 10 m across. In contrast, the platforms are raised circular features, with the majority measuring some 15-20 m in diameter or larger. Their general appearance as low mounds resembles highly-eroded funerary barrows, consistent with the earlier interpretations of such features on the Rudele and Meleia hills, where subsequent excavation confirmed their role as stances for round houses.

Not all terraces would have been used for human habitation. Even allowing for erosion, some of the narrower terraces may not have been able to host constructions and, even where traces of buildings or building platforms are visible on terraces, not all such buildings were houses. Where building platforms survive on terraces, in most cases there are two such structures present, probably including domestic and ancillary structures (Oltean 2007, 69).

In general, artificial terraces lie on steeper slopes, while circular platforms are present either on or close to hilltops, or on artificial terraces. Despite the added building effort however, most identified settlements lie on hillsides rather than hilltops. Nevertheless, with few exceptions, most settlement enjoys a southern and south-eastern aspect and is only rarely found at altitudes higher than 1200 m. A few exceptions however occur, most notably on the Pustiosu and the Gerosu hills, where settlement terraces face north and northeast towards

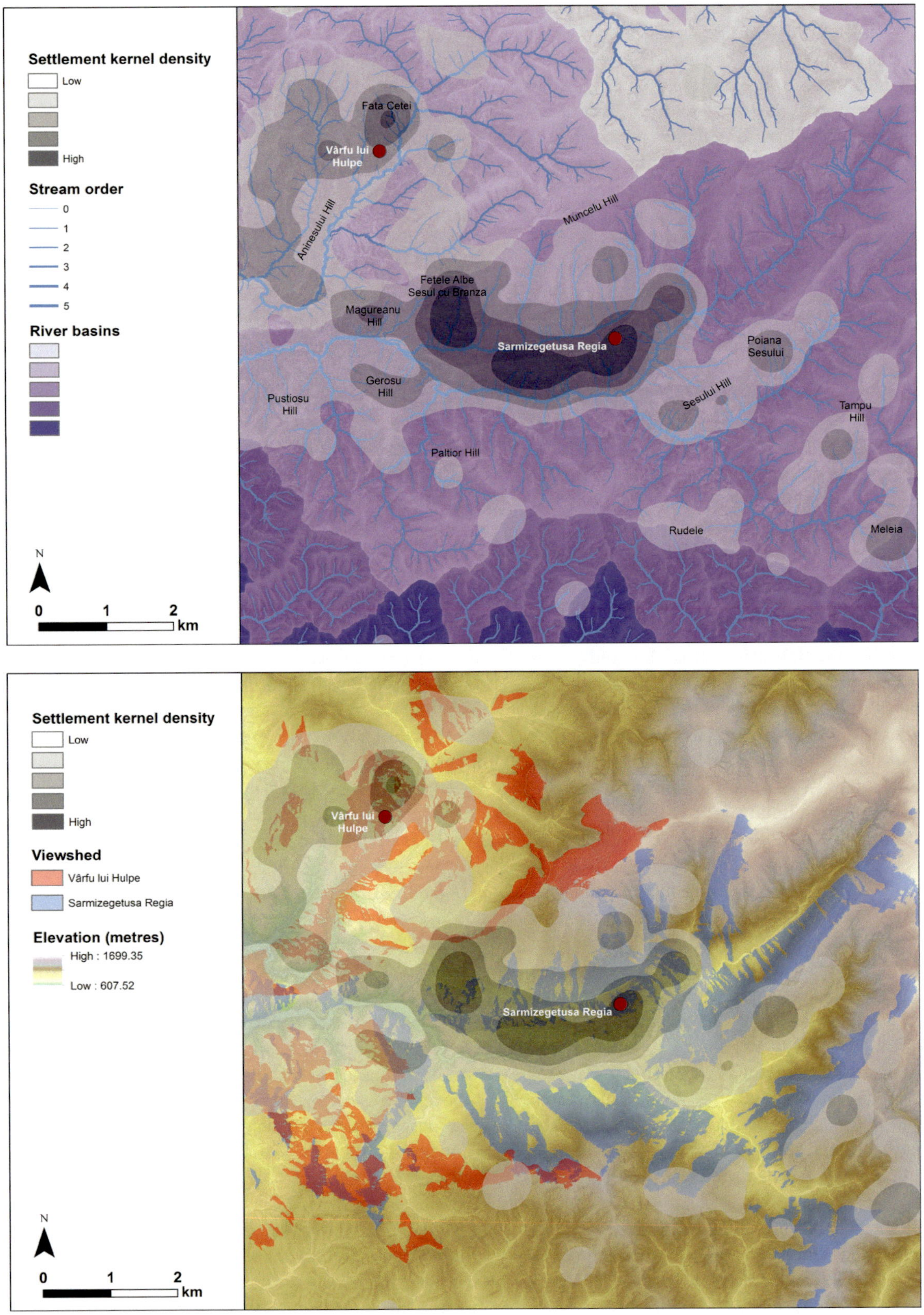

Figure 4: Settlement density distribution in relation to hydrology (above) and visual coverage from hillforts (below).

the Grădiştea valley. These choices highlight a natural avoidance of hilltop wind exposure and the generally more challenging environment of altitudes above 1200m, while at the same time maximising sunlight available. The exceptions therefore should be seen as deliberate actions where cultural or economic reasons may have superseded the ecological rationale for settlement. Accordingly, this may lend further support to metallurgical activities noted at hilltop settlements on Rudele Tâmpul and Meleia (Gheorghiu 2005, 72) where the additional wind action could have assisted furnace reduction. Similarly, it may further indicate that the settlers on Pustiosu and Gerosu Hills favoured visual connectivity to the main settlement agglomeration on Gradistea Muncelului to better use of environment for their own benefit.

25.3.2 Spatial analysis

Unsurprisingly, given the local topography and the previous knowledge of ancient and modern settlement patterns (Apolzan 1987; Oltean 2007), the spatial distribution of settlement across the study area is far from even. The majority of settlement is scattered across the hilly landscape, but the kernel density analysis identified several areas of increased settlement aggregation (Figure 4). According to this, the densest area of occupation is on the Grădiştea Muncelului hill, where previous research already noted the presence of the largest aggregated settlement of pre-Roman Dacia with in excess of 100 artificial terraces estimated to the west, south and east of the area occupied by the hillfort (see above). Our dataset indicates however that as many as some 430 terraces and house platforms were located on the Grădiştea Muncelului hill alone, expanding significantly the earlier estimates of the extent and density of this settlement. The Kernel density analysis demonstrates not only that by far the greatest concentration of activity was in the area to the west of the hillfort, but also that this area of high density settlement extends further north beyond that hill, on the southern slopes of Muncelu hill in the area of Feţele Albe and Şesul cu Brânză. The extension of the settlement from the Grădiştea Muncelului hill onto Muncelu is further supported by the internal morphology and spatial distribution of archaeological features on the latter, including some possible east-west oriented internal roads facilitating access from Feţele Albe and Şesul cu Brânză to the settlement on the eastern part of Grădiştea Muncelului hill. This potentially brings the total extent of Sarmizegetusa Regia to some 650 ancient settlement terraces and platforms. Beyond these, a zone of lesser settlement density links it to a smaller nucleus further to the west on Muncelu hill and extends further onto Gerosul hill to the southwest. Interestingly, this analysis does not support the extension of the main settlement to include the small cluster at Căprăreaţa, to the northeast of the hillfort at Sarmizegetusa Regia, previously assumed to be part of the main settlement (Glodariu 1975).

The kernel density analysis also indicates for the first time the presence of a second area of greater settlement density further to the northwest, including some 95 terraces and platforms in the area of Vârfu lui Hulpe hillfort. The relationship between the hillfort and its terraced settlement contrasts with that at Sarmizegetusa Regia. While at Sarmizegetusa Regia the hillfort is in a core location with the largest proportion of its open settlement occupying the same hill spur around it, at Vârfu lui Hulpe the highest settlement density is to be found on the neighbouring Faţa Cetei hill (where previous research had already noted the presence of 30-40 terraces, Oltean 2007, 69), with the hillfort positioned on the edge of the raised settlement density zone. A smaller pocket of higher aggregation of 34 terraces can be found at least 400 m to the west on Anineşului hill. Here again, the two clusters are connected by an area of medium aggregation which extends considerably farther to the west to Cornu Petrii Hill and onto the southern part of the Anineşului Hill.

The dual settlement polarity noted above is confirmed by the hydrology analysis which establishes the presence of two distinct hydrological basins within the study area, one centred on Sarmizegetusa Regia and the other on Vârfu lui Hulpe (Figure 4a). Within these hydrological basins, other distinct pockets of medium aggregation have been identified on Meleia, Şesului hill, Poiana Şesului, Tâmpu and Muncelu hills in the proximity of Sarmizegetusa Regia, on Magureanului hill further downstream along Grădiştea Valley and on the hill immediately to the East from Vârfu lui Hulpe across the Aninesului Valley.

25.3.3 Movement in the landscape

The spatial aggregation trends discussed above can help identify potential communities through space-sharing but, as stated earlier, this may not be the only factor in operation. Other links between various pockets of scattered settlement and the two hillforts could have been constructed either by sensorial (*e.g.* visual) connectivity (Figure 4b), or through pathways of physical movement through the landscape (Figure 5). Based on the local topography, the Least Cost path analysis identified the potentially most efficient pathway between the two hillforts. According to this, an ancient traveller between the two hillforts was likely to have moved from Vârfu lui Hulpe through Faţa Cetei and across the Anineşu stream onwards to the Muncelu hill. A slightly different approach to climbing the Muncelu hill would have been more efficient on the way back. For most of the way this path leads through an area of low to no aggregation, but would have started by crossing through the settlement at Faţa Cetei first and would have approached Sarmizegetusa Regia's hillfort from the northeast passing through

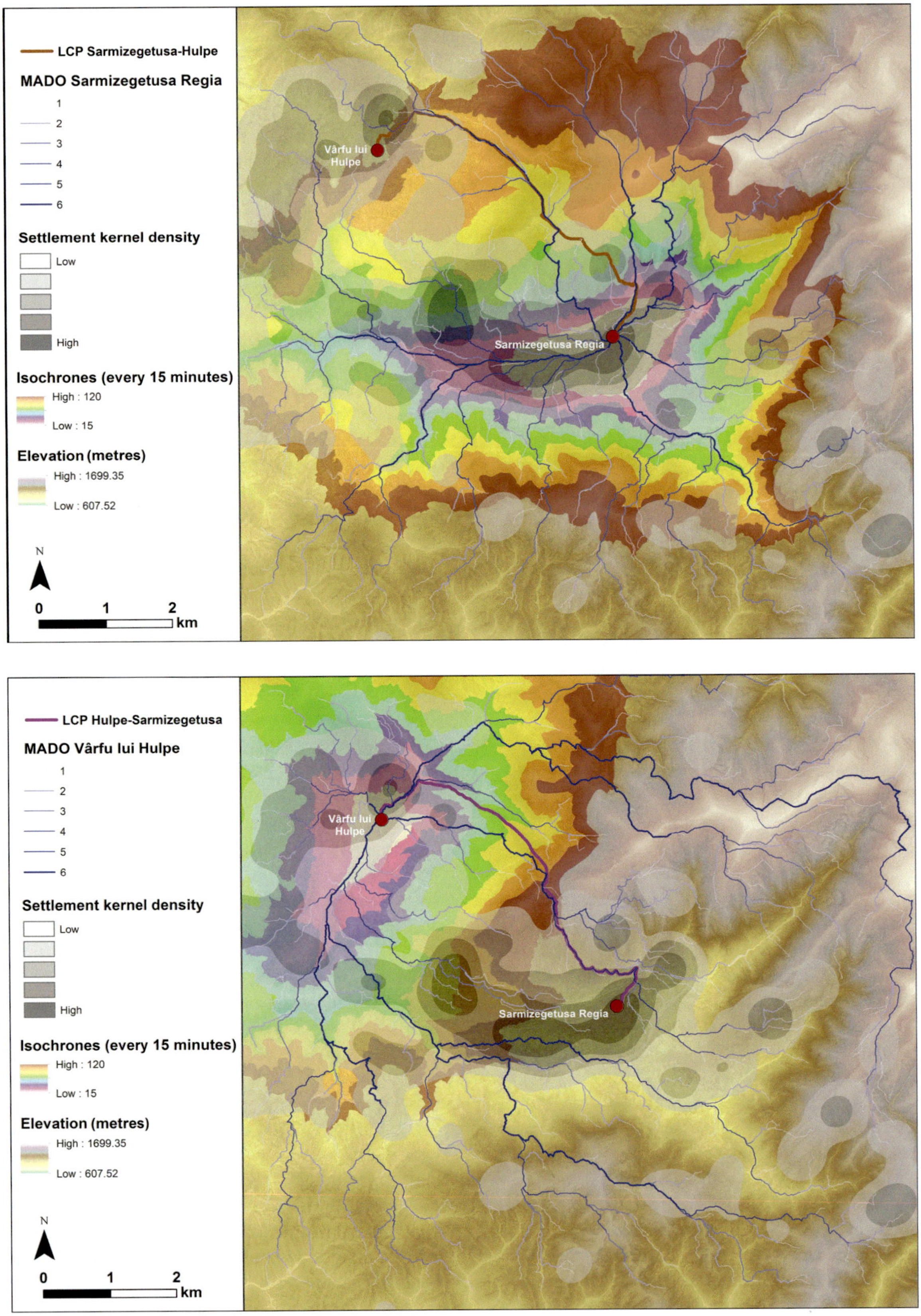

Figure 5: Mobility pathways towards Vârfu lui Hulpe (above) and Sarmizegetusa Regia (below).

its religious quarter. This indicates that, although the proximity to this route may not be of primary concern to a more distanced settlement, this could have nevertheless enhanced considerably the relative position and the potential significance of the dense settlement at Faţa Cetei. Also, given the positioning of the sacred area before reaching the hillfort rather than behind it, this lends more weight to a potentially higher relevance of that approach to Sarmizegetusa Regia when compared to the alternative (modern) approach along the Orăştie/Grădiştea valley and across the western side of the hill.

The Focal Mobility Network (MADO) analyses allowed us to assess the extent to which various settlement locations might have natural access on the ground from/ to each of the two hillforts. These indicate that all areas of aggregation were located on one or more major axes of natural movement towards at least one of the hillforts. Interestingly, neither hillfort is located on each other's natural pathway, indicating perhaps that the two hillforts emerged independently from the other. Furthermore, isochrones calculated in ArcGIS to help define those areas reachable from a given location in 15-minutes intervals indicate that virtually all settlement within the study area was reachable in no more than two hours from at least one of the two hillforts (Figure 5). Also, it became apparent that, although both hillforts were located outside the range of that time limit from each other, it would have taken longer to travel from Sarmizegetusa Regia to Vârfu lui Hulpe than in the opposite direction.

25.3.4 Visibility in the landscape

Viewshed analyses, performed from a series of evenly spaced points along the ramparts and an observer point height of 6 m (the estimated mean height of Dacian citadel walls), indicate that only a partial visual command of the surrounding landscape was possible from either Sarmizegetusa Regia or Vârfu lui Hulpe hillforts. A fair level of visual coverage is achieved only from both locations, but this occasionally extended beyond the area which could be easily reached on foot in two hours or less (Figures 4b & 5). As in the case of hydrology, the main physical entity dividing the visual landscape between the two centres is Muncelu hill. Some areas of visual overlap occur, on and to the south of Gerosu Hill where several locations were visible from both hillforts. However, if scattered settlement foci are potentially well connected on the ground to both hillforts, only some of those in the immediate spatial proximity were connected visually to the hillforts. Accordingly, Vârfu lui Hulpe enjoyed good visibility to virtually all terraces in its immediate proximity and to those on Faţa Cetei hill or to the small cluster on the hill to the east. However, the larger aggregation 500 m west of the hillfort to the north of Aninesului hill is outside its visual range. Assuming that visual connectedness was a prime factor in defining communities within this landscape, its absence in this instance therefore raises doubts whether this cluster was indeed part of the same community. Similarly, Sarmizegetusa Regia's viewshed illustrates variable degrees of visual connection to the larger and medium aggregation zones on the southern slopes of Muncelu and on Gerosul hill, but stops short of covering other aggregated nuclei such as those on Şesului hill, Poiana Şesului, Tâmpu and Meleia to the southeast. In terms of visual control of their main access paths, Vârfu lui Hulpe generally has an excellent command, with access from the south and from the east covered for the better part and to a distance of at least 3 km away. By contrast, though it had partial visual access to short stretches of some of them, the hillfort at Sarmizegetusa Regia could generally see poorly its main access routes, with only that from the northeast covered for just over 2 km all the way to the Roman fortification on Muncelu Hill. Much of the optimal paths between the two hillforts are visually controlled for 3.5 km by Vârfu lui Hulpe, with only the last 1.5 km stretch visible from Sarmizegetusa Regia. This seems to suggest that, although visual control could have strengthened Sarmizegetusa Regia's community ties with neighbouring aggregation clusters (*e.g.* Feţele Albe), visual command over access routes was of a lesser concern there than in the case of Vârfu lui Hulpe.

25.4 Conclusions and further implications

The present study is part of the most complete, to date, assessment into the extent, distribution and structure of ancient settlement at the core of Dacia immediately preceding its conquest by the Roman Empire in 101-106 AD. Although a sample of the newly-mapped features should be subjected to future systematic checks on the ground to confirm their validity and to provide in-depth insight into their nature and chronology, it is now clear that the area was far more intensely occupied in later prehistory than previously assumed. Almost 2000 artificial terraces and platforms related to open settlements apparently in varying degrees of aggregation, ranging from isolated homesteads and hamlets to larger aggregations have been identified.

The spatial and statistical analyses described above support an explicit assessment of the networking potential within the study area, with obvious implications for a better understanding of community aggregation and agency across landscape. The known settlement gravitated around two local elite fortified sites, Sarmizegetusa Regia and Vârfu lui Hulpe. Both affected community aggregation trends to a variable degree; the former was by far the most successful in attracting settlers, but nevertheless, the impact of the latter on the settlement pattern can now be finally acknowledged. Both also could have the ability to connect either visually and/or through physical movement with settlement in the surrounding area which may have been relevant to building communities beyond the spatial limits of aggregated pockets of settlement. Nevertheless, the lower potential for visual control from inside its newly-confirmed hillfort seems to indicate that the importance of Sarmizegetusa Regia as a space of worship and congregation may have superseded the strategic relevance of the site (see also Oltean 2012). These types of sites were important in the European Iron Age for the construction of collective identities and for strengthening ethnic links (*e.g.* Fernández-Götz 2018 with extended bibliography). There, religion and ideological mechanisms could have acted as activators of more complex forms of social organization and as elements of cohesion in the processes of aggregation, urbanisation, and centralisation.

The present study provides a foundation for further assessment of to what extent (and if so in what way) this core area remains exceptional within ancient Dacia and beyond. Better dating will be required to explore whether the settlement patterns outlined above represent a settlement 'explosion' or whether the identified density is the result of gradual development. Finally, and given that only 597 of the 2203 features recorded are in areas currently protected by the Romanian state under the WHS framework, it is hoped that the present study will allow for more effective cultural heritage protection strategies to be implemented.

25.5 Aknoweldgements

The LiDAR dataset was made available to IO via the BBC, with the initial processing and interpretation possible as part of the ArchaeoLandscapes Europe EC funded project (Culture programme 2007-2013; Agreement Number: 2010-1486).

JF received a three year postdoctoral research grant under a contract between the Galician Innovation Agency (GAIN) and the Spanish National Research Council (CSIC) at the Institute of Heritage Sciences (Incipit), including a two year research stay at the Department of Archaeology, University of Exeter, within the project "The archaeological landscapes of the Roman frontier: comparative perspectives on resources exploitation, social change and imperialism through a non-invasive methodology" (IN606B-2016/002).

25.6 Bibliography

Daicoviciu, H., Ferenczi Ş. & Glodariu, I. 1989. *Cetăţi şi aşezări dacice în sud-vestul Transilvaniei.* Cluj-Napoca: Editura Ştiinţifică şi Enciclopedică.

Doneus, M. & Briese, C. 2006. Full-waveform airborne laser scanning as a tool for archaeological reconnaissance. In S. Campana & M. Forte (eds). *From Space to Place 2. International Conference on Remote Sensing in Archaeology. CNR, Rome, Italy, December 2-4, 2006.* 99-106. Oxford: Archaeopress.

Doneus, M. & Briese, C. 2011. Airborne Laser Scanning in forested areas -potential and limitations of an archaeological prospection technique. In D. Cowley (ed.). *Remote Sensing forArchaeological Heritage Management.* 59-76.EAC Occasional Paper No. 5. Budapest: Archaeolingua.

Fábrega-Álvarez, P. 2006. Moving without destination. A theoretical GIS-based determination of movement from a given origin. *Archaeological Computing Newsletter* 64, 7-11.

Fábrega-Álvarez, P. & Parcero-Oubiña, C. 2007. Proposals for an archaeological analysis of pathways and movement. *Archeologia e Calcolatori* 18, 121-40.

Fernández-Götz, M. 2018. Urbanization in Iron Age Europe: Trajectories, Patterns and Social Dynamics. *Journal of Archaeological Research* 26, 117-62.

Floca, O. 1957. *Regiunea Hunedoara. Ghid turistic.* Deva.

Gheorghiu, G. 2004. *Dacii pe cursul mijlociu al Mureşului,* Cluj-Napoca: Mega

Gillings, M. 2012. Landscape Phenomenology, GIS and the Role of Affordance. *Journal of Archaeological Method and Theory* 19(4), 601-11.

Glodariu, I., 1975. Un atelier de făurărie la Sarmizegetusa dacică. *Acta Musei Napocensis* XII, 107-34.

Hanson, W.S. & Oltean, I.A. 2002. Recent aerial survey in Western Transylvania: problems and potential. In R.H. Bewley & W. Rączkowski (eds). Aerial Archaeology: Developing Future Practice. 109-15. Amsterdam: IOS Press.

Hanson, W.S. & Oltean, I.A. 2003. The identification of Roman buildings from the air: recent discoveries in Western Transylvania. *Archaeological Prospection* 10, 101-17.

Harris, O.J.T. 2014. (Re)assembling Communities. *Journal of Archaeological Method and Theory* 21(1), 76-97.

Herzog, I. 2014. A review of case studies in archaeological least cost analysis. *Archeologia e Calcolatori* 25, 223-39.

Hesse, R. 2010. LiDAR-derived Local Relief Models – a new tool for archaeological prospection. *Archaeological Prospection* 17, 67-72.

Kavruk V., Stefan, M.M., Buzea, D., Stefan, D. & Bordi Z.L. 2017. O analiză arheologică şi etnografică a rutelor de aprovizionare cu sare din sud-estul Transilvaniei. *Istros* XXIII, 381-430.

Kokalj, Ž. & Hesse, R. 2017. Airborne laser scanning raster data visualization: A Guide to Good Practice. Ljubljana: Založba ZRC.

Kokalj, Ž., Zakšek, K. & Oštir, K. 2011. Application of Sky-View Factor for the Visualization of Historic Landscape Features in Lidar-Derived Relief Models. *Antiquity* 85, 263-73.

LAStools, n.d. *Efficient LiDAR Processing Software*. rapidlasso GmbH®, Version 171231, http://rapidlasso.com/LAStools.

Llobera, M., Wheatley, D., Steele, J., Cox, S. & Parchment, O. 2010. Calculating the inherent visual structure of a landscape ('total viewshed') using high-throughput computing. In F. Nicolucci & S. Hermon (eds). *Beyond the Artefact. Digital Interpretation of the Past. Proceedings of CAA2004, Prato 13-17 April 2004*. 146-51. Budapest: Archaeolingua.

Llobera, M., Parcero-Oubiña, C. & Fábrega-Álvarez, P. 2011, Order in movement: a GIS approach to accessibility. *Journal of Archaeological Science* 38(4), 843-51.

Llobera, M. & Sluckin, T.J. 2007. Zigzagging: Theoretical insights on climbing strategies. *Journal of Theoretical Biology* 249(2), 206-17.

Luca, S.A. (ed.) 2008. *Repertoriul arheologic al judetului Hunedoara* (2nd ed.). Muzeul Naţional Brukenthal: Sibiu.

Oltean, I.A. 2007. *Dacia. Landscape, colonization, Romanization*. London, New York: Routledge.

Oltean, I.A. 2012. Sarmizegetusa Regia, In R. Bagnall, K. Brodersen, C. Champion, A. Erskine & S. Huebner (eds). *The Encyclopaedia of Ancient History*. Blackwell.

Oltean, I.A. & Hanson W.S. 2007. Cropmark formation on "difficult" soils in Romania. In J. Mills & R. Palmer (eds). *Populating clay landscapes*, 73-87. Stroud: Tempus.

Oltean, I. & Hanson, W. 2017. Conquest strategy and political discourse: New evidence for the conquest of Dacia from LiDAR analysis at Sarmizegetusa Regia. *Journal of Roman Archaeology* 30, 429-46.

Parcero-Oubiña, C. & Fábrega-Álvarez, P. 2006. Diseño metodológico para el análisis locacional de asentamientos a través de un SIG de base Raster. In I. Grau Mira (ed.). *La aplicación de los SIG en la arqueología del paisaje*. 69-91. Alicante: Universidad de Alicante.

Risbøl, O. 2013. Cultivating the wilderness – how lidar can improve archaeological landscape understanding. In R. Opitz & D. Cowley (eds). *Interpreting Archaeological Topography. 3D Data, Visualisation and Observation*. 51-62. Oxford: Oxbow.

Ştefan, M. M, Ştefan, D. & Buzea, D. 2015. From Sites to Landscapes in Late Second Iron Age Eastern Transylvania. New Perspectives on the Fortified Sites from Jigodin. *Ephemeris Napocensis* 25, 21-42.

Verhagen, P. 2012. Biting off more than we can chew? The current and future role of digital techniques in landscape archaeology. In S.J. Kluiving & E.B. Guttmann-Bond (eds). *Landscape Archaeology between Art and Science. From a Multi- to an Interdisciplinary Approach*. 309-20. Amsterdam: Amsterdam University Press.

Verhagen, P. 2018. Spatial Analysis in Archaeology: Moving into New Territories. In C. Siart, M. Forbriger & O. Bubenzer (eds). *Digital Geoarchaeology. New Techniques for Interdisciplinary Human-Environmental Research*. 11-25. Cham: Springer.

Verhagen, P. & Jeneson, K. 2012. A Roman Puzzle. Trying to Find the Via Belgica with GIS. In A. Chrysanthi, P. Murrieta Flores & C. Papadopoulos (eds). *Thinking Beyond the Tool. Archaeological Computing and the Interpretive Process*. 123-30. Oxford: Archaeopress.

Wheatley, D. 1995. Cumulative viewshed analysis: a GIS-based method for investigating intervisibility, and its archaeological application. In G. Lock & Z. Stancic (eds). *Archaeology and Geographic Information Systems: A European Perspective*. 171-86. London: Taylor and Francis.

Chapter 26

A structured Iron Age landscape in the hinterland of Knežak, Slovenia

Boštjan Laharnar, Edisa Lozić & Benjamin Štular

26.1 Introduction

The Iron Age of Knežak and its neighbouring regions (Figure 1) is defined on the basis of a set of common characteristics as gleaned from the cemeteries, settlements, hoards and stray finds recovered across an area extending from the north-eastern coast of the Adriatic to the foothills of Snežnik mountain (1796 m a.s.l.) (Guštin 1979; Gabrovec 1999, 154-5). The characteristic features of the pre-Roman landscape are the fortified hilltop settlements or hillforts, which are often identified today with *gradišče* or *kaštelir* place names. Investigation of the hillforts in the regions of Kras and Istria (Figure 1) shows that they were first inhabited in the Early Bronze Age (Maggi *et al.* 2017, 59; Hänsel *et al.* 2015). None of the hillforts around Knežak has witnessed large-scale systematic investigations and it is therefore not possible to make the same observation.

The chronology of the Knežak hillforts is based on small-scale trial trenching conducted decades ago (Battaglia 1927; Urleb 1960) and on stray finds recovered in or near hillforts either by chance or by amateurs using metal detectors. These indicate the beginning of permanent habitation in the Late Bronze or the transition to the Early Iron Age, *i.e.* towards the end of the 2nd and in the early 1st millennium BC, and a peak in habitation, construction and fortification activities during the Iron Age, between the 9th/8th century BC and the arrival of the Romans in the last decades of the 1st century BC. These long centuries of the Iron Age surely bring up numerous questions as to the settlement dynamics, relationships between the hillforts, their hierarchy, evolution, use and function, as well as the development of the wider hillfort landscape.

The introduction of Airborne Laser Scanning (ALS, also known as LiDAR) technology to archaeology has opened up the hillfort landscape to study. The striking density of archaeological features at Knežak hillfort landscape contains cairnfields, banks and linear earthworks, enclosures, linear boundary earthworks and hollow ways. The hillfort landscape is not the result of a single event, but rather a palimpsest of multi-period activity. Our research has shown that we may reliably date this activity to the Late Bronze and in particular the Iron Age. The Knežak study area thus represents a unique landscape document that offers an insight into the late prehistoric field distribution and land use.

In D.C. Cowley, M. Fernández-Götz, T. Romankiewicz & H. Wendling (eds). Rural Settlement. Relating buildings, landscape, and people in the European Iron Age (Leiden 2019: Sidestone Press): 263-271.

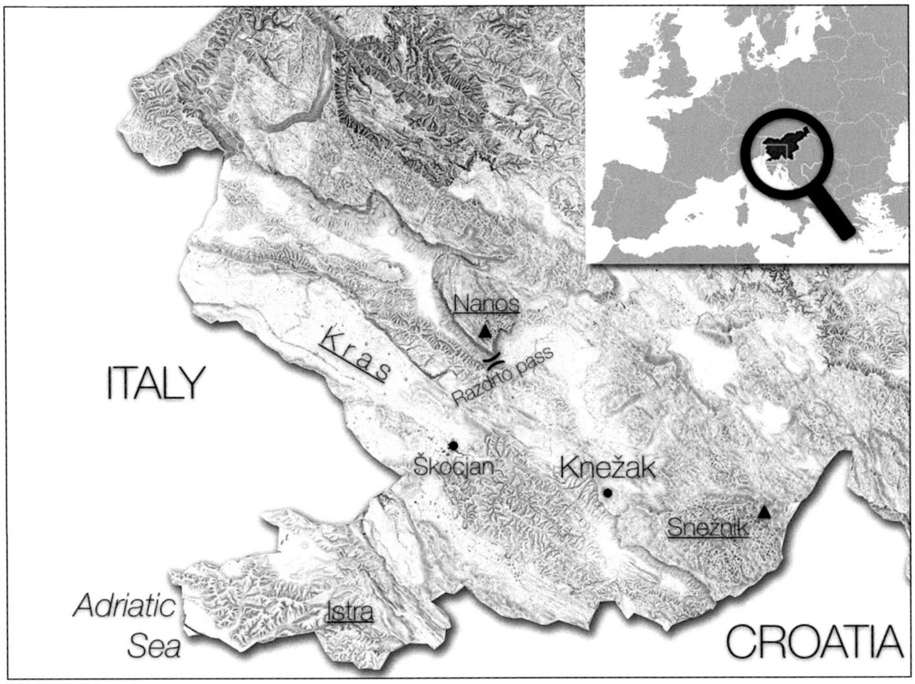

Figure 1: Location of the study area.

26.2 Methodology

One area of archaeological prospection that has been revolutionised by the development of ALS applications in archaeology is the capacity, with the appropriate data, to create high resolution digital elevation models (DEMs) under dense forest canopy (Doneus & Briese 2008; Lasaponara *et al.* 2011, 2061-70). For the Knežak study area we used data acquired in 2014 and 2015 within the nationwide aerial laser scanning of Slovenia (©ARSO, Slovenia). This approach has provided a detailed view of the micro-topography of the 12 km^2 densely-forested Knežak study area, developed through the following workflow: data processing, data visualisation and interpretation. In the first step, the ALS point cloud data was processed and optimised for archaeological interpretation with the processing approach developed specifically for the Slovenian raw ALS data (Štular, Lozić 2016, 157-66; cf. Triglav-Čekada *et al.* 2016). Point cloud filtering and classification approach has been designed to extract optimal archaeological information from raw Slovenian ALS data. The resulting point cloud ground data was interpolated into a high-resolution DEM with a 0.5 m x 0.5 m spatial resolution (Štular & Lozić 2016, 162-3). Next, the DEM was visualised using several well-known visualisation methods (cf. Štular *et al.* 2012; Kokalj & Hesse 2017) and an additional custom method based on the standard deviation of elevation (cf. Lindsay *et al.* 2015). Finally, advanced image fusion techniques (cf. Zhang & Huang 2015, 6828-61) were used to create visualisations suitable for fieldwork and publication (Figure 2). This technique was used in order to increase visibility and to enhance the detection of archaeological remains. The resulting visualisations were used in a GIS environment for interpretative mapping. Aerial photographs from the 1950s to 2015 and a cadastral map from 1828 were also used to inform mapping. Archaeological features were mapped at a scale of 1:2,000 to an accuracy of 10 cm as points, lines and polygons, each with essential metadata such as the visualisation used, feature type, confidence level, and name of interpreter, attached. Selected features were then excavated to further explore their character, in a programme of work that is ongoing.

26.3 Survey Results and Dating Evidence

While there is a wider landscape study underway, this paper will focus on the survey results from the hillfort at Gradišče above Knežak (Figure 2 a & Figure 3) and its territory (Figure 2 and Figure 4). Perhaps the most striking archaeological evidence at Knežak plateau (600-750 m a.s.l.) is the density of archaeological features beyond the hillfort rampart. These features are cairnfields, banks and linear earthworks, enclosures, hollow ways and linear boundary earthworks. Dating the mentioned archaeological features at the current stage of the research is challenging. From the body of evidence already available a general picture of the chronology can be painted, albeit with broad strokes.

26.3.1 Hillfort

The Knežak hillfort (Figure 3) is well preserved and has a double rampart (Figure 3 a, b), an annexe (Figure 3 c), three open squares (Figure 3 d-f) and at least 49 buildings with 109 or more individual building-parts, most likely rooms

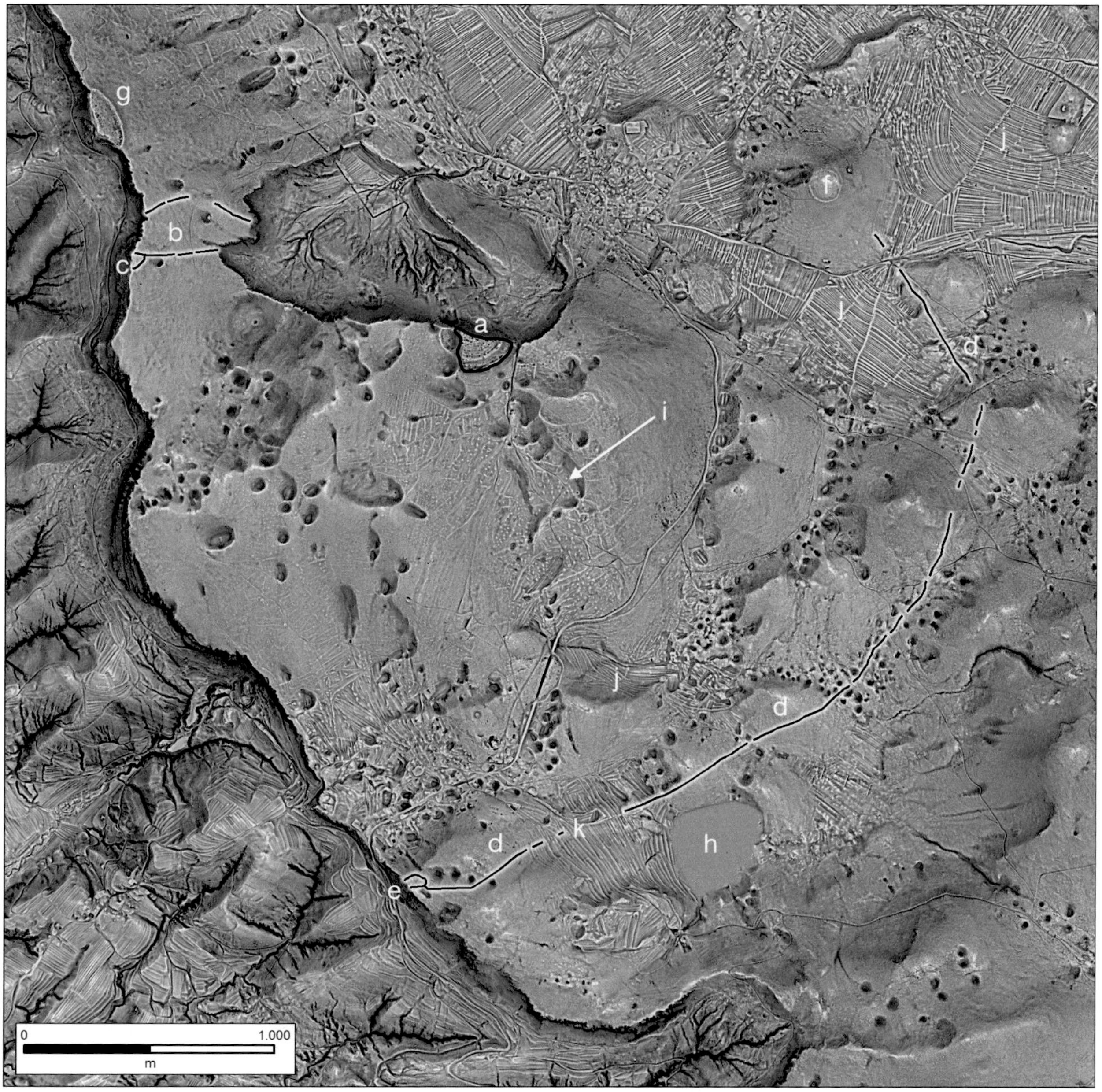

Figure 2: a) Gradišče above Knežak hillfort; b) & d) linear earthwork boundaries; c & e) enclosures; f) Obroba hillfort; g) Gradišče at Čepna hillfort; h) Šembije intermittent lake; i) cairn excavated in 1950s and the adjacent location of the 2016 excavation; j & k) high and post-medieval ploughing. Advanced image fusion visualization, see text.

(average building size 195.3 m^2, average building-part size 37.7 m^2). The entrance is in the south and is visible as a break in the inner and outer ramparts.

The chronology of the hillfort is based on the stray finds recovered by chance or by amateurs using metal detectors, as well as on the trial trenching performed in the 1920s and 1950s. These date the beginning of permanent habitation to the Late Bronze or the transition to the Early Iron Age, *i.e.* towards the end of the 2nd and in the early 1st millennium BC. Having said that, it is not clear whether the stonework ramparts built in the drystone technique coincide with these early habitations. The hillfort witnessed its peak in habitation, construction and fortification activities during the Iron Age, between the 9th/8th century BC and the arrival of the Romans in the last decades of the 1st century BC. According to small finds (*e.g.* numerous brooches and coins) the hillfort continued to be occupied after the arrival of the Romans and the parallels of contemporary hillfort architecture in the neighbouring Kras region (e.g. Mušič 1999, 356-70) moreover show

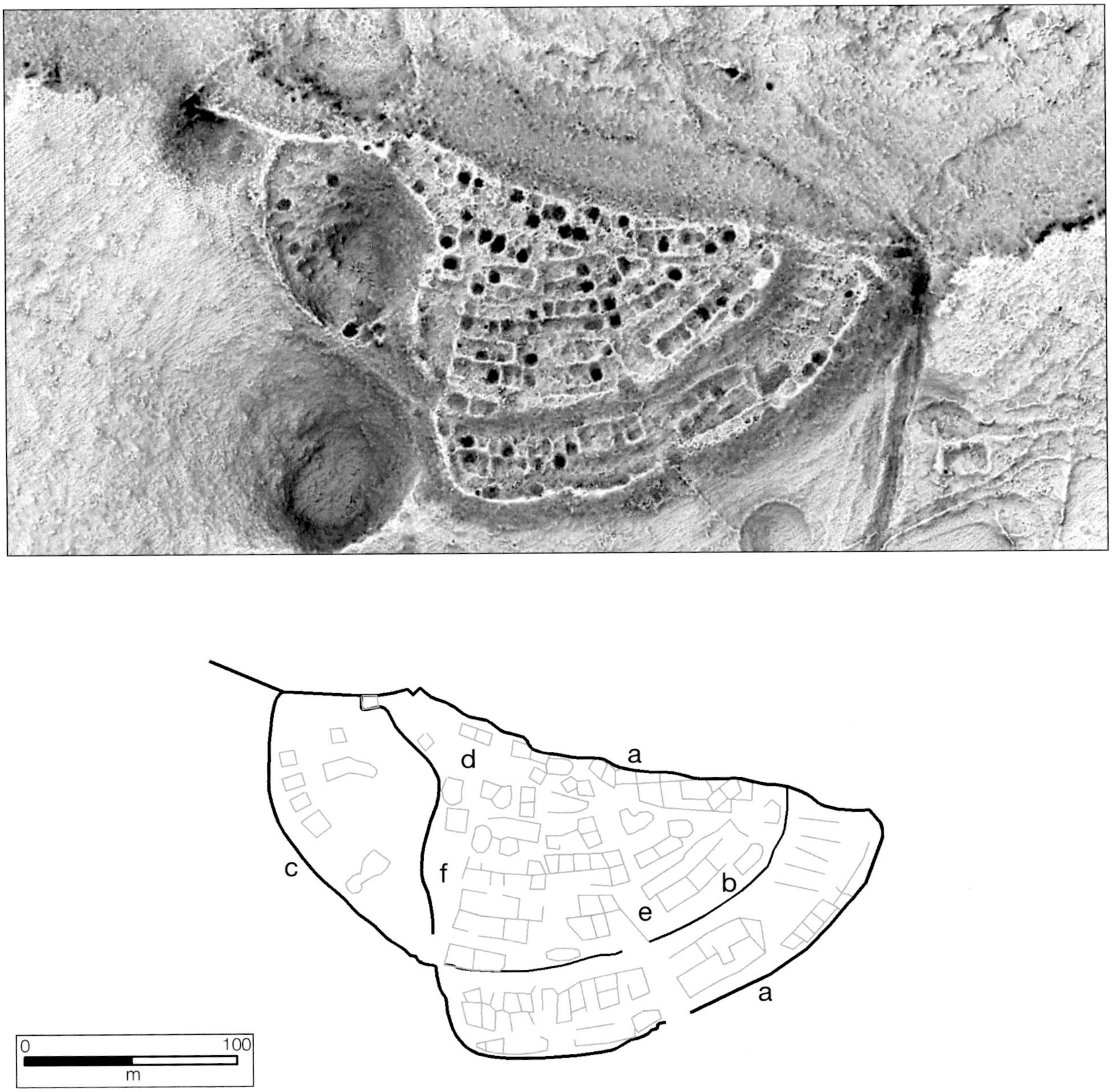

Figure 3: The Gradišče above Knežak hillfort: a) outer ramparts; b) inner ramparts; c) annex; d – f) open square spaces. Advanced image fusion visualization, see text.

that the interior layout of the hillfort, with its remains of buildings, squares and streets, was modified during the last habitation phase dated to the Late Roman period.

26.3.2 Cairnfields

There are four cairnfields and several dispersed cairns discernible on the Knežak plateau. The closest to the settlement is the loosely clustered Cairnfield a with 72 cairns (Figure 4 a) that are adjacent to, but also interspersed with banks and linear earthworks. Further south, Cairnfield b with 164 cairns is the largest and boasts some of the largest cairns measuring up to 7.5m across (Figure 4 b) that are partially interspersed with rectangular enclosures. West of it is Cairnfield c comprising 53 of the smallest cairns (Figure 4 c). Southwest of the hillfort is Cairnfield d with 123 similarly sized cairns (Figure 4 d). At the southern end of the plateau there are also two small cairn groupings (Figure 4 e). Cairnfields are located on gentle predominantly south facing slopes (average 10.85 degrees) – both factors that predispose agriculture in this particular environment. There is an absence of cairns at the bottom of the valley, which may be the result of destruction through intensive

Figure 4: The Gradišče above Knežak hillfort territory: a – e) cairnfields; f & g) linear earthworks – possibly terracing; h) enclosure; i) rectangular enclosures; j – m) hollow ways; n) funnelled way.

arable farming practised here from the medieval period to the recent past (Figure 2 j). The cairnfields are interspersed with banks and linear earthworks (Figure 4 f and features marked in grey).

At least two of the cairns have been excavated so far. One of them was among the largest cairns of the site and investigated in the 1950s (Figure 2 i), yielding small shards of exclusively prehistoric pottery of the *kaštelir* type (Urleb 1960, 284). During our non-invasive field survey, we examined the cairns and documented pieces of *kaštelir* type pottery in several holes left by uprooted trees. This type of pottery, usually unearthed in a very fragmented state, is common on the prehistoric hillforts in SW Slovenia and can only broadly be dated to the Late Bronze and Iron Ages.

Apart from those at Knežak, several very similar cairns have been excavated in SW Slovenia from the second half of the 19th century onwards. Up to now, they were believed to be burial mounds. Excavators unearthed no graves, but consistently reported on dispersed shards of prehistoric pottery, burnt earth and in some cases charcoal (Müllner 1880, 23; Urleb 1974, 74-5; Osmuk 1988, 196-7; Turk 1994). The pottery shards date exclusively to the Late Bronze and Iron Ages, which is consequently also the date for the cairns. Our investigations have confirmed these findings and also yielded no later pottery (Roman, medieval). The cairns at Knežak, but also at other sites in southwest Slovenia, are located in a karst and predominantly sub-Mediterranean environment, on slopes and plateaus covered by a thin layer of soil and with the bedrock lying at shallow depths. The soil here was never ploughed and manured. The agricultural activities of the people living in the hillforts, either in late prehistory or in the Roman period, were limited to the thicker and more fertile soils in the dolinas (Slapšak 1995; 2003; Novakovič & Simoni 1997), while the high and post-medieval ploughing took place in lowland areas and was connected with the beginnings of the present-day villages dating back to the 11th/12th century AD.

26.3.3 Banks and linear earthworks

Banks and cairns are represented in approximately equal shares in Cairnfields a and b, cairns represent a minority in Cairnfield c and a marked majority in Cairnfield d (Figure 4). An area between Cairnfields a and c is occupied solely by banks perpendicular to the slope (Figure 4 f), which appear to be more structured, *i.e.* parallel or perpendicular to each other, than others. Close to the hillfort is an area of just over 133,000 m^2 enclosed with and divided by parallel banks in a manner reminiscent of a field system (Figure 4 g); the parallel earthworks are perpendicular to the gentle slope (average 5.77 degrees). East of this is a kidney-shaped enclosure (Figure 4 h) devoid of any features or finds and separated from the hillfort by a hollow way and by rough terrain (Figure 2). A group of rectangular enclosures (Figure 4 i) represents the easternmost features on the plateau that are situated on steeper slopes (above 10 degrees). Another group of enclosures is intersected by a funnelled way (Figure 4 n).

Several banks and linear earthworks, which were partly damaged by modern forestry works, and produced shards of the *kaštelir* type prehistoric pottery, have been examined. One of the banks (Figure 5) has recently been trial trenched and positively identified as anthropogenic in origin as its central layer consisted of medium- and small-sized stones mixed with earth. The deposit also revealed the odd shard of the *kaštelir* type prehistoric pottery. An important find there was a Roman footwear hobnail discovered in a layer superimposed on the earthwork, which supports our assumption of the bank being contemporary with the prehistoric occupation of the hillfort.

26.3.4 Linear boundary earthworks

A short double earthwork (Figure 2 b) is blocking the natural bridge that crosses the precipice and delimits the territory to the neighbouring hillfort on Gradišče at Čepna (Figure 2 g). The earthwork closer to the Knežak hillfort terminates in the west in a small enclosure (Figure 2 c). A significantly longer linear boundary earthwork (Figure 2 d) delimits the territory to the south and east. At its south-western end, it terminates in a small enclosure (Figure 2 e;), while at its northern end is oriented towards the hillfort on the Obroba hill (Figure 2 f).

The linear boundary earthworks have never been trial trenched and we have no reliable data as to their dating, though they do seem to be remnants of the hillfort landscape. We can trace the modern land division on cadastral maps from the early 19th century onwards; it is identifiable on the ground as a system of drystone walls that are not constructed with respect to these linear features and clearly follow a different logic. The longer linear boundary earthwork (Figure 2 d) is connected at both ends to an oval enclosure, one of which represents the hillfort on the Obroba hill from the Late Bronze and Early Iron Ages (Turk 1996, 109-10; Bratina 2006, 72-3). Ploughing destroyed a section of its southern part (Figure 2 k). It seems that the linear boundary earthwork was a poorly visible and overgrown ruin already when the medieval and post-medieval fields were created (present state: approx. 4.0 m across and 0.25-0.30 m high) and did not have any bearing on the human activities of the day.

26.3.5 Hollow ways

The most prominent hollow way leads to the hillfort from the southwest, along its eastern rampart and then forks: the short northwest way leads to the water spring and the northeast way traverses the steep slope in the direction of the Obroba hillfort (Figure 4 j). At both ends, the traces of the hollow way are lost in the arable fields of the valley bottom.

There are other paths that we deem contemporary with the hillfort landscape based on the relationship with other features, more precisely based on the fact that these pathways do not cut banks and linear earthworks, but rather that the banks and linear earthworks are positioned so as to leave empty space measuring 17 m or more on each side of the pathways (Figure 4 k-m; l). It would appear that the main supra-local south-north route forks just south of our study area, creating two pathways (Figure 4 j, k) connected by a local communication (Figure 4 l). The rest of the pathways (Figure 4 m, n) would appear to be local communications.

The dated cairns and a bank in turn help us to determine at least some of the pathways as contemporary as well, because at the minimum four of the paths (Figure 4 j, l, m, n) are fully incorporated into the cairnfield and banks landscape, *i.e.* the latter was shaped so as to make room for the paths.

26.4 Concluding remarks

The ALS data have revealed numerous traces of the field system of the hillfort Gradišče above Knežak, surprisingly well-preserved archaeological features that include cairnfields, banks and linear earthworks, enclosures, hollow ways and linear boundary earthworks.

In a seemingly confusing mass of archaeological features there is order in the disposition and location of the differently sized groups of cairnfields and in the differently shaped banks and linear earthworks. The features appear to be complementing and upgrading each other. Paths are cleverly positioned to lead among the features and into the main line of communication below the hillfort. The features form a cohesive hillfort landscape and represent the remains of land use and field distribution. They are believed to be what remained of the field system that was created, used, managed and clearly delimited with linear boundary earthworks. In the north, the system is bordered by a double linear boundary earthwork adapted to the uneven terrain (Figure 2 b), in the south and east by a boundary earthwork connected with an enclosure (Figure 2 e) of a prehistoric appearance and with the Late Bronze and Early Iron Age hillfort at Obroba (Figure 2 f). The Knežak hillfort landscape was not created in a single campaign, but is rather the work of generations of inhabitants; we can view it as a palimpsest of multi-period activity. The collected archaeological evidence suggests this activity spans late prehistory. The main indicator for such dating is the shards of the *kaštelir* type pottery unearthed during excavations and field surveys of some of the cairns, as well as banks and linear earthworks. Later finds, from the Roman and the Middle Ages, are absent. However, the hillfort itself was inhabited until the late 4th century AD, indicating that the hillfort field system or at least part of its features were still in use in the Roman period. The period after the decline of the hillfort (late 4th/early 5th century) and up to the 11th/12th century AD, when the present-day villages in the lowland begin to take shape, has yielded no archaeological or historical data. The beginnings of these villages can be inferred from documents on the construction and later development of the churches, but also the creation of the lowland fields connected with ploughing using the heavy plough from the 11th/12th century onwards. The plateau holding the hillfort above Knežak (600-740 m a.s.l.) with poor and shallow soils is unsuitable for heavy ploughing; there were no fields on the plateau at this time, only pastures and forests of the people living in the lowland villages. This is also the reason why the hillfort field system survived as well as it did, as fossil landscape from the time when the hillfort was inhabited. The available data have not, however, revealed the exact types of agricultural activities connected with the features of the field system.

The recent excavation of a bank (Figure 5) revealed individual stones laid in an upright position. The stones were interlaced with soil, *i.e.* stones and soil were found alternately over and under each other, as if woven together. This is evidence of this not being a simple clearance cairn where stones would be heaped into a pile and the soil would subsequently form from *e.g.* decaying tree leaves in the empty spaces between the stones.

The current working hypothesis is that the banks, linear earthworks and cairns were constructed with the aim of fostering the growth of certain types of plants (hoe farming) or agroforestry. These earthworks indeed compensate for two of the main shortcomings for agriculture on the Knežak plateau: very shallow soils and proneness to summer drought. Concentrating soil into earthworks creates more room for root systems and stones help retain soil moisture. This effect is clearly visible on the aerial photographs showing cairns overgrown with healthy grass in the time of summer drought. On the other hand, the system of enclosures with funnelled and enclosed pathways suggests manipulation of herds of grazing animals.

The remains of the linear boundary earthworks are a unique monument without parallels in the wider area of central Europe, and presumably represent the boundary of the territory of the Knežak hillfort community. Parallels can be found in Dalmatia, Croatia (cf. Chapman *et al.* 1996) and farther away in Western Europe, mostly in Great Britain (*e.g.* Oswald 2011), where such earthworks delimit the areas of certain activities rather than the territories of individual communities (Johnston 2001).

Such boundaries are physical evidence of a territorial organisation of the Iron Age communities living in the area. This is particularly true of the area of Knežak where the landscape is very well preserved and affords an insight

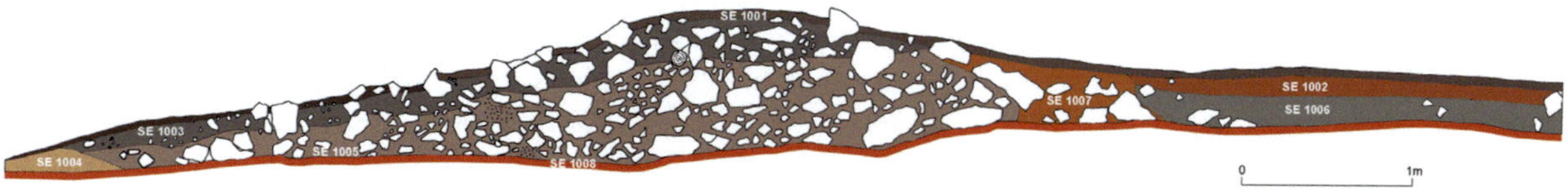

Figure 5: A section of the linear earthwork excavated in 2016.

into its structure in late prehistory. The hillfort territory is delimited by precipices on the northern and western sides, while the remaining sides are encircled with linear boundary earthworks. The Knežak case study can therefore serve as a starting point for future verifications of the numerous theoretical models for delimiting the Iron Age communities that have been proposed in the past decades, but could not be verified by material evidence (Slapšak 1995; Novaković 2001; Bintliff 2014).

26.5 Acknowledgement

The authors acknowledge the financial support of the Slovenian Research Agency (research core funding No. P6-0283).

26.6 Bibliography

Bratina, P. 2006. Knežak – Knežak – gradišče Obroba. *Varstvo spomenikov* 39-40, 72-3.

Doneus, M. & Briese, C. 2011, Airborne laser scanning in forested areas – potential and limitations of an archaeological prospection technique. In D. C. Cowley (ed.). Remote sensing for archaeological heritage management. 59-76. Budapest: Archaeolingua.

Chapman, J., Shiel, R. & Batović, Š. 1996. *The Changing Face of Dalmatia. Archaeological and Ecological Studies in a Mediterranean Landscape.* Leicester.

Battaglia, R. 1927. Necropoli e Castellieri dell' età del ferro del Carnaro. *Bulletino di paletnologia Italiana* 47, 93-15.

Bintliff, J. 2014, Settlement Patterns. In P. Horden & S. Kinoshita (eds). *A Companion to Mediterranean History*. 203-18. Chichester: Wiley-Blackwell.

Gabrovec, S. 1999. 50 Jahre Archäologie der ältern Eisenzeit in Slowenien / 50 let starejše železne dobe v Sloveniji. *Arheološki vestnik* 50, 145-88.

Guštin, M. 1979. *Notranjska. K začetkom železne dobe na severnem Jadranu / Zu den Anfängen der Eisenzeit an der nördlichen Adria.* Katalogi in monografije 17. Ljubljana.

Hänsel, B., Mihovilić, K. & Teržan, B. 2015. *Monkodonja. Istraživanje protourbanog naselja brončanog doba Istre / Forschungen zu einer protourbanen Siedlung der Bronzezeit Istriens. Knjiga. 1 / Teil 1, Iskopavanje i nalazi građevina / Die Grabung und der Baubefund,* Monografije i katalozi 25. Pula: Arheološki muzej Istre.

Horvat, J. 2005. Poselitev na Pivškem in ob zgornjem toku Reke od pozne bronaste dobe do pozne antike / Settlement in the Pivka Area and along the upper Course of the Reka River from the Late Bronze Age to the Late Antique Period. In *Kras: voda in življenje v kamniti pokrajini / Kras: Water and Life in a rocky Landscape,* 220-48. Ljubljana: Založba ZRC, ZRC SAZU.

Johnston, R.A. 2001. *Land and Society. The Bronze Age cairnfields and field systems of Britain.* Unpublished PhD thesis, Department of Archaeology, University of Newcastle upon Tyne.

Kokalj. Ž.& Hesse, R. 2017. *Airborne laser scanning raster data visualization. A Guide to Good Practice.* Ljubljana: Založba ZRC.

Laharnar, B. 2015. The Roman Army in the Notranjska Region / Rimska vojska na Notranjskem. In J. Istenič, B. Laharnar & J. Horvat (eds). *Evidence of the Roman Army in Slovenia / Sledovi rimske vojske na Slovenskem, Katalogi in monografije 41*. 9-42. Ljubljana: Narodni muzej Slovenije.

Lasaponara, R., Coluzzi, R. & Masini, N. 2011. Flights into the past: Full-waveform airborne laser scanning data for archaeological investigation. *Journal of Archaeological Science* 38(9), 2061-70.

Lindsay, J.B., Cockburn, J.M.H. & Russell, H.A.J. 2015. An integral image approach to performing multi-scale topographic position analysis, *Geomorphology* 245, 51-61.

Maggi, P., Pieri, F. & Ventura, P. 2017. *Monte Castellier: le pietre di Elleri narrano la storia.* Trieste: Edizioni Università di Trieste.

Mušič, B. 1999. Geophysical prospecting in Slovenia: an overview with some observations related to the natural environment. *Arheološki vestnik* 50, 349-405.

Müllner, A. 1880, Archäologische Excurse nach Süd-Steiermark und Krain. *Mittheilungen der K. K. Central – Commission, NF* 6, 21-6.

Novaković, P. & H. Simoni 1997. Archaeology of the Kras dolinas. *Annales: Series historia et sociologia* 7/10, 19-36.

Novaković, P. 2001. Detecting territoriality and social structure in the Bronze and Iron Ages: GIS and the hillforts in the Kras region. In B. Slapšak (ed.). *On the good use of geographic information systems in archaeological landscape studies.* 101-15. Proceedings of the COST G2 WG2 Round Table, Ljubljana, l8 to 20 December 1998, Ljubljana: Office for Official Publications of the European Communities.

Oswald, A. 2011. *Prehistoric Linear Boundary Earthworks.* Introduction to Heritage Assets. English Heritage:Swindon.

Osmuk, N. 1988. Goriče pri Famljah. *Varstvo spomenikov* 30, 196-7.

Slapšak, B. 1995. *Možnosti študija poselitve v arheologiji.* Arheo 17. Ljubljana: Založba ZRC.

Slapšak, B. 2003. O koncu prazgodovinskih skupnosti na Krasu / The end of prehistoric communities in the Karst region. *Arheološki vestnik* 54, 243-57.

Štular, B., Kokalj, Ž. Oštir, K. & Nuninger, L. 2012. Visualization of lidar-derived relief models for detection of archaeological features, *Journal of Archaeological Science* 39 (11), 3354-60.

Štular, B. & Lozić, E. 2016. Primernost podatkov projekta Lasersko skeniranje
Slovenije za arheološko interpretacijo: metoda in študijski primer. In R. Ciglič, M. Geršič, D. Perko & M. Zorn (eds). *Digitalni podatki.* 157-66. Ljubljana: Založba ZRC SAZU.

Turk, P. 1996. Datacija poznobronastodobnih depojev (The dating of late bronze age hoards). In B. Teržan (ed.). *Depojske in posamezne kovinske najdbe bakrene in bronaste dobe na Slovenskem / Hoards and individual metal finds from the eneolithic and bronze ages in Slovenia.* Katalogi in monografije 30, 89-124. Ljubljana: Narodni muzej.

Triglav-Čekada, M., B. Barborič, Ferk, M. & Zorn, M. 2016. Nationwide aerial laser scanning reveals relict rock glaciers and protalus ramparts in Slovenia. *The Cryosphere Discuss.*

Urleb, M. 1960. Gradišče nad Knežakom. *Varstvo spomenikov* 7, 282-4.

Urleb, M. 1974. Križna gora pri Ložu: halštatska nekropola / Hallstattzeitliches Gräberfeld Križna gora. Katalogi in monografije 11. Ljubljana: Narodni muzej.

Zhang, H. & Huang, B. 2015. A New Look at Image Fusion Methods from a Bayesian Perspective. *Remote Sensing* 7 (6), 6828-61.

Chapter 27

Around the Münsterberg

How online tools help us to rethink our data

Loup Bernard

27.1 Introduction

This paper presents a short case study of how online data from French and German archaeologists can help the reconsideration of a so-called *Fürstensitz*, the Münsterberg, in a broad context. In the framework of a web-GIS archaeological evidence, palaeo-environmental data, and topography are easily combined for analysis.

27.2 The ArkeoGIS project

The ArkeoGIS project, which has been online since 2011 (http://arkeogis.org/en/), is a web-GIS which aggregates datasets originating from different institutions dealing with the past and the environment. Every contributor shares part or all of the spatial data, with at least one classification (*e.g.* settlement, grave...) and one period. While the chronological system is based on absolute dating, the interface allows inclusion of dates such as the traditional Hallstatt/La Tène system. All or part of the available data can then be queried inside the application and displayed in the browser on a map. The result of every query can be retrieved as a text file (.csv format) that can be re-used in any other software, database, or GIS, for example.

From the beginning, the project has tried to draw in colleagues from geographical studies, with pollen analysis and soil mapping listed, for example, with associated literature. While it is more and more difficult for researchers to stay up-to-date with literature in their own field of research, maintaining an awareness of associated disciplines is even harder, especially if that spans several countries and languages. Indeed, mapping of these archaeological and associated data in a common framework is important as the combination of knowledge produced by different researchers opens new questions, as well as informing planning of rescue archaeology and infrastructure projects.

In D.C. Cowley, M. Fernández-Götz, T. Romankiewicz & H. Wendling (eds). Rural Settlement. Relating buildings, landscape, and people in the European Iron Age (Leiden 2019: Sidestone Press) 273-275.

27.3 The Münsterberg case study

The ArkeoGIS project in the upper Rhine Valley originated in 2008 as a collaboration between the Universities of Strasbourg and Freiburg-in-Breisgau, together with the regional archaeological services and companies, to share data around the river. To date this has supported the compilation of many databases describing several thousand sites that are now available for professional researchers wishing to work on this area. In illustrating the potential that this presents, two queries relating to the regional context of the Münsterberg are presented.

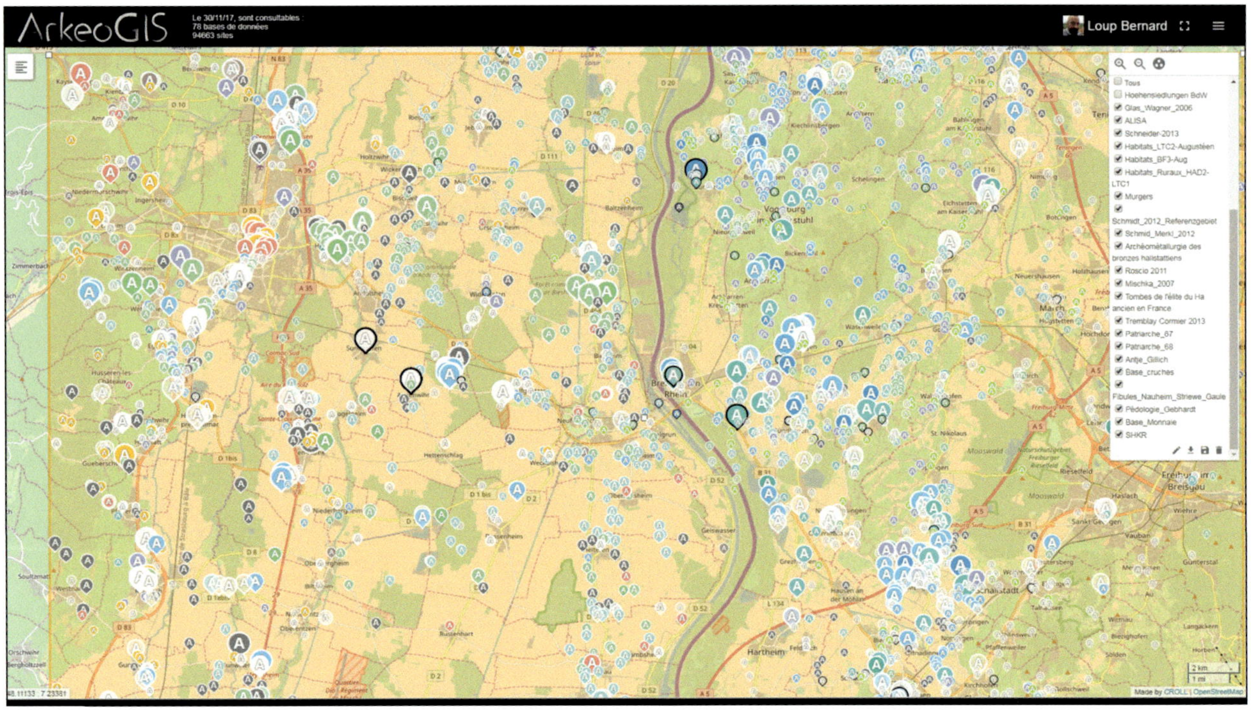

Figure 1: Archaeological and environmental data available around the Münsterberg (L. Bernard).

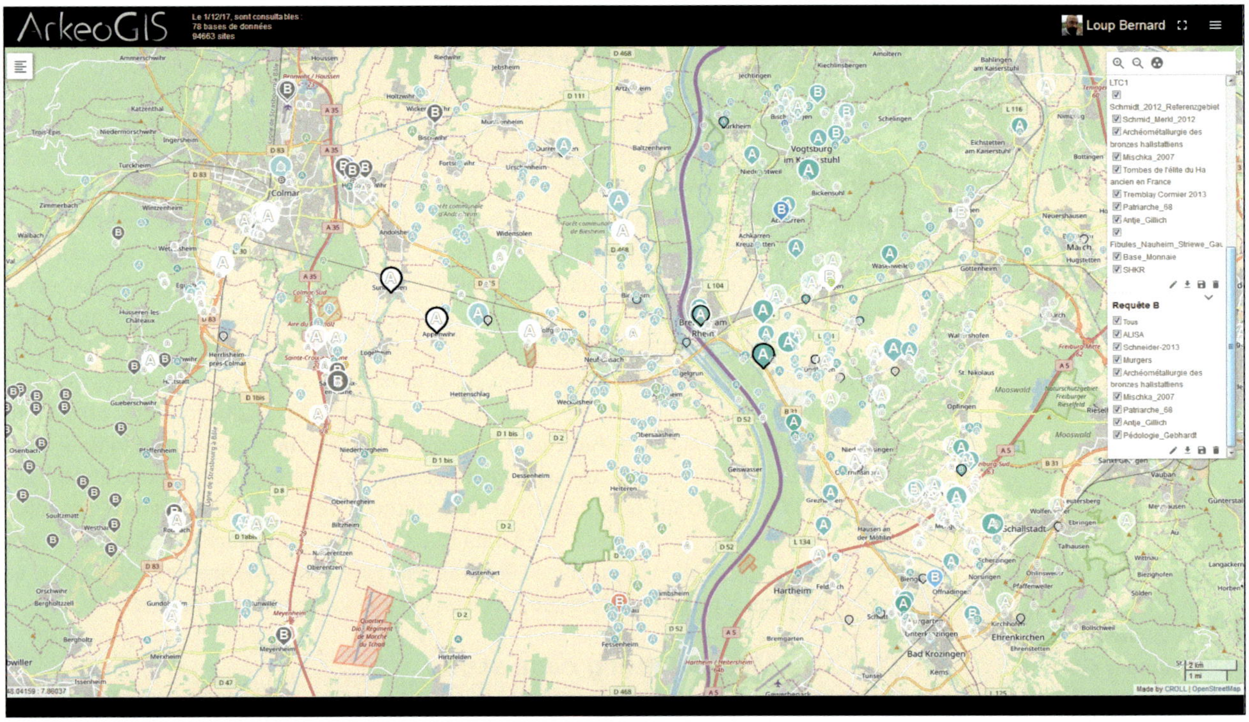

Figure 2: A) Map of Iron Age sites between the Vosges and the Black Forest, and B) the available environmental data. The queried databases are listed in the box on the right of the map. (L. Bernard).

The first query requests all available data in the area (Figure 1). The result is difficult to read because data can be redundant in ArkeoGIS if a site is present in different datasets. Nevertheless, it provides an excellent immediate picture of the current state of knowledge in the study area, depending on the available datasets. Information on the database records and the metadata for each dataset, including a digital original identifier, is available. In this example some 9,838 lines of information drawn from 22 datasets are available.

In this case the history of research introduces complex bias that needs to be taken into account. For example, the area surrounding Freiburg-in-Breisau has been examined in several PhDs and research grants (the SHKR, for example: Siedlungshierarchien und kulturelle Räume, https://www.jma.uni-kiel.de/en/research-projects/data-exchange-platform/shkr) over the years. Thus the density of Iron Age sites (blue dots) is because Iron Age datasets were the first to be integrated in ArkeoGIS, and because of the long tradition of pre- and protohistory (*Vor- und Frühgeschichte*) study in the city. On the left bank of the river, the rapid development of the French city of Colmar is evident, with the clear contribution that rescue archaeology provides in several transects following the lines of road development around the city. More interesting, the amount of data makes the empty gaps between site distributions significant, as these can correspond to forested or ploughed areas, in contrast to areas of known settlements or cemeteries. Cross-referencing of datasets, such as soil mapping and pollen analysis, is easily undertaken with the map interface being the key medium for integration. The distribution of archaeological sites also clearly indicate where and when the channel of the Rhine riverbanks has migrated.

The second query (Figure 2) of Iron Age sites between the Vosges and the Black Forest provides 2,637 returns from 20 different sources. However, only 618 sites from nine datasets provided a more precise date range (Ha D3/LT A), due to the precision of the original databases which were not all designed by protohistorians.

Any user can get direct access to the coordinates, characteristics and literature for the area within a few mouse clicks. This represents a huge improvement compared to the situation a few years ago, when researchers would have needed several months of work going through French and German literature in different libraries and institutions in order to get the same information (see the maps in Brun & Chaume 1997, 377-8 for example). This integration within a common web-GIS also supports a better understanding of the data that has become available over the last few decades, as the databases from the different PhDs for example, each reflect the state of knowledge at a given time.

27.4 Discussion

Moving back to the two examples of the utility of ArkeoGIS, for the Münsterberg, it is clear that the hillfort is definitely not only surrounded with sites on the right riverbank (as it appeared in Pauli & Stork 1993, 103, 104), but also by dozens of farms, villages and several productions sites in the mountains and on the left riverbank. Although the state of research in the Vosges area is comparatively poor and is mostly from 19th century investigations , new work is starting to provide more data (Walter 2016), such as the large number of open settlements, such as in Geispolsheim, on the west riverbank (Landolt & Fleischer 2011).

The cooperation with palaeo-environmentalists (Bernard *et al.* 2015) also opens new possibilities, as human impact can be read in some areas at certain scales. Having a mapping of known sites can help to understand taphonomic processes (*e.g.* selective erosion or burial of sites) which are vital elements in attempting to understand Iron Age landscape and society.

Note: All detailed metadata regarding the datasets will be online in arkeogis.org as soon as this paper is published. The shared databases are open to any professional archaeologist on request at http://arkeogis.org/demande-dacces/.

27.5 Bibliography

Bernard, L., Ertlen, D. & Schwartz, D. 2015. ArkeoGIS, Merging Geographical and Archaeological Datas Online. In F. Giligny, F. Djindjian, L. Costa, P. Moscati, & S. Robert (eds). *Concepts, methods and tools. Proceedings of the 42nd Annual Conference on Computer Applications and Quantitative Methods in Archaeology.* 401-6. Archaeopress: Oxford,

Brun, P. & Chaume B. (dir.) 1997. *Vix et les éphémères principautés celtiques : les VIe et Ve siècles avant J.-C. en Europe centre-occidentale. Actes du colloque de Châtillon-sur-Seine (27-29 octobre 1993).* Paris: Errance.

Landolt, M. & Fleischer, F. 2011. Les occupations d'Entzheim " In der Klamm " et de Geispolsheim " Schwobenfeld " (Bas-Rhin) du Hallstatt C à La Tène B (fouilles 2006 à 2009). *Bulletin de l'Association française pour l'étude de l'âge du fer*, AFEAF, 29, Paris, 13-7.

Pauli, L. & Stork, I. 1993. *Der Münsterberg in Breisach. II / Hallstatt- und Latenezeit.* München: C.H. Beck Verlag.

Walter, M. 2016. Les sites de hauteur du massif vosgien. Actualisation des données et modalités d'implantation (Néolithique récent – Xe siècle), Archimède 3, 20-36.

Chapter 28

Archaeology, landscapes, and heritage in the southeast Iberian Peninsula

The *ALHIS* project

Leticia López-Mondéjar

28.1 Introduction

This paper presents a brief summary of the ALHIS (Archaeology, Landscapes and Heritage in the southeast Iberian Peninsula) research project, based at the Institute of Heritage Sciences of the Spanish National Research Council. The project deals with the Late Iron Age in the southeast Iberian Peninsula and focuses on both archaeological study and heritage management issues. The first part of the project seeks to explore, through the study of the landscape and the broad archaeological record of this area, the socio-political transformations experienced by the local communities during this period, such as the consolidation of elites and the symbolic appropriation of territory. On the other hand, the project seeks to enhance the value of the sites from this period for cultural heritage management and development. This short paper focuses on the archaeological study of the region.

28.2 Spatial and chronological context

The study area takes in the territories of the present-day Region of Murcia and the Segura valley, from the end of the 5th century through to the 1st century BC, dealing with the development of Late Iron Age communities (the so-called Iberians) and their transformation with the expansion of Roman occupation (Figure 1). A series of fortified settlements (*oppida*) dating from the 5th century BC have been documented in the area, including some of the most important Iberian Iron Age sites, such as El Cigarralejo and Verdolay. Moreover, from the end of the 3rd century BC, the development of these territories was marked by the founding of *Qart Hadasht*, a city which became the Punic capital in the Peninsula. Its establishment and conquest by Rome in 211 BC under the name of *Carthago Nova*, are crucial to understanding the transformations that took place in the area during this period.

Despite the interest of the area for exploring the socio-political and territorial processes that took place during this period, Iron Age studies have usually examined the main fortified sites and their necropolises, focusing attention on their rich burials. Moreover, there has not been any attempt to explore the area in a Landscape Archaeology framework, which has demonstrated its value in helping to understand questions such as the rise of social complexity and the strengthening of socio-political elites (Falconer

In D.C. Cowley, M. Fernández-Götz, T. Romankiewicz & H. Wendling (eds). Rural Settlement. Relating buildings, landscape, and people in the European Iron Age (Leiden 2019: Sidestone Press) 277-280.

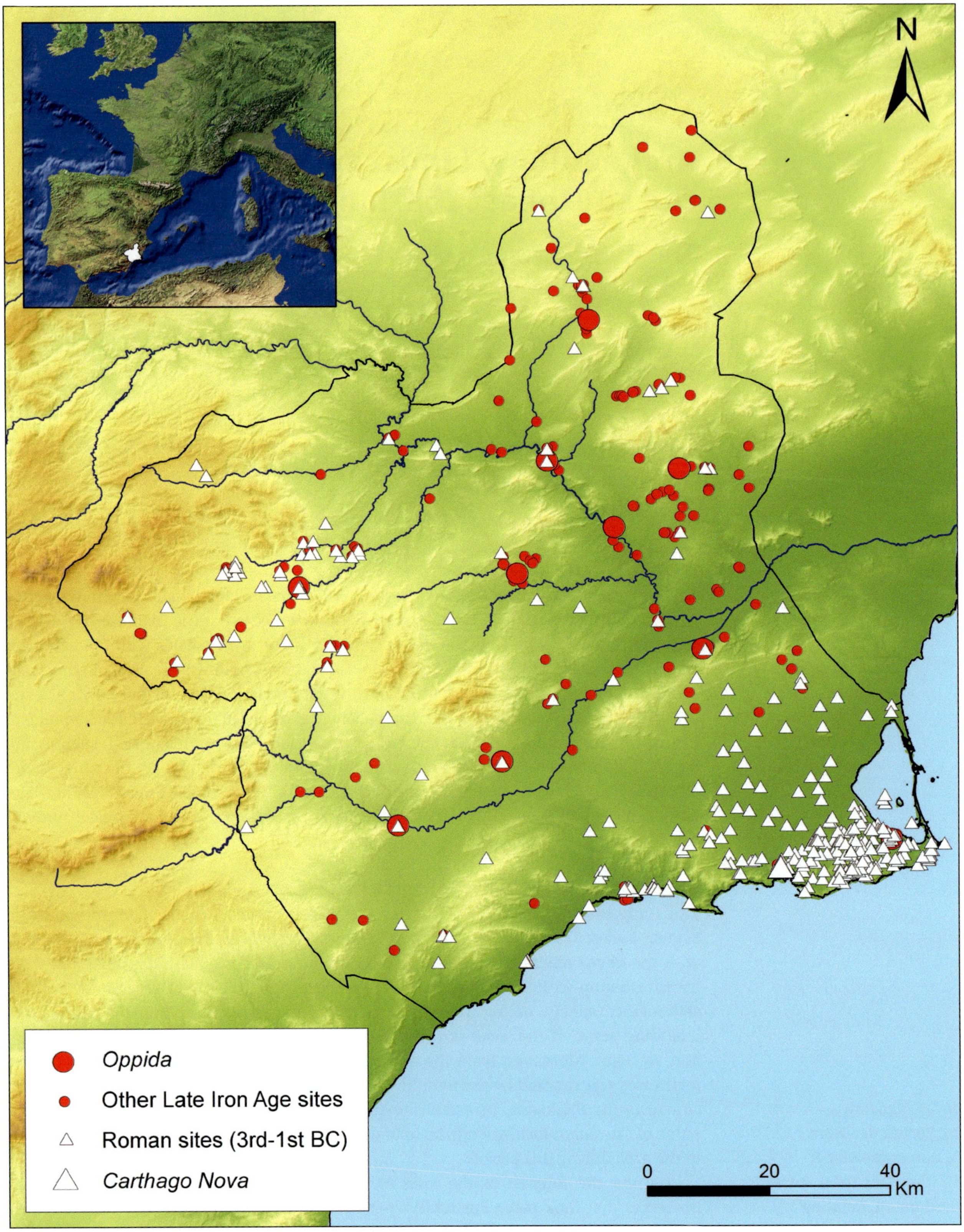

Figure 1: Study area and the main Iron Age and Roman sites known in the analysed territory (Graphic: López-Mondéjar).

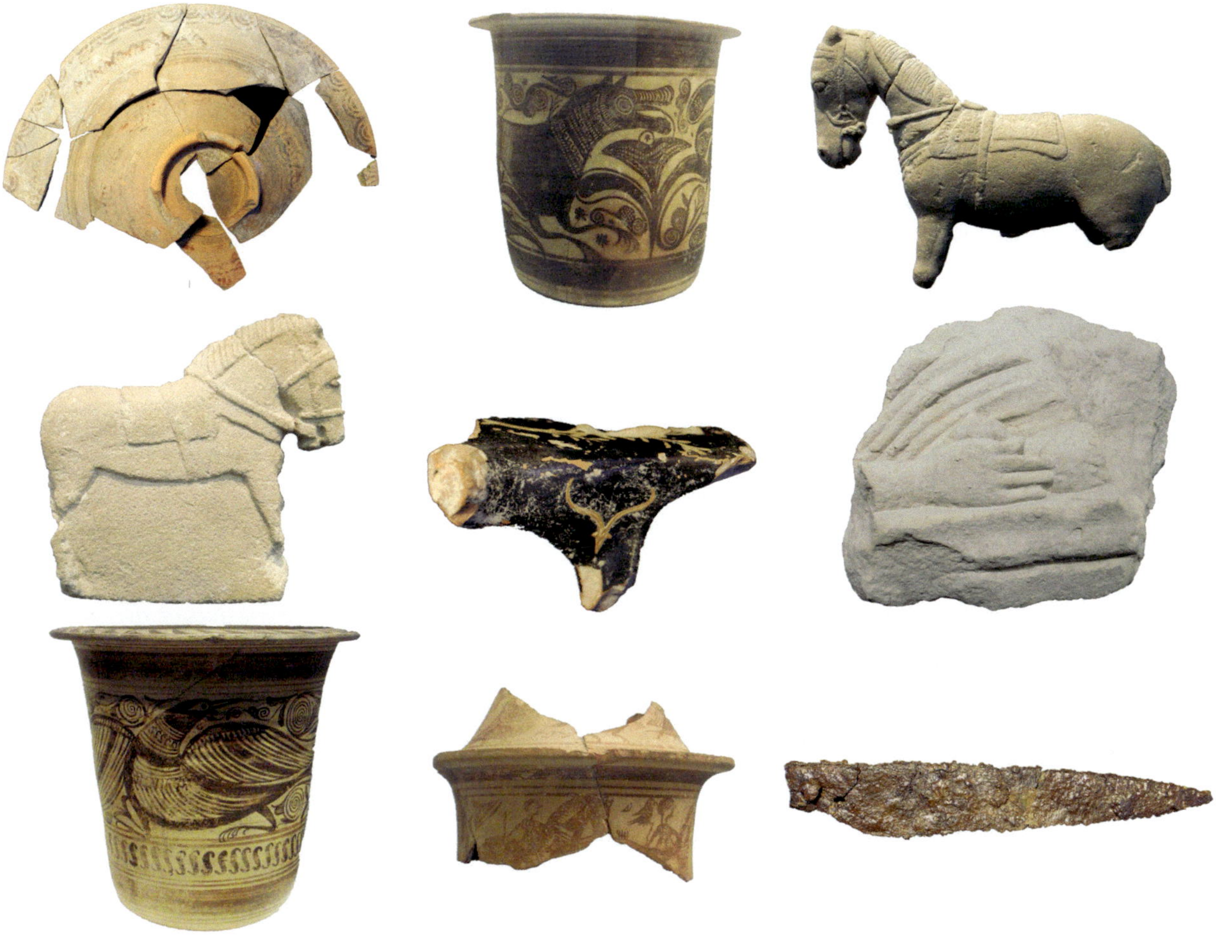

Figure 2: Examples of the material record dated to the period of study (Image: López-Mondéjar).

& Redman 2009; Fontijn 2008). For example, studies in Catalonia, Andalusia and Valencia have helped to understand how socio-political systems operated in the area, and to address issues such as spatial expressions of power, productive uses of the land (intensive or extensive crops, livestock, etc.), and the symbolic appropriation of the landscape (Grau-Mira 2014; Mata-Parreño *et al.* 2012; Ruiz-Rodríguez & Molinos-Molinos 2007). This interesting perspective and methodology has barely been applied in Murcia, where major sites and burials have attracted archaeological attention, but little is known of other secondary settlements. However, over the last few years this situation is changing, and a dense network of sites and a more complex settlement pattern have been detected.

28.3 Research methodology and approach

The research methodology of the project is interdisciplinary and comprises four main strands of work. Firstly, the compilation, review, and analysis of the heterogeneous archaeological and historical data for the area (structures, ceramic production, weapons, sculptures, grave goods, etc). These data have been compiled from different sources, including bibliographic sources, unpublished data from the Regional Archaeological Service, ancient textual sources, and fieldwork, producing a comprehensive database of the Late Iron Age and Roman sites in the region. Secondly, all this information has been integrated into a Geographic Information System (GIS). The third stage of the project has been dedicated to the analysis of the compiled data. This has covered formal archaeological analysis (chronologies and typologies from contexts, stratigraphies, comparative analyses), cross analyses (including documentary, archaeological and geographic data to identify and to define new evidences), and spatial analyses (GIS analyses and LiDAR-derived visualisation) approaching issues such as territorial control, exploitation, spatial articulation and territorialities, the study of continuities and transformations in the settlement patterns, and the hierarchies of sites. Here, GIS is the key tool for queries, analysis, data exchange, and the production of thematic maps. Finally, a crucial aspect of the methodology is the contextualization and comparison of the results from the analyses. This helps to more clearly define problems and similarities between the southeast Iberian Peninsula, nearby areas, and the processes operating in other parts of the western Mediterranean (Figure 2).

Throughout, the project takes a broad, diachronic, interrelated and contextualized approach based on different scales of observation – the local (*oppidum*) and supra-local (regional).

28.4 Preliminary results and perspectives for the future

The preliminary outcomes of the analysis of Late Iron Age and Roman sites in the area, especially in the Middle Segura valley, in the period from the 5th to the1st century BC have identified some key issues. Firstly, within the Iberian and Roman landscapes regional cult places played a key role in both the integration of local communities in broader geopolitical territories and their incorporation to the Roman landscape, through key sites such as Cueva Negra and the Roman baths in Fortuna and Archena. Secondly, socio-political transformations are clearly visible in both settlements and funerary practice, identifying the need for a holistic approach. Moreover, the need to rethink the models of evolution applied to other Iberian territories, and the role played by social groups apart from aristocracies is evident. This reveals the heterogeneity of the Iberian communities and the particularities of the socio-political processes in every area, demanding that every territory requires specific study. The study has also highlighted the importance of the Punic world in the development of regional settlement, revealed by the presence of Punic coins in local contexts, the reinforcement of certain fortifications, and the destruction evidenced at a number of sites.

In summary, the ALHIS project is providing a research framework, and territorial models and settlement patterns for Protohistoric and Roman sites in the area, an important contribution to helping the understanding of socio-political dynamics, which are otherwise not included in the general summaries for this period (Berrocal-Franco *et al.* 2013; Díaz-Andreu & Keay 1997). And specifically for Murcia, the project is for the first time developing a diachronic, broad based, socio-political study of the landscape during the second half of the first millennium BC.

28.5 Acknowledgments

This project has been funded from the European Union's Horizon 2020 research and innovation programme under Marie Skłodowska-Curie grant agreement No 654906.

28.6 Bibliography

Berrocal-Franco, M.C., García-Sanjuán, L. & Gilman, A. (eds) 2013. *The Prehistory of Iberia. Debating Early Social Stratification and the State*. London: Routledge.

Díaz-Andreu, M. & Keay, S. (eds) 1997. *The Archaeology of Iberia. The Dynamics of change*. London: Routledge.

Falconer, S.E. & Redman, C.L. (eds) 2009. *Polities and Power. Archaeological perspectives on the Landscapes of Early States*. Tucson: University of Arizona.

Fontijn, D. 2008. Everything in its right place? On selective deposition, landscape and the construction of identity in Later Prehistory. In A. Jones (ed.). *Prehistoric Europe: Theory and practice*. 86-106. Chichester: Wiley-Blackwell.

Grau-Mira, I. 2014. The Iron Age landscape of Alcoi Valley, eastern Iberia: Agricultural intensification and socio-political dynamics. *Journal of Field Archaeology* 39 (2), 124-33.

Mata-Parreño, C., Moreno-Martín, A. & Quixal-Santos, D. 2012. Estrategias de ocupación y explotación del entorno periurbano de Kelin'. In M.C. Belarte-Franco & R. Plana-Mallart (eds). *El paisatge periurbà a la Mediterrània occidental durant la protohistòria i l'antiguitat*. Tarragona: Institut Català d'Arqueologia Clàssica.

Ruiz-Rodríguez, A. & Molinos-Molinos, M. 2007. *Iberos en Jaén*. Jaén: Universidad de Jaén.

Chapter 29

Rural domestic patterns in northwest Iberia

An ethnoarchaeological approach to Iron Age household layout

Lucía Ruano & Luis Berrocal-Rangel

In D.C. Cowley, M. Fernández-Götz, T. Romankiewicz & H. Wendling (eds). Rural Settlement. Relating buildings, landscape, and people in the European Iron Age (Leiden 2019: Sidestone Press) 281-287.

29.1 Introduction

This paper presents preliminary results of research on households and domestic space in north Iberia during the Iron Age, which draws on Archaeology of Architecture and Ethnoarchaeology. The current focus of our analysis is the fortified villages, known as *castros*, in the provinces of Asturias and Lugo, as well as the north of the province of León. Our principal interest is studying settlement using meso- and micro-spatial approaches, focusing on the domestic layout inside the settlement and also within the domestic structures, based on a corpus of sites where domestic structures have been identified. Traditional approaches to such material have a tendency towards descriptive texts, with functional or typological approaches, where forms, architectural evolution and cross-cultural influences are the main interests. There has been less attention paid to contextual factors that might influence domestic architecture and, as a result, house features and the distribution and use of space have not been deeply studied. Furthermore, the lack of standardised documentation in existing studies has made this study of different architectural possibilities more difficult.

The domestic sphere, with its expression in architectural structures and material culture, is very significant as a reflection of the social and cultural processes which are our focus. We approach this from the premise that domestic architecture and its associated elements respond to specific meanings, as well as conditioning behaviour. Thus, we have to be able to access the social, political, economic, symbolic and functional contexts where they developed, both within the household and the settlement. In undertaking this research we have built on work produced during the last twenty years in other areas (Ayán Vila 2005; 2012; Ayán Vila *et al.* 2003; 2009; González Álvarez 2016; Mañana *et al.* 2002; Marín Suárez 2011; Sastre *et al.* 2010). Following these studies, we have defined two objectives in re-examining the data from past archaeological interventions. Firstly, the review of published articles and monographs, amongst a range of sources including diaries, excavation reports, historic photographs and drawings, informs an understanding of how our current knowledge of domestic architecture has been produced, and what its limitations are. Our second, and main objective is to maximise the information from these archaeological remains, applying different theoretical and methodological tools from Archaeology of Architecture and Ethnoarchaeology. This approach has already supported the recognition of models of occupation and social and symbolic aspects of domestic space (Ruano 2016).

29.2 Methodology

Our methodological framework applies integrated analyses from Archaeology, Architecture, Anthropology and Psychology, following an approach developed by Galician researchers, who have termed it *Archaeotecture* (Ayán Vila *et al.* 2003; 2009). The first step in this method is the *formal analysis*, the study of the physical characteristics of the archaeological remains, which can be divided in to several stages. Firstly, constructional and stratigraphic analyses characterise building materials, their origins and qualities, different architectural techniques, and phases in the different stages of construction, abandonment and collapse of structures, as well as processes such as building tasks, resource investment, and the different stages of life of a building. Secondly, through *functional analysis* we try to identify the activities that took place in the different domestic spaces, followed by the study of *typological and morphological* aspects of constructions. Finally, we perform *spatial analyses* to try to understand the relationships between different spatial areas within household layouts and the settlement. As we believe that the organisation of household space is also related to human perception, *syntactic analysis* or *perception analysis* are undertaken using tools to analyse movement and visual perception (Hillier and Hanson 1984). Movement analyses are used to analyse spatial relationships within a building, with circulation analysis and gamma analysis to study permeability between spaces. On the other hand, analysis of visualisation conditions aims to study personal space inside and between structures to identify public and private spaces, as well as analysing perceptions of the settlement layout, trying to understand the landscape that is created within the settlement.

This methodology has allowed us to describe and systematically analyse architectural elements and associated material culture, as well as the organization of spaces, for the whole area of study. While this approach is helping to reconstruct the original context of the domestic sphere, we have found several limitations. These include a lack of scientific rigor in many archaeological interventions, a biased archaeological record, compartmentalised studies of domestic architecture and its material culture, lack of accurate plans and surveys and of extensive excavations, and, also, our contemporary western vision of some concepts, such as house, family, privacy, intimacy, and relations between people and animals.

29.3 Ethnoarchaeological approaches

The problems raised by a contemporary western ethnocentricity for our study prompted us to develop a study of traditional architecture. We believe that an ethnoarchaeological approach is fundamental to understand the potential of a study like ours to comprehend past societies (González-Ruibal 2003, 12). It can provide interpretative tools that help re-think our object of study, allowing us to consider a broader range of interpretations and meanings for the different patterns of architecture and domestic space amongst Iron Age communities. In this, an ethnoarchaeological approach challenges the role of preconceived concepts, about family, privacy and so on, to explain the archaeological record and past societies (González-Ruibal 2001)

For these reasons, we have studied the traditional architectures of southwest Asturias, northwest León and eastern Lugo, keeping archaeological research problems in mind. Here, in historically isolated regions, many traditionally built constructions have survived. However, profound socio-economic changes in these areas during the last fifty years are dismantling the traditional system of life, with negative consequences for this type of architecture. For example, in the recent past there were many structures with thatched roof used as houses, while today they are used as stables, garages, warehouses, ethnographic museums, temporary refuge, and haylofts, for example – if they are not completed abandoned. Although they have received economic support from The Office of Education and Culture of Asturias, the result of these efforts has not been so positive, since there has not been any further monitoring (Graña y López 2007; Menéndez 2008). This situation highlights the pressing need to document these traditional architectures and techniques.

Despite these circumstances, we have been able to identify different types of traditional buildings and structures (Figure 1). In southwest Asturias, and between León and Galicia, large round byre-houses were built of stone and wood and thatched with rye straw. On the other hand, in Asturias, in the municipalities of Somiedo and Teverga, there are better preserved examples with roofs made of stone or broom, in this case related to transhumance and seasonal livestock activities. In seeking to develop our integrated methodology and looking for fresh insights from the ethnoarchaeological perspective, we have applied our archaeological methodology to the study of these structures, though the progressive changes have limited us to a formal analysis of constructional features. Nonetheless, the observation of the structures that still remain standing has given us important architectural knowledge about the different possibilities that these materials offer as building elements. This is illustrated with reference to two types of structures in the municipalities of Somiedo and Teverga.

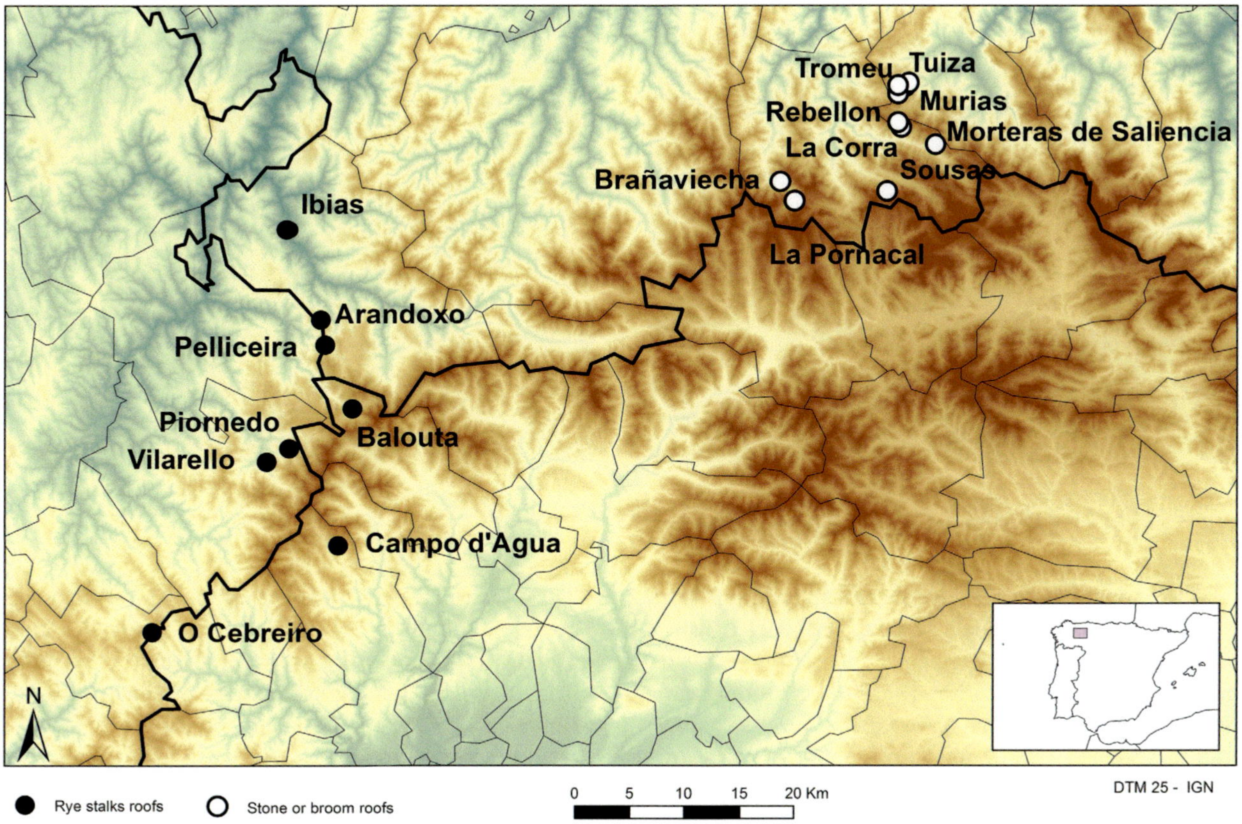

Figure 1: Ethnographic sites in Asturias, León and Lugo. (© Lucía Ruano).

29.3.1 Type I: Simple structures

In areas of grazing meadows in higher ground there are architecturally and typologically simple structures, used by herdsmen and the youngest cattle (Figure 2). These can be grouped into two types of building.

Firstly, there are circular structures, known as *corros*, that are built with dry-stone walls of limestone and sandstone, without foundations. They have a stone corbelled roof usually covered with turf which improves insulation. The majority have an earthen floor, with only a few examples of paved floors. The buildings measure between 2 and 3 m in overall diameter, with walls between 0.50 and 0.80 m thick and up to 3 m in height. They have a single small door of some 0.65 m width and 1.5 m height, whose jambs and lintels are usually made of large blocks of stone dressed around the door opening. There are no windows, or other fittings beyond an outer shelf or aumbry to store tools and cool milk overnight. There are some examples of conjoined pairs of structures while, in other cases, the internal area has been divided in two.

The second type of simple structure are also circular on plan with stone walls and a thatched roof of broom (*Cytisus scoparius*) known as *chozos*. These have an average diameter of 5 or 6 m and the drystone walls also do not have foundations and are no more than 1.5 m high. Some structures have an enclosure at the entrance, where the cattle were milked. The beech or oak timber frame of the roof is conical, with the rafters set directly on the wall and reinforced with subsidiary ones. The point of the roof is protected with turfs and large stones, which prevent water from seeping through the thatch. In some cases, it is also secured with forked branches. There is only one small entrance, which measures no more than 1.3 m high and 0.7 m across. The floors are earthen and there are usually timber mangers and the bed of the herdsman in the interior. Those types of buildings have close parallels, possible precedents, in Iron Age domestic architecture such as that excavated in the hillfort of Castiellu de Llagú, Oviedo (Berrocal-Rangel *et al.* 2002, 124).

*29.3.2 Type II: Structures with hayloft thatched with broom (*Cytisus scoparius*)*

Buildings with haylofts are the most abundant structures, and while they may be rectangular or circular on plan, the vast majority are rectilinear (Figure 3). They are usually found amongst meadows on valley bottoms or lower and medium slopes, and are used by herdsmen in spring and autumn enroute to and from higher meadows. Since the cattle are stabled at night, there is a need to store hay.

Figure 2: Simple structures (type I) at Somiedo, Asturias. Left: chozo; Right: corros. (© Lucía Ruano).

The circular examples are significantly larger than type I, measuring between 6 and 9 m of diameter, with a conical thatched roof. The rectangular structures measure between 6 and 10 m in length and 5 and 6 m across including the walls. Both of them have two floors – the ground level used as a stable with a hayloft above supported by a wattle floor. Today, the rectangular buildings have an attached structure housing the herdsman's bed and hearth, although previously these were in the stable. These buildings are always located on sloping ground, which provides easy ground-level access to the hayloft from a second entrance in rear of the building, which is levelled into the slope.

They are mainly dry-stone constructions of limestone or sandstone, although soil and dung mortar has been observed. The roof structure is made of oak or beech, with principal and subsidiary rafters, laths and purlins. These are joined with wood pegs or metal nails, with evidence also of different joining techniques, such as scarf joints, half-lap joints and mortice and tenon joints. A thin layer of brushwood or heather provides a base-layer for the roofing, over which is laid the broom thatch. With renew or repair, usually every year, old phases of thatching often survive below the most recent overcoat. These types of roof can provide a large capacity for storing hay as they can measure more than 10 m in height and a roof pitch of 55-60°, which has a positive influence on the roof's lifespan. Channels to carry surface water away from the building are sometimes protected by irregular masonry walls, which also keeps the cattle away from the thatch.

29.3.3 Type III: Round structures with hayloft thatched with rye straw

There is another set of structures in the southwest of Asturias and on the mountain range known as Sierra de los Ancares. These are large circular or oval byre-houses permanently occupied by people and animals together (Figure 4), which may measure up to 20 m in diameter. These buildings have dry-stone walls of regular masonry, on which is set a conical wood roof frame constructed using the same joining techniques outlined above in Somiedo and Teverga. The main difference is that the thatch is of rye stalks tied to the wood frame. Generally, these structures do not have windows, although there may be ventilation holes in the thatch. They do not have chimneys, as the smoke can seep through the rye stalks, while helping to preserve the organic roof and to cure foodstuff such as meat or chestnuts.

29.4 Possibilities of an ethnoarchaeological approach

The ethnoarchaeological approach to vernacular buildings has offered information about some important aspects of traditional architecture, which we believe is relevant to Iron Age archaeological research. Firstly, it has provided insights to the range of materials utilised to build structures, as well as different architectural techniques and the distribution of their internal building space. Comparing across each area it is evident that environmental, social and economic factors, among others, are fundamental to understanding how domestic spaces were built and articulated in the past.

Secondly, it provides a perspective on regional variability. For instance, the same material can be used in different ways more related to identity than practical or economic considerations. This is evident in the ways in which the plant matter is secured to the roof, as in Somiedo and Teverga, each valley has their own ways to secure the thatched roof. These include the use of turf to hold down the thatch, the use of beech or holly planks hung over the top with a little crosspiece, all of them joined by mortice and tenon, the use of forked sticks or branches, and beech bark placed over the apex. So too,

Figure 3: Structure with hayloft thatched with broom (type II) at Teverga, Asturias. (© Lucía Ruano).

Figure 4: Round structure with hayloft thatched with rye straw (type III) at Piornedo, Lugo. (© Lucía Ruano).

in the southwest of Asturias and in Sierra de los Ancares, there are several ways to secure the thatch. One is called *a paleta* and uses a wooden legget to work the bundles of rye stalk thatch that have been tied to the wooden frame with ropes of twisted straws. A second method is known as *a baguna*, and sees the stalks fixed to the roofing timbers with a braid of sticks.

The ethnoarchaeological evidence has also provided information about meanings and decoration. Although these structures are little ornamented, the good stonework around doors and external shelves, the apparently deliberate use of different colours of stones in the walls, and the carvings found on two rectangular structures at Somiedo provide insights into the ornamentation of structures. At Somiedo blocks of stone flanking the doorway bear two pairs of carved faces (Figure 5), whose different carving techniques could indicate two different dates. They may represent the owners of the structure, and while these are recent, they bear certain similarities with Celtic style and can be compared with similar finds of Late Iron Age or Early Roman date documented on several archaeological sites, such as Barán (Lugo) or San Chuis (Asturias) – (Álvarez Núñez 1991; Villa Valdés 2006, 334; Marín Suárez 2011, 446).

Figure 5: Carved faces from La Pornacal, Somiedo, Asturias. (© Lucía Ruano).

Finally, the varying states of abandonment, decay and collapse of many of these structures provides data that can help to better understand the post-abandonment processes that have affected archaeological structures.

29.5 Conclusions

The theoretical and methodological approach outlined above aims to offer new ways of looking at and thinking about household, domestic space and architecture of past societies. This approach takes a cross-disciplinary, integrated and holistic approach to the analysis of all the domestic excavated remains in a standardised manner, which facilitates comparison between sites. For the domestic archaeological record of the Iron Age in the north of Iberia, the ethnoarchaeological evidence can be extremely helpful to reconstruct aspects of the domestic environment, which is otherwise notably difficult to infer from the archaeological record alone. Indeed, there is a large amount of relevant ethnographic and ethnohistorical work on traditional architecture, and while little of this has been undertaken with archaeological problems in mind (Politics 2015, 43) it could provide a rich source to illuminate the range of potential practices that produce the archaeological record.

29.6 Bibliography

Álvarez Núñez, A. 1992. Castro de Barán, 91 (informe de la primera intervención arqueológica). *Boletín do Museo Provincial de Lugo* 5, 153-78.

Ayán Vila, X. 2005. Arquitectura doméstica y construcción del espacio social en la Edad del Hierro del NW. In A. Blanco, C. Cancelo & Á. Esparza (eds). *Bronce Final y Edad del Hierro en la Península Ibérica. Encuentro de jóvenes investigadores*. 34-54. Salamanca: Ediciones Universidad Salamanca.

Ayán Vila, X. 2012. *Casa, familia y comunidad en la Edad del Hierro de NW*. Thesis, Universidad de Santiago de Compostela.

Ayán Vila, X., Blanco Rotea, R. & Mañana Borrazás, P. 2003. *Archaeotecture. Archaeology of Architecture*. Oxford: BAR International Series 1175.

Ayán Vila, X., Mañana Borrazás, P. & Blanco Rotea, R. 2009. *Archaeotecture: Second Floor. Papers from the Archaeology of Architecture sessions held at the EAA Meetings in St Petersburg (2003) and Lyon (2004)*. Oxford: BAR International Series 1971.

Berrocal-Rangel, L., Ruiz Triviño, C. & Martínez Seco, P. 2002. *El Castiellu de Llagú: un castro astur en los orígenes de Oviedo*. Madrid: Real Academia de la Historia.

González-Ruibal, A. 2001. Etnoarqueología de la vivienda en África Subsahariana. *ArqueoWeb. Revista sobre Arqueología en Internet* 3(2).

González-Ruibal, A. 2003. *La experiencia del otro. Una introducción a la etnoarqueología*. Madrid: Akal.

González Álvarez, D. 2016. *Poblamiento y antropización de la montaña occidental cantábrica durante la Prehistoria reciente: una aproximación desde la Arqueología del Paisaje*. Unpublished thesis, Universidad Complutense de Madrid.

Graña García, A. & López Álvarez, J. 2007. *Los teitos en Asturias. Un estudio sobre la arquitectura con cubierta vegetal*. Gijón: Red de museos etnográficos de Asturias.

Hillier, B. & Hanson, J. 1984. *The social logic of space*. New York: Cambridge University Press.

Mañana Borrazás, P., Blanco Rotea, R. & Ayán Vila, X. 2002. *Arqueotectura 1: Bases teórico-metodológicas para una Arqueología de la Arquitectura, TAPA 25*. Santiago de Compostela: Universidad de Santiago de Compostela.

Marín Suárez, C. 2011. *De nómadas a castreños: El primer milenio antes de la Era en el sector centro-occidental de la cordillera cantábrica.* Unpublished thesis, Universidad Complutense de Madrid.

Menéndez, C.O. 2008. *Teitos. Cubiertas vegetales de Europa Occidental: de Asturias a Islandia.* Oviedo: Colegio Oficial de Aparejadores y Arquitectos Técnicos de Asturias.

Politics, G.G. 2015. Reflections on Contemporary Ethnoarchaeology. *Pyrenae* 46(1), 41-83.

Ruano, L. 2016: *Arqueología de la Arquitectura aplicada a la Protohistoria del Occidente de Asturias (ss. I a. C. – d. C.): el hábitat doméstico en Coaña y San Chuis.* Madrid: Servicio de Publicaciones, Universidad Autónoma de Madrid.

Sastre, I., Currás, B. & Alonso, F. 2010. Parentesco, desigualdad y formas de identidad en la Edad del Hierro del Noroeste. *Arqueología Espacial* 28, 169-86.

Villa Valdés, A. 2006. El Pico San Chuis: reseña de un yacimiento pionero en la investigación castreña en Asturias. *Sautuola: Revista del Instituto de Prehistoria y Arqueología Sautuola* 12, 112-9.